Marching On...

125 YEARS OF
THE ST MIRREN FOOTBALL CLUB

1877-2002

Jack Paterson and Bob McPherson
with Brian Wright

FIRST EDITION
OCTOBER 2005

Published by Saltire Graphics
on behalf of
The St Mirren Football Club Limited

© JACK PATERSON and BOB McPHERSON

Marching On... 125 Years of St Mirren Football Club

First published in 2005
by Saltire Graphics
Brook Street Studios, 60 Brook Street, Glasgow G40 2AB

The St Mirren Football Club Limited 2005

Designed and Printed in Scotland by Saltire Graphics/Print • Glasgow

All rights Reserved

No part of this publication may be reproduced,
stored in a retrieval system, or transmittted in any form or by any means without
the prior permission in writing by the publisher.

ISBN 0-9543647-0-8

CONTENTS

The Authors 4

The Chairman 5

This is your Club 7

CHAPTER ONE
    The 1870s, Getting Started 9

CHAPTER TWO
    The 1880s, A Period of Progress 13

CHAPTER THREE
    The 1890s, Leagues and Love Street 19

CHAPTER FOUR
    The 1900s, Limited Company, Unlimited Ambition 27

CHAPTER FIVE
    The 1910s, Conflict, Cochrane and a Cup 40

CHAPTER SIX
    The 1920s, Consistency and Success 51

CHAPTER SEVEN
    The 1930s, Decline and Fall 62

CHAPTER EIGHT
    The 1940s, Struggling, Winning, Thriving 73

CHAPTER NINE
    The 1950s, Highs, Lows and Hampden 84

CHAPTER TEN
    The 1960s, Going, Going, Gone,... Then Goals Galore ... 98

CHAPTER ELEVEN
    The 1970s, Nadir to Zenith... Thanks to Fergie 112

CHAPTER TWELVE
    The 1980s, Triumphs... and Trophies at Last 132

CHAPTER THIRTEEN
    The 1990s, Struggles and Champagne 159

CHAPTER FOURTEEN
    The New Millennium, Still Marching On 180

Dedications and Memories 188

Acknowledgements and Thanks 191

THE AUTHORS

Jack Paterson

Bob McPherson

Jack Paterson has been a St. Mirren supporter since being lifted over the turnstiles as a youngster by his father back in the 1960s.

A Paisley Buddie born and bred, he is co-owner of his own graphics and print business and is editor and designer of both the 'Black & White' magazine and 'The Saint' newspaper.

A Saints' shareholder, some years ago he re-designed the Club crest after St. Mirren had received a request from the Lord Lyon's office to make changes to the badge. Jack's re-design had only one aim - "to keep the logo as close to the original as possible".

He lives in Lochwinnoch with his wife Elaine, daughter Kirsteen and son Ross, who like his father and grandfather is a fervent supporter of the Club.

Bob McPherson, by contrast, is something of a mixture when it comes to the great game. A keen Third Lanark supporter until the Hi-Hi's sad demise in 1967, he then followed Clyde home and away for the next nine years before moving to Dundee in 1976.

Since then, Dundee United have very much claimed Bob's allegiance but he also has a decade-long admiration for Charlton Athletic, a soft spot for Workington and a general interest in all levels of football.

In short, the complete football fan, and one who enjoys contributing to a variety of Scottish football club publications, not least of which are 'Black & White' and 'The Saint'.

Married to Ann, they have two daughters - Claire and Laura - and the family home is in Broughty Ferry.

Brian Wright

Now retired from teaching, Brian Wright is most certainly steeped in Saints tradition, having supported St. Mirren man and boy. He feels that he was 'fated' to be a Saints fan, and not only because his father, Alex, managed the Club to the old Second Division Championship 1967/68.

Rather it's due to the fact that the first game he can ever remember being taken along to was at St. Mirren Park, in the far off days of his childhood back in 1962!

Brian contributes to the Club match programme and writes a regular column in The 'Black and White' Magazine. An enthusiastic follower of football in general, he is keen on all aspects of the game. First and foremost though he is a 'St. Mirren man'.

He lives in Johnstone with his wife, Cheryl and their two St. Mirren supporting sons, Calum and Andrew.

THE Chairman

Stewart Gilmour
Chairman

As Chairman of The St. Mirren Football Club, it is my privilege to offer some words of thanks to all who hold this great institution close to their hearts.

Reaching our 125th anniversary is an achievement which should not be underestimated. However, it has only been made possible by the support, affection and fortitude which the people of Paisley have shown for their football club.

Therefore I would like to acknowledge the efforts of every supporter, every player and every official from the founders in 1877 to the present day. They were, and you are, the Club, the links which have held firm over these one hundred and twenty-five years.

From times of great joy through days of despair, in war-time and periods of great uncertainty, our chain has remained unbroken. Indeed it has been forged from so much pride and commitment, both to and from its community, that it is our greatest wish that it will remain thus for as long as football is played.

But that does not mean we can be complacent. Others have failed to travel so far and these pages remind us just how perilous the great sport of football can be.

This history records the exertions and accomplishments of our Club over the first one hundred and twenty-five years. I trust it will provide an inspiration for those yet to come.

On behalf of St. Mirren FC, I would like to record my thanks to the authors, Jack Paterson, Bob McPherson and Brian Wright for their excellent efforts. I hope all Saints supporters enjoy the book; after all, each of us is part of its continuing story...

BOARD OF DIRECTORS 2002

George Campbell	*Kenneth McGeoch*	*Bryan McAusland*	*Roger Lucas*	*James Purves*
Vice-Chairman	*Director*	*Director*	*Director*	*Director*

Football. One small word, but a huge part of everyday life in today's Scotland. No: make that the world! It captivates the fans, assaults the senses, and shatters dreams, while firing bullets of elation, disappointment, hope, and frustration in equal measure. No again: make that unequal measures!

Even in today's global village of computers, instant communication, and hi-tech gadgetry, this simple game with simple rules provides a focus for a huge part of Scotland's, and in our case Paisley's, sporting life.

Which brings us neatly to...

St. Mirren. Two words, but what words! They encapsulate all the aforementioned multiplied by one hundred, one thousand, a million! Why? Because they represent pride, determination, sense of place, sense of community. We are the Buddies!

In 2002 this Club, our Club, became one hundred and twenty-five years old. One hundred and twenty-five years old! Saints were formed thirteen years before structured football came into being. Indeed we were founder members of the League.

This book will show that St. Mirren remain one of the truly great names of Scottish football. With a history just bursting to get out and impress.

A history second to none.

THIS IS Your Club

A proud history, peppered with proud men, great players, loyal supporters, determined directors, and, in the early days, visionary committee men. Men who, through good days and bad, through war years and peacetime, sought and fought to ensure this Club's survival. Sometimes against great odds, which all too often must have seemed insurmountable, especially with Paisley being situated only seven short miles from Scotland's biggest city and the football giants within.

Countless great players have come and gone. Sad times and bad times have passed and been recorded for posterity in Saints' own record books. Great games, exciting European adventures, cup victories, breathtaking performances, nail-biting replays, relegation despair, the unexpected, the unforgivable, the downright unbelievable!

When all mixed together, stirred, and allowed to settle, this recipe makes for a history, life, and story of St. Mirren which is inextricably interwoven with that of Paisley and its environs. As has been recorded elsewhere, it is often said that "Paisley is St. Mirren and St. Mirren is Paisley"! In what other town would its local football club receive such an accolade?

That this bold statement is true is undeniable, and will probably be so for as long as the beautiful game is played and the world exists. The game gives the town, the team, and the people - Buddies all - the opportunity to continue a great tradition and ensure the survival of values which even today's modern world cannot destroy in this, the early years of the 21st century.

In compiling and researching this book we, (the authors) could have (and almost did) lose ourselves in the Club's historic documents, share registers, and minute books. We were sidetracked left and right. Each time we turned another page of a minute book, each time we looked at a photograph, something new would come to light. Which in turn would lead to discussion, puzzlement, amazement, and amusement.

These records and others we have accessed have proved only one thing: that a history as colourful, complex, and surprising as that of The St. Mirren Football Club cannot hope to be fully recorded in a book such as this. There is no doubt that we will have left out more than space will allow us to include. We apologise for the many omissions, players, personalities, and incidents that we have been forced to leave aside, perhaps for others to record in another book in another time. We have done our best.

So to work... This is St. Mirren, one hundred and twenty five years on... This is your Club...

CHAPTER ONE
The 1870's

The 1870s - Getting Started

1877-78

In common with the lives of many Saints, the story of 6th century St. Mirin is riddled with "reputed", "now thought", and "it would appear" references. An absence of records in a much later era relating to the football club which bears the name of Paisley's Saint have ensured that St. Mirren FC's early years are also destined to remain imprecise, and this has manifested itself most obviously in the conflicting information which surrounds the number of grounds the Club used before finally settling at Love Street in 1894.

More of that later, but chroniclers of St. Mirren's history are more fortunate than most in one respect: St. Mirren have an undisputed starting point in 1877. "6th October, 1-0 win over Britannia, Goold scored" has been repeated so often down the years that these accepted facts could easily have formed part of a St. Mirren creed. A check of this primary data was considered unnecessary until the earliest history of the Club was uncovered. Written just seventeen years after St. Mirren were formed, it tells quite a different story of the Club's first match.

A short series of St. Mirren recollections was published in the 'Glasgow Echo' on the first three Thursdays of March 1892, and the author, "Old Internationalist", made no mention of Britannia as he asserted that "the first match (for St. Mirren) under the new auspices (Association football) was a disastrous one, as their opponents, the Ailsa, gave them a severe baptism, seven goals to one being the adverse result of their first association game."

First game or not, a 7-1 defeat is certainly a disaster, but Old Internationalist managed to convey a level of optimism which has been the hallmark of St. Mirren supporters ever since. "Such a result as this at once did them a power of good", he claimed, "as it showed the weak points in their defence and attack and paved the way for better displays eventually". Treating disaster and triumph in similar vein may have started with Rudyard Kipling, but Old Internationalist was clearly an adherent.

But was he accurate? Did Saints start with a 1-0 triumph or a 7-1 drubbing? Were years of extolling Saints' ruling of Britannia misplaced? Was Old Internationalist so old that his recollections of just seventeen years previous were unintentionally misleading? An early task was simply to establish if the Ailsa match took place before or after 6 October 1877.

It transpired that the match against Ailsa was indeed a first for St. Mirren, but the Pollokshields club were Saints' first away opponents on 20 October, two weeks after the Britannia match. Thus the issue was settled, and the 'Paisley Daily Express' report of the match against Britannia which begins with "The opening match of the St. Mirren came off on the grounds of the former at Shortroods" was once again the authorised version of the Club's beginnings.

It had been an early warning. If Old Internationalist could be wrong about something as basic as the first match so soon after the event, it was clear nothing could be taken for granted. Next in line was the St. Mirren legend which states that, back in 1877, some rugby players preferred the round ball game to the rugby code, and decided to form an association football club called St. Mirren.

Old Internationalist was in no doubt about St. Mirren's pre-1877 rugby connections: "Not a few of our leading Scotch clubs made their first bid to football notoriety by following the rugby game and amongst those whose initial attempts led in that direction may be numbered the Paisley Saints. The foundation of the Club was laid as far back as 1876 when the fortunes of the carrying game was sought after by the fifteen who constituted the Saints' team".

The swing from other sports towards football had been happening for a few years prior to 1877, and this trend wasn't occurring entirely by chance. Four years before St. Mirren were formed Mr. Archibald Rae, Secretary of Queen's Park Football Club, became the first-ever Secretary of the Scottish Football Association. His appointment was an acknowledgment not only of his contribution in convincing eight clubs to form the national body for football in Scotland in 1873, but for the indefatigable manner in which he undertook, in person and in writing, to convert cricket and rugby clubs throughout Scotland towards the eleven-a-side football game.

It is known that Mr. Rae, in his self-appointed role as football's first marketing manager, had made contact with clubs in Paisley and, indirectly or not, his efforts soon bore fruit. By the time St. Mirren took the field against Britannia on 6 October 1877 there were twelve association football clubs in membership of the Renfrewshire Football Association. These were Greenock Southern, Kennishead (Thornliebank), Levern, Morton, Port Glasgow Athletic, Renfrew, Thornliebank, 17th Renfrewshire Rifle Volunteers (Lochwinnoch), and the 23rd Renfrewshire Rifle Volunteers. By then there were also plenty of other clubs, such as St. Mirren and Britannia, who were active but not members of any association.

Old Internationalist provides some specific details of the St. Mirren rugby experience: "Their first year as Rugbyites gained them an income of little over two pounds sterling. A combination who could work smoothly and successfully on such a modicum surely gave promise of future success. Their expenditure was not affected by ground outlay, as they 'took possession' of their first playing pitch and consequently 'paid no rint'".

The authors of this history have been able to find only one match report of the St. Mirren Rugby Club, but it's enough to confirm that such a team did exist. On 26 February 1877, St. Mirren played Regent at

MEADHRAN, MIRIN, Paisley MIRRIN AND MIRREN

All early references to Paisley's Saint use the spelling "Mirin", although the Gaelic form is Meadhran. His connection with Paisley continued from the 6th century, and if the events of his life are uncertain, the impact of Mirin was not, and we do know for certain that an altar and tomb were erected to his memory in Paisley, that a small burn in the town was named after him, and for many years a fair was held in Paisley on his festival day, the fifteenth of September.

In King James IV of Scotland's Charter of 1488 raising Paisley to the status of a burgh, one of the main reasons for doing so was "the singular respect we have for the glorious confessor, St. Mirin" and this traditional spelling of the name continues to this day in Paisley's St. Mirin's Cathedral, in Paisley Abbey, which contains a St. Mirin Chapel, and in schools throughout the West of Scotland.

In David Cameron's 'Calendar of Scottish Saints', Mirin is "renowned in the provinces", which suggests his work took him to other parts of Scotland, and variously spelled place names would appear to confirm this: St. Mirron's Wall in Kilsyth, Kirkmirran in Kirkcudbrightshire, Knock Mirren at Coylton in Ayrshire, and Burn of Mirran at Edzell in Angus. In the 'New Statistical Account of Scotland' of 1845, mention is made of "Inchmurrin, the island of St. Mirren, tutelar Saint of Paisley" in Loch Lomond.

This spelling of "Mirren" appears to be the first time the name has been shown in the way most football supporters would recognise, but by the 1870s, local newspapers in Paisley included mention of at least two organisations which used "St. Mirren" in their title, although the spelling seemed to change from week to week, depending on who was the compositor! By then of course, there was the newly completed St. Mirren Street, and the formation of St. Mirren Football Club coincided with a trend toward spelling "Mirren" that way.

The advent of St. Mirren Football Club certainly increased the likelihood of the "Mirren" form being adopted in the Paisley area, but the name has now come full circle. Anyone searching for "St. Meadhran" on the Internet will immediately produce the following description: "Meadhran was active in Strathclyde; Mirren is the patron saint of football". The latter half of that phrase would find few dissenters in Paisley!

Greenock, and "after a well contested match, resulted in the favour of the St. Mirren by one disputed goal, dropped by McLardie, one touch to nothing".

Unfortunately the teams are not given, but the reporter noted that "for the St. Mirren, McLardie, Inglis and Galt worked hard", and these three names are prominent in the early years of the football club, and this is regarded as sufficient to make the link between the one-season rugby club called St. Mirren and the football club which started the following season.

St. Mirren's cricket connections are an altogether different matter, and are well documented. The St. Mirren cricket team had been formed in 1875 and played all its home matches at Shortroods. In the 28 August 1875 edition of the long-since defunct 'Western Standard' (and 'Paisley & Renfrewshire Observer'), generous space was given to St. Mirren cricket team's match with Blythswood which had been played the previous Saturday, and the listed St. Mirren side included the names of J. Fisher, J. Galbraith, F. Muir, and J. Paterson. Two years later, all four of these cricketers played in the first football match against Britannia.

The 'Western Standard', just a week before Saints' first-ever football match, also recorded that the previous week St. Mirren had beaten Thistle from Port Glasgow at Shortroods by 52 runs to 32, and "for the St. Mirren team J. Galbraith had 29 in fine style and J. Walker bowled well". J. Muir and six of this September 1877 Saints cricket team, Galbraith, Fisher, Graham, Paterson, Reid, and Drennan would play in the first ever St. Mirren football match, and it was J. Galbraith's name which featured prominently in the 'Paisley Daily Express' genuinely exclusive match report - none of the other local papers were present to record the proceedings.

Origins of the Club Crest... 1

The Great Seal of the Abbey.

"On the ball being started, it was soon carried into the strangers' ground, and it was more than once that the strangers' goal was in danger. Galbraith for the home team, had some good shots, which only passed a foot wide. Half-time being called, ends changed with the ball well down the field.

"On it being passed to Muir, who had a good run in front of the strangers' goal, he, on being charged, passed it to Graham, who shot at the goal. Unfortunately it only lay on the line with the goal, but Goold, coming up, put it through between the posts, thus securing a goal for the home team. Time was then called, the St. Mirren winning by one goal to none."

The 'Express' report suggests a deserved if narrow victory, with T. Graham coming tantalisingly close to scoring Saints first-ever goal, an honour that was secured by the alert J. Goold. The odds on the scorer having the initial "J" were fairly high, as the full team on that historic occasion indicates: J. Adam; J. Fisher and J. Stewart; J. Goold and W. Reid; J. Shearer, Johnny Paterson, J. Galbraith, F. Muir, T. Graham, and David Drennan.

St. Mirren missed the first week of the 1877-78 football season because of their over-lapping cricket commitments, but played at least sixteen matches between 6 October 1877 and 6 April 1878. Their second recorded win was also a 1-0 victory over Britannia just five weeks after the historic opening game, although the return match also deserves to be remembered, if only for its strong claim to be Saints' shortest-ever match, as the match report states that "after half an hour's play resulted in favour of the St. Mirren by one goal to nothing, when darkness put an end to the game".

In the second half of the inaugural season two excellent wins were recorded. On 19 January 1878, the Second Eleven of the Paisley (Rugby) Football Club came to Shortroods, and the match report included the following: "The 2nd Paisley won the toss and chose to play with the wind in their favour. About 3 o'clock Goold kicked off against a rather strong breeze, the ball being well returned by Murray and, after some good play, the St. Mirren wore their opponents up the field and Muir, getting the ball, made a good run and passed to McKechnie who strongly put in between the posts.

"Nothing further occurred except some good runs, but nothing came of them. Darkness coming on, time was called, leaving the St. Mirren the victors by five goals to nothing. The play on both sides was good but the superior passing and dribbling of the St. Mirren accounted for the easy defeat of their heavy opponents".

The reference to the bulk of their normally rugby-playing opponents is significant. It is not a charge levelled against the former rugby-playing St. Mirren in any of the early season reports, and right from the start it seems the Association game was well-suited to the active sportsmen who formed the first St. Mirren team.

The second impressive score took place on 16 February, when they met another new Paisley team called Abercorn who had been formed just a month after St. Mirren on 10 November 1877. The "Abbies" were to remain active for the next forty-two years, but, due to a combination of circumstances, would eventually lose out to Saints in the battle to win the support of the Paisley people. In February 1878 no one connected with the St. Mirren Club was contemplating civic supremacy, but if they had they couldn't have made a better start - they trounced Abercorn 7-0!

It was Abercorn's first recorded match, and they in turn couldn't have made a worse start. Perhaps Old Internationalist was right to claim that good can come from such defeats, because Abercorn would certainly prove to be formidable opponents for Saints in the years to come.

All in all it was not a bad start for The St. Mirren Football Club. It is not clear if they played every week because match reports may not always have been submitted to the local papers, but the absence of the name "St. Mirren" in the "Fixtures For Saturday" feature in the local

Origins of the Club Crest... 2

The Common Seal of the Burgh of Paisley. Last used officially 1912.

press suggests that they may have been left with some blank Saturdays in their first season.

Sixteen Saints matches have been identified during 1877-78, of which six were won and four were drawn, but some of the local opposition was not of the best. The wholesale adoption of association football, so obvious in Glasgow and Dunbartonshire thanks to the earlier pioneering work of Queen's Park, still had some way to go in the Paisley area, and the 'Western Standard' was typical in its sports coverage. Cricket was given considerable prominence in the 'Standard's pages throughout its six month season, and during the winter months any substantial match reports on "football" were always of the fifteen-a-side game. The 'Paisley Herald' was more likely to carry reports of matches played under "Association rules", but details were very brief. It was a situation which would change in two short years to reflect the fast-growing popularity of football in the county.

1878-79

The St. Mirren cricket team had played all their home matches at Shortroods, and the phrase "at the ground of the former at Shortroods" is consistently used throughout 1877-78 to describe the location of Saints' home football matches. Unfortunately, there are no maps in existence which show the exact location of the cricket and football field of that name, but the Shortroods area name will give many readers an understanding of its general location. Unfortunately, the same cannot be said for Abingdon Park, the ground which St. Mirren used throughout the 1878-79 season.

This second season is the least well documented of Saints' early years, but it is known that on 21 September, the day the 1878-79 football season opened, St. Mirren's players were still finishing their cricket fixtures. As things turned out, there wasn't much football played between then and the 1879 cricket season, as local newspaper reports suggest that St. Mirren's footballers played in just eight games all season.

St. Mirren were destined to move again at the end of 1878-79, and it must be assumed that the Abingdon Park lease was

Origins of the Club Crest... 3

Paisley Burgh Coat of Arms granted by the Lord Lyon King of Arms, 1912.

for just twelve months. If that is the case, Saints certainly didn't get their money's worth! A newspaper report of Saints match against Regent FC of Glasgow on 21 September confirms that "this match was played at Abingdon Park", but this was one of only four matches which appears to have been played by Saints on their second ground, and it is little wonder that doubts have persisted over the years about this ground's very existence!

The late start due to cricket commitments meant Saints had barely got into their stride before the press began to make mention of local ponds being "all iced over" on 15 December 1878. It was the beginning of a long freeze, and the first match report after the thaw is dated 15 February 1879, when they travelled to play old friends Ailsa, who by this time were playing out of Buckingham Park in Govan. The far-from-match-fit Saints lost 3-2, but it was noted that "best for the St. Mirren were Fisher (back), Duncan (half-back) and Grant and Hawthorn also showed well".

In their second season St. Mirren were still playing at a very basic level of football, and this is indicated by the report of their away match to Kilbarchan on 23 November 1878: "the above match was played on Saturday and, after an hour's play, resulted in a victory for the St. Mirren by two goals to nothing". Matches failing to last the full ninety minutes seems to be an acceptable part of the late 1870s scene, but if this particular report is accurate the visitors certainly dominated the game's sixty minutes: "the St. Mirren, playing with ten men, kept the ball throughout the whole game within twenty yards of the Kilbarchan's goal". With such territorial dominance, even with just ten men, the surprise must be that Saints only scored two!

In 1878-79 there was mention in the press for the first time of a St. Mirren 2nd Eleven, but otherwise there is scant evidence of the non-stop growth which the Club would demonstrate in the subsequent thirty years. That growth was set to begin during the 1879 close season, when St. Mirren moved to their third ground on the eve of their third year as a football club.

1879-80

Thistle Park, Greenhill was Saints new home, and they would remain there for four years. Around this time there was a Paisley Thistle Cricket Club who played out of Greenhill, and it is likely that Saints' new football pitch was part of the same "field".

Origins of the Club Crest... 4

The St. Mirren Crest dropping the Abbot used from the 1950s onwards.

There are no maps which show where Thistle Park was, but it was later described as being "within a few minutes walk" of their fourth ground Westmarch, the location of which is shown on page 23, and it is likely that Thistle Park was situated just to the south of Westmarch.

On 6 September 1879, John Elder FC from Govan became the first visitors to what the 'Paisley Herald' described as "the fine new ground of St. Mirren". The report continued that "after a very pleasant and well-contested game it resulted in a win for the strangers by two goals to nothing". The opening game was one of eleven defeats sustained by Saints in a twenty-three match season in which they earned eight victories and four draws. At the end of season 1879-80, St. Mirren would also declare to the SFA that they had "obtained" fifty-nine goals and "lost" forty-nine.

Three of these reverses were significant because they indicated that standards still needed to be raised if the Club was to have any hope of competing at a higher level. A week after the opening game at the new ground they travelled to Alexandria, where Vale of Leven's Second Eleven reminded St. Mirren of their cricketing heritage and hit them for six. Six weeks later on 25 October the return fixture took place at Greenhill, and this time the Dunbartonshire club's reserve side won 8-1.

It was by far the worst result of the season, but it seemed to do little damage to Saints' confidence because two weeks later they won

Origins of the Club Crest... 5

1970s version – Following a competition, a player was depicted. Although used in the match programme, this crest was never used on the playing kit.

5-1 against first-season conquerors Ailsa, by then in their last-ever season. Quality opposition returned to Greenhill on 15 November in the shape of the great Queen's Park, and although the fixture was against the Spiders' third team, the Hampden XI, the Glasgow visitors were still strong enough to concede none and score three.

It would be another ten years before Paisley was considered a major football centre, but in 1879 it wasn't even considered the focal point of the game in Renfrewshire, as the 'Paisley and Renfrewshire Gazette' pointed out on 22 November 1879: "football is becoming very popular in the Upper Ward of the County, especially is this the case in the vicinity of Johnstone where at a contest between 2nd Johnstone and the 1st Johnstone Rovers no less than 2,000 spectators were present".

That same day, Johnstone FC, formed a year after St. Mirren and themselves destined to become a Scottish League club, were beaten 2-1 by Saints at Thistle Park, and three other teams from Paisley - namely Victoria, Rangers, and Paisley - also put teams on the park that afternoon. It was this local competition, particularly between Saints and Abercorn, which would soon lead to increased publicity and bigger crowds for the game in Paisley.

On 17 January 1880, after inclement weather had interrupted Saints' fixture list, the 'Gazette' reported that "notwithstanding the hard nature of the ground on Saturday, the matches played were numerous and the play keen on all sides". Saints' opponents that day were the Good Templars Harmonic in a match played at Onslow Park, Dennistoun, and it was reported

Origins of the Club Crest... 6

1980s roundel version.
The Lord Lyon objected to the use of the old burgh crest "crown" device and instructed the club to drop it.

that "a hard and well-contested game resulted in a draw". Meanwhile, at Thistle Park, Saints' second team found some disharmony in the Harmonic rearguard, which was breached five times without reply.

Two weeks after the Harmonic match, and after an existence of less than three years by both clubs, a match took place which would nowadays be called "the big one". St. Mirren were at home to Abercorn, and the 'Gazette' reporter did it justice: "These clubs met on Saturday. The occasion had been looked forward to with great interest in local football circles and the turn-out at Thistle Park, the St. Mirren Grounds, was the largest which has yet favoured the game in the town". The 'Gazette' continued, "The game resulted in the favour of the Abercorn by four goals to two. These two clubs are pretty equally matched. On a former occasion this season, they met when the game was drawn - two goals being scored by each club."

Another aspect of the sport's increasing popularity, the advent of the travelling supporter, was mentioned in the 'Gazette' of 21 February 1880 in their report of Saints' match with Johnstone Athletic: "A match between these clubs came off on Saturday last at Mossbank Park, Johnstone before a good number of spectators, a few of whom were from Paisley".

The report of Saints' match at Mossbank against Johnstone Athletic is very typical of the style and vocabulary adopted at the time: "The ball was kicked off by the St. Mirren captain against a strong breeze and was well retained by the home back and carried over the strangers' (Saints) lines. Some stiff encounters took place, both strongholds being repeatedly endangered, especially that of the strangers; but all attempts proved futile up to the call of half-time.

"On ends being changed, the Paisley players soon assumed the offensive and, by a kick splendidly placed by Wilson, Davis sent the ball flying between the posts. On the ball being centred, the St. Mirren forwards were again on the alert, their right wing having a good run, and Anderson by a pretty piece of play right in front of the goal, kicked the leather under the bow.

Origins of the Club Crest... 7

Final amended version designed by Jack Paterson in 1996.
The aim was to keep as close to the original as possible, using the five vertical stripes to mimic the crown device.
Although simple in appearance, this was the 6th version submitted, and was finally accepted by the Lord Lyon.
It now appears on all kit and printed matter.

"The ball being again sent away, some play of a give and take nature occurred in midfield. The St. Mirren forwards again broke away and added another goal (number three) by a long shot from the feet of Goold. The play now became very fast all round, both sides showing some good play.

"A corner kick now fell to the Paisley men which was nicely placed by Muir. The ball was sent in by Anderson but it struck the cross-bar and rebounded back into play and was smartly pounced on by Muir and sent into the desired haven.

"On the leather once more being set a rolling the Johnstone team invaded the St. Mirren territory by some good forward play and the scene of the action was now in front of the strangers' fortress, where shot after shot was sent in by the busy feet of the home team, all of which was parried by Burgess, the St. Mirren goalkeeper. At last one took effect which he failed to stop; this after a hard struggle, the Athletics got their first and only goal, having worked very hard to get it.

"On the resumption of play time was soon called, with the ball in neutral ground. The St. Mirren were thus left the victors by four goals to one"

Four goals to one is a good result by any standard, but St. Mirren still lacked status in the eyes of some, and the vast majority of the twenty-three games played in 1879-80 were against the lesser lights of the locality's football clubs. The positive response St. Mirren had received from both Queen's Park and Vale of Leven had been a step in the right direction but Saints had yet to play in the Renfrewshire Cup let alone the national competition. The aim of the enthusiastic St. Mirren members at the beginning of the 1880s was to play regularly against the better teams in their own county. By the beginning of the 1890s, St. Mirren Football Club would be playing against the best teams in the whole country.

The 1880s - A Period of Progress

1880-81

It was obvious from the start that the men behind St. Mirren were ambitious to provide Paisley with a club to be proud of, and the founding fathers could be content with their progress in three short years. However, it had been clear for some time that the only way Saints were going to improve the standard of their play was by competing more frequently against Scotland's top teams, and with that in mind they made their debut in the Scottish and Renfrewshire Cups during 1880-81.

CHAPTER TWO
The 1880's

In truth they couldn't have made an earlier first appearance in either competition, because the normally well-organised St. Mirren FC, with committees for every facet of the Club, inexplicably failed to apply to join the SFA until their fourth year of existence! By then the Club had 100 members, and their first registered colours were "scarlet and blue one inch stripe jerseys and hose (stockings) and white knickers".

St. Mirren's long and successful connection with the Scottish Cup began on 4 September 1880 with a 3-0 victory over Johnstone Athletic at Thistle Park. They enjoyed a second home draw against the 17th Renfrewshire Rifle Volunteers, who, as their name might suggest, put up considerable resistance before going down 3-2.

Ultimately, what counted most was not Saints' luck but their opponents' experience, and the 3,000 crowd saw Arthurlie take a 2-0 half-time lead. Saints did hit back through the prolific Goold, but Arthurlie got a third to win the competition for Barrhead. The losing Saints team that day - the club's first-ever finalists - were J. Burgess, J. Fisher, Allison, Johnny Paterson, Arrol, A. Muir, David Drinnan, Davis, Wallace, Gorman, and Goold.

It was just four years after the original six "cricketers" had played in St. Mirren's first-ever match, but such was the rate of change that only Fisher and Paterson still survived.

At the beginning of the 1880s the Renfrewshire Cup attracted an

Paisley Skyline circa 1887, ten years after the Club was founded. A town of industry, weaving mills and... St. Mirren.

The desire of St. Mirren to be exposed to football of a higher calibre was fulfilled in the next three rounds of the Scottish Cup as they were drawn against a trio of teams - Abercorn, Cowlairs, and Dumbarton - who ten years later would, like the Buddies, be Scottish Football League founder clubs.

Saints eventually went out of the national competition, convincingly beaten 5-1 by leading club Dumbarton, but they departed from the tournament with the consolation of a good debut cup run and the civic satisfaction that they had inflicted a comprehensive 4-1 away win over Abercorn, their closest rivals.

Saints had an even better cup run in the Renfrewshire competition and reached their first-ever final in only their fourth year of existence. En route to the county cup final they beat Glenkilloch 5-0 in the first round, and were given a bye in the second. Perhaps it was just as well, because they then took part in a four-match marathon against Barrhead, in which a third game 2-1 defeat was successfully protested following two draws. The fourth game was lost 3-2, but for reasons now unclear Saints still proceeded to the semi-final, where they met and defeated Shawlands Athletic 2-0.

If reaching a cup final despite losing twice en route can be considered fortunate, the choice of St. Mirren's Thistle Park as venue looked to be another advantage for the Saints' cause. There was just one exception to all this apparent good fortune when influential half-back Bob Whyte sustained a fractured leg at work and missed the final.

entry of at least twenty clubs, a reasonable reflection of the extent of St. Mirren's county opposition. These neighbouring clubs provided the majority of the twenty matches played during 1880-81 and Saints' record of played 22, won 9, lost 9, and drawn 4, with 44 goals scored and 47 conceded indicates they were, at best, county class in 1881. The strides that St. Mirren would make during the 1880s can be measured by the large scores they began to run up against local rivals, and within ten short years St. Mirren and Abercorn would be a class apart from the rest.

1881-82

By the beginning of 1881-82 season, St. Mirren had a declared membership of 230 and their blue and red colours remained unchanged. In the 1881-82 Scottish Cup a 5-1 home victory over Johnstone Rovers in the first round on 3 September augured well for a run to emulate their debut cup season, but Paisley Athletic put an early October end to such aspirations with a 3-1 win.

Saints fared little better in the county cup. A 5-3 home win over the same Paisley Athletic was some consolation for the Scottish Cup result, then a 5-1 Thistle Park defeat of Pollok led to an away tie against Johnstone at Cartbank Park. Saints were beaten 3-0 in apparently clear-cut fashion, but a successful protest led to a second game, watched by 3,000. Johnstone again prevailed, this time by 4-2.

Saints' fifth season, like the preceeding four, would have finished trophy-less but for the intervention of Mr. T. C. Barlow, a London-based pyrotechnic artist. Mr. Barlow provided an impressive silver cup for the winners of a challenge match which was played on Guy Fawkes Night at Thistle Park, and 5th November is the easy-to-remember date when Saints won their first-ever trophy.

Their opponents were the Glasgow-based Alexandra Athletic, who had been formed in 1873, and by 1881 were a prominent side with an attractive fixture card. Other clubs would soon eclipse them, and Saints' 5-1 Barlow Cup victory was early evidence of this.

The Barlow Cup match was just one of twenty-nine games played by Saints that season, and their record of 17 wins, 6 defeats, and 9 draws showed a considerable improvement on the previous season.

1882-83

In the 1882-83 edition of 'Watson's Directory for Paisley', the St. Mirren entry stretched to seventeen lines, an eye-catching way to eclipse their local rivals. By then Saints were also placing adverts in the local papers and sports journals advertising each forthcoming "Grand Football Match", but on 14 April 1883 the Club came up with a more obvious way to be noticed by Paisley people; they won the Renfrewshire Cup.

It was St. Mirren's second county cup final appearance in three attempts, but their final opponents again had the edge where experience was concerned. This was Thornliebank's third final, and they had already won the trophy twice in its four year existence. What Thornliebank couldn't match was St. Mirren's support, as crowds of never less than 3,000 had watched Saints progress through the competition. In the first round, Cartvale from Busby were beaten 5-1 at Thistle Park, local rivals Paisley Athletic were defeated 3-0 away from home, and Greenock Southern succumbed in an 8-0 Thistle Park mauling.

As the season unfolded there was general agreement within the Club that real progress was being made, and the only major concern was that by the end of the season the Club might need to find a new ground if the lease for Thistle Park could not be renewed.

In the county cup semi-final, also at the St. Mirren ground, Johnstone Rovers fared little better, as they conceded five goals without reply, and on 14 April 1883 Saints headed to East Park in Paisley in assured mood. Their confidence proved to be well founded, as Thornliebank were defeated 3-1. To the delight of the majority in the 6,000 crowd, a trophy was bedecked in St. Mirren's scarlet and blue colours for the first time. The club's first medal winners were G. Drinnan, D. Marshall, D. McPhee, Johnny Paterson, James Kerr, Andrew Wallace, George Watt, Robert Fairlie, James Imrie, Tom Johnstone, and Aird.

Back on 9 September, there was more high scoring by Saints in the first round of the Scottish Cup as Yoker were soundly beaten 8-0 at Thistle Park. The second round sent Saints to Cappielow, where the tie produced a further six more goals. Unfortunately, five of these were credited to Morton, who were beaten in the next round by Johnstone.

It wasn't just in cup ties that goals were plentiful. In between the Morton cup-tie and the Renfrewshire Cup success there was a full fixture card of pre-League era challenge matches, and Saints managed to score 102 goals whilst conceding 80, an average of six goals per match in the thirty-two game season.

1883-84

By August 1883, Thistle Park in Greenhill - as a home ground at least - became part of St. Mirren's history, as Olympic took over the Thistle Park lease and St. Mirren set up new headquarters just slightly further north at Westmarch in a spacious ground "bounded by an orchard on the west side" which would later afford Saints the opportunity to run prestigious athletic meetings and bicycle races.

Confusingly, the 1883-84 registered details with the SFA do not mention Westmarch, and the St. Mirren ground was still described as "Thistle Park, Greenhill Road, Paisley, half a mile from railway station and St. James Park, five minutes from St. James Station". It must be assumed that SFA Handbook print deadlines and prolonged lease discussions about Thistle Park combined to produce this misleading information.

It is unlikely that visiting teams would have got lost as a result of this erroneous entry. Thistle Park and Westmarch weren't that far apart, and although the location of the Westmarch ground is traditionally given as "the junction of what is now Clark Street and McKean Street", we know that St. Mirren described the new ground as being "off Greenhill Road Paisley, about one mile from Gilmour Street Station and two minutes from St. James Station". We also know that in 1890 "a barricade with gate was to be erected along Greenhill Road", which indicates that the ground may have been a bit further west than had previously been assumed.

What is clear from the 1883-84 SFA Handbook is that black and white formed part of Saints colours for the first time, and these are intimated as "black and white jersey, three-quarter inch stripes, white knickers and hose one inch stripe blue and red".

Despite the confusion of the SFA entry, Queen's Park found the new ground without any reported difficulty, and St. Mirren could not have wished for more auspicious visitors than the Spiders for the inaugural Westmarch match on 25 August 1883. A 2-1 home win set the seal on a great day for Saints, and was achieved against a club who, later that season, would score no less than forty-three goals in their six-match journey to the English Cup Final.

The Scottish Cup dominated the early part of the season, with a convincing 6-0 home win over Caledonian being followed up three weeks later on 29 September with a 7-0 away win to Woodland. Saints' third round opponents were better known and much more formidable. Arthurlie in the pre-League mid-1880s enjoyed their peak period as a senior club, and they certainly spoiled an otherwise excellent season for Saints when they won 3-1 at Barrhead.

Renfrewshire Cup Medal awarded to R. Gilmour 1883-84.

Saints recovered from this disappointment, and such was the improving quality of their fixture list with opponents such as Cambuslang and St. Bernards that they were regularly attracting crowds of 2,000 to 2,500 to their new Westmarch ground. When the visitors were as famous as the 3rd LRV (Third Lanark) the crowds rose to 3,000.

Such gates weren't just restricted to St. Mirren, and the influential 'Scottish Athletic Journal' of 4 January 1884 noted that "the advance of the game in Renfrewshire has been remarkable".

Local rivalry was a key to that advance, and in January the 'Journal' noted that although St. Mirren v Clyde at Westmarch was expected to be an attractive game, more interest would be centred on the meeting the same day of the Second XIs of St. Mirren and Abercorn, "the two principal Paisley clubs", in the fourth round of the Second Eleven Cup competition.

Underlining the equality of St. Mirren and Abercorn at this time, it was reported that "two big events came off at Paisley on Saturday. At Blackstoun Park the Abercorn and the Arthurlie met in the third round of the Renfrewshire ties and also St. Mirren and Cartvale met at Westmarch. At both grounds attendances were about equal, each match being witnessed by about three thousand spectators".

Swelled by a healthy contingent from Port Glasgow, this was only half the number who had turned up at Westmarch to see Saints defeat Port Glasgow Athletic in the first round of the Renfrewshire Cup by three goals to nil. That proved to be seven fewer goals than the unfortunate Glenpatrick conceded in round two.

The Cartvale county cup match on 4 January was the first of three third round matches between the sides, and it finished at 2-2. Interest in the result was high, and a large crowd of people assembled opposite the Globe Hotel in the High Street anxiously awaiting word from Busby.

A 3-3 draw at Westmarch followed before Saints triumphed 3-1 to move into the semi-final. This meant a return to Thistle Park to meet

Olympic, a Paisley team made up exclusively of teachers. The 6-1 scoreline in Saints' favour suggests that on this occasion at least it was the teachers who were given a lesson.

Waiting for Saints in the final for the second successive year was Thornliebank, and the appeal of the repeat confrontation was underlined when 8,000 spectators turned out at Abercorn's Blackstoun Park. Thornliebank provided much more determined opposition than they had in 1883, and the game ended at 1-1.

This determination produced a much more physical encounter than twelve months previous, and this continued in the second match. 2-2 after extra time was the score in the second and third games, which were also played at Blackstoun. The fourth game moved to Rangers' Kinning Park ground, and, as can so often happen after such a hard-fought series, one team won emphatically. In this case the emphasis was 7-1 for Saints.

The Renfrewshire Cup had been won and now it had been retained. 30,000 people had watched the four-part final, and the Saints team selection showed only one change, apart from at half-back where Hutchison replaced Bob Whyte in the third and fourth games after the latter suffered a broken leg in the second game. Contemporary match reports suggest he had enjoyed an outstanding season, and although he had previously broken his leg in 1881, sadly this time he never played again.

The season had thrown up some brighter news on the player front as the Club's second team began to produce players who could make the transition to first team football. Notable amongst these were Robert Fairlie and Andy Brown, who would later win two caps for Scotland.

Bob Whyte was not alone in severing his active connection with St. Mirren. Match Secretary Walter Craig, who had performed the task since 1880, had also been the Club's representative on the SFA committee, and in 1884 he resigned from both posts owing to ill-health. Right from the start St. Mirren had been fortunate to have men of real quality behind the scenes, and the 'Scottish Athletic Journal' was in no doubt about Walter Craig's credentials: "No more popular or gentlemanly representative sits on the (SFA) committee or one who understands the game better. He is an enthusiast about football and indeed all kinds of indoor and outdoor games have his support".

How could Saints fail to prosper with such people at the helm?

1884 -85

No team is guaranteed success, but after three seasons of trophy-winning, 1884-85 proved to be something of a disappointment.

The usual September start to the Scottish Cup produced a 4-3 win at Westmarch, but this was the era of protests which were many, varied and imaginative, and a Neilston appeal not only produced a replay but the match was moved "up the hill" to Neilston. This time there was no dispute, and the match ended in a 4-1 win for St. Mirren. Nor was there any argument when Johnstone came to Westmarch on second round business and were beaten 3-0. The same could not be said of Renfrew, who in just one cup round over sixteen days managed to play St. Mirren three times at Westmarch, courtesy of two protests, and lose each game.

The sequence started on 25 October with a 1-0 win for Saints, and ended on 11 November with a 6-3 win. In between, Saints also inflicted a 3-0 defeat. They had by then played and won six cup ties, and had only completed three rounds! After five ties at Westmarch and a visit to Neilston, Renton's Tontine Park beckoned on 15 November, just four days after the last of the Renfrew matches had finished. Renton won 2-1, and for some with a St. Mirren allegiance there was disappointment after putting in so much effort for such little advancement. For others, such a result represented progress. Renton were one of Scotland's top sides; they would win the Cup that year, and a 2-1 away defeat to them was no disgrace. Saints had shown they could compete with the best.

As interest in one cup disappeared, Saints' defence of their county cup-winners title began, and they got off to the usual comfortable start as Johnstone Rovers were beaten 6-1 away from home. Then a 4-3 win over Greenock Northern took Saints through to the third round, where they met Morton in front of 4,500 at Westmarch. Suffice to say, Morton won 4-3, but they returned to Westmarch on 21 March to face the then more successful and all-amateur Port Glasgow Athletic. It was to be no happy return for Morton, as the team from "the Port" won 2-1 in front of over 7,000 spectators. It would be 1893 before the Cappielow club would finally win the Renfrewshire Cup.

1885-86

Arthurlie were to feature prominently during 1885/86, and clashes between the two clubs were becoming increasingly intense. In a second round Renfrewshire Cup tie which Saints won 3-1 at Barrhead, the Paisley players endured considerable physical intimidation by a crowd of home supporters who were apparently incensed by an incident in which it appeared one of the Barrhead team had been struck by a St. Mirren player. The Renfrewshire FA ordered the match to be replayed in Johnstone where Saints won 4-3.

The county cup proved to be a controversial competition that year. In the third round Saints met Port Glasgow Athletic and lost the match 4-2 in front of 2,000 spectators. St. Mirren immediately lodged an appeal on the very reasonable grounds that the referee had failed to appear. Saints' protest was upheld. The replay crowd doubled to 4,000, but they fared no better, going down 4-1 to Athletic.

Saints reached the final tie of the four-team invitation Charity Cup, where it was reported that Saints and Arthurlie, "before a large crowd", fought out a vigorously contested first half in which the Barrhead team took the lead with two goals which lacked a certain subtlety. For the first, Saints 'keeper Cameron was bundled over the line, and in what was described as a "scrimmaged goal", Arthurlie made it 2-0. St. Mirren scored near the end of the match, but could not prevent Arthurlie again prevailing in cup football that season.

The Arthurlie result typified what had been a frustrating season. The first team had won just thirteen of thirty-four matches played, and for the second successive season no cups had been captured. The early exit from the Scottish Cup - a 2-0 away defeat at the hands of Abercorn in the First Round - was particularly painful.

"Frustrating" was an inadequate description of the season as far as long-serving Match Secretary John Orr was concerned, and at the 1886 AGM he did not pull his punches. It had been "the worst season we ever had", and Mr. Orr attributed it partly to "the want of enthusiasm and the players not agreeing amongst themselves". No doubt thinking of two other defeats inflicted on St. Mirren by a more competitive Abercorn

Winners of Renfrewshire Challenge Cup 1882-1883
W. Craig (Secretary), D. Marshall, J. Kerr, J. Paterson, G. Drennan, J. Davies (Umpire),
J. Imrie, T. Johnstone, G. Watt, A. Brown,
D. Macfee, A. Wallace, R. Fairlie.

that season, he expressed the hope that St. Mirren would not lose "the high position they had gained in the three preceding years" and looked forward to everyone pulling together to enable the Club to regain "their former position".

With an eye to the continuing development of the Club, Mr. Orr also remarked that "the want of a third eleven was a great drawback as all clubs generally got the best players for their first team out of their 3rd Eleven". He added, "as an instance in our history", that the first year the Club won the Renfrewshire Cup the team was "remodelled almost wholly from the 3rd Eleven".

It's a confident football club which can talk about history after just nine years of existence, and that assurance extended to the Club's financial position.

The ground was being used for various sports where possible, but some were less profitable than others. Income from a Spring Bike Race had been £54.11s.11d, but the profit had not exceeded £7. Overall, St. Mirren's income during the twelve months to May 1886 had been £334. 0s. 3 1/2d, with expenditure totalling £338. 0s. 10d. The Club, which was still amateur at this time, owed £420. 10s. 10 1/2d, but St. Mirren were still growing and no-one expressed undue concern.

Cup was impressive by any standards, but it was not enough to inhibit Pollokshaws, who came to Westmarch in the second round and won 5-3.

One of the nineteen victories that season took place in January 1887, when Saints went down to the "Five Towns" of Stoke to play Burslem Port Vale and won 5-1. Vale's official history 'The Valiant Years' confirms the impressive scoreline for the visitors, but rather spoils it by referring to "Scottish side St. Merrin's", a new variation of old Mirin's name!

During the 1887-88 season, St. Mirren decided to return to their roots. On 7 March 1887, a deputation was received from Gleniffer Cricket Club requesting use of the Westmarch ground for cricket. Two weeks later a meeting held in the Club House agreed "that we take steps to the formation of a cricket club". The proposal extended to taking over, "at a valuation", the cricketing material of the Gleniffer C.C., and that it be handed over to the St. Mirren Cricket Club, whose members must belong to the parent St. Mirren Football Club.

Nearer home, the local battle for supremacy with Abercorn was again not going Saints' way in 1886-87 as "the Abbies" won all three encounters - including a decisive 7-2 victory - but Saints' triumph in the final of the Paisley Charity Cup for the first time gave everyone at the Club a boost

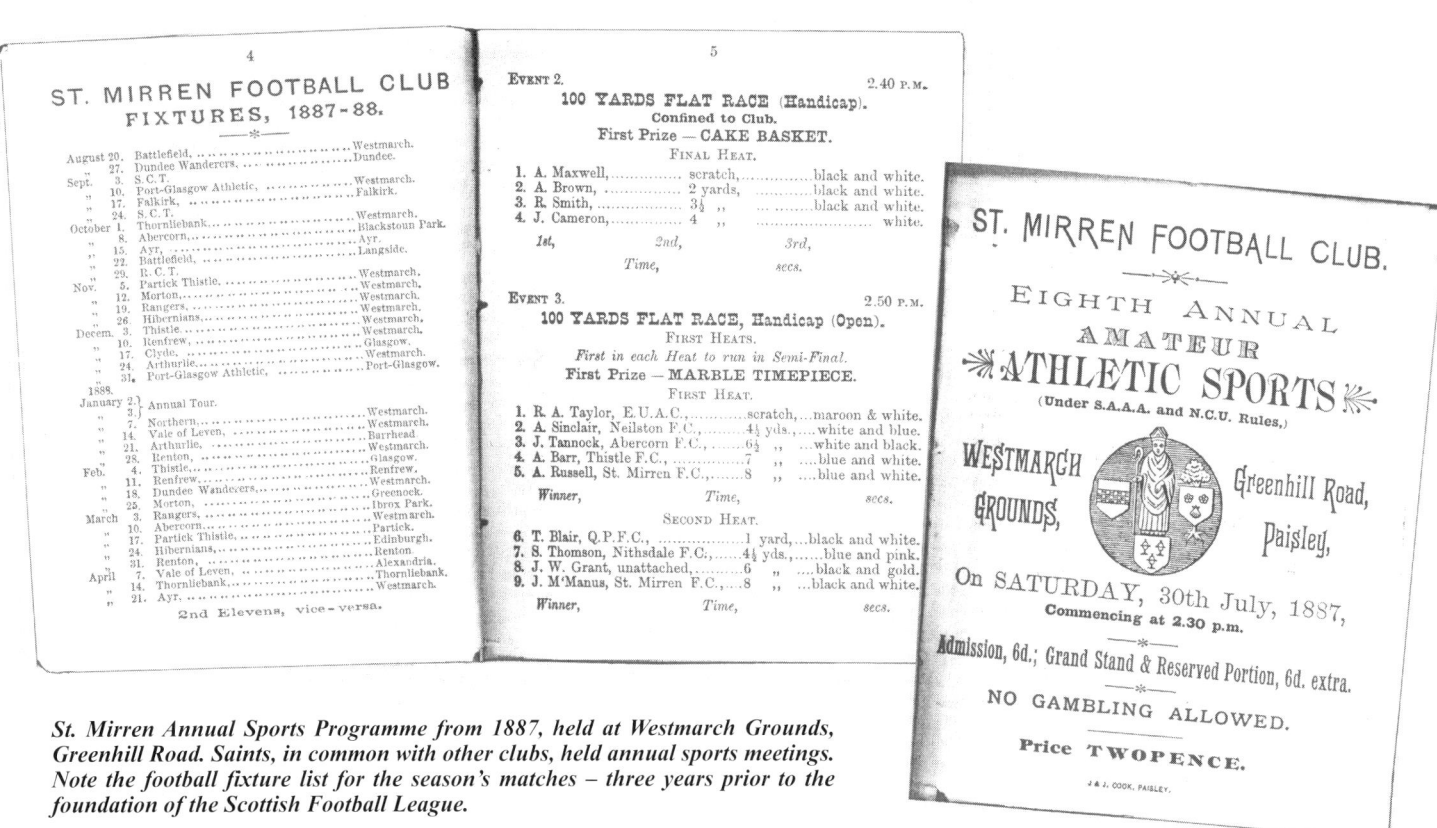

St. Mirren Annual Sports Programme from 1887, held at Westmarch Grounds, Greenhill Road. Saints, in common with other clubs, held annual sports meetings. Note the football fixture list for the season's matches – three years prior to the foundation of the Scottish Football League.

1886-87

Amongst the names of new members hidden away in the minutes of a committee meeting held on 6 September 1886 was a modest mention of a sixteen year old called James Dunlop. No one that night could have envisaged that, in just over three years time, the same James "Daddy" Dunlop would share with Andy Brown the distinction of becoming St. Mirren's first full internationalists for Scotland, and tragically, by January 1892 he would die from an accident incurred while playing for Saints.

Representation at Scotland level was certainly not on the agenda when Saints started their 1886 Scottish Cup campaign. In the first round they won 5-3 against Arthurlie on 18 September at Westmarch, and the margin could have been greater but for two late goals by the Barrhead side. Incredibly, this match was the first of seven consecutive seasons in which Saints and Arthurlie were drawn together in the Scottish Cup. Two weeks later the highly respected Port Glasgow Athletic were the second round visitors, and they lived up to their reputation when they departed from Westmarch as 3-2 victors.

A 9-0 away win over Dykebar in the first round of the Renfrewshire

as Thornliebank were beaten 5-1 on 28 May. The victorious team were Cameron, Maxwell, McHardie, Hutchison, Cheyne, Graham, Harper, Fairlie, Morton, Bain, and Brown, with Alex Fairlie and a Saints' player called Morton each scoring two goals.

It was decided that medals would be awarded to the eleven players who featured in the final, and in the absence of a secure trophy cabinet the Charity Cup would circulate amongst committee members and club patrons.

In June 1887, moves were begun to increase subscriptions, with the addition to the fees being used to pay for a boiler built at the back of the Club House to enable the players to have hot baths instead of going to the public baths. Player patience was required, because it was not until November 1888 when a Mr. Boyd offered to provide a boiler that it was agreed to have it built "as quickly as possible".

Also in June 1887, the Club agreed to get bandages, plasters, and ointment to be kept in the Club House in case of emergency. Things were looking up!

1887-88

During Season 1887-88, Saints played 38 matches, of which twenty-four were won, only five were lost, and in the process they scored 122 goals. It's an impressive record by any standard, and yet the season is mainly remembered for just four games, the quartet of Scottish Cup ties at four different grounds which it took to separate Saints and Hearts in the competition's fourth round.

The nine-match cup campaign began with two local ties - an away match on 3 September at Thornliebank which was narrowly won 1-0, followed by an equally daunting visit to Dunterlie Park in Barrhead on 24 September where Arthurlie and Saints drew 3-3. In the replay at Westmarch, Saints triumphed 4-1. The third round draw gave Saints a third away tie, but they came away from Hurlford's Corsehill Park with a comfortable enough 4-2 win.

Heart of Midlothian were Saints' famous and formidable fourth round opponents. A 1-1 draw at Tynecastle began the sequence and was followed by a 2-2 draw at Westmarch. Falkirk was the neutral location for the second replay, but the two sides produced another 2-2 draw, a scoreline which hides the fact that Saints were two goals down and fought back through goals from Tom Johnstone and Alex Fairlie. It was only when the scene moved to Cathkin in Glasgow for the third replay that Saints finally went through by 4-2 on 26 November.

The elimination of Hearts encouraged optimistic claims in some quarters that Saints were now favourites to lift the trophy, but the standard of opposition was not going to get any easier as Saints progressed through the rounds. Just a week after finally disposing of Hearts, Renton were fifth round visitors to Westmarch with a side containing some of the best footballers of the day. They narrowly won 3-2.

Saints' achievement in beating Hearts and running Renton so close was a measure of what the Club was capable of. It had shown Paisley people that they had a team that could compete with the best, and much of the credit for that went to the methods of Saints' trainer and groundsman, Bob Hindle.

Although a League set-up was still over two years away, there was an income guarantee system in operation, and in December 1887 it was revealed that the guarantee for the First Eleven's New Year matches away to Dundee Harp, Forfar Athletics, and Fair City Athletics (Perth) was £22.10s.0d. Fortunately, in a festive financial balancing act which would have pleased all but a treasurer with Micawber-like tendencies, the cost of the trip was precisely £22.10s.0d.

During December and January, the Club had a series of meetings with the landlord regarding the lease of the Westmarch field. The upshot was that a new four year lease at £50 per annum was agreed. This was good news for St. Mirren. Westmarch had good facilities, and the Club were keen to upgrade them to ensure maximum use was made of the ground.

The question of an inadequate water supply was addressed at this time, and on 10 February it was proposed that the Club should have a forty-yard square cricket pitch costing no more than £20, with the Cricket Club being asked to contribute to this cost. The condition of the running track was a major factor in attracting more sports, and on 5 March 1888 it was intimated that a pony plus harness had been bought to assist in the rolling of the track.

Saints' successful Scottish Cup exertions deserved to be recompensed, and that reward came in the shape of the Renfrewshire Cup. They were given a welcome bye in the Second Round, having beaten Johnstone Harp at home by 5-0, and in the third round 4,000 at Westmarch saw Saints defeat Morton by 2-0. A crowd of 5,500 assembled for the semi-final at Dunterlie to see an Arthurlie team comprehensively beaten 4-0.

Saints' fellow finalists were none other than Abercorn. It represented a chance to win back some local pride and it was an opportunity partially taken on 24 March 1888 at Cappielow, when 5,000 saw Saints manage a 2-2 draw, a good result compared to some against Abercorn in the previous couple of years. The replay was also in Greenock, and this time the attendance had grown to 6,000. Saints' confidence also grew after an Abercorn lead was nullified and the final outcome of 4-1 was achieved by the following side: Cameron, T. Brandon, Maxwell, McHardy, McBain, Patterson, R. Brandon, J. Brandon, Dairlie, Brown, and Johnstone.

1888-89

The record books show that St. Mirren were out of the 1888-89 Scottish Cup before 1888 was finished, but that only tells part of the story. They also reached the tournament's quarter-final stage for the first time, and took leading team Dumbarton, who two years later would share Scotland's first-ever League title, to three games.

The cup campaign commenced for the second time in four years with a trip to Neilston, and this time Saints came away with a 4-3 victory. It proved to be the most difficult of the early ties, and each of the next three rounds, scheduled at three week intervals, were also played away, but these games proved to be something of a procession with nineteen goals scored and only two conceded.

The goal blitz began on 22 September at Saints' former home Thistle Park, where Dykebar were beaten 6-1. Another away draw took Saints to Arthurlie's Dunterlie Park, but the 7-0 win for Saints highlighted that the Barrhead club were beginning to fall behind the standard of the best, and this would ultimately lead to them missing out on attaining League status in 1890.

On 3 November, Saints were on their travels again as they headed over the Ayrshire border to meet Kilbirnie. Another 6-1 victory ensued. The results in the first four rounds had not only been pleasing, but had again underlined that Saints were pulling away from most of their local competitors and were being increasingly judged by how they performed against Scotland's leading clubs.

In the fifth round the Westmarch team finally got a home tie when Queen of the South Wanderers were beaten 3-1, and then Saints drew Dumbarton: exactly the calibre of club to test St. Mirren's progress.

On 15 December 1888, Saints came back from Boghead Park with a 2-2 draw, and seven days later that score was repeated at Westmarch. The second replay took place on 29 December at Ibrox Park, but this time Dumbarton prevailed by three goals to one.

Tom Brandon, one of the first St. Mirren players transferred to an English Club.

Eight years earlier Saints had been convincingly beaten 5-1 by "the Sons" in the Cup. The evidence was compelling; the gap between St. Mirren and Scotland's top teams was closing.

If the national cup had shown that an elite was quickly developing in late 1880s Scottish football, the Renfrewshire Cup merely confirmed it. Records show that a first round match against Kilbarchan ended at 1-0 for St. Mirren, but they also indicate that the match was stopped. When the full ninety minutes took place the score was 11-0.

In the second round Saints' opponents were Clippens Thistle, who had beaten Mearns 12-0 in the first round. Saints put up a somewhat better show than Mearns and beat Clippens 14-1, prompting the thought that a Mearns v St. Mirren tie might well have eclipsed the famous 1885 Arbroath-Bon Accord result!

The wide disparity in the competing teams' abilities was doing nothing for the reputation of the county cup, and the competition was now only beginning to take on any significance in the latter stages. In the semi-final Saints and Morton drew 3-3 in front of 4,000, but Paisley triumphed over Greenock in the replay as 5,000 watched Saints win 3-1.

The 1889 final was a repeat of the final twelve months earlier. Cappielow was again the venue, Saints and Abercorn were the repeat participants. Only the poor weather was different, and this kept the crowd down to just 2,500. Tom Johnstone and Andy Brown scored in the first half to give Saints a 2-1 lead, but "the Abbies" came back in the second half to clinch a 3-2 win and make up for Saints' win the previous season.

If clubs like Dykebar and even Arthurlie were beginning to find their own level in the game, it would take the establishment of League football in Scotland to assess the role to be allocated to St. Mirren. That was two years off, but other influences were already coming into play.

Professionalism had been legalised in English football in 1885, but football in that country remained chaotic, with games often cancelled at the last minute. The introduction of League football in England in 1888 changed all that. Arranged football matches became "fixtures" in the true sense of the word, and as a result the leading English professional clubs quickly prospered, often leaning heavily on the main contemporary source of football talent - Scotland.

St. Mirren Football Club would not be alone in having to adjust to this new order, and within five years professionalism and other unique influences in Scotland would further clarify the extent of the challenge to be overcome.

They were given an early example. At the end of the 1888-89 season right-back Tom Brandon joined the growing Scottish contingent being assembled by Blackburn Rovers, with whom he was to win two F.A. Cup medals in his first two seasons. He had only joined St. Mirren on 6 June 1887 with his two brothers, and within two seasons he was gone.

Apart from a brief spell with the then non-league Sheffield Wednesday, Brandon remained with Blackburn until 1899, and his ten years at the top of English football was a first for Paisley's latest manufacturing industry - footballers.

Renfrewshire Challenge Cup, Won by St. Mirren F.C., 1887-88
Robert Hindle, Thomas Brandon, Robert Lang, John McManus, James Maxwell,
Robert Fairlie, John Paterson, James Cameron, Hugh McHardy, Alex McBain, John Harper,
James Brandon, Thomas Johnstone, Robert Brandon,
Edward McBain, Andrew Brown. With cup – Robert Allison.

1889-90

For the third year in a row St. Mirren reached the fifth round of the Scottish Cup, and as plans to instigate a Scottish league unfolded during this historic season, the timing of this successful sequence could not have been bettered. They were pulling away from the majority of their local rivals, and in three cup runs had shown themselves to be a match for Hearts, Dumbarton, and in 1889-90, the mighty Queen's Park.

In the first round, St. Mirren travelled to Barrhead on 7 September where they defeated Arthurlie by four goals to two. At three week intervals after that, Kilbarchan and Pollokshaws were beaten at Westmarch in rounds two and three respectively by 6-0 and 5-1 margins.

On 9 November 1889, Saints travelled to play a team called Lanemark from a hamlet just outside New Cumnock in the fourth round and won 8-2. So far their Scottish Cup run had been untroubled, but in the fifth round their name was drawn out of the hat with Queen's Park, record eight times winners of the trophy, and almost the full Scotland side. On 30 November Saints made their way to Hampden to face the famous amateurs - the first time the two clubs had met on Scottish Cup business. Saints lost 1-0, but the general consensus was that, at the very least, Saints' fine exhibition deserved another match with the Spiders, who went on to win the trophy for a ninth time that season.

In August 1889, it had been decided to erect a new pavilion at Westmarch, and by December it was ready. The 3rd LRV (Third Lanark) were asked to switch a fixture due to be played at Cathkin on 28 December to Westmarch, and thus become St. Mirren's honoured guests at the opening of the new facility. The switch of venue was agreed, and after the match both teams enjoyed a celebratory dinner at the Globe Hotel in Paisley.

The scores in the early rounds of the Renfrewshire Cup continued to reflect the varying degrees of development amongst the county's football clubs. Perhaps Clippens Thistle officials recognised that they were now out of their depth. Beaten 14-1 by Saints in 1888-89, the two teams were due to face each other in the first round of the 1889-90 tourney, but Clippens decided to scratch. It may have been a wise decision. In the second round St. Mirren travelled to Busby, conceded two but scored eleven.

In the third round a once-again competitive Arthurlie were narrowly beaten 3-2 in front of a 5,000 crowd. A thousand more were at Underwood Park to see Abercorn soundly beat Saints by six goals to one and remind Paisley football fans that there were two clubs worthy of support in the town. A narrow 5-4 win by Saints over "the Abbies" in the final of the Paisley Charity Cup that year was further evidence of just how well matched the two clubs were as League football beckoned.

The two Paisley teams may have been of an even standard at that time, but when Abercorn's Underwood Park was chosen by the SFA ahead of Saints' offer to use Westmarch as the venue for Scotland's full international against Wales on 19 March 1890, it was two St. Mirren players who added local interest to the prestigious match. Andy Brown lined up at right half, whilst the clever play of James Dunlop had earned him the inside left berth in a Scotland team which won 5-0. A week later Saints' left back Richard Hunter wore his country's dark blue against Ireland.

The 1880s had witnessed ten years rate of progress which remains unrivalled in St. Mirren's history. Three of their players had been selected by Scotland, they won the Renfrewshire Cup three times in ten attempts, and reached the quarter-finals of the Scottish Cup. They had proved they could compete with the best and the best had taken note.

On 21 February, Renton FC wrote asking St. Mirren to "join a League", and also asking the Club to call a meeting of Renfrewshire clubs. It was immediately proposed that "we join same and the Match Secretary write to Abercorn asking them to join". St. Mirren then received another letter from Renton FC on 13 March asking that the Club send two representatives to a meeting in a Glasgow hotel on 20 March to discuss the formation of a league.

Events were moving fast, and by 1 April the St. Mirren committee were considering and approving league rules which had been drawn by, amongst others, St. Mirren's Mr. Archibald Towns. Particular mention was made of Rule 15, which proposed "that two-thirds of the gate would be retained by the home club and one third would go to the away club with a guarantee of £10 if one third is under that amount". Saints sent two representatives to a further meeting with full powers to vote on this and other matters.

The League was inaugurated on 30 April 1890, and St. Mirren were one of just eleven founder member clubs. The great Queen's Park didn't want to join, neither did Clyde. Both quickly realised their mistake. Hibernian - Scottish Cup winners just three years earlier - weren't even invited, and neither were St. Bernards. St. Mirren were now part of an elite, a privileged group, and the 1890s would see them begin to leave behind their opponents of the early years. Only Abercorn would continue to accompany them in their bid for national prominence, but they too would fall away, to be replaced eventually by Morton as Saints' only county challengers.

As the new era edged nearer, the Club's Annual General Meeting acknowledged the achievements of the past, and in particular the outstanding contribution made by captain Johnny Paterson. His name had first been connected with St. Mirren back in their 1875 cricket days, and continued with St. Mirren Football Club from the first match in 1877. He was the only man at the Club to have played in the three Renfrewshire Cup-winning sides, and for his service and outstanding leadership qualities he was unanimously made a life member of the Club. He would be one of the last of the Club's great amateurs.

The 1890's - Leagues and Love Street

1890-91

A St. Mirren FC minute of June 1890 notes that "a quotation for the supply of St. Mirren membership cards was unanimously accepted from stationers McDougall Brothers". This firm was for many years the oldest booksellers in Paisley, but alas they no longer exist. Few in 1890 would have predicted that an amateur football club like St. Mirren, even one on the edge of a new era for football, would have outlived such a respected local business.

CHAPTER THREE

The advent of League football in Scotland was not universally welcomed, but such critics were easier to shake off than the problem posed by professionalism. The payment of players had been legalised in England in 1885, but in late 1880s Scotland there was sufficient evidence to suggest that professionalism was not going to disappear, and St. Mirren were not immune from the sport's continuing dilemma.

At St. Mirren's AGM on 9 May 1890, just four days after the new Leagues rules had been ratified, leading Club member A. McKechnie moved that a fellow member Mr. Edward Wright "was trying to induce players to leave the club and go to England as professionals, that he be expelled from the Club and further that he be not allowed to enter the field." There was also an amendment that Mr. Wright be asked to apologise.

Mr. Wright was duly removed from the assembly, but appears to have been unmoved by the sanction imposed. It was not until 1 December 1891 that the Club received a letter of apology for "introducing Mr Thomson to Accrington FC", and on receipt of his apology it was decided to reinstate him as a member of the Club. The "Mr Thomson" was S. Thomson, who made a total of 31 appearances and scored eight goals between 1890 and 1892 for the ill-fated Accrington club, who ironically had been expelled from the English League in 1884 - for paying their players!

There were signs of football's festering sore much further north than Accrington. Hibernian had won the Cup in 1887, but there was strong evidence that they had been involved in preparing a set of records which hid the fact that at least one player was being paid, and although the advent of the League also coincided with Hibs being at a very low point, following the defection of most of their players to Celtic, it is far more likely that it was for the former reason that they received no invitation to join the new League.

In September 1890 another east coast club, St. Bernard's, were suspended by the SFA for concealing professionalism, and previous suspicions regarding the Edinburgh Saints in this regard was also likely to have been the cause of them not being invited to take part in the League. Despite their non-involvement, St. Bernard's still managed to have an early impact on the new set-up and the League history of St. Mirren.

Saints' first-ever league game, a creditable 2-2 draw away to Renton, was erased from the record books along with the Dunbartonshire club's four other league games after the Tontine Park club were banned by the SFA from all football that season after playing a friendly against the suspended St. Bernard's in defiance of an SFA ruling. As a result, Saints' second League game on 30 August 1890 - a 5-2 home win against Cowlairs - officially became their opening match, and the first of the five goals scored for Saints that day by the season's top scorer Morrison gained a significance which was not appreciated at the time.

Three weeks earlier, St. Mirren's pre-season preparations were rocked when it was announced that the well-known figure of trainer and groundsman Bob Hindle would no longer be seen around Westmarch. The St. Mirren committee had been dissatisfied with Mr. Hindle's explanation about why he had left the ground some days earlier, and during the discussion Mr. Hindle expressed some reservations with his overall situation. The Club's committee decided it was in everyone's interest that he be given a month's notice to leave, and immediate arrangements were made to advertise the vacancy in three newspapers. A week later on 12 August 1890 and just eleven days before the start of the season, Mr. D. Whitehill was appointed as trainer and groundsman.

At Renton three days after the season started, the St. Mirren committee agreed that there was a need for "a dozen new shirts and a dozen pair of knickers to be got for the first team". Long-time official James Bryce agreed to supply the cloth for the knickers, and tailor-to-trade Archibald Towns, who two months earlier had helped draft the first-ever rules and regulations of the Scottish Football League, showed that he could shape more than laws; he agreed to make the knickers! Renton's disqualification meant the League became a ten-team competition, and in nine home games Saints drew once and won five, including a first-ever victory over Celtic. They were much less successful away from Westmarch, as nine straight defeats were suffered, including a 4-2 defeat at the hands of bottom club Cowlairs who only won two other matches all season. Three weeks later, Rangers beat Saints 8-2 at Kinning Park, and it took another eight fixtures before they won their third league game of the season.

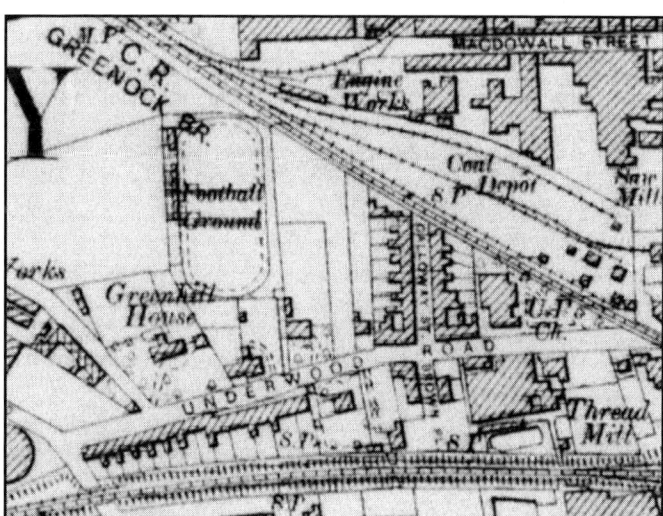

Abercorn's Underwood Park, where Saints first ever Scottish Caps were won by James Dunlop and Andy Brown.

There was genuine St. Mirren concern for Renton's plight, and it was agreed on 8 October 1890 that at the first League meeting St. Mirren's representatives should propose that "a petition got up and signed by all the League clubs is presented to the SFA asking them to allow the Renton FC to resume playing on 1 November 1890". The League were also supportive, and intended raising the issue with the SFA at the first opportunity. There was widespread unease that Renton had been suspended by the Association without a proper hearing. The decision would be challenged in the courts and eventually resolved to Renton's satisfaction, but the first League season was lost to them and Saints' first League match in effect never happened.

In the middle of the eight-match unsuccessful run, and despite a first-half lead courtesy of a 'Daddy' Dunlop double, Scottish Cup participation ended in the fifth round of the then eight-round tournament when Queen's Park came to Westmarch on 6 December 1890. Perhaps Saints thought they had it won, and by all accounts Dunlop's rocket shot for Saints' second goal certainly deserved to win a match, but the Cup holders had other ideas. The Spiders may well have been 'non-league', but they were virtually unchanged from the mighty side of twelve months earlier and they headed back to Hampden with a 3-2 win.

The Renfrewshire Cup was providing a bit of respite from the pressures of the new League, and Saints reached the semi-final where they were due to meet Arthurlie in January. In advance of the game the St. Mirren committee agreed that "our team do not take tea with Arthurlie, seeing they had never apologised for ejecting our President and Treasurer from their Club House on 6th September". Nine days after the unfortunate incident St. Mirren had written to the SFA requesting an apology from the Barrhead club, but none had been forthcoming. The action of ejecting the St. Mirren President and Treasurer had taken place during the latest in a seven-season series of Scottish Cup ties between two clubs who normally enjoyed excellent relations. The last thing anyone wanted was for such familiarity to breed contempt - particularly for each other.

The Club was honoured when Andy Brown won his second full Scotland cap, again against Wales, on 21 March 1891, but it had proved to be a difficult inaugural league season. St. Mirren finished in eighth place with eleven points, having scored 39 goals and conceded 62. Abercorn, Paisley's other standard bearers, had gained one more point than Saints to finish one place ahead. It was a situation that would be repeated in 1891-92 and would then never happen again.

This single point of a difference between the "two principal Paisley clubs" was a continuation of the 1880s pattern where "the Saints" and "the Abbies" not only enjoyed equal status but maintained excellent relations. On 1 July 1890, as the new League set-up became clearer, the St. Mirren committee agreed that "Mr. Towns be empowered to bring up at the first League meeting that the Abercorn FC have arranged fixtures in Paisley with non-League clubs on dates which we play league matches at home". The two clubs had an agreement about gates, and Abercorn were adjudged to have broken it "without our sanction", but by September the desire to maintain good local relations prevailed and it was agreed to discuss the matter directly with Abercorn.

1891-92

In mid-June, the St. Mirren Match Committee recommended "the advisability of engaging a (new) trainer for the team for next season as after the last years experience of Mr. Whitehill they do not consider he is qualified for the position nor yet has he the necessary experience". This submission begs the question why he was appointed in the first place. The General Committee's members decided they would meet with the team to establish if they were satisfied with Mr. Whitehill's performance. The response from the playing staff was sufficiently negative that, on 10 July, the committee decided to terminate Mr. Whitehill's connection with St. Mirren, and the whole process of advertising the vacancy began again.

Following a successful court action, Renton were reinstated to the Scottish League, and with a new addition in Leith Athletic the League increased to twelve teams. It made little difference to Saints, and the second league season was much the same as the first. Five wins were again achieved, although this time two were away to Third Lanark and Rangers. The home form was less impressive, and the upshot was that although the League had been enlarged, Saints remained in third bottom spot and Abercorn were again one place above and this time two points better off.

The Scottish Cup and St. Mirren were kept apart for the first three months of the season as Saints received a bye in each of the first four rounds. When it was announced that they were due to play Celtic in Paisley on 28 November, the Glasgow club immediately tried to get the tie switched to Celtic Park. Saints decided the game should go ahead at Westmarch, but on this occasion home advantage made no difference and Celtic won 4-2.

Although the League continued to expose Saints to the highest available opposition in Scotland, it was Abercorn who featured most prominently in Saints' season. In addition to winning three of the four league points, Abercorn beat Saints 2-1 in the Renfrewshire final, and they also captured the Paisley Charity Cup at Underwood Park when they triumphed 5-3. It was quite a one-sided story, but it all paled into insignificance by a single incident which overshadowed the second half of the season and will never be forgotten by St. Mirren supporters.

In a friendly match against Abercorn on New Year's Day at Underwood Park where James 'Daddy' Dunlop played the first of what should have been many international games, Saints' gifted inside left fell on a piece of broken glass thought to have been thrown onto the field by a spectator. He injured his knee, and from this cut he contracted tetanus and died on 11 January 1892. He was only twenty-two, yet he was known throughout the football world by the nickname 'Daddy', given to him almost from the moment he broke into the first team because of his natural leadership qualities.

James Dunlop was that unusual combination, a skilful player who brought out the best in his colleagues, and one who could score as well as make goals. The tragic circumstances of his death shocked the citizens of Paisley, his home town. On 10 February, the Club's President Mr. James K. Horsburgh presented the Club with a "handsome" photograph of "our late esteemed member James Dunlop", and two weeks later St. Mirren agreed to raise a monument to Dunlop. Subscriptions were to be confined to members and supporters, and five designs were submitted to the Club. It was left to James Dunlop's former colleagues to make the final decision at the Club's AGM.

1. James Dunlop's monument at Woodside.
2. Enhanced detail SMFC on reverse of the monument.
3. The wording on the monument plaque.

An impressive broken pillar monument, signifying a life cut short, was chosen by the St. Mirren players and erected in Paisley's Woodside Cemetery, where, over one hundred years after his premature death, a steady stream of Saints supporters still make their way to pay tribute.

On 12 January 1892, a special committee meeting of The St. Mirren Football Club was held with Mr. Horsburgh in the chair: "Owing to the death of Mr. James Dunlop, no business was transacted and on the motion of Mr. Horsburgh, seconded by Mr. Alexander Towns, the following special minute was recorded, expressing the Club's sincere sympathy with Mrs. Dunlop and family in their very sad bereavement".

The special minute read as follows...

JAMES 'DADDY' DUNLOP

"Before proceeding with the ordinary business of the meeting perhaps you will allow me to say a few words of reference to the recent mournful death of our late esteemed member Mr. James Dunlop.

"Although from Saturday last little hope of his recovery was held out, at the same time the serious development of the injury that led to his death and the ultimate termination of his life yesterday morning was sufficiently sudden and startling to make a very painful impression upon the wide circle of friends by whom Mr. Dunlop was esteemed and loved.

"The injury Mr. Dunlop received although serious enough was not at first supposed to be likely to lead to fatal results; but as the worst has happened, it is at least some relief to our feelings to reflect that no direct blame is attached to anyone engaged in the match in which the injury was received. I think it is generally admitted that it was a pure accident of a nature quite unusual and unexpected.

"Apart from Mr. Dunlop's position as a distinguished football expert he will be much missed in business circles in which, as you know, he was fast making a name and position for himself, as he could not have failed to do from his energetic and pushing disposition. In this connection I am sure you are ready to add to mine your sincere expression of sorrow at the untimely death of a young gentleman of so much promise.

"It was however as a football expert and enthusiast that Mr. Dunlop was best known to us and the public. His career as such was not a long one, unfortunately, but short as it was he had already made a name for himself such as few young men of his age has ever attained, and there can be no question that had he been spared, the highest honours that can fall to the amateur football player were in store for him.

"Mr. Dunlop's connection with the St. Mirren Club was honourable alike to himself and the Club. As a player there was not a trace of anything unsportsmanlike or unfair in his style, indeed it always seemed to me that he was an ideal football player, and one who would rather suffer defeat than resort to any tactics in the least degree suspicious or objectionable. He had a genius for the game: he initiated a style which the younger generation of players will remember and imitate for years to come.

His removal is a heavy blow to the St. Mirren Club, by every member of which Mr. Dunlop was highly respected and loved. I can pay no higher compliment to the memory of our young friend than is conveyed in the expression of what we feel and I am sure you are pleased to have this opportunity - mournful as the occasion is - of thus expressing through me your heartfelt sympathy for the loss of our young friend with his bereaved relatives and friends."

A copy of this minute signed by the President and a letter of condolence signed by the officials of the Club were sent to Mrs. Dunlop.

1892-93

If the 1880s were a period of steady progress, the 1890's were characterised by turning points, and none was more dramatic than 1892-93. In terms of position, it was a League campaign which has never been bettered, but Saints' seven defeats included 6-1 and 5-1 scorelines, and two 4-1 reverses. A team doesn't gain third spot with that kind of form, and Saints also managed to hit eight past Clyde at Westmarch, and a week later Abercorn conceded four at the same venue.

It was a helter-skelter of a season, but no point was lower than 21 January in the Scottish Cup. Away victories in the first two rounds over the original Aberdeen club and Leith Athletic took Saints to a less-than-green Shamrock Park in Broxburn, where they struggled in the mud and lost 4-3 to the least known of the West Lothian town's three senior sides, Broxburn Shamrock.

Saints bounced back from that disappointment to record five League wins in a row, their best sequence of the season, and top scorer James McLean would eventually score ten of the team's forty League goals. Five wins also stood out for Abercorn; it was the total of their wins all season and along with bottom club Clyde they became the first two Scottish clubs to experience relegation when the League split into two Divisions at the end of the 1892-93 season.

The new Second Division would include a Morton team which beat Saints 3-0 at Underwood Park to finally win the Renfrewshire Cup and begin their eventual role as Saints only county challengers. Abercorn would return briefly to the top Division in three years time, but May 1893 was to prove the turning point in the fortunes of the two Paisley rivals, as Saints maintained continuous top league status until 1935, by which time Abercorn had been out of existence for fifteen years.

1893-94

In its fourth season the League was changed for the third consecutive year, thus establishing early-on that Scottish football's appetite for reconstruction was ravenous. This time at least the development was generally seen as strengthening the base of the game, but the main decision at the SFA's 1893 AGM would, in the longer term, severely restrict the competitiveness of many of the League's new clubs.

In May 1893, on a motion from Celtic, Scottish football's problem of illegal professionalism was solved by the inevitable solution of making it legal. A year earlier in a similar vote, St. Mirren's representatives were instructed to 'vote for amateurism'. Now the Club had to embrace the concept of professionalism, and with Abercorn seemingly settling for life as a Second Division side, the timing certainly suited Saints.

It was unlikely that the Paisley public were alone in noting that the quality of the St. Mirren players was on the increase, and the main problem St. Mirren would face was whether they could hold on to their star players now that money was officially involved in the game. On 2 March 1894, Saints' clever right back David Crawford repeated his public statement that he "intended to play for a city club next year".

On 24 March, Crawford won his first Scotland cap in a match against Wales at Rugby Park in Kilmarnock, and playing immediately in front of Crawford at right half, also making his international debut, was his Saints colleague Edward McBain. It was the second time in two years that St. Mirren had two players in a Scotland team; a week later Crawford doubled his caps tally.

More caps would follow, including John Patrick, Saints regular 'keeper during 1893-94, but his chances of winning a cap that season were not helped by a less-than-impressive performance in the Scottish Cup against Third Lanark. Saints had already eliminated Hearts in the first round on 25 November, but three weeks later Christmas came early at Cathkin when the normally reliable Patrick had a real off-day. Third Lanark took the lead when Patrick rushed out of his goal and completely missed the ball. For Third's second goal he gave a repeat performance, but this time injured his full back David Crawford in the process. It was 3-1 at half time, and finished 3-2 for Thirds, despite all Saints' efforts to retrieve the situation.

Saints' League record of seven wins, three draws, and eight defeats was marginally poorer than the previous season, although their goal difference improved, increasing from one to two! One match which undoubtedly helped Saints figures took place on 17 February at Westmarch, when the newly amalgamated Dundee showed they weren't completely as one by conceding ten goals in a 10-3 win for Saints which set a new League record. The goals started as early as the second minute, and it was 4-1 by half-time.

Saints scored a further six, and as the afternoon developed the main surprise was that top scorer James McLean didn't get any. Despite the scoreline, the press reckoned veteran centre-half Andy Brown had been Saints inspiration! Brown was certainly playing as well as ever, and there was considerable surprise, in Paisley at least, when he was overlooked for that season's internationals.

The rout of Dundee on 17 February proved to be St. Mirren's last-ever League game at Westmarch. A week later it was reported that Saints' lease was due to run out in May. There seemed to be no chance of it being extended after a further report stated that "no effort will be made to renovate the stand at Westmarch", and that "the unsettled nature of the tenancy, together with a protest lodged by the railway officials will stop operations in the meantime".

A St. Mirren sub-committee had been busy inspecting suitable sites in the surrounding district but at the end of February 1894, according to reports, "had not yet settled on their future home." That didn't stop press speculation. "It is not improbable," claimed the 'Paisley Daily Express', "that the old brickfield at the foot of Love Street will be their ultimate choice. The nature of the ground forbids building extensions for some time, which fact will render the chance of securing a lengthy lease more probable. The removal will probably cost the club £500, but the central situation of the proposed new field will ensure the return of that sum in a few years".

It was hardly a ringing endorsement of the Love Street site, but for all the practical reasons given in the 'Express' it was the choice of the committee in March 1894. They had just six months to get the new venue ready for League football, but before that there was still some football to be played and one last match at Westmarch. Incredibly, Saints scored ten again!

On 9 June 1894, their opponents in the Paisley Charity Cup Final were Abercorn, who had won just five League games, but this time these were Division Two matches. Few expected anything other than a win for the home team, but no one predicted a 10-0 margin in St. Mirren's favour. It was a result which would have been unimaginable just two years earlier. Remarkably, two years hence Abercorn would be back in Division One, but they would never again be pre-eminent in Paisley. Saints were moving to a new ground, but they were already at a different level.

SFA medal awarded to J. Scouller.

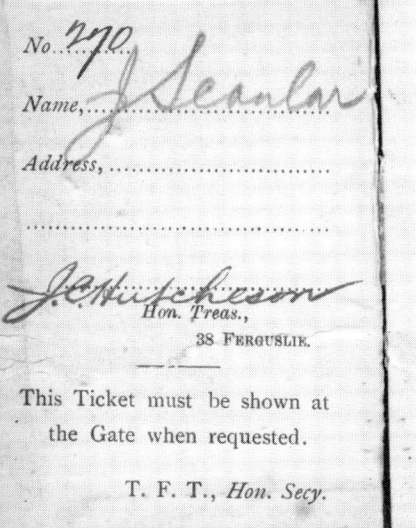

Season ticket in the name of J. Scouller for the 1892-93 season at Westmarch.
Mr Scouller went on to serve the Club over the forthcoming years as Treasurer, Director, and Chairman.

J. Scouller

1894-95

Westmarch had been purchased by a Glasgow syndicate for trotting purposes, but by the end of July 1894 the former St. Mirren Grounds were "dilapidated" and being used by just children and sheep. During June the stand had been removed, and the handsome pavilion which had been opened just five years earlier had been demolished, although both were expected to be re-erected at Love Street. It had become increasingly deserted over the previous weeks, and it was commented that "old Bob Hindle wouldn't recognise the place".

Meanwhile, the new St. Mirren headquarters were taking shape on schedule for an 8 September opening match against Celtic. The newly-sown grass had taken, the track had been marked off, and the press box was in position.

Ground matters had naturally dominated St. Mirren's thoughts, but by early June the rumours were rife as to "many prominent players leaving the team next season". Internationalist David Crawford had signalled his intentions and his move to Rangers surprised no-one, but the rest of the hearsay proved to be equally accurate. The most notable other defector was Crawford's full back partner James Mirk, who moved to Gorgie Road where he played sixteen League matches that season and won a championship medal with Hearts.

Despite the changes in personnel, Saints had already had a 2-1 win at Hawkhill Recreation Ground against Leith Athletic, and a narrow 1-0 defeat by the champions-to-be at Tynecastle by the time the big opening day arrived. Considerable publicity was given to the fact that, to begin with at least, "the only entrance is by Love Street" and in anticipation of a big crowd the gates were opened at 2.30pm for a four o'clock kick off. 8000 spectators were in the ground on 8 September 1894 to see Mr.

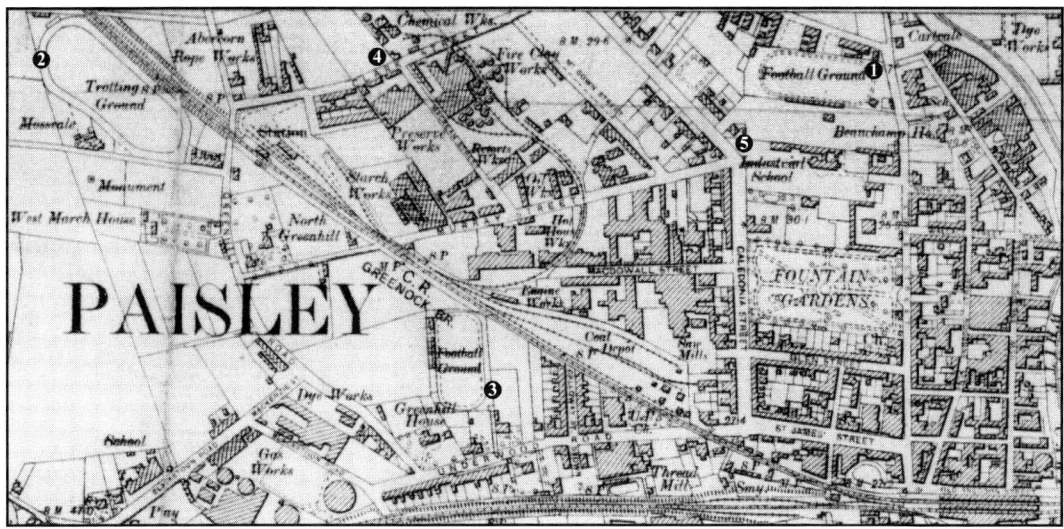

Late 1890s map showing:-
1. *"St Mirren Grounds" at Love Street.*
2. *Trotting Ground at Greenhill Road, site of Westmarch.*
3. *Abercorn's Underwood Park.*
4. *Site in Clark Street often thought to be site of Westmarch.*
5. *Industrial School.*

Note: Width of St Mirren Grounds, later to be extended to accommodate terracing by expanding towards the "Industrial School", which was cleared to make way for Albion Street and housing.

Archibald Sliman, President of the SFA, formally open the grounds by kicking off at the start of the game.

Fifteen years earlier, almost to the day, St. Mirren had lost their opening match at Thistle Park when John Elder FC spoiled the party with a 2-0 win. History was to repeat itself as Celtic left the un-named new ground off Love Street with a deserved 3-0 victory. The SFA records of 1894 show that St. Mirren's registered ground was given as "Fullerton Park", and this ground name has worked its way erroneously into several histories of the Club. It is likely to have been merely a local reference to the fact that the proprietor of the site was a Mr. John Fullerton.

The Celtic match was the first of three consecutive home games, and after all the excitement of 8 September, there was an encouraging 5-1 win over Dundee which was followed by a much closer 4-3 victory over Dumbarton. After that things settled down, and the team finished in fifth position having won nine and drawn one of their eighteen fixtures. The 5-1 win over the "Dundonians" proved to be Saints' biggest League score of the season, while no team managed more than four past 'keeper Patrick.

On 24 November, the SFA President made a return visit to Love Street, but this time Mr. Sliman was wearing his Battlefield FC hat. He watched as his team were beaten 5-0, but the visitors successfully protested and the game was replayed at Love Street on 8 December. This time the score was 8-1 for St. Mirren. In the next round Saints travelled north-east to play a Dundee team who had conceded fifteen goals to Saints in the two previous competitive matches. A 2-0 win for the Carolina Port club on 15 December ended the sequence and Saints' Scottish Cup involvement.

Saints returned to League business with a 2-2 draw at Celtic Park and a 4-2 win over Rangers in Paisley, but less than usual significance was attached to these two results, as Hearts were clearly the best team in Scotland. St. Mirren were just four places behind, and considering the upheaval the Club had experienced during the previous fifteen months it was a cause for some satisfaction, and there was a further boost for St. Mirren when right-winger and top scorer John Taylor played in Scotland's 3-1 March win over Ireland in Glasgow. This added to the earlier selection of Saints' forward J. Connelly and half-back H. Goldie for the Scottish League against their Irish counterparts.

1895-96

A promising 2-1 opening win against champions Hearts, who were to finish fourth, proved no more than early-season enthusiasm, and when Saints met Hearts in the return fixture in October 1895 they left Tynecastle with a 5-1 defeat. This deficit underlined the gap between Saints and the top four throughout this very disappointing season, and a week later a visit to the east end of the Capital produced the same result as Hibs added to their earlier 3-1 win in Paisley.

St. Mirren... early winners of the Paisley Charity Cup circa 1890.

Celtic, who also won 3-1 at Love Street and had scored four without reply at Parkhead in August, were undefeated throughout 1895-96, and were Champions elect when Saints travelled to Ibrox on the third last Saturday of the season. This scenario as much as anything else helped Saints take home a surprise point from ten-man Rangers in a 3-3 draw, but the real difference in the sides was perhaps more accurately reflected in the earlier fixture at the St. Mirren Grounds where Rangers won 7-1.

Rangers also took five goals off Saints without reply at Ibrox to end Paisley's interest in the Cup after just two rounds. It was a result which was not well received by St. Mirren's General Committee, who insisted that two members of the Match Committee were present at training nights "to see that the training of the team is duly attended to".

Saints' final points total of thirteen could have been worse. With two games to go, both against Third Lanark, they had only nine points and were looking likely to finish in second bottom place. Mid-table Thirds, with little to play for, were beaten 3-2 in Paisley and 2-0 at Cathkin, and the season was given a better complexion than perhaps it deserved.

At the end of a poor season in the early days of the Club, the benefits of running a third team had been extolled. In August 1895 the Club had decided not to run a Second XI for reasons of finance and with a view to protecting the field. The St. Mirren Westmarch XI FC and the St. Mirren Victoria XI FC both immediately requested that St. Mirren accept them as "a junior combination to replace the Second XI", but both were turned down. In view of the poor season, it was a policy which might need to be reconsidered. Despite the disappointing season, there was plenty happening off the pitch. During May 1895, draining and resoiling of the field had taken place as ground upgrading work continued, and the Club were once again getting requests from various organisations to use St. Mirren's facilities. The Victoria and Fereneze Bicycle clubs and the Glenkilloch Cycling Club had made enquiries, and it had been agreed to host a ladies cycling meet and a ladies football match.

John Patrick (St. Mirren & Scotland)

"St. Mirren Grounds, Love Street" was registered with the SFA - no "Fullerton Park" this time - and its central location was certainly raising the profile of the club with non-football people in Paisley, but it had also brought some new problems. There was some concern about the number of non-members using the field to play football during the day, and this was to be prohibited. In addition, complaints had been received about damage being done to property adjoining the ground "caused by the habit of some people climbing upon it to gain a view of the field or free access to the field".

One of the adjacent buildings was a slaughterhouse, and this was seen as a possible source of Club income. It was agreed that the Treasurer should interview the superintendent of the slaughterhouse "as to letting to him the field for the accommodation of sheep brought into the slaughterhouse and to report terms he is prepared to offer". The Provident Cooperative Society had offered £10 for the same privilege, and if successful in their bid, their representative was given the use of the field "on condition that the sheep be removed from the field during all matches"!

In the end, it was agreed to let the Slaughterhouse have use of the field on the same terms, and in a season which had seen St. Mirren beaten 7-1 at home, it was the earnest hope of all with St. Mirren affiliations that the Slaughterhouse would be the Love Street area's only place of carnage in the seasons to come.

Revenue-raising and sheep was something of a recurring theme in Saints' first year at Love Street. At the end of the season a Mr. James Wood requested delivery of a sheep won by him as a prize at the Club's fund-raising bazaar. The Secretary was instructed to do so!

1896-97

The poor showing in the League during 1895-96 meant that it was the other clubs who would decide in which Division Saints would be playing during 1896-97, so on 19 May the Club's Match Secretary wrote to all the leading clubs in the League asking them to support the inclusion of St. Mirren in Division One the following season. On 2 June, it was reported to the committee that a Mr. T. McKaig was willing to provide additional access to the ground via a 15 foot passage through his property from Caledonia Street at the rent of £6 per annum, provided the Club erect a gate and barricade. The enterprising Mr. McKaig later added that he had wood for sale which would be suitable for the construction of the barricade, and the Club agreed to purchase the wood. The new access point from Caledonia Street would be ready by the start of the 1896-97 season. Around this time, the Club also decided to erect barbed wire around the field which would be put up with iron standards. Things were beginning to take shape, and this coincided nicely with the news that Saints would be remaining in a Division One which would also that season contain Abercorn.

The first fixture did Saints no favours as they went down 5-1 at Ibrox, but they recovered well in week two with a 5-0 win over Clyde. There then followed a six-match alternate sequence of lose-win before the wins and losses started to come in batches. The opening two matches apart, there were no dramatic scorelines, and in general it was a much steadier campaign, with nine wins and one draw making up the nineteen points which gave Saints sixth spot.

The season, of course, contained two clashes with Abercorn. In the first match Saints had a 4-2 home win, but in the return fixture at Underwood the "Abbies" triumphed 3-2. It was to be the last of just eight League matches between the two clubs. Abercorn had struggled all season, and finished bottom with just one draw plus that solitary win at Love Street to their credit.

Credit is what they got from St. Mirren, and on 25 May Saints voted for Third Lanark to stay up, Partick Thistle to be promoted, Clyde to be demoted, and Abercorn to remain in Division One. The last choice, if made public at the time, would certainly have confounded those critics who claimed that St. Mirren's one aim was to close down Abercorn. Saints were keen to help local football as much as possible, and earlier in the season three local clubs - St. Mirren Thistle, St. Mirren Victoria, and St. Mirren Westmarch - had all approached Saints asking for the use of the field to run a Junior XI, and the Thistle team were selected.

In the first round of the Scottish Cup Saints fans were also reminded of former days when Renton returned to Love Street, but by then they were a mid-table Division Two side, and it showed as Saints enjoyed a convincing 5-1 victory with Sandy Wylie hitting a hat-trick. The next round took Saints to the Old Gymnasium in Edinburgh, home of St. Bernard's. Despite the name of the venue, the match took place outside and on a pitch which by all accounts was near to unplayable. Certainly Saints couldn't play on it, and they lost 5-0.

There was something re-assuring about the way St. Mirren operated at this time, and in October 1896 the Club showed a respect for order and rules that the Club's founding fathers would have applauded. An SFL proposal to pay a five shillings railway fare per match to neutral linesmen who were engaged in important league matches was opposed by the St. Mirren committee, not because they were against the idea, but because it was a proposed change of rules during the playing season - and that would never do! On 9 March 1897, it was agreed that The St. Mirren Football Club should be formed into a limited liability company, and a week later there was a further recommendation that the capital should be fixed at £2000 at £1 per share. At the AGM on 13 April 1897, the Club's General Committee made their recommendation to this effect. A vote was then taken and the motion was carried. There had also been an amendment that the club remain as constituted. The AGM was adjourned, but when it reconvened on 13 May a motion to rescind the former motion was carried by a large majority. The Club's General Committee would not suggest another change in status until 1904.

John Hindle (Trainer)

St. Mirren was set to remain the same type of football club it had been since 1877, although twenty years on, the quality of players had certainly improved. On 20 March 1897, John Patrick became the seventh St. Mirren player to be capped for Scotland when he played in the match against Wales at Wrexham in a 2-2 draw. Two weeks later he performed brilliantly in a 2-1 winning Scottish team at Crystal Palace.

The rejection of floating the Club as a limited liability company was not to be misinterpreted as lack of ambition. There was an enthusiasm to raise playing standards, and the limited number of League games was restricting that improvement. On 18 May 1897, St. Mirren decided to make contact with several members of the Glasgow League, which was formed in 1895 and comprised the six Glasgow clubs, i.e. Celtic, Clyde, Partick Thistle, Queen's Park, Rangers, and Third Lanark.

The Glasgow League was one of a number of local leagues formed to supplement their season, because Scottish League fixture lists only ran for 18 to 22 games and were often finished by February. Unfortunately, the Glasgow League was not going to be the answer. Within a month of St. Mirren's approach, Clyde FC wrote to inform them of the winding up of the Glasgow League and the possible formation of a new league of which Saints might wish to be a member club.

1897-98

St. Mirren Trainer James McWilliams gave notice that he was resigning and would leave the Club's employment on 9 August, and John Hindle was selected from four candidates to replace Mr. McWilliams. As on a previous occasion when Bob Hindle left, there seemed to be an unseemly rush to fill a vacancy which had such important implications for the whole club. The terms of John Hindle's employment included a rate of twenty-two shillings per week: he was expected to keep the grounds and pavilion in order, including the cutting of the grass; he was to have the use of the house in the field free of rent. At the beginning of September, John Hindle rescinded his claim to "use of home", and in lieu of this his wages became twenty-five shillings per week. Immediately an application to take possession of the house was received from John Patrick, Saints international goalkeeper. It was agreed to grant the 'keeper's request for so long as he was in St. Mirren's employment but the Club's property committee were asked to put the house in a "tenantable condition".

On 11 September, St. Mirren beat Partick Thistle 1-0 at Love Street to begin a five match undefeated run which included a 7-2 home win over St. Bernard's and a 4-2 defeat of Hearts at Tynecastle. Four days before the Thistle game, the first home game of the season, the Committee unanimously decided to give the long-serving but by then retired Andy Brown a player's ticket for the season. At the 1898 AGM they extended the honour, when it was unanimously agreed to elect Mr. Andrew (Andy) Brown, "an old and faithful player", to be a life member of the Club. 1897-98 was generally a good season for Saints, and when the last match was completed on 12 February 1898, St. Mirren were the sixth best team in Scotland. They had scored thirty goals, eleven of which came from the boot and head of top scorer Sandy Wylie, and had conceded just thirty-six. Nine of those thirty-six came in one match at Ibrox, and it remains a mystery why a defence which conceded just twenty-seven goals in seventeen matches should malfunction in such dramatic fashion over ninety minutes. The 9-0 score remains St. Mirren's biggest defeat.

The Scottish Cup campaign was also a disappointment because it lasted just two weeks in January. It began well enough, with a 7-2 win over the little-known Dumfries Hibernian, but for the second time in three years the second round draw took Saints to Carolina Port and a 2-0 defeat by Dundee.

On 24 February 1898, the Renfrewshire FA selected St. Mirren Grounds for a county cup replay between Morton and Port Glasgow Athletic, but while St. Mirren were trying to increase access points to the ground and improve viewing points within, it was disappointing to note that some damage was caused to the gates and barricade during the match. St. Mirren considered a charge of £3 to defray the damage, but decided to take no further action. St. Mirren minds were soon considering normal football matters, and on 19 March there was great delight when Hugh Morgan was capped for Scotland against Wales in the 5-2 win at Motherwell. Hugh Morgan would move to Anfield at the end of that season, and during the 1898-99 season he became joint top scorer for Liverpool with ten goals, and won the second of his two caps against England on 8 April 1899 at Birmingham.

Not put off by the Glasgow League experience, on 12 April 1898 St. Mirren discussed a suggestion made by seven clubs to form a "combination" to be known as "The Western League". The League's headquarters were to be in Paisley, and the other six clubs were Abercorn, Kilmarnock, Linthouse (Glasgow), Morton, Partick Thistle, and Port Glasgow Athletic. The St. Mirren committee approved the idea, and in addition to the previously mentioned seven clubs, applications to join were to be received by the Ayr and Ayr Parkhouse clubs. It was agreed to support the latter for admission.

1898-99

The Western League wasn't the only local league being promulgated. On 5 July 1898, Partick Thistle FC wrote regarding formation of a 'Scottish Federation' and called a meeting to inform and discuss. Mr. W. Maxwell attended the meeting on behalf of St. Mirren, returned with a list of clubs likely to join, and gave details of the financial arrangements and a commitment by all clubs involved to appoint two referees. It was agreed that St. Mirren would join, but would be represented by the 'A' team.

The highlight of the season was Saints' Scottish Cup run. In 1898-99, Kilmarnock would win the Division Two championship for the second year in succession, and do so without losing a game. In Division One, Rangers would go one better than Killie and take the title without dropping a point! Leith Athletic were also enjoying a good season as runners-up to Kilmarnock, and Third Lanark would finish in a comfortable mid-table position in Division One.

St. Mirren Football Club 1899 Winners of The Paisley Charity Cup and The Renfrewshire Cup
J. Blane, J. Patrick (Goalkeeper), R. Binnie,
J. Hindle (Trainer), E. McBain, D. Greenlees, M. McAvoy, D. Fairlie (Secretary),
Alex Chalmers, W. Steel, Adam J. Monro (President), M. Mullen, R. Orr, A. Wyllle.

On the face of it, not the easiest four clubs for St. Mirren to be drawn against in the Scottish Cup, but they did so well that they reached the Cup semi-final for the first time in the Club's history. A 7-1 first round win suggests that the Leith team were easily dismissed, but the next round gave Saints the difficult-sounding task of crossing swords with the 3rd Lanarkshire Rifle Volunteers. They came away from Cathkin with a 2-1 win, and in the third round they headed down to Ayrshire to take on a Kilmarnock team that had forgotten how to lose. St. Mirren reminded them, and another 2-1 win for Saints took them into the uncharted waters of the semi-final stage.

It was the biggest game yet in Paisley and the St. Mirren fans in the 10,000 crowd saw their team put up a tremendous display, despite being a goal down. Then star man Donald Greenlees got them back into the game when he scored, and it stayed at 1-1 until five minutes from time, when Rangers grabbed the winner. It was a performance which matched the occasion from the following eleven: Patrick, McBlane, Jackson, Greenlees, Bruce, McAvoy, Chalmers, Steel, McNeilly, Orr, and Wylie.

Sandy Wylie, with nine League goals, would be Saints' top scorer for the second year in a row, and the name 'Jackson' was now featuring regularly in the Saints line up. Young Tom would go on to eclipse the international record of all his St. Mirren predecessors.

In the eighteen-game League campaign, Saints won eight and drew four to finish in fifth place. The six matches lost were, perhaps understandably, against top four finishers Rangers and Hearts on two occasions each, and once by Celtic and Hibs. At St. Mirren Grounds Hibs were beaten 2-0, and in one of the best results of the season Saints recorded a 4-0 home victory over Celtic. In a season which went largely to form, Saints' fans might have expected the team to beat bottom club Dundee, but the 5-1 romp at Love Street was none the less welcome. Those who travelled to Dens were even more delighted by a thumping 7-1 win which completed spectacular back-to-back victories.

St. Mirren Football Club Five-A-Side Tournament medal won by J.C. Hunter 1899.

During the season it was noted that two Railway timetables had for years been allowed to be placed on the boundary wall of the ground facing Love Street. Not any more! The Railway company were asked to removed them or pay rent on the spaces taken. They responded by agreeing to pay £1 per annum in rent. The St. Mirren Commercial Department was born!

Back in October, Mr. W. W. L. Coats of Paisley and President of the Craigielea Rugby Football Club had written on behalf of the Scottish Rugby Union requesting the free use of the St. Mirren Grounds for an inter-county rugby match, North v South West District. St. Mirren agreed to the request, and Mr. Coats wrote back on behalf of the SRU thanking

that he was in the course of moving to another house. It was not clear if he would have stayed but for the inspector's report!

News of a different nature reached St. Mirren in January 1900, when the Club were advised that the West of Scotland League and the Scottish Federation combinations were defunct. It was another local league disappointment, but the problem of insufficient fixtures would be addressed within the Scottish League, as Division One was quickly enlarged from ten clubs in 1901 to eighteen clubs by 1906.

In 1899-00, eighteen league games were proving difficult enough. By the end of that season St. Mirren had won just three league games. They had beaten bottom club Clyde 3-0, narrowly defeated second bottom team St. Bernard's 4-3, and hit four past Dundee without reply. They had also drawn six matches, but their twelve points meant they finished third from the bottom of the Scottish League Division One for the fourth time in the League's ten year history.

They had the same number of points as St. Bernard's, but there was no application of goal average or difference. The 1899-00 relegation system still had an old boys' network aspect to it, but compared to 1895-96 there was at least some bite to the process. Bottom club Clyde were already dependent on the votes cast by the other Division One clubs but a possible second reversion depended on a play-off between St. Bernard's and St. Mirren.

The two Saints' sides and their supporters travelled to the newly opened Dens Park on 7 April 1900, and after a goalless first half St. Bernard's took the lead. Sandy Wylie equalised for Saints and then scored the all-important winner. 'All-important' because both Clyde and St. Bernard's failed to be re-selected, and were replaced in the First Division by Morton and Partick Thistle. It was not until the 1921-22 season that automatic promotion and relegation came in.

The League campaign had been undeniably disappointing, but the Cup competitions can often provide some respite and that looked to be happening on 13 January when Saints travelled through to Tynecastle, and, in one of the season's best results, came away with an excellent no-scoring draw. Scottish Cup glory was short-lived, however, as the Maroons won 3-0 in the Paisley replay.

The temporary relief of the cup is even more likely in county competitions, but Johnstone didn't oblige. In the second round of the Renfrewshire, they came to Love Street and won 2-1, with match reports suggesting the extent of their victory could have been more.

"Westmarch Grounds"... with the railway line to the left and St. James Station visible beyond the goal, across Greenhill Road.

the Club for the 'cordial and courteous manner in which you have considered the application of the Rugby Union'. Sadly after all that inter-sport fellowship, it has to be added that when the rugby folk put the "footie" posts back after the match they were found to be 'defective'.

It wasn't just the goalposts which were defective. At the beginning of the season the condition of the terracing on the north side of the field was discussed, and it was agreed that considerable improvements were needed. Additionally, the trainer was also instructed to remove an accumulation of ashes lying at the rear of the pavilion. There was still much to be done.

1899-00

By October 1899, goalkeeper John Patrick had been living in the house within the ground for two years. At the beginning of that month, the Club received a letter from the Sanitary Inspector clarifying that the house was unfit for habitation. This shocking news was immediately brought to John Patrick's attention, but he calmly informed the Club

Morton's promotion would provide a different angle on local rivalry, and although the Greenock club would provide growing county competition, it would not be until 1967 that Morton would play in a higher Division than St. Mirren. That was a situation rectified twelve months later, and one which occurred again in three disastrous seasons between 1972 and 1974. It has not been repeated.

In 1900, the changing face of football in the county was also reflected when Arthurlie and Johnstone joined Saints and Abercorn in the Paisley Charity Cup competition as the other senior sides in Paisley began to vanish from the scene. Soon only one would be left.

During the first ten years of the Scottish Football League, St. Mirren had been 3rd once, 5th twice, 6th three times, 8th three times, and 10th once. Along the way they had matched and beaten Scotland's best, and had reached a Scottish Cup semi-final for the first time. As they entered the twentieth century they formed part of Scottish football's elite.

They did not look out of place.

The 1900's - Limited Company, Unlimited Ambition

1900-01

After ten years of trying to come to terms with the advent of League football and the adoption of professionalism, the amateurs of Queen's Park finally applied to join the Scottish League in 1900, and in recognition of their status the Spiders went straight into Division One. This increased the League to an awkward eleven teams, but Queen's provided an additional two fixtures and that was at least a step in the right direction for St. Mirren and others.

CHAPTER FOUR
The 1900's

The play-off scare of the previous season had been a timely reminder that St. Mirren's place at the top was not guaranteed, and the message seemed to have been taken on board in the first game of the first season of the new century with a 5-2 victory over newly-promoted Partick Thistle at Love Street. Two of the goals were scored by Ronald Orr, who would be top scorer with ten league goals that season. Orr's goal-grabbing did not go unnoticed, and he joined Newcastle at the end of 1900-01, winning two Scotland caps during his seven years on Tyneside. He later moved to Liverpool, where he equalled his Saints' record by being top scorer in two successive seasons.

J. K. Horsburgh (President)

A week after the Partick opener, Saints met the other promoted club at Cappielow for the first time in a League game. In a closely contested match Morton won 1-0, but by 10 November, when Queen's Park were beaten 4-3 in Paisley, Saints had won five and drawn one of their first nine fixtures, and looked set for a good League campaign.

Off the field the news was also good. At the half-yearly General Meeting on 16 November, the Treasurer's statement showed the Club to be "slowly but gradually getting clear of its debt" and the Match Secretary, with only three matches lost, "read his report to date which gave every satisfaction". There would be less satisfaction in the months to come, as the team failed to win any of their remaining eleven matches and slumped to ninth in the final table.

It was not a decline which was meekly accepted by Saints fans, and on 14 March 1901 the Club's much-respected President, Mr. James K. Horsburgh, called a special meeting "owing to the comments that had been passed on him by members of the Club and the general public who seemed to think that he alone was responsible for the teams that had been put on the field on the previous Saturdays". It would be three years before the Club appointed a "Manager", and even longer before his duties included team selection and coping with supporters' aspirations.

The League results in the second half of the 1900-01 season certainly pointed to some bad selections by the Match Committee, but that picture improved when the Scottish Cup was taken into account. In the first round Kilwinning were thrashed 10-0, and that win boosted confidence to the extent that Celtic only narrowly defeated Saints 4-3 the following week in the League. Second round opponents Ayr were defeated 3-1 away from home, then came a quartet of matches against Third Lanark in the third round.

The first match at Love Street on 16 February ended goalless, although Thirds did most of the pressing during the last twenty minutes. In the replay at Cathkin a week later it was Saints who had the better of a very tough match which finished 1-1. Seven days later at neutral Hampden, Saints took the lead three times in a 3-3 draw that owed as much to "extremely weak" goalkeeping by Saints' Maxwell than any brilliance on the part of the Crosshill club. A second replay at Hampden finally resolved the matter with a single goal victory - "a victory for Paisley" the local 'Express' called it. The four ties with Thirds had each been watched by good crowds, and Saints had gained a welcome £550 from the series. St. Mirren's second Scottish Cup semi-final awaited, and this time their opponents were Celtic.

This was a game St. Mirren should have won against a less-than-impressive Celtic side. The Paisley defence and midfield excelled, but the forwards, particularly Hay, failed to take a number of chances, or as one reporter saw it, "bungled things that any junior would have converted into goals". Centre-forward Cowden's poor quality distribution also drew critical comments, and Saints eventually paid the usual price for not turning pressure into goals when Celtic's Campbell scored the only goal of the game in the first half. A first-ever appearance in the Scottish Cup Final would have to wait.

At the April 1901 AGM, the President Mr. Horsburgh, proposed that Rule 1 of the Club be altered to read that "the Club shall be called 'The St. Mirren Football & Athletic Club' with uniform of cream jersey and knickers and black hose". The team's colours had been black and white since Season 1883-84, but there seemed to be no sentiment attached to them, because the motion to change the title and colours "was carried by a large majority": an unthinkable development at any time since.

Another equally important vote was due in May, and for the second year in a row the Secretary was instructed to write to all the Division One clubs "asking them to bring before their committees the position of St. Mirren in the League and asking for their support at the election for places in the League for next season". The Club again received the required level of support, and Division One football was assured for 1901-02.

1901-02

Scottish Football continued to grow, and this was reflected in the admittance of another club to the League, Arthurlie. The Barrhead club joined Saints, Abercorn, Morton and Port Glasgow Athletic to give Renfrewshire five of the Scottish League's twenty-two places, although only Saints and Morton were in a Division One which had reverted to ten clubs.

A 5-1 home defeat by Rangers in September was the one dent in an otherwise very controlled set of League statistics. Only twenty-three goals were conceded in the other seventeen games, with twenty-nine goals scored. As a result, eight games were won and three drawn out of eighteen, giving Saints an improved fifth top finish. Morton, who had impressed with a fourth top start the previous season, finished bottom with just one win.

Sandy Wylie

Saints' reputation as a good cup side was consolidated around this period with a third semi-final appearance in just four years, but the run to the semis had one notable incident. Airdrieonians from Division Two were beaten 1-0 in Paisley with a goal scored "half a minute from time", according to the referee in evidence to the S.F.A. after the Lanarkshire side had claimed the referee had "exceeded time prior to the goal being scored".

A strong-going Stenhousemuir, enjoying "perhaps their best-ever season" according to their centenary history, came to Paisley in the second round but were hammered 6-0. In the next round, a goal in each half at Brockville was sufficient to overcome Falkirk in front of 5,000 spectators, before Saints faced Celtic at home in the Scottish Cup semi-final for the second year in a row.

Stark in the Saints' goal was deemed to be at fault as Celtic went two goals up after fifteen minutes, but Saints "played a strong, bustling game" and scored before the interval. Another goal by each side in a hard-fought second half watched by 12,000 meant that there was no place for St. Mirren in the 1902 final, and that honour remained an unfulfilled ambition for everyone connected with the Club.

On 4 February, Rangers FC intimated that they "were willing to place the services of their team free of all charges" for a benefit match for Mr. Alexander (Sandy) Wylie of St. Mirren on 15 May 1902. Just three weeks before the match was due to take place came the sad news that former left-winger Sandy Wylie had passed away peacefully in his sleep at the early age of twenty-nine. St. Mirren was Wylie's only senior club and his skillful and spirited performances led to a Scottish League cap against the Irish League in 1893. He was also Saints top scorer in 1897-98 and again in 1898-99. The beneficiary of the Rangers match became Sandy Wylie's widowed mother and a good crowd saw the pride of Paisley beat a ten man Rangers by 4-3.

A month before the Wylie match, Scottish football was shocked when part of the Ibrox Park terracing collapsed during a Scotland v England international on 5 April 1902. Twenty-five spectators were killed and several hundred injured. Three days later the St. Mirren committee were moved to record a "Special Minute with reference to Ibrox Disaster":

> "This meeting of the Committee of The St. Mirren Football Club desires to record in its minutes its most profound regret at the terrible catastrophe which befell the football public attending the International Match at Ibrox Park on Saturday 5th April. It extends its sincerest sympathies to those who are mourning for lost ones so suddenly cut away in the fullness of life and also to the very large number who are suffering from so severe injuries and earnestly hopes for their speedy recovery."

The milestones in the football calendar continued, and at the Club's AGM on 11 April members were told that income in the previous twelve months had been £3,444 5s 3d, and expenditure during the same period was £3,321 16s 0d, giving the Club a small operating profit of £122. This was a satisfactory enough state of affairs, but it meant that the purchase of a ground was not feasible, and there was no option but to continue to lease the Love Street site. Since December 1900 there had been discussions with proprietor John Fullerton regarding the question of renewing the lease, which was costing £60 per year to rent "the field". The aim was a further three year lease on the same terms.

For many years St. Mirren had played friendly matches against a wide range of English clubs, usually around Christmas or at the end of the season. Although these games offered different and usually attractive opposition, Saints were often left with a deficit, and for the game against the Newcastle United on 30 April 1902 it was decided that members would have to pay if they wanted to watch the match from the Stand, as their tickets were now only valid for the rest of the ground. It would not be long before members would have to pay to watch English teams no matter what part of the ground they accessed.

No matter whether the opposition were English or Scottish, some people persistently tried to gain free admission to the ground, and in June 1902 local company Messrs. Winning & Fulton wrote to ask if St. Mirren could protect their property as supporters were scaling the ground's perimeter walls from their property at 3 & 4 Springbank Road. St. Mirren wrote back denying any responsibility, but, in the Paisley fashion, offered to meet them "in the matter of expense of erecting a barrier sufficient to keep the public from getting into the field".

At the beginning of July 1902, the Club did agree to meet one important expense when the offer of a new three year lease at a rent of £65 per annum was accepted. On a smaller scale during July and August, a WC was to be located inside the pavilion and a shower bath was to be "fitted up in the clubhouse". The great Methodist John Wesley had once written "cleanliness is indeed next to godliness". From now on at Love Street even the non-Saints were going to be clean!

1902-03

There were now twelve clubs in each Division, but only five finished above Saints at the end of 1902-03. One of them was Celtic, who finished in fifth position, and the two clubs' well-matched League records were reflected in the trio of matches it took to separate them in the first round of the Scottish Cup.

16,000 spectators at Celtic Park watched as Saints, but for poor shooting, should have at least been a couple of goals ahead by half-time, and by the end Celtic were rated lucky to have kept it to a no-scoring draw. A week later on 31 January 1903, Saints got off to the best possible start when Wilson beat McPherson in the Celtic goal "with a swift shot". During the first half tempers became a little heated, and some of the players had to be separated following an incident when Celtic's Watson got a slight cut to the head, then just a minute before half-time McDermitt scored for Celtic "from the midst of a scrimmage".

There was no further scoring and a second replay was required. Back again to Celtic Park, Saints failed to take advantage of the wind in the first half, and Celtic scored near the interval. They scored a further three as Saints' play continued to disappoint the Paisley fans in the 35,000 crowd. St. Mirren just could not get by Celtic in the Scottish Cup!

Some honours did come Saints' way that season. Right-winger David Lindsay became the ninth St. Mirren player to be capped for Scotland when he lined up against Ireland on 21 March 1903 at Celtic Park, and centre half Wattie Bruce, who also doubled as an emergency centre-forward, won the first of his two Scottish League caps when he was selected to play against the Irish League who were also the opponents when he won his second League cap the following year. Many felt that both Bruce and his two wing-halfs, Donald Greenlees and Mick McAvoy, should have gained more international recognition. Donald Greenlees was to win just one League cap, which was one more than McAvoy.

Opinion in Paisley was obviously at odds with those who selected the international teams of the day, but for a time as a half-back line unit they were unrivalled, and that at least wasn't a view confined to Paisley. For much of the time, playing behind them were international full backs John Cameron and Tom Jackson, so it's little wonder that for the first few years of the new century St. Mirren were consistently well-placed in the League.

Twenty-two league matches and a guarantee of just one cup tie was still proving insufficient for the needs of the leading clubs. During 1902-03 and the following season St. Mirren took part in an Inter-City League competition which ran for four years and over that period included Hearts, Hibs, Dundee, and Saints as well as all but Clyde of the six Glasgow clubs. The next few seasons would see unprecedented growth in the size of Division One to meet the needs of these top clubs.

The SFA were changing too, and at their AGM in May it was to be decided whether the Association should become a limited company. To that end Mr. Horsburgh, the Club's representative to the SFA, was instructed to vote in favour of the change of SFA status "on the understanding that the liability of each club in the Association be restricted to five shillings".

Behind the scenes, trainer John Hindle was proving to be a man of many parts. In December 1902, the Committee accepted an application from him to run a small refreshment stand inside the grounds, provided this would not interfere with his normal duties, and in May 1903 he was given permission to use the ground to run a dog handicap race.

Also in May, the Club decided to support the inclusion of Greenock Morton and Port Glasgow Athletic in the following season's Division One. It was becoming the committee's practice to support all county rivals in such votes. St. Mirren may have been the biggest and best football club in Renfrewshire, but they harboured no plans to be the only one.

1903-04

St. Mirren's consolidated position as a top side was reflected in a healthy representation in Scottish League and Scotland teams at this time. When the "St. Mirren Grounds" were chosen as the venue for the match between the Scottish and Irish Leagues on 27 February 1904, Saints' left back John Cameron and wing-half Donald Greenlees were both picked to play. Two weeks later at Dens Park, Tom Jackson won the first of three caps in four weeks when he was selected for Scotland to play Wales.

Wearing the cream shirts, cream shorts and black socks in 1903/04.
Top Row: J. Hindle (Trainer), J. Cameron, F. Rae, J. Scouller (Treasurer), W. Bruce, M. McAvoy, R. Smith (Secretary). Middle Row: T. A. Jackson, D. Crawford, J. K. Horsburgh (President), D. Greenlees, Robertson, G. Reid, J. Smith. Front Row: H. McDonald, D. Lindsay.

non-League St. Johnstone proved even easier opponents in the second round when they crumpled to a 4-0 defeat in Paisley. Rangers came back to the St. Mirren Grounds on 20 February and this time there wasn't a penalty in sight. Some people argued there wasn't even a goal, such was the disputed nature of Rangers' winner, but the goal stood and the cup drifted away for another year.

History continued to be made off the pitch. Mr. Alexander D. Boyd proposed at the April 1904 AGM "that the offices of Match Secretary and Honorary Secretary be done away with and that a Club Manager be appointed". A ballot showed 259 members in favour of having a "Manager" and 121 against. At a separate committee meeting on 3 May it was agreed to advertise the post of Manager/Secretary at the salary of £150, but this was carried by just five votes to four. The job was to be advertised in the 'Record' four times, 'Referee' two times, and 'Athletic News' once. Amongst the St. Mirren committee some doubts may have persisted about the value of such a post, because an amendment was then passed reducing the salary to £130.

John Cameron then topped his Scottish League selection when he and Tom Jackson were named as Scotland's full-back partnership for the match with Ireland in Dublin at the end of March, and in April Tom Jackson retained his Scotland right-back position when he lined up against England at Celtic Park. Within the space of 42 days in 1904, Tom Jackson became the most capped St. Mirren player, a title he would retain for seventy-six years. It was an unprecedented flurry of international recognition for St. Mirren players.

At the end of 1903-04, John Cameron followed the Tom Brandon trail of fifteen years earlier by joining Blackburn Rovers. At Ewood Park Cameron formed an outstanding full-back partnership with the much-capped England internationalist Bob Crompton. Cameron later joined Chelsea, with whom he won a second cap in the April 1909 match against England played at Crystal Palace. In April 1906, St. Mirren made an unsuccessful bid to Blackburn Rovers to obtain John Cameron's services on a loan basis.

By mid-March, a top six finish was achieved for the third year in a row. Twenty-six League fixtures had been played as the First Division grew to twelve clubs in 1903-04, but one game stood out, and by the end of it one St. Mirren player had made history.

On 9 January 1904 Rangers came to town, but got an early shock when Saints scored after five minutes' play. The Ibrox team recovered well enough to go in at half-time 2-1 up, but shortly after the resumption Saints equalised with the first of four penalties, an aspect of the game introduced only two years previously. From three of these internationalist David Lindsay scored for Saints, and in doing so became the first-ever player to score three penalties in a match. Rangers converted another penalty, and before the end both teams scored again to make the final score 5-4 for St. Mirren, while the profusion of penalties earned David Lindsay a place in the history books.

By December 1903 the Ibrox Disaster was still a recent memory, and thoughts turned to the provision of emergency services. St. Mirren received a letter from the St. Andrews Ambulance Association re: "sending of men to all matches at the grounds who would be prepared to render first-aid in cases of emergency." The suggestion was adopted. At the same meeting, a letter came from the secretary of a memorial fund which had been set up to establish a school in memory of Queen Victoria, and as a monument to Scottish Soldiers and Sailors who died in the South African War, "asking that a portion of the proceeds from some popular matches be handed over to this fund". This was a typical example of the diverse nature of requests for assistance that the Club had been asked to consider since the early 1880s.

In a season where one League game included an international football first for St. Mirren, there was nothing historic about the three Scottish Cup ties. Ayr were beaten 2-0 away from home in the first round, and

Another major step was also being considered at this time. Seven years after an abortive attempt had been made to form the Club into a limited liability company, a Mr. Gavin Chittick raised the topic again at the 1904 AGM, and proposed the setting up of a sub-committee "to enquire into and report on the advisability of forming the Club into a limited company". The sub-committee got the go-ahead by 227 votes to 127, and a few days later it was agreed that seven Club members should form the rather grandly titled Limited Liability Enquiry Committee.

Within two weeks of advertising the new Secretary/Manager post sixty applications had been received. About forty were put aside as not being suitable, and the balance was

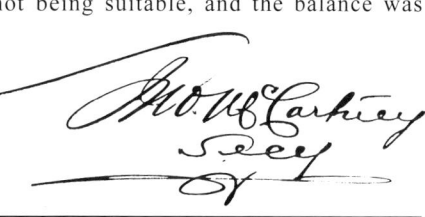

Signing for Saints – John McCartney the first ever Secretary/Manager.

considered on 19 May, where the process eliminated all but four candidates: Mr. J. S. Ferguson and Mr. George Morrell, both from Glasgow, Mr. John Richardson of Edinburgh, and Mr. John McCartney of Barnsley. Three of the four attended for interview on 26 May, but the unfamiliar recruitment process slightly faltered when they were all asked to arrive at the same time!

After the three interviews a discussion followed on the merits of each gentleman, but the fourth candidate, Mr. McCartney, would have to be seen before a final decision was taken. Immediately following John McCartney's interview, Messrs. Morrell and Ferguson dropped out of the reckoning, and in a straight vote between Messrs. McCartney and Richardson the former received nine votes to the latter's three. On 1 June 1904 John McCartney was "elected for one year" as the first Manager of St. Mirren Football Club, but he would stay much longer and be much appreciated.

John McCartney was thirty-eight when he joined St. Mirren, and had been secretary-manager of Barnsley FC for three years prior to coming to Paisley. His playing career as a full-back had commenced with the Busby-based Cartvale FC before joining Rangers in 1886, where he endured a less-than-happy two years. In 1888 he moved on to Cowlairs, and stayed with the Springburn club until the end of the 1892/93 season. He then played twenty games for Newton Heath (Manchester United) during 1894/95 before serving Luton Town for three years. In 1898 he joined Barnsley as a player, but graduated to trainer in 1901, and finally manager in a six year stay in South Yorkshire. St. Mirren had appointed a much-travelled and widely experienced football man; it proved to be an inspired appointment.

1904-05

John McCartney was responsible for everything from negotiating players wages and transfers to travel arrangements. Everything, that is, except team selection. On 9 August 1904, it was the Match Committee who selected wing-half Mick McAvoy as captain for the season, and it was they who picked the team to play the opening game against Dundee at Dens Park. On match days McCartney's job was to manage the resources he was given.

Despite these apparent restrictions, no one was in any doubt that McCartney was in charge of the team, and in September 1904 he devised a set of "bye-laws" which clearly defined the players' obligations to the Club, following the action of David Lindsay "crying off twenty minutes before the start of the home game against Port Glasgow Athletic on 10 September". Around this time, David Lindsay and team captain Mick McAvoy challenged the practice of paying bonuses of ten shillings only to those players who played in the relevant matches. The committee agreed to pay bonuses to both players for one game in which they did not play, but this was a one-off gesture, and the new Secretary was instructed that the two players in dispute "should be shown their agreements".

The early part of season 1904-05 was not a particularly happy time for David Lindsay. On 24 September, he reported twenty-five minutes late for a match against Morton, and the following week his attention was drawn to the official "bye-laws" which had been instigated, in part at least, by his previous misbehaviour. Even his playing form was not appreciated at this time, and his September 1904 reprimand also carried a warning "against his careless play on the field". On 30 May 1905, penalty record-breaker Lindsay moved to Hearts for £100.

One man who would not be around to give John McCartney the benefit of his experience was long-serving St. Mirren committee member, Club President, and for many years the Club's active representative to the S. F. A., James Kay Horsburgh, who during the 1904 close season had decided to retire. A deputation from the General Committee had "endeavoured to induce that gentleman to reconsider his position", but he had "a fixed determination to adhere to his letter of resignation". It was accepted with regret, but Mr. Horsburgh's departure may have been timely. As his era was ending, St. Mirren were on the brink of big changes.

On 3 October 1904 another link with the old St. Mirren ended when the Chairman announced the sad death of Andy Brown, "an old and valued playing member of the Club". In March 1890, Andy Brown had, along with James Dunlop, been the first two St. Mirren players to be capped for Scotland, and it was difficult to comprehend that within fourteen years both had died. It was unanimously agreed that the committee, representing the Club, should record the following resolution in its minutes and that a copy be sent to Mrs. Brown: *"The members of this committee desire to record their deep sense of regret at the death of Mr. Andrew Brown, who for many years was a trusted and tried friend of The St. Mirren Football Club. His period of brilliant service as a player; his unfailing courtesy and geniality; his many self denying and kindly actions are forces that will live long in the hearts of his innumerable friends. The earnest, sincere and universal sympathy of this Committee is extended to Mrs. Brown and family in their great loss."*

On 28 February 1905, an episode began which was a world away from the St. Mirren of Andy Brown and James Horsburgh. Dundee FC offered £100 for Jack Fraser, who had been with Newcastle United for two seasons prior to joining St. Mirren in the summer of 1901. Saints had valued him at £200, and the Paisley response to the Dens proposal was that "we amend the figure and solicit £150". By 11 April, Fraser was looking for "a consideration" from St. Mirren if he were to sign for Dundee. He was advised by St. Mirren to do his best in his negotiations with Dundee, but Saints "might give him £25 out of the (already reduced) £150 transfer fee".

On 18 April, Dundee repeated their offer of £100, and although this time Saints accepted the proposal it wasn't the end of the matter. On 13 June, Fraser wrote insisting on gaining £25 from the transfer fee, and his demand was accompanied by a letter from his solicitor, who forwarded a second threatening letter a week later. The dispute was due to reach the courts on 8 August, but Saints approached Fraser's agent with the compromise that, as the fee between the two clubs had been lower than originally envisaged, he "might be persuaded to accept a sum pro-rata".

On 8 August, the day the case was due to be heard in court, a payment of £20 was made and accepted. Jack Fraser, who later gained a Scottish cap and a cup-winners' medal with Dundee, had been with several clubs in England before joining Saints and was familiar with the developing transfer process, but it was an early lesson for a Club, which for the next 100 years proved to be extremely fair to all their employees when it came to transfer fee benefits.

The Fraser episode should not be taken to suggest that the Club were naive in their transfer market dealings. In October 1904, Fraser's old club Newcastle United had asked St. Mirren to name a figure for their new centre-forward G. Reid, and although Reid was sounded out about a move to the North East of England, the timing of the Geordies' request did not suit St. Mirren. Six months later a similar enquiry from Sunderland was more favourably received, and at the end of April a fee of £325 was agreed. By 9 May no money had been received from Sunderland, so Middlesbrough, who were closely monitoring many of the Saints' team at this time, stepped in and immediately sent a cheque for the asking price. The transfer was completed to St. Mirren's satisfaction, and Reid became a "Boro" player to end his Tyne-Wear-Tees saga.

Tom Jackson (St. Mirren & Scotland)

The Club's most capped player, Tom Jackson, increased his Scotland appearances to four when he played at Wrexham on 6 March 1905. Twenty-two days later he "absented himself from training", and the directors demanded to know why. On 4 April he was informed "that regular attendance was necessary for decorum amongst players. He "promised to amend", but Jackson had been called before the committee already that season. He had been late in arriving for training the previous October, and "a falling off in play" had also been noted. He was advised that "a change is desired at once or steps will be taken to enforce club requirements."

"No man is bigger than St. Mirren" appeared to be the message, but this man Jackson was exceptional in many other ways. He not only left the 4 April 1905 meeting in the company of Secretary/Manager McCartney to jointly arrange a date for his benefit match against Rangers at the end of the season, but a fortnight later he was offered a new contract: the best paid player at the Club!

On the field, Saints won nine and drew four of their twenty-six matches. They then slipped to tenth out of the fourteen teams in the League, but interest in the Club remained high, as was shown by the 18,000 people who watched them beat Hearts 2-1 in the second round of the Scottish Cup, having disposed of Clyde with a single goal victory in the previous tie. Airdrieonians, whose form was consistently better than Saints or Hearts that season, put an end to hopes of Scottish Cup glory with a 3-1 win at Broomfield after a 0-0 draw in Paisley.

It was events off the park which dominated season 1904-05. The Limited Liability Sub-Committee met on 7 October 1904, and were told that the selling price of the Love Street Grounds "would not be less than £5,500", and that an alternative fifteen year lease with gradually increasing rent was also on offer. The sub-committee decided that this purchase price was "outwith the ability of the Club to pay and that further enquiry be made regarding an extended lease and the rental". Thirteen days later the Club were asked to make another offer to purchase the Love Street Grounds, and it was indicated to St. Mirren "that if purchase was not effected a new lease would only be obtained on much different terms and conditions".

This hard bargaining stance on behalf of the Love Street site proprietor was having its effect. It was increasing the chances of the Club moving to a new ground, and on 4 October the Secretary was asked to "ascertain the best terms upon which the Club could purchase Shortroods Estate. The Secretary was also to see bank officials and obtain some idea of what they might be prepared to do in the way of assisting the club in a purchase scheme." By the end of October, the sub-committee decided to draw up more details of the Shortroods site, including a pitch measuring 120 x 72 yards.

As an outcome to the two separate lines of enquiry, the sub-committee recommended to the General Committee that the Club go ahead with the purchase of Shortroods Estate, as per a rough sketch showing just over five acres at £720 per acre, and that the best means to secure this objective was the formation of the Club into a Limited Liability Company. They also recommended "that the members be post-carded for the half-yearly meeting to be held on 11 November at 7.30 pm in the Minor Town Hall to discuss the question of the ground and the Limited Company recommendation."

At the November meeting there was unanimous support for the motion "that the Club go on with the purchase of Shortroods Estate, as per plan produced, showing five acres 937 at £720 per acre, and that best means to secure this object would be the formation of the Club into a Limited Liability Company".

Saints minute their first ever meeting as a limited company, Friday April 21st 1905 in the Good Templar Hall, Paisley.

The last-ever meeting of The St. Mirren Football and Athletic Club took place on 6 February 1905, and seventeen days later the first meeting was convened of the new company's Directors. Five hundred and fifty-four members were each given two shares, and 339 other subscribers bought 2,231 shares between them. Some things didn't change with the metamorphosis from Committee Members to Directors. During March the Directors were still undertaking the spying missions for new players and selecting the team.

On March 21 1905, it was confirmed that St. Mirren's offer of £4,000 to purchase the Love Street site had been accepted, and that a considerable part of the purchase price could be deferred at 33/4% rate of interest. The offer, which was to remain open until 15 May April 1905, was to be considered by the Club's shareholders. The possibility of purchasing the Love Street site had caused the Directors to take up again with the executors for the late Mr. T. McKaig the question of adjacent land. In May 1905, the McKaig Trust "seemed disposed" to favour the Club's move to purchase two acres, at £350 per acre, of adjacent land bounded by Love Street and Greenock Road, and the "proposed new street" (Albion Street).

On 21 April 1905, the first-ever Chairman of The St. Mirren Football Club Limited, Mr. Archibald Towns, welcomed shareholders to the inaugural meeting of the Company, and Secretary John McCartney informed them that negotiations for the purchase of the Shortroods plot had fallen through, due to the fact that the share capital had not been fully subscribed and the sale could only be carried out on cash terms. There had also been difficulties with regard to the removal of the sitting tenant from Shortroods, which had not been foreseen when the original offer was made to St. Mirren. There was now the possibility of protracted negotiations.

On March 30, St. Mirren had written to the sellers of Shortroods regretting "our inability meantime to negotiate further" due to the uncertainty of timing, but the more encouraging events connected with the Love Street option were of considerable financial benefit to the Club, compared with the cost of moving to a new district. Love Street it was; there would be no return to Shortroods for St. Mirren.

A shareholders' meeting in July was needed to endorse it, and it would be 8 August before the deeds of purchase were signed, but on 15 May 1905, the "St. Mirren Grounds" effectively became St. Mirren's property on payment of £1,000 in cash and the balance of the purchase price, £2,900, on Bond at 33/4% rate of interest. Meticulous as any of their predecessors, St. Mirren's new Board confirmed that the cost of converting from "club" to "company" had been £124 3s 11d. St. Mirren now had a full-time manager, they were a limited company, and they owned their own ground. It had been an extremely productive twelve months.

1905-06

Prior to the start of the season, it was confirmed that Saints would continue to wear cream shirts and white pants. They also decided on a change strip of blue and black stripes during a season which would typify a very successful decade. They garnered thirty-one points from thirty League fixtures as Division One was again enlarged, and their thirteen wins and five drawn matches put them in a respectable eighth place in the final table. In the Scottish Cup they reached their fourth semi-final, and although they just failed to overcome the penultimate hurdle, the national tournament again proved to be financially rewarding.

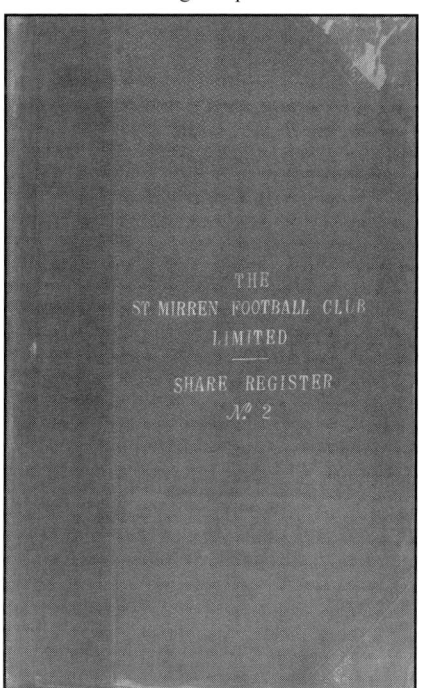

Saints had to unravel the mysteries of Limited company status and the issue of shares.

Eleven of Saints' forty-one League goals were scored by leading marksman David Wyllie, and he was also prominent with a home hat-trick in the first round of the Cup against a Black Watch side crushed 7-2 on 27 January. It should have been an away tie, but St. Mirren suspected the Black Watch didn't have a private ground which complied with the cup rules. After some one-way correspondence from Saints, and the Club paying the not inconsiderable sum of £1 1s for the delivery of a letter to the home of the Black Watch secretary, the S.F.A. reported back to St. Mirren that the Black Watch would play at Paisley.

A home draw in the second round ensured no such ground problems, and Division One Morton were eventually overcome 3-1. Saints were then called upon to travel to meet a very strong-going Airdrieonians side who would finish third top that year. An excellent 0-0 draw at Broomfield took the tie back to St. Mirren Park, where a 2-0 win for Saints saw the Waysiders fall in round three.

There were 16,000 at Love Street on 31 March 1906 to see the first of three semi-final clashes with mid-table Third Lanark. What turned out to be a "fast and stubbornly contested game" ended in a 1-1 draw, and St. Mirren drew most credit from the result as centre-half Robertson and left back Crawford received injuries in the first half "which practically rendered them useless", according to one contemporary report.

A week later, the replay at Cathkin was played in splendid weather before a crowd of 20,000, but it was a disappointingly poor game and ended goalless. Again, Saints were adjudged to have been the superior side, despite the absence of Robertson and Crawford, and the no-scoring outcome was mostly attributed to the performance of the Hi-Hi's 'keeper, James Raeside, and Saints' poor shooting.

The series was losing none of its attraction as another 20,000 turned up at neutral Ibrox. Two days earlier, Crawford and Robertson had undergone "severe tests" and declared themselves fit to play, and Robertson took the trouble to confirm this by telegraph. Finally there was a winner: unfortunately it was Thirds' with a single goal.

One noticeable feature of the change in the Club's status was that the Directors took an even keener interest in the team's performance, and they were not slow to confront Secretary/Manager John McCartney with their opinions. The fitness and condition of Saints' international full-back Tom Jackson was a typical subject of discussion, and at the Board meeting held on 14 November several "expressions of dissatisfaction were given". As a result of this, the Manager arranged for Jackson to undergo two medical examinations, and he was declared fit for the home match the following Saturday against Dundee.

Around the same time, the Directors gained the impression that there were "differences on the field of play between Crawford and Jackson", and John McCartney was asked to ascertain if such was the case. Jackson wasn't interviewed, but Crawford confirmed that no differences existed. That denial didn't stop the Directors making similar assertions in the future!

The Board also had a softer side and on 23 January St. Mirren sent ten shillings to the Dundee-based Lochee United who had written asking for financial assistance as their pavilion had been destroyed by fire. At the beginning of the season a St. Mirren shareholder, a Mr. B. Devaney, made an application for a half-price ticket on behalf of a thirteen year old "delicate lad". The Board decided that the circumstances were exceptional and immediately agreed to the request.

As owners of the ground, one of the Directors' main tasks was the continued improvement of St. Mirren Park. By the end of the season plans had been drawn up for a new stand and terracing, and one hundred railway sleepers had been bought at 6d each for banking purposes. The St. Mirren Directors had consulted other clubs, and were especially grateful to Rangers, who allowed Saints to inspect their own ground improvement plans, an example of the inter-club co-operation which was prevalent at the time.

Insuring the Club's most valuable assets had become another priority, and in March 1906 they accepted an offer from the Scottish Burglary and Fidelity Insurance Company Limited to insure the pavilion for £100 at five shillings per annum. The new insurance company's name may have been on the lengthy side, but few things were as long as the time it was taking to negotiate with the McKaig Trust regarding the buying or leasing of a strip of land 160 yards by 160 yards by an area between the St. Mirren Park boundary and the proposed new (Albion) street frontage.

The Trust's previously positive disposition toward St. Mirren's proposal to buy the land had disappeared by 11 July 1905, and they were refusing to make an offer or suggest a price. St. Mirren obtained a revised valuation which was £650 an acre, almost double what had previously been offered to the Trust.

By 29 March 1906 the Club had weighed up the pros and cons of leasing and buying, and decided to offer £450 per acre, but the McKaig Trust responded that they "would not entertain the price quoted for a moment", and stated that unless St. Mirren met their valuation the negotiations must drop. The price quoted by the Trust was quite out of the reach of St. Mirren, and attempts to buy the land were suspended as the season closed.

1906-07

The black and white St. Mirren flag flew at half-mast from the pavilion on 9 July 1906 when the Club learned of the death of David Fairlie, who had been Club Secretary in the early 1880s, and Saints' sympathy was conveyed to his brother Robert, who had been a member of the first St. Mirren team to win a competition when the Renfrewshire Cup was captured on 14 April 1883.

It was the beginning of a season where personalities were to the fore. Full back Tom Jackson won his fifth and sixth caps, and it was the final season in St. Mirren colours for one of the Club's finest-ever servants. Wing-half Donald Greenlees, who had enjoyed an expenses-free benefit game at the beginning of

Robert Robertson confirms his fitness by telegraph from Renfrew: "No ill effects quite sound" April 1906.

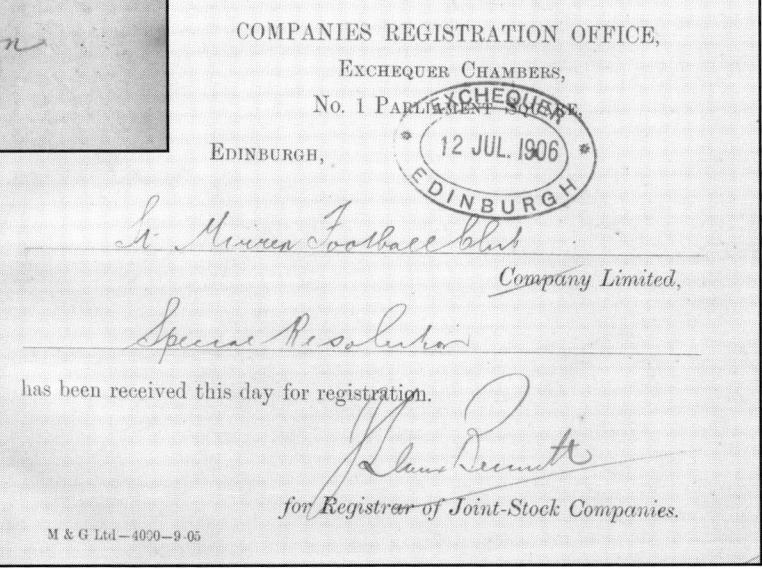

Company business well under way... Special resolution acknowledgement for the new limited company from Companies House in Edinburgh, July 1906.

the season, had been regularly selected throughout, but the prevailing opinion was that he was slightly past his best, and on 6 May 1907 he expressed a willingness to consider a reduction in wages.

The player himself had recognised his career was coming to an end, and in the same discussion he informed Secretary John McCartney that he had the possibility of a job in Southampton. The Club decided to defer making an offer until it was learned how his job offer turned out, but on 16 May it was decided to grant him "a free League transfer", and he was given "a present of £5 in recognition of services rendered and general good conduct". He played for Morton the following season, but continued to train with St. Mirren.

A less satisfying time with Saints was experienced by highly-regarded goalkeeper Livingstone Rae, and on 24 July 1906 he was brought before the Directors and warned as to his conduct, and that any breach of training regulations in the future would be met "by stern measures". Rae had previously been warned back in December 1904 about his misbehaviour and a breach of training rules. On 31 July, Rae was suspended for a fortnight by the Club for failing to keep himself in a fit condition. His wages were cut to two shillings and

Donald Greenlees One of the Club's finest ever servants

Team Group 1906-07
D. Crawford, T. Hart (Vice-Chairman), L. Rae, R. Robertson, R. Fisher (Chairman), D. Greenlees, T. A. Jackson, J. Scouller (Director), A. Kirk (Director)
D. Wyllie, T. Carr, M. McAvoy, A. Anderson, A. McCulloch
G. Hamilton, J. Wilson.

sixpence during the period of suspension, and this decision was upheld despite an expression of regret for past conduct from the player.

Rae's troubles continued, and on 25 September he was reported, not for the first time, to be "the worse for drink". He was again called to appear before the Directors, strongly censured, and told to appear twice daily at the ground. Rae continued to be selected, but a month later the Secretary watched goalkeeper James Grant of Vale of Carron, and he was signed on 5 November 1906. By mid-January Rae was back in the spotlight "for misbehaviour and inattention to training", and on 16 May the almost inevitable happened, and Rae was placed on the transfer list at £200.

By putting Rae up for transfer the Club, by implication at least, were recommending him to other clubs. The same could not be said for R. McLean. Owing to repeated reports of McLean's deterioration in play, not helped by his failure to train every day, it was decided to dispense with his services at the beginning of October. Towards the end of November, Ayr Parkhouse approached Saints asking for the conditional transfer of R. McLean. John McCartney responded by suggesting that the Ayr club should have nothing to do with McLean, and asked if they would not prefer a player called Lynch instead! McCartney must have been persuasive, because on 24 December Lynch was transferred to Parkhouse on condition that they paid £1 of his thirty shilling wages, that he remained a Saints player until the end of 1906/07 season, and that he was available for selection by Saints for the forthcoming Second Eleven Cup Final.

John McCartney and the Board certainly had their standards, as outside left Andrew Wilson from Vale of Clyde discovered. Less than two months after being given a signing on fee of £5 10s 0d in December following a trial against Alloa Athletic, he was "reported again for feeble play at Dumbarton". On 18 February the Board decided enough was enough, and "orders (were) given to hand him his papers"!

In the middle of October, G. Hamilton reported ill with inflammation of the kidneys and this was backed by a medical certificate. A week later the Secretary called on Hamilton at his home, and reported that he was "undoubtedly in a bad way but making a turn for the better." On 12 November, two Directors asked the unfortunate Hamilton for his agreement to accept a cut in wages for the remainder of his illness, because his wages, for no play, "were causing hardship to the Club". The player stated that he was going to Wales for three weeks, but would consider the wage-reduction request on his return.

On 18 December Hamilton resumed training, but on Christmas Eve the Secretary was instructed to "see Hamilton and endeavour to arrange for half wages during the five weeks previous to his resuming training". A week later it was confirmed that Hamilton had "voluntarily remitted £5 from his wages which were due to him during his illness"

Lowering the St. Mirren flag for a former member showed that there was still some sentiment in the game, but it appeared to be diminishing. When Leeds City wrote to St. Mirren in November 1906 to ask for assistance for the widow of D. Wilson, who had been fatally injured in a match for Leeds against Burnley on 27 October 1906, the sum collected at the matches against Dundee and Celtic was just £6 6s 1d. Wilson had been transferred from Saints to the Leeds club at the end of the 1900-01 season, and perhaps five years on few remembered him as a Saints player. For whatever reason, there was disappointment within the Club about the amount to be sent to Leeds, but it is noted that the question of the Club adding to the total didn't arise.

The Hamilton incident showed that the Club, as a limited liability company, were determined to keep their costs under control. They weren't alone in that aim. On 29 November 1906, the Club wrote to the tramway company regarding the number of cars in service on match days and the stopping places at the entrance. By 10 December the tram company had agreed to five stopping places, but this would be monitored for viability.

St. Mirren certainly appreciated that transport had to be profitable. On 19 November, the Club was asked to guarantee a minimum travelling figure as part of the "Football Special" train arrangements. The Board decided to guarantee 200 places for the journey to Greenock. In the event, a total of 497 people made the trip, and the Club earned commission amounting to £1.2s 9d. On 24 December, one Director wanted to know why 500 were guaranteed instead of 200 for the "Kilmarnock Special" It was a legitimate concern, but there was delight after the event when it was learned that the "railway statement showed that 583 passengers had travelled to Kilmarnock and the Club received £1 16s 5d as commission'.

Income arrived from the most unlikely of sources. On 29 May it was advertised in the 'Paisley Daily Express' that part of the ground would be opened as a coup, with St. Mirren charging 3d per load. Seven days later 738 loads had been deposited, giving a total income of £12 5s 9d, and even after purchasing railway sleepers for banking and paying wages a profit of £5 14s 9d was achieved! It wasn't all about money; Paisley didn't regard St. Mirren Football Club as a mere commercial organisation. The Club were in constant demand to aid the community, and when an organisation such as the Wellmeadow Bowling Club asked Saints to play a benefit match in aid of their funds, the Club were delighted to help. Such links with the town could only increase Paisley's goodwill towards the Club.

On the pitch throughout 1906-07 Port Glasgow Athletic always looked likely to end up near the bottom of the League, and it was no real surprise when they finished in eighteenth place in a Division One reconstructed for the fifth time in six seasons. The team from "the Port" survived the vote and remained in the top Division, but at the other end of the county Arthurlie were enjoying their best-ever season in the Scottish League, and were always in contention for a top spot and the possibility of becoming the fourth club to represent Renfrewshire in Division One.

The Barrhead club finished joint second with Vale of Leven, and were a confident lot, particularly at Dunterlie Park, which was the venue for Saints' first round tie in the Scottish Cup. Any doubts about Arthurlie's ability to compete with their more illustrious rivals disappeared at half-time as the home team went in 1-0 ahead. A shock looked on the cards when Tom Jackson missed a second-half penalty, but Crawford scored with another opportunity from the spot after sixty minutes. David Wyllie later scored what proved to be the winner, but it was Arthurlie who emerged from the tie with great credit.

It was another Renfrewshire derby in the second round when Port Glasgow Athletic came to town, but they left Paisley with the League campaign their only concern as Saints eased through with a 4-0 victory and faced up to Hibernian in the third round at Easter Road. The two clubs had matched each other throughout the League campaign, and were equally difficult to separate in "the Scottish". A 1-1 draw in Edinburgh was followed by a repeat of that scoreline in Paisley. Tynecastle was eventually chosen as the venue for the second replay, and the Gorgie ground made Hibs happy in extra time as they scored two without reply from Saints, who were without regular back Crawford and consistent scorer David Wyllie.

The absence of Wyllie was particularly hard to overcome, and the quality of his play attracted the attention of others. On 2 October 1906, Manchester United asked about Wyllie but their enquiry "was not entertained". Two weeks later Stoke City made contact, but "the Potters" were told that St. Mirren "were not disposed to deal". In March 1907 Derby County made an approach for Wyllie's services but "the Rams" were merely "declined".

Throughout the season there was evidence that the bonus scheme had its inconsistencies, this stemmed from a decision taken on 9 October "that each match be judged on its merits". The players were told in advance of the match at Ibrox on 3 November that the bonus to beat Rangers was ten shillings. In the event they drew 1-1, so the Directors decided to grant them five shillings, but to make up the ten shillings offered for a win against Rangers "should they beat the Clyde". There was no separate bonus for beating Clyde - which they did! On 3 December, the bonus decision suggests that the possibility of beating Celtic was already considered something special: "Decided to give the players £1 bonus should they beat Celtic", read the less than confident minutes!

No bonuses were paid out for the match against Aberdeen on 31 December for the simple reason that the Dons didn't appear! As a result, the St. Mirren Secretary produced a statement of the cost to the Club in preparing for the non-event. It totalled £10 16s 11d, and it was decided to ask Aberdeen FC for £15 to settle without going to the League, but "if they offer half we decide to accept". Aberdeen wrote declining to entertain the claim for £15, so St. Mirren turned to the League, and at an SFL meeting on 7 February 1907, it was intimated that £5 had been awarded to St. Mirren by Aberdeen and the matter was closed.

After the excitement of the previous couple of seasons, it had been a "steady as you go" type of season, but at least one decision at the Directors Meeting on 29 April 1907 would prove to be significant. For no apparent reason, they decided to "re-introduce the black and white striped shirt with knickers and stockings as at present". To this day, it's a decision which has never been bettered!

1907-08

The season was just two weeks old when Secretary John McCartney reported on the very unsatisfactory quality of the new black and white shirts, and that they had been returned to the suppliers. Mr. McCartney had contacted Newcastle United regarding their suppliers, and was informed that their shirts had fast colours and were dry cleaned. As a result of this advice, the St. Mirren Secretary was asked to find out the costs associated with the dry cleaning process.

This did not appear to be the solution, and by 12 January the black and white jerseys had washed in so much it was decided to obtain yet another set. This time Notts County were consulted, after which the problem seemed to be solved. It was not the best re-launch of the black and white stripes, but at least there was no mention of returning to cream!

On the field, Saints started the season with a 3-2 win over Motherwell at Fir Park, and by the morning of 26 October the records showed that they had played eleven, won eight, and drawn three to give them their best-ever start to a League season. They had conceded just thirteen goals, but on the afternoon of 26 October they contrived to lose 6-0 away to Dundee.

Two draws and a win followed the Dens debacle, but then Saints really hit trouble with six defeats in a row, during which 19 goals were conceded and only three scored. A New Year draw at Rugby Park signalled the beginnings of an inconsistent second half of the season in which four games were lost, four won, and five drawn. Thanks to their superb start they still managed to finish seventh, but that accomplishment was soon to be re-categorised as peripheral. Squeezed in among these last twelve League fixtures, Saints also played six Scottish Cup ties, and the outcome was an appearance in the final at Hampden for the first time.

It was Division One opposition all the way to the final, and the campaign started with a 3-1 home win over Third Lanark. Fir Park hosted the next tie, but mid-table Motherwell were good enough to fight back from being 2-0 down to claim a 2-2 draw, but they didn't repeat the feat at St. Mirren Park as Saints held their 2-0 lead. In the third round Saints faced a Hearts side which was not enjoying the best of seasons, St. Mirren lived up to their favourites tag by beating the Maroons 3-0 at home.

Saints were now in familiar but unsuccessful territory, and Kilmarnock were their semi-final opponents. A disappointing 0-0 draw at Rugby Park could and should have been different as both sides missed penalties. White was the penalty "sinner" for Saints when the prolific David Wyllie seemed to be the more obvious choice to be spot-kick taker. He underlined this claim in the replay, when his two goals gave Saints a 2-0 win. At the twenty-seventh attempt Saints had reached their first Scottish Cup Final!

The 'Glasgow Herald' greeted the win with the headline "A New Finalist", and paid tribute not only to Saints' achievement, but to the overdue nature of the breakthrough: "After many years of striving St. Mirren have achieved one ambition in reaching the final of the Scottish Cup. That they will do credit to the position we have no doubt. In the present season St. Mirren have experienced acutely the joys of success and the pains of defeat but within the last two months they have maintained a consistency that is strongly reminiscent of that joyous period at the opening of the season."

When the great day arrived on 18 April 1908 one of the local papers reported that "the tie has aroused enormous interest in the community and the exodus city-ward by train, car and brake promises to be a record". Another paper talked of thousands and thousands of Paisley folk "of all classes" who were Hampden-bound. The team would be taking a different route to Mount Florida, their post-lunch departure point would be Waddell's in Union Street, Glasgow, where they would also dine after the match.

Manager John McCartney reported that all his men were fit, so there were no excuses. That was fine, because no one expected to need any excuses. 55,000 spectators were present as the following eleven represented the hopes of Paisley in the town's biggest football event up until then: goalkeeper James Grant (first season in first team), right back Gordon (pre-season signing from Falkirk), left back White, right half William Key (promising pre-season signing from Queen's Park), centre-half Robertson, left half Mick McAvoy, right-winger Clements (previous season signing from West Bromwich Albion), inside right Jimmy Cunningham, centre forward David Wyllie, inside left Tom Paton (pre-season signing from Sheffield Wednesday), and left winger Anderson. It proved too big an occasion for the newly-assembled team, as Celtic ran out convincing 5-1 winners. No excuses; Saints just hadn't performed to their capabilities.

The following Monday's 'Paisley Daily Express' reflected a town's disappointment: "At Hampden on Saturday the St. Mirren sadly belied their reputation when they crumbled away before Celtic and were four goals behind at the finish. Warm supporters of the Paisley club could hardly recognise in Saturday's victims the same team as ousted Third Lanark, Motherwell, Hearts and Kilmarnock in the earlier ties, all after strenuous struggles."

The 'Express' looked for the slightest signs of consolation: "There were isolated good things in the play of certain of the men but all in all they were off their game, apparently quite unnerved by the greatness of the occasion. On the other hand the Celtic were at the top of their form and the marvel is that the score was not bigger."

Even the Celtic players afterwards agreed that the real St. Mirren hadn't been seen at Hampden, but the game turned on the minutes immediately before and after half-time. Celtic's second goal near the end of the first half was scored by Jimmy Quinn from a suspiciously offside position, and Celtic's Rangers-bound Bennett added a third right

By mid-October 1907, the Directors had twice expressed dissatisfaction with the displays of the Club's best paid player, and they decided that "if a very decided improvement is not shown both in play and tactics in the next match" he would be suspended. The "next match" was the calamitous 6-0 defeat by Dundee at Dens on 26 October, and Jackson was again at the centre of the Directors' censure. He was reported to have been "much under the influence of liquor on the return journey despite the fact that he had a facial injury requiring abstemiousness"

Due to the number of repeated warnings the Saints' internationalist had received, he was suspended for one week and his wages reduced to two shillings and sixpence. Jackson was included in the party but not the team for the game at Ibrox two weeks later. He turned up late and was in further trouble with the Board. The public's view of the treatment of Jackson had led to considerable criticism of the Board in the letters' column of the 'Paisley Daily Express', but a subsequent interview with John McCartney in that paper, at the Board's behest, was regarded as having set the record straight.

Jackson was late in turning up for the home match against Morton on 16 November and gave fog as his excuse, but in addition to being admonished for his tardiness he was ordered "not to interfere or shout at other players in the team". On April 30 1908, Jackson was informed that

Team Group 1907-08 with Club Directors
Mr M. Laidlaw (Director), Mr J. Scouller (Director), T. A. Jackson, R. Robertson, J. Grant, D. Gordon, M. McAvoy, Mr W. Blackett (Director),
Mr J. Kilpatrick (Director), Mr A. Kirk (Director), Mr T. Hart (Vice-Chairman), J. Hindle (Trainer), Mr J. McCartney (Secretary),
H. Clements, J. Cunningham, Mr R. Fisher (Chairman), T. H. Paton, A. L. Anderson, W. Key, T. A. Milne.

after the interval. After that Saints looked a beaten side, and Jimmy Cunningham becoming St. Mirren's first-ever scorer in a Scottish Cup Final was the only other incident worthy of note.

Worthy of note throughout the season was the spectacular fall from grace of Tom Jackson, St. Mirren's most capped player in the Club's first one hundred and three years. He had been given permission to go to New York during the close season on condition that he returned to Scotland in time for pre-season training on 23 July.

On July 29 it was reported that Jackson had not put in an appearance for training, and by 6 August, nine days before the start of the season, there was still no sign of him. Jackson was "suspended forthwith sine die and fined all wages from 23 July". The Club's decision was forwarded to the S.F.A, and Tom Jackson was informed of the Club's decision in writing. Jackson reported for training on 14 August, the day before the opening fixture at Fir Park. He was informed that, due to his failure to report for training on 23 July, his suspension began from that date. Within a week he was back in the team.

"the Directors regretted their "inabilty to re-engage him"and three weeks later he was placed on the open-to-transfer list at £200. Jackson immediately offered to play for £3 instead of £4 per week, and as the season ended the matter remained unsettled, but it looked unlikely that Tom Jackson's relationship with St. Mirren Football Club could be redeemed.

Tom Jackson was not alone in being admonished by the Board, and throughout the 1907-08 season at least two players per week were hauled in front of the Board to be told that they weren't playing well or they were giving half-hearted displays. Like school children, each pledged to play better in future, knowing that if they didn't a series of penalties right up to dismissal awaited them.

This period underlined that the manager's role remained that of implementing the policies of the Club. It was the Board which decided which players were to be retained or transferred, and there were times when Secretary John McCartney, wearing his managers hat, had to force the issue as to whether a player was to be left on the transfer list. There wasn't much happening at the Club which didn't involve the Board, and this was underlined when it was decided in October 1907 that from that point on the Chairman would act as linesman! In such circumstances it was no real surprise when they decided that, in addition to a team photograph featuring the players, Trainer, and Secretary, a second group photograph should be taken which included the Directors.

The Board had real ambition for St. Mirren, but their representative at a Scottish League meeting observed at first hand how others already had the power and influence. On 1 March 1908, there was considerable concern about the manner in which Rangers and Celtic had arranged fixtures between themselves without consideration for others. Appeals for fair play were ignored, and some clubs walked out in disgust before the vote was even taken. A 'Paisley Daily Express' editorial the following day strikes a prophetic note: "The League, it was loudly trumpeted, was formed for mutual success, interest and profit but this latest success of Celts and Rangers seems to make for monopoly."

Tom Jackson was not in the cup final team, but even if he had been included he may not have been given a medal, because the Club initially decided to buy just eleven commemorative medals in lieu of a bonus, and present them to those players who not only played in the final, but who were to be retained by the Club the following season. It was then agreed that a further four medals should be given to Mr. Laidlaw the linesman, players Milne and Wilson, and the Secretary/Manager Mr. McCartney, who was also given a grant of six guineas for his part in steering the Club to its first ever Scottish Cup Final. The medals were to have black and white flags in enamel with the inscription "Scottish Football Association Cup Finalists 1907-08". On the other side, "St. Mirren FC Ltd." and the Burgh Coat of Arms in enamel.

Despite the season's problems with the black and white striped shirts, the design of the medals suggested these were now regarded as the Club's colours, and this view was strengthened when Director Thomas Hart declared on 12 June 1907 that " black knickers were decidedly more preferable than white with the black and white striped shirts." The shirts weren't even mentioned. The stripes, dry-cleaned or not, Newcastle or Notts, were here to stay.

1907-08 had started with a record-breaking undefeated run in the League and ended in a historic Hampden appearance in the Cup. Despite the eventual result, making their Scottish Cup Final debut was Saints' first honour, and 18 April 1908 was the greatest day in Saints' first thirty years. The frequency of their participation in Scottish football's showpiece was set to rise as the twentieth century unfolded.

1908-09

There was unanimous agreement amongst the Board on 10 June 1908 to re-engage Tom Jackson and accept his offer of a reduced pay, but he was no longer to be featured in an advert on the Season Ticket. Jackson's strained relationship with the Club was becoming well-known, and on 30 June 1908 Preston North End wrote asking for particulars about Jackson and the amount of transfer fee St. Mirren required, but no move materialised. Jackson himself made a move at the beginning of August 1908, when he applied for a free transfer "to assist him in his efforts to obtain the Secretaryship of Third Lanark FC". No contact was received from Third Lanark.

Saints began 1908-09 with two away defeats at Pittodrie and Cathkin, but the 2-0 home victory over Hearts on 29 August marked the start of a ten-match unbeaten run which included seven victories. One of the drawn games in this sequence came against Queen's Park on 10 October 1908, in a game which had crowd trouble, an incompetent refereeing display, and a show of indiscipline by Saints' two wing-halves.

The worst offender of the pair was right half William Key, playing against his former club, who took exception to some of the comments directed at him from the crowd and proceeded to strike a spectator. The Board severely censured Key, and instructed him that no matter what provocation he received in future he must not "take that course again". They weren't much happier with the dissent shown by the team captain. Left-half Mick McAvoy was told after the game that "he must not argue points on the field with the referee as such conduct is resented by the Directors". It would not be the last time McAvoy would displease the Board during 1908-09.

The behaviour of the two half-backs was bad enough, but the throwing of various sizes of stones and ash at Referee Edward by a section of the crowd after a particularly contentious incident in the Queen's match was enough to have the ground closed by the S.F.A. for two weeks. The Directors considered and then rejected thoughts of an appeal against closure, and also decided to take no further action on the question of the referee's competency, but they did request "as a favour" that Mr. Edward was not sent to Paisley again that season, although the Club would be happy to accept him officiating at away games. The home match against Hibs on 31 October was forced to take place away from Love Street, and Dunterlie Park in Barrhead was the choice, with Arthurlie charging a £5 ground fee.

A week after the 1-0 win over Hibs at neutral Dunterlie, a narrow 3-2 defeat by Airdrieonians at Broomfield on 7 November saw them falter, but they then had another five game run without failure, which gave them a highly impressive record of played 18, won twelve, drawn four, and lost just two by the time they headed to Dens Park on 19 December. This was championship-winning form, but for the second successive year an away match against Dundee proved to be the season's turning point. The Dark Blues won 4-1, and only three more matches were won all season, a record not helped by the prolonged absence of inside right Tom Paton due to a broken collar bone suffered during the Dundee defeat. Five days earlier, prolific scorer David Wyllie was transferred to Fulham for £300, with the player gaining £200 as his part of the move.

The loss of two important players may not have been the only factor which contributed to the team's drastic dip in form. On 25 January 1909, the Board discussed the need to settle on who should be the responsible

Letter from the Abercorn Football and Athletic Club to the Committee of St. Mirren Football Club Limited, bemoaning Saints arranging fixtures in opposition to their home matches. A compromise was reached.

D. Crawford

party to talk to the players on points of play during the course of matches. Complaints had been made "of too many interfering and upsetting the men". The Board were of the opinion that only the Director in charge should give orders or instructions as circumstances required, a ruling which throws further light on the peripheral influence John McCartney was permitted to bring to the "Manager" side of his Secretary/Manager job title. The Board continued to reprimand players for all manner of misdemeanors. Amongst those facing a Directors' rebuke was a player called Gourlay who was challenged "over his back-heeling proclivities"!

In the first round of the Cup in January 1909, St. Mirren offered non-league Alloa Athletic £50 and half of the gate money exceeding £100 as an inducement to switching the tie to Paisley. The Clackmannanshire club were happy with the £50, but wanted half the total gate money. St. Mirren withdrew the offer and the game went ahead at Recreation Park, resulting in a 2-2 draw. The difference in the two teams' status was more obvious in the replay, as Saints ran out 5-0 winners. In the second round another non-league outfit, Beith, were beaten 3-0 at home, but when the third round took Saints to Shawfield on 20 February to face a Clyde side enjoying their best-ever League campaign, a 3-1 reverse put an end to Saints' cup interest.

A cup exit is always difficult to bear, but five days after the Shawfield defeat the Directors gave consideration to a topic they considered even more important. They had for some time been receiving numerous reports of "loose conduct on behalf of several players", and decided that "suspensions would certainly follow on all well authenticated cases". They felt that "the credit of the Club was at stake and strong measures were necessary to combat their evil influence".

There was no shortage of examples of this "loose conduct". Harry Ross, right back and captain of Fulham and previously of Burnley, had been signed in mid-October, having been rated by two Directors as being "certainly a great player who appeared sound in mind and limb". A fee of £275 was agreed with the Craven Cottage club, with Ross receiving £100 plus £6 removal expenses. By 26 December, his play was regarded as showing "great deterioration", and by 11 January he had been placed on the transfer list. A week later, the Directors "forbid his action in raffling and selling jewellery amongst the other players".

By 22 February, Ross was regarded as being "out of condition". Reports mentioned "secret drinking", and following the Clyde cup tie he did not contact the Club until 8 March. By then the Board had "undoubted proof of his hard drinking for a period", and as a result Ross was suspended without pay until the end of the 1908-09 season.

Tom Brown, signed at the end of the 1907-08 season from Sunderland, was another who was causing problems. According to John McCartney, shortly after he signed there had been "much talk of a cruel kind" regarding Ross, but Sunderland AFC had verified that "the rumours were entirely false". The rumours weren't specified, but Brown was one of two players who had been seen by the Board in mid-December "about their moral character", and to the great annoyance of the Directors, Brown himself did a bit of talking when he "publicly declared before the third round cup-tie that he had no intention of trying". He was also reported for drunkenness, and there had been complaints about his behaviour at the Paisley Theatre.

The bad behaviour could not just be attributed to a failure to check on the character of new signings. Team captain Mick McAvoy, fine player though he was, was also proving to be a poor role model. In May 1907 he had been offered a reduced wages deal at the same time as Donald Greenlees, and then surprisingly the following season was made captain. Already in 1908 he had been accused of using bad language as he left the field of play following a 3-1 home defeat by Rangers on Boxing Day, but matters came to a head on 8 March 1909 when Chairman Mr. John Scouller reported that, after the home win over Aberdeen on 6 March, the player had "in the presence of witnesses made use of insulting and obscene expressions regarding the Club". He had also shown "insubordination towards the officials at the cup tie against Clyde".

It was felt that "in the interest of decorum something must be done to protect the players and officials". The Directors unanimously decided to dismiss McAvoy from the service of the Club. He was to be paid his wages up to the end of his engagement, and a letter to that effect was forwarded to McAvoy along with a cheque for £24 for wages. The loss of inside right Tom Paton during the Dundee defeat may have been the only public explanation for the team's slump in form, but unprofessional behaviour by a number of players was also taking its toll, and the Directors had begun to re-establish the standards they expected from St. Mirren players.

At the end of March 1909, Secretary John McCarthy reported that he had had a meeting with Mr. Stevenson, the editor of the 'Paisley Gazette', regarding stories appearing which were "detrimental to the club's best interests". These stories were not detailed, but the Directors' dissatisfaction with the antics of Ross, Brown, McAvoy, and others suggests that there was recognition within the Club that the main fault did not lie with the messenger.

Off the field problems weren't confined to the players. Trainer John Hindle, warned on two occasions the previous season about "failing to turn up for duty", was accused of being economical with the truth over his involvement in a drinking bout with Harry Ross on 24 February 1909. He was put "on probation" until the end of the season, but Mr. Hindle's entrepreneurial leanings were a constant source of concern to the Board, and on 12 April 1908 he was asked the exact nature of business he intended to carry-out during his meal hour. It transpired that the trainer's aim was to "make a few shillings" by making a few calls and taking a few bets for a certain Mr. Thomas Bonar.

The Board were unhappy with this response, which, from their knowledge of events, fell some way short of the whole story. One director produced a business card bearing the name "John Hindle" which advertised the soliciting of bets. Back in April 1907, Hindle had been instructed to give up all gambling and devote his time to club business or he would lose his position as trainer. In April 1909, two Directors, Messrs. Laidlaw and Kirk, both claimed to have been grossly insulted by Hindle. They complained about "his language and bearing towards them in the presence of visiting officials", but the Board deferred taking action. In May the Club drew up an agreement with Mr. Hindle, and pointed out to him that only due to his domestic position was he retained at all. For a group of Directors never slow or unwilling to be critical of players' performances, they showed remarkable patience and understanding in their dealings with John Hindle.

Mick McAvoy

A month after the Shawfield defeat a sad little episode began to unfold. Former Saints and Scotland goalkeeper John Patrick, who between 1897 and 1899 had been willing to live for two years in a house on the club grounds which was eventually rated "unfit for habitation", had written to the Club on 23 March 1909 asking for assistance as he was unable to work due to illness. Saints regretted that they couldn't help, but it wasn't a definite 'no', because they decided to find out whether Patrick's application was genuine! John Patrick wrote again a week later, and this time Saints opted to send him thirty shillings to meet his unfortunate circumstances. In response, Patrick, who only twelve years earlier at Crystal Palace had played a starring role in Scotland's 2-1 win over England, wrote and thanked the Club for their kindness.

St. Mirren Park had greatly improved since John Patrick's time, and now that it was owned by the Club there was even greater emphasis on enhancing its facilities. In mid-April the Board were looking at ways to improve the pavilion and the perimeter barricades, and two Directors had also visited the Airdrieonians' pavilion to inspect their heating system in action with a view to up-grading the Love Street equivalent. These remained minor adjustments. It was the acquisition of some adjoining land owned by the McKaig Trust which would enable St. Mirren to maximise the Love Street location, but discussions on this topic were intermittent and frustrating. To enable the Trust to decide on a price, nine months earlier a ground plan had been prepared on behalf of St. Mirren using part of the McKaig land, and the adoption of this plan would enable the playing pitch to be brought up to "international requirements" and a grandstand could be built.

In February 1909 talks with the Trust re-opened. By 5 April 1909 they looked to be closed again, as the Club received advice from the Trust "that the lowest price for ground is £8,350, with payment on previously quoted terms". John McCartney was instructed to advise the Trust "the price is so ridiculously high that the Directors find it utterly impossible to consider the question of relieving the Trustees of their ground."

The season finished on 24 April 1909 at Clune Park, Port Glasgow. There was apparently no appetite to extend it, as a short-notice request from the then-struggling Woolwich Arsenal to play a "guarantee match" near the end of April was deemed 'unable to arrange'. It is unlikely that the declined response to Arsenal was because of the Paisley Charity Cup, because the competition seemed to be struggling through the apathy of some of the expected participants. An eleven-a-side tournament was a non-starter with Johnstone, Arthurlie, and Academicals, and eventually Saints agreed to host a five a side tournament at St. Mirren Park.

At the end of the 1908-09 season Tom Jackson's name was again included in St. Mirren's open-to-transfer list, but the fee was now reduced from £200 to £100. The previous September, Clyde FC had asked for the player on a month's trial, but it was not a success. Clyde expressed their thanks to St. Mirren for the loan of the player but "decided to have nothing further to do with him". A few days later on 16 October, John McCartney confirmed he had re-registered the player with the League, but in an incident-packed season the former internationalist remained curiously detached, seldom selected by St. Mirren and unwanted by others.

1909-10

The hard-line taken by the Directors towards those St. Mirren players with wayward tendencies had its effect, and the 1909-10 season was free from such diversions. By Christmas, the team had recorded a respectable nine wins and four draws in eighteen fixtures, but on 20 January 1910, Secretary/Manager Mr. John McCartney intimated that he had been approached by Heart of Midlothian, who "desired his services".

Mr. McCartney had decided to accept the "first class terms on offer" from Hearts, subject to obtaining release from his contract with St. Mirren. Saints immediately made him an improved offer in an attempt to keep him, but to no avail. Mr. McCartney thanked his directors "for their very kind and substantial terms", but felt that he had gone too far with the Edinburgh club to withdraw honourably. Mutual regrets were exchanged, and St. Mirren decided to advertise for a replacement immediately. After he departed for Tynecastle, the Board voted John McCartney an honoranium of £10 for his services. They also decided to write to Heart of Midlothian about the calibre of the man who was about to become the Edinburgh club's new Secretary/Manager:

> We have the pleasure of bearing testimony to Mr. John McCartney's qualifications. For six years he has been employed here as Secretary and Manager, and now, of his own account, leaves us to take up another post of a like nature in Edinburgh. Shortly after Mr. McCartney's advent to Paisley, our Club was converted into a Limited Company, and the many duties of an exceptional nature arising at that time of transition were by him efficiently carried through. As a secretary his work has always been of the most satisfactory nature due in a large measurement to the careful and methodical manner in which his clerical duties have at all times been performed. In the management etc. of players and in the general conduct of our business, he has carried into these his wonted enthusiasm and has devoted himself absolutely to the furtherance of our interests. We should have only been too pleased to retain his services, but in knowing that in doing so his advancement would be retarded, and accordingly we part with him regretfully at the same time feeling certain that with the qualities displayed by him while in Paisley, his success in football management is secured.
>
> For THE ST. MIRREN FOOTBALL CLUB LIMITED
> John Scouller
> Chairman

John McCartney's resignation proved to be the decisive act of a season which had opened with optimism. By the time the season ended, only four more wins had been gained and only one win in the last eight. Mr. McCartney's successor lasted just over two months in the job.

McCartney may have left St. Mirren's employment, but his name immediately featured in the St. Mirren minutes as manager of Hearts. On 24 February, he restated his new club's interest in centre forward George Buchanan, whose chequered career would have been well known to McCartney. Buchanan had been put on the open to transfer list on 19 May 1908 for a fee of just £25, but was later taken off. In early November 1908, Liverpool expressed an interest, and the Anfield club were told that his fee was now £350! They had him watched but felt he was over-valued!

Buchanan continued to catch the eye and in March 1909 Rangers expressed an interest, but on 10 January 1910, another side of him emerged when he was suspended for a month after being asked to play for the "A" team. He "religiously refused to make any effort on the field", and "the offence was aggravated by his declaration to several players and in the hearing of officials that he was not going to try a leg". Furthermore, "his conduct on the field was the cause of an unprecedented demonstration at the close of the match".

By February 1910, Saints were asking Hearts for £150 with a further £50 if the Maroons re-signed the player for the following season. St. Mirren also demanded a percentage of any subsequent transfer fee received for Buchanan by Hearts. In the end, George Buchanan was transferred to Hearts, and the following season he was the Gorgie club's top scorer.

During the 1909 close season there had been considerable activity around the ground, and plenty of evidence that the Club was important to the commercial life of the town. No less than twenty-nine offers were received by 11 June 1909 to carry out improvement works on the pavilion. They were predominantly local, and eventually the brickwork was awarded to G. Robertson of Love Street, A. Keith of St. James Street did the joinery, and Hunter & Gourdie of Causeyside did the plumbing. When the work was completed, the pavilion balcony's forty-four seats were made open for the public at twenty-one shillings for the season. The remaining fourteen seats were for the exclusive use of home officials and visitors.

Director Thomas Hart attended the League meeting of 13 July and reported that "kick offs at 3.30pm were to be considered universal", which would end the staggered nature of start times. Perhaps more controversially for a sport which was always looking for good press coverage, it had also been decided "that clubs decline to give gate and stand drawings for press purposes".

The benefits which football gets from media exposure were more appreciated at Club level when St. Mirren invited the press to view the new pavilion on 19 August, and the revitalised pavilion was topped off with a new black and white striped flag which included "St. M.F.C. Ltd" as a prominent and proud feature. In another positive note in the run up to the new season, sales of ten shilling season tickets were reported to be "phenomenal".

At the end of July 1909, Division Two champions Abercorn asked Saints to open their new ground, New Ralston Park, on Tuesday 31 August. Saints replied that they were unable to do so at the start of season, but would consider doing so later. The fixtures congestion excuse to Abercorn had been genuine, and during early August Saints played two practice matches where a total of £33 11s 3d was collected, these funds were distributed to local worthy causes. Abercorn had three months earlier offered Saints a match at (Old) Ralston Park on a "1/2 gate and Stand" terms. It didn't take place either, which was a pity, because in the previous twenty-four months the growing gap in status between the two clubs had been arrested, and Abercorn still believed an Abbies/Saints match had considerable public appeal.

They persisted in that view, and in mid-December Mr. Hamilton Neil, Chairman of Abercorn FC, visited St. Mirren and asked for a "benefit match" to be played on 31 December, but the request was declined due to fixture congestion. Mr. Neil expressed his disappointment and hoped a match could be arranged later in the season. The Abercorn Chairman wrote again on 21 February for a "benefit game in aid of their New Field Fund". Saints had hoped to find a suitable date sometime in March or April, but Abercorn finally got a game with St. Mirren when the two met in the two-legged Renfrewshire Cup Final.

3,000 were at New Ralston on the evening of 26 April to see Paton and Millar give Saints a 2-0 first leg lead. Four days later, the replay coincided with Saints' last League game at Shawfield against Clyde. The following full-strength team was selected to play Abercorn: McBurnie, Reid, Featherston, Harvey, Allan, Weir, Clements, Miller,

Paton, Milne, and Cunningham, who was Saints scorer in a 1-1 second leg draw. It was the same team which had played in the first leg, and was a clear indication that Saints considered the County trophy to be important, and that Abercorn were still worthy of their respect.

The Scottish League must have taken a similar view, because St. Mirren's action in sending the Reserves to play at Shawfield went unpunished. Clyde won 2-1 and finished fifth top, so the Saints' Reserves must have given a good account of themselves!

Saints' first match of the season was due to take place on 21 August, and the players had been instructed to appear for pre-season training at the end of July. All turned out except for Grant, Reid, and White. Goalkeeper James Grant, outstanding during the previous season, asked to train at Falkirk, which was much nearer home. Grant had done this in previous seasons, but he was informed that meantime "he must turn out on Tuesdays". He did not respond. Right back Reid had trained with St. Bernards in Edinburgh without permission. He was told to "train here until further orders", which he did. White "could not turn up before 16 August".

There were no repercussions to the three players missing the first pre-season training session, but the Club's Directors were determined that discipline would be tight. The player registration system meant that clubs held the power, and the everyday presence of under-used players like Jackson, McAvoy, and Ross was a constant reminder of what could happen if a player stepped out of line. At the start of the 1909-10 season Tom Paton was unanimously chosen to replace Mick McAvoy as first team captain, and McAvoy joined Jackson and Ross in the retained-but-surplus-to-requirements category, despite the Club's earlier intentions to dismiss him.

Jackson began a second season facing the prospect of being severely under-utilised, as all his plans to move elsewhere had floundered. In late December, the Club noted that the 'Weekly Record' had carried what it considered to be "untrue and unfair statements as to the Club's dealings with Jackson. The Club decided to put their version of events to the editor in order to "having our position made right with the public" and this appeared in print on 25 December 1909. The Board considered this outcome to be satisfactory.

In May 1909, Harry Ross remained on the transfer list and was valued at £400, £125 more than he had cost. By 28 September, when Burnley enquired about the fee required to buy back their former player, they were told that St. Mirren would consider any reasonable offer, which is exactly what the player was told a month earlier. This did not satisfy the player, who applied to the League in late October to have his transfer fee reduced, but the League "declined to interfere". By the end of the season the player was again asking the Club to reduce his transfer fee, but the request was ignored and there were no further enquiries from Burnley or anyone else.

In Tom Brown's case, there was a definite intent to employ his talents, but injuries were disrupting such plans. By 24 January he had played in eleven Saturdays out of twenty-three, taking part in four first team matches, seven "A" team games, and a county cup tie. In June 1910, Woolwich Arsenal asked about Brown and were told that St. Mirren's selling price was £150. By 4 July there was no response from the South London club.

In September 1909 there was no response from the hot water tap in the home dressing room, because the Clyde trainer had drawn off too much for the visitors. Trainer John Hindle was told to liaise with his opposite numbers in future, but it was a message he failed to heed, because three weeks later the unsupervised Partick Thistle trainer emulated his Clyde counterpart, and the result was that the Saints players again had no hot water in the home dressing room. To prevent a recurrence, St. Mirren put a stop valve on the visitors pipe which forced them to seek out Trainer Hindle before hot water could be drawn from the boiler.

Problem fixed? Alas, no. On 20 November there was again no hot water for the home team, despite the stop valve. This time Hindle had gone to retrieve the match ball from over the wall in the adjoining McKaig Trust ground. He left the cold water running and spoiled the bath!

These minor inefficiencies were emanating from a man who had a catalogue of much more serious misdemeanors behind him, and he was adding more. Hindle and hot water seemed made for each other. In July 1909 several of the Directors were far from satisfied with the general appearance of the ground, and Mr. Hindle was informed "to complete his requirements at once". Two days after the November no-water incident, he was accused of again being involved with gambling, and this time five different people accused him of not paying out monies owed. He emphatically denied all the accusations, and amazingly the Board took no further action. On 29 June he was yet again called before the Board regarding his non-attendance at the ground. It was yet again impressed upon him that on no occasion must he leave the grounds other than at hours arranged for meal times.

One of John McCarthy's last tasks at Love Street involved the home fixture with Celtic, due to be played on 29 January. Always lucrative, it was in danger of postponement due to snow covering the ground. Between Thursday morning and Saturday at 2pm, 620 loads of snow had been cleared and 24 tons of sand spread at a cost of £18 14s 7d. The effort proved to be worth it. Not only were the gate receipts £228 3s 3d, plus stand takings of £14 18s 6d, but Saints beat ten-man Celtic 2-1.

A week prior to the Celtic match, Saints had beaten Highland League Elgin City 8-0 in the first round of the Scottish Cup. Their next cup opponents were Hearts. The first game ended in a 2-2 draw after Saints had been two in arrears, and for the replay Saints arranged a special saloon to be fixed to the players train. They would lunch at the Corn Exchange and would take tea in Bissets after the match. Some of the other replay arrangements went less well. Hearts would not agree to Saints' nominees for a match referee. They in turn asked St. Mirren if they would contemplate an Englishman, but Saints replied that no English nominee should be considered, and if Hearts wouldn't accept this then they were to apply to the SFA.

After all the pre-match fuss the game ended goal-less, although Hearts did miss a penalty, and neutral Ibrox was the location for the second replay. After an early injury to Saints influential defender Bob Robertson, the increased win bonus of £2 on offer for the Ibrox game was never in danger of being paid out, as Hearts ran out convincing 4-0 winners. Club minutes show that the Chairman of Hearts wrote later congratulating St. Mirren on the "sportsmanlike manner we took our defeat in the Scottish tie," and "hoped that the good friendship existing between the two clubs be long maintained".

The Club, keen to attract the widest possible support, tried to improve the supporters' behaviour on a regular basis, and an incident which took place in the Stand on 26 February highlighted this. A shareholder named James Russell was assaulted by a ticket holder named Adam for reproaching him for using bad language. The Board sympathised with Mr. Russell, and supported him "in charging the party to the Police and hoped that the sentence on Adam at the Police Court on Monday morning would be a lesson to others whose conduct is objectionable." Violence should never be condoned, but in Mr. Adam's defence it seems only fair to point out that watching St. Mirren has always been a passionate business, and on the day in question St. Mirren were beaten 6-1 by Rangers!

The Rangers match was the third match under the stewardship of Mr. W. Barrie Grieve. Although the managerial vacancy was advertised, there is no record of any other candidates being interviewed, and Mr. Grieve was unanimously appointed Secretary and Manager on 15 February 1910. By 1 March he had moved from Kilmarnock to a house in North Street in Paisley, and seven weeks later he was asked to leave.

On 23 April 1910, a meeting was held to discuss Mr. Grieve's conduct. "The condition of affairs were such that drastic measures would have to be taken at once," summarised the temporary minute recorder: "It was agreed to consult the company's solicitor regarding the dismissal of the said official. The solicitors advised that based on what he had been told dismissal was an appropriate action, and so it was done. Mr. Grieve wrote to the Board asking to be given another chance, and on 30 May he again asked the Board to reconsider their decision. This was declined, and he was asked to return all papers belonging to the club.

St. Mirren ended in thirteenth place in the League, their worst finish in twenty years of League football, but it was not part of a trend. They had finished 9th, 5th, 6th, 6th, 10th, 8th, 7th, 7th, and 7th in the other years of the 1900s, and had reached the final of the Scottish Cup. Beyond dispute, they were the leading club in the county and were widely recognised as one of Scotland's best teams. The "Club" had become a company, but their identification with the community was stronger than ever. The 1910s could be faced with confidence.

The 1910's - Conflict, Cochrane and a Cup

1910-11

Throughout 1910-11, St. Mirren advertised their home matches on a regular basis in the 'Evening Times', 'Evening News', and 'Daily Record', but it was for the more specific purpose of providing details of their Secretary/Manager vacancy that the Club used the pages of the 'Glasgow Herald' and the other three newspapers on 20 June 1910.

CHAPTER FIVE
The 1910's

A week later four candidates were interviewed, in the second round of voting Mr. Hugh Law attracted four votes to Mr. Hugh Spence's three, and Mr. Law was duly appointed Secretary/Manager of St. Mirren with the one proviso that he must reside in Paisley.

After a decade of consolidation as one of the top clubs in Scotland and a six year period of continuity under John McCartney, St. Mirren had experienced a period of relative uncertainty, with three Secretary/Managers in less than five months. Mr. Law's tenure would eventually equal that of Mr. McCartney, but one of his earliest thoughts must have been how fortunate he was to have inside-right Jimmy Cunningham in his team.

Cunningham, who had received £36 from a benefit game at the beginning of the season, would end up as top scorer with eighteen goals, and during the season his signature would be sought after by Third Lanark, Celtic, Rangers, Woolwich Arsenal, Kilmarnock, and Partick Thistle. He was undoubtedly the star man of the team in 1910, and such was his consistency of performance that he even managed to draw favourable post-match comments from the usually hard-to-please Directors.

Also drawing a compliment from a Board member was the high-scoring inside forward's younger brother Robert, who made a favourable first impression following his home debut against Queen's Park on 12 November. "Best outside right we have tried this season", was one Director's verdict, but the new winger's contribution was eclipsed by the elder Cunningham, who scored twice in a 3-1 home win over the League's bottom club.

It was only Saints' third victory in eleven League matches, and this one-win-in-three return was set to continue throughout the season. Such form didn't suggest a home win when League leaders Rangers were the visitors on 17 December, but two goals from that man Cunningham were sufficient to give Paisley's pride a 2-1 victory.

On 8 December, two days before a home match with Morton, goalkeeper James Grant reported that he was unfit to play due to a sharp attack of pleurisy. The Club immediately made arrangements to secure the services of William Duncan from Airdrieonians for £75, and a further £25 if he was signed for the following season. Although Grant was much improved by the time of the Scottish Cup first round match against Celtic on 28 January, it was Duncan who lined up at Celtic Park in a Saints' team without Jimmy Cunningham, and the injured forward's goal threat was greatly missed as Celtic went through 2-0.

A month before the Celtic cup-tie, former Sunderland player Tom Brown, whose three and a half year stay at Paisley had been less than successful, was transferred to Hamilton Academical until the end of the season. If the move became permanent then the "Accies" would pay a transfer fee of £75. Two days after the Celtic cup tie, it was decided that Clyde would be allowed to approach recent first choice 'keeper James Grant with a view to transferring him to the Shawfield side until the end of the season.

Saints' League form continued to disappoint in the second half of the season, and they finished in twelfth place - just one position better than the previous season. This wasn't what Saints' fans had been used to in the previous ten years, but there was some consolation for them and the new manager when the Renfrewshire Cup was captured for the tenth time when Johnstone were beaten 3-2 in Johnstone and 1-0 in Paisley.

One surprising aspect of the County Cup success was that Jimmy Cunningham failed to score in any of the three matches. Perhaps he had used up his season's quota. In a noteworthy friendly match against Airdrieonians just three days before the second leg of the Renfrewshire final, three penalties were awarded to Saints in the first half, and they were all for handling offences. St. Mirren eventually won 4-2, all four goals were scored by the Cunningham brothers, with right-winger Robert getting one and Jimmy claiming a hat-trick.

A week before the Airdrie match, Saints had squeezed in another friendly when they responded to a press advertisement commissioned

1910, and the club agree that a 'Mirror of Life' photographer may 'take snapshots at the ground". This cutting from the same publication, dated December 1910 versus Hearts, shows the small space for spectators on the site of today's North Bank. The terraces were later built up and the ground widened towards Albion Street.

by Glentoran to play an Easter Tuesday match at the Oval in Belfast. Saints offered to make the trip for £35, which was accepted by the East Belfast club, and a full-strength squad plus two Directors headed across the Irish Sea on 17 April 1911. The game ended in a 3-1 win for the home team, a suitable reward for the enterprise shown by the up and coming "Glens".

Earlier in the season, the enterprise of local firm Stewarts Tailors was less appreciated by the St. Mirren Board. Stewarts had devised an offer called "Overcoats for Goals" which was intended as an incentive for the players, but the scheme was publicised without authority from the Club, and Saints' players were advised that any involvement with this would be seen as a serious misdemeanor. The firm were further warned not to use the Club's name in advertising without permission.

When re-signing talks commenced in April, Jimmy Cunningham

refused the terms on offer and Woolwich Arsenal re-stated their interest in the player. Ultimately he signed for Kilmarnock for a fee of £250, with Cunningham getting £40 as his share of the move. At the same time as open-to-transfer and retention lists were being prepared, one of Saints' forgotten men finally looked as if he was going to get a move. It was announced that record cap Tom Jackson would be loaned out to St. Johnstone during the 1911-12 season if the Perth club managed to gain admittance to Division Two. Although the Perth Saints failed to attract enough votes Jackson's temporary move went ahead, but St. Mirren retained the right to transfer Jackson "to any other club, at any time during the season".

Prior to the vote St. Johnstone had written to their Paisley namesakes seeking support at the League meeting, but there were a constant stream of clubs writing to St. Mirren Park and they were usually looking for more than a vote. During 1910-11, financial assistance was requested from Moorpark Crusaders, Newmilns FC, and Workington AFC. Unfortunately St. Mirren couldn't help all who applied, although there was no doubting such clubs were genuinely struggling. At the end of that season Workington proved the point by going into voluntary liquidation.

The Renfrewshire Cup success had been pleasing, but the Directors continued to harbour higher ambitions. On 7 June 1911, the Secretary was asked to invite representatives from three companies to visit Love Street to advise on what they could provide in the way of stand accommodation, all three firms were asked to submit sketches and quotations at once.

The erection of a new grandstand had been discussed two years earlier, but this time there was no talk of purchasing adjoining land; the proposal was to build on the site of the existing stand. However, the Directors' enthusiasm for the project was thwarted when the shareholders voted that "nothing be done meantime". This would prove to be a fortuitous deferment, as the tragic events in the middle of the decade ensured that such a construction was no longer financially feasible, or a priority.

1911-12

The first game of the 1911-12 season, a 0-0 draw with Partick Thistle, was an inauspicious start to a season that threatened to end Saints' continuous presence at the top level of Scottish football. Two days after the opening match at Firhill, on 21 August trainer John Hindle prompted the start of a series of unwelcome distractions from on-field matters when he was yet again reported as "having absented himself from his duties". Once more he apologised, and for the umpteenth time he was told that any recurrence would mean instant dismissal. It was an annual and apparently hollow threat, and had last been delivered ten months earlier, following Hindle's part in a disturbance which occurred in the pavilion.

The Board's decision in late September to enrol Hindle and his assistant Peacock at the Club's expense at a weekly ambulance class held in the North School must have been further evidence to John Hindle that he had survived again. He had escaped more often than Harry Houdini, but in mid-November a further instance of his misconduct was discussed at Board level, and the Club placed newspaper adverts for a new trainer. Applications were received, but Hindle not only stayed on but in January he was given a bonus in recognition of his service! Less than a month later he was called in front of the Board to answer further charges of absenting himself from his duties without authority, and was asked to explain incidents of misconduct which had taken place earlier in the month at Aberdeen. He was severely censured but he still kept his job!

The Board certainly had other things to think about. By 20 September the team had played four games and won one, but the issue of missed penalty kicks was already deemed sufficiently important for the Board to decide that inside right Archibald Kyle, signed in the summer from Clyde as part of the deal which permanently transferred goalkeeper James Grant to Shawfield, would be first choice to take all penalty kicks from that point on. The Board also suggested that the players should practice taking penalty kicks during training. It is not known to what extent penalty practice took place, but the problem of missed penalties persisted, and not one of the many penalties awarded was converted by Kyle, his deputy John Baird, or anyone else in the thirty-four League games.

There were signs that Saints fans' patience with the team's performances was certainly being tested, and towards the end of October Club Secretary Hugh Law interviewed Captain Duncan of the local police regarding the best way to stamp out swearing during games. Several solutions were discussed, but the police officer did not think it was advisable to have plain clothes men in the stand! Less direct action was adopted, and billposters were to be up around the ground warning spectators against swearing and seeking their assistance to "stop this disorder".

There was disorder of a different kind during November 1911 following the decision to upgrade walls and brickwork in and around the ground. There had been confidence that the improvements would be concluded in time for the home match against Clyde on 11 November, but Abercorn, aware of their neighbours' tight timescale, contacted St. Mirren and offered the use of their Ralston ground. Saints thanked their fellow Buddies for their "kind offer". A fortnight later Abercorn approached Saints for the transfer of a player called Harvey until the end of the season. Perhaps as a gesture of thanks to the "Abbies", Saints quickly agreed.

By 16 December 1911, St. Mirren had played eighteen of their thirty-four League fixtures and had won only two. The Directors were growing increasingly concerned about the team's poor position, and had travelled all over Britain looking at players who could improve the situation. On

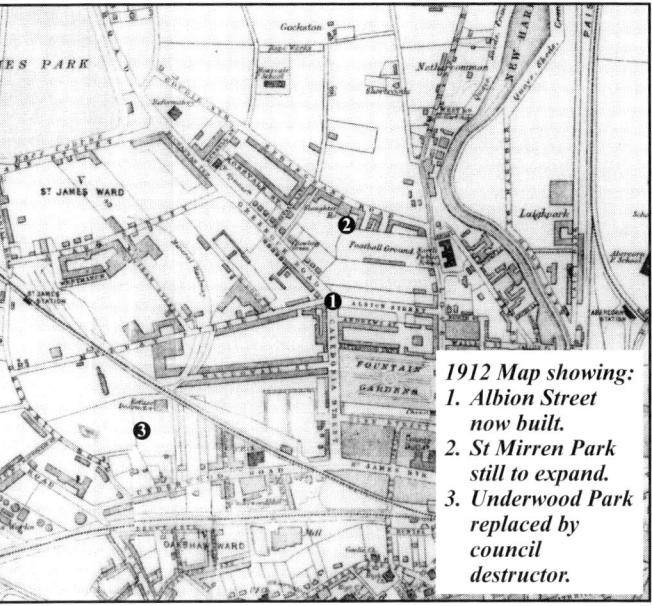

1912 Map showing:
1. *Albion Street now built.*
2. *St Mirren Park still to expand.*
3. *Underwood Park replaced by council destructor.*

22 January they signed Ted Magner from Everton for £200, with a further £100 to be paid to the Goodison Park club if Magner was signed for the 1911-12 season. In a comprehensive deal, Everton were to receive 50% of any amount exceeding £300 if Saints transferred Magner on to another club, and if the player was not re-engaged by St. Mirren for the 1912-13 season he was to be regarded as the property of both clubs!

Ted Magner went straight into the team on 27 January 1912 and was an instant hit, scoring two of Saints' three goals in the drawn home cup tie against Aberdeen. He also scored one of Saints two goals in a 2-1 win over Airdrie the following week, but there was no Magner magic three days later at Pittodrie, as the Dons hit four Scottish Cup goals without reply.

A month later Saints found themselves dumped out of a second cup competition. By 1911, the Renfrewshire Cup was seen by the majority of the county clubs as an annual opportunity to put up a good show against the three Scottish League teams, but on 9 March 1912 Arthurlie exceeded that limited ambition. The Barrhead team's main tactic was to ensure that Saints' centre Magner, who had scored in the three preceding Division One games, was deprived of service. The Arthurlie approach was successful, and their one goal was enough to take them through to the final against Morton.

The acquisition of Magner meant Saints showed a marginal improvement in form, but no club accumulated less than seven wins and ten draws, and St. Mirren finished bottom. On 6 May the Board discussed a letter from the President of the Scottish League (Second Division), which proposed amending the rules to allow automatic promotion, and therefore relegation, to be introduced.

There was a widespread belief that the Division Two champions, newly amalgamated Ayr United, were poised to replace Saints in Division One, and even St. Mirren's position as the pre-eminent Paisley club was under threat. Abercorn had played Saints three times during the season in the Charity and Renfrewshire Cups, and the "Abbies" had won twice and drawn the other. More importantly, they had finished as Division

Two runners-up, and there was a chance that they could swap Divisions with Saints. Considering what was at stake, it is remarkable that the Board gave no voting instruction to their Scottish League representative, and "the matter was left in Mr. Hart's hands". Fortunately for St. Mirren, the motion was defeated and neither Ayr United or Abercorn secured sufficient votes, but it had been a close run thing.

There was nothing close about the vote to remove one of the Directors at the Club's AGM on 12 June 1912. The extremely active Dr. Andrew Richmond was accused of providing "indiscreet publicity of the company's private affairs" and the demand for his resignation was unanimous. Despite the vote, Dr. Richmond was in his usual place when the first meeting of the new Board took place one week later! Discretion appears to have been the theme of the 1912 meeting, and prior to the main business of the evening, a majority of shareholders reversed a Board decision by voting that the press should not be allowed to record the proceedings, and thus the press people were asked to leave.

Also leaving was Trainer John Hindle, finally dismissed on 6 May 1912 after an incident-packed fifteen years. The post was advertised immediately, and by 30 May the large number of applications was reduced to a short leet of seven trainers. It eventually came down to a choice between Mr. Charles G. Durning of Petershill FC, and Mr. R Davidson of Annbank FC, with Charles Durning eventually being appointed Trainer and Groundsman at £2 10s per week.

Between 1910 and 1912 the Club had finished thirteenth, twelfth, and eighteenth, and the Directors bore direct responsibility for this unsatisfactory state of affairs. No one was yet questioning their qualifications for the task, but shareholders clearly suspected that any recipe for success was being spoiled by too many cooks. Less than two years after the appointment of a new Secretary/Manager, the 1912 AGM decided that a sub-committee of just three Directors was to be formed, and this trio would choose the team for each game. It was a step in the right direction, but the Secretarial side of the Secretary/Manager Hugh Law's job was set to prevail for some time yet.

1912-13

During the 1911-12 season, Derry Guilds FC had won the Irish Intermediate Cup, and much of the credit for that success was attributed to their goalkeeper William O'Hagan. He had been one of St. Mirren's many signing targets during that disappointing season, and he was signed just in time to play in the last League game of 1911-12 against Third Lanark at Cathkin on 27 April 1912. O'Hagan's fellow 'keeper William Duncan had no way of knowing just how successful O'Hagan's career with St. Mirren was going to be, but the immediate inclusion of the Irishman in the first team was enough of a message for Duncan, and he

Renfrewshire Football Association Victoria Cup Winners Medal won by Fred Blanchflower of St Mirren Football Club.

asked to be put on the transfer list within a month of O'Hagan's arrival.

The close season was marked by some hectic activity in the transfer market as the Directors took action to ensure that St. Mirren would not feature anywhere near the 1913 relegation area, and a typical 1912-13 team underlined the extent of the changes: goalkeeper William O'Hagan (late 1911-12 signing); right back Andy Reid (long-serving); left back Tom Snoddy (close season signing from Raith Rovers); right half Thomas Pearson (close season signing from Wemyss Athletic); centre half Fred Burden (close season signing from Hearts); left half Hugh Stevenson (close season signing from Blackburn Rovers); Fred Gray, (close season signing from Clyde); George Elmore (close season signing from Partick Thistle); Ted Magner (previous mid-season signing); inside left Archibald Kyle (previous season signing from Clyde); and left winger Fred Sowerby (close season signing from Hearts).

It had taken quite a lot of money to assemble this new team, and there was some evidence to suggest that the outlay was more than the Club could afford. Hugh Stevenson had joined St. Mirren in June, but his previous club Blackburn Rovers had still not received their £200 transfer fee five months after the move. Saints apologised for the delay and offered to pay interest on the sum owed, and for the first time were forced to state that "the fee will be paid as soon as finances permit". On 13 January, in an attempt to raise some revenue, a list of several unwanted players was advertised as "open to transfer" and circulated to all English League clubs.

Finances may have been tight, but one of the Board's priorities was to re-engage centre forward Ted Magner, even if it did mean paying Everton a further £100 under the original transfer deal. He had scored in five League games and twice in a Scottish Cup tie, and it was considered money well spent. Magner began the 1912-13 season with two goals in two games, and would eventually finish up as top scorer with nineteen League goals and twenty-three in all competitions.

Magner's goalscoring exploits had made him very popular with Saints' fans, so it was something of a shock when it was disclosed on 10 March that he had asked to be put on the transfer list, and a fortnight later Leicester Fosse FC offered a player exchange involving the centre. If Magner was unsettled by transfer speculation it didn't show, and on 15 March he scored all of Saints' five goals against the shaky defence of bottom club Queen's Park. A month later he hit a hat-trick in the last League game of the season, a 4-4 home draw with Raith Rovers. Suitably impressed, the Kirkcaldy club made immediate enquiries about Magner's signature and were told that he could be bought for £500. That ended the enquiry!

Despite all the changes, the season was proving to be only slightly better than 1911-12, and by the mid-point in the season crowd unrest was manifesting itself in swearing, barracking of players, and stone throwing, and all three problems were addressed. From mid-December 1912, police began to patrol the front of the stand "in an endeavour to get spectators to refrain from using obscene language towards the players", and a month later an appeal to end this "disorder" was placed in the 'Paisley Daily Express'. By the end of January attempts to encourage the ending of such behaviour were escalated, and such misdemeanors would be punished by immediate ejection from the ground. At the same time the Chief Constable was asked to place one or two Constables among the crowd to watch for stone throwing at the finish of matches.

A reasonable run in the Scottish Cup brightened the scene somewhat, and following a 0-0 home draw against Third Lanark in the Second Round on 8 February, innovative Director, Dr. Andrew Richmond suggested that the team, Secretary, and Trainer should spend Tuesday to Saturday at Seamill Hydro in preparation for the replay. It certainly worked, and two goals from George Elmore saw Saints into the next stage. Each team member was given a bonus of £1 for beating Thirds, and it was explained to the players "that it would have been more but for the special training expenses at Seamill". In the third round Saints were given another home tie, this time against Airdrieonians. A return visit to Seamill also proved successful, with a goal from left-winger Fred Sowerby being sufficient to give the players a bonus of £2 and take Saints through to a fourth round tie against Raith Rovers in Kirkcaldy on 8 March. The Board repeated the idea of sending the playing staff and team management to a seaside retreat, and this time they stayed at the Wemyss Bay Hydro. The change of scene again proved beneficial for second top scorer Elmore, who produced another cup goal, but it was not enough as the Rovers ran out 2-1 winners.

By the end of the season Saints had accrued ten wins and ten draws, which was just three more wins than the previous season. On the positive side, those six extra points were enough to move St. Mirren up to twelfth place in the eighteen team League, but they had conceded sixty goals, one more than when they had finished bottom the previous season. It was an improvement of sorts, but it was still a poor position by the standard of the 1900s.

1913-14

1913-14 offered the prospect of a bigger-than-ever safety net as Division One grew to twenty clubs, but it merely increased the number of teams who were better than Saints that season. Only eight of their thirty-eight League matches were won, and for the second time in three seasons St. Mirren finished bottom of the League.

For the first League game of the season at Dens Park, the inclusion of Saints' two close season signings from Everton, left back Walter Holbem and left winger William Davidson, were the only changes to the team which had been re-assembled the previous season. The Dens game ended in a 1-0 defeat, and the following week Saints suffered a second reverse when they lost 2-1 at Ibrox. In the third League encounter, a Ted Magner goal was enough to give Saints a share of the points with Dumbarton at St. Mirren Park, but he would not score another goal until New Year's Day, and would score just one League goal after that.

Interest in obtaining Magner's signature had persisted during the close season, and Partick Thistle made an early £350 offer. This was at least £50 less than the Club were willing to consider, and the valuation of the forward increased by a further £100 when Stockport County were quoted the price five weeks later! Around 6 October 1913, it looked as if he was heading for Grimsby's Blundell Park for £350, but some of the Directors insisted on the £400 base figure being met, and the Mariners were unable to pay the upper figure.

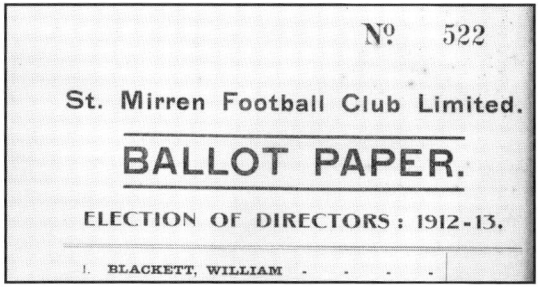

Limited company activity... Ballot paper for Election of Directors 1912-13.

By this stage of the season Saints had won just three games, and George Elmore, who had scored twenty goals the previous season, was also struggling to find the net, and had scored only his third goal on 11 October. Ted Magner was not having a comfortable season, and the transfer speculation continued on 10 November when Brighton and Hove Albion were advised that Saints wanted £500. The very same week as the Brighton bid, Raith Rovers were told "that the St. Mirren Board are not meantime desirous of parting with Magner", but that message had not been made public.

On 15 November, Brighton had Magner watched, but their representative considered the asking price was much too high. The Brighton man may not have picked the best day to study the centre forward, as Saints were beaten 6-0 by Hearts. Bristol Rovers asked about Magner in late November, and Motherwell were next to have a look on 15 December when a Fir Park deputation saw him play but not score against Hibs in a 3-3 draw. They reported that they were "not pleased with his display and couldn't make an offer".

It wasn't clear whether the Club wanted to sell or keep him, but one Magner goal in four months was neither helping St. Mirren to win matches nor adding to his value. However, Magner's situation was not the major behind-the-scenes irritant.

Left back Walter Holbem had been valued at £250 by Everton, but the Liverpool club had agreed that payment could be deferred until 15 March 1915. The full back had made 89 appearances for Sheffield Wednesday between 1906 and 1911, and played eighteen times for Everton between 6 September 1911 and 12 March 1913, but within six weeks of becoming a St. Mirren player it was clear that his Scottish stay was unlikely to be long term.

At the end of August he intimated to Secretary Hugh Law that he "wanted to go home to Sheffield as he did not like the place". Holbem had an interview with Saints' Directors on 4 September 1913, and as a result he was allowed to go home to Sheffield for the weekend after the match with Third Lanark on 6 September. He didn't return on the Monday and was advised in writing he must return to Paisley by Friday 12 September. This he did, and was included in the team which surprisingly defeated Celtic at Parkhead on 13 September to give Saints their first win of the season.

Walter Holbem wasn't the only unsettled player, and in September two regulars from the previous season asked to be put on the transfer list. Tom Snoddy, unable to get into the team at left back since Holbem's arrival and left winger Fred Sowerby, replaced by another ex-Evertonian William Davidson, were told their requests were refused. Meanwhile Holbem continued to be unhappy with life at Love Street, although every effort was being made to understand his position.

On 13 October it was agreed that after each match Holbem would be allowed to travel to and from Southport at the Club's expense. Two weeks later – coincidentally the day that Dr. J D Holmes was appointed the Club's new medical advisor, the homesickness bug was threatening to become an epidemic – and William O'Hagan applied to travel to and from Londonderry every weekend: he was refused!

Right half Thomas Pearson's problems went beyond homesickness. During October 1913 he had been examined by his doctor and the Club's Trainer and was found to be suffering from a very infectious skin disease. He was suspended until "he gets a certificate from his doctor to say that he is thoroughly cured", and until his suspension was lifted he was "not to be paid and he was prohibited from training with the other players". He would return to training within one month, but Walter Holbem was going to take much longer to deal with.

Despite Holbem's off-the-field complaints, he was an experienced and effective full back who had maintained his playing standards, but in late October the Board expressed considerable dissatisfaction with two of his displays. There were signs that their patience was coming to an end, and the player was told he must train and reside in Paisley. In the meantime, there was a suggestion that Rangers were interested in him, and the Club made it known they would accept the Ibrox team's highest bid for the full back.

On 30 October, Rangers stated they were willing to pay £400 to £450 for the unhappy Holbem. The player, who was in Lancashire at this stage, advised St. Mirren by postcard that he would play that week if chosen, but that he could not get back to Paisley before Friday night! On 3 November he was formerly put on the transfer list at his own request, and thereafter continued to be selected. The Rangers offer had been well in excess of what Saints were due to pay Everton, but when Preston North End wanted to know Saints' price for Holbem they were told on 17 November that they would be required to pay £850!

The inflated selling price quoted for Holbem came just three days after the six-monthly meeting of shareholders on 14 November 1913, when satisfaction was expressed at the news that the latest balance sheet showed the Club had reduced its debt from £1,400 to £565 in the previous six months. The team had played fifteen League games by this stage, and had won six and drawn one. They would win just two more games all season, and the Holbem and Magner sagas seemed to be unnecessary diversions from the overall needs of the team.

By 27 November, Holbem's refusal to report for training as requested led to him being suspended "sine die", but by 8 December, in an attempt to be rid of the problem, Preston North End were asked to submit their best offer. Preston confirmed they would pay £300, which was acceptable to Saints, who in turn lifted Holbem's suspension on 29 December 1913. The player then advised PNE that he was only willing to sign for them if the Deepdale club offered him a three year contract! This was an unacceptable condition, and Preston threatened to stop their cheque! The matter was eventually resolved on 29 January 1914 when Everton agreed to let Preston have all the necessary documentation.

A week after the Holbem issue was finally settled, Bernard Callaghan lined up in the left back position, and Fred Sowerby had reclaimed the left wing berth from William Davidson, the other 1913 Everton signing, as Saints took on Dundee at Love Street on Scottish Cup business, having disposed of Caledonian FC by five goals to one in the first round. In what was an otherwise woeful second half to the season, a cup run looked a possibility when Dundee were beaten 2-1, with Fred Sowerby scoring the winner from the penalty spot.

On 14 February 1914 Saints had a welcome League win at home against Clyde, and the same eleven players were chosen to face Aberdeen the following week at Pittodrie in the Cup. Included at outside left was an amateur called James Hodge Speedie, and it was twenty year old Speedie, on loan from Hearts, who scored both Saints' goals to take them through to the fourth round. Speedie was selected again for the fourth round match with Partick Thistle, and, despite Saints' terrible League form, a huge crowd turned up at St. Mirren Park to watch as the unlikely figure of centre half Fred Burden scored the only goal of the game to take St. Mirren to their sixth Scottish Cup semi-final.

Hibernian were Saints' opponents in the penultimate round, and the match was played at Tynecastle. Wilson put Hibs ahead with a long shot after fifteen minutes, and although Saints equalised through Scottish Cup specialist Speedie, a further goal from Wilson and a third by Williamson put the game beyond Saints reach.

Ultimately, it was a very disappointing season on the pitch as the Directors allowed peripheral issues to drift. For one season at least they appeared to lose their focus on what really mattered in football terms. What really mattered beyond football would soon become all too apparent, and there would be at least one sad link with the season just ended. An unexpected Saints hero in the Scottish Cup run had been James Speedie. Just seventeen months after scoring twice at Pittodrie for his adopted team, on 25 September 1915, Private J. H. Speedie would be killed during the battle of Loos.

1914-15

In the mid 1910s extending the Love Street site remained a core ambition of the St. Mirren Board, and talks with the McKaig Trust had resumed in November 1913 after a four year break. Nothing had changed. The two parties could not agree on a price, whether they discussed outright sale or lease arrangements, and St. Mirren regarded the sums quoted as "prohibitive". In April 1914 it was decided the best way forward was to extend the then-existing stand at either or both ends, and by mid-June this had been priced at £683, with half payments deferred until 30 April 1915 and 1916.

By 21 June 1914 it was the improvements to the stand itself which were being deferred, owing to the short time left before the new season was due to start. At the same time, the Club contacted football's most famous stadium architect, Mr. Archibald Leitch of Glasgow, "to submit a plan of the best stand accommodation he can suggest on our ground as it presently stands". Within six weeks Mr. Leitch submitted his plans, and these were considered by the Club's property committee and put before the shareholders on 27 November, but matters would not progress until after the War.

Of at least equal importance to the upgrading of the ground's facilities during the 1914 close season was the need to carry out improvements to a team which had finished bottom of the League. The side had only one player of real quality, and when Tottenham Hotspur expressed an interest in goalkeeper Willie O'Hagan it prompted the Board to offer the 'keeper a new deal which made him, at £5 per week throughout the year, the Club's best-paid player. Once St. Mirren had decided that O'Hagan was staying they remained resolute in that view, and a month later when Bradford (Park Avenue) FC offered £250 plus two players, the St. Mirren Board told the soon-to-be promoted Avenue that "O'Hagan has signed for us and we have no wish to part with him".

The rest of the team which regularly lined up in front of O'Hagan was much changed from the previous season. Experienced right back Andy Reid and eventual Scotland cap John "Jock" Marshall shared the role of partner to Bernard Callaghan at left back. Right half Thomas Pearson and centre half Fred Burden were replaced by Hughie McGrory and Bob Reid, who joined Saints from Blackburn Rovers and Portsmouth respectively. Completing the changed half-back line, Hugh Stevenson's place at left half was taken by a former Saint, Andrew Davidson, who returned to St. Mirren Park from Celtic.

Fred Gray in uniform. He gained the rank of Lieutenant and was awarded the Military Cross.

More changes up front meant there wasn't much left of the previous season's forward line. At outside right, Fred Gray still played, but his appearances were subject to his military commitments, and in his absence Fred Sowerby switched from his more usual left wing role. The rest were new. Inside left Archibald Kyle had joined Hamilton Accies in late January 1914, and the other regulars, George Elmore, Ted Magner, and William Davidson remained on the books but were seldom in contention. In came Tom Page, John Clark, James Brannick, and Andrew Brown.

Saints' recent series of buys from Everton - Ted Magner, William Davidson, and Walter Holbem - had produced mixed results, but two more were fixed up on 27 April. Toffees' inside forward Tom Page signed for Saints for £50, and as part of the deal Saints would pay for his furniture removal. At the same time, a further £75 was spent on James Brannick, another inside forward from Goodison. Centre forward John Clark, secured from Lincoln City, would prove a more than useful signing, with nineteen League goals spread throughout the season, and left winger Andrew Brown joined Saints from Rangers for a fee of £150.

Saints' financial situation in mid-1914 can be illustrated by the deals struck with Everton and Rangers. Everton agreed that payments for Brannick and Page could be deferred until 30 September and 31 October 1914 respectively, while Rangers were even more accommodating, and were willing to wait until 7 January 1915 for Andrew Brown's transfer fee. Rangers' remuneration for Brown was still not paid by 25 February 1915, and there was some relief when the Ibrox club generously allowed the fee "to lie over until finances are in a healthier state".

Times could not be more difficult. Following Germany's invasion of Belgium, the United Kingdom had entered the First World War at midnight on 4 August 1914. Most people thought it would "be over by Christmas", and football folk were no different. Two weeks after the War started, the Scottish football season kicked off with twenty clubs in the re-titled "A" Division and fourteen in the "B" Division, making the Scottish League bigger than ever.

On 12 September 1914 at Tynecastle, "John McCartney's Hearts", to use the contemporary idiom, defeated St. Mirren 5-0. It was Hearts' fifth game of the season and their fifth win. By the end of November the Maroons had played another eleven matches, and had dropped only three points out of a possible thirty-two. The 1914 group of players were reckoned to be the greatest-ever Hearts team, and looked set to dominate Scottish football for many years to come.

Chairman Thomas Hart

Those with other affiliations might have debated that claim, but no-one would dispute that they were a remarkable group of young men: at the end of November the entire team enlisted for military action. Players from other clubs followed the Hearts example in varying degrees, as many felt uneasy about continuing to play football when friends and family were fighting for their country on the other side of the English Channel. Seven of the Hearts team – including temporary Saint James Speedie – were killed in action and very few of the survivors ever played again.

There was a strong body of opinion opposed to the playing of football during wartime, but at the Club's half-yearly meeting on 27 November 1914, St. Mirren Chairman Thomas Hart expressed some concern about what he regarded as the "present crusade against football". He considered the criticism "quite unwarranted", and it was his view that "the game was the means of huge sums being collected on behalf of the various War Relief Funds. All the clubs have given their players every encouragement to enlist and no obstacles were put in their way".

The facts backed up Mr. Hart's claim. To assist the Forces' recruitment drive, the Club offered to placard St. Mirren Park with posters, and during the 1914-15 season there were collections for the Red Cross Society and the Belgian Relief Fund, a large number of footballs were sent by the Club as part of the Football for Soldiers Scheme, and a St. Mirren XI met a Scottish Junior XI on behalf of the Serbian Flag Day.

Soldiers in uniform and wounded soldiers were admitted free to Saints' home games, and when three non-shareholder season tickets were returned to the club in mid-September by men who had "gone to the front" the Club decided to remit the full value of these tickets. There had to be a limit to this community involvement, however, and when it was suggested that spectators pay a little extra at the gate which would be donated to some of the war funds, the majority of the Board, no doubt with one eye on the Club's already diminishing attendances, felt that "spectators were already contributing very handsomely in various ways".

The drop in war-time attendances was inevitable as money and time became more scarce, and the Board met on 30 November 1914 to consider the Club's financial position. After a long discussion it was decided to meet the players on 7 December to discuss a reduction in wages. The players were willing to accept a drop in pay of up to 15%, whereas the Board were looking for reductions of up to 50%, and both parties agreed to seek further direction from the League. A League-wide solution was devised, and this allowed Chairman Thomas Hart, at the Club's 10th AGM on 9 April 1915, to report that the players "agreed without demur to accept the reduced wages as agreed to by the Scottish League".

On Saturday 26 December, St. Mirren had a 2-0 home win over a good Falkirk team to give a playing record to that date of won seven, drawn six, and lost seven. Twenty points from a possible forty showed that the wholesale changes to the team had been effective, but the Club endured another financial blow when a Board meeting held prior to the Falkirk match was advised that the often lucrative Scottish Cup competition had been suspended.

Things were now becoming extremely difficult for clubs, so bad that St. Mirren's S.F.A. representative, Mr. John Scouller, had been recommended to support a motion at the Association meeting to suspend all senior football, but the vote was to carry on. It would not be the only time that season that the Board would consider asking the League "to discuss the question of curtailing the season".

A week before the Scottish Cup decision, the Club had resigned from the Reserve League when the "A" Team was disbanded as an economic measure, and seven players had been given free transfers, but the loss of Cup revenue would force the bank, who had been supportive and sympathetic, to express some concern about St. Mirren's overdraft level.

The Club pointed out that with the players' wage reduction and the Reserve team savings, the overdraft would certainly get no worse. They did, however, rejoin the Reserve League later in the season, but there was another saving when the League decided to dispense with neutral linesmen after 16 January. Eventually the overdraft facility was continued, but only after the Directors had signed guarantees to cover the amount in question.

Money had never been tighter for Saints, so any reduction in costs was welcome. On 25 January, Private Fred Gray suggested that the Club could reduce his wages by the amount of his military allowances when not playing if they would agree to give him full wages when playing. The Club agreed, giving him a vote of thanks for his loyalty to St. Mirren, but Saints didn't get the benefit of Gray's skills too often, as his regiment's needs and an injury sustained in March meant he made few appearances in the second half of the season.

It may have been war-time, and football was certainly in a financial straight-jacket, but the game still generated passion. On 6 April, the Club was forced to carry out an investigation into half-time and full-time incidents that had taken place in the pavilion at Brockville the previous Saturday. All the players were interviewed and warned about a repetition. There wasn't one.

The season finished with Saints winning fourteen and drawing eight of their thirty-eight matches to finish in ninth place, but it was a sign of the times that every player was included in the transfer list produced at 30 April. Everyone had their price, from the little-used Fred Blanchflower at £25 right up to former Spurs' target Willie O'Hagan at £2,000.

The validity of results during the First World War have been questioned many times, but in the case of 1914-15, the top four of Celtic Hearts, Rangers, and Morton was unchanged from pre-war 1913-14 season, and on that basis Saints' ninth place finish must be recognised as a genuine improvement on the immediately preceeding years.

1915-16

Financial pressures in 1915 meant that for the first time in fourteen years the Scottish League had only one Division, although for the third consecutive year Division One would contain twenty teams. On 29 April, the Board met with all the First Eleven players to clarify the Club's financial position. It was explained that the payment of wages was dependent on new arrangements with the Clydesdale Bank, and on 5 May 1915 it was minuted "that only those in need were to be paid".

During 1915-16, there would be no Reserve League and on 26 July 1915, the Scottish League imposed a maximum wage of 20 shillings per week, although clubs were to be allowed to pay an extra 20 shillings per week up to 40 shillings, provided that at the end of 1915-16 their audited balance sheet showed a profit after all expenditure had been deducted.

Saints had been lucky in the first war-time season with few absentees due to military service, but there were some prominent players missing more often than not throughout 1915-16. Top scorer John Clark was stationed near Bristol, and most of the football played by him was in the red of Bristol City as an amateur. Top 'keeper Willie O'Hagan played when home on leave, and although right winger Fred Gray was available for a few weeks from mid-October onwards it was a constant struggle to obtain his release.

A further loss was experienced when the Board noted on 17 August that inside right Tom Page had intimated "that he didn't want to play for us again even although we got him a good job". In a further note, the player explained that his wife was unwilling to reside in Scotland. Page remained a St. Mirren registered player, but was loaned back to Everton.

Inconsistencies in team selection were reflected in Saints' scores. They made a good start to their League fixtures, losing one and winning four of their first five fixtures. Then, between 25 September and 16 October, they lost four-in-a-row to Motherwell at Fir Park, and Morton, Dundee, and Dumbarton at home. A week after the Dumbarton defeat, Saints headed for Celtic Park with a line-up which was not far short of being the first choice: O'Hagan, A. Reid, Callaghan, McGrory, R. Reid, Davidson, Gray, Bruce, Clark, Sowerby, and Brown. The presence of the high-scoring John Clark and always dangerous Fred Gray made all the difference, and both scored in a 2-0 victory which was a highlight of the season.

The Celtic result had been pleasing, and although the playing of football was one way to keep life as normal as possible, there were constant reminders that far from home more important activities were being undertaken by the nation's young men. On 13 October 1915 the Board's sympathy was extended "to the relatives of our late player Private James Armstrong who had died of wounds received in action". Five days later the Directors wrote to their Heart of Midlothian counterparts expressing "their sympathy regarding the late James H. Speedie and ask them to convey same to Mr. Speedie's people".

Such news had a saddening effect on everyone, but against the backdrop of such sacrifice the Directors were determined to insist on high standards at St. Mirren Park. In mid-October inside right Robert Hannah was suspended "sine die", as his physical fitness was regarded as unsatisfactory due to "his own misconduct"; on 6 December he was given a free transfer. A week earlier the Board decided to see every player and convey their disappointment with displays in the previous few weeks, and on 10 January 1916 the Directors expressed dissatisfaction "at the laxity of training and urged the strictest supervision by the Secretary".

1. *William O'Hagan lines up for Ireland 1919.*
2. *A wartime cigarette collector's card showing the keeper in Saint's colours while on active duty.*

On 8 November the St. Mirren Directors resolved to present silver cigarette cases in The Royal Oak Tearooms to Private John Clark, Lance Corporal Fred Gray, and Trooper Willie O'Hagan "in appreciation of their patriotism in joining the colours". Left half Andrew Davidson would take part in a similar ceremony a few months later, but in mid-October he had accepted a position in Greenock Infirmary, and Morton were agreeable to provide Davidson with training facilities.

Morton's immediate co-operation was greatly appreciated by the player and Saints at a time when clubs went out of their way to help each other, and loan deals were a notable feature of the season. There had been problems earlier in 1915-16 with cross-border loan deals, and the S.F.A. had sought clarification regarding the position of any players from English League clubs appearing for Scottish clubs. On 13 December an S.F.A. circular included the following: "Any club signing English professionals shall have an agreement stating that no remuneration shall be given to said players for their services".

Agreement or not, one player who was proving difficult to acquire was centre-half Andrew Jackson of Middlesbrough, whose father Tom remained Saints' most capped player for seventy-six years. Several attempts were made to get the younger Jackson on loan. In mid-September "Boro" agreed that Jackson could play as an amateur, but it wasn't until the last couple of months of the season, and subject to being released by his regiment, that he managed to play two games for his father's old team.

Permanent moves also took place, and by late December 1915, as John Clark's appearances at centre forward grew less likely and in the end totalled just three matches, Saints decided to sign George Philip from Sunderland. He scored the only goal in the game against Clyde on 12 February, but he netted only three more goals and made a limited impact. By the end of the season it was James Bruce, with ten goals from twenty-eight starts, who was the Club's top scorer.

On 15 January 1916, Saints' goalkeeper Dan Hillcoat, who was to play thirty-eight matches during 1915-16 after being so long in the shadows of William Duncan and Willie O'Hagan, conceded three goals in an away match against Hearts, and, perhaps to his relief, was blamed for none of them. Prior to the Tynecastle match, Hillcoat had received a letter asking him "to let his team down in the Hearts match," as the writer "had backed the Hearts heavily to win".

The 'keeper had sensibly handed the letter over to Secretary/Manager Hugh Law, and it was passed on to Mr. MacAndrew, the League Secretary, for investigation. Meanwhile, St. Mirren Director Thomas Hart and Hearts Vice-Chairman Mr. Lorimer had interviewed the referee, linesmen, and players of Hearts before the game in Gorgie, but all declared they had not received a similar letter. It was a strange and non-recurring incident.

The Scottish Junior Leagues were still operating in 1915-16, and, as always, their ranks included players who were capable of playing at a higher level. In late January, each of three Junior matches were watched by a pair of St. Mirren Directors. They had specific targets based on reports received, and while some were found to be "outstanding", others received less complimentary comments. An inside right of Rutherglen Glencairn was described as "of no use, too light, too small", but Harry Higginbotham, the outside right of Kilsyth Rangers, must have been rated a bit higher, because he was offered League terms on 24 April.

On 17 April, left half Andrew Davidson and right half Hugh McGrory were each presented with a suitably inscribed silver cigarette case "as an appreciation of patriotism in joining His Majesty's Forces", and a week later inside right James Brannick was given the same recognition.

Thanks to control of costs, such as the cancelling of the November meeting of shareholders "owing to the abnormal season and unnecessary expense", and above all the ceiling on wages, the financial situation had improved to the extent that by the end of the season some players were named in a retained list, in contrast to the previous April when every player was available for transfer!

Chairman Thomas Hart reported to the AGM on 28 April 1916 that "over £200 had been collected at St. Mirren Park for various war funds and charities and that fully 100 footballs had been dispatched to soldiers on active service". He also gave a list of players who had joined the colours. It was a list which at once honoured the brave volunteers and recognised the extent to which the war effort was by then having on a normal peacetime activity such as running a football club.

Mr. Hart also spoke of the loss sustained by the death of the late Mr. Robert Fairlie, "an old player and official of the Club". Robert Fairlie had been a member of the first St. Mirren team to win the Renfrewshire Cup back in April 1883. He would no doubt have joined with those who empathised with the sport's attempts to carry on in difficult circumstances, but in the midst of a War which was about to enter its third year, no-one would claim that St. Mirren's playing statistics of thirteen wins and four draws from thirty-eight games was of any real consequence.

1916-17

In retrospect, May 1916 doesn't seem a suitable time to consider starting a football team but, on 2 May two St. Mirren Directors met with a Mr. W. H Lamond and his sub committee regarding the proposed letting of St. Mirren Park for a junior team to be run from 1916 onwards. The

Team Group 1916-17
G. B. Riddell, W. R. Cook, C. Durning (Trainer), J. Cochrane (Secretary and Manager),
Cadet F. Gray, J. Scouller, J. Inglis, A. Reid, D. Hillcoat, B.Callaghan, J. Walls, Wm. Farmer, Jas. Fleming,
H. Higginbotham, C. Pringle, Thos. Hart (Chairman), A. Dixon, A. Brown,
J. Marshall, W. Brown.

fee for the use of the ground was to be £36 per annum, reduced to £28 after negotiations, plus one third profits. The team was to be known as St. Mirren Juniors, and the new club's organisers asked that a St. Mirren Director should act as President of the fledgling Junior club.

St. Mirren not only provided a Director, they also gave complimentary season tickets to the Juniors' six-man committee. Ten months later at Firhill, a goal from Dorward after a 0-0 draw was enough for St. Mirren Juniors to defeat Renfrew Juniors and win the Scottish Junior Cup!

There were no such high points in Hugh Law's six year association with the senior St. Mirren, and a fortnight after the launch of St. Mirren Juniors, Mr. Law resigned his position as Secretary/Manager, having been offered a "commercial position that would demand his full-time attention". The club accepted his resignation with regret and the parting was certainly amicable, and long after he left St. Mirren Park, Hugh Law continued to bring new players to the attention of the Club.

On 6 July 1916, three candidates were interviewed for the Secretary's vacancy. Club minutes indicate that the Directors' main consideration centred on the hours and salary for which each candidate was prepared to work. Mr. John Cochrane of Johnstone stated that he would undertake the job in a part-time capacity and for only twenty-five shillings, which was fifteen shillings a week less than his nearest competitor.

Cochrane got the job. The evidence suggests that Paisley parsimony strongly influenced the appointment, but the following years would show that it was one of the best decisions taken in the Club's history. At the same meeting as John Cochrane was selected, the Directors agreed to sign James Lindsay of Burnley. Typical of the time, and showing no change from the days of John McCartney, Mr. Cochrane was expected to do all the administrative work during the week, and on match days make the best of the resources put at his disposal. The Directors not only continued to pick the team, but they made any last minute changes right up to kick-off.

On Saturday 19 August 1916, John Cochrane watched as his new team were beaten 5-1 by Celtic at St. Mirren Park, but victories eventually outnumbered defeats by 15 to 13, as a respectable seventh place in the final league table - the best for eight years - was achieved. It could have been even better, but the team saved their worst run of form for the last seven games between 10th March and 28th April, when a meagre two home points were gained.

This disappointing spell coincided with the reversion of Jock Marshall from centre-forward to his more familiar full-back role. Back on 16 November, a special Board meeting had been convened because right half Bob Reid could not travel to Dundee, and an unexpected injury to inside-left James Lindsay had further upset the previously selected team. Veteran Andy Reid was recalled at full-back, and regular right back Marshall lined up at centre forward.

Marshall was an instant hit as he scored both Saints' goals in a 2-0 win. He then scored in four of the next seven games as they embarked on their best spell of the season, taking thirteen points from a possible fourteen. The emergency centre forward remained in the position for three months, and ended up as top scorer, as he converted fourteen of Saints' forty-nine league goals that season. He finished the season as a full-back, and although he continued to demonstrate prolific powers as a goalscorer in Saints colours, it was his defensive qualities for Middlesbrough and Llanelli which would eventually earn him seven full caps for Scotland.

Marshall found himself in what had been quite a changed team, and with the exception of inside left James Lindsay from Burnley and centre half William Brown from Everton, the rest of the incomers – centre half Robert Sim (Petershill), left-half Louis Gordon (Ashfield), outside right Robert Blackwood (Johnstone), inside-right Charles Pringle (Maryhill), centre forward John Inglis (Kilbarchan Athletic), and Harry Higginbotham (Kilsyth Rangers) – had all made the step up from Junior football and had generally coped well with the higher grade.

Other matters were never far away, and Chairman James Fleming, speaking at the 1917 AGM, reported that close on £700 had been collected to date as war tax, and that nearly £400 had been collected at St. Mirren Park for charitable purposes. A vote of thanks was moved by Mr. Adam to the Chairman and Directors, and "all who had assisted in these strenuous times". By the time of the 1918 AGM the "strenuous times" would be nearing their end.

1917-18

There were bigger than usual changes in the opposition Saints would face, as Aberdeen and Raith Rovers, the two bottom teams at the end of the previous season, and fifth bottom Dundee, were asked to withdraw from the League at the end of 1916-17 because of war-time travel difficulties. Hearts and Hibs remained, but the eighteen club League effectively became a West Central Scotland competition as Clydebank were invited to even up the numbers.

The co-opted club made a highly respectable debut, finishing in ninth place; two ahead of Saints, who won eleven and drew seven of the thirty-four fixtures but never managed to string together more than two consecutive wins all season. Team selection during the first half of the season was remarkably consistent, and although far more players were used and more positional changes made after January, particularly in the forward line, the pattern of results remained obstinately erratic.

Long-serving right back Andy Reid joined Airdrieonians during the close season, and for the first half of the season it was a surprise if the first three names on the team list were not Dan Hillcoat, Jock Marshall, and Bernard Callaghan. However, for the opening match of the 1917-18 season at Tynecastle, Jock Marshall was back at centre-forward, and from the penalty spot he scored Saints' only goal in a 2-1 defeat.

Marshall's prowess in two positions posed a continuing dilemma for the Directors, and for the second game against Thistle he was co-listed at both centre and right back. By mid-November, the purchase of Bobby Orrock from Falkirk meant that Marshall could be moved forward without significantly weakening the defence, and by the end of the season he had been selected as a forward on eleven occasions. From those eleven starts he managed to score eight times, making him Saints' top scorer for the second successive year.

In early December, goalkeeper James Doolan was signed from Pollok FC, and he retained the position for much of the second half of the season. The half-back-line was also a steady part of the team, with ex-Evertonian William Brown a virtual ever-present at right half, as was left-half James Walls, signed from Bathgate in November 1916. The centre half position was filled by the versatile Charles Pringle in the early part of the season, until James Logan was signed from Rangers in mid-October. He then became the preferred pivot.

Logan's signing from Rangers freed Pringle to play much of the season at inside right, whilst James Lindsay filled the other inside forward position more than anyone else. Amongst those who did play at inside left was Fred Gray, who turned out twice for Saints during March. Back in October 1917, the Club had learned with considerable pride that former Private, by then Lieut. Fred Gray had been awarded the Military Cross for distinguished and meritorious services in battle.

At the same time as news broke of Fred Gray's award, the Club was advised by Saints' Liverpool-based registered player Tom Page that his team-mate James Brannick had made what was termed "the supreme sacrifice", and Page asked if the Club could do something for the late player's mother. As a first step, a cheque for £3 3s was forwarded to Mrs. Brannick with a message of condolence.

The Club also showed some sympathy in a very different situation. Right winger Harry Higginbotham continued to be regularly selected throughout the season in spite of a highly publicised sending off incident during the first game of the season against Hearts at Tynecastle, in which Higginbotham climbed into the crowd to chase a spectator who was taunting him.

It is just possible that the haranguing of Higginbotham and his subsequent foray amongst the fans had something to do with his surname, but there was no obvious explanation for an equally bizarre incident which happened during a Saints match on 9 March 1918, when a Canadian soldier ran onto the Rugby Park pitch and tried to fight with some of the players.

On the opposite wing from Higginbotham was William Dorward, who had scored the goal which won the 1918 Scottish Cup for St. Mirren Juniors. He had turned senior during the 1917 close season, and was an ever-present on the left wing for the first half of the year, in addition to scoring four Division One goals. In the second half of the season the left wing berth was occupied by Jamie Thomson, who had scored once in his six appearances for Manchester United in the English First Division during the 1913-14 season.

Thomson remained registered with the Old Trafford club when he made his Saints' debut against Kilmarnock on 1 January 1918, and signed for St. Mirren on "League terms" in April 1918. He had also played for Clydebank, Renton, and Dumbarton Harp in the past, but his career was to be dominated by the ten years he would wear the black and white stripes of St. Mirren. In his first half-season he scored six goals, including a hat-trick in the last League game of the season which enabled Saints to defeat Hearts by three goals to two.

The problem position remained centre forward with John Clark on loan to Linfield for the season. One of the players who had temporarily led the line, and to some effect, was Partick Thistle's Neil Harris. Harris hit seven goals in five games during his loan spell, and another centre called Reid also came from Firhill for two games in February. The Club wrote to Partick Thistle thanking them for the loan of Reid, but they had even greater reason to thank Celtic.

Left half Andrew Davidson had been brought back to Love Street from Parkhead in June 1914, but his £100 transfer fee was not paid to Celtic until September 1917. Celtic's forbearance was greatly appreciated by the St. Mirren Directors, and they expressed to them "our sincerest thanks for allowing us this time to pay". The war had brought communities together, and the football community was no different.

1918-19

St. Mirren recorded their "gratification of the allied troops at this time", and at the eleventh hour, on the eleventh day, of the eleventh month of 1918 the First World War finally came to an end. Wherever possible attempts were made in every sphere of life to quickly get back to normal, and for Scottish football part of this normalisation process took the form of a special national cup competition which was called the Victory Cup.

After details of the competition were announced, St. Mirren Director Thomas Hart expressed some concerns on 4 December about the proposal, and raised the question of "whether cup-ties might be the means of disorganising our League programme". At that point Saints had played fourteen League matches and had only won three, with five drawn. St. Mirren decided they would go ahead with the competition and Mr. Hart's concerns didn't materialise. Of the four League games played during the cup competition, Saints won two and drew one.

A more fundamental question was discussed by the Board on 8 January, and the Directors reaffirmed that there was no lack of ambition at St. Mirren Park. "The question of ways and means of strengthening our team was considered," recorded the minutes, "and an assurance was given that if any player was brought forward as being a suitable candidate for our team the Directors would raise the necessary cash to secure him."

Harold McKenna

They had made some earlier signings, and none were better than left half or centre half Harold McKenna and inside left Charlie Sutherland. McKenna had made twelve appearances for Rangers during their 1917-18 championship-winning season, and joined St. Mirren on loan for 1918-19, and would remain for the following season. For five months in 1918-19 he was a permanent fixture at left half, but moved to centre half when left half Harry Anderson was signed on loan from Raith Rovers at the beginning of March. Anderson would sign permanently for Saints on 20 June 1920.

Sutherland had joined from Third Lanark for just £35 at the end of August 1918. He and ever-present Jamie Thomson were the first choice left-wing partnership, although Sutherland also played at inside right if circumstances demanded. By the end of the season his goals would help make St. Mirren history.

Goalkeepers O'Hagan and Hillcoat were still unavailable for much of the season, and John Richardson, signed from Queen's Park in August 1917, had become first choice goalkeeper. By 8 February 1919 the newly demobilised Willie O'Hagan was back in the team, and sadly young Richardson would never play again. On 19 February 1919, by which time the sudden deaths of young men should again have become a rarity, Chairman James Fleming announced that John Richardson had died and the Club's deepest sympathy was conveyed to Mrs. Richardson.

The first round of the Victory Cup was a home tie with Dumbarton on 1 March. It remained goal-less even after extra time, and the replay took place the following Wednesday at Boghead. Before the first match, Trainer Charlie Durning was instructed to be early at the Dumbarton ground with a view to having the boots studded to suit ground conditions. One of the players who would benefit from this professional approach was inside forward Frank Hodges, who had been signed on loan from Birmingham City on 24 February 1919. The West Midlands club were "on no account willing to transfer him", and the Blues' high regard for Hodges was borne out on his debut in the replay when he scored the game's only goal.

Hodges was one of three short-term loan players in the team, and contrary to what his Birmingham bosses had told St. Mirren, he was destined to join Manchester United at the beginning of the 1919-20 season, and would play 20 games for them. At the end of that season Saints would make strenuous efforts to sign him permanently.

Saints and Clyde had already drawn 1-1 on two occasions in the League before they were drawn together in the second round in Paisley on 15 March. The Bully Wee, who were not enjoying the best of seasons and would finish second bottom, faced a St. Mirren team in the third match which included a forward line of Hodges, Page, Clark, Sutherland, and Thomson.

The much-missed John Clark had been released from the Army in mid-January and he brought back some fire power to the team, but it was Tom Page at inside right, so seldom available for selection, who gave the team's play an extra dimension. Page made the extra effort to play for Saints in the Victory Cup and the impact of his playmaking was obvious. Two goals from John Clark and a third from Jamie Thomson were enough to put Saints three up after eighty minutes, and although Clyde pulled two back there was no doubt which team was heading for the quarter-finals.

Champions elect Celtic were one of the seven other teams to have reached the last eight, and the Parkhead men were paired to meet Saints in Paisley on 29 March. In preparation for what was expected to be a big crowd the terracing was to be repaired "where the earth had been washed hard against the boarding". It proved to be a sensible precaution, because a crowd of 24,633, a record at that time, paid a total of £613. 12s 9d to watch a very keenly contested cup tie.

Secretary John Cochrane was to have some influence on the outcome of the match. He had learned on 25 March that highly-rated Morton left back John Fulton had just been demobilised from the Armed Forces, and just before the Celtic match, with the permission of Morton, Fulton was signed on loan, and would be the first choice in that position for the rest of the season, although the St. Mirren Board accepted that Morton could recall Fulton for Renfrewshire Cup ties.

Fulton's short-term signing meant that Bernard Callaghan, for so long Jock Marshall's full-back partner and a Motherwell signing target at the beginning of the season, missed out on the latter stages of the Victory Cup, and did not even get a medal as a reserve. The "ways and means of strengthening our team" as considered earlier in the season by the Board meant the best available players were selected, and sentiment was a secondary consideration.

At the same time as Fulton arrived, R. Perry replaced regular right half William Brown to become the third of the three short-term loan players who would be in the team for the rest of the season, before returning to Bury in the summer.

The turning point in the Celtic match, and perhaps of the Victory Cup campaign, came in extra time when the Glasgow team's Patsy Gallacher missed a penalty and Jamie Thomson later scored for St. Mirren for a 1-0 passport to the semi-finals. The team which had beaten Celtic was O'Hagan, Marshall and Fulton, Perry, McKenna and Anderson, Hodges, Page, Clark, Sutherland, and Thomson, this side would also represent Saints in the penultimate and final rounds.

There had been comments that the competition lacked credibility because many clubs still had players in the Armed Services, but, as the attendance for the Celtic tie had shown, it was certainly a competition the public took seriously, and in the semi final, despite St. Mirren facing a Hibernian team which had used thirty-five players that season and finished bottom of the League by a clear seven points, a crowd of 30,000 assembled at Easter Road

Prior to the semi-final, the Club invested some of the Celtic tie takings by arranging for the team to spend a few days at Wemyss Bay Hotel for "special training", and each player was given an allowance of 10/- per day. It was a preparation they would repeat if they got to the final.

Victory Cup Winners 1918-1919
C. Durning (Trainer), W. R. Cook, J. Scouller, W. Farmer, G. Riddell, T. Hart,
J. Cochrane (Secretary & Manager), J. Granger, R. Perry, J. Marshall, W. O'Hagan, J. Fulton, H. McKenna, S. Coyle (Groundsman), W. H. Lamond,
F. Hodges, T. Page, J. Clark, J. Fleming (Chairman), H. Anderson, C. Sutherland, J. Thomson.

At Easter Road Hibs' Williamson headed the home team into a 1-0 half-time lead, but in the second half Saints were superior, and it was no surprise when they equalised through a scrambled effort from the head of Jamie Thomson to take the game to extra time. Right at the start of the additional period, Hibs' top scorer Bobby Gilmour broke his collar bone, and thereafter the ten man Easter Road side struggled. A second goal by Thomson was consolidated by a third from John Clark to take Saints through to their second national cup final, where they would meet Hearts.

Squeezed in between the semi-final against Hibs and the final with Hearts was a home League game against Partick Thistle. Missing from Saints' line-up on 19 April was Jock Marshall, who had been selected to represent Scotland against Ireland at Windsor Park. It was an international match which was included in the official centenary book of the S.F.A., but it is one classified as an "Unofficial Victory Match", so Marshall was (and then wasn't!) the twelfth St. Mirren player to be capped by Scotland.

Despite Saints' elimination of Celtic, it was Hearts who were the pre-final favourites, if only because of their higher League position throughout the season, and none but the Paisley partisans in the 60,000 crowd at Celtic Park on 26 April expected a St. Mirren victory. True to form, it was the Edinburgh side who dominated proceedings for ninety minutes, particularly in the first half hour when it was one-way traffic towards O'Hagan. Try as they might, the Maroons just could not break down a well-organised St. Mirren defence, and another cup game required to be extended. The determination which had defeated Dumbarton after a replay and both Celtic and Hibs in extra time came to the fore again as Hearts' offensive efforts caught up with them in the extra period.

St. Mirren were by then clearly the stronger side, and went ahead in the 99th minute from a Charlie Sutherland header. Two minutes later, right winger Frank Hodges made it two and Hearts were broken. A third from bargain-buy Sutherland completed the victory. St. Mirren had won their first national competition, and their success in the Victory Cup would provide Paisley with the perfect excuse for another post-war celebration.

"Victory Cup 1919" has since become a familiar entry in the list of St. Mirren honours, but it's a fact that some of the best histories of Scottish football fail to even mention the tournament, and others claim that assessing the calibre of the competition is difficult due to the absence of so many players who were still conscripted at the time. The same situation prevailed between 1914-15 and 1918-19, when the Scottish League Championship was won by Celtic on four occasions and Rangers once. These championship wins are included in all Scottish football records without qualification or reservation. In 1919 St. Mirren won the equivalent of the Scottish Cup; it's an achievement which deserves similar recognition and respect.

1919-20

As life slowly returned to normal in July, St. Mirren FC had never been bigger or more ambitious. There was much to look forward to, but they also permitted themselves a backward glance at what had just been achieved. On Tuesday 8 July in the George Temperance Hotel in Paisley, medals were presented at the Club's Victory Cup "Presentation and Social" to reserves William Brown and John Granger, as well as the eleven players who had played with such determination in the cup ties against Celtic, Hibs, and Hearts. Secretary/Manager John Cochrane, Trainer Charlie Durning, and the Club's seven Directors also received medals.

The sense of optimism was further conveyed when it was announced on 24 June that Secretary/Manager John Cochrane had been appointed on a full-time basis at an increased salary of £6 per week, but not everyone was happy. There was to be no wage increase for Trainer Charlie Durning, and he ended his eight year connection with the Club. The post of Trainer/Groundsman was advertised immediately, and on 4 September Mr. Archibald McGregor was appointed at £4 per week.

Five of the cup-winning eleven - O'Hagan, Page, Clark, Sutherland, and Thomson - would feature prominently in 1919-20, but the three short-term loan players in the triumphant team reverted to their registered clubs. Left back Fulton returned to Cappielow, and despite efforts to sign the other two, right half Perry and outside right Hodges headed back to Bury and Birmingham City respectively. In the case of Hodges, attempts to capture him continued even after he joined Manchester United on 1 August, and although records show Hodges bracketed with Denis Lawson on the right wing for the Ayr United game in February, the story ended there.

Two of the vacancies were filled, when left back William Lavery was signed from Raith Rovers on 24 June, initially on loan, and thereafter he played in almost every match. A fortnight earlier, Queen's Parker Archie Cowan, with three full seasons of Division One football under his belt, was signed and would become the regular right half. In between these two signings, centre half James Riddell was bought from Rangers for a £100 fee, he would also win a regular place in the team.

In the early part of the season, the third vacancy on the right wing was mainly covered by Thomas Nuttall, a July signing from Everton, and occasionally by re-signed war hero Fred Gray. At the beginning of November, Denis Lawson was signed from Kilsyth Emmet and went straight into the team against Hearts, with Nuttal as his inside right partner. Lawson excelled on his debut and retained the right wing berth, but Nuttall fared less well and didn't play again. On 23 December he was reported "as having gone home so that his agreement now terminates". No attempt was made to persuade him to stay.

A week before Nuttall played his last game for Saints, his fellow summer signing and ex-Everton colleague W. Wright also made his last appearance for St. Mirren. Wright had featured at centre or inside forward in most of the games up to 1 November, but had only managed to score one goal. At the beginning of November, Dunfermline asked for him on loan, but he refused to go and John Cochrane reported on 9 December that Wright also "had gone home," and thus "his engagement had now terminated".

The Everton connection was continuing to prove less than successful, and the biggest disappointment was the talented Tom Page. Signed in April 1914, his failure to make a domestic move to Paisley kept his appearances in a St. Mirren shirt to a minimum. By August 1915 he informed the Board that he didn't want to play for the Club, although nearly four years later he did make some effort to play in the latter stages of the Victory Cup.

Under pressure from the Board, he was directed to "take up residence in Paisley" at the end of September 1919, and he played in over twenty-five games during 1919-20, but Page continued to have a strained relationship with St. Mirren, and matters came to a head on 12 April when he "refused to strip" for the home match against Aberdeen. He later advised the Club that it was "not his intention to return to Scotland". As a result he was suspended the following week, and every English League team was informed of his availability.

Some of the Everton intake, such as full back Walter Holbem, had proved to be time-consuming distractions, and it was not as if there was insufficient talent closer to hand. Back in September, young local lad John Buchanan had been given a brief taste of first team football, and he scored the only goal in a 1-0 challenge match win over Morton. By 29 November, after various other forward combinations had been tried, he was back in the team, and in an away match against Partick Thistle he scored Saints' first goal in a 3-3 draw. The following week he retained the centre forward position at Airdrie, where his goal was enough to win another away point. By the end of the season, John Buchanan had scored thirteen League goals to become Saints' top scorer, and he hit nineteen in all competitions.

Although young Buchanan had scored in Jock Marshall's benefit match, their St. Mirren careers would only slightly overlap. On 28 October, Marshall's request to be put on the transfer list was refused, but within a week Middlesbrough enquired about Saints' star full back and were invited to make an offer. By 8 November, it was agreed to accept £1,750, with the player's share of the fee not to exceed £350, but Marshall was still listed with Walter Sneddon at right back for the match against Falkirk at Brockville on 15 November, but he didn't turn up.

At a Board meeting on 18 November it was unanimously agreed to suspend Marshall "for failing to appear on Saturday last and until he apologises we do not do anything with Middlesbrough". The player then explained that his non-appearance "was due to illness", and he stated that "he was sorry for his action". As a result of this apology, the Board agreed to again take up the matter of Marshall's move to Teesside, and the outcome was that he joined the Ayresome Park club for £1,400, with £400 going to the player.

It was an unfortunate final episode to a great St. Mirren career. John Marshall had been in the first team for five seasons, automatic choice at right back for four years, and for two years in a row had been the Club's top scorer. He had already worn the dark blue of Scotland in an "unofficial" international, and would be capped six times whilst with Middlesbrough, and once with Welsh club Llanelly.

If Marshall's Scotland connection as a St. Mirren player was not quite the genuine article, Willie O'Hagan's two Irish caps were real enough. On 25 October 1919, O'Hagan swopped the atmosphere of a Morton derby at Love Street for an Ireland v England clash at Windsor Park, and helped his countrymen to a creditable 1-1 draw. He played again for Ireland at the Linfield FC ground on 14 February 1920 when Wales were the opponents, and this time the outcome was a 2-2 draw.

Competition from the great Elisha Scott kept Willie's caps to just two, but O'Hagan was left with the satisfaction of being one of the very few Irish international goalies not to have suffered defeat. It was a record he maintained on 20 April 1920, when he wisely opted to play for a St. Mirren select in preference to the team of Irish internationalists who provided the opposition for his testimonial match, as St. Mirren won by six goals to three.

Marshall's right back position was set to be taken over by Third Lanark's George Lennon, a £500 signing in mid-January, but the immediate replacement was the versatile Charlie Pringle, who had returned to the team in October at left half following his demobilisation. On Christmas Day 1919, it was as a right back that he joined the twenty-one other St. Mirren and Albion Rovers players who emerged from the temporary huts which were used as dressing rooms for the inaugural match at Rovers' new and almost-ready ground at Cliftonhill. Sunny weather blessed the big day for the "Wee Rovers", but, as so often happens on such occasion, the visitors avoided all the distractions – including an enthusiastic 8,000 crowd – and Saints came away with a 2-0 win.

In January, the first round of the Scottish Cup took Saints to Warner Park in Stevenston to play the local United, who were known by the less-than-attractive nickname of "The Lousies", but there was certainly nothing lousy about the home team's play, as the close 2-1 win for Saints accurately reflected. Ayrshire beckoned again in the second round and 2-1 was the repeat scoreline, but this time it was in favour of the United from Ayr, and Paisley hopes of back-to-back national cup glory vanished at Somerset Park on 7 February.

St. Mirren Juniors had also found it difficult to match the glory which accompanied their sensational capture of the Scottish Junior Cup in 1917. Although they had provided three players to their Scottish League counterparts during the 1919 close season, most notably left half Alf Leslie, relations between the two "St. Mirrens" had become strained following a series of minor incidents, and on 17 February the Juniors advised the senior club that "in future they will make their complaints to the press". It was not a threat or a tactic which greatly impressed the directors of St. Mirren. They had their minds on the creation of an improved St. Mirren Park, so on 11 May 1920 the Juniors were advised the future arrangements would "preclude them from being tenants in our ground".

After years of unavoidable delay, some decisions could finally be made to create a Greater St. Mirren Park. During 1919-20, leading football stadium architect Archibald Leitch had stated that the price for building a new stand, as per his original drawing and within the existing ground boundaries, would be £4,500. At the Club's AGM on 15 April 1920, the shareholders decided that ground extension rather than just a replacement stand was needed. A mandate was given to the Directors to signify the Club's intention to purchase the extra ground, provided that the vendors were prepared to grant extra time for the raising of the necessary capital. By 4 May, steps began to finally purchase the required land from the McKaig Trust, and although Saints had won just fifteen and drawn eight of the forty-two League fixtures, the season ended as it had begun; with considerable optimism.

The final game of the season, for the Paisley Charity Cup, proved to be Saints' last-ever game against Abercorn. On 15 May the "Abbies" had no answer to goals from top scorer John Buchanan and Hugh McIntosh, and within months Paisley's blue and whites - founder members of the Scottish League, twice Scottish League Second Division Champions, and five times winners of the Renfrewshire Cup - had disappeared from the scene. In the ten meetings between the two Paisley sides in national competitions, St. Mirren held the narrow advantage of five wins to four, with one game drawn. From now on "the Buddies" would mean just one team.

The 1920s - Consistency and Success

1920-21

The 1920s compare favourably with any other decade in the Club's first 112 years of League football, yet the start in 1920-21 couldn't have been worse. Records for 1920-21 show that not only did Saints finish bottom of the League for the third time in thirty years, but they suffered more defeats - thirty-one - than in any other season.

CHAPTER SIX

The 1920-21 performances meant that for sixty-seven years Saints had sole rights to the title of "most defeats in a single Scottish season", which led to an undesirable entry in the 'Guinness Book of Records'. Thankfully, another club had an equally awful season in the 1987-88 Premier League, losing thirty-one of their forty-four games, so there's at least one reason to be grateful to Morton! By 1993 the names of both St. Mirren and Morton were finally deleted, when Cowdenbeath managed to lose thirty-four times.

One unwanted record may since have gone, but 1920-21 remains littered with dreadful statistics. Saints lost fourteen of the nineteen home games in the League, yet for much of the season somehow managed to stay just ahead of Dumbarton until a complete collapse in their last fifteen games produced thirteen defeats. They finished six points behind the "Sons" in last place, and the ninety-two goals conceded was worse than any other team in Scotland or the three English Divisions.

It is too much of a simplification to claim that the decade's disastrous beginning can be attributed to the Directors' preoccupation with ground improvements. Records show they were as active as ever in the transfer market, but with most available finance set aside to pay for the construction of a new stand the quality of the players brought to the Club may have been lower than usual. In the same season that the first team finished bottom of the League, the reserve team, with a side full of players with first team experience, romped away with the Alliance League. The Club had too many players of a certain standard, and not enough who matched the demands of Division One.

Charlie Sutherland, two goal hero of the Victory Cup Final.

Some previous season regulars had gone. Reserve 'keeper Dan Hillcoat had been sold to Kilmarnock for £150 in July, and inside forward Charlie Sutherland, hero of the Victory Cup final, was transferred to Millwall for £250 in early June. Wing half or centre half Harold McKenna, who had been with Saints for two years but was in fact still a Rangers player, had been recalled to Ibrox, and also wearing blue would be inside forward Tom Page, whose future was finally settled when he joined English League newcomers Cardiff City in June 1920 for a fee of £300.

Despite these departures there remained a core of good players. Willie O'Hagan was still in goal, Jamie Thomson for the fourth season in a row proved that wingers don't necessarily have to be inconsistent, and on the opposite right wing Denis Lawson was also a terrific performer. Charlie Pringle was to divide the season between right half and centre half, and was accomplished enough to win a cap later in the season, an honour which would also soon be conferred on Lawson.

Right half Archie Cowan found himself out of the picture during the season, and by 6 January the former Queen's Parker "had left with a free transfer". His right half position would be taken in spells by Charlie Pringle, Richard McAvoy, Alf Leslie, John Buchanan, Alex Duff, and finally William Clunas. As results failed to improve, such lack of selection continuity was not just restricted to right half!

Although ground development was a priority, normal Director duties continued, and on 30 October two of the Board attended a cup tie between Renfrew and a Paisley side called Vulcan, and were impressed with their first sight of Love, the Vulcan centre forward. The following Saturday, George Love scored two of Saints' three goals against Raith Rovers in what was only Saints' third League win of the season. He remained at centre forward for the rest of the season and his eight League goals made him the Club's top scorer. Less than a year after his last game for Vulcan, George Love was given a free transfer by St. Mirren.

By the turn of the year, team performances couldn't have got much worse, but the Directors weren't taking any chances! They warned the players not to attend the Brake Club Dance on Friday 7 January or any function on a Friday before a game. Defeats continued, and on 15 January, Third Lanark left Love Street with a 3-1 win. It was Saints' nineteenth defeat from twenty-eight games, and although it hadn't been a good team performance, Saints' goalkeeper Willie O'Hagan received more criticism that most.

O'Hagan hadn't missed a game up till then, and although his performances had led to two meetings with the Directors, he was listed for the Scottish Cup visit of Armadale on 22 January. Perhaps he shouldn't have been. Following his January interview with two Directors, Willie O'Hagan asked to be placed on the transfer list "owing to financial and other troubles". His request "was not entertained".

At 11.50 on the morning of the cup tie, a telegram was received from the 'keeper stating that he was confined to bed. When John Cochrane called at O'Hagan's house and tried to induce him to play, O'Hagan stated "that his bones were sore and he had pains in his ankles". According to Cochrane, "he refused to play even after being told that (reserve keeper Richard) Toole was unfit". O'Hagan's reserve was forced to play, and although St. Mirren took the lead twice in the match, it was the West Lothian side who eventually won through by 3-2 to pull off the shock of the round.

The result did nothing to ease the Club's ragged relationship with O'Hagan, who just one year earlier had enjoyed his best-ever season. Following a visit to the 'keeper's home by two Directors, the Board decided that "had the player been anxious to comply with his contract he could have been present to play here on Saturday last and furthermore the Directors express their strongest disapproval of the attitude taken up by the player". O'Hagan was to be given no pay until a previous loan from the Club was re-paid, and he was placed on the transfer list at his own request.

Young Richard Toole, signed in the summer from Musselburgh Comrades, would continue in goal, but the search began for O'Hagan's long-term successor. On 17 February, John Cochrane left a note for the Directors stating that "he had gone to Bo'ness for John Bradford". Four days later it was confirmed that goalkeeper "Jock" Bradford had been signed for £25, and he made his debut the following Saturday in a home match against Albion Rovers. By this time O'Hagan was again being paid, but had been told that his presence at training or on match days was not required. He was transferred to Airdrieonians at the beginning of May 1921.

In the middle of Saints' most disappointing set of results, there was brighter news in November regarding the long-awaited ground development. Mr. J Gilchrist Bennett CE, and not the previously involved

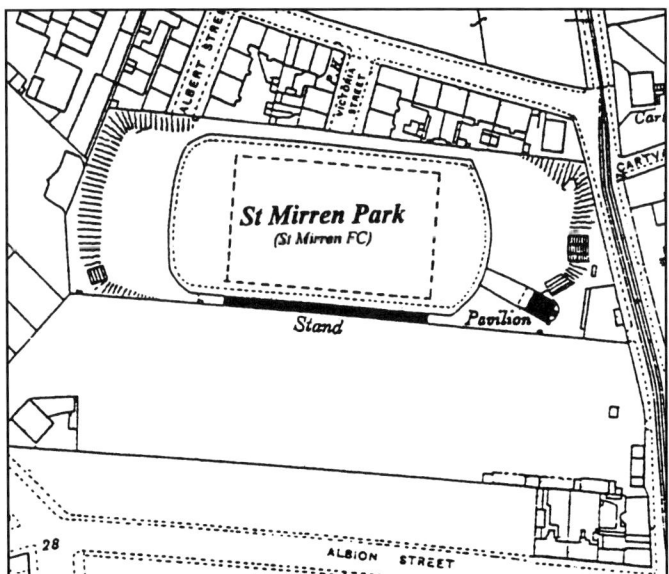

As the map circa 1913/1914 shows, the purchase of land between the stand and the boundary with Albion Street allowed the club to widen the ground and build terracing embankments and a new stand.

famous football ground architect Archibald Leitch, was the man appointed as project engineer, and at the same time Mr. MacRobert of the Club's lawyers MacRobert, Son, and Hutchison was instructed to purchase the additional land required to accommodate the new stand.

By 30 November, St. Mirren had signed a cheque for £2,525 to purchase the land, and Mr. Bennett's plan for the new stand was approved. The land purchase and all the improvements were to be funded by a new share issue, and the Secretary reported in December that almost 15,000 new shares had been applied for and this had raised £4,602, but it soon became obvious that buying the land would be the least of the costs. On 8 February 1921, Mr. John R Stutt's offer to lay a new pitch, track, and barrier fence at a cost of £5,076 18s was accepted on the understanding that the work was to be completed within twenty weeks.

Schedules were issued and estimates sought on 1 March, but it was as late as 14 April before information such as steel work costs were known. By 5 May the question of funding the building of the new stand was revisited, and a meeting of Club Directors, the project engineer, and the Club's lawyer unanimously decided to issue debentures (which would pay interest to investors) up to a total of £10,000.

On 23 May the Directors confirmed that "we regretfully are compelled to modify our ideas meantime and propose to proceed with a stand at a cost of about £7,000". As far as positioning the revised stand was concerned, the Club agreed to see Mr. Bennett regarding "having the stand in the middle". Such enforced changes were disappointing, but the newly opened "Greater Love Street" would be a source of pride in a few short months.

There was a major on-field investment at the beginning of April when the Club completed the transfer of Dumbarton centre forward Dunky Walker and left back Joe Till for a joint fee of £1900. Both went straight into the team against Hearts on 15 April, and endured a 4-0 defeat in a match played at neutral Easter Road. Authority had been given by the League to play their three remaining League home fixtures on neutral ground, and this allowed the Club to "take down" the old stand and advertise it for sale after the home game against Hibs on 26 February.

The first of the three games was against Ayr United on 19 March, and although serious consideration was given to using Celtic Park or Cappielow, the problem was simply solved by Saints playing their home match against Ayr United at Somerset Park! Two days later, Saints' ground was closed as the contractor started to "cut up the ground".

The "Ayr" arrangement was somehow not permitted for Saints' match with Hearts on 15 April and the game took place at Easter Road. Things were not being made any easier for the groundless St. Mirren when they opted to "motor through" to Edinburgh to avoid a possible rail strike. The third of the three neutral venue matches was against Rangers, and the match went ahead on Thursday 21 April at Hampden. It was Dunky Walker's second game for Saints, and he also played in the last League game of the season at Dens. Neither he nor the team would score in these matches, but it would be a different story the following season!

1921-22

Chosen by Barcelona's Swiss-born founder and President, Hans Gamper, St. Mirren had the honour of taking part in the first match played at FC Barcelona's new Les Corts ground, which quickly became known as "the cathedral of football". The match with "Barca" on 20 May 1922 marked the beginning of an eventful Spanish tour, and came at the end of a memorable Scottish season for the Buddies.

Hans Gamper, Barcelona President, who personally corresponded with St. Mirren.

Precisely nine months earlier on 20 August, St. Mirren had taken part in another stadium ceremony when the reconstructed "Greater Love Street" was opened by S.F.A. President Mr. Tom White of Celtic in front of 12,000 supporters. St. Mirren Chairman Mr. George B Riddell acknowledged the work of the contractors and others in getting the ground ready, "considering operations had only commenced a few months ago". Unfortunately the new grandstand was not completed, but it was hoped to have it finished for the match against Rangers a fortnight later. Meanwhile, spectators were advised "to keep clear of the stand in its present unfinished state".

Debenture trustees who had helped finance the ground improvements, the Project Manager, the Club's lawyers, the various contractors, representatives from every League club, the S.F.A., the Scottish League, and the Renfrewshire F.A. had all been invited to attend the opening, and three specially ordered cases of "Auld Scottie" were also on hand to assist any visiting dignitaries who might need some encouragement to enter into the spirit of the occasion!

The team played their part on the big day as five shots were hit past the Queen's Park goalkeeper without reply. Four of the Saints' goals came from centre forward Dunky Walker, and one from Robert Stevenson. The following Tuesday, a crowd of 11,000 watched Walker and Stevenson repeat their goalscoring feats as Hamilton Accies were also beaten 5-0. The third game was at Easter Road, and the same Saints eleven lined up for the third time. A 1-1 draw resulted and Walker scored again.

It was the unprecedented consistency of team selection which was to transform the team's fortunes. Goalkeeper Jock Bradford had been in the team since his February debut, and after just two games the Directors decided that Bradford "will do for next season". At right back, William McAllister had joined from Johnstone in mid-March and played four games near the end of 1920-21, and his left back partner Joe Till had signed from Dumbarton on the same day as Walker. Right half William Clunas, from Kilbarchan Athletic, had featured in 1920-21's last six games, completing the half back line were centre half Willie Summers and left half James Miller, signed from St. Bernards towards the end of the 1920-21 season.

A forward line of Lawson, Pringle, Walker, Stevenson, and Thomson would, injuries apart, show only one change all season. Right winger Denis Lawson was one of Scotland's best, and Charlie Pringle would once again show the form which in the previous season had not only earned him a League cap against the Irish League, but also a full cap against Wales at Pittodrie on 12 February 1921 - an outstanding achievement for a player in a struggling club side.

Willie Summers

At centre forward was Walker, and on the left wing for the fifth consecutive year was Jamie Thomson. Filling the inside left berth was Robert Stevenson, who had been part of a double transfer involving 1919-20 hot shot John Buchanan. The following season Buchanan scored just five goals and played wing half as often as centre forward, which may have prompted his November transfer request, but he got his wish when he moved to Morton on 17 May 1921 for £200, with Stevenson making the opposite journey on the same day for a fee of £250.

The new grandstand, with accommodation for 2,000 spectators, was officially opened on 3 September 1921, and for Saints' second gala occasion in three weeks a marquee was erected adjacent to the stand.

Work in progress on "New Greater Love Street Grounds" clearly showing the old pavilion still in place behind the Love Street End goal.

The match against Rangers attracted a then-record crowd of 35,290, and produced gate and stand receipts of £1,852 1s 6d. This time the guest list included Mr. J. Oscar Clark, who opened the stand, Lord Glentanar, Mr. Harold Coats, Provost Lang, Baillie Glover, Renfrewshire FA representatives, three trustees, and a number of former players.

An injury to left half James Miller just prior to 1 October caused the first disruption to the team, and allowed Alex Duff the chance to stake his claim. Duff had been signed in October 1920 from Kilsyth Rangers, and had played over twenty games at centre half and left half before being replaced at the beginning of March 1921. He was rejoining a much more confident first team, and by the end of September Saints had won three and drawn five of the nine games played. Only a narrow 2-1 home defeat by Rangers on 3 September spoiled a solid start, and Walker had already scored thirteen times!

Although the new stand was now in operation other ground improvements were still required, and in the previous December three Directors had visited Ibrox and Firhill to assess the cost of "laying and banking" of terracing. Parts of the ground were established as a "free coup", but the Club were specific about what could be deposited. On 31 October, the groundsman was instructed that "nothing but clean rubbish be allowed on our banking" and the laying down of "the clean rubbish" finally ended on 28 January 1922.

Alex Duff at left half remained the only change until 5 November, when newly signed Curran from Shawfield took over at inside right, with Pringle moving back to left half. Curran would play just four times, but a summer signing from Duntocher Hibs, Archie Gillies, would take over the inside right position on 3 December and remain there for the rest of the season. The match on 5 November underlined Saints' improvement, and the 4-1 win over Clydebank gave Saints nineteen points, one more than the previous season's total.

Dunky Walker

The Scottish Cup draw meant a journey to Annan to play Solway Star was in prospect, but in return for £140, a half share of the gate, and a friendly match before the season's end, the game was switched to Paisley. At either location the Star defence would be required to face Walker, who by then had scored thirty-four goals in all competitions. By 4.40pm on Saturday 28 January, he had hit another five in a 7-2 first round win.

In the Cup's second round on 11 February, the only other significant team change occurred when Andrew Findlay, signed earlier in the week from Roslyn Juniors, lined up against Kilmarnock at Rugby Park. Findlay was part of a second emphatic cup win, and there was another hat-trick from Walker as Saints won 4-1. Two weeks later, two more goals from Walker and one from the impressive Stevenson was enough to defeat Airdrieonians by 3-0 in the third round.

For the fourth consecutive Scottish Cup round, Dunky Walker scored for Saints as the Buddies and Rangers drew 1-1 at Ibrox. Hopes were high of further Saints' progress as the tie switched to St. Mirren Park three days later, but two goals from the visitors ended Paisley's expectations. Despite the cup disappointment, Saints held their form to finish in eighth place with forty-six points. By the end of the League campaign, Walker had scored forty-five goals, two more than the previous season's whole team, and in doing so scored twice in each of four games, four times on three occasions, and hit two hat-tricks. He also created a Club record which is unlikely to be surpassed.

Also creating a club record of their own were Morton FC, and on 3 April the St. Mirren Board agreed "to offer Morton FC our congratulations on entering the Scottish Cup Final". Morton would of course go on to win the Scottish Cup that year, but they would not be the only Renfrewshire club to capture a prestigious trophy

In mid-February 1922 it was agreed that the Club would make a tour of Spain during the close season, "provided we make not less than £200". This assurance was received in a letter from Barcelona President Hans Gamper at the beginning of April, although as late as 9 May Director Mr. Hall and Secretary John Cochrane were delegated to visit Williamson's Tourist Agency, and "it was to be left with them to decide whether or not we are going".

They decided Saints were going and would be represented by most of the first choice team, but the Spanish party also included Birrell, Hamilton, Barclay, Dodds, and Leslie, and they had hardly played a game between them all season. It remained to be seen whether the notable absence of Willie Summers and Charlie Pringle would be felt.

The first match of the tour was the historic first-ever game at Camp de Les Corts. Saints lost 2-1 to a Barcelona side who scored first through an unfortunate own goal by Saints' left back Robert Birrell. The following day at Les Corts, Saints lost 1-0 to a Barcelona side showing only two changes from the previous day. A four day break gave the Saints players time to become more acclimatised for a challenge match against the world's oldest football club, Notts County, who had beaten Barcelona three times during 1914, and two days later would defeat them again by 4-2.

At stake, in addition to the reputations of Scottish and English football, was a specially commissioned, one-off trophy which is still referred to by Catalans as the Copa Inauguracion Les Corts, but it was to become familiar to St. Mirren supporters as the Barcelona Cup. After a goal-less first half, Saints took the lead ten minutes into the second half through Walker, but they were forced into extra time when County hit a late equaliser. Both sides had it all to do again in difficult conditions, but with time running out it was that man Walker who grabbed the winner. Les Corts had had its "inauguracion" and now the "Copa" belonged to Paisley.

From Catalonia the cup-winning Saints travelled east to Santander in Cantabria, where they defeated a North Spain Select 3-2 on 28 May. Two days later they drew 2-2 with another local select team in Santander, before moving further east to Gijon in Asturias where they finished the tour on 4 June with an emphatic 7-3 win. Dunky Walker, who had started the season with four goals, ended it by scoring six!

The 1922 Saints would be coming home with a cup to keep, and their inaugural match with Barcelona would earn St. Mirren a permanent place in the FC Barcelona story. If the previous season had been one to forget, 1921-22 would always be recalled with relish.

The opening of Barcelona's new stadium, Camp Des Les Corts.

Below: The Copa Inauguracion Les Corts, better known as the Barcelona Cup.

1922-23

Three of Saints' leading players, Lawson, Summers, and Pringle, refused the resigning terms offered in early May 1922, the latter two missed the Spanish tour. Of the three, Pringle was furthest ahead in negotiations, and his refusal to sign was deemed "tantamount to requesting to be placed on the transfer list", and Saints made it known that they were willing to listen to offers for the versatile Pringle. It was also agreed that the same approach was to apply to Lawson and Summers should they again refuse to re-sign.

Notts County immediately expressed an interest in Pringle, but on 26 June Secretary John Cochrane confirmed that the Scottish internationalist had been transferred to Manchester City for £1,410, with the player receiving £300 as his share of the deal. Charlie Pringle had been in the Saints' first team for five years, and had served the Club well in a number of positions. He was to be no less successful at Maine Road, where he went on to become team captain. Denis Lawson re-signed in time to join the tour party, but Willie Summers was just too late to be included in the Spanish adventure. Saints' first-ever foreign trip was described in great detail by the Secretary at the Board meeting of 12 June, during which Chairman George Riddell accepted the splendid Copa Inauguracion Les Corts on behalf of the Club. The trophy was immediately referred to as the Barcelona Cup, and that has been the practice ever since. It was agreed to exhibit it in Director Mr. Hall's window "for a week or so", and thereafter two-goal hero Duncan Walker was to receive it. This circulating of the cup continued for some time until the insurance company objected to it being "shifted from shop to shop".

Trainer Andy Reid attends to star inside right Archie Gillies.

Although Charlie Pringle had gone, there was a comforting continuity about the rest of the team as the 1922-23 season began. Jock Bradford remained the undisputed first choice 'keeper throughout his second full season with Saints apart from a five match spell in September, and the 'keeper was made team captain for the last three months. Retaining the right back berth was Andrew Findlay, while future Scotland internationalist James Hamilton, signed in mid-April 1922 from Vale of Clyde, was Findlay's regular partner.

Two of the three half back positions were almost automatic selections. The constructive William Clunas was at right half for a second season, team captain Willie Summers continued to be a calming influence at centre half, and the left half position was predominantly taken by John Scott, who had been signed from Manchester United at the beginning of July for £225.

Of the established "Lawson, Gillies, Walker, Stevenson, and Thomson" forward line, only Robert Stevenson was challenged in any way for his position, and the benefits of a settled team were again shown by the results as forty-two points were gained from thirty-eight games. Fourteen teams in Division One again finished below St. Mirren, but a reduction from twenty-two to twenty clubs meant that Saints not only consolidated their improved form but moved up two places for a top six finish.

The Scottish Cup was Saints' only real disappointment: it was all over within a fortnight. On 13 January they travelled to Borough Briggs in Elgin where goals from Clunas, Thomson, and Walker qualified them to make the much shorter journey to Lanarkshire in the second round. Motherwell's League form had not matched Saints all season, but two goals from the Fir Parkers was one more than Saints could score, and the Buddies were out. Saints' generally improved form over the 1921-23 period was beginning to attract attention, and when centre half Summers was placed on the transfer list at his own request in early February 1923, both Stoke and Burnley showed immediate interest. At the same time Leicester City enquired about Denis Lawson, and a month later Chelsea put in a £2000 bid for Lawson's services, but their offer was unanimously rejected as insufficient. The two English clubs were not alone in admiring Saints' speedy winger, and the Scotland selectors named him in the team to play England at Hampden on 14 April 1923, and thus Denis, deservedly, became the thirteenth Saint to play for Scotland.

Chelsea FC were nothing if not determined, and in mid-April they made a £4000 joint bid for Lawson and Clunas, but the St. Mirren Board intimated they had no wish to sell more than one of these leading players. One Saint who seemed an obvious transfer target was Duncan Walker, but his name had not been mentioned in this regard until he asked to be put on the transfer list at the end of April.

No one had expected Walker to repeat his record-breaking scoring feats, but his total of twenty-one League goals was still more than anyone else had ever scored for St. Mirren. Off the pitch it had been a strange, and perhaps strained, season for him. At the beginning of October he was brought before the Board and asked to explain his poor physical condition and his reasons for missing training. A fortnight later and just five months after securing his place as a Club legend, it was agreed "that we try and dispose of Duncan Walker". For the immediate match against Airdrieonians at Broomfield on 21 October and the following week he played for the "A" team.

A couple of months later a strange sequence of events indicate a less than harmonious second season. On 4 December the Secretary reported that he had received various complaints about Duncan Walker's behaviour "on Friday and Saturday last just prior to the Clyde game", and requested that action be taken against Walker. Following a Directors' discussion, John Cochrane was instructed "to secure someone to shadow Walker on Tuesday, Wednesday and Thursday of this week". A week later the Board confronted Walker with a report of his movements, but the player "denied most of our evidence". By 11 December Trainer Andy Reid was instructed "to record any observations in his training book", but after that matters settled.

Four months later, no sooner had Walker put in his transfer request than Everton made enquiries about him and within a fortnight similar letters were received from Tottenham, Burnley, and Nottingham Forest. On 28 May 1923 John Cochrane reported that Duncan Walker had been transferred to Forest for £2,225, and the player's share of the transfer was £250, subject to League approval. Dunky's spell with Saints was a short and mostly sweet spell, and his scoring record of sixty-six League goals in just two seasons makes him one of the outstanding players in the story of St. Mirren.

During the 1922-23 season ground upgrade work continued. Three telephone boxes for newspapers were installed, and the Club investigated the cost of installing electric light into each telephone booth, appropriately from a Mr. Bell! Work continued on improving the terracing, and having asked in the past for "clean rubbish", it was decided in December that as soon as the two banks at the Love Street end met "we will close the grounds and take only clean ashes to dress the banking all round".

The most obvious change to the ground was the replacement of the old pavilion. On 17 July, Messrs. Black and Morton's bid of £1033 7s 6d to build the new pavilion was accepted, but they eventually promised not to exceed £903. Within a week the work was started, and another £40 came off the cost when the old pavilion was sold for that amount to Messrs. R & G Gilmour.

St. Mirren's efforts to give Paisley a top-class stadium were rewarded when, for the first time in thirty-three years, international football came to town. Wales, as they had been in 1890, were the visitors, and on 17 March 1923 a crowd of 25,000 at St. Mirren Park saw Scotland win 2-0. A month earlier St. Mirren announced that they would only accept ashes from the council's cleansing department base, which ironically was located on Abercorn's original ground at Underwood Park, site of the only other international played in Paisley.

At the 1923 AGM on 15 May, Chairman George B. Riddell paid tribute to Mr. John Scouller, who had announced his retirement from the Board after twenty-six years of continuous service. "St. Mirren Football Club has never had a more whole-hearted worker," said Mr. Riddell, who advised the meeting that steps would soon be taken "to signalise our appreciation of Mr. Scouller".

As John Scouller was bowing out St. Mirren had just completed a successful foreign tour and had hosted a full international match; they were also in the midst of an unprecedented period of consistency. The Buddies had come a long way in twenty-six years, and John Scouller could content himself with the thought that his many admirers greatly valued his contribution to that progress.

1923-24

At a testimonial tea held in his honour in the Royal Oak Restaurant, John Scouller was presented with a watch, a wallet, an umbrella, and an amount in cash in recognition of his service to the Club. Despite watching St. Mirren over many years, even Mr. Scouller would have had difficulty recalling two consecutive seasons as similar in outcome as the 1922-23 and 1923-24 seasons.

Both produced fifteen wins, twelve draws, and forty-two points from thirty eight games to give two sixth top finishes; even the "goals for" and "goals against" figures differed by just one goal. The separating factor was the team itself. Although "Bradford, Findlay, and Hamilton" continued to be the first three surnames on the team sheet, and Summers and Thomson were also still there, the rest of the team was to evolve as the season progressed.

Right half Clunas and right winger Lawson had been the subject of previous transfer speculation, and on 13 August Sunderland FC enquired about Lawson. They were advised that he was not for sale, but phone calls from Liverpool and Newcastle United in mid-October regarding the same player forced the issue, and "after considering the whole business it was resolved that we are agreeable to transfer Lawson for £2000". On 23 October, every English League club was circulated regarding the winger's availability.

On 5 November the Secretary reported that Sunderland AFC had watched Lawson the previous Saturday, but had ended the game more interested in Clunas. This conclusion galvanised the Board, and the Secretary was instructed to immediately telephone all the leading English clubs about Clunas's availability. At the same time the Board's plans to raise money were delayed "until we see if anything arises out of some of the players transfers".

Scottish internationalist Lawson was transferred to Cardiff City on 12 November for £2,050, and the player's share was £500. There had been talk at the time of Charlie Pringle's transfer that the cost of enlarging the ground would lead to an exodus of the Club's leading players. Certainly there is no evidence that any great effort was made to retain Pringle, Lawson, and later Clunas, but the records show that such transactions were executed with great reluctance. On the day of Lawson's transfer, the Secretary was instructed to write to the Commercial Bank and state that "we are strongly of the opinion that the short-sighted policy they have pursued had forced us to sell at an inopportune time and the price accruing from players is only a fraction of what we expected".

William Clunas was transferred to Sunderland at the end of November, and for the rest of the season his place was taken by Thomas Barclay, a former Stewarton centre half who was signed in March 1921 but had seldom featured in the first team. Willie Summers remained at centre half, Saints' having rescinded previous plans to transfer him, and he would remain at St. Mirren Park long enough to become a cup-winner. John Scott was replaced at left half by William McDonald, a summer signing from Irvine Meadow who would also become a permanent fixture in the side.

The transfer of Lawson allowed Sam Evans, signed from Clydebank on 13 June, to take over the outside right position, and he did so well that by March 1924, Liverpool FC wanted to know Saints' asking price for him. Archie Gillies remained at inside right, and only a November injury which required him to have a cartilage operation allowed John Whitelaw, signed from Shettleston on 8 October, to cover most of Gillies' four month absence.

Centre forward Dunky Walker was going to be a hard act to follow, and early in the season the task fell to Alex Merrie, who had signed from Saltcoats Victoria at the end of July. Merrie scored six League goals and was succeeded by John Wood, who joined from Manchester United for £500 in late December 1923. Wood hit fourteen goals, including five against bottom club Clydebank on 8 March, but a couple of weeks later Walker's true successor was discovered when Davie McCrae made his debut against Hibs. McCrae would score three goals in his first five League games, and in his first full season would become, to that point, second only to Walker as Saints' top scorer.

Regular inside left Robert Stevenson had refused to re-sign in July, and the dispute wasn't settled until 27 August. He was immediately reinstated to the first team, but was dropped to the "A" team at the beginning of November. Such was the play of William McIntosh, a September 1922 signing from Strathclyde, that Stevenson didn't get back into the first team for the rest of the season. There were no such problems for Jamie Thomson, who continued to excel on the left wing.

The parallels with the previous season continued, with Saints' Scottish Cup campaign again lasting just two weeks. Their first round opponents were mid-table Division Three Beith, who, despite losing 3-2, gave a performance which belied their status. Particularly impressive was visiting centre Davie McCrae, and St. Mirren wasted little time in signing him a few days later.

In the Cup's second round, a visit of Rangers again broke the ground attendance record when 40,291 packed St. Mirren Park on 9 February, but one goal by the visitors was enough to give them victory. Such crowds vindicated the decision to enlarge the ground, and if there was frustration about having to sell current and future Scotland players, the Club gained great satisfaction on 1 March 1924 when full back James Hamilton lined up for Scotland against Ireland at Celtic Park to become the fourteenth Saint to represent Scotland. Less than two years earlier Hamilton had been playing for Vale of Clyde. He had benefited from playing in a very good St. Mirren side, and that standard would remain high for the rest of the 1920s.

1924-25

Hopes that Jock Bradford, Andrew Findlay, and James Hamilton would form the basis of Saints' defence for the 1924-25 season were dashed when Hamilton was admitted to the Royal Alexandra Infirmary in mid-September suffering from a leg fracture. St. Mirren's latest internationalist returned for the first-ever New Year's Day derby match with Morton, but was spoken to by the Secretary "regarding his rough play" following the match against Third Lanark on 31 January. Hamilton continued to play right up to the Raith Rovers match on 18 February, but was cautioned by the S.F.A. at the end of February following a complaint by Third Lanark.

Hamilton didn't play for the first team again in 1924-25, but his absence was covered at the beginning of October when Saints signed William Newbiggin on loan from Motherwell for just £50. The deal included an option of paying a further £150 before 26 April 1925 for Newbiggin's outright transfer, or the player would have to return to Fir Park. Such was Newbiggin's impact that he never again wore claret and amber.

Davie McCrae

Another significant Saints' signing took place at the end of August when right half Tom Morrison was recommended to the Club by a Troon Athletic official. Secretary John Cochrane was aware that the player was already involved with Morton FC, and responded to Troon "that St. Mirren would do nothing until the business with Morton was finished". Morrison then informed Morton that he would not be joining them, and Saints swiftly stepped in. Morrison was to be St. Mirren's right half for the rest of the season in a half back line which again featured Willie Summers and William McDonald.

For the third season in a row, St. Mirren would finish as the sixth best team in Scotland, but it was the Club's Scottish Cup run which caught the public's imagination. Excellent crowds watched Saints' progress in the competition, and this interest culminated in a new record attendance when 47,428 people packed into St. Mirren Park on 7 March 1925 to see the Scottish Cup fourth round tie with Celtic.

The cup campaign had commenced on 24 January with a 3-1 win over the then - Highland League Peterhead, with Saints' three goals coming from Davie McCrae, Archie Gillies, and John Whitelaw. In the second round, Division One strugglers Ayr United were narrowly beaten 1-0 thanks to a McCrae goal, and making his debut at outside right was Matthew "Mattha" Morgan, who had come from Renfrew Juniors at the beginning of January. Morgan's arrival as the regular right winger signalled the end for Sam Evans, who had made such a good impression the previous season.

Arriving a month before Morgan was inside forward Allan Gebbie from Muirkirk Athletic. Gebbie also secured an immediate place in the team, but an injury ruled him out of the home cup tie against Partick Thistle in the third round. The increasingly influential John Cochrane secured Gebbie's replacement from St. Johnstone with the loan of James Howieson "for all our Scottish Cup ties" for a fee of £100. Howieson played against Thistle, but the arrangement was only implemented on this one occasion.

By the following season Howieson would be a permanent Paisley Saint, but his one-off appearance in 1924-25 was in front of an enthusiastic 30,205 fans as Paisley and Partick cup optimism began to grow. Davie McCrae again grabbed all the headlines when his two goals were enough to take Saints through to the last eight.

Quarter final opponents Celtic were to finish just four points and three places ahead of the Buddies in the League, and a close match was anticipated. Additionally, in the midst of a period of championship domination by Rangers, the Cup represented Celtic's best chance of a trophy, and both these factors contributed to the record crowd. Unfortunately for Saints, danger man McCrae had sustained an injury in an earlier League match which required infirmary attention, and it not only blunted his menace in the first match but meant he was unable to take part in the further two games needed to settle the tie. McCrae's place on both occasions was taken by Douglas Thomson, another on-loan player from St. Johnstone.

The first game was devoid of incident and ended in a disappointing 0-0 draw, but the next two ties contained moments of real controversy, and Saints were the sufferers. Celtic went ahead in the Parkhead replay through top scorer Adam McLean, but Saints fans in the Celtic Park crowd disputed the legitimacy of this particular "goal", as Jock Bradford, still holding the ball, was charged over the line by McLean. A chance to fight another day came when the temporary Thomson headed in a corner from his left-wing namesake, Jamie.

If the St. Mirren players felt hard done by at the end of the first replay, it was nothing to the anger they showed at neutral Ibrox. A McGrory header had earlier separated the teams, and as the game entered the final minute, Saints' Gillies was brought down as he made for goal. To the Buddies' dismay, only a free kick was awarded. Incensed at being deprived of a penalty, they refused to take the free kick from the spot identified by referee Peter Craigmyle, and the stand-off was only ended when the referee blew for full-time. Two days after the third Celtic tie St. Mirren complained about Mr. Craigmyle's handling of the game.

Davie McCrae had been missed in the Celtic games. He would finish the season with forty goals in all competitions, and 1924-25 signalled the start of a seven year St. Mirren goalscoring record which is unlikely to be matched. His twenty-nine League goals included seven doubles, and he scored all four goals in a 4-1 home win over Motherwell. He also hit home four goals in the Scottish Cup, but that was merely an appetiser; the following season he would be fully fit to face Celtic, and his goal would help, at last, to bring the Cup to Paisley.

1925-26

On 24 April 1926, St. Mirren completed their League fixtures with a 3-1 home win over Aberdeen. It was their twentieth win, a result which ensured that they finished fourth in the League and their best performance for thirty three years. At one stage it looked as if they could win the Championship, but it was triumph in another competition which would bring unprecedented football joy to Paisley.

In the first sixteen fixtures the team lost only once, but an unexpected 1-0 defeat at Muirton on 14 November from St. Johnstone was the first of seven losses in eight weeks which put paid to the Buddies' title chances. Prominent again was centre forward Davie McCrae, who scored twenty-four times in the League including twelve goals in ten consecutive League matches!

It was far from being a one-man team and there was quality and experience throughout the side, but that quality did not include international full back James Hamilton, who despite barely featuring in the first team for six months was attracting the attention of other clubs. On 30 September it was confirmed that Hamilton had been transferred to Rangers for a fee of £2,300, with £300 going to the player.

Hamilton was nearly followed through the exit door by James Howieson, who had only joined the Club from Dundee United on a permanent basis on 26 October for a fee of £1000. He was not an instant success. On 18 November Howieson was part of Saints' strongest available team, which travelled to Liverpool to take part in a benefit game for football's first superstar, Billy Merideth of Manchester City, Manchester United, and Wales, who was retiring that year. After the Merideth match St. Mirren received enquiries about Summers and Howieson, and within a month the Club agreed to transfer Howieson on the grounds that "although he is a good player he is not fitting into the side". No transfer took place, but he remained in the Reserves until 9 February 1926, when he returned for the cup replay against Arbroath.

A fortnight earlier, there was no McCrae in the team to face Division Three strugglers Mid-Annandale in the Cup, and for the third week running he was playing for the Reserves. His place was taken by James McDonald, signed from Johnstone in May, who scored one of the four home goals which took Saints through to the second round. Two of the other goals came from inside left Hugh McCrindle, who had joined from Rutherglen Glecairn in August, and Jamie Thomson scored the fourth.

The Cup... Object of desire and finally won by Saints in 1926.

Jock Bradford leaps to clear Cup Final danger.

In the second round Saints travelled to Gayfield, and found themselves facing a ten-man Arbroath side after just thirty minutes. Even a Tom Morrison penalty kick failed to alter the 0-0 scoreline, but in the replay Saints won 3-0 with goals from Mattha Morgan, Jamie Thomson, and James McDonald.

For the second year in a row Partick Thistle were third round visitors, and another 20,000 crowd watched an evenly-contested match. A James Howieson shot cancelled out an earlier converted penalty by Thistle before an incident occurred which turned the game. Following the withdrawal of a Thistle defender through injury, the referee bounced the ball to re-start the game. There was no question of passing the ball back to the team in possession, and when the ball broke to Saints' Mattha Morgan he unhesitantly hammered the ball into the Thistle net, and Saints were through to the quarter finals, where they met Airdrie at home.

This was an Airdrieonians side which had finished second in the League for the three previous seasons, and would do the same in 1925-26. The quality of both sides attracted a crowd of 25,000, but for over an hour it was the Saints defenders who took most of the honours before McCrae put the Buddies ahead in the sixty-fifth minute. The normally reliable McCrae then missed a penalty, but Allan Gebbie was on hand to follow up and enable Saints to overcome Scotland's second best team.

In the semi-final at Celtic Park on 20 March, Saints faced a Rangers team which had finished one place ahead of Airdrie in the League for three previous years, but who had fallen from that high standard throughout 1925-26. However, they were still formidable opponents, as the 61,000 crowd could see, and they dominated the first half without scoring against a Saints defence superbly marshalled by Willie Summers. After the break, it was Saints who took the lead when a Tom Morrison free kick was not cleared properly, and a returned lob from long-serving Jamie Thomson was enough to take St. Mirren to their second Scottish Cup Final. The players were awarded a £4 bonus for the semi-final triumph, and three days later in a League game at St. Mirren Park Saints beat Rangers again.

Between the Semi Final and the Final on 10 April, Saints also managed to win their other two League games, despite considerable pre-Final distractions. The Secretary was instructed to purchase eighty tickets for the Final to be distributed amongst people who from time to time had served the Club without payment, and in a nice touch some tickets were also sent to former Chairman, Mr. John Scouller. It was an occasion which was to involve the whole town, and in recognition of that an invitation to accompany the team was sent to the Provost, the Magistrates, the Town Clerk, and his Depute.

Saints' opponents were to be Celtic, and with a 6-1 win over St. Mirren's cup final team just five weeks earlier, the Parkhead team were pre-match favourites. When the match commenced it was Saints, in their familiar black and white stripes, who immediately established their supremacy, and their attacking policy paid off as early as the third minute, when McCrae was brought down and Howieson's free kick was deflected for a corner. When Tom Morrison's accurate flag kick came over, the Celtic 'keeper Shevlin failed to reach it, but McCrae had no such problems and his header put Saints one up. It was a dream start, but it was a goal many Buddies missed as they arrived belatedly following a disruption of rail services on the Cathcart Circle.

Twenty-six minutes later, most had arrived to swell the crowd of paying customers to 98,620. They were in time to see Saints take a deserved two-goal lead. Although Shevlin had been much the busier of the two goalkeepers, a long-distance shot from the industrious Howieson appeared to catch him unexpectedly, and the ball finished high in the back of the net. The second goal at once strengthened Paisley confidence and reduced Celtic's resolve. For the remaining sixty-one minutes the Saints' defence was more than capable of snuffing out any isolated signs of a Celtic revival, while the tireless McCrae and his fellow forwards made it a busy afternoon for the Parkhead defence.

Saints finished the game in convincing fashion, and were still well in control when Referee Peter Craigmyle - not, it will be remembered a favourite of Paisley just one year earlier - blew the final whistle. Much of the credit went to the highly competitive half back trio of Morrison, Summers, and McDonald, but the team hadn't a weakness. They had been the most constructive team throughout, and after the match their superiority was sportingly recognised by Mr. Tom White, President of the SFA and Chairman of Celtic FC. "Without question," said Mr. White, "the better team won and the better team deserved the Cup". Mr. White added that he had seen Saints defeat Airdrie, Rangers, and now Celtic, and on each occasion they had deserved to win.

It was a result that everyone connected with the Club believed was achievable, although St. Mirren Chairman Mr. James Hall did admit he had prepared two post-match speeches! Saints' capture of the Cup was perhaps more of a surprise for the Town Council, and the Civic Reception

Scottish Cup Winners Medal awarded to Director George Riddell.

on the Saturday night was later described as a "hastily got up affair". It may have been all done in a rush, but the population of Paisley quickly found out about it, and they turned out in their thousands to welcome the team back from Hampden. The victorious St. Mirren party were met by the Town Band on Hawkhead Road, and captain Jock Bradford was seen waving the cup from a taxi cab. Eventually the trophy was placed on top of one of the cabs as they slowly moved through the dense crowds towards the Town Hall. Everyone spoke about Paisley's joy. The old adage "Paisley is St. Mirren and St. Mirren is Paisley" had never been better illustrated.

The Club ordered medals for the Cup-winning eleven; Trainer Andy Reid, Secretary/Manager John Cochrane, and players William Hay, Tom Barclay, James McDonald, Archie Gillies, and Hugh McCrindle. The cup-winning bonus was fixed at £8, and the Directors added that "Gillies to be included". It was only right. Archie Gillies had been a permanent fixture in the side since December 1921, and would surely have played in the Final had he not sustained an injury against Hibs on 27 February which put him out for the rest of the season. Gillies had his medal and his bonus, but he unfortunately missed the chance of a lifetime.

Team Group 1925-26
Thos. Hart, Geo. Riddell, Jas. Fleming, Thos. Craig, J. Cochrane (Secr & Manager),
W. F. Walker, T. Morrison, A. Findlay, J. Bradford, W. Newbiggin, W. McDonald, A. Reid (Trainer)
M. Morgan, A. Gebbie, D. McCrae, J. R. Hall (Chairman), W. Summers, J. Howieson, J. Thomson.

Much luckier were Jock Bradford, Andrew Findlay, Willie Newbiggin, Tom Morrison, Willie Summers, William McDonald, Mattha Morgan, Allan Gebbie, Davie McCrae, James Howieson, and Jamie Thomson, and it was a cheering thought that their names would always be recalled whenever talk came round to St. Mirren and the Cup.

The Cup may have been won, the trophy may have been on show all over town, but the season wasn't finished. There were still two League games to go and a short Irish tour to be undertaken. The Cup was presented to the fans at the last home game of the season against Aberdeen and then it was off to Ireland, where the short tour consisted of a match against Bohemians in Dublin on 28 April and the following day a journey north to Belfast to face Linfield. Not only did Saints beat the "Bohs" 2-1 and draw 1-1 with Linfield, but the visit produced a profit of £175 17s 2d. The tour was considered "very satisfactory". It was an apt description for the whole season.

1926-27

Seven days after winning a cup medal, Saints' centre half Willie Summers was capped by Scotland against England at Old Trafford. It was undoubtedly the best week of his football life, and the honours looked set to continue when he was named to play for Scotland against Wales at Ibrox on 25 October 1927. Two days before the international during a match at Muirton Park he suffered a bad knee injury, and missed this second chance to play for Scotland. He was also badly missed by Saints for the next four months.

Before Summers' injury, St. Mirren had won seven and drawn one of their eleven League games played. By the end of December, Summers had missed ten games and Saints had won just three of them. Tom Barclay was an able deputy, but such was Summers' importance to the team that the Directors asked the Secretary on 27 December to speak to Summers "to explain that we are very anxious for his return to the team".

Summers would miss another nine games, and unfortunately he wasn't the only long-term absentee. During the summer, left back Willie Newbiggin contracted rheumatics in his knee and was sidelined until the turn of the year. He played a handful of matches during January and February, but became unavailable again until mid-April. In January, just as Newbiggin returned, right winger Mattha Morgan had an operation on a perforated stomach and wasn't back in the team until 9 April, with just four games to go. His place was taken by Donald Henly, who had been signed from Ardrossan Winton Rovers in late August.

Not once in the whole season did the cup-winning team play together, but only Willie Summers and Jamie Thomson were missing from the victorious eleven when Saints played Rangers in the second round of the Cup, having beaten Arbroath 2-0 in the opening round. On 5 February at Ibrox, Saints faced a Rangers team that had won the October League encounter in Paisley by 7-3, and few backed Saints to repeat the semi-final win of eleven months earlier. These predictions proved accurate as Rangers rattled in six for no reply, and Saints' reign as cup-holders ended in a most disappointing manner.

Three days after the cup exit Saints played Clyde at home. It proved to be Jock Bradford's last game for St. Mirren. A week after the Clyde game, on 12 February Saints played Rangers again at Ibrox and were soundly beaten 4-0. The 'Paisley Daily Express' of 14 February mentioned that it had been the first instance of a match commentary being broadcast on radio, and a repeat of the experiment was entirely a decision for the clubs. As far as the match report was concerned, the same newspaper commented "that a notable absentee was Bradford who was suffering from a cold". Behind the scenes his absence had not been appreciated, "and after hearing the Doctor's certificate it was unanimously decided to censure Bradford for failing to appear for training last Thursday and also not sending us notice".

Later on at the same Board meeting prospects for the following season were discussed, and "after considering the question of the goalkeeper it was decided not to re-sign John Bradford and the manager was instructed to make the best bargain possible with him in our interest with a view to releasing him". On the same day goalkeeper David Robertson was signed from Rosslyn Juniors, and the following Saturday for the home match against Dundee, St. Mirren fielded goalkeeper Tom Boyce, who had joined in August from Ardrossan Winton Rovers. By 7 March, "John Bradford had received his papers and £21 in final settlement of all claims against us", and a great St. Mirren career was over.

Bradford, whose place was taken by either Boyce or Robertson for the rest of the season, was the first of the cup-winning team to leave, but he was to be closely followed by Cup Final hero James Howieson. Despite the indifferent results, Howieson was one of a number of Saints players who were highly rated, and his reputation in the game was sealed when he was capped in Belfast against Northern Ireland on 26 February 1927. He was amongst illustrious company that day. To his right at centre forward was the great Hughie Gallacher, and on his left was the extraordinary Alan Morton.

St. Mirren were aware that Howieson's value had increased since joining from Dundee United for a £1000 fee sixteen months earlier, and the possibility of transferring him was discussed five days before he played for Scotland. On 2 March, English Division Two side Hull City were told they could have the inside left "for £2000 clear". Five days later he was transferred to the Boothferry Park club for £3,200, with Saints' share recorded as £2,705 2s 11d.

If the two main departees were notable, two new arrivals would also make an impact on St. Mirren. In October, Robert Rankin of Strathclyde Juniors was beginning to attract attention from the senior ranks, and Saints were one of the clubs he impressed. After speaking to Rankin, the player in turn wrote to St. Mirren and stated that, owing to the number of clubs interviewing him, he desired to be registered with the Buddies at once. On 18 October he was signed, and on 13 November he played the first of his many games for St. Mirren.

From mid-February onwards, Robert Rankin would form a very youthful left-wing partnership with Jimmy Connor, who had joined from Glasgow Perthshire FC on 21 June. Connor made what was described as "a promising debut" against Dundee on 22 February, and both youngsters would eventually play for Scotland, a sign of the calibre of player the Club was able to attract in the wake of their cup win.

The team's wing halves Tom Morrison and William McDonald were two islands of continuity in a sea of transition, and so good was Morrison's

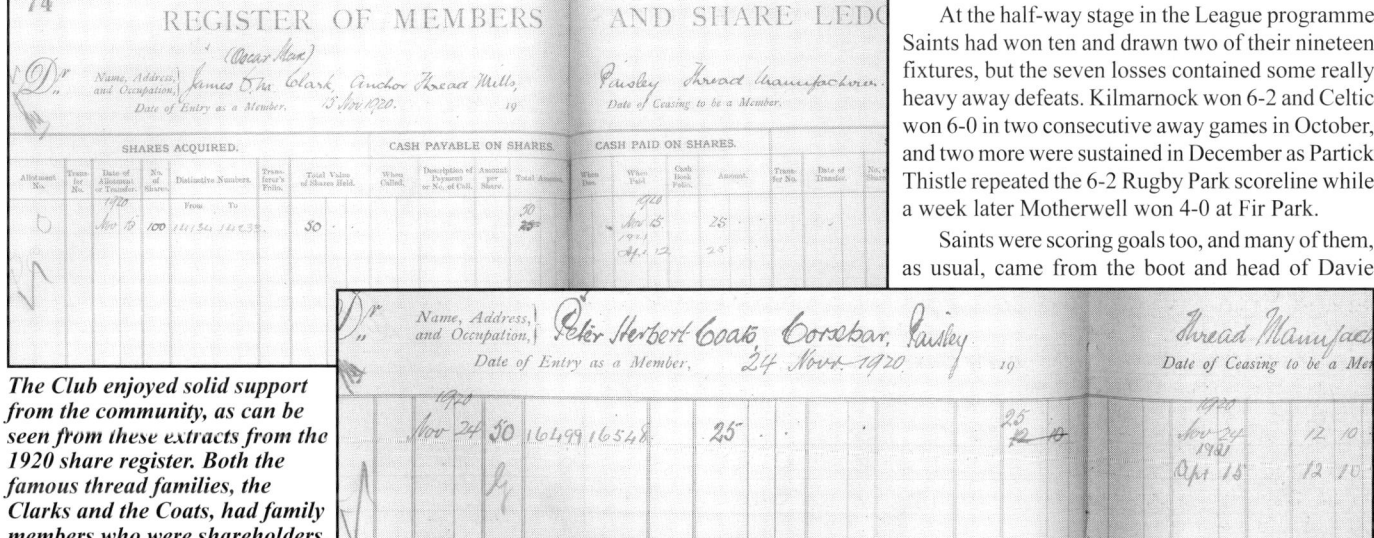

The Club enjoyed solid support from the community, as can be seen from these extracts from the 1920 share register. Both the famous thread families, the Clarks and the Coats, had family members who were shareholders.

form that in October he was chosen to represent the Scottish League against the Irish League. Morrison then became the sixteenth Saint to play for Scotland when he faced England at Hampden on 2 April, and William McDonald was named as a reserve for the same match.

During the 1926-27 season, Tom Morrison became the third of three Saints players considered good enough to be picked for Scotland, and yet the Club finished in only tenth place. It would prove to be a mere blip as Saints returned to the top six the following season.

1927-28

After protracted pay negotiations, Willie Summers re-signed for Saints on 27 June, and at the same time received permission to work in a public house on Saturday evenings, provided it did not interfere with his football duties. A month later the Club advised Sheffield Wednesday that "we are prepared to receive their best offer" for Summers, and on 4 August the player was asked how he viewed a transfer.

The Wednesday enquiry ultimately came to nothing, but a Summers transfer had become a possibility. The centre half was still considered a very important player, but there was a bigger picture to consider. On 1 September it was decided that "with a view to helping us meet our liabilities we endeavour to sell Barclay, Hay and J. McDonald". Nine days later, on the morning of the home match with Raith Rovers, talks began with Bradford City regarding the transfer of Willie Summers.

Summers was involved in these negotiations, but by then was so unsettled that he advised the Board that "in future he would be a non-trier". In a further discussion he withdrew his "non-trier" utterance and was in his usual position at 3pm on 10 September. He gave an outstanding performance, but it proved to be his last League game for Saints, and he became the third of the cup-winning team to leave the Buddies when he was transferred to Bradford City for a fee of £1620.

Saints at that stage had played five, won four, and drawn one; the team was looking good. A piece of initiative shown by John Cochrane had brought experienced 'keeper Willie Fotheringham from Morton for a fee of £275, and once again the two full backs were Findlay and Newbiggin. The Morrison, Summers, and McDonald half-back line was as good as any in the League, while all eyes would now be on replacement centre half George Walker, who had been signed the previous November from Rosslyn Juniors.

Up front Mattha Morgan held the right wing berth, but his new inside man was William Cowan, capped three years earlier whilst with Newcastle United and signed from Manchester City in May for £700. Davie McCrae was unchallenged at centre, and at inside left Charlie Sutherland, two-goal hero of the 1919 Victory Cup, had been re-signed. Jamie Thomson, Sutherland's left wing partner of nine years earlier, was still in contention, but would lose out to young Jimmy Connor as the season progressed.

Charlie Sutherland did not enjoy a happy return, and by the end of October the Board's view was "that we consider the question of cutting our loss with Sutherland". Within three weeks he had been released, and from 14 January onwards the inside left position was filled by the promising Robert "Bobby" Rankin, who would spring to prominence in the second round of the Scottish Cup.

At the half-way stage in the League programme Saints had won ten and drawn two of their nineteen fixtures, but the seven losses contained some really heavy away defeats. Kilmarnock won 6-2 and Celtic won 6-0 in two consecutive away games in October, and two more were sustained in December as Partick Thistle repeated the 6-2 Rugby Park scoreline while a week later Motherwell won 4-0 at Fir Park.

Saints were scoring goals too, and many of them, as usual, came from the boot and head of Davie McCrae. On 21 January, the Buddies' top scorer gave a classic demonstration of the centre forward's art when he scored five of Saints' goals in a 6-1 Scottish Cup home win over Clyde. In the next round a fortnight later McCrae hit two more, while inside left Bobby Rankin scored his first hat-trick for the Club in a 5-1 victory over Vale of Atholl FC.

Things were not so rosy off the park. The Club's revenue account at 30 November showed a loss of £3,440, and there had been discussions about the best way to raise £4000. It had been agreed that "should we receive a good offer for the transfer of Morrison we would consider it favourably". This willingness to consider such a transfer was significant and in stark contrast to a decision taken at the beginning of September, when Sheffield Wednesday had been told that Morrison was not for sale.

On 6 February it was disclosed that revenue from the thirteen League matches was £1,854 down on the corresponding period in the previous season. The following day, "in view of the embarrassed financial position of the Club", it was decided to transfer international right half Tom Morrison to Liverpool, by 13 February the fee was agreed at £4,100, with £400 going to the player. His place was taken for the rest of the season by Davie Colquhoun, who had been signed in April 1926 from Blantyre Victoria.

Mid 1920s...
From left to right:
John Cochrane
(Secretary and Manager),
W. F. Walker (Director),
James R. Hall (Director),
Thos. Craig (Director)
Barlow Cup 1881,
Barcelona Cup 1922,
Paisley Charity
Challenge Cup ,
Victory Cup 1919.

Now two-thirds of the Saints' formidable half-back line had gone, and prospects for the remainder of the season looked poor when Partick came to Paisley in the third round of the Cup and won 5-0. Thereafter Saints won just four of their last ten League games, but the Club's excellent early season form ensured a creditable fifth top finish for John Cochrane's team.

The following season "John Cochrane's team" would mean Sunderland. On 24 April 1928, Cochrane resigned after nearly twelve years as Secretary/Manager. He had considerably developed the "manager" side of the job, and during his tenure Saints had enjoyed unprecedented consistency, and, of course, the capture of two cups. Also departing was left winger Jamie Thomson, who had been given a free transfer. He had served the Club well over the same twelve years.

The Club regretted Mr. Cochrane's decision, but congratulated him on his appointment to Sunderland AFC, where he would also make a lasting impression. He was given a £50 gift to purchase a memento which would bear the following description: "Presented to John Cochrane in recognition of his services to the Club". It was recognition he thoroughly deserved.

1928-29

One of John Cochrane's first acts as the Secretary/Manager of Sunderland was to bid for St. Mirren's promising centre half George Walker. On 25 May his offer was refused: "At present we are not transferring Walker or any other first team player" was a policy statement which would be reiterated throughout the season.

Three days later Cochrane's old job was offered to Partick Thistle Assistant Manager Donald Turner for a period of one year at an annual salary of £364. The proposal was accepted by Mr. Turner, and his official appointment commenced on 1 July. He made a good start. At the end of the first half of the season, the Buddies had won ten and drawn four of the nineteen fixtures, and a team along the lines of Page, Findlay, Hay, Colquhoun, Walker, McDonald, Morgan, Gebbie, McCrae, Rankin, and Connor could be rattled off with confidence by Saints supporters.

Willie Fotheringham had been ill at the beginning of the season and was expected to take a few weeks to recover . His eve-of-season replacement was Sam Page, signed from St. Johnstone for £230 and destined to remain first choice 'keeper right through to 26 January 1929, when he fractured a finger in a match against his former club. This allowed Fotheringham to regain his place.

Andrew Findlay was at right back, and his new partner was Walter Hay, signed back in August 1924 from Petershill, but finally making a first team place his own. The long-standing Findlay/Newbiggin full back partnership ended when Willie Newbiggin was granted a free transfer at the beginning of October, thus becoming the sixth member of the cup-winning team to leave the Club. From mid-November onwards, the regular full backs became Hay and Thomas Lilley, who had come from Sunderland on 1 August for £350.

The half-back line of Davie Colquhoun, George Walker, and William McDonald was unchallenged all season, as were Allan Gebbie, Davie McCrae, Bobby Rankin, and Jimmy Connor from inside right to outside left. Connor was, however, missing from 26 January to 6 April due to pneumonia, and one of his replacements was none other than Jamie Thomson, who had been given a free transfer eight months earlier. Uniquely, he would also be given another one in April 1929.

At outside right the continual selection of Kenneth Dyer, signed from Govan High School on 9 January 1928, prompted Mattha Morgan to ask to be put on the transfer list, but his 8 October request was turned down and he featured a bit more often in the season's second half. It was a period when nine of the nineteen games were lost. Incredibly, seven of these defeats came in consecutive matches as the team's form dipped alarmingly during the January to March period. The bad run started with a 6-0 hammering at Pittodrie on 12 January, and in the following six matches Saints scored just once while conceding seventeen goals.

After the seventh defeat on 9 March, a 3-0 loss to Hamilton Accies at Douglas Park, the run of poor displays was discussed at some length by the Board. The Secretary was asked to convey a message to the effect that the Board viewed the present situation with "extreme concern". They felt that "our closeness to relegation demanded drastic changes and that unless an improvement in the spirit and play of the team in the game tomorrow was forthcoming these changes would be made".

There were eight League games left. The "game tomorrow" was a home match against mid-table Falkirk on 12 March, and Saints convincingly won 5-0. Four days later, Third Lanark were also beaten 5-0 at Love Street. On 9 April there was another burst of home goals as the Buddies defeated Raith Rovers 5-2, and the scoring continued the following week with a 5-3 victory at Easter Road. The final game of the season against a strong Queen's Park side was the only game of the eight which was lost. The Board's threatening noises had worked and the Club would finish eighth top, but the Directors' intervention may not have done much for the self-confidence of the Club's new Secretary/ Manager!

Almost unnoticed in the midst of the disastrous run of League defeats, Saints began to put together an excellent Scottish Cup run. It started with a 4-0 away win against former League club Nithsdale Wanderers at Sanquhar. The Wanderers opened strongly but soon faded, and although both teams missed penalties, Saints ran out comfortable winners.

In the second round Cathkin Park was the venue as Saints were drawn against Division One strugglers Third Lanark. McCrae scored after just three minutes, but the Buddies looked less likely to extend that lead than Third Lanark did to equalise. Such a chance was lost when Thirds missed a penalty, and McCrae's early strike proved sufficient for St. Mirren.

Ayr United at Somerset Park provided another stiff test in the third round. At half-time honours were even and the outcome uncertain, but a Gebbie goal thirteen minutes into the second half gave Saints the edge, and McCrae clinched a place in the last eight with a goal twenty minutes from the end.

A 20,000 home crowd saw Saints take the lead through Rankin in the third minute of the quarter final, thereafter it was action all the way. Aberdeen equalised in the twentieth minute, and then took the lead before Gebbie made it 2-2 by half-time. A second goal from Rankin gave Saints the lead for a second time, but with just six minutes to go the tie looked Pittodrie-bound when Aberdeen came back yet again to level at 3-3. In the very last minute the journey north became unnecessary when Morgan grabbed the winner in what had been a sensational match.

Semi-final goals from Morgan and Rankin allowed Saints to come back and then take a 2-1 lead against Rangers at Hampden, which remained the score twenty minutes into the second half. Then Rangers equalised, and five minutes later they scored what proved to be the winner. The Buddies had played well, but not well enough to appear in another final.

The season ended as it began. A Sunderland offer of £3000 for George Walker was refused, and the Club had a vacancy to fill when Donald Turner resigned on 6 May as Secretary/Manager.

1929-30

In five full seasons to the end of 1928-29, Davie McCrae had scored one hundred and ninety one goals in all competitions for St. Mirren, an average of thirty-eight goals per season. He deservedly, and perhaps belatedly, was included in an SFA continental tour party and won caps against Norway and Germany. To no-one's surprise at St. Mirren Park, he scored two goals in Oslo for his country.

There was nothing belated about Bobby Rankin's rise to fame. He had only been playing senior football since November 1927 but he not only lined up alongside McCrae in two of Scotland's games, but also won a third cap against Holland. A third Saint in the party was former player Andy Reid, who had been the Club's trainer since the dismissal of Archibald McGregor in February 1920. On his return from the tour, Reid accepted an invitation to join John Cochrane at Sunderland, and on 22 June he resigned from St. Mirren. He was replaced by David Allison.

McCrae would score a further twenty-eight goals during 1929-30, his first two coming against a Morton side whose promotion had prompted St. Mirren to send "heartiest congratulations on their return to the 1st League". Such friendly sentiments were no doubt sincere, but that might not have been the Cappielow conclusion, coming as they did immediately after Morton had suffered a 7-2 aggregate defeat from Saints in the final of the Renfrewshire Cup! Morton would find life very difficult in the higher division, but Saints, with a new Secretary/Manager, would enjoy another fine season and would finish fifth for the second time in three seasons.

The new Secretary was John Morrison, who had held the same post with Third Lanark. The Club had received a number of applications, but had "sounded out" only two, the other being Willie Reid of Albion Rovers. Both men were interviewed and Mr. Morrison emerged as the preferred candidate, but his appointment was only confirmed after comprehensive discussions were held with leading Third Lanark officials. St. Mirren were happy with what they heard, and Mr. Morrison's initial appointment was for one year from 1 June at a salary of £300.

Robert Rankin

Throughout the season, John Morrison would receive detailed reports and instructions from the Directors regarding individual and team performances, but he was not exposed to his predecessor's experience of an alarming dip in form. The longest losing streak of three games was matched by the best winning sequence, and as wins continued to outnumber losses, the Buddies occupied a respectable position without threatening to overtake the top four of Rangers, Motherwell, Aberdeen, and Celtic. Saints' worst result was a 5-0 defeat at Tynecastle on 31 August, but typical of the season it was countered on 11 January when the "Maroons" were beaten 6-2 at St. Mirren Park.

The following week the team were in confident mood when they made the three hour train and car journey to Kirkcudbright to meet non-League St. Cuthbert's Wanderers in the first round of the Scottish Cup. Saints returned as 5-1 winners, but a fortnight later Division Two Forfar Athletic provided stiffer opposition, and held the visitors to a 0-0 draw at Station Park before losing 3-0 in the Paisley replay.

In the third round Saints were paired with a Celtic team seemingly in decline, and although the tie was to be played at Celtic Park, the Paisley players drew confidence from their excellent 3-0 victory there the previous season. Such assurance was to be well-founded, and two goals from new boy Alex Stewart and one from Rankin helped the Buddies to a 3-1 win in front of 32,000. Almost 30,000 less were present for a fog-affected farce of a fourth round tie against mid-table Hamilton at Love Street. Saints lost 4-3 in the most frustrating circumstances, and such was the Club's disappointment that they asked the S.F.A. to amend the rule governing postponements to include fog.

The team that eliminated Celtic had become the first choice over the season, namely Fotheringham, Hay, Lilley, Colquhoun, Walker, Miller, McCrae, Gebbie, Stewart, Rankin, and Connor.

The effective Colquhoun-Walker-McDonald half-back line of the previous season had ceased to exist. At the beginning of June, the Secretary reported that William McDonald was seriously ill with pneumonia, and within a fortnight it was intimated that only members of his family were being allowed to see him. By the end of June the news was much better as he was reported to be improving slowly, but his fitness didn't improve sufficiently to allow him to play football, and at the end of the season he was given a free transfer.

William McDonald would always be recalled as a member of the 1926 cup-winning team, but he deserved to be best remembered as a skillful and versatile footballer who was St. Mirren's first choice left half for six years, coinciding with some of the most successful of the Club's first one hundred and twenty-five years.

The left half position was taken by John Miller, who had been signed from Yoker on 16 February 1925. Miller had waited patiently to become a first team regular, but a much more instant promotion came to Alex Stewart, who had played six times in the previous season for Queen's Park and was recommended to St. Mirren by his father. After playing a trial, he joined Saints as an amateur on 6 August.

Later in the season he became the first of only three St. Mirren players to be capped for the Scottish Amateur International team when he lined up at outside left against Ireland in Londonderry. He signed professional forms with St. Mirren on 4 November, and by mid-December such was his form for the Reserves that he was drafted into the first team at centre forward, with top scorer McCrae moving to outside right to accommodate him.

As Alex Stewart came into the team, one of the 1926 cup-winners left. The establishment of the Hay-Lilley full back partnership greatly restricted Andrew Findlay's first team opportunities, and after nearly eight years service his "engagement with the Club" was terminated on 23 December. The number of surviving cup-winners would drop to two at the end of the season when Morgan and McDonald were given free transfers.

The Twenties had proved to be a decade of consistency, capped players and a cup; the Thirties would be very different.

The 1930s - Decline and Fall

1930-31

For much of the 1920s St. Mirren's attendances were at least two thousand people short of break-even point, and from time to time there were public statements to the effect that, without increased support, Saints would have to sell a leading player. It was a pattern of professional football not exclusive to Paisley, and most Buddies understood that the transfer of top players was as often as not, at the behest of the Club's bankers.

CHAPTER SEVEN

The seemingly never-ending supply of talented Scottish footballers meant that life went on; despite the loss of quality players such as Pringle, Lawson, and Morrison, Saints had continued to be successful. Since 1922 they had sold an internationalist most seasons, but by 1930 two years had elapsed since a major player had been transferred. No one expected it to last, and it didn't.

Outside left Jimmy Connor had been the subject of previous bids from English clubs, but had shown a marked reluctance to leave Scotland. John Cochrane's Sunderland, with its colony of Scots, was a much more attractive proposition to Connor, and on 12 May it was confirmed that the winger had moved to Roker Park, where he was to enjoy great success and gain four caps for Scotland. Alex Stewart took over as Saints' left winger, and the rest of his colleagues were usually Fotheringham, Hay, Ancell, Colquhoun, Walker, Miller, Meechan, Reilly, McCrae, and Rankin.

The side contained three newcomers. Bobby Ancell, who had been signed from Mid-Annandale FC on 17 February, made his debut at left back on 13 September in an away match against Falkirk. At outside right was John Meechan, who had played a dozen games the previous season and had come originally from Maryhill Hibs in August 1928. The third new member of the side was inside right J. Reilly, formerly of Celtic. The trio's new side had made a good start, winning eleven and drawing four of the twenty-four games played up to 24 January, and

Saints seemed to be heading for yet another top six finish. Inexplicably, they slumped to sixth bottom – the worst finish in ten years.

This change in fortunes was completely unexpected. On 10 March 1931 the Club's financial position – no doubt helped by the Connor cheque – was described as "greatly improved", and the Directors took the opportunity to recognise "the special services rendered by Secretary/Manager John Morrison and Trainer David Allison during the present season to date". They were given bonuses of £50 and £25 respectively, with more to come if Saints reached the Scottish Cup Final and won it. Within four days the Club were out of the Scottish Cup, and would score just two goals in the last eight league games.

In the previous two months the deterioration in League form hadn't been reflected in the Scottish Cup. Clydebank were Saints' first round opponents and, unlike Nithsdale Wanderers and St. Cuthbert's Wanderers in the two previous seasons, the Clydeholm Park club were agreeable to move the match to Paisley in return for a generous compensation package. Two goals from the versatile Allan Gebbie, who during the season would play at right back and centre half as well as various forward positions, set Saints on their way, and McCrae added another for a 3-1 win.

It was the first of seven cup ties that season. A 1-1 draw at Shawfield brought Clyde back to Paisley for a second round replay, and it was 1-1 again after the second ninety minutes. In extra time it took another two goals from Davie McCrae to separate the sides, and Saints moved on to meet Falkirk. St. Mirren's Directors expected another hard game, but were clear on the route to the third round. "Falkirk's inside forwards were to be stopped by Colquhoun and Miller", was the suggested strategy. They were stopped, and another McCrae double meant Saints won 2-0.

Crowds had been good in all the previous rounds, but an excellent 36,000 supporters turned up at Cathkin Park to see if Division Two runaway leaders Third Lanark could add cup glory to their successful League campaign. It looked as if they would when Thirds took the lead in the second half, but that man McCrae equalised to take the tie back to St. Mirren Park. This time Saints made the task even harder when top scorer McCrae was sent off in the first half, but two quick goals from left winger Alex Stewart and one from his inside man Rankin took Saints to a semi-final place.

Saints' only excuse for their late season League form was a longer than usual injury list, but it was a full-strength team which was selected

---

CHARITY HAT-TRICK

Saints were often invited to compete in local charity competitions during the twenties and thirties. In 1928/29, Third Lanark were beaten 6-1 in the Paisley Charity Cup, and St Mirren defeated Kings Park 4-1 in the Stirlingshire Charity Cup.

A year later the Stirling Charity Cup was retained, and the Mayor of Wolverhampton's (charity) Cup was captured with a 2-0 win over Wolves. This Wolverhampton Charity Cup medal was awarded to Saints Manager John Morrison in 1929/30.

---

to meet one of the best-ever Motherwell sides in the semi-final. Unfortunately, the "Steelmen" took the lead after thirty minutes, and despite all Saints efforts the final score was 1-0.

The Buddies were out of the cup, but there had been an earlier distraction from the wretched League results. Much-in-demand centre half George Walker won his second Scottish cap when he played at Windsor Park in Belfast on 21 February, and left half John Miller became the twenty-first Saint to be capped for Scotland when he helped beat England by 2-0 at Hampden on 28 March. For the first time ever the Club had four full internationalists in the team. It was four more than most teams, and the Directors weren't alone in looking for a greatly improved set of results in the forthcoming season.

1931-32

Ten years after the opening of "Greater Love Street" there was a need for the Grandstand to be re-roofed, the work was done during the close season. Unfortunately it wasn't the only roof threatening to cave in, as the nation's economic recession increased its effect at St. Mirren Park.

A major problem arose in May when Colquhoun, Hay, Rankin, Stewart, and Walker indicated that they couldn't accept the pay being offered. George Walker told the Board that his refusal to re-sign was because his wages had been reduced for the previous two years, "and he didn't think his play warranted the reduction". The Board were unmoved: there would be no increase for Walker or anyone else.

Walter Hay re-signed on 6 July, while Tottenham Hotspur were making enquiries about Davie Colquhoun. Three weeks later Colquhoun moved to Spurs for "£1800 clear to the Club", with the right half receiving £450. His place would be taken by long-serving Allan Gebbie, and to Gebbie's left would be Walker, who re-signed on the eve of the opening game against Clyde at Shawfield on 8 August.

By the end of the month, Spurs were actively trying to sign Bobby Rankin, who had reiterated to Saints that he was only willing to re-sign "on his own terms". On 7 September the North London club confirmed that they were unable to find a job for Rankin, and "unless he dropped the employment part of the transfer" the deal was off.

It was off! On 22 September, Bobby Rankin re-signed and went straight into the Reserves' game against Hamilton Accies four days later. One week on he was back in the first team, so Fotheringham, Hay, Ancell, Gebbie, Walker, Miller, Knox, Workman, Meechan, McIndoe, and Rankin became the first choice eleven for most of the season, with only Meechan dropping out in mid-February when McCrae fully recovered from an injury.

Six of the opening twelve fixtures up to 26 September had been lost, but with Rankin back in the team the situation immediately improved. For the next eleven games Saints lost only to champions-to-be Motherwell, and picked up eighteen points from a possible twenty-two. The team was playing well, and apart from Saints' tendency to ease up in games, even the hard-to-please Directors thought so!

Rankin's re-signing meant that Alex Stewart was the lone pay dissident. His original note to the Board had been regarded as "impertinent", and in September the Secretary was instructed to "get as much publicity as possible for Stewart with a view to a transfer". Morton asked for the player's services until the end of the season, but were advised that "while we are willing to assist Morton at any time, in this case we would be assisting Stewart, and we have no intention of doing so".

St. Mirren's response to Morton indicated just how much the relationship between player and Club had deteriorated, Stewart's continued omission was one of four changes from the previous season. Gebbie for Colquhoun was the only change in defence or midfield, and the season's three newcomers were Jimmy Knox, Tommy Workman, and Robert McIndoe.

Outside right Jimmy Knox was a free transfer signing from Charlton Athletic. He joined on 11 May, and would score thirty goals in his first season. Knox's inside right partner would be Tommy Workman, who had previously been on St. Mirren's books before joining Arthurlie during the 1928-29 season. Workman played a trial at the beginning of August, and was signed from Bridgeton Waverley for £75 in time to make his debut in the first home game on 15 August against Queen's Park. Both he and Knox scored the goals. The new inside left was Robert McIndoe, who had been signed from Troon Athletic for £55 on 10 August, he made his debut against Dundee on 26 August, 1931.

On 5 January a request from a Mr. Yuill to hire St. Mirren Park for greyhound racing was unanimously refused, but it would soon be seen as a possible income stream for the Club. In the meantime, St. Mirren were losing money most weeks, and when the Board discussed the financial position on 25 January they concluded that "the only hope of making ends meet at the end of the season was at least one transfer".

Such a transfer would not just be about money, as the Board had already shown. In a succession of discussions between 23 November and 7 December, John Cochrane's offers to sign George Walker for Sunderland went from £2000 to £4000, but they were all refused: Walker's contribution to the team was seen as more important than his immediate sale value.

A good Scottish Cup run would have helped the income situation, and although Saints did visit Hampden again it was only a first round match against Queen's Park, where they lost heavily by 4-1. It was the first time the Buddies had failed to reach the second round since the embarrassing defeat by Armadale eleven years earlier. By mid-April St. Mirren faced such serious financial difficulties that the Directors, the Secretary/Manager, and the Club's legal adviser each lent the Club £25 to help pay the wages and fund a short and profitable Irish tour. Some much-needed finance was finally received when the unhappy situation with Alex Stewart was resolved. On 27 April, Sheffield United bought him for £900, and would make a further £100 payment if he signed for season 1933/34.

Jimmy Knox featured on a cigarette Collectors Card circa 1955.

Money worries apart, it hadn't been a bad season. Expectations of an improved League campaign had been satisfied as Saints finished fifth for the third time in five years, and the team also proved to be the best in two counties in a new end-of-season competition. Two years' efforts to launch an inter-counties trophy came to fruition when St. Mirren, Morton, Kilmarnock, and Ayr United took part in the South Western Counties Cup. Saints, the form team, became the first winners when they beat Kilmarnock 2-0 and thrashed Ayr United 7-1 in the final.

1932-33

Saints started the season with four international players on their books. If none were transferred, the Club would have every chance of a successful season and every likelihood of a worsening financial situation. That's the way it turned out. Walker, Miller, McCrae, and Rankin were still prominent on the last Saturday of the season as the team secured seventh place in the League by winning 3-1 at Airdrie. As anticipated, the overdraft almost doubled.

A review of the Club's financial position had taken place on 14 June, when it was decided to borrow £1000 from the Burnbank Trust Ltd. Each Director also loaned the Club a further £20. In the course of the meeting the topic of greyhound racing was raised. Within a fortnight St. Mirren were considering offers from two greyhound racing companies.

A Director was charged with gathering all the relevant information on the sport, and a special meeting of shareholders on 22 July authorised the Board to proceed with negotiations "at best offer and a five year lease". The best offer came from a Clydebank group who offered a minimum of £2,600 per annum for the use of St. Mirren Park. It was just the additional income stream that St. Mirren needed.

Alterations to the ground were made, and considerable time and effort was expended to ensure that the racing venture was a success. The first races were held in mid-October, but by 7 November the S.F.A. had issued a ban on greyhound racing at football grounds. St. Mirren and fourteen other clubs intended to argue that at the very least they should be allowed to complete their contracts, but in Saints' case the dispute quickly became academic. On 7 December the Secretary/Manager John Morrison informed the Board that the Clydebank Greyhound Company had closed down for an indefinite period.

A letter was then received from the greyhound company on 30 January 1933 requesting termination of the contract, and there followed extensive legal activity regarding the non-payment of rent and a ban on Clydebank Greyhound Company removing any property from the St. Mirren Grounds. It transpired that the greyhound company were in a very bad financial state and could only repay St. Mirren at £5 per week.

It had been an imaginative attempt to balance the books, but such income generation would inevitably need to revert to the selling side of the transfer market. Saints certainly had good players, and the team showed all its qualities on the first day of the season, when Rangers came to town on 13 August and left with a 2-0 defeat. The following week against Falkirk at Brockville Saints won 3-2, and their 100% record was maintained when Third Lanark were beaten 3-1.

The team became temporary table-toppers, this impressive early season record of eleven wins from the first sixteen fixtures being achieved by a team of Kenny, Hay, Ancell, Gebbie, Walker, Miller, Knox, Workman, McCrae, Rankin, and McIndoe which had changed little from the previous season.

Willie Fotheringham had started the season in his usual place, but after being declared unfit on 3 September he was replaced by William Kenny, who had been signed from Burnbank Athletic on 23 April, 1931. Within five weeks the veteran keeper was fit again, but young Kenny had done well enough to retain his place, and was first choice goalkeeper until 3 December, when he was injured in a match against Ayr United.

Fotheringham came back but only remained in the first team until Kenny had proved his fitness. By 2 January Kenny was back in the first team, and there he stayed until the end of the season. During the second half of the season some of Willie Fotheringham's performances for the reserves suggested that time had caught up with him, and following a testimonial game he was granted a free transfer at the end of the season. He moved to Queen of the South and retired in 1937, but would return to the Club as Manager in 1942 to guide his team to a memorable Summer Cup triumph.

The side remained on consistent lines until an injury to Davie McCrae meant his place at centre forward was taken by John Meechan on 3 January, 1933. McCrae was still injured at the end of January when a specialist confirmed, contrary to earlier fears, that Saints' top scorer did not need an operation and his outlook was good. John Meechan would continue at centre until McCrae returned on 11 March against East Stirlingshire. Saints won 3-0 and McCrae got all three!

Goalkeeper and centre forward apart, the only other change of personnel was at outside left, where Robert McIndoe fell out of the picture. On 7 January he was replaced, initially by Farmer, in the midst of the team's worst period of the season, as Saints won only three of eleven fixtures between 19 November and the first round of the Scottish Cup on 28 January. The cup draw had linked Saints with Division Two King's Park. John Morrison, watching them in advance, concluded that they were "very ordinary and with due care we shouldn't have much difficulty winning the tie". The tie on 21 January ended in a 0-0 draw, and Saints' post-match verdict gave a bit more credit to the Stirling club after what had been "a hard game under very bad ground conditions". The subsequent 5-1 win in the Paisley replay was to justify John Morrison's original assessment.

The Buddies played St. Johnstone at Perth in the League before the next round. They lost again as their dip in form continued. The official match summary didn't pull its punches: "Very poor display, players apparently not taking any risks. Forwards with exception of Meechan, poor; inside ones especially. Only Walker and Miller of others really good".

Kilmarnock, who had been beaten 1-0 at home by Saints on 2 January, were Saints' second round visitors, and on 4 February the Ayrshire team reversed the scoreline. The general consensus was that it had been a very close game with Saints very unfortunate to lose.

Four days before the Kilmarnock tie news had reached the Club of the death of Mr. John McCartney, the much-admired first Secretary/Manager of St. Mirren Football Club. It wasn't the only reminder of the past. The previous season a Mr. James Imrie of Govan had written to say that he was an old Saints player who could no longer pay his way into the games. The Club had granted him a complimentary ticket for each home game until the end of the 1931-32 season, and they were delighted to repeat the gesture during 1932-33.

Saints' financial problems meant they weren't always able to respond to pleas for help in the way they would have liked, but some requests just couldn't be turned down. James Imrie had worn St. Mirren's original scarlet and blue colours on 14 April 1883 when he became one of the Club's first-ever medal winners as the Renfrewshire Cup was captured. Men such as James Imrie and John McCartney had helped make St. Mirren. No matter the prevailing difficulties, they would never be forgotten.

1933-34

After prolonged negotiations, George Walker was transferred to Notts County on 20 June, with the Club receiving £2,000 and the player £600. Arrangements were immediately made to use Walker's transfer fee to clear the overdraft. A credit of £600 was left, but such were the weekly losses sustained by the Club that this credit would be wiped out by 23 November.

Centre forward John Meechan, whose first team appearances had been restricted by Davie McCrae's exceptional goal-scoring, was next to go when he joined Burnley on 4 July for a fee of £180, with the player receiving £30. Ironically for Meechan, McCrae was one of three pay rebels, and didn't re-sign until 2 September. He then went straight into the team against Queen's Park and scored the only goal in a 2-1 defeat. Full back Walter Hay, who had intimated on 14 August that he thought the wages offered were inadequate in view of his years of service, followed McCrae's example and re-signed on 5 September.

For the second time in three seasons Bobby Rankin held out for more money, and by the end of November there was little sign of the two parties being reconciled. Indeed, Rankin was told that if he wanted to see the match "admission is one shilling"! On 18 January, Bobby Rankin was transferred to Dundee for a quarter of the fee the Club had received for fellow internationalist George Walker. Dundee FC would pay just £650, with the player getting £150 of that amount.

Any team would be affected by the transfer of two internationalists, and the loss in quality was apparent right from the opening game of the season at Tynecastle, where Hearts hammered Saints 6-0. "Very indifferent display," was part of the official verdict, and perhaps something of an understatement. Thereafter, the number of goals conceded returned to normal dimensions until the very last game of the season. Bottom club Cowdenbeath, with a defence which by then had conceded one hundred and eighteen goals, were the Buddies' opponents. Saints failed to add to the Cowden "goals against" column, but the Central Park side hit Saints for another six.

In between the two 6-0 hidings, Saints won nine and drew nine of their other thirty-six fixtures to finish seventeenth. It was the Buddies' worst League performance since 1913-14. No team scored less than their total of forty-six goals, and more than once the Directors described them as "hopeless at finishing".

Davie McCrae had never been "hopeless at finishing". He had been the Club's top scorer in eight of the previous nine seasons, demonstrating an unprecedented and unlikely to be surpassed display of consistent goalscoring. In a season where goals were so hard to come by, it was all the more perplexing that for two months the Club suspended their most likely source of goals.

Following a 7-2 win over Third Lanark on 28 October, and two months after re-signing, McCrae was very upset about being barracked, and intimated that he would never play for the Club again. He later explained in writing that he felt the barracking was unjustified, as were rumours about him not trying. He felt it would be better for the Club and himself if he were to be put on the transfer list or have his registration cancelled. Both suggestions were rejected. Two weeks later, on 11 November, McCrae's "indifferent" display at outside left was strongly criticised, and he was consequently suspended for "misconduct during

Collectors Pin Badge from 1934 featuring Johnny Latimer.

TOMMY WORKMAN

On 9 January 1934, the Club were stunned to learn of the sudden death of inside right Tommy Workman. The twenty-four year old had played against Hamilton at Douglas Park on 30 December, but by 5 January he had been moved to hospital, diagnosed with appendicitis. Three days later he passed away.

St. Mirren Chairman Thomas Hart paid tribute to Tommy Workman's services to the Club, and at his funeral six Saints players, Hay, Gebbie, Wilson, Miller, Knox, and McCrae, acted as pall bearers. More sad news was received a fortnight after the funeral, when the Club learned that Tommy Workman's young daughter Margaret had also passed away. The Club continued to pay Tommy's full wages for some time after his death, and football people throughout Scotland generously supported the fund set up in his name by St. Mirren. From the money raised a "broken column" memorial was erected at his grave in Woodside Cemetery in April 1934.

Tommy Workman's memorial at Woodside. A broken column design representing life cut short.

put this intention in writing. "At a time like this," he wrote, "I am willing to let bygones be bygones if you can see your way to raise my suspension and I will come back and do my best for the old club."

On 15 January, McCrae's suspension was lifted, and he rejoined a team which was normally on these lines: McCloy, Hay, Ancell, Gebbie, Wilson, Miller, Knox, Latimer, McCrae, McGregor, and Phillips. Goalkeeper William Kenny had quickly confirmed that he was not going to be Willie Fotheringham's long-term replacement and was blamed for losing a number of goals. After a short trial, Jimmy McCloy was signed from Clyde for £150 on 30 October.

The only other change in defence was at centre half. Fulton Wilson – who had signed from Coats' Juniors on 30 June 1930 for £10 – had taken over from the departed Walker. Despite a shaky start in August when his ability to perform adequately at centre half was being questioned, Wilson made the position his own.

Johnny Latimer had been signed from East Stirlingshire on 27 June for £200 and made his early appearances at outside right whilst Jimmy Knox underwent an operation to remove a growth which had formed when a previous injury caused blood to clot. This had become bone, and threatened Jimmy's football future. Fortunately Knox – scorer of forty-seven goals in the previous two years – recovered well, but Latimer's re-entry into the team at inside right arose from more tragic circumstances opposite.

During Davie McCrae's two periods of absence his place at centre was taken by a number of players, but mainly by inside forward Jimmy McGregor, who had been signed from Benburb in December 1932. When McCrae was available McGregor lined up at inside left, and in both positions enjoyed a successful first full season, becoming Saints' top scorer with thirteen League goals. At outside left, John Phillips had taken over on 25 February, and he retained the position throughout 1933-34. It was a team which needed to be strengthened, according to the Directors, yet somehow Saints managed to intersperse League mediocrity with a cup run that went all the way to Hampden!

That eventuality would have surprised most of those present at Hays Park in Penicuik on 20 January, as St. Mirren struggled to draw 2-2 with their East of Scotland League opponents, Penicuik Athletic. Saints put their display down to "ground difficulties", and duly won the replay by 4 goals to 1, with McCrae and Phillips scoring two each.

Struggling Division Two side Brechin City were the next opponents, and goals from Phillips, Latimer, and another two from McCrae gave the Buddies a fairly easy 4-0 win at Glebe Park. In the third round Saints received a bye, and were then drawn against holders Celtic. A crowd of 33,434 spectators assembled at St. Mirren Park on 3 March where they saw three penalties being missed, including one from Jimmy Knox, but goals from McGregor and Latimer gave Saints a 2-0 win and a place in the semi-final.

Prior to the Celtic tie, and in the interests of economy, the Club had given a miss to their usual big match preparations at Seamill Hydro, and decided that the only variation in training would be a day on the "Braes" and lunch at Fereneze Golf Club. The routine worked so well it was repeated for the semi-final against Motherwell.

The Lanarkshire club's wonderful consistency in the League around this time made them much more difficult opponents than Celtic, and for the second round in a row few fancied Saints to progress. The 30,000

Why waste words when you've lost the Cup Final...
1934 Saints official minutes sum up the 5-0 defeat from Rangers in one word... "Bad" That's the whole official report!!!

and after the Third Lanark game, being insubordinate and failing to give his best service to the Club".

On 27 November, the Manager was asked "to get publicity that we are willing to receive offers for McCrae and Rankin". By 9 January, Dens Park was beginning to beckon for Rankin, but nothing had materialised for McCrae. At that point the centre expressed a willingness to come back and do his best for St. Mirren. The Board requested that he

crowd at Tynecastle saw a very different performance than the one given by the Buddies back in August. Jimmy Knox hit a hat-trick to give Saints a deserved 3-1 win and a third Scottish Cup Final appearance. The Chairman commented on how important the Motherwell win had been, and just how much it meant to the Club financially.

The town was also delighted, and gents' outfitters McArthur's offered each player an overcoat if they won the cup! The commercially-minded

Mr. McArthur added that the offer was conditional on him being given the cup to display in his shop window! The local Rotary Cub invited the players to lunch on the Wednesday prior to the final, and the Town Clerk's office, maybe with the 1926 "hastily got up affair" in mind, made plans for a reception in the event of a Saints' win.

The Cup Final team which faced Rangers in front of a massive crowd of 113,403 was McCloy, Hay, Ancell, Gebbie, Wilson, Miller, Knox, Latimer, McGregor, McCabe, and Phillips. Thoughts of Paisley celebrations quickly disappeared, as Rangers began to construct a convincing 5-0 victory. "Bad" was the one-word verdict in the Club's minutes, and in typical Paisley fashion the Board simply moved on to the next business.

A week before the Cup Final, left half John Miller had played for Scotland against England at Wembley. It was his fifth cap, and he became the second most honoured St. Mirren player up to that point. Few could have predicted that it would be nineteen years before another St. Mirren player wore Scotland's dark blue as the Club headed into a period of decline.

1934-35

Any demonstration of county supremacy is normally welcomed by Saints supporters, but not even an early season 8-0 hammering of Morton in the delayed final of the Renfrewshire Cup was enough to stifle growing criticism of the Board's stewardship of the Club in 1934.

By 1 October, the team had lost six of the ten League games played. Two weeks later a four-man delegation from a shareholders-formed "Vigilance Committee" met with four of the Club's Directors. The delegation referred to Director Mr. James Fleming bringing honour to the Club in his role as President of the S.F.A., and suggested that every assistance should be given to Mr. Fleming to help him carry out his duties. This could be best achieved, the delegation argued, by co-opting three shareholders onto the Board.

The four shareholders also mentioned the fall in gates and the dissatisfaction among the Club's leading players, which was shown by the fact that more of them than ever had been in dispute over re-signing terms. Such dissatisfaction, they claimed, was not helped by the players not being given any bonus for playing in the previous season's Scottish Cup Final. The delegation went into specifics about various players who should and shouldn't have been sold and signed, and were critical in general of an apparent policy of buying other teams' "cast offs". They also wanted Manager John Morrison to "retire".

The delegation's remarks concluded with a demand that, unless the Vigilance Committee had satisfaction from the Board, and in particular their request for three new Directors to be co-opted, they would make a requisition for an Extraordinary General Meeting. They demanded a reply within ten days.

The Board's response was sent to each member of the delegation and to the local press: "Regarding the proposal to augment the number of Directors by the co-option of three shareholders, the matter was carefully considered at this week's meeting of the Board and it was unanimously agreed not to accede to this request. The Directors are so firmly convinced that a board of seven is adequate for the effective conduct of the company's business that they are resolved rather than submit to this proposal to retire en bloc".

An Extraordinary General Meeting took place on 5 November to decide whether the Directors retained the confidence of the shareholders to manage the affairs of the Club. The meeting lasted nearly three hours, but turned on an element of rigmarole involving proxy votes. The Board survived, but could not have been comforted by their reception.

From the 1880s, onwards, the Buddies regularly featured on the original football cards produced by Baines of Bradford.

During the close season it had been obvious that better quality players were needed if 1934-35 was to be an improvement on the previous year's disappointing League performance. That search for new talent became even more pressing when five of the first team refused the terms on offer. Unprecedented activity in the transfer market was undertaken, but it was to prove singly unsuccessful.

Goalkeeper Pat McMahon, formerly with St. Anthony's before moving to West Ham United, was signed on 14 May, and replaced the unsigned Jimmy McCloy. McMahon didn't make the best of starts, and took much of the blame for a 4-1 defeat by Queen's Park on 18 August. More criticism followed. When Saints were beaten 4-2 at home by Hearts on 6 October it was described as the "best display this season". Tellingly, the official verdict on the match added, "McMahon's display being largely to blame for the defeat".

When the new keeper was also implicated in a 3-1 defeat at Dunfermline on 17 November it was obvious he was not going to last the season. During a 5-2 defeat by Clyde at Shawfield, McMahon sustained injuries to his thumbs and shoulder. Two days later Jimmy McCloy was re-signed, and McMahon never played again for St. Mirren: on 18 March he was give a free transfer.

Right back Walter Hay had been a short-term pay rebel the previous season, but this time he didn't re-sign at any stage and didn't play for Saints at all in 1934-35. His replacement, Tam Baird, was an internal promotee who had been signed from Lugar Boswell on 1 December 1930. This was the first season Baird had been given a run in the first team, and it was an opportunity he relished. It was also one set to continue. Walter Hay had been in the first team for six years, having been signed back in August 1924 from Petershill, but on 7 January 1935 he was transferred to Rangers for £850.

Right winger Jimmy Knox and international left half John Miller had periods of dispute which were short-lived. They were both back in the team by the third League game, but left winger John Phillips, a virtual ever-present the previous season, never played again: on 14 December he was transferred to East Fife for £75 "clear to the Club".

No one satisfactorily took over the left wing position. Stoddart, signed from Wishaw on 18 September for £40, went straight into the team, but lost his place when William Dowall joined from Motherwell on 10 December. Dowall played for the rest of the season, but his first few displays were a disappointment. Less than a month after joining Saints, the former Fir Parker had to be spoken to "regarding his lack of spirit".

Centre forward was an even bigger problem. The Club's greatest-ever goalscorer, Davie McCrae, had been given a free transfer at the end of 1933-34, but in the first half of the season none of the Board's replacements measured up to the task. On 5 November £350 was spent on Dick Black from Manchester United. Black made an instant impact when he scored the only goal on his debut five days later to give Saints two much-needed points. He then failed to score or impress in his next six games, and didn't make another competitive appearance.

Saints lost 3-2 at home to Queen's Park on 29 December. By then the team had played twenty-three League games, and had accumulated just nine points. St. Mirren were bottom of the League, and even with fifteen games to go there was talk of relegation. For the Queen's match, Dick Black had been replaced by John McKenzie, who had been secured from Ross County on 1 October for the much more modest outlay of £37.

McKenzie would score eleven League goals between 29 December and 20 April, but until the beginning of February he found himself in a team still subject to constant change. A line up of McCloy, Baird, Ancell, Gebbie, Wilson, Miller, Knox, Latimer, McKenzie, McGregor, and Dowall came to be regarded as the first choice. It wasn't lost on some that, after all the chopping and changing, the most successful eleven of the season was mainly comprised of players who were on the Club's books during the previous season.

Points-gathering greatly improved in the last two months, but other teams' results meant Saints gained limited League advancement from their more settled team and improved form. Home wins in April over bottom-half Dunfermline Athletic and Partick Thistle meant that Saints' final game at Celtic Park fell into the "must win" category. They lost 2-1.

At the end of the 1934-35 season only five points separated the bottom five teams, but Saints had left it too late. Falkirk finished bottom with twenty-four points. St. Mirren gained twenty-seven points for the second year in a row, but this time ended second from bottom. Seven other defences had conceded more than Saints' seventy goals, but crucially every other side exceeded the Buddies' forty-nine goal tally.

The writer Sir Max Beerbohm once wrote that "there is much to be said for failure. It is much more interesting than success." During 1934-35, there were precious few St. Mirren supporters who agreed with that particular assertion. After three bottom of the League finishes in their forty-four year League history, Division Two awaited for the goal-shy Saints and bottom club Falkirk. Both clubs had been relegated for the first time in their respective histories but were destined to immediately re-discover their way to goal, and in record-breaking fashion too!

1935-36

Chairman George L. Gilmour announced at the 1935 AGM that he and fellow Director Mr. James Wilson "were not accepting nomination and that the five gentlemen who had been duly nominated would not be opposed by the present Board". The five nominees, all prime movers behind the Vigilance Committee, were James Adam, Thomas Campbell, Allan McLean, Malcolm McPhail, and James Hunter Peacock. They were duly elected to the Board. One by one the other members of the previous Board would resign.

The Vigilance Committee had prevailed, but there was appreciation of the work done by their immediate predecessors, and, on the motion of James Adam, "the Chairman and retiring Directors were accorded a hearty vote of thanks for their services". Once installed, the new Board would specifically write to Mr. Thomas Hart "thanking him for his long and loyal service to the Club".

The new Board met for the first time on 29 May, and Mr. Adam was elected Chairman. They faced familiar problems. Bobby Ancell intimated that he had "no intention of signing at present terms", whilst, for the second year in a row, John Miller and Jimmy McCloy had also rejected the terms offered. Within a week all three had re-signed, but a condition of Ancell's re-signing was that "he was to be transferred if a suitable offer was made"

A "suitable offer", as far as the Club was concerned, was £3000. Plenty of clubs had shown interest in Ancell, but only Sunderland came near to St. Mirren's valuation of the full back. After prolonged negotiations, Sunderland Manager John Cochrane offered St. Mirren £2,700, with the player receiving £300.

The deal was struck on 23 October, but Ancell had missed that day's match against Raith Rovers, and the transfer was subject to the player showing satisfactory form the following Saturday against Brechin City at Glebe Park. Sunderland's Scottish scout, Sam Blythe, intimated that he wouldn't attend the game at Brechin because "he didn't think the game was a stiff enough test".

After that, Sunderland's interest in Ancell petered out. However, Blythe's less than complimentary comment about the quality of some of Saints' Division Two opponents was not without foundation. Five of the top clubs in the Division would score over one hundred goals, and the Club's own match verdicts confirmed the League's inequality. When the Buddies blasted Dumbarton 8-0 at Love Street on 4 January the game was unavoidably described as "one-sided", and a 5-0 win over Edinburgh City on 15 February was said to be "too easy".

No matter the standard of some teams, every game had to be approached professionally if Saints were to be promoted. To achieve this, the Directors wisely decided to stick with a winning team and McCloy, Baird, Ancell, Gebbie or Cunningham, Wilson, Miller, Latimer, Knox, McGregor, McCamon, and Gall were the core twelve who would win far more than they would lose.

It wasn't a markedly different line-up from the team which had done well in the closing stages of the previous Division One season. Allan Gebbie, sole survivor from the 1926 Cup Final team, and Finlay Cunningham, signed from Baillieston Juniors in May 1932, had equal claim to the right half position over the season. Only on the left wing was there any real change. Inside left McCamon had joined Saints on 9 September from Largs Thistle for £20, while the new outside left was William Gall, who had been signed on 9 July.

Back where they belong... the eleven who won promotion for St Mirren during 1935-36, sending the Buddies back to Division One.

Left to right, back row:- T. Baird, R. Ancell (Captain), J. McCloy, F. Cunningham, T. Wilson, J. Millar, D. Allison (Trainer).

Front row:- J. Latimer, J. Knox, J. McGregor, J. McCamon, W. Gall.

St. Mirren began their Division Two campaign on 10 August with a 6-1 win at Methil. It was the first of many decisive away victories, but a 3-2 defeat by Edinburgh City on 7 September gave Saints an early warning that not every lower division team would be a pushover.

Disappointment at City's East Pilton Park was followed by five wins on the trot. Saints then travelled to Cappielow on 19 October to meet a Morton side who had also started well and were matching Saints' goal-scoring feats. The Greenock team won 1-0, but Saints responded the following Saturday with a good all-round display and scored six goals against a poor Raith team. A further four points were picked up against Brechin and Alloa before a visit to Falkirk halted Paisley progress; East Stirlingshire won 3-2. Then it was Morton again.

On 26 November, Jimmy Knox hit three of the nine goals scored in a Renfrewshire derby match that simply thrilled everyone who saw it. The final score was 5-4 for St. Mirren, and, unusually for those times, a player from each side was ordered off. Even the Club's normally detached and sober match summary reflected the excitement. "Best game seen at Love Street for a long time," exclaimed the minute. A more typical tone returned with the additional comment, "although our team took a long time to settle"!

Following the Morton game, Saints made their second visit to Falkirk within two weeks. This time it was for a top of the table confrontation at Brockville. A crowd of 10,000 saw the "Bairns" deservedly win, although most observers felt the 5-0 margin exaggerated their superiority on the day. It was a temporary setback. Saints won their next seven League games before Scottish Cup business intervened on 25 January.

A 3-2 away win against Division One Ayr United led to Saints being drawn against Dalbeattie Star in the second round. The Club immediately appealed to the S.F.A. that Star's ground didn't have a barricade around it and therefore didn't conform to the competition's rules. The appeal was turned down, and the tie went ahead on 8 February. Despite ground conditions which were said to be "terrible", it turned out to be a fairly easy game. A Jimmy McGregor goal, one of his forty-six in the season, was enough to take Saints through.

The third round brought Rangers to St. Mirren Park and gave Saints the chance to measure themselves against a leading Division One team. The clash was sufficiently intriguing to attract a crowd of 43,308. John Miller was made for such a match, and he scored Saints' only goal in a close 2-1 defeat. St. Mirren had played well, and many considered that they had been a little unfortunate not to at least draw.

There was still plenty to play for. A draw and two wins between 29 February and 14 March meant that a home victory over Brechin City on 21 March would clinch promotion. After the first of seven goals hit the Brechin net celebrations were never in doubt. Third Lanark FC wasted no time in congratulating Saints "on regaining your First Division status".

The supporters had played their part too. Plans to establish a St. Mirren FC Supporters' Club had been announced half-way through the relegation season. On 3 September 1935 it was agreed to give official recognition to the new Supporters' Club, whose members were keen to stress that their sole aim was to assist St. Mirren FC; they had no desire to interfere with the Club's management.

Rooms at St. Mirren Park were provided for the supporters' organisation at the beginning of October, and permission was given to sell the Supporters' Club Federation paper at the ground. In January 1936, the Supporters' Club made their first donation when they gave £50 to St. Mirren and also presented a set of red and white jerseys. It was the start of a long-running partnership.

Club accounts for the period 16 March 1935 to 30 April 1936 showed a loss of £318 17s 1d, which was considered "very satisfactory" in view of the wages paid and heavier travelling costs. On the field the season had been more than satisfactory. Saints had won twenty-five of their thirty-four Division Two fixtures, and along the way had scored one hundred and fourteen goals. They had proved themselves to be too good for Division Two; they were heading back to where they belonged.

1936-37

On three separate occasions during 1936-37 the Club were approached about leasing St. Mirren Park for Greyhound Racing. None of the propositions were entertained. Indeed, turning down such offers had become a matter of principle. "The present Board are set against anything like that," stated Chairman James Adam. The Directors certainly weren't resistant to change, as the Club's Trainer and Manager were to discover.

After nine years with St. Mirren, including seven as Trainer, David Allison was asked to leave. He resigned on 23 May to be replaced by Motherwell-born Hugh Good. The new Trainer had previously been Glentoran's Player-Coach and his assistant was to be none other than Saints' legend Davie McCrae.

A bigger change was to follow on from a 2-1 defeat by Hamilton at Douglas Park on 10 October. The team's five wins and a draw from twelve League games wasn't a bad record for a promoted club, and a continuation of this form would produce a mid-table finish. However, the Directors weren't satisfied, so two days after the Hamilton match they discussed the management of the Club.

Versatile Allan Gebbie, who played in both the 1926 and 1934 Cup Final sides.

By a majority decision, Secretary/Manager John Morrison was asked to tender his resignation with effect from the end of October. Perhaps the request was inevitable. Exactly two years earlier, some members of the Board, as Vigilance Committee representatives, had demanded that Mr. Morrison should be asked to "retire". John Morrison had been Secretary/Manager since 1 June 1929. His spell as Manager had undeniably coincided with a deterioration in results, but he could cite in his defence that it was also a time of great financial difficulty, which had forced the Club to part with some of their best players.

On 20 October it was decided to appoint Paisley man Sam Blythe as John Morrison's successor. Mr. Blythe had been John Cochrane's assistant at St. Mirren Park before becoming Sunderland's highly regarded scout in Scotland. By the time Blythe arrived at St. Mirren Park a third of the season had elapsed, but the changes in playing personnel were set to continue apace.

Jimmy McCloy remained the first choice goalkeeper. The right back position was less straightforward. In the first half of the season the role moved between Tam Baird and close season signing Arthur Tonner, who had been with West Ham United for three years. Neither player completely satisfied the Board, and on 18 January Bill Murray was signed from Sunderland for £300. He would retain his place at right back for the remainder of the season.

At left back, Bobby Ancell was finally sold for £2,450. The classy defender moved to Newcastle United on 1 September, within thirteen months he would win his two caps for Scotland. Ancell was initially replaced by international left half John Miller, until the middle of October when Joe Craven took over the position, having been signed on 26 September for just £15. Craven was a former Parkhead and Partick Thistle player who had spent the previous season with Northampton Town from Division Three South in England.

There would be no Allan Gebbie at right half in 1936-37. For twelve years the creative and versatile Gebbie had been a cornerstone of successive St. Mirren sides at inside forward and wing half. He had often appeared alongside Saints players who had, or would, play for Scotland; he had never looked out of place in such company. Allan Gebbie, acclaimed rescuer of several children from the 1929 Glen Cinema disaster when seventy youngsters perished, played in two Scottish Cup Finals, and in his last season was associated with more success as Saints gained promotion. He left on a free transfer, joining Aldershot on 19 June 1936. He would be fondly remembered at St. Mirren Park.

Within two weeks of the season starting the right half position became the property of Willie Kelly. He had been signed from Maryhill on 15 October 1934, having then been described as "very promising, good size and strong". Kelly had been one of a number of young players who were tried in the relegation season, when he played six times during November and December 1934. He was now ready to fulfill his promise.

Willie Kelly's inclusion in the first team meant that Cunningham moved to centre half at the expense of Fulton Wilson, the half-back line being completed by John Miller, who had ended his early season stint as Ancell's interim replacement.

Twenty year old local lad Robert Ferguson, who had previously been with Hearts and Yoker, was the undisputed outside right. More often than not Ferguson's inside partner was fans' favourite Jimmy Knox, although Knox had a few games at centre and a few weeks in the Reserves early in the season. The previous season's inside right, Johnny Latimer, had joined Dundee on 28 July for £325. Signed from East Stirlingshire on 27 June 1933 for £200, Latimer had scored twenty goals in his time with St. Mirren.

No one really claimed the centre forward spot, with Dick Black, Jimmy Knox, Jimmy McGregor and John McKenzie each having a run. Knox would end up as the team's top scorer with twenty League goals, although ten of these were scored on two separate occasions when he hit five! Meanwhile, nine-goal Black was transferred to Morton for £150 on 2 March 1937.

The inside left position was split between P. McCamon and newcomer Alex Callan. Callan had been much sought-after when he was signed on 16 June from Morton Juniors for £20. On the left wing, William Gall eventually lost his place to Alex Hanlin, who had joined Saints on 1 December 1936 from Burnbank Athletic for £40.

By the time the Scottish Cup was due to start on 30 January, Saints had won seven and drawn seven of their twenty-four League games. They were still on schedule for a respectable first season back in Division One. The cup campaign began with a home tie against non-League Beith, with centre half Cunningham the unlikely source of a hat-trick in a 4-0 victory.

The second round brought another home match. This time Brechin City were beaten 1-0. That score was repeated in the third round against Cowdenbeath in yet another home tie. Saints then hit their worst form of the season, and would lose five of their last seven League fixtures. Clyde came to Paisley for the fourth round of the Cup in the middle of this bad run and left with a 3-0 victory.

By the end of the season, Saints' total of eleven wins and seven draws from thirty-eight League games gave them sixteenth place, though earlier form had pointed to a more satisfactory outcome. Although the defence took shape from mid-January onwards, most of the forwards were unconvincing, and the team at no point had a settled look. The quality of the side would need to be improved if Saints were to repeat the regular top six finishes of the 1920s.

1937-38

In the summer of 1937 it was the contention of the Directors that a place within the top six of the Scottish League was entirely appropriate for a club of St. Mirren's standing, so they agreed to pay the players a New Year's bonus if there were no more than five teams above Saints by 31 December.

The Board's top six target, even for half a season, was nothing if not ambitious. The team had finished in sixteenth place the previous season, yet for the opening match at Pittodrie on 14 August only one new player had been added. That "new" player was Saints' former internationalist Bobby Rankin. The Club had previously made a couple of enquiries to Clyde FC about buying back Rankin, but had been unable to meet Clyde's valuation. By 23 June the asking price was £500. Manager Sam Blythe was authorised to talk to the Shawfield club again and "go the length of £400 for Rankin's transfer".

Blythe must have been persuasive, because he announced on 20 July that Clyde had accepted an offer of £350! There was delight that Bobby Rankin was a Saint again, but he was no miracle worker. Opening opponents Aberdeen had finished in the top six for the previous five seasons and would do so again in 1937-38. Saints' aspirations were given an early dent as the "Dons" won 4-0.

Better form was shown a week later in a home draw with Hearts, the improvement continuing on 22 August with a fine 2-1 home win over Aberdeen. The unbeaten run was extended with a creditable 1-1 draw with Clyde at Shawfield, followed by a clear-cut 4-1 home win over Queen's Park on 4 September. The next week a second new player was fielded in an impressive 3-0 win over Kilmarnock. Making a scoring debut that day at Rugby Park was left winger Johnny Deakin, who had been signed on 10 May from Johnstone Juniors. He would impress enough to remain automatic choice on the left wing until 19 February.

For the second time in seven games, Saints were beaten 4-0 away from home when they received a mid-week mauling from Hearts on 15 September. They recovered the following Saturday to win 4-2 over Queen of the South at home and after eight League games Saints had won four and drawn two. This opening sequence turned out to be the most productive points-gathering part of the season.

The ninth game, a visit to Ibrox on 25 September, produced a third 4-0 away reverse which led to goalkeeper Jimmy McCloy being dropped for the next match against Queen's Park at Hampden on 27 September. Taking over in goal was eighteen year old Gordon Rennie, who had been signed from Banks o' Dee on 7 September for £31. Four regulars were missing from Saints' line up against Queen's as the Buddies suffered yet another 4-0 away defeat.

Jimmy McCloy was clearly unhappy about his reversion, and, not for the first time, asked for a transfer. The 'keeper played for the Reserves for the next eight matches but was recalled after a 3-0 defeat at Muirton against St. Johnstone on 20 November. McCloy was to remain first choice until the last League game of the season on 30 April.

Despite the early season 4-0 defeats, the defence was regularly praised in the official minutes. The choice from goalkeeper to left half was normally Jimmy McCloy, Bill Murray, Joe Craven, Willie Kelly, Cunningham or Wilson, and John Miller. Apart from goalkeeper, the only other defensive change all season happened after the Perth fixture on 20 November, as Fulton

Wishaw born Willie Kelly, signed from Maryhill Juniors.

Wilson began to be considered more than Finlay Cunningham for centre half.

Selection of the forward line in the first half of the season was also consistent, but this unit was never lauded. Comments ranged from "forwards disappointing" to "forwards utterly hopeless near goal", but the most common criticism was "forwards failed us badly at goal." Despite these aspersions, Rankin and Deakin were the left wing pairing every week, and Robert Ferguson was undisputed outside right to the end of the year and beyond.

Much of the expressed dissatisfaction with the forwards was aimed at Jimmy Knox and John McKenzie. At the end of the year Knox had scored just five goals, a disappointing figure not helped by being dropped from mid-October to mid-November. He had been played at centre forward a couple of times, but usually lined up at inside right with John McKenzie as first choice centre. In the first half of the season McKenzie scored nine goals, and, like Knox, two of his goals were scored in a 6-1 rout of Clyde on Christmas Day.

By the end of 1937, Saints had won five and drawn three of the fourteen games played, usually by fielding a team of McCloy, Murray, Craven, Kelly, Cunningham, Miller, Ferguson, Knox, McKenzie, Rankin, and Deakin. This eleven had produced mid-table form, quite a bit short of a top six finish.

The Board were undeterred. Inside forward John McMenemy's displays for Partick Thistle suggested to them that he was just the player to invigorate the forward line. His £500 transfer went through in time for him to play in the 1-1 draw against Rangers on 15 January. In his second game, a winning cup tie against Dunfermline Athletic on 22 January, he sustained an injury which not only caused him to be hospitalised but, it was feared, could have permanently incapacitated him from football.

John McMenemy's injury was a real blow, because the Club's financial position, whilst not in debt, didn't permit them to re-enter the transfer market. By 22 February, McMenemy's news was good, and he got the go-ahead to re-commence training. Meanwhile, all efforts to secure the loan of an experienced forward proved unsuccessful.

During McMenemy's absence, the Club signed William McLintock from Dunipace Juniors on 8 March for a £40 fee. McLintock's debut against Partick Thistle on 2 April coincided with McMenemy's return. The youngster scored in an unlucky 3-2 defeat, but by then Saints had been knocked out of the Scottish Cup in the second round by Falkirk on 12 February, and were dropping dangerously close to the relegation zone.

It was a serious situation, and one which may have increased Club sensibilities. Earlier in the season St. Mirren had allowed the 'Daily Record' to install broadcasting equipment in the ground. All was going well until a match with fellow-strugglers Ayr United on 19 February, when the announcer chose to broadcast some jokes. The Club took a dim view of this, and the Manager was instructed to "write to the 'Daily Record' expressing our disapproval of this sort of thing and asking them to be more careful in future".

Two weeks before the Ayr United fixture, however, there had been considerable laughter at Love Street. A hat-trick from Knox, a double from McKenzie, and one each from the left wing pairing of Rankin and Deakin not only brought some relief to the much-maligned forward line, but also produced a score-line for Saints' supporters to savour. On 5 February, the Buddies scored seven against a defence which would eventually concede one hundred and twenty-seven League goals and be relegated. It was not the best of seasons for Morton!

Saints had only four League games left to play when they gave a glimpse of what might have been. A superb performance, with goals from McLintock, McMenemy, and Knox, earned a 3-0 win over a strong Motherwell side. Then the Buddies slipped back, losing two consecutive away games against Hibs and Celtic. Despite these defeats they were safe. On the last Saturday of the season Ayr United met Dundee, which meant one of these sides couldn't match the thirty-three points collected by Saints.

The Buddies had finished four points and two positions better off than the previous season. At first glance it was an improved performance, but in fact they had come much closer to relegation. A top six finish still looked a long way off.

1938-39

Although the Board was set against using St. Mirren Park for Greyhound Racing, they were always willing to consider other ways of bringing money into the Club. When they received an application from a Mr. George Bingley at the beginning of May 1938 to stage a World Boxing Flyweight Championship between Glasgow's Benny Lynch and the American Jackie Jurich they quickly agreed to the suggestion. St. Mirren would receive 3.5% of the gross drawings.

On 3 June, the Directors were advised that the boxing contest had been deferred from 15 June until 29 June. The reason soon became obvious. Benny Lynch, way past his best and soon to retire, weighed in at seven pounds over the weight limit and in doing so automatically forfeited his title. The fight went ahead, but its importance had been diminished. An expected 30,000 crowd failed to materialise, and St. Mirren's share of the income was just £128 4s 9d.

The sale of centre forward John McKenzie proved to be more profitable than the boxing venture. McKenzie, a £37 buy from Ross County in 1934, was transferred to Manchester United for £225 on 3 June. He had scored forty-one goals in all competitions since his debut on 29 December 1934.

There was no fee for goalkeeper Jimmy McCloy, whose six year connection with Saints ended during the close season:

Keeper Jimmy McCloy, who left Saints during the close season.

Gordon Rennie took over in goal. The remainder of the team for the opening game against Clyde on 13 August, with the exception of outside left Stead, would be on familiar lines from the previous season: Rennie, Murray, Craven, Kelly, Wilson, Miller, Knox, Rankin, McLintock, McMenemy, and Angus Stead, who had been signed on 8 February.

After the opening League match, Chairman James Adam proposed that the Manager be given a free hand in team selection for a trial period of eight matches, or until Saints played Albion Rovers in Paisley on 24 September. Manager Sam Blythe thanked the Board for the faith placed in him.

The team selection experiment didn't last long. On 6 September the Manager informed the Board that "it was very awkward for him to select the team when he could only see one of St. Mirren's two teams at a time". He asked the Board to reconsider its position! By this time the Club were bottom of the League, having lost four and drawn one of the five matches played. Responsibility for team selection reverted to the Board, but Sam Blythe remained part of the process.

The first side chosen by both Board and Manager lost 1-0 at home to Kilmarnock on 10 September, but there was some relief three days later when Saints finally won a game; a 2-1 victory over Queen's Park at Hampden. It was followed by the 3-1 defeat of Raith Rovers at Kirkcaldy, a result which lifted Saints off the bottom of the table.

Form in October improved as six points were gained from five matches. November's return was more mixed, and on 26 November a 6-1 defeat at Easter Road from mid-table Hibs hinted at a long, difficult season for Saints. It wasn't entirely unexpected. During the close season plenty of acquisitions had been made for the future, but the side which had ended the previous season just one point above relegation hadn't really been strengthened at first team level. The Board faced a dilemma. They were trying not to plunge the Club into debt by spending heavily on transfer fees, yet at the same time were attempting to avoid the perceived mistake of their predecessors by taking on other clubs' "cast-offs".

The Directors stayed optimistic and team selection remained consistent. Rennie was unchallenged in goal, and the same could be said of his two full backs, Bill Murray and Joe Craven. In the half-back line, right half Willie Kelly had been switched to left half due to an early season injury to John Miller, and Kelly's place at right half was taken by William Young, a £100 buy from Blackburn Rovers on 23 June 1937. John Miller had resumed playing on 8 October with a game against Aberdeen Reserves, though he would be unable to regain a regular place in the team.

At centre half, Fulton Wilson held the position until 3 December, when two bad slips by him in the home game against Falkirk allowed the "Bairns" to score twice and win the game 2-1. Finlay Cunningham took over and retained his place until 11 March, when Wilson returned for the rest of the season.

Robert Ferguson was again the regular right winger, and his inside man was Jimmy Knox, who would score fifteen of the team's fifty seven League goals. Top scorer, however, was nineteen-goal William McLintock. To his immediate left was usually Bobby Rankin.

Only the outside left position changed hands on a frequent basis. Johnny Deakin, one of seven to be tried in that position, played in fifty per cent of the games. Making half that total was Alex Kinnaird, who had been signed from Third Lanark for £650 on 29 November. Dan Wood played only four times in the first team, but at the very least he impressed the Motherwell FC management. Signed from Renfrew Juniors on 16 August for just £20, he was sold to the Fir Park club for £250 at the end of November.

Two errors by centre half Wilson had been blamed for the loss of one match, but generally the unsuccessful trend of the season was ascribed to being "unlucky", and consecutive defeats by Celtic and Rangers during December were categorised thus. However, fortune did not feature anywhere in a 7-0 home win over East Stirlingshire in the first round of the Scottish Cup on 21 January.

Edinburgh City provided a much more formidable obstacle in the next round, but two goals from McLintock and one from Knox eventually gave the Buddies a 3-1 win. Plans were immediately made in anticipation of Saints drawing Celtic, Hearts, or Rangers at home. At this time, Third

Lanark's request to receive the balance of the Alex Kinnaird fee was deferred until "our Third Round opponents are known". Any extra money generated from such a cup tie was going to be welcome.

The third round opponents turned out to be Motherwell. Sadly, they proved to be too good for Saints at Fir Park, where they won 4-2. Arrangements were made to pay Third Lanark immediately after the tie. More worryingly, when the cup results were stripped away, the months of January and February had brought only two wins. St. Mirren were just four points above the relegation area.

March was even worse. "Played four, lost four" was the summary. The month ended with the departure of one of the team's steadiest players, when Bill Murray asked for his release from the Club to enable him to take up his new post as Manager of Sunderland AFC. Despite Saints' predicament, the Directors agreed to the request. Murray played his last game for the Club on 1 April, just three League matches before the end of the season, then moved south to Roker Park where he succeeded ex-St. Mirren Secretary/Manager John Cochrane as Manager of Sunderland. Like Cochrane, Bill Murray would be hugely successful on Wearside.

Three weeks after Murray's move, two goals from Robert Ferguson and one from William McLintock were enough to give Saints a 3-2 win at Somerset Park. The Ayr victory meant that one more point would ensure Division One safety. A home match against second placed Celtic, trailing Rangers by nine points, was all that remained. By the end of the day that gap had become eleven, as Saints won 2-1. Top scorers McLintock and Knox got the goals.

Saints finished eighteenth out of twenty teams to complete three seasons of mediocrity since they had returned to Division One. More important considerations than football would soon demand that there would be no League football for another seven years. When it returned, Saints would recover from their Thirties' decline.

1939-40

At the 1939 AGM, Chairman James Adam referred to "the unsatisfactory position of the Club in the Scottish League", and attributed this to "a lack of scoring forwards". This had certainly been the Board's consistent view for two years, but it was also borne out by the facts; only one team in the 1937-38 and 1938-39 seasons had scored less goals than Saints.

Mr. Adam moved on to a happier AGM topic when he paid generous tribute to the career of John Miller, which had ended in April after fourteen years at St. Mirren Park. The Chairman spoke of John "serving the Club faithfully and well", and stated that the Directors had offered, and John Miller had accepted, the post of Assistant Trainer. Loud and prolonged cheers greeted this statement – a testimony to John Miller's popularity. His position as St. Mirren's second most capped player would not be beaten until 1980, and indeed at the end of St. Mirren's first one hundred and twenty five years he remained the Club's fourth most honoured Scot with five caps.

Two weeks after the AGM, Davie McCrae wrote to the Board thanking them for the confidence placed in him following his appointment as Trainer in succession to Hugh Good, and expressing his willingness "to give all he had". John Miller wrote in similar vein. St. Mirren now had a Paisley man as Manager and two St. Mirren legends on the training staff. It was no guarantee of success, but it could only add to Club spirit.

For the opening game of the season on 12 August the following team was chosen: Rennie, Bruce, Craven, Young, Wilson, Kelly, Ferguson, Brady, McLintock, Steel, and Deakin. Only three names were unfamiliar. Sunderland-bound Bill Murray's place at right back had been taken by D. Bruce, a £50 signing from Bristol Rovers on 12 August 1937, and inside right Tom Brady had joined Saints from Aberdeen for £550 on 16 May.

The third new name, at inside left, belonged to a sixteen year old amateur called Billy Steel. Events elsewhere determined that Steel's debut, the opening 5-1 defeat by Rangers, and the four subsequent results would all be erased from the record books within three weeks.

Director Mr. Malcolm McPhail, having attended a special meeting of the S. F. A., advised the Board on 6 September that "owing to Britain having declared war, the decision was that football was to be suspended as from 3rd September 1939". All contracts between clubs and players were to be suspended as from the same date. St. Mirren's players would be paid wages, expenses, and bonuses due up to and including 2 September.

This initial ban on competitive football was lifted, and permission was given to play Morton in the Renfrewshire Cup Final on 27 September. The match ended in a 1-1 draw. The replay was arranged to take place at Cappielow on 7 October, despite the fact that Saints were already scheduled to play a friendly against Hibs at Love Street that day. The decision was to play both games!

Saints allocated most of their first team players to the county match with Morton, but it's worth noting that the Board resisted the temptation to play two guest players. Manchester City's centre half and captain Les McDowall, and left winger Jimmy Caskie, who had joined Everton six months earlier from St. Johnstone, both appeared for Saints at Love Street against Hibs in a 3-3 draw.

The new pair avoided a fiercely contested tie, which the minutes later described as "a little rough" due to "a weak referee". Four players were sent off and ten goals were shared! One of Saints' remaining nine players on the pitch was Johnny Deakin who squared the game at 5-5 in stoppage time after Saints had been 4-2 ahead at half-time.

Cappielow was again the venue for the third attempt to settle the outcome of the 1939 county cup. This time Tom Brady gave Saints the lead, but two goals from Morton were sufficient for them to prevail.

The 6 September decision to abandon League football was reviewed, and after consultation with the Home Office it was agreed that the continuation of football could be a morale booster. Two geographical Divisions of sixteen teams were established by the Scottish League on 21 October 1939. Such was the West of Scotland's dominance at the time that only four of the clubs in the new Western Division were drawn from Division Two of the Scottish League. Players were to be paid £2 per week, and some travelling expenses were to be allowed. Gate drawings were to be equally divided, with a guarantee of £50 to visiting clubs.

John Miller, Saints second most capped player in the first 73 years.

In the thirty Western Division games and the three Emergency War Cup ties, Saints fielded thirty-seven different players, nearly half of whom were guest players. Many were England-based Scots like Caskie, whilst others such as McDowall were leading English players who were "in the district" due to work or military commitments. Some played just once, but no guest player could become a short-term Saint until proper insurance had been arranged and permission to play had been authorised by their registered club and the S.F.A.

Despite all the changes, a first choice team emerged and was as follows: Wilson, Logan, Craven, Mooney, McDowall, Kelly, Brady, Yorston, Linwood, Stead, Caskie. The team won eleven and drew four of the thirty Western Division matches.

Goalkeeper Gordon Rennie was serving with HM Forces, and played only when leave permitted. His place was initially taken by James Bayne, a Saints' signing on 25 May from Bradford City. From 4 October onwards, Greenock-born Alex Wilson of Arsenal became first choice, and he remained in that position until 16 March 1940, when Johnstone from Aberdeen FC took over.

At right back, David Logan was signed from Hibs on 28 October and for the rest of the season he worked in partnership with regular left back Joe Craven. Ahead of them, William Young kept his place at right half until 21 November, when Stenhousemuir were given permission to play him. He was initially replaced by Tom Ashe, who had been signed from Johnstone Juniors on 11 October 1938. From the middle of October the position went to John Mooney, who had joined Saints from Edinburgh City on 21 February.

From the second game of the season, the centre half position was taken by William Milliken, a £40 Saints' signing from Kilbirnie Ladeside on 4 January 1938. At the end of January, the Manager informed the

Board that Milliken had been "called to the colours", and "he had seen the lad and wished him God-speed". The pivot for the remainder of the season was Les McDowall of Manchester City. He had shown his versatility earlier in the season by lining up for Saints at centre forward when Linwood was unavailable.

Work commitments limited right winger Robert Ferguson's appearances, so inside forward Tom Brady was moved to the wing to cover the enforced absence. At inside right was ex-Scotland internationalist Benny Yorston of Middlesbrough, who was in Saints' side until 5 March. He then had to return to England to undergo an Army PT course, after which he played just once.

At the beginning of November, King's Park FC were granted centre forward William McLintock's services, and Saints' previous top scorer was replaced by Alex Linwood, who had played four games during 1938-39 following his signing from Muirkirk Juniors on 4 October 1938 for £40. Linwood would score nineteen goals in the Western League and two in the Emergency Cup. On Alex's left hand side would be Angus Stead, who made the inside left position his own.

Outside left Johnny Deakin reported on 21 November that he too had been called up to the Forces, but was still available for selection. By that time Saints also had Jimmy Caskie, and on more than one occasion Caskie played outside right while Johnny Deakin appeared on the left flank. Caskie was to prove an outstanding success, and every effort would be made during the close season to retain his services.

There would be no Scottish Cup throughout the war years, but a replacement "Emergency War Cup" was introduced in 1940. The first round was a two-legged affair, but a 6-0 home win over Queen of the South made the second leg almost an irrelevance. A 10-1 aggregate took Saints through to the second round, where they defeated Hamilton Accies 2-0 at Douglas Park.

Saints then drew Rangers in the third round. Fears that football crowds could become bombing targets meant that restrictions were placed on all grounds, although the figure could be adjusted for special games, such as the New Year's Day fixture with Kilmarnock when the crowd maximum was raised to 15,000.

By the time the authorities had decided that no more than 25,000 people would be allowed to assemble at St. Mirren Park for the Rangers tie on 23 March, the Club had issued 25,000 tickets for the ground, plus 4,000 for the enclosure and 1,225 for the stand. The directors were left with no option but to transfer the match to Ibrox Park, where Rangers won 3-1.

The financial benefits from a tie with Rangers could not have been more timely. In January 1940 it became known that the income tax authorities were pressing St. Mirren for payment of £175. Costs were again reviewed, and not only were Saints' normal contributions to the community greatly reduced, but Trainer Davie McCrae's wages were brought down to fifteen shillings per week, while Assistant Trainer John Miller was to be released. The latter decision by the Board was greatly regretted, "but owing to the war had no option."

Adverse weather conditions caused the postponement of several matches between 13 January and 10 February, and caused considerable damage to the dressing rooms due to burst pipes. It was another unwanted expense, but the Club's financial difficulties were compounded on 20 February when the Town Chamberlain insisted on full payment of local rates and taxes by 31 March 1940.

Saints began to pay the Chamberlain's office £25 per week, but Manager Sam Blythe informed them that "no promise of clearing the entire account by March could be given". At the same time, they were also paying the same amount to the Collector of Taxes.

The Town Chamberlain was dissatisfied with the repayment rate, and instigated the arrestment of St. Mirren's share of the gate following the home match against Hamilton Accies on 9 March, which amounted to £143. The Club's lawyers, MacRobert Son and Hutchison, immediately provided an advancement of £100 to cover the week's wages.

In the same week, the Paisley Charity Cup Committee sought immediate payment of £189 4s 9d due to them for a Charity Cup game against Clyde. Chairman James Adam immediately offered to pay this amount from his own pocket, on the undertaking that the Board would repay him from the takings of the third round of the Emergency War

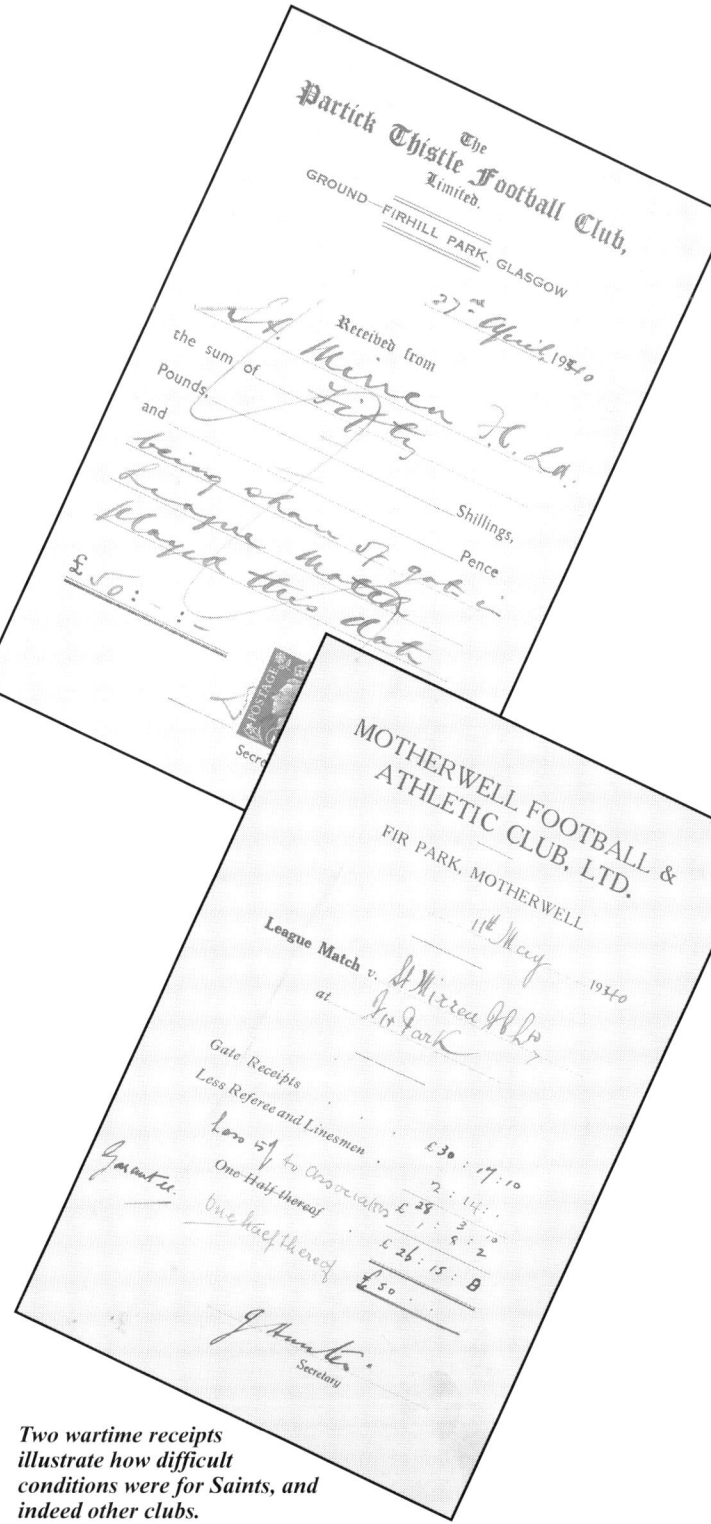

Two wartime receipts illustrate how difficult conditions were for Saints, and indeed other clubs.
The first is from Partick Thistle to St Mirren for a match played at St Mirren Park on 27th April 1940, which ended in a 3-1 victory for the Saints. The Club paid Thistle their guarantee of £50.
The second is from Motherwell F. C. for a match played on 11th May 1940 at Fir Park, Saints winning 4-1. This shows total receipts of £30 17s 10p, but the Motherwell club still had to pay Saints their £50 guarantee! The receipt is signed by famous 'Well Manager John (Sailor) Hunter.

Cup match against Falkirk or Rangers. Should the takings not meet the amount owed to Mr. Adam, the other Directors and Manager agreed to share equally the amount owed.

There simply wasn't enough money coming into the Club. Two home games in April against Queen of the South and Hamilton had combined takings of £96. After paying both visiting clubs their £50 guarantee, St. Mirren made a loss of £6 before taking into account any of their own wages and other expenses.

The Rangers cup tie alleviated Saints' problems, but it is little wonder that some clubs like Dundee FC eventually shut down for the duration of the war. It says much for everyone connected with St. Mirren that they were prepared to keep marching on.

The 1940s - Struggling, Winning, Thriving

1940-41

In June 1940 the Scottish League decided to disband League football for season 1940-41, but stated that "district competitions would be in order". By the beginning of July, Rangers FC had convened a meeting to discuss the formation of a new competition, the result being the Scottish Southern Football League.

CHAPTER EIGHT
The 1940's

The 1939-40 season in the Western Division had certainly been a real struggle financially, but the Club regarded an operating loss of £123 3s 7d for the year to 30 April 1940 as "quite satisfactory", and were delighted to participate in the new League, which would contain the thirteen leading West of Scotland clubs, plus Falkirk and the two main Edinburgh teams.

Just as things looked promising, the Club received a letter from the Chief Constable of Paisley "informing us he could not grant permission for football to be played on our grounds this season". The Chairman reported that the Chief Constable had confirmed that his decision was "absolutely final". Rangers FC were approached regarding the use of Ibrox, and this was agreed along the usual lines, with the Glasgow club retaining the stand and enclosure drawings.

After just two Southern League games, Manager Sam Blythe offered to resign on 19 August. Due to the Club's financial situation his own position had been very difficult in previous months. Back in May he had been asked "to finish up full time on Saturday 18th", and was then asked "to find a situation in the close season". The Manager's August request prompted another re-think, and the Club offered him a full-time situation, which he accepted.

At the same time Groundsman Malcolm McAulay intimated his resignation. St. Mirren Park was still closed by order at this point but Mr. McAulay's situation had also been insecure for a number of months. Although not directly employed by the Club during the close season, he had agreed "to do his best to keep things in order in his spare time". The Groundsman's resignation was accepted with regret. He would be replaced in October by Mr. Ralph Liddell of Kelburne Cricket Club.

The playing squad presented a much more stable picture, particularly in the forward line. Only the early January 1941 acquisition of the great Bob McPhail, who filled the three inside forward positions on eleven occasions, disrupted the usual five of Caskie (Everton), Brady, Linwood, Stead, and Deakin.

Jimmy Caskie's selection was automatic, and, thanks to the availability of Johnny Deakin on the left wing, he usually lined up at outside right. Caskie's inside man was Tom Brady, who scored twenty-six goals in all competitions. This was a distinction he shared with Alex Linwood, who hardly missed a game all season at centre forward. Linwood, for the second year in succession, was top scorer in the League with nineteen goals. Angus Stead was again the regular inside left, his wing partner being either Deakin or Caskie.

This lack of opportunity for others to break into the forward line frustrated one young forward. At the beginning of October Sam Blythe reported that promising amateur player Billy Steel was dissatisfied with not getting a game, and had asked for his "freedom from the Club". Young Steel's self-confidence paid off, and not only was he subsequently selected six times, but he was offered professional forms on 26 November. However, he wasn't prepared to sign them, stating that he intended remaining amateur "until the war was over".

The choice of the team's defence, goalkeeper apart, was also quite consistent. In the first half of the season James Hall, signed from Third Lanark, was Saints goalkeeper, until Bobby Johnstone was signed from Motherwell on 16 October. Johnstone was then the preferred option, although Arsenal's Alex Wilson was re-employed for seven weeks when Johnstone was injured.

At right back was William Savage, who had been signed on 6 August from Queen of the South. Savage would be unchallenged in that position all season, as was Joe Cavan, who completed his fourth season filling the left back berth.

The half back line began the season as Kelly, Clark (Plymouth Argyle), and McDowall (Manchester City), but on 1 October James Clark advised the Club that he had joined the Forces, and would no longer be available for selection. From mid-October to mid-December Willie Kelly took over as pivot, then Les McDowall switched to the centre of the defence for the rest of the season. George Urquhart, a former Saint on temporary loan from Arbroath, was ahead of the rest for appearances at wing half.

Jimmy Caskie

The ban on the use of St. Mirren Park was lifted on 12 October when Hibs were the visitors. By then repairs to various exits had been completed and "everything was fixed for the requirements of the Chief Constable". Saints had played three "home" games at Ibrox. After that unforeseen problem was overcome it turned out to be a moderately successful season, with the team winning twelve and drawing eight of their thirty fixtures to finish seventh out of sixteen.

The Directors, not for the first time, weren't satisfied. On 28 January 1941, Manager Sam Blythe was asked to resign his position and took charge of his last St. Mirren team on 15 February in a 1-0 win over Celtic. Donald Menzies was his immediate replacement.

The season also contained eleven cup ties in two competitions which both lacked a straight knock-out ingredient in the opening stages. The 1940 Emergency War Cup had given way to the 1941 League War Cup, the new competition commencing in March with four sections each containing four teams. St. Mirren's reward for winning eleven points out of a possible twelve was a semi-final tie with Rangers on 19 April. The match was lost 4-1 at Hampden, but the consolation was that Saints' share of the gate amounted to a much-needed £705 16s 3d.

There was also a "Summer Cup" tournament, the early rounds of which were two-legged. In the first round Tom Brady scored five times in a 6-2 aggregate win over Partick Thistle, but Hearts then won 3-2 in Paisley and 3-1 at Tynecastle on 28 June. It was the end of a season which had begun way back on 10 August; the Saints' players had less than three weeks before pre-season training began!

Before that, though, they would all be in for a shock. St. Mirren's Secretary and Chairman had been asked to appear before the Scottish Southern Football League on 18 April to assist an investigation into alleged irregularities regarding payments to certain players. All books and records relating to the Club were to be examined by League officials in conjunction with the S.F.A.

The outcome of a subsequent investigation by the S.F.A. Council, which was made public on 6 June 1941, stunned Saints supporters. The Club was found guilty of payment irregularities and fined £100.

Consequently, five Directors – Messrs. J. Adam, J.S. Gladstone, S. MacDonald, T. Campbell, and M. McPhail – were suspended from taking any further part in football management, and a similar ban was directed towards former Manager Sam Blythe. Two other Directors, Mr. W. Small and Mr. W.W. Waters, were allowed to continue their connection with St. Mirren.

It wasn't just the management side of the Club which felt the repercussions of the S.F.A. judgement: Everton's Jimmy Caskie was fined £20 and prohibited from playing for St. Mirren again, whilst Manchester City's Leslie McDowall was fined £5 and his St. Mirren connection was also involuntarily severed.

Other players were also implicated by the Association. Tom Brady was severely censured, and Bob McPhail, John Mooney, and D. Alston were severely censured and warned. Nine other first team squad members were warned that if they were involved in any similar case severe action would be taken.

Many observers believed that such payment irregularities were not confined to Paisley's club, and that the S.F.A. punishment was not only intended as a deterrent to St. Mirren but to other teams. Such sentiments were of no comfort to the St. Mirren men. The outgoing Directors' undoubted ambitions for the Club had tarnished the Buddies' sixty-four year reputation. Their actions may have been well-meaning, but they did not reflect the spirit of the Club developed by men like former Club President Mr. James K. Horsburgh. It was to be hoped there would never be a recurrence.

1941-42

St. Mirren's Articles of Association required that there must be a minimum of five Directors. The upheaval caused by the S.F.A. Report meant that the two remaining Directors, Mr. W. Small and Mr. W. W. Waters, had to increase their number without delay. On 10 July, former Chairman and ex-President of the S.F.A., Mr. James Fleming, who was keen to help the Club out of its difficulties, accepted an invitation to return to the Board.

The minimum five Board members was restored when Mr. Dan McKinlay and Mr. Robert (Bobby) Rankin, still a registered player, were co-opted on 31 July. At the same time, Mr. Small was appointed Chairman. It was a return to some kind of normality in the running of the Club.

Mr. Fleming's return as a Director was not intended to be a long one. He resigned on 2 September, but stated that "he would help the Club in any way that was within his power". His place was taken by Mr. Harry West, but his tenure was also to be brief, and he resigned on 23 February to be replaced by Mr. John Lang.

The support staff continued to change. Groundsman Ralph Liddell's services were terminated after less than a year, and Davie McCrae's stint as Trainer was also brought to an end. Former player and trainer Andy Reid replaced both of them on 25 September. Meanwhile, Secretary Donald Menzies was expressing concern about "the onerous and worrying nature of his duties". His February 1941 appointment had certainly coincided with considerable activity both on and off the pitch, which may have been the reason why no-one at the

John Deakin

Club followed-up Sam Blythe's repeated attempts to sign seventeen year old Billy Steel.

On his eighteenth birthday, 1 May 1941, Billy Steel signed professional forms with Morton. At Cappielow he was to win three of his thirty caps, and his £15,000 transfer from Morton to Derby County in 1947 was a British record. That same year his status as one of Scotland's greatest-ever players was confirmed when he was selected and scored for Great Britain against The Rest of Europe at Hampden on 10 May. Many Saints fans followed his career with considerable interest and not a little frustration.

Some emphatic defeats in the early part of the season resulted in three goalkeepers being tried before 4 October. At that point the Board brought in David Stevenson from Hearts on a temporary transfer. He remained first choice until Hearts recalled him on 11 April, but occasional heavy defeats still occurred in a season where one hundred and eight goals were conceded in all competitions.

It would be less than fair to blame any of the custodians. The team simply did not have a settled look at any time, and in one match against Airdrieonians at Broomfield on 10 January Saints fielded a side with four players listed as "Newman". Despite such obvious consequences for teamwork, Saints won 2-1! Nine other games of the thirty League matches were won and seven were drawn.

At right back, David Logan was out of contention by the beginning of October. Selection then rotated between Sam Smith, guest player Holliday of Newcastle United, and latterly Alex Sheir. Joe Craven completed his fifth season at left back.

The half-back line throughout the season was Stenhouse, Kelly or Simpson, and Martin. Jimmy Stenhouse, signed on 11 August from Lochgelly Violet for £15, was the most consistently selected of the four. At centre half, Willie Kelly was superseded in the middle of January by ex-Ranger Jimmy Simpson. Left half Joe Martin, signed from the Junior ranks in early September, held his position for most of the season.

Saints' enforced loss of Everton's Jimmy Caskie was very much Hibs gain, and Caskie's place on the right wing was taken by Dan McGarry, who had been temporarily transferred from Barnsley FC on the last day of July.

Tom Brady was at inside right until Jimmy Drinkwater was signed from Northwich Victoria in November. Drinkwater went straight into the team which drew with Falkirk on 8 November, and remained at inside right for the following six weeks before proving that he was nothing if not versatile. In the second half of the season he featured at right back, centre half, left half, centre forward, and inside left! Meanwhile, Brady went back to inside right.

Alex Linwood was selected at centre whenever he was available and he was again the top scorer with nineteen goals. For the third year in a row his inside left was Angus Stead, until 13 April, when Stead was transferred to Partick Thistle for £350. Meantime, Johnny Deakin was in his usual left wing position, although he moved to inside left on occasion to allow McGarry to switch wings as attempts were made to find a longer-term right winger.

There was considerable evidence that money was tight. On 15 December it was revealed that eighteen months after Tom Brady had been transferred from Aberdeen for £550, the Pittodrie club were still owed £326 13s 9d. Director Mr. Dan McKinlay agreed with the Aberdeen board to pay the outstanding amount back at £25 per month. Mr. McKinlay also solved another problem when he agreed on 5 February to sign a personal cheque for £100 "to bridge the difficulty at the moment". The "difficulty" was that the S.F.A. had warned St. Mirren on 2 January that, if the overdue £100 fine wasn't paid by 2 February, the Club would be suspended.

Directors Small, Waters, and Rankin each advanced £25 to the Club on 18 February, and at the same time an unsuccessful attempt was made to have the S.F.A. fine reduced. On 2 March, the monthly "Brady" payment to Aberdeen only went ahead because Chairman Mr. Small loaned the Club another £25. New Director John Lang also gave the Club an interest-free loan of £25 shortly after his appointment, but such financial difficulties were not exclusive to St. Mirren. Club correspondence of the time reveals that other clubs were in similar difficulties.

The League War Cup, which had been such a financial bonus the previous season, began on 28 February. However, Saints won just six points out of twelve and failed to progress to the semi-finals. The last home match of the season, a Summer Cup tie against Hearts, was as good as any match seen at St. Mirren Park all season. It ended 3-3, but the return was less close as Hearts ran out comfortable 4-1 winners to end Saints interest in the 1942 competition.

The 1943 Summer Cup would be a different story, not least for Willie Kelly. He had been the team's centre half and his usual competitive self until 22 December. Manager Menzies then reported that Kelly "was laid up with diphtheria and not likely to play for ten weeks". His recovery was quicker than anticipated, being named as first reserve for the away game against Celtic on 31 January.

He was listed at left half in the team to play Partick Thistle on 7 February but the game was postponed. Two weeks later there was a suggestion by both the Trainer and Manager that Kelly hadn't been applying himself during training in advance of the game against Falkirk on 28 February. By 9 March, Willie Kelly wrote to the Board asking to be granted a free transfer "through having lost his place in the team". Donald Menzies confirmed to the Board that Kelly had lost his place "through not training properly".

On 11 April a poor Saints team lost 5-1 at home to Morton in the final League Cup sectional tie. By this time Willie Kelly had not played for the first team since 13 December. Morton learned after the 5-1 match that Aird, their regular centre half, was incapacitated through injury, and St. Mirren were asked to temporarily transfer Willie Kelly to the Greenock club. Saints were willing to help Morton, but were looking for some financial recompense for such a loan. If the terms were right they would even contemplate making such a move permanent.

A temporary transfer was arranged, and Willie Kelly joined Morton for what remained of the season. Twelve months later, with any problems between the player and the Club long since resolved, Willie Kelly would prove to be the inspiration behind Saints' run to another Hampden cup final and the capture of the 1943 Summer Cup. After all Saints' war-time problems, the winning of a major trophy would never be more deserved.

1942-43

The season had barely begun when Secretary/Manager Donald Menzies intimated on 31 August his wish to resign, "owing to the fact that he couldn't cope with the work delegated to him". The Board acknowledged Mr. Menzies' heavy work-load and appointed Mr. William Scott to take over the secretarial work. The Club's filing system was also to be re-organised so that the Directors would know "at a glance the entire working of the Club".

Just two weeks later the Manager's position became vacant when Mr. Menzies was "called up". A note of appreciation for his services to St. Mirren FC was recorded, and he was wished "good luck and a safe return". On 12 October, Mr. W.C. (Willie) Fotheringham, Saints' former goalkeeper, emerged from six candidates as the unanimous choice to be appointed Manager, and at the same time Mr. Scott was confirmed as Secretary.

In November, the Board were advised that Mr. Thomas Hart, a former Director and Chairman of the Club and President of the Scottish Football League had died. Chairman Mr. Waters made reference to "the active interest he had taken in the affairs of the Club and football in general". Similar sentiments had been expressed six months earlier when the Directors stood in silence in memory of Mr. George Riddell, another St. Mirren FC stalwart and former Chairman.

The contribution of both men to St. Mirren set a standard for those who followed, but their 1943 successors were operating in difficult times. They were, however, able to confirm that the Club's finances were in better shape than for many years, the Directors considering a profit of £673 for the year ending 30 April 1943 to be "very satisfactory".

Less satisfactory was Saints' playing record. By the time the 1943 Summer Cup competition commenced on 29 May, they had already played thirty-eight competitive matches since the season started on 8 August. An unprecedented number of enforced changes in team selection contributed to a very moderate set of League results, winning only eight and drawing five of the thirty matches played. Three games accounted for twenty one of the seventy-seven goals conceded.

The Summer Cup, although under the auspices of the S.F.A., was still exclusively a Southern League affair, although there had been an unsuccessful attempt in April 1942 by members of the North Eastern League to be included. St. Mirren had opposed the April 1942 move owing to "the difficulties in raising teams to travel such distances", and that was the prevailing view. It was still a competition which included most of Scotland's top teams, and in the first round Saints were drawn against Third Lanark.

In the first leg at St. Mirren Park on 29 May, Saints were represented by Cowan, Drinkwater, Howe, Mooney, Kelly, Colquhoun, Jess, Stenhouse, Linwood, Deakin, and McGarry. The team had been selected solely by Willie Fotheringham, a responsibility he had first been given on 24 May 1943. He included Paisley-born Jimmy Cowan for his seventeenth game of the season; a remarkable achievement for a sixteen year old.

The uncompromising Jimmy Drinkwater had shown his versatility in his first year as a Saint, but in his second season he displayed his expertise in one particular position as he settled in as the Club's undisputed right back. At left back, Joe Craven was given a free transfer at his own request, and Drinkwater's partner was Jack Howe of Derby County, who was to play thirty-four times for Saints but miss out as the Summer Cup run climaxed. Three years later he would be an English F.A. Cup winner with Derby, and thereafter an England internationalist.

Jack Howe
Left Back
(Derby County)

Arthur Housam
Right Half
(Sunderland)

Dan McGarry
Outside Left
(Barnsley)

Until 4 January the regular right half had been Tom Ashe, but in the second half of the season Arthur Housam – a temporary signing from Sunderland AFC – became the regular choice. Housam was unavailable for the first leg against Thirds, and John Mooney, out for so long through injury, took his place. Willie Kelly had covered both wing half positions in the first half of the season, but from January onwards was at the heart of the defence as centre half and captain.

Left half proved to be a problem position in the first half of the season, with no fewer than twelve players used. Twenty-one year old James Colquhoun, a £30 signing from Carluke Rovers, took over in early February, and would be playing against Stanley Matthews five months later!

Right winger Tommy Jess, formerly of Third Lanark, was signed after he had advised the Club in April that he was a free agent. To accommodate the inclusion of Jess, the industrious Jimmy Stenhouse moved to inside right for the last eight games of the season, having played the first seven matches at right half. In between these two spells Jimmy lined up at outside right, and missed only two of Saints' thirty-eight games.

Alex Linwood continued to be first choice centre forward, but was unavailable during September and for much of the January to May period. Despite this he still ended up as the Buddies' top scorer for the fourth year in a row, with thirteen Southern League goals and twenty-eight in all competitions. To Linwood's left, Johnny Deakin missed only three matches and more often than not was at inside left, with Dan McGarry on the left wing.

A minute into the second half of the first match with Third Lanark, the Crosshill club scored direct from a corner to lead 3-1, having missed a first half penalty. Forty-four minutes later a Linwood hat-trick, a penalty from Kelly, and goals from Howe and Deakin gave Saints an amazing 6-3 first leg lead. The same Saints' eleven, their confidence boosted by a three goal advantage, convincingly won 3-1 at Cathkin on 5 June to go through on a 9-4 aggregate.

In the first leg of the second round at Love Street on 12 June, an unchanged Saints team were 5-0 up at half-time against Dumbarton before slackening off in the second half. They eventually won 6-3 for the second time in a row, with Alex Linwood scoring five of the goals.

Arthur Housam returned at right half for the second leg, the only other change being in goal. After the first Third Lanark tie an attempt had been made to re-sign goalkeeper David Stevenson of Hearts, who was again available, but the S. F. A.'s rule that "no temporary transfers are to be allowed in the Summer Cup" precluded this move. Jack Weare, a free agent who had previously served West Ham United, had made his Saints debut on 28 November against Dumbarton, and played right through to 1 January 1943. He was re-engaged for the 1-1 draw against Dumbarton, and would play a significant role in the Summer Cup story.

Willie Fotheringham's first-choice team was beginning to emerge. In the semi-finals Rangers were paired with Hibs, and Saints were drawn to meet Morton. This was a Morton team which had beaten Saints 8-0 on New Year's Day at Cappielow, and had also triumphed in May with a 10-7 aggregate in the Renfrewshire Cup. It was also a Morton team which was benefiting from the Greenock club's important war-time location by gaining access to guest players of the highest calibre. The great Stanley Matthews of Stoke City and fellow English internationalist Tommy Lawton of Everton added ability and glamour to a team which already contained the increasingly influential ex-Saint Billy Steel, and former temporary Saint Leslie McDowall of Manchester City.

The Summer Cup...
Still on display at St Mirren Park

The S. F. A.'s Emergency Committee had recommended that the game be played at Greenock, and not unnaturally Morton concurred, with their spokesman claiming that Cappielow would be "the best drawing venue". Mr. Waters of St. Mirren favoured a ballot for the venue, and stated that "there was still an element of sport in the game as far as his club were concerned". Failing a ballot, the Paisley view was that the match should be played at Hampden one week after the other semi-final. The two clubs reached deadlock, so the S. F. A. called a meeting and decided that the venue would be Ibrox!

Willie Fotheringham was unable to announce his team until just before kick-off on 26 June, but all the predictions were that it would be Weare, Drinkwater, Howe, Housam, Kelly, Colquhoun, Jess, Stenhouse, Linwood, Deakin, and McGarry. Saints' three guest players, Howe (Derby County), Housam (Sunderland), and McGarry (Barnsley), were all excellent players, but Morton's star imports were widely expected to take the Greenock side into the final.

It transpired that neither left back Howe nor inside left Deakin were available, so their places were taken at the last minute by McLatchie and Thomson. Nineteen year old Dick McLatchie had previously been attached to Hibs, but was signed for £10 on 19 March in time to play against Queen's Park Reserves the following day. He had played three times for the first team before the Morton semi-final tie. Alf Thomson had made his Saints' debut at Easter Road on 6 March, and the Morton match was only his third game for the Buddies.

Thomson was an instant hero to the Saints' fans in the 20,000 crowd when, after eighteen minutes, he took advantage of space provided by the Greenock defence to put the white-shirted Saints ahead with an unsavable shot. The maroon-clad Morton were not dominating in the expected fashion, mainly thanks to Kelly and McLatchie's efforts in nullifying the threat of Lawton and Matthews, but goals in the thirty-second and thirty-fourth minutes gave Morton a half-time lead that most commentators had anticipated.

Left half James Colquhoun had done much to assist McLatchie in dealing with the wiles of Matthews in the first half. So successful had the Saints' pair been that shortly into the second half the Stoke City winger moved to inside right in an effort to make a more telling contribution to the game. However, it was Jimmy Stenhouse who caught the eye half-way through the second half when he latched onto a weak pass back to square the match at 2-2.

Two minutes later the opportunist Alf Thomson hit a second goal to give his new Buddies a 3-2 lead! For a while after that Morton's spirits noticeably dipped, but a goal from Lawton seven minutes from the end meant the two sides had to do it all again at Hampden.

The enthralling first game had generated even more interest in the tie, and 40,000 were attracted to the replay. When the team was announced, two-goal Thomson dropped out to make way for the available Deakin, and Jack Howe was preferred at left back to young McLatchie, despite the latter's excellent showing against Matthews. At the last minute Howe was again unavailable, so McLatchie remained in a team which read Weare, Drinkwater, McLatchie, Housam, Kelly, Colquhoun, Jess, Stenhouse, Linwood, Deakin, and McGarry.

Morton went ahead through Tommy Lawton after seven minutes; one of the few times he escaped the attentions of Kelly. His shot from fifteen yards had been well covered by Weare until it was deflected off the leg of McLatchie. For the rest of the half the Buddies few chances were of the high and wide variety.

Saints equalised through an Alex Linwood six-yarder in the fifty-second minute, but parity didn't last long. Two minutes later, Billy Steel restored Morton's lead when he placed the ball in the net as Weare, who had hurt his shoulder in a fall in the preceding sequence of play, lay injured.

Weare returned to action with his shoulder strapped, but after a couple of minutes it was obvious he was no longer fit for the task. An immediate re-shuffle of the side took place with Kelly taking over in goal, Housam moving to centre half, Stenhouse to right half, Jess to inside right, and Weare moving to the right wing.

Two-one down, no goalie, and thirty-one minutes still to play. The prospects for Saints looked bleak. However, in the sixty-eighth minute a cross from Drinkwater was met by Linwood, who flicked his twelve yard header beyond the reach of Morton 'keeper McFeat to make it 2-2.

Nine minutes later Johnny Deakin hit a slow, back-spinning shot which gradually moved across the goalmouth from the left. The ball evaded the Morton 'keeper and, from what had seemed an impossible position, just crept across the line at the far right hand side by the width of the ball.

Against all the odds Saints were ahead, but there were still thirteen minutes to play! Morton pressed for a third goal, and three minutes from time the Cappielow club's Adams seemed to have scored with a well-directed header, until "stand-in" Kelly pulled off a miraculous cat-like save at his low left hand corner to take Saints, instead of the much-fancied Morton, through to the final

It may have been war-time, but Saints' fellow finalists on 10 July were not going to be "Rangers" in name only. The Ibrox side had been fortunate in having most of their key players available during the war years, so Saints were going to have to repeat the heroics of the semi-final against another team of internationalists.

Willie Fotheringham opted for the eleven which had won the replayed semi-final. His confidence in the team was well-founded, as his men in white attacked with determination throughout a first half in which they showed themselves to be at least the equal of Rangers in every facet of the game.

The closely contested nature of the match continued into the first fifteen minutes of the second half, when the defensive qualities of Willie Kelly and his men were given the stiffest of tests. Rangers appeared to have made the breakthrough when Weare was adjudged to have brought down Torry Gillick, but George Young's spot kick went yards wide.

The penalty reprieve didn't change the pattern of the game. Rangers were well on top, but hearteningly the Saints defence remained resolute, with Willie Kelly coolness personified. With fifteen minutes to go, Arthur Housam momentarily relieved the pressure when he broke upfield. Carrying the ball forward, he reached a position on the right side and crossed with power. The ball reached the ever-alert Deakin, who deflected it to Linwood. Saints' top scorer, who had come closest to scoring in the first half with a header, this time hooked the ball into the corner of the net. 1-0 Saints!

Linwood was mobbed by his team-mates, and it was only now that the true number of Buddies in the 46,000 crowd became obvious! With fifteen minutes to go there was still much to do. Corner after corner threatened Saints' lead, but when Weare made a great save from Duncanson with just three minutes to go it began to look as if it was going to be Saints' day.

When the final whistle blew, the pleasure felt by the Saints' fans could not have been imagined by their Ibrox counterparts. The Buddies had been struggling for a number of years, and had been little better in the preceding ten months of the 1942-43 season. The brilliance that the team had shown throughout the Summer Cup campaign had been completely unexpected, and was all the more enjoyable for that.

Every member of a team described as "makeshift" had played to their capabilities, and the cup win was thoroughly deserved. The trophy was presented on the field to St. Mirren's captain Willie Kelly, a leader of men who just did not know when he was beaten. It was probably his finest hour. Jimmy Drinkwater had also been a tower of strength, and in the stylish Alex Linwood Saints possessed someone who could score against any defence. Along the way they had unearthed heroes in Thomson and McLatchie.

The Summer Cup victory of 1943 was not only a reward for Saints' fans who had stuck by the Club through difficult times, but after four long years of war-time deprivation it was a refreshing reminder to the people of Paisley of the better times they hoped to enjoy again.

1943-44

At the beginning of the 1943-44 season, St. Mirren's finances were much improved. The operating profit from the previous season, plus the additional income generated by the successful Summer Cup run, meant that the Club could repay the various loans which the Directors had made in the more difficult financial times which prevailed at the beginning of the War.

Other clubs reported a similar story, as the imposed wages cap kept football's major cost under control. Just before the new season started, another means of restraint was added when the rules regarding players from other football associations playing for Scottish clubs were clarified.

The imported players had added glamour to Scotland's war-time football scene, but under the revised regulations those in the Armed Services could only play for a specific Scottish team if their unit was posted to that club's district. Non-Scottish League footballers who were civilians could, from then on, only play for Scottish clubs if their places of employment were in Scotland.

In Saints' case, only Howe, Housam, and McGarry fulfilled the amended conditions. However, the Club hadn't been over-dependent on guest players, and the Buddies' nucleus of home-grown players suggested that a respectable set of results was a realistic prospect for the season to come.

Just five weeks after the triumph of the Summer Cup at Hampden, St. Mirren returned to the Mount Florida stadium for their opening Scottish Southern League match against Queen's Park. They left with a 3-1 victory, but unfortunately it was not a prelude to a procession of victories. The result against the "Spiders" was one of only nine wins in the season's thirty Southern League fixtures.

The unavailability of players was a recurring war-time problem, but it was to worsen for Saints in the second half of the season. Unsurprisingly, results deteriorated. It was a disappointing situation made all the more frustrating because good judges could see that a team of some potential was patiently being assembled at St. Mirren Park.

Eighteen year old goalkeeper Malcolm Newlands, who had been signed from Carluke Rovers on 30 August for £35, made his debut on 9 October in a home match against Third Lanark. Newlands' displays ensured that he quickly became the first choice 'keeper, but one side-effect of his excellent form was that "J. Cowan" was amongst the eleven names on the list of players who were to be given free transfers on 24 April 1944.

Jimmy Cowan, who had played five times in 1943-44 before Newlands' arrival, was promptly snapped up by Morton. In his first match for the Cappielow club he saved two penalties! He quickly gained prominence as an outstanding goalkeeper, and his abilities were brought to a wider public thanks to his display in the 1948 Scottish Cup Final; a week later he won his first cap.

Eventually, Jimmy Cowan amassed twenty-five appearances for Scotland, and was so highly rated that he continued to be capped even when Morton were relegated. His performance against England in 1949 was the undoubted high point of a marvellous career, the Paisley man playing so well that the Wembley match has been known ever since as "Cowan's Game". Truly, as far as Saints are concerned, he is the one that got away!

Jimmy Cowan

Another player destined to attain legendary status was signed by St. Mirren on 7 August 1943. Seventeen year old right back Willie Telfer joined from Burnbank Athletic for £25, and was selected for the first match of the season against Queen's Park. He immediately established himself as a first team regular.

On 13 September it had been agreed to release left back Jack Howe of Derby County, so when an injury was sustained by Dick McLatchie at the beginning of October it provided an opportunity to field new signing Davie Lindsay, who had joined Saints from Benburb on 2 August. Lindsay's tough-tackling style not only kept him in the team at left back, but soon endeared him to the Saints' support, if not to opposing forwards!

For fifteen matches Sam Cowan was Saints' right half. During the rest of the games, the position was equally shared between George Urquhart, James Colquhoun, Jimmy Stenhouse, and Bobby Scott, a £40 signing from Armadale Thistle who had joined on 13 December. Willie Kelly was a permanent fixture at centre half, with only injury or suspension causing him to be omitted from the team's line up. To his left was either James Colquhoun or Tom McKenna, an unattached left half who had been signed for just £5 on 30 August.

Tommy Jess and Jimmy Stenhouse were the regular right wing pairing, and Alex Linwood managed to appear in three quarters of Saints' matches. He was again the Club's top scorer, with sixteen goals in the League and twenty-two in all competitions. From mid-January, Johnny Deakin was unavailable for selection, his usual replacement being Bobby Kennedy, an inside left who had been signed from Ashfield on 14 February 1944. It was a similar story for outside left Dan McGarry, whose place in the second half of the season was usually taken by James Murdoch, another capture from Carluke Rovers.

Enforced team changes had been the least of Manager Willie Fortheringham's worries earlier in the season. On 13 September he advised the Board that his employers had dispensed with his services. The Club's Directors decided to employ Mr. Fotheringham on a full-time basis, but his extended duties were to include providing assistance to the groundsman! This increased focus on football matters produced at least one result: on 29 November the Manager included in his weekly report to the Board a request that "the players should be permitted to come to the ground on Tuesday next so that they might have a little discussion on the tactics of the game".

Increased tactical awareness or not, the poorer post-New Year form carried forward into the other two competitions. One win and two draws was insufficient to take Saints beyond the League Cup sectional stage, and although Queen's Park were overcome in the first round of the Summer Cup, a 7-2 aggregate defeat at the hands of Motherwell ended Saints' chances of back-to-back wins in the end of season competition.

Compared to 1942-43, the season had proved to be unspectacular, but at the very least St. Mirren were continuing to provide thousands of Paisley people with a diversion from war-time concerns. The Directors however, had one minor concern of their own, involving a possible loss of Club income. On 20 September it was revealed that 25% of the 8,000 crowd at the previous home game had gained admittance via the boys gate. The Board agreed that the figure could be right but there was a strong suspicion that more than just a few of the 2,000 boys might be "hairy-faced"!

1944-45

League and club officials who worked so hard to ensure that senior football in Scotland continued throughout the Second World War deserve the utmost recognition for their efforts, but a review of Saints' 1944-45 season is as good a time as any to emphasise that none of the matches in the six year series of Scottish Southern League matches, and its one-off 1939-40 predecessor, appear in the record books.

Some cynics may argue that for some clubs, in some war-time seasons, it's just as well! Such commentators imply that the off-the-record status of these matches merely obscures some embarrassing defeats. Other observers acknowledge that the unofficial label is appropriate because clubs had no real control over the availability of their players. For St. Mirren, 1944-45 was such a season. Saints won just seven league fixtures and two cup ties out of thirty-eight matches. In addition, the quality of football on view was often disappointingly low.

Right back Jimmy Drinkwater didn't make a single appearance, Johnny Deakin was able to play just twice, and long-term loan star Dan McGarry played only four times. Their places, and those of other regulars, were taken by a succession of first or second season ex-Juniors who simply could not match the calibre of the absentees.

Saints suffered a further reduction in the standard of the team in the second match of the season against Rangers at Ibrox on 19 August, when Willie Kelly was "ordered off the field". The following week his place at centre half was taken by Willie Telfer, and Director Bobby Rankin proposed that Kelly be put on the "open to transfer" list.

Willie Kelly was subsequently transfer listed at £750, but there would be no immediate interest in him. He had been suspended for six months, a period imposed as much for his disciplinary record as for the particular misdemeanor at Ibrox. Kelly's presence would be sorely missed by St. Mirren.

Malcolm Newlands with twenty-one appearances was again the most regular goalkeeper, but James Kirk, a £40 signing from Annbank United on 13 December 1943, was selected on twelve occasions before joining the Forces in mid-November. The keeper's jersey was also worn five times by Allan Blacklaws, who had been signed from St. Anthony's on 4 December 1944, and home-on-leave Gordon Rennie turned out three times.

The two full back positions were held by Willie Telfer and Davie Lindsay, although Willie was moved to centre half for five matches in August and September as a temporary substitute for Kelly. It was perhaps too demanding a role for an eighteen year old in only his second season, but it was one he would soon make his own. Meanwhile, Telfer and Lindsay represented a continuity of selection which was not typical of the season.

Bobby Scott, signed from Armadale Thistle on 13 December 1943, and Sam Cowan shared the right half position, although the promising Jim Taylor of Fulham also played there on eight occasions. Willie Kelly's place at the heart of the team was originally taken by Telfer until the experienced Third Lanark centre half Jimmy Blair was signed on 27 September. Blair played right through to 1 January, until the pivot became William Roy, who had joined Saints from Shettleston Juniors at the end of 1944. Roy played in eleven consecutive matches until 7 April, when Jimmy Blair returned to the position and remained there until the end of the season.

Jimmy Blair hadn't been Saints' first target to fill the void left by Willie Kelly. On 11 September 1944, Albion Rovers FC were approached for the transfer of their centre half, but the Coatbridge club's directors were not willing to sell to Saints. The pivot in question was a twenty-one year old called Jock Stein.

Bargain buy Tom McKenna was not destined to match Stein's status in the game, but he was certainly an effective performer for Saints, and was chosen at left half on twenty-five occasions. James Colquhoun and David Cabrie, signed from Arthurlie on 19 June 1944, were McKenna's most likely substitutes.

Outside right George Hunter, who had been signed on 20 November for £40 from the splendidly named Ayrshire Junior outfit Scottish Stamping and Engineering Athletic FC, played in more than one third of Saints' matches. Tommy Jess was the other right winger most likely to be selected. To their right, the inside right and centre forward positions were rare 1944-45 examples of selection stability, with Jimmy Stenhouse and Alex Linwood each exceeding 25 appearances.

Inside left was regarded by the Manager and the Board as one of the team's weak points throughout the season. Bobby Kennedy and David Cabrie were the players most frequently selected, but plenty of others were tried without much success.

As soon as Dan McGarry became unavailable for the left wing berth after just two games, James Murdoch was reinstated for five matches in the early part of the season. Then various short-term solutions were tried before Andrew "Gunny" Hunter was signed from Kilmarnock Juniors on 11 December 1944. Hunter played nine times, but he lost his place when Feehan, the outside left of Clydebank Juniors', was signed for £40 on 28 February. Feehan went straight into the team, playing in each of the last twelve matches.

Feehan's one dozen appearances included the only Scottish Southern League Cup sectional tie which Saints won, a 3-1 home victory over Dumbarton, in which he scored two goals. He also netted in the 4-2 home leg victory over Hibs in the Summer Cup, but Saints' two goal first leg advantage was submerged in an avalanche of seven Hibernian goals, a poor 9-4 aggregate ending to the season on 2 June.

By that time Director Bobby Rankin was running the team as interim manager for the second time during the season. After sixty-eight years the Club were still evolving the role of Manager! The precise nature of the job had been raised by Manager Willie Fotheringham back on 30 October 1944 when he sought clarification on the division of duties between himself and the Secretary. At the same time the Secretary, on account of additional work, asked for an increase in salary!

Both Manager and Secretary were informed that the Manager, from that date onwards, would be responsible for writing to officials and visiting clubs; the completion of team lines and the referee's report; making application for clothing, petrol, and soup coupons, etc. Any other duties were to be mutually agreed with the Secretary.

Between that October meeting and March 1945, the Manager had not kept well. On 26 March the Chairman suggested that Mr. Fotheringham be given a month's holiday to enable him to regain his health. In anticipation of this proposal being accepted, it was decided that Mr. Rankin would replace him temporarily.

Willie Fotheringham returned to his duties in mid-April, but intimated on the seventeenth his preference that Mr. Rankin should choose the team for his first match since his return. After that all responsibilities returned to normal, but on 14 May 1945 Willie Fotheringham tendered his resignation as "the Directors' policy did not coincide with his own". Mr. Fotheringham's resignation was accepted, and Mr. Rankin again looked after the team in a temporary capacity.

Willie Fotheringham had served the Club well as player, scout, and manager. In the most difficult of circumstances he had brought cup success and joy to Paisley in 1943. Ironically, he departed from St. Mirren Park just seven days after the War in Europe had officially been declared won. The Club would soon begin the task of identifying when Saints' registered players in the Armed Forces would be released. In some cases it would be six months, but after six long years it was at least a sign of a return to normality.

1945-46

At the beginning of June with Director Bobby Rankin continuing as temporary part-time Manager, St. Mirren prepared for one more season of Scottish Southern League football. A large number of applications for the full-time manager's post had been received, but the Directors deferred making an appointment.

The reason for the postponed decision became obvious on 28 August, when Mr. Rankin advised the rest of the Board that he "had obtained his release from the railway company". He was immediately and unanimously appointed Manager of St. Mirren, and at the same time he resigned from the Board.

St. Mirren were getting a man with considerable football knowledge, and one well aware of the strengths and weaknesses of the playing staff he was inheriting. He was also a manager with an unrivalled appreciation of the financial constraints under which football clubs must operate.

On 10 July, Saints lost the services of Dan McGarry when the left winger's request to be released was granted. Still a registered Barnsley FC player, McGarry had been with St. Mirren since 31 July 1941, and

Playing Days... Willie Fotheringham pictured in Saints colours in 1930-31.

for much of that time had formed a highly effective left wing partnership with Johnny Deakin. He would be missed, but an even greater loss would be centre forward Alex Linwood, who a week earlier had been the subject of an uninvited transfer enquiry from Motherwell FC.

Six days after the departure of McGarry, Linwood submitted a written transfer request which was refused. Meanwhile it was revealed that the Club had received an enquiry from Dundee United regarding centre half Willie Kelly. The Tannadice club were informed that the transfer fee would be £450.

Tensions between the player and the Club became evident on Tuesday 7 August, when Kelly turned up for the Club's trial match but refused to play. This action resulted in him being suspended "sine die", although the suspension didn't last. On 21 August, Kelly joined United for the quoted fee. The trial match incident was an unfortunate end to Willie Kelly's eleven year Saints' career, but the episode would not be allowed to detract from countless inspiring performances from a player whose commitment to St. Mirren has seldom been equalled.

The new Manager wasn't having his troubles to seek. By 11 September, Johnny Deakin and Malcolm Newlands both asked to be released. Both applications were rejected, but Saints' enthusiasm to retain the services of Deakin was underlined on 15 October when the Chairman, Mr. J. M. Lang, Director Mr. Waters, and the Manager agreed to travel to Northern Ireland to discuss his future after he was demobilised.

The meeting proved to be fruitful, and a number of issues concerning the soon-to-be married Deakin were eventually sorted out to the satisfaction of both parties – so much so that it was agreed that the Manager and Mrs. Rankin would return to Belfast on 7 November to attend Johnny Deakin's wedding!

On 28 August 1946, Bobby Rankin was appointed Manager of St. Mirren - and simultaneously resigned as a Director. Five years earlier he had been appointed to the Board whilst still a registered St. Mirren player!

Malcolm Newlands' request to leave coincided with the signing of former Hearts 'keeper David Stevenson, who had played for Saints during the War. Manager Rankin would later show that in the absence of Stevenson Allan Blacklaws was the preferred deputy. Newlands was apparently dropping down the pecking order.

To make Newlands' situation worse, Gordon Rennie had still to return from the Forces, and Jack Weare, a hero of the 1943 Summer Cup, made it known in early November that he wished to rejoin Saints. The Club were keen to use Weare, at least until Rennie became available again.

The War may have been over, but access to St. Mirren's full squad of registered players only marginally improved. Despite that, the new Manager did his best to give the team a more settled look, although he wasn't too successful when it came to the goalkeeping position!

Newlands began the season as the man in possession, and played in four of the first five games. Then Stevenson was signed and took over on 8 September in a 1-0 League win over Morton. Stevenson played right through to 3 November when he became unavailable and Blacklaws played for one match.

Weare then took over in goals for two weeks, before Rennie made a brief appearance on 17 November. Newlands then returned and was regularly selected until 4 February 1946, when Rennie confirmed that he had been demobilised. Adjudged to be the Club's best 'keeper, Rennie went straight into the side on 9 February, but he only lasted two weeks! He broke a small bone in his right arm in a match against Hibs on 16 February and the following week Newlands was back!

Malcolm Newlands held his position as first team goalie until the end of the season, although Rennie returned for the Paisley Charity Cup match held on 8 June. On 3 June, Newlands repeated his transfer request. It was again refused.

At right back, the highly rated Willie Telfer began the campaign in the first team, but by mid-October the more experienced Jimmy Blair was preferred. In the second half of the season, as Blair was utilised elsewhere in the team, Sam Smith made a welcome return to action. From 2 January 1946 onwards Smith missed few games as full back partner to Davie Lindsay. Occasionally, Colin McCalman, who had been signed from Arthurlie on 14 September 1944, deputised at full back.

The defence greatly benefited from the presence of centre half Jim Taylor of Fulham FC, who later captained the "Cottagers" and won two England caps. In September he unfortunately had to move back to London and wasn't successfully replaced. The versatile Jimmy Blair also made a number of appearances at left half, but the half back line evolved into a first choice of Bobby Scott, William Roy, and Tom McKenna.

Selection at outside right was less clear-cut. David Cabrie, George Hunter, and Tom McIntosh, a February 1945 signing from Lobnitz Amateurs, each played five times, Jimmy Stenhouse appeared on nine occasions, and Walter Kane, who arrived from St. Anthony's on 29 January 1946 for £75, played twice more than Stenhouse.

From mid-December, onwards Jimmy Stenhouse also made nine appearances at inside right, but W. Stewart, signed on 27 September 1944, came in for ten consecutive matches from the beginning of the season to 20 October, when he was called up to the Forces. In the second half of the season Johnny Telford took over for seven games in a row.

At centre forward Alex Linwood hardly missed a game, and for the seventh successive season was the Club's top scorer. His "business as usual" record belied a difficult period for the much admired goalscorer. At the end of November the Club received enquiries from Leicester City and Middlesbrough regarding his availability for transfer.

On 11 December Linwood was asked to attend the Board meeting "in view of his repeated requests for a transfer". Alex made his statement to the Directors and was then given the Club's point of view. After discussing the situation, the Board advised the player that they had decided to let him go "as soon as they had another player for his position". It was the Board's intention to make such a signing "as quickly as possible". Typically, Linwood scored two of Saints' three goals the following Saturday.

The Board soon realised that finding a replacement for a player of Linwood's prowess would not be easy, and a week after agreeing to transfer him "as quickly as possible" they decided to have another discussion with him "regarding the advantages of remaining in Scotland".

Wolverhampton Wanderers then expressed an interest on 4 February. On the same day a letter was received from Tom McKenna in which he stated that he was "dissatisfied with conditions at Love Street", and wished to be given a free transfer. McKenna had been chosen to travel with the Reserves to Kilmarnock the previous Saturday but had not done so. The left half later apologised for his non-appearance; in turn he was advised that the Board would consider offers for him. On 3 June, Reading FC signed McKenna for £250, a profitable return on a player who had cost just £5 three years previously.

Willie Telfer

Inside left Willie Reid, signed on 21 May 1945 from Dumbarton for £430, was the man in possession until mid-November when he became unavailable. In the second half of the season the most frequently selected player at inside left was Johnny Telford, who turned out on eleven occasions in addition to his run at inside right.

On 5 November the Board concluded that the loss of McGarry meant the team "badly needed to obtain a good outside left". Jackie Gillies was signed from Clyde on 9 November for £530, plus a £20 signing-on fee for the player. This total was £200 less than Clyde had originally quoted, and Gillies played in almost every remaining game of the season. However, his St. Mirren career was not destined to be long-lasting, transferring to Brentford on 8 May 1946 for his purchase cost of £550.

As Alex Linwood was refusing to re-sign for 1946-47, it was decided to circularise all the clubs who had previously shown an interest in signing him. It was also agreed to do nothing meantime about Stenhouse, who had also declined to re-sign. It was an unfortunate situation. Players' careers had been marking time for six years and some, understandably, wanted to move on while they could.

More importantly from St. Mirren's point of view, nine League wins was only a slight improvement on the previous poor season. A recurring theme in the Directors' reports about the Reserves' performances throughout the season had been that, Willie Telfer apart, the majority were incapable of challenging for a regular place in the first team. That was the underlying problem which required to be addressed by Bobby Rankin.

1946-47

One significant name missing from the Saints' team which lined up on 10 August at St. Mirren Park for the first Scottish League fixture for seven years was Alex Linwood, who had been transferred to Middlesbrough for £6000 on 3 June.

Signed on 4 October 1938 for £40, Linwood had been a first team regular and top scorer for seven consecutive years, a record shared with the great Davie McCrae. In all competitions, the ever-alert Alex scored 169 goals for Saints during the seven year War period.

No one, however, should doubt the quality of his goals or his pedigree as a player. After returning to Scotland from Tees-side, Alex won a Scottish League cap and a championship medal with Hibs, and a Scotland cap and a Scottish Cup runners-up medal with Clyde. It's a personal honours list which would surely have been longer had the bulk of Linwood's career not coincided with the War.

Two months after he joined Middlesbrough, the St. Mirren Board gave their ex-player a wedding present of £10. This was followed at the beginning of September by the Saints' Directors donating £20 to Muirkirk Juniors, Linwood's first club. Both gestures reflected the esteem and affection in which Alex Linwood was held in Paisley. The succeeding years never diminished that respect.

Linwood had to be replaced and other positions strengthened. Enquiries were made about several players including right half Bill Shankly of Preston North End. Of these transfer targets, Saints signed centre forward Archie Aikman of Hearts for £650 on 19 July. On the same day another centre forward, Alex Crowe of Polkemmet Juniors, was recruited for what would prove to be a bargain £20. Crowe appeared at outside right, inside right, and inside left for a total of twenty-nine games and scored six League goals. Free agent Reg Gore, formerly of West Ham United, also joined the Club, but made little impact.

For the first match – a 3-1 home defeat by Clyde – Aikman and Gore were added to seven more familiar names in the following line up: Malcolm Newlands, Sam Smith, Davie Lindsay, Bobby Scott, William Roy, Jimmy Drinkwater, Johnny Telford, McLaren, Archie Aikman, Reg Gore, and Johnny Deakin. The other newcomer was inside forward McLaren, who had been signed from Blackpool for £500 at the beginning of July. He would play sixteen times in four different forward positions without being conspicuously successful in any of them, and he was transfer-listed at the end of the season.

Saints' second League game, away to Queen's at Hampden, came just four days after the Clyde defeat. It was also lost, this time by 3-2, but there was some good news immediately after the game, when Jimmy Stenhouse agreed to re-sign on the originally offered terms.

Stenhouse started the season switching between right half and inside right, but he experienced some difficulty in getting away from his work on time and for this reason, on 29 October, he requested to be put on the transfer list. Coincidentally, a Bradford City official contacted St. Mirren a week later regarding Stenhouse, but the "Bantams" terminated their interest when they were informed that the fee would be £6000.

By the time the new Scottish League Cup got underway on 21 September, Saints had played ten Division "A" League fixtures, gaining just two wins and two draws. Archie Aikman, who had got off the mark during the Hampden defeat, seemed to be the ideal replacement for Linwood when he hit all four goals in a 4-1 away win at Hamilton in mid-August. It was not to be. Despite twenty-two appearances, most of them in the first half of the season, he hit only three more League goals and was placed on the transfer list at the end of the season.

On 9 September the Manager enquired about the versatile forward Arthur Milne of Hibs. After negotiations with the Hibernian board about the £2000 price tag, Milne was signed for a fee of £1650 and made his debut against Rangers at Ibrox in a 4-0 League Cup defeat on 14 September. Arthur took over on the right wing, but towards the end of the season was played at centre. He was equally at home there, or indeed on either wing.

Saints' results in the six League Cup section ties were a continuation of their League form. Only three points had been gained, all from Queen's Park. The forwards' play had improved since the arrival of Milne, but two 4-0 defeats from Rangers and a 6-1 hammering at Cappielow confirmed that the team's main deficiency was at the back, particularly at centre half. Several player-swops involving established pivots proved to be unsuccessful.

Davie Lindsay featured on a collectors card of the day.

William Roy had begun the season at centre half, then Jimmy Drinkwater took over for the third match, where he stayed until 19 October when a combination of injuries resulted in J. Henderson taking over. Incredibly, he had been signed on the morning of the match from Yoker Athletic! Morton won 6-1!

After the Morton result, Roy was recalled on 26 October, and played until 23 November when left back Davie Lindsay took over the problem position, with deputy Jimmy Drinkwater lining up beside regular right back Willie Telfer. By this point the search for a centre half had taken St. Mirren representatives up to Inverness, down to London, and to many points in between.

Twelve days before making his centre half debut, Davie Lindsay had been suspended "until further notice" for refusing to train. In what was turning out to be an eventful season for Lindsay, he wrote a letter of apology to the Board a week later. He had already had a transfer request declined on 1 July; on 2 December he advised Manager Bobby Rankin that he didn't like playing at centre half and didn't think he should have been dropped from full back. He also reiterated his desire for a transfer, and expressed a wish to speak directly to the Directors. Such a meeting took place, but the player was informed that it was not for him to make a judgement about his abilities or where he should play in the team! He was also told he would not be transferred.

Johnny Deakin was also not to be transferred. On Christmas Eve Deakin's request to move was refused, but his concern was not directly football-related, as became apparent on 14 January 1947 when he became the second player, along with Drinkwater, to be made an assistant groundsman employed on ground maintenance duties at £4 per week. Deakin would hardly miss a match in 1946-47, most of his appearances being on the left wing. He ended the season as the Club's top scorer with nine League goals.

The New Year began with a second comprehensive defeat at Cappielow, but the 4-0 reverse was followed the next day by a 1-0 home win over Hamilton Accies. On 4 January, Saints pulled off their best result of the season when they were fortunate to defeat Rangers 1-0 at Paisley. After the Rangers result, Bobby Rankin declared himself "quite satisfied with the play of the team although one or two positions still need to be strengthened".

Right half was one of the positions where standards were not good enough, as the season-long efforts to lure Bill Shankly away from Preston indicated, but there were some encouraging signs. Newlands had consolidated his position as No. 1 goalkeeper, and had only lost his place to Rennie for eight consecutive games after he had taken a head knock in a League Cup tie at Ibrox back in September. David Cunningham, a 1946 summer signing from Army football, had done likewise at left half, and would miss only two games after making his first team debut on 5 October in a League Cup tie against Queen's Park.

The Manager's optimism proved to be premature. On 25 January, a Dumbarton side destined to finish second bottom of Division "B" came to Love Street on Scottish Cup business and left with a shock 3-2 victory. Throughout this period and right up to 22 February, Davie Lindsay remained at centre half. However, in Manager Rankin's report for the Board meeting held three days later he mentioned that he was "having trouble with Lindsay". The player was advised by the Directors of the "serious consequences if he continued in his present attitude".

Lindsay was injured for the match at Somerset Park at the end of March and Roy returned. League results had continued to disappoint, and it took until the fifth last match, a 5-1 win over fellow-strugglers Kilmarnock at Rugby Park, to give Saints some breathing space. Three of the Club's five goals that day were scored by Drinkwater, his only League goals of the season.

On 16 April, Lindsay submitted another request to be placed on the transfer list. This time it was not completely turned down, but he was advised "it may be implemented at a time which suited the Club". Roy retained his place at pivot until the last game of the season when an increasingly experienced Willie Telfer again filled the jersey.

The Buddies eventually finished third bottom, just one point ahead of relegated second bottom club Kilmarnock. Nine wins from thirty fixtures was in line with results in the preceding two seasons in the Southern League. There would be a marked improvement in 1947-48.

1947-48

Three St. Mirren players who had been placed on the open to transfer list for a total of £2000 were all reclassified as free transfers by the League Management Committee on 4 June. It was a decision the Club objected to, but one which allowed no appeal.

The ruling was particularly difficult to accept in the case of centre forward Archie Aikman, who had cost the Buddies £650 just twelve months earlier. The Falkirk-born player joined the "Bairns" to become not only one of that club's best-ever centre forwards, but Scotland's leading goal-scorer during the season. St. Mirren made an attempt to change the rules at the 1947 S.F.A. AGM, but to no avail.

The season opened on 9 August with a narrow 1-0 League Cup defeat by Aberdeen at Love Street. Four days later Saints were considered unfortunate to lose 3-2 to Hearts at Tynecastle in the first League fixture. On the same day, for St. Mirren Reserves, the name "Lapsley" appeared at right back for the first time. Davie Lapsley had joined Saints in the summer of 1946 as a centre forward, and made his first team debut on 4 September 1946 against Partick Thistle. During the 1946-47 season he played twice more at centre and once at inside left.

Gerry Burrell, top scorer in all competitions.

At centre forward against Heart's first team on 13 August was debutant Willie Jack, who had been signed on 26 June from Shawfield Juniors for £75. He played in seventeen of the first twenty matches and ended the season as Saints' top League scorer with eleven goals. Arthur Milne was the preferred centre in the second half of the season, scoring six League goals.

After just two matches, qualification for the League Cup knock-out stages began to look unlikely when Saints succumbed in a disastrous 8-1 hammering by Queen of the South on 16 August. Four days later, Johnny Telford, who had made over twenty appearances in various forward positions in the previous season, scored all three of Saints' goals in a 3-1 victory over Morton at Cappielow in the final of the 1947 Renfrewshire Cup. In the same game Davie Lapsley made his right back debut in the first team. It was, as usual, a welcome victory over the Greenock side, but St. Mirren's main objective remained unaltered: the League form must improve.

Two days after the Dumfries debacle, the Manager made two significant captures when he signed Gerry Burrell, outside right of Dundela FC of Belfast, and left winger Alfie Lesz, who had originally been in the Polish Army. Neither played in the third League Cup tie on 23 August – a 3-1 defeat at Motherwell – but both played three days later in Saints' first victory of the season, a 3-0 League win over Aberdeen in Paisley.

Gerry Burrell would play thirty-five consecutive games in his first season, and was the Club's top scorer with seventeen goals in all competitions. Alfie Lesz also became an automatic choice, and was the second top scorer with sixteen goals. In his first nine games, Alfie played at inside left with Arthur Milne on his left, but at the end of October Lesz moved to the left wing, with Johnny Deakin to his right.

By 23 August, Willie Telfer was the Club's recognised right back, however on that day he made the permanent positional change which would not only solve one of Bobby Rankin's biggest problems but would establish Willie as one of Scotland's best centre halfs for the next fourteen years.

Telfer, whose usual half back partners were Wattie Reid and Joe Martin, missed very few games in his first season as pivot. Following the 4-2 home win over Motherwell on 6 December it was announced that Willie had broken his nose during the encounter, "but was expected to be fit for Saturday first". He fulfilled that expectation and many others over the years.

After Telfer's re-assignment, the right back berth belonged to the versatile Jimmy Drinkwater from 23 August until 4 October. Then Sam Smith was moved from left to right back and the vacant left back position was initially taken by Joe Martin.

On 25 October, reluctant pivot Davie Lindsay regained his favourite left back position and held it until May, apart from a seven match interruption around January when Drinkwater took over. Lindsay's impressive displays at left back won him his desired move, subsequently on 24 May 1948 he was transferred to Luton Town for a fee of £7,700.

Saints' return League Cup tie match at Pittodrie on 30 August was lost 2-0, but in the fifth League Cup tie the Buddies gained revenge over Queen of the South in spectacular fashion by winning 7-1. A 3-0 defeat from Motherwell rounded off the League Cup sectional ties. By this time Saints' League record stood at played two, won one.

On 1 September, Deakin and Newlands not for the first time asked to be placed on the transfer list. The Board decided that nothing would be done "unless and until they could be replaced", but they changed their mind about Malcolm Newlands. Goalkeeper James Kirk, signed from Annbank United for £40 on 13 December 1943, was highly regarded, so it was decided to advertise Newlands' availability.

On the other hand two enquiries regarding Deakin were given short shrift. It was then decided to award him the sum of £550 in respect of his ten years with Saints. On hearing of the award the Club's undisputed inside left "expressed his sincere appreciation".

Chairman Mr. W. J. Walker had a mid-September meeting with the players, who told him that they felt the gymnasium was inadequate and efforts should be made to improve it. They also wanted a masseur. The Club agreed and an appointment was made. The Chairman also agreed to the suggestion that a twelfth man should be present as first team reserve and should qualify for first team wages.

The players intimated they were keen to report half-an hour earlier on match days to discuss tactics, and their interest was soon rewarded. In discussions with the Board after the 1-0 home defeat by Queen of the South, Manager Bobby Rankin explained that the half-time team changes had been made at the request of the players, and Mr. Rankin "thought they might play better in their new positions since it was their own request".

One player who was certainly taking up a new position was Jimmy Stenhouse, when it was confirmed that he had been transferred to Aberdeen for £6,000. Stenhouse had joined St. Mirren on 11 August 1941 for just £15, and in the intervening period had not only included some spectacular efforts amongst his thirty eight goals but had shown himself to be an industrious, competitive, and unselfish player for the Club. Nevertheless, the transfer fee seemed to be a good bit of business for a player who had featured in only seven of the first seventeen matches in what was to be a better than average season.

By the time Saints comfortably defeated Shawfield Amateurs 8-0 at Love Street in the first round of the Scottish Cup on 24 January, they had won seven and drawn three of their seventeen League fixtures and were on schedule for the required improvement. Two weeks later, on 7 February 1948, East Stirlingshire were Saints' round two opponents. They arrived in the midst of an excellent season in "C" Division, but the narrow margin 2-0 win for the Buddies owed more to poor play by Saints – particularly in the second half, than to the competence of the "Shire".

In the third round the Club received another home draw, but this time it was Division "A" opposition in the form of a Clyde team enjoying a similar season to Saints. A crowd of over 20,000 anticipated a close encounter, and that's what they got as Saints fell behind in the fourteenth minute but were back on equal terms just two minutes later.

Right on the half-time mark Saints scored a second goal, which took them through to a fourth round away meeting with high-flying Hibernian. Hibs were at the beginning of their greatest-ever period and proved too strong. Two goals from Alex Linwood, by then in the Easter Road ranks, helped Hibs to a 3-1 win.

The remaining thirteen League fixtures saw Saints win on six occasions and draw twice. The resultant points total of thirty-one and a slightly better goal difference than Clyde was sufficient to push St. Mirren into fifth place. It was the Buddies' best finish since 1929-30, and a League position much more in keeping with the aspirations of most Saints' supporters. The next challenge was to maintain that standard.

1948-49

Johnny Deakin's displays for Saints during 1947-48 earned him selection for the Scottish League's match in Dublin on 24 April, and he returned to the Emerald Isle with his Saints' team mates for an end of season tour to Lurgan and Belfast, which the Chairman later claimed had been "a great success, and that the players would probably reap the benefit in the new season".

The Manager agreed with these sentiments, and early season form – three consecutive 2-1 League victories and a 6-1 win over Morton in the 1947-48 Renfrewshire Cup Final – suggested both men were right.

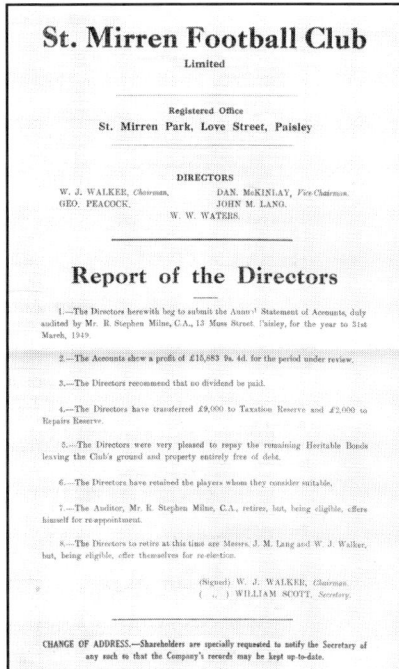

The Annual Report confirms a good financial year for Saints.

In the fourth League match, newly promoted East Fife ended the run of wins, but Saints recovered immediately with a 3-1 home victory over Aberdeen on 31 August. Four days later they produced the same scoreline against Hearts at Tynecastle to begin their League Cup campaign with a confidence drawn from an excellent League record of played six, won five.

This good form was less in evidence in a League Cup section which also included Aberdeen, Morton, and Third Lanark.

The Buddies' two wins, two draws, and two defeats gave them six points, the same total as the other three teams, but Saints' superior goal average was sufficient to take them through to a quarter-final tie with Rangers at Ibrox on 30 October. A first half goal from Rangers ended Paisley participation in the competition.

During November and December, two wins from eight games saw Saints begin to drop out of the Championship race. By 22 January, when the strong-going Stirling Albion from Division "B" were defeated 2-0 in the Scottish Cup, ten wins and three draws had been achieved from the nineteen League matches played.

On 5 February the second round of the Cup took St. Mirren to Dens Park where they fought out a no-scoring draw with Dundee. Three days later an unchanged Saints side lost 2-1, leaving the team to focus on equalling or bettering the previous season's fifth top finish.

Form worsened, but there were frustrating glimpses of what a good team they could be. At the end of February, Saints played well but lost 2-1 at Ibrox in controversial circumstances. The manner of the defeat led the Manager to pen a letter of protest to the S.F.A. regarding the referee's action in allowing the game to continue three minutes after the regulation time had elapsed, a decision which enabled Rangers to clinch the winner right on the final whistle.

Perhaps fired up by a sense of injustice, Saints completely out-played league leaders Dundee the following Saturday and won 6-1. The only other highlight in a disappointing second half of the season was a fine 2-0 home win over third-placed Hibernian. The fans were left with thoughts of what might have been as the team finished ninth in the final table.

Financially the Club had never been in better shape, and accounts showed a profit of £18,883 for the year ending 31 March 1949. It was a happy state of affairs, and it looked like Morton would help it continue. On 22 February the League intimated that Cappielow had been closed for the remainder of the season, and Morton would have to play their home games at Paisley. It was extra income for Saints, as the ground-sharing arrangements permitted all stand and enclosure drawings for Morton's "home" games to be retained by St. Mirren.

The Club also benefited from several profitable transfers, but another hallmark of Bobby Rankin's management style was continuity of selection. Goalkeeper James Kirk's consistently good displays meant he didn't miss a match, apart from a six week period after he broke his finger in the game against Morton on 21 August. Kirk's fine form led to the sale of former first team 'keeper Newlands, who joined Preston North End for £2000. He would later serve Workington with distinction for eight years.

During 1948-49, Davie Lapsley made his breakthrough as St. Mirren's right back. On 14 September his request to be released or transferred was refused, but his action was timely as right half Wattie Reid had been criticised for his performance the previous week in a 3-1 defeat from Aberdeen. On 18 September 1948, Lapsley replaced Reid at right half for a League Cup tie against Morton at Cappielow: the path to legendary status was begun.

Davie remained at right half until 16 October, when he moved to right back in a straight swop with Sam Smith, who had played there for all twelve matches up till then. The popular Sam was set to leave the Club due to his occupation as a cattle auctioneer, which dictated that he moved to Forfar. He later became one of the Angus town's best known characters and a very successful chairman of Forfar Athletic.

After Smith left, Lapsley didn't miss another game at right back all season. His partner at left back was the long serving Joe Martin, who took over the jersey on 23 October from the ubiquitous Jimmy Drinkwater.

"Drinkie" moved to right half, and a typical 1948-49 half-back line became Drinkwater, Telfer, and Willie Reid. Another Reid – Wattie, a £40 signing from Neilston Juniors on 25 June 1947 – had made twenty-three first team appearances in his initial season as a Senior. Wattie was right half at the beginning of the campaign, and played in seven of the first eight games until 18 September, when Lapsley took over for four weeks. For the rest of the season the position belonged to Drinkwater. On 22 February 1949, Wattie was given a free transfer.

After just one season at centre half Willie Telfer had become the linchpin of the whole defence. To his left, the wing half role was shared between Joe Martin and Willie Reid, with Joe Martin in possession from 14 August to 6 November when he switched to left back. Willie Reid was selected thereafter.

Injuries upset a forward line which all season should have read Burrell, Stewart, Milne, Deakin, and Lesz. At outside right Gerry Burrell not only made chances for others with his speedy play, but was again Saints' top scorer with twelve League goals and twenty-one in all competitions. Gerry's inside man was Willie Stewart, who from 31 December 1947 had made just a handful of appearances for the Reserves the previous season. Willie had indirectly replaced the injured Deakin for the first match against Clyde in mid-August, and kept his place for most of the season.

At centre forward was the clever, if not prolific, Arthur Milne. Only illness or injury prevented Milne from being selected during 1948-49, and that made progress difficult for another centre forward, Willie Jack. On 19 October, Jack asked to be put on the transfer list. He had been the Club's top League scorer in 1947-48, but had originally refused to re-sign on 19 April 1948, when he stated that he "did not think he would settle at Love Street and wanted away". His October request was turned down, but he finally got his wish in April 1949 when he was given a free transfer.

The injury sustained by Johnny Deakin in the pre-season trial match kept him out of the team until 26 February. His inside left position was most frequently filled by the stylish Willie Davie, who had been demobilised on 22 September 1947 but had been unable to regain a regular first team place.

A specialist's report on Johnny Deakin at the beginning of September indicated that he required to have a cartilage removed. The operation successfully took place that month, but the surgeon discovered signs of arthritis and was not too hopeful for the future. However, a further report in early October gave a much a more optimistic outlook, which was good news for the player and the Club.

Left winger Alfie Lesz, injured in the same trial match as Deakin, had a less prolonged absence, and he returned on 2 October. Up till then his place had been taken by Johnny Telford, who was then transferred to Third Lanark for £2,500, with the player awarded £500 in lieu of service. The financial security such transfers brought to the Club was a very pleasant change after years of Directors' loans and war-time worries, but no one was losing sight of the fact that for St. Mirren football always came first: it was goalnets and not bank balances which the supporters wanted to see bulging!

1949-50

A season which promised much began with the League Cup sectional ties. In Saints' section not too many problems were anticipated from Aberdeen, and few observers regarded Celtic's team as markedly superior to the Buddies. The biggest obstacle to Saints' progress in the competition was expected to be reigning champions Rangers, and so it proved.

A fine 3-1 home win over the "Dons" on 13 August was followed seven days later by a 1-0 victory over Celtic at St. Mirren Park, watched by a new record crowd of 47,438. This total exceeded by just ten the ground's previous record, established on 7 March 1925 for a fourth round Scottish Cup tie, also against the "Celts".

Unfortunately, sandwiched between these two victories was a 5-1 defeat at Ibrox, a result which emphasised that qualification from this group was not going to be easy. In the return tie Saints played well to draw 1-1 with Rangers, but sadly the other two ties were lost and Saints were out.

The League campaign opened with an encouraging 3-2 win at Pittodrie, Saints' third match against Aberdeen in only six weeks. By the time the "Dons" were beaten 4-0 on their League visit to Love Street on Christmas Eve, Saints had won six and drawn six of their sixteen League fixtures, and indeed had at one point led the League. They were playing a brand of football which few others could match or better, but an inability to convert chances was producing draws instead of merited wins.

Of the six games played between Hogmanay and the first round of the Scottish Cup on 28 January, Saints won two and drew one. This was evidence of a deterioration in form, but Saints' previous supremacy in tussles with Aberdeen provided some confidence for the Buddies when the "Dons" visited Paisley on Scottish Cup business.

This optimism, though justified, was not rewarded and the 2-1 cup defeat was a prelude to seven consecutive League defeats during February and March, before a 1-1 draw at Palmerston in the last game of the season broke the unhappy sequence. It also ended another inexplicable collapse in the second half of a season. This time Saints finished eleventh out of sixteen with a team which had again promised so much more.

Willie Miller, a 1948 close season signing from Irvine Meadow, had replaced James Kirk in goal for the second game on 17 August. Miller had played six times during the previous season when Kirk broke his finger, and was first team 'keeper in all but one match right through to 3 December. Kirk was then reinstated, although Miller later featured in some of the end of season friendlies.

The reliable full back partnership of Davie Lapsley and Joe Martin was much in evidence throughout the season. They missed an early season Renfrewshire Cup final, when Saints fielded a virtual Reserve team, but otherwise were ever-presents right through to 3 January when Martin missed his only other competitive match.

One of Lapsley's only two absences at full back lasted a mere ten minutes! On 25 February in a home match against Partick Thistle, he was selected to fill the problematic centre forward position. Unfortunately after ten minutes play Jimmy Drinkwater was injured and had to go to outside right, Arthur Milne was re-positioned at centre, and Davie reverted to right back. The result of the Drinkwater injury was that "no judgment could be given on Lapsley as a centre forward". Lapsley, signed as a centre, was not tried again, and missed just one more game at right back for the rest of the season!

Drinkwater, Telfer, and Reid remained the first choice half back line, with Willie Telfer missing only two League games due to an injury sustained in February. The versatility of Drinkwater and Reid meant the preferred half-back unit was quite often disturbed, as the two wing halfs were utilised to meet needs elsewhere in the team.

After two seasons of scintillating performances, right winger Gerry Burrell hit a loss of form. On 10 September he lost his place in the team to twenty-three year old Amateur Internationalist Eddie Blyth, who had joined Saints from Babcock & Wilcox on 19 April. After a couple of weeks in the reserves, Burrell had a meeting with the Board on 20 September when he requested a transfer, as he could not see himself regaining his previous form with the Club.

The Directors, for their part, expressed their enthusiasm to retain Gerry's services, and the player eventually agreed that a spell in the reserves was the best way forward, and so it proved. By 22 October he was back in the team, scoring two goals on his return against East Fife. He then missed only one game until 25 March, when injury kept him out for a few weeks.

Willie Stewart filled the inside right berth until 10 September, when Johnny Deakin replaced him against Aberdeen at Pittodrie. A month later Manager Bobby Rankin reported that Deakin was not happy being asked to play at inside right, and Willie Davie had requested a transfer. After some discussion the Board agreed that both players were "essentially inside lefts", and that "as Deakin was thirty years old the Club could afford to let him go if a suitable offer was received".

Directors William Walker, W. W. Waters, and John Lang pictured at the mouth of the tunnel, 1949.

On 24 October it was confirmed that Johnny Deakin, after twelve years of sterling service to Saints, had been transferred to Clyde for £7000, with the player receiving £350. Following Deakin's departure, Willie Stewart and Eddie Blyth shared the inside right position throughout the season.

Arthur Milne continued at centre forward until Alex Crowe took over on 10 September. Crowe retained his place with some excellent performances and a contribution of seven goals until 12 November 1949, when he was carried from the field at Ibrox with a fractured leg. He would not play again until 23 December 1950, and would be sorely missed.

Crowe's injury focused attention on the requirement for a new centre forward and several names were discussed. The following Saturday against Partick Thistle at Firhill that need was underlined when the Club fielded left half Willie Reid at centre. The position appeared to have been filled on a more permanent basis on 23 November, when George Henderson was signed from Dunfermline Athletic for £5000. Three days later, George scored on his debut against Dundee in a 1-1 draw.

Henderson also hit the net in his second match, and by 7 January his goals total had risen to six following a double against Clyde. His efforts were apparently not deemed good enough. On 28 February, Stirling Albion offered £1000 plus their centre forward Jack Jones in exchange for Henderson. The Stirling offer was accepted.

In many ways it was a perplexing deal. Henderson was being allowed to go within three months of being bought, and for £4000 less than he cost. His replacement had been the Annfield club's top scorer as they stormed to promotion the previous season, but he had done nothing exceptional in "A" Division as Albion struggled. Jones, who made his debut for Saints at Dens Park on 4 March, scored just once in Saints' last five league games. Just three weeks after Jones arrived another centre forward was set to depart. The name of Arthur Milne, who had started the season at centre, was included in the 28 March list of seven players who were to be given free transfers.

On the left wing, Willie Davie took over from Johnny Deakin at inside left on 3 September, and only an eight match absence through injury kept him out of the team. During this time his place was taken mainly by young Jackie Neilson, who had been signed from Newtongrange Star for £100 on 18 October. At outside left, Alfie Lesz was again first choice, testimony to his consistency.

The season ended with the news of Trainer Andy Reid's retiral, severing a St. Mirren connection as player and trainer which spanned over forty years. It didn't take someone of Andy's considerable football experience to identify that Saints' lack of firepower was their main problem. The Buddies' total of forty-two goals was the lowest of all but the two relegated clubs. Perhaps more tellingly, Saints' top scorer was right back Davie Lapsley. If the main problem was obvious, the challenge was to rectify it!

Highs, Lows and Hampden...

1950-51

The 1950 League Cup competition got under way on 12 August with a 1-1 draw at Falkirk, but that experience did nothing to prepare Saints for the visit of Hibernian three days later. A Buddies' defence which in later games was to prove itself to be a reasonably efficient unit was simply bemused by the brilliance of Hibs' "famous five" forward line, and it was widely acknowledged that the 6-0 margin in Hibs' favour in no way flattered the Edinburgh side.

CHAPTER NINE
The 1950's

The performance of Hibernian's attack would long be remembered by all who saw it, but the game also provided a footnote for another forward. It was Saints' centre Jack Jones' seventh, and, as it turned out, final match for St. Mirren before being transferred to Kilmarnock. Six other Saints would be tried at centre throughout the season, including George Stewart, signed on 27 October from Dundee for £2250. Stewart's eventual position as the Club's leading scorer with just seven League goals illustrates that none of Jones' successors were a conspicuous success.

The next opponents were an excellent Dundee side, who won 3-1 at Dens. After four sectional ties, Saints had won only three points, all from Falkirk. The fifth tie was at Easter Road, and Hibs again won convincingly by 5-0, further damaging Paisley's early-season optimism. It was the Buddies' misfortune to be in the same section as a Hibs team in a class of their own, and one which would eventually win the League by ten clear points.

The sectional ties ended with a welcome 3-1 home victory over Dundee. The team's shaken confidence was then given a further boost when they defeated Clyde at home and Falkirk at Brockville in the first two League fixtures. Both these teams would be amongst the League's poorest sides, and tougher tests awaited. Before that, however, there was the pleasant interlude of a testimonial match against Sunderland in honour of retired Trainer Andy Reid, who had been succeeded by Jimmy McGarvey.

The third and fourth fixtures were lost, but in the fifth League match the Buddies displayed commendable spirit, winning 4-2 at home versus Aberdeen. These two points were to be the last Saints would collect for the next five matches, during which they scored just one goal, at home to East Fife.

Ex-Polish Airman, Alfie Lesz

Despite these poor performances some players continued to interest other clubs. On 31 October, Chelsea asked St. Mirren to name their price for left winger Alfie Lesz. Chelsea's enquiry wasn't discouraged, and Saints' apparent willingness to part with such an effective performer could in part be explained by the excellent form shown by Jimmy Ritchie, signed from Lanark United during the 1950 close season. The Chelsea approach eventually came to nothing, leaving the two players to share the left wing duties throughout the season.

On the same day Chelsea enquired about Lesz, Manager Rankin concentrated on more urgent business when he stated that "it was essential to sign a centre forward and an inside forward". Days earlier, Stewart from Dundee had been picked up, but in the eyes of Manager Rankin he was essentially an inside man. The real problem was at centre. The capture of Stott of Partick Thistle or the re-signing of Alex Linwood from Clyde were just two of many attempted transfer moves made around this time. The Thistle price for Stott was regarded as too high, whilst Clyde refused to contemplate selling Linwood. These replies were typical of the twin responses Saints would receive throughout 1950-51.

The next victory, over Partick Thistle on 18 November, was another comeback win. It was also equally isolated, the following seven matches producing just two points and four goals. The last two of those four goals came in a 5-2 defeat by Morton at Cappielow on New Year's Day, which sent Saints to second bottom in the League with just ten points to their name.

One of the defeats during this six week period was a 4-0 drubbing from Third Lanark at Cathkin on 2 December. The following Monday, Chairman William Walker spoke of the Club's serious position, and suggested that the poor results owed much to a lack of discipline, particularly in defence. The Manager was asked to speak to the players regarding the need to be more focused.

This Mr. Rankin did, but the defence were in fact doing reasonably well! Fifty-two goals would eventually be conceded, just two more than the previous season, and a better "goals against" figure than seven other teams. Bobby Rankin's usual policy of selection continuity, where possible, was again evident in defence.

Keeper Jimmy Kirk missed just one competitive match, and Davie Lapsley was unchallenged at right back. Willie Cunningham would take over from Joe Martin at left back from 2 January, after which he didn't miss a game. Indeed, such was Cunningham's early impact that he was selected by Northern Ireland to play against Wales in Belfast on 7 March 1951.

Willie Reid was the regular right half until mid December when the determined Jackie Neilson took over. Jackie played in every match thereafter, whilst to his left at centre half was the ever-present Willie Telfer. The half back line was completed by Willie 'Togo' Johnston, signed from Strathclyde Juniors on 19 October 1948 for £100. "Togo" took over at the end of August and played in all matches bar two until the end of the season.

For the second season in succession defensive frailties were not the team's main deficiency. There was an absence of craft up front, and the side desperately needed a proven goalscorer. During November and December a succession of enquiries was made regarding centre and inside forwards, but mostly to no avail. There was one exception: on 21 November the elegant inside forward Jimmy Duncanson was signed from Rangers for £2,500. He went straight into the team!

Coinciding with Duncanson's arrival was the departure of unsettled inside left Willie Davie, who joined Luton Town for a fee of £7,500 on 9 December. Davie made only five first team appearances for Saints during the season due to an earlier re-signing dispute, but in his absence no one had laid a regular claim to the inside left position. Duncanson took over on 2 December and played there for twelve consecutive games until he moved to inside right in mid-February, with the versatile Willie Reid re-assigned to inside left for the last ten fixtures.

As part of the Davie deal with Luton Town, St. Mirren gained outside right Tommy Kiernan. He made his debut on 30 December and played nine times on the wing and once at inside right, having taken over the right wing berth from Eddie Blyth, who was usually preferred to Gerry Burrell. Kiernan wasn't a success, and after the Partick Thistle game on 24 February he was replaced by Peter Rice, who had been signed from Aberdeen for £750 on 9 January. The Club was well covered at outside right. As a result, at the end of the season Kiernan was placed on the transfer list.

The next three games at the beginning of the new year produced a 1-0 home win over Hearts and two successive 1-1 draws. The Scottish Cup then intervened, and Saints' improved form continued with a 1-1 home draw with high-flying Hibernian in front of a crowd which included four prominent members of the government. In the replay at Easter Road, Hibs hit five goals past Saints without reply for the second time in the season, ending Saints' last distraction from the main task of surviving in Division "A".

Three more draws followed that Scottish Cup exit, including a point taken from Ibrox. When Third Lanark were beaten 2-1 at Cathkin on 10 March it gave Saints nineteen points and eight consecutive League games without defeat. It was certainly an improvement, but at a Board meeting on 6 March concern was expressed about the goalkeeping position. These reservations about keeper Kirk, which centred on a number of misunderstandings with Telfer, manifested themselves at the end of the season when the goalie's earlier request to be transfer-listed was granted.

Successive defeats in the remainder of March by Celtic at Parkhead and Hibs at home dragged Saints back into the danger zone. Two home wins – 3-2 over Airdrieonians and 3-0 against Motherwell – meant that with just one fixture to play both Saints and Clyde had twenty-three points, just one ahead of Airdrieonians, Third Lanark, and Morton.

In their last match – against Raith Rovers at Love Street – Saints won by two goals to nil. It was a momentous victory, achieved despite the absence of the suspended Lapsley, and it gave Saints twenty-five points; enough to ensure that it was Clyde who joined the already relegated Falkirk in the drop to Division "B".

The St. Mirren side had only scored thirty-five goals, which made them, along with the bottom of the table "Bairns", the League's lowest scorers. Had it not been for the comparative efficiency of the defence, the Buddies would not, for the second season in a row, have finished in eleventh place. That final placement belied what had been a nail-biting end to the season. No one with St. Mirren affiliations had any wish to repeat the experience!

1951-52

Since the advent of professionalism St. Mirren had always had players who were the object of other clubs' interest. On 29 May 1951, as far as Everton were concerned the targets were Davie Lapsley and Willie Telfer. The Goodison Park club were advised that Telfer was not for sale, but offers in the region of £20,000 would be considered for the then unsigned Lapsley, who looked very unlikely to resolve his contractual differences with the Club.

Everton wished to see Lapsley play before submitting an offer, and this of course could not be achieved until the full back re-signed. There was, however, an early opportunity to bring matters together. As part of the 1951 Festival of Britain, Glasgow Corporation initiated the summertime St. Mungo's Cup, a knock-out tournament for Scotland's Division "A" clubs.

On 14 July in glorious weather a 17,000 crowd watched Saints defeat Partick Thistle 2-1 at St. Mirren Park. Aberdeen, who had eliminated Rangers in the first round, did likewise to Saints at the second stage on 21 July, winning 4-2 at neutral Hampden. It was, however, a defeat

All at sea...
The North Bank looks on as only Dunky McGill seems to be heading in the right direction in this 1952 league clash with Third Lanark.

caused more by defensive blunders than any brilliance on the part of the "Dons".

The same Saints' eleven played in both St. Mungo Cup matches, but apart from Lapsley three other regulars from the previous season were missing. Left back Willie Cunningham's unavailability due to National Service would not be long term, but left winger Jimmy Ritchie's similar situation forced him to miss the whole season. The fourth absentee was transfer-listed keeper Jimmy Kirk, who would join Bury on 14 August for £850.

Kirk was succeeded by the experienced, if injury-prone, John Lynch, who had been given a free transfer by Dundee at the end of the previous season Lynch became the regular goalie, although Len Crabtree, signed from Cumnock Juniors, played thirteen times in two spells. During the season Lynch would be credited with reducing the previous season's repeated confusion between goalkeeper and centre half, but in the opinion of some was said to lack mobility. Regrettably, at the campaign's end he would be given a free transfer for the second time in twelve months.

The League Cup tournament opened with a creditable 2-2 home draw with Dundee, but a 3-2 defeat by Raith at Kirkcaldy meant that a win against Hearts on 18 August was essential if Saints were to be sure of staying in contention for the competition's knock-out stages. The scene, albeit a very wet one, was set for one of the most sensational matches ever seen in Paisley!

Hearts went ahead in the very first minute through Willie Bauld. Two more goals from "the King of Tynecastle" and one from Saints' Alex Crowe took the score to 3-1 in Hearts' favour before Saints' 'keeper Crabtree, playing only his second game for the first team, collided with the great Jimmy Wardhaugh and had to play on the wing. The redoubtable Joe Martin took over in the home goal, whilst his resilient fellow-Saints stormed back with a second goal from Crowe and one from Gerry Burrell to cancel out Bauld's first half hat-trick: 3-3 at half-time!

Bauld took his personal tally to an incredible five with two more strikes in the sixtieth and sixty-fourth minutes, and the score remained at 5-3 for Hearts with just ten minutes to go. It looked all over for Saints, but Crowe struck again to complete his own hat-trick and six minutes later he scored Saints' fifth to level the tie at 5-5! The drama continued to the last minute when Burrell was brought down in the penalty area, but Saints' appeals were turned down by a referee who clearly felt that ten goals in one match was more than sufficient!

The League campaign began on 8 September with a 3-0 defeat at Pittodrie. That same day Irvine Meadow were eliminated from the Scottish Junior Cup, and this enabled Manager Rankin to call up an inside right who had already been signed for £200 by Club Secretary William Scott and Director Mr. Waters on 26 June 1951. That player's name was Tommy Gemmell.

A week later Saints' second League game ended in a 3-0 home win over Raith Rovers, one of the scorers being Davie Lapsley, who, despite all predictions, had re-signed on 20 August and declared himself "happy with the terms". There was no subsequent Everton bid. Davie had missed nine matches, a duration lengthened by the excellence of deputy Jimmy Drinkwater. Lapsley would also endure a frustrating finish to the season when he was replaced by the wonderfully named Armour Ashe, who also covered for Willie Cunningham in the left back position for eight matches at the beginning of the season.

On 20 October, following a suspension incurred by regular right winger Burrell, Saints' reshuffled forward line for the match against East Fife at Methil included young Tommy Gemmell, who made a scoring debut in a 3-1 win. He would go on to play at inside forward in every game excepting the last two; a remarkable run for a newly-signed ex-Junior.

Gemmell joined a team whose inconsistent but reasonably satisfactory form was about to take a worrying dip. On 24 November Saints began the day with twelve points from eleven games, but one point taken from the next five games meant that they slipped below the safe point-per-game ratio. That ratio worsened in four consecutive lost matches between 13 February and 1 March. By then twenty-eight of thirty fixtures had been played, and only twenty one points had been collected.

In the penultimate match – "vital" according to the Club's minutes – Queen of the South were defeated by three goals to one, and a third of Saints' goals was scored by youngster Sammy Wilson, who would also score in the final game. Signed from Renfrew Juniors on 28 August, he played six times at inside right from the beginning of February onwards and scored four important goals.

It was an unrivalled scoring rate. The excellent Eddie Blyth, for example, missed just five matches in the three main competitions, played in every forward position except centre, yet scored only two League goals. In the critical centre forward position, George Stewart made eighteen appearances and was again the Club's top scorer in the League with six goals, just two more than Wilson!

Even less successful was Alex Crowe, who led the line sixteen times, interrupted by a two month period from mid-September to mid-December when he was not selected and unsuccessfully asked to be transfer listed. Crowe's four-goal burst in that memorable League Cup tie against Hearts suggested that he had regained his pre-injury form, but his League total of just two goals continued to disappoint his many admirers.

On 20 February, St. Mirren's determination to avoid relegation was stressed when centre forward Billy Williamson was signed from Rangers for £4000, earning Director Mr. Waters much praise for his part in securing the player's release after lengthy negotiations. Williamson was to play in each of the remaining four League games, twice at centre forward and twice at inside left. He scored only one league goal, against Queen of the South, but it was the acclaimed quality of his play – particularly in combination with Jimmy Duncanson in the last two games against Queen of the South and Celtic – which alone made his signing worthwhile.

The victory over Queens had given Saints the most fragile of lifelines. Some of the other relegation candidates still had up to five games to play, and one of these rivals was Celtic. At 3pm on 15 March 1952, Saints and Celtic both had twenty three points, but the Glasgow club had played only twenty-six games. A huge 37,000 crowd turned up to witness a fixture where the threat of relegation unusually applied to both sides.

St. Mirren triumphed 3-1, reached the twenty-five point mark, then had to wait and hope that none of the other clubs by-passed their points total. It was a long wait. Motherwell, the team which had beaten Saints 3-2 in the first round of the Scottish Cup on 9 February, were Cappielow's last visitors of the season on 12 April. The "Steelmen" won 2-0, and in doing so ensured that Morton remained on twenty-four points and thus were relegated along with the badly adrift Stirling Albion.

Three days after the Celtic encounter a request from Jimmy Drinkwater to be given a free transfer was granted. From his very first season in 1941-42, Jimmy had shown that he was not only a highly effective wing half but also the most versatile player at the Club. During the early part of his tenth season as a Saint he played fifteen times for the first team, but was gradually slipping out of contention. Regular reserve football was not for Jimmy Drinkwater! The Club would later present him with £400 "in lieu of benefit". It was richly deserved.

For a third successive season Saints finished with twenty-five points; for a second year in a row they escaped relegation by one point. Being Scotland's fourteenth best club might have been acceptable to the eighteen teams below St. Mirren, but it certainly wasn't good enough for the Buddies. Remarkably, the improvement would be immediate.

1952-53

By mid-July, the unexpected news that goalkeeper Len Crabtree was due to undergo a cartilage operation meant that the inexperienced James Lornie, a Scottish Junior International cap who came from Aberdeen St. Clements on 1 April, was the Club's only keeper! Andrew Pirrie, himself just nineteen years old and an ex-Schoolboy Internationalist, was signed on 17 July and selected to face Celtic in the opening League Cup tie. Although performing well, an unfortunate mistake by the young 'keeper provided Celtic with the only goal of the game.

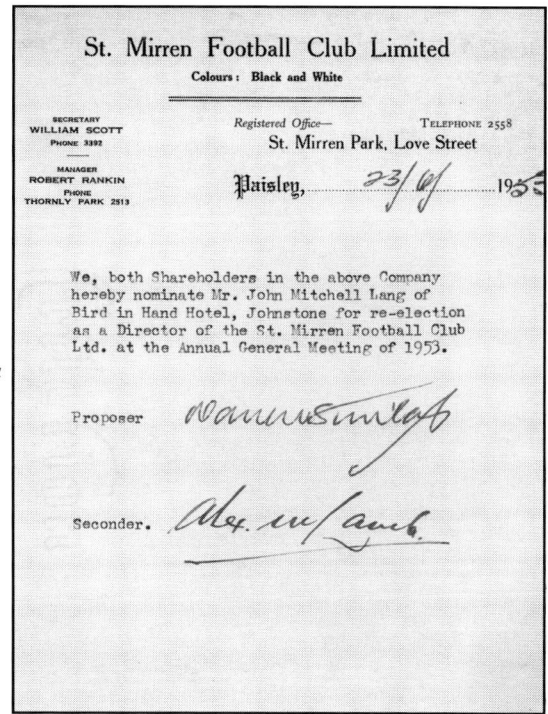

Letter nominating John Lang of the Bird in Hand Hotel, Johnstone for re-election as a Director at the 1953 Annual General Meeting.

Lornie then took over in goals to face two-in-a-row Champions Hibs at Easter Road on 13 August. The resultant 5-2 defeat was conclusive enough in the end, but there was no sense of the complete mis-match of two years earlier. After that the forwards had continued to be held mainly responsible for Saints' poor results, but encouragement was taken from the third tie as Partick Thistle were beaten 5-1 with a goal from Sammy Wilson, two from centre George Stewart, and another double from the small but stylish inside forward Dunky McGill, who had joined Saints from Duntocher Hibs on 2 August 1951 for £200.

A second defeat at the hands of Celtic prompted a reshaped attack and an impressive 3-1 home win over Hibernian on 27 August. Confidence at the Club was sky-high after that, but irrespective of a 2-2 draw with Thistle, insufficient points had been acquired to stay in the competition.

The goalkeeper problem continued as the League Championship got underway. In the first fixture, a 3-2 home defeat by Rangers, Lornie was clearly at fault for the second goal, underlining the urgent need for an experienced goalie. So the Club turned to Queen of the South's Bob Park, who was signed for £400 just in time for the away match against

Hearts on 13 September. He would play in all but two of the remaining matches.

That Tynecastle match, a 2-1 victory for Saints, was the start of a seven game unbeaten run. When they lined up to face Celtic on 1 November they had played eight, won five, and drawn two. The Buddies were second top of the League, and George Stewart typified the improvement. The under-fire centre had scored six League goals, the equivalent of his previous season's total. Perhaps George wasn't aware of it, but his goals and the team's good results were being appreciated by an even larger number than the thousands at Love Street, as permission had been granted in October for the Supporters Association to broadcast home games to local hospitals.

Interestingly, the line-up for the Celtic match was not Manager Bobby Rankin's precise choice. It was normal practice for the Manager to select the team, but the Board reserved the right to over-rule his selection: for the game on 1 November they exercised that right!

Rankin wished to revert to the forward line of Rice, McGill, Stewart, Gemmell, and Blyth, which had been selected in seven consecutive games up to 4 October. The Board preferred that Tommy Anderson be retained at outside left with Eddie Blyth taking over the right wing at the expense of Peter Rice. Both nominees for the outside right spot had often played there since Gerry Burrell's £4,000 transfer to Dundee eleven months earlier. It was a rivalry which continued throughout 1952-53.

In effect, the difference in team selection was a minor matter. The three inside forwards, McGill, Stewart, and Gemmell played together in the vast majority of the games, and, although dissatisfaction with Stewart continued, there was nothing but praise for Gemmell, who had quickly established himself as the team's playmaker. By the end of the season Anderson had played on the left wing twice as often as anyone else. Refreshingly it was a season of front line selection continuity!

The team lost 2-1 against Celtic, but bounced back with two draws and a victory before heading for Easter Road to face Hibs for the third time. A brilliantly executed opening goal by Tommy Gemmell and Telfer's mastery of Hibs' inside forward trio provided the platform for a notable 2-0 victory. Again spirits were high: after thirteen fixtures, Saints were top of the League with eighteen points from a possible twenty-six. The general feeling prior to the Hibs victory was that the football being played was less attractive but obviously more successful than in the previous two seasons. If no one was complaining about that, the belief persisted that too many scoring opportunities were still being scorned.

The display and result against Hibs was the high point of the season. The following week's match against a strong Airdrie side at Broomfield on 6 December was not just the end of a fourteen match unbeaten run, but the season's turning point. Saints lost 3-1, and centre half Willie Telfer was sent off early in the second half for a second bookable offence. Telfer's dismissal was regarded as undeserved, so the Club sent a letter of protest to the S.F.A.

One week later, Saints – including Telfer – drew 1-1 at home against new League leaders East Fife. Despite the Club's appeal, Telfer was then suspended for three weeks, covering four matches. Willie had played in each of the twenty-one competitive games to that point; indeed, it had been three years since the Manager had been faced with the prospect of nominating a substitute centre half.

Regular right half Jackie Neilson, who had taken over from Telfer at Broomfield, was moved to centre half for the away match at Ibrox. The Directors also decided that "a change at centre forward was essential". As a result, Stewart was replaced by former Rangers player Billy Williamson. There was further upheaval to the team's normal formation when left back Willie Cunningham and left half Willie Reid were declared unfit to play.

Rangers defeated the weakened Saints side by 4-0, with their centre forward Simpson scoring all four goals. At the following Monday's Board meeting it was admitted that "a mistake was made in playing Neilson at centre half". Jackie had looked uncomfortable throughout, and his limitations in the air had been particularly exposed.

The Neilson sideways shift meant that none of the half-back line of Neilson, Telfer, and Reid, which for the second season on the trot was the mainstay of the team, was in their normal position. The choice at right half of debutant Neilly Moore, a start-of-the-season signing from Muirkirk Juniors, was a big gamble which didn't come off. Saints were also weaker at left half where Willie "Togo" Johnston lacked the influence of Willie Reid.

Hearts came to Paisley on 27 December and a goal by Billy Williamson saw Saints back to winning ways. It didn't last long, form thereafter became patchy, but as the Scottish Cup approached there was some satisfaction that the team were only two points short of the twenty-five which had been garnered by the end of each of the previous three seasons.

Joe Martin

Brechin City were Saints' first round opponents on 24 January, when the little Angus side took all the plaudits with a brave second half performance and equaliser which secured a 1-1 draw at Love Street. In the replay a Sammy Wilson goal after fourteen minutes was just enough to take the Buddies through to a second round tie at Pittodrie.

Tommy Gemmell was declared unfit for the early February match, as much a boost for Aberdeen as it was a blow to St. Mirren. There was a further setback after thirty-two minutes when Neilson, who had played in every match until then, was carried off with a serious leg injury. By half-time it was 2-0 for Aberdeen, and that's the way it finished. Thankfully, Neilson would return to the team for the last five League matches.

In the seventeen games between the Hibs top-of-the-table clash and the end of the season only twelve points were collected. During this time the team reverted to its form of the previous two seasons; excellent approach play, but scoring opportunities galore squandered. Latterly, the defence – with Lapsley an ever-present, but injury restricting Cunningham to just twelve appearances – began to show the strain of supporting a forward line whose lack of physical presence contributed to its poor strike rate. The team finished in sixth position with thirty points; at one stage much better had been expected.

The course of the season also saw some notable departees. Left winger Alfie Lesz, who had made just fifteen appearances during the previous season, had been transfer listed at £3000 the previous April. Alfie then appealed against the amount in July 1952, but the problem was circumvented when he joined Worcester City, whose non-League status meant that no transfer fee could be collected.

There was no such complication with Joe Martin. On 11 November 1952 it was agreed to give the wholehearted Martin a free transfer. Left half Joe had been with the Club since September 1941, but like many others was unfortunate that the war years meant that he played far fewer games for Saints than he should have. After the War he turned out at left back as often as left half, but wherever he was asked to play he did so without fuss and with dedication.

There were also four free transfers. Able deputy Armour Ashe, single appearance goalkeeper Andrew Pirrie, and veteran forward Jimmy Duncanson were listed, but perhaps the saddest departure of the four was Alex Crowe, whose career had promised so much until injury intervened. His contribution to Saints, not least his four goals against Hearts, ensured he would never be forgotten.

1953-54

Over the close season Manager Bobby Rankin had been incapacitated, but he returned in time to attend the first Board meeting of the new season on 4 August. There it was agreed that "as the Manager has happily recovered from his illness, team selection would now be his responsibility again".

He didn't have an easy start. For the third time in four years, Hibs were one of Saints' sectional rivals in the League Cup. However, this was a less formidable Hibernian than before, and the known capabilities of the other two teams – Falkirk and Queen of the South – permitted thoughts of progression. That possibility continued after the Buddies drew three times and won once, but away defeats by Hibs and the "Doonhamers" saw Saints bid goodbye to League Cup involvement after just three weeks.

Following yet another demonstration of missed chances on 22 August from basically an unchanged team from the previous season, the Directors felt the implications for the term ahead were already obvious: new forwards were urgently needed. Partick Thistle's Stott was again a signing target, and enquiries were also to be made about Motherwell's Aitkenhead.

Before those moves took place, Bobby Rankin acquired former Celtic centre half Jimmy Mallan for a four week trial, as there was an obvious lack of experienced cover for this position. The Manager was then informed that 'Well's Aitkenhead was not for transfer, and that Thistle's price for Stott was £2500. This was considered too high, and an offer of £1500 was made. Partick acknowledged the bid, but stated that meantime, owing to their small staff, they were not transferring Stott.

By this time the League programme was underway. The Club made a good start with a 3-0 win in Aberdeen and a 3-2 home victory over Hamilton. Peter Rice and Dunky McGill were then declared unfit to face Queen of the South for the September clash at St. Mirren Park. Their injuries weren't the reason for Queen's emphatic 4-0 win, described by the Manager as "too bad to be true", but it was the beginning of an unprecedented spate of injuries. It was also the commencement of a results sequence which ensured that, although there was no real prospect of relegation, a repeat top six finish was equally unlikely.

It was a mostly mid-table existence, but the season was not without incident! For the match at Methil against East Fife on 31 October, Saints listed Jimmy Mallan and not Willie Telfer at centre half. Four days later the Club were asked by the League to comment on the accuracy of a press report which claimed that Telfer had been rested from the side in view of his selection for the Scotland versus Wales match, due to be played on 4 November.

The Club replied on 2 December that "the Directors felt that if Telfer were chosen for the Scottish team, it would be strengthening our team at Methil to leave him out and play Mallan. If any further information was required Mr. Waters would supply it verbally". The response wasn't convincing. As a result, the Scottish League advised that the Management Committee considered the explanation "unsatisfactory", and the Club were fined £20 at the end of December.

Willie Telfer, easily Saints' most dominant personality on the pitch, was becoming increasingly prominent off it. 12th December saw the Buddies make the short trip to Parkhead where Celtic won just as convincingly as the 4-0 scoreline suggests. Saints still had a reasonable fourteen points from thirteen fixtures, but two days later an unusually agitated Mr. Rankin stated that he was "ashamed of the exhibition given at Celtic Park by the whole team, with the exception of Park and Gemmell". He was particularly critical of centre forward Stewart and pivot Telfer.

If the centre forward position could not be improved from outside the Club, then he proposed that, for the next match against Aberdeen, Mallan should be played at centre half and Telfer at centre forward. The Directors indicated that, in the main, they shared his feelings about the Celtic Park performance but could not support all his suggestions. They did, however, agree that if Telfer was asked to play centre forward and he was willing, they would have no objection, but if he did not agree he was to be played at centre half.

When Willie was approached about playing at centre he was less than keen, and responded with "not this week at least", so he was in his usual position for the home game against Aberdeen on 19 December and the team lost 4-1. The following week, on Boxing Day at Hamilton, Jimmy Mallan was the pivot and Telfer played at centre. Success! The team won 2-0, both strikes coming from Tommy Gemmell.

Queen of the South had hit form, and as League leaders were attractive New Year's Day visitors to Paisley. Their presence, together with the intriguing sight of Telfer at centre, attracted a crowd of 20,000. Saints won 5-3 and Telfer hit a hat-trick! The next day at Kirkcaldy, Telfer scored again in a 2-1 win, a third successive victory, and the season's best run. Willie's three goals in three matches was proving heady stuff for at least one local football commentator, who suggested that Telfer was just the man to lead Scotland's attack in the World Cup matches!

That wasn't the way Willie saw it. Two days after a struggling performance against Rangers on 9 January, he informed the Board that he didn't like playing centre forward. He had taken ten years to establish himself as a top central defender, and all that effort was "in danger of being thrown away" because "the Club cannot get a centre". He felt it was unfair to him to be asked to play centre forward and stated that he would rather sit in the stand than do so, as his international position was being prejudiced.

The Chairman advised him that the Board thought he was the man to solve the long-standing centre forward problem, but Willie pointed out that if that was the case then the Board must be satisfied with the centre half now playing. If so, he reminded them of their promise to transfer him if he could be replaced! The Board were not to be diverted, and asked him to carry on at centre forward "for a few games yet". He reluctantly agreed.

The next day's newspapers made fascinating reading as Willie went public regarding his feelings. The lack of goals from the forward line was set to continue, but the Telfer experiment had back-fired and was becoming a source of friction between the player and the Club. He played at centre once more, against Hearts, before returning to central defence, with Mallan replacing Willie Cunningham at left back for the remaining thirteen League matches.

In the midst of the Telfer furore, it was reported that Bobby Rankin had been re-admitted to the Royal Alexandra Infirmary on 5 January for further treatment, on the same day Peter Rice was transferred to Raith Rovers for £500.

Time for the Cup, and Saints were drawn to meet Division "B" leaders Motherwell in the first round. The Fir Parkers arrived at St. Mirren Park just a week after winning by an incredible 12-1 against Dundee United. Saints improved on the Tannadice team's performance by ten goals, but still found themselves out of the tournament, with the first of the visitors' goals being scored by Aitkenhead, a previous Saints' transfer target.

Bobby Rankin by this time had returned home from hospital, but was able to follow Saints' progress against Motherwell courtesy of regular fifteen minute phone calls from groundsman Malky McAulay. The Manager's disappointment at the cup exit may have been tempered by the fact that his team had amassed a respectable twenty points from twenty games as they entered the final third of the League programme.

Jimmy Mallen

During this time, Saints accepted a number of invitations to take part in floodlit matches. This followed a successful venture during the previous season when they met Drumcondra, then a top League of Ireland side, in what was reputed to be Dublin's first floodlit football event. In fact, during the course of 1953-54 Saints played Derby County, Falkirk, Hull City, Kilmarnock, Leeds United, Liverpool, Portsmouth, West Ham United, and Rochdale under floodlights. Extra income of £2764 was generated from such matches, as well as providing the players with additional income and invaluable experience.

In the last part of the season the injury situation worsened, and, following a match against Thistle on 24 March, the Club had sixteen players out of action from a playing staff of thirty-six. This made it impossible to field two teams the following Saturday, so a Reserve League Cup tie had to be postponed. Despite the difficulties, the team managed to pick up eight points from the final twenty available to finish two points and five places less than the previous season.

In the middle of the last ten matches, on 25 February came the news that, after a spell of two months illness, Bobby Rankin was gradually getting back to good health and "getting up for short periods each day". However, less than a month later it was announced that he had been re-admitted to the Royal Alexandra Infirmary for further treatment.

Bobby Rankin had been unable to attend a Board meeting since the turn of the year, the loss of his expertise and advice being a bigger blow to the Club than any of the injured players. As an interim measure, it was confirmed on 14 June that left half Willie Reid had agreed to become Coach and Assistant Manager. As far as the Directors were concerned, "there had been no more loyal player than Willie Reid". Bobby Rankin's actions, as usual, spoke louder than words: Willie had been his first signing as Manager back in May 1945. Reid's promotion would no doubt delight his long-time Manager.

1954-55

BOBBY RANKIN

Bobby Rankin died on 25 August 1954. He was only forty-nine years of age. Tributes by Chairman Mr. Dan McKinlay and his fellow Directors were immediately paid to the unwavering loyalty Mr. Rankin had shown towards The St. Mirren Football Club. Throughout Scotland, Bobby Rankin had enjoyed the highest reputation as a skilful player, and later as a manager of considerable integrity, but it was in his native Paisley that he was most appreciated. The Chief Football Correspondent of the Paisley Daily Express captured the essence of the man:

"One of the finest and best of sportsmen - Bobby Rankin - has passed to his rest after a long illness. Bobby, as a football player and manager never fought a harder battle than he did with his last adversary.

"It was my privilege to know this slight and pawky person somewhat better than others, being a visitor made welcome to his office at Love Street, his home at Lochfield and his bedside in the Royal Alexandra Infirmary.

"Never have I seen a man who bore misfortune more cheerfully. He had a heart many times bigger than his body and a spirit to match.

"When his team had done badly, he never, in all the times I knew him, was disturbed. He gathered his thoughts calmly and arranged them accordingly. When the strain was on, as it was so often with St. Mirren, his was the calm figure that remained unruffled.

"So it was in his illness. He was cool in the midst of pain; and while those who saw him in these spasms, which twisted and wracked his frail body, winced and looked away, he would dismiss them as of slight consequence.

"There are many in this town who will miss Bobby's helping hand. Many a pensioner and invalid would never have seen a match at Love Street had it not been for Bobby Rankin.

"He was kind and courteous to the end, and imbued with a cheerfulness that triumphed in the face of death. He played the game fairly until the final whistle."

Bobby would be a hard act to follow, but on 31 August Willie Reid was appointed Manager, and he assured the Board of his "utmost endeavour". Reid's close connections with Bobby Rankin would ensure there was a strong element of continuity in the management of the team, but he had already shown, since his appointment as Assistant Manager in early June, that he had many ideas of his own regarding training and playing methods.

The team had already played four League Cup ties by the time Willie took over. The last two games, at home to Raith and Killie, were both won, but it wasn't enough for Saints to reach the quarter-finals. On a more positive note, the team had scored fifteen goals, and six of these had been executed by the big new centre forward, John McGrory, who had been signed from Celtic on 11 May for £750.

The League programme began in spectacular fashion, with a stunning Tommy Gemmell-inspired 7-2 win over Queen of the South. The result was all the more impressive when it was later learned that, due to the late running of the train to Dumfries, the players had been forced to change in the guard's van!

The triumphant team at Palmerston was to form the basis of Willie Reid's side throughout his first season in charge. Goalkeeper Jim Lornie was still in the Services but was now available for selection. He was preferred to Bob Park, who was given a free transfer at his own request on 23 November.

Davie Lapsley remained at right back, turning defence instantly into attack with his powerful clearances, but his left back partner fluctuated between Jimmy Mallan and Willie Cunningham during the first half of the season. "Togo" Johnston held the position from January onwards.

Johnston had moved to left back from left half. In January, Willie Reid's former position was inherited by twenty-year old Bobby Holmes, signed from Kilsyth Rangers as a centre half on 7 March. Holmes completed a formidable half back line, with Scottish League cap Jackie Neilson and internationalist Willie Telfer to his right.

The forward line, inside right apart, was much more straightforward than usual. Billy McMaster, who joined the Buddies from Blantyre Vics as a centre forward on 3 March 1953, was installed on the right wing, but he had six different partners at inside right, four of whom each made at least six appearances: Neilly Moore, Bobby Holmes, Sammy Wilson, and eighteen year old David Laird, a close season capture from Cambuslang Rangers.

6ft $1^{1}/_{2}$ins, centre forward John McGrory replaced George Stewart, who, like Alfie Lesz before him, had joined English non-League club Worcester City. This time the Board raised the matter of losing out on a transfer fee with the League and the Association, the case eventually being brought before a meeting of the International Association in Switzerland! The problem was resolved on 28 September, when Stewart joined Accrington Stanley from Worcester and Saints received £1000.

McGrory played twenty-one times right through to the Scottish Cup tie on 5 February. The following week he asked to play for the Reserves, and the week after that he broke his right leg. Tommy Anderson then took over for four weeks before Telfer was again brought in as a stop-gap centre for five fixtures to 16 April.

At inside left, Tommy Gemmell missed just one competitive match all season, while to his left was seventeen year old Brian Callan, a player with previous Queen's Park connections who had been signed on 11 May. He missed just one match until 12 March, when the Manager decided to rest the youngster. He remained in the Reserves for the rest of the season.

After the fireworks at Palmerston Park, five points were picked up in the following three games. Then two consecutive 4-0 defeats, from Raith at Stark's Park and champions-to-be Aberdeen in Paisley, took the shine off that excellent start. It became three League defeats in a row when the side lost 1-0 to Falkirk at Brockville on 23 October, but this dip in form was interrupted five days earlier by a Monday night visit to Peel Park in Accrington for one of the season's floodlit friendlies.

Manager Reid was keen to take St. Mirren to a new level. Three days after the Brockville set-back he proposed that the Club "would greatly benefit if he could have fifteen or sixteen players training on a full-time basis". The Board did not quite agree with the new Manager's contention, and the decision was deferred until a modified lighting system was installed, which the Directors believed might offer a flexibility which could be just as effective as full-time training.

Programme for Saints only League Cup Final appearance of their first 125 years. 1955-56 versus Aberdeen

Saints played on, and Willie's side began a five match unbeaten run on 30 October with a 2-1 victory over Rangers at St. Mirren Park, followed by a 1-1 home draw with Celtic. Dundee were then defeated at Dens, before Saints hit seven for the second time in the season as Stirling Albion were hammered 7-1 at Love Street, with Gemmell hitting a hat-trick.

The sequence continued with a 3-2 home win over Partick Thistle, but came to an end with a 2-1 defeat by Hibs at Easter Road on 4 December. Three days earlier, left back Willie Cunningham signed for Leicester City for a fee of £4,750, but it was not the last that Saints' fans would see of the man they always called "Irish".

Following the Hibs result, another undefeated run began with three wins and three draws. This gave the Buddies a very healthy twenty-five points from the eighteen games played, moving them up to third in the League.

Such a lofty position would certainly have pleased Mr. W. W. Small, who had been St. Mirren Chairman in the early years of the Second World War. In early December the Club learned of his death, and there was ready acknowledgement of the valuable service, financial and otherwise, that he had provided at a very critical time in the Club's history. Mr. Small would also have been delighted to learn about plans to erect a covered enclosure to run one hundred and twenty yards on "the side of the ground opposite the stand", the North Bank. The go-ahead for this proposal was eventually given on 9 February 1955.

Results from the last twelve fixtures were a disappointment, and just seven points were won. The previous good work was particularly dented during February and March when only one point was collected from five fixtures. This run included a shock 2-1 defeat at Annfield, one of only two wins secured by bottom club Stirling Albion all season. Playing in the winning Albion team that day was former Saint Dunky McGill, who had moved to Stirling for a fee of £1,500 on 22 September. It wouldn't be long before he was a Saint again!

During the final twelve-match decline, Saints were beaten 2-1 by Hamilton Academical in the fifth and Saints' first round of the Scottish Cup. That February result sparked off what had developed into an annual discussion on the urgent need to obtain an experienced centre forward. Despite this continuing weakness, the team not only finished in sixth place for the second time in three seasons but achieved their best points total since 1938.

Willie Reid's "utmost endeavour" had made an impact. It was an achievement which would not have surprised his much-admired predecessor.

1955-56

During the close season the Club showed they were in accord with those concerned about television's effect on attendances when they opposed a request by the BBC to televise six League matches. As the season progressed, the Board would find that nothing affected attendances more than the quality of football on view.

There wasn't much quality in evidence from Saints as they crashed 3-0 to Dundee in a home League Cup tie on 3 September, but thankfully other results in the competition were better. Two wins over Airdrieonians and three points from Kilmarnock weren't quite enough to take Saints through to the knock-out stage, but they got there courtesy of the slightest of superior goal averages.

The Buddies were more convincing at the next stage, defeating Division "B" Dumbarton 5-1 at Love Street and drawing with the "Sons" in the return leg at Boghead. Motherwell, though, provided much stiffer opposition in the Semi Final at Ibrox on 1 October. A second and late goal from Tommy Gemmell took the tie to extra time. Gemmell then grabbed a third, but the Fir Parkers got their own late equaliser to take the Semi to a replay at Celtic Park seven days later.

The Parkhead game became "Rodger's Replay", as right winger Jim, freed by Rangers at the end of the previous season, hit outstanding form, notably in the first half. Goals from Davie Laird, who played a big part in Rodger's performance, and Jackie Brown, who had been signed from Queen of the South in late September for £1700, took the Buddies through to their first League Cup Final.

22 October 1955 was a proud day for the Club. Prior to the big match, the official party lunched at the Brabloch Hotel. If the team were successful, it was planned to return there "for a victory dinner via the main streets of the town", although few outside of Paisley considered it likely. Opponents Aberdeen were the Champions, and playing well. Indeed, they had comfortably beaten Saints, without an indisposed Gemmell, by 3-0 in a League encounter at St. Mirren Park just seven days before the final.

That Aberdeen match was Saints' third League fixture, having drawn the other two. Paisley form was undeniably indifferent, but there was a recognition that, at their best, Saints could match the Dons from goalkeeper to left half. No such claim could be made when the respective forward lines were compared: Saints problem of having a pretty but punchless attack force had been with them since 1947!

The North Bank awaits its cover... St Mirren Park circa 1955.

Willie Reid selected Lornie, Lapsley, Mallan, Neilson, Telfer, Holmes, Rodger, Laird, Brown, Gemmell, and Callan. These eleven St. Mirren players, as if stung by the widespread "no chance" predictions, came straight out of the blocks and took Aberdeen by surprise. Paisley's team were winning every ball, each of the ten outfield players tackling, chasing, and intercepting all over the pitch. For the first thirty minutes Aberdeen weren't in it!

By half-time Saints were well ahead on points, but then an anticipated aspect of the game emerged. For all Saints' efforts, they weren't getting beyond the well-organised Dons defence to put pressure on Fred Martin in the Aberdeen goal. Much of Saints' physical presence in the forward line was expected to be provided by young Davie Laird at inside right, but he had been injured during the first forty-five minutes. The other inside man, Tommy Gemmell, had been suffering from a cold, which gradually reduced his effectiveness.

Although there were no goals it had been a great first half, and those who had chosen not to join the 44,106 assembled at Hampden had made the wrong decision. Of the two sets of supporters, it was the far larger Paisley contingent who had most to look forward to as the second half began. Two minutes later Aberdeen took the lead.

A loose ball was chased and caught by Dons' left winger Jackie Hather. His cross was out of reach for Saints' goalie Jim Lornie, and appeared to be heading for the opposite corner flag. Just as the ball was crossing the goalmouth it seemed to swerve, and struck Jimmy Mallan. The Saints' left back was standing just five yards from goal, and the ball rolled slowly into the net. It was an own goal; it was also a complete fluke!

Despite the goal, the pattern of the game remained the same as the Buddies went all out for an equaliser. It was all St. Mirren. By then, Aberdeen's back division had lost their earlier composure and were beginning to give away fouls, which proved their undoing. In the fifty-seventh minute a Jackie Neilson free kick found Bobby Holmes, whose great diving header from the midst of a crowded defence looked a great goal all the way.

Completely against the run of play, a swerving cross from Hather is missed by 'keeper Lornie, before hitting the unfortunate Mallan (extreme left) for a forty-seventh minute own goal in the League Cup Final.

Bobby's dazzler lit up the game. It was the least Saints deserved. They were by then effectively playing with ten men, as Laird's worsened condition saw him only able to limp along on the right wing, but there was no discernible drop in their efforts. With eleven minutes to go and the game finely balanced, disaster again struck the Buddies. From twenty-five yards out, a seemingly innocuous left foot shot from Aberdeen's international right winger Graham Leggat suddenly posed a real danger to 'keeper Lornie, whose positioning meant he could only paw the air as it floated over his head and dropped behind him into the net.

Saints supporters could hardly believe it. At no time had St. Mirren been second best to Aberdeen, and Holmes' header was a goal fit to win any final, yet two harmless crosses, two preventable goals, meant they had lost a game they should have won.

In the practice of the day, the Saints players lined up to applaud the "Dons" from the field, but there was no doubting the disappointment felt by everyone at the Club. Reassuringly, there appeared to be no lasting adverse effects. Within seven days a first League victory was achieved with a 3-1 home win over Hearts, the fourth of thirty-four games in a Division "A" extended to eighteen teams.

The playing squad was augmented in an unusual way when Stirling Albion admitted that their financial position precluded them from paying the balance of the transfer fee for former Saint Dunky McGill. The Annfield club suggested transferring McGill back to Saints; the St. Mirren board accepted the proposal and McGill returned in October. A month later, left winger Ally MacLeod of Third Lanark, a long-time transfer target, was bought for £4000 and went straight into the team against Partick Thistle on 5 November at Firhill. The unorthodox Ally produced no fireworks as the team lost 2-0. It would be March before he displayed his Thirds' form in a Saints shirt.

In another team development at the end of November, 'keeper Jim Lornie asked to be played in the Reserves. His first team place against Falkirk was taken by Campbell Forsyth, signed from Shettleston Juniors in mid-April. Forsyth would win a more permanent place in the team by the end of the season.

A run of ten games by £1700 purchase Jackie Brown found him wanting as a Division "A" centre forward, so Bobby Holmes was switched to centre from left half, where "Togo" Johnston took over. The experiment of playing Holmes at centre worked initially. He had strength, a necessary burst of speed, and was a clever ball player, but right from the start many felt a highly effective wing half had been sacrificed in the process.

Those reservations grew as Holmes began to show his limitations as leader of the attack. The question of getting an experienced centre forward had been aired yet again at the beginning of the season, but the dilemma remained the same: securing the signature of such a player cost much more money than the Club had.

A convincing 3-0 home win over fellow strugglers Clyde on 28 January completed the first half of the fixture list: Saints had accrued seventeen points from the seventeen games. The Clyde result, together with a 6-0 Scottish Cup fifth round win over Division "B" side Third Lanark the following Saturday, were expected to be confidence builders. Unfortunately, the next game was a visit to Pittodrie, where Aberdeen showed their superiority with a 4-1 win.

There was still confidence amongst the Saints' support as over 5,000 Buddies formed part of the 20,620 crowd at Airdrie for the next round of the Cup. They saw a thrilling 4-4 draw which neither side deserved to lose, but in the replay the "Waysiders" proved worthy winners, posting a 3-1 victory.

The second half of the League programme saw only ten points gathered. St. Mirren entered March with nineteen points from twenty one games. It was to prove to be the worst month of the season. Without the injured Gemmell and Holmes, Saints were beaten 3-1 at home by fellow strugglers Partick Thistle. For the first time all season the will to win seemed absent. A 4-1 defeat by Queen of the South the following week was more of the same. There was an obvious lack of fighting spirit, and calls grew louder for major team changes. Additionally, without Holmes and Gemmell the side appeared to have no guile. Saints dropped to fourth bottom.

By the time they lost 4-1 at Ibrox on 21 March, real concern was being expressed about the defence. After years of carrying the team, the back division were showing signs of wilting under pressure, ascribed to the fact that they were all nearer thirty than twenty. The team continued to struggle, and the 2-0 defeat by Celtic seven days later was widely regarded as the worst display of the season. By then the team seemed to have lost all self-confidence, and looked to be depending on the results of others for their salvation.

Some fighting spirit returned as Falkirk were beaten on the last day of the month, the first win in five matches, but the struggle wasn't over. On 18 April, for the second season in a row the Buddies lost 2-1 at Annfield against doomed Stirling Albion. In a lethargic display they had thrown away the two easiest points in the whole League programme after being one up after just two minutes! Four days later, and in the knowledge that Clyde were almost certainly relegated with Stirling, Saints showed excellent form to defeat Dundee 3-1 at St. Mirren Park. They were safe!

Twenty-seven points and fourth bottom! What was so nearly the story of a League Cup triumph became a season of poor displays, reflected results, and supporters so disgruntled that crowds went as low as 5,000. Five times that number had been at Hampden. By the end of March, 100,000 less people had watched Saints' home matches compared to the same point in the previous year. It was a drop of 23%, and a trend which had to be reversed.

1956-57

In the Paisley Charity Cup match against Leicester City on 12 May, two former internationalists lined up in Saints' colours for the first time. Twenty-seven year old inside forward Wilson Humphries had been freed by Motherwell, and was signed immediately by Manager Willie Reid; thirty-four year old centre forward Bobby Flavell, a Kilmarnock "free", signed on 28 June. Both would play over twenty times in the coming season.

Heading in the other direction was left winger Ally MacLeod, transferred to Blackburn Rovers for £6,000 at the end of June. By that time left back Jimmy Mallan had also gone, being the best known of the thirteen players "freed" at the end of 1955-56. Two centre forwards were also released. John McGrory had failed to recapture his pre-injury form, whilst Jackie Brown's purchase had been an unsuccessful gamble.

Bobby Holmes

In July the Club declared a loss of £5729, compared to the previous year's profit of £5456. The deficit was mainly due to a drop in attendances, although the profitable MacLeod fee would claw back the amount of the loss. "Gates" were falling everywhere as leisure-time patterns changed due to the introduction of the "five-day week". Specific to St. Mirren, fewer people lived within walking distance of Love Street as outlying areas were developed, so increased travel costs had become a consideration.

League Cup ties with Queen of the South, Kilmarnock, and Dunfermline were the season's opening attractions. Three draws and two wins was a decent start from the first five ties. In the fifth match at Rugby Park, Willie Telfer played at centre forward following evidence from earlier games that Flavell was no longer mobile enough to play in that position. In the final sectional match Saints seemed content to coast towards qualification with a 0-0 scoreline, but opponents Dunfermline required more. Within thirty seconds of the eightieth minute they got it by scoring twice, and the too-casual Saints were out.

The opening League fixture, at home to Aberdeen in front of 15,000, was lost 2-0, but the Buddies battled well. Similar spirit was shown in the second match, a draw at Tynecastle against a Hearts team superior to the "Dons". The signs were good, and they continued in an extraordinary match at Brockville on 29 September when Saints came from behind three times: 3-2 down at half-time, Humphries scored his first goal for the Club, before inside right Flavell, whose flicks throughout the game had been a joy to watch, put the Buddies 4-3 ahead with a superb eighteen-yarder. Dunky McGill extended the lead, but Falkirk didn't give up either, and got a fourth with minutes to go.

A 2-1 home defeat by Rangers at the beginning of October was a set-back, then Queen's Park won 5-0 at Hampden, a margin that didn't flatter the Amateurs. Recriminations followed, and claims were made that certain players seemed to be selected on reputation only. Gemmell, Neilson, and Holmes were the off-form players most people had in mind.

One week later, Saints hammered Queen of the South 7-1 in Paisley after a 1-1 half-time scoreline! Winger Willie Devine, signed from Whitletts Victoria and destined to cover the right wing berth vacated by RAF airman Jim Rodger, was in sparkling form, but the result owed more to Doonhamers' defensive lapses than Buddies' brilliance.

That Hampden horror show apart, the side could not be faulted for effort, and this continued in a 3-3 home draw against a competitive Raith Rovers on 27 October. Unfortunately, right half Neilson was badly injured in this match and would be out for the rest of the season. His replacement, until the arrival of Archie Buchanan from Hibs at the end of February, was inside forward Sammy Wilson, who had just completed his National Service.

A faultless display by 'keeper Campbell Forsyth went a long way to securing two points against Dunfermline at East End Park on 3 November, followed by a 2-1 victory over bottom club Ayr United which took Saints to the season's culmination of fourth from top. Perversely, the Somerset Park performance underlined the side's weaknesses. Throughout the first half Saints were under pressure and indebted to Willie Telfer. Telfer apart, the half-back line still wasn't functioning properly. Industry alone would not be enough to keep Saints in the League's top six.

Between 17 November and 22 December, just one point was taken from six League matches. Talk of bad luck abounded, but the New Year began with Saints being completely outplayed at Kilmarnock, where Forsyth somehow kept the defeat to 3-0. The next day Saints produced a totally disjointed performance against Hearts and lost 2-0 at home. A trio of defeats in five days was completed at Pittodrie, when the Buddies were given a lesson in chance-taking and lost 4-0.

Then followed a 0-0 draw against Falkirk which was poor fare for the fans. Enough was enough, so another attempt was made to fill the troublesome centre forward position when 5ft 5ins Peter McKay was signed from Burnley FC on 24 January for £3000. Thirty year old McKay certainly had pedigree. He had been the English Division One club's top scorer in the previous season and had also hit a record 185 goals in 158 appearances for Dundee United in Division "B". Two days later McKay would score two debut goals in a flattering 4-1 home win over Queen's Park, but in another eleven League games he would add only three more goals to his total.

Willie Telfer was dropped against Queen's and promptly submitted a transfer request, which was accepted the following week. There had been some criticism of his play in a narrow 1-0 defeat by Rangers at Ibrox the previous week, but up to this point Telfer had only missed three games, including short spells at right back and centre forward. He would quickly be recalled in that latter position when McKay couldn't play in the Cup.

Left winger Willie "Cowboy" McCulloch, who joined Saints from Airdrieonians in mid-January for £2000, would stay in the team until 8 April, but with just one League goal he failed to live up to his reputation as a "strong shooting" winger. Willie did, however, make an early Cup contribution to Saints when his corner was powerfully headed in by Holmes to give Saints a rather fortunate 1-1 home draw against an injury-hit Partick Thistle on the second day of February.

John "Cockles" Wilson

For the Firhill replay, Willie Reid included John "Cockles" Wilson at left back. Wilson's reserve team switch from centre forward to left back had allowed his strength and ability to flourish. In the 2-2 draw he proved to be a real find and would be Lapsley's full back partner for the rest of the season. The other notable contributor to a much improved performance was Bobby Holmes, back to his outstanding best.

A third tie beckoned, but before that Saints lost a League game 2-0 at Palmerston Park to a poor Queen's team. St. Mirren didn't have one shot on goal in the game, the players giving every impression that they were saving themselves for the second Cup replay. The Dumfries defeat sent Saints to fourth bottom, only three points ahead of the last two teams. In the second replay the match was tied at 1-1 after ninety minutes, but a tremendous Lapsley free kick in extra time turned the game in Saints' favour and it ended in an emphatic 5-1 win.

In the next round, 20,865 assembled at St. Mirren Park on 16 February to watch Saints and Dunfermline Athletic battle for a place in the last eight. The breakthrough came in the fifty-ninth minute, thanks again to a typically powerful Davie Lapsley free kick. It was just enough to separate two well-matched sides.

The low point of the season came at Stark's Park on 23 February when Raith Rovers won 7-0. Raith, with a team which had finished in mid-table the previous year, were second top of the League by the end of that match, while third bottom Saints were just two points ahead of the second bottom club. Rovers' improvement was attributed to their decision to go full-time, but whatever the reason the part-time Saints had been cut to ribbons.

In the quarter final away to Celtic, Saints produced a strange, listless performance, and were lucky to be only two down at half-time. They got a goal back through Holmes in the second half, but never looked like winning. It was a disappointing end to a good cup run.

On a brighter note, Willie Reid re-introduced seventeen year old Tommy Bryceland at inside left in place of the indisposed Holmes for the match against Motherwell at the end of March. Bryceland had been a much sought-after inside forward with Gourock Juniors when he signed for Saints on 19 March 1956. He was an instant hit, and nine days later played against Celtic at Love Street. He had since made two League Cup appearances in August and the game against the Steelmen was intended to provide some further experience. He scored twice as Saints' 4-0 triumph gave them seven points out of eight in an inconsistent series of displays since the Scottish Cup exit. Bryceland stayed in the team for the remainder of the season.

The fourth last League fixture, a 4-2 home victory over Hibs on 13 April, ensured that there would be no relegation for St. Mirren. Four days later at Celtic Park, with Willie Telfer celebrating his 500th league and cup appearance, Saints defeated Celtic 3-2, with young Bryceland grabbing the first goal. After that, the season petered out.

Despite the acquisition of some well-known names, the season-on-season improvement was a marginal three points and three places to seventh bottom and thirty points. Tommy Bryceland and "Cockles" Wilson had, on the other hand, been discoveries of note; finding more young players of that calibre had to be the target.

1957-58

On the eve of the new season, an unfortunate dispute between Tommy Gemmell and the Club over a benefit payment meant that Saints' best forward for the previous five years was refusing to re-sign. Happily, the problem was resolved at the end of July, when £1500 was received from Wrexham FC for the transfer of half back Willie Dallas.

Dallas, a £500 signing from Luton Town twelve months earlier, had played twenty-eight times for Saints, and at one time was envisaged as Willie Telfer's eventual replacement. Also departing after just one season was Wilson Humphries, who joined Division Two Dundee United on a free transfer. Sammy Wilson, six years a Saint, was also given a "free", but was quickly snapped up by Celtic.

The season started with a confidence-sapping 6-0 League Cup defeat at Ibrox, but two 1-0 home wins within seven days, over Raith and Thistle, restored spirits. Rangers then came to Paisley, won 4-0, and clinched qualification with two rounds of matches still to play. In the last of the ties, a 2-0 victory at Firhill, Tommy Bryceland was injured. He was not expected to be indisposed for long.

League fixtures began at Motherwell, where two McKay goals after twenty-five minutes should have set Saints up for a comprehensive win, but from 2-2 onwards the team seemed resigned to the 4-2 defeat which befell them. Within seven days, only the brilliance of Falkirk 'keeper Bert Slater kept the score to 2-1 for the Buddies, as the same eleven Saints demonstrated improved team-work in this second fixture. Another roller-coaster season had begun!

Team-work, in defence at least, was noticeably absent on 21 September as 'keeper Forsyth and pivot Telfer's converged off-day gifted Killie a 4-2 victory. Two days later, it was discovered that Bryceland's continuing discomfort was due to a broken leg, which was only detected after a second x-ray!

Tommy Gemmell

A visit to Stark's Park on 5 October surprisingly produced another off-day from Willie Telfer. Although only one goal was conceded to Raith, thanks to 'keeper Jim Lornie, the match raised the question of the lack of cover for Telfer's position. It was a quandary which would soon need to be addressed.

One week later, direct comparison was made between the two pivots on show at St. Mirren Park. For Rangers, ex-Queen's Parker John Valentine was nervously struggling to fill the void left by George Young; Telfer was said by one commentator to be "streets ahead". This time a makeshift Saints' team matched Rangers for effort, with the link play between Gemmell and Neilson being an effective feature of the side's play, but Saints still lost 3-1.

The Buddies' defence was stretched to breaking point at Firhill on 19 October, when only poor finishing by Thistle capped their 3-2 win. Meanwhile, seven miles to the south of Maryhill, the same ninety minutes saw Celtic annihilate Rangers 7-1 in the League Cup Final. Someone always gets the blame when a match is won by such a wide margin; on this occasion it was Rangers' centre half Valentine, whose place the following week was taken, in the interim, by Willie Moles.

Saints, by then, were in the midst of a five-match losing run. Clyde, with a late Archie Robertson header, beat the Buddies 2-1 at Shawfield to send them to joint bottom with just four points from eight games. This desperate situation was compounded when a ten-man Hibs team left Love Street on 2 November with two points from a 3-2 win. Hibs had a new young centre called Joe Baker, and he scored a hat-trick. "Where could we get a centre like that?", was the question Saints supporters were asking as they left the ground. Unless they followed the fortunes of Chelsea FC's reserve side, they were not to know that Joe Baker had a brother called Gerry.

The rot finally stopped when fellow strugglers Airdrieonians were soundly beaten 5-0 on 9 November. It was the first victory of a six-match unbeaten run. Willie McCulloch, who had promised a lot but had failed to deliver since his signing ten months earlier, showed his Airdrie form against his old team when his crosses provided Peter McKay with four of the five goals.

Saints' other goal was scored by Willie Telfer. It was his last goal, and game, for St. Mirren. On the following Thursday he was transferred to Rangers. "Willie Telfer of St. Mirren" was no more, and a section of the Saints' support were less than happy about that fact. "Big Wull" had been Saints' centre half since 23 August 1947, and in that time had seldom missed a game. His popularity with Saints supporters was undisputed, but the more objective Buddies pointed out that he had asked for a transfer on three occasions during his Saints' career, and no one had forced him to accept the Rangers offer! Life would go on for St. Mirren.

Saints' first match following Willie's transfer was a visit to Celtic Park, and the experienced Buchanan took over at centre half. This was a Celtic team and support still buoyed by the League Cup massacre of Rangers. Against all the odds, St. Mirren played with a team spirit which often surfaces only at such times. The whole side were constructive, pacy, and skilful. The forwards bombarded the Celtic goal and were ably supported by an excellent half-back line. The Buddies scored twice to earn a draw; it could have been more.

Two points were gained on St. Andrew's Day with a 3-1 away win over Third Lanark, and seven days later Saints were impressive 3-0 winners when East Fife's defence cracked under constant pressure. Bottom of the League Queen's Park were then beaten 3-1, to move Saints to ninth top after fifteen games with a team which had been unchanged for five games in a row: Forsyth, Lapsley, Wilson, Neilson, Buchanan, Johnston, Devine, Gemmell, McKay, McGill, and McCulloch.

Flu victim John Higgins should have been at right back amongst these familiar names from the previous term. Picked up on a free transfer from Hibs during the summer, Higgins had been in the team since August. Davie Lapsley's appearance against Queen's was only his third of the season, and all three displays seemed to suggest that his long run in the team was coming to an end.

Just beginning was a major development of the ground. St. Mirren Secretary, Mr. Willie Scott, announced on 18 December that "thanks to the efforts of supporters in backing the St. Mirren Development Club", work would begin in January 1958 to erect a covered enclosure along the North Terracing to accommodate 16,000 supporters. The work was expected to be completed by the end of the season. Plans to install floodlighting would follow.

The Queen's Park performance, although successful, was barely Division One standard. Starting with the late December meeting with Hearts at Tynecastle, the team's uncompetitiveness was underlined by the loss of six of the next seven matches. Hearts won 5-1 as the Maroons' forwards rained shots in on Forsyth for the whole ninety minutes. The efforts of the visiting forward line drew unfavourable comparison.

A 2-1 victory over Kilmarnock at St. Mirren Park in atrocious conditions on New Year's Day was the only halt in a seven match deterioration which reached its low point when Raith Rovers came to Paisley and won 4-0, in front of only 5000 spectators. The emerging combination of a punchless forward line and a weak defence was proving disastrous.

The Club were looking likely candidates to be at the wrong end of a Scottish Cup shock when they were drawn away to Division Two Ayr United. Perhaps with that in mind, the experience of Davie Lapsley was re-employed at right back. A soft penalty award, converted by McKay, was enough to give Saints a second chance, and the following Wednesday, due to three goalkeeping errors, they scraped through by 2-1.

The second round draw linked Saints with promotion-chasing Dunfermline Athletic, who made a nonsense of their lower Division status with a well-merited 4-1 win. A feature of the game was the prominence of Pars' centre forward Andy Dickson, who repeatedly exposed the limitations of Buchanan as a centre half.

Out of the Cup, there were twelve fixtures left to reverse the slide towards relegation. Inside right Vincent Ryan, signed during the previous week from Celtic for £2000, started the away match against Hibs on 22 February, and to his left was John "Cockles" Wilson, signed originally as a centre forward. Fit-again Tommy Bryceland was also in a revamped attack: would the changes help?

The North Bank watches marching pipe bands shortly before the new cover is constructed.

The answer appeared to be 'yes'. Gemmell and Ryan scored once each and Bryceland hit a double to give Saints the lead on four occasions; Cockles Wilson got Saints' first equaliser, the all-important fifth. Saints had scored five away goals, yet only earned one point! It was not a day of efficient defending, but the fans loved it!

Left winger Alistair Miller, signed from Third Lanark on 19 July, was included the following week against Airdrieonians. Saints won 3-2, with Bryceland, Wilson, and Miller grabbing the goals in what was a second-rate game. That was no fault of Cockles Wilson, who was continuing to add some much-needed vitality to the front five.

The beginning of March saw the first three matches drawn, followed by a crucial victory over second bottom East Fife at Methil on 29 March. This left the Fifers seven points behind Saints with just five games left. The Buddies were as good as safe.

The following Saturday, Saints played considerably better yet lost 3-2 to Hearts, whose win gave them the Championship in front of over 20,000 at Love Street. No one could have predicted that twelve months hence five times that number would be at Hampden to watch the Saints go marching in!

1958-59

There was a new pressure on Scottish football at the beginning of the 1958-59 season. The World Cup Finals had been televised, and the wonderful Brazilians, Pele and all, had set new standards. After the summer of '58, Scottish football fans began to make comparisons with the fare offered at local football grounds; the challenge facing St. Mirren was thus increased.

Fortunately, Saints were in an attractive League Cup section with Airdrieonians, Celtic, and Scottish Cup holders Clyde. For the opening game against the "Waysiders", Manager Willie Reid named Forsyth, Lapsley, McTurk, Neilson, Leishman, Gregal, Bryceland, Ryan, Wilson, Gemmell, and Miller.

Cup winning Manager Willie Reid behind his desk at St Mirren Park 1959.

Johnny McTurk was at left back for the first fourteen matches, allowing Cockles Wilson to continue at centre forward. Wilson scored a hat-trick in the opening match, but most people felt he was much better at full back. It was a situation set to continue when centre forward Peter McKay was transferred to English non-League club Corby Town for £1000 on 14 August.

At centre half was Tommy Leishman, who had joined St. Mirren in August 1955 from Camelon Juniors. His National Service call-up in March 1956 restricted him to a mere seven appearances, but he was seen as the long-term replacement for Willie Telfer. Regrettably, he suffered a bad leg injury in the Airdrie tie and would be out for six months. It meant that Jackie McGugan, signed from Pollok Juniors during the 1956 close season, replaced him in the second game and didn't miss a match at centre half for the rest of the season.

At left half was Tony Gregal, signed from Benburb in 1957. The position was available after Bobby Holmes broke his leg in training at Love Street early in May, just prior to his planned departure with the Scotland team on a continental tour. Bobby was expected to miss much of the 1958-59 season, and his absence was a major blow to Manager Reid's plans. Gregal would play eighteen times before losing out to Tommy Leishman.

The opening game at Airdrie was won 4-3, although the team faltered after a confident start. A close affair with Clyde in Paisley was lost 2-1 then, at Parkhead, Celtic scored three for no reply from a Saints' team which appeared to lack determination. In the return set of sectional ties, a wonder Davie Lapsley goal from thirty-five yards out turned the second Airdrie game for Saints, who won 3-2.

Then it was back to square one with a vengeance. A consolation goal was scored against Clyde at Shawfield, but only after the home team slackened off at six! It was only the fourth match of the season, yet the team already looked demoralised. The last tie was against section leaders Celtic at home. Saints, being Saints, followed up the Shawfield debacle with a 6-3 win over the 'Celts'!

By the end of the second League game, a 2-0 home defeat by Killie, the old failing of having all the play but not being able to finish had returned. In that context, Wilson was reckoned to have speed but little else to offer as a centre forward, whilst Vince Ryan, deemed to be ineffective at inside right, swopped places with outside right Tommy Bryceland. The defence were not immune to criticism, and Campbell Forsyth, for all his strong points, was accused of making some terrible gaffes.

Two weeks after the Killie match, Ryan moved to centre forward against Dunfermline, allowing Wilson to return to left back. Ryan looked a different player at centre and scored one in a 3-2 win. Parts of the team were looking good, but the balance still wasn't right.

In mid-November Saints drew 3-3 with Celtic at Parkhead. By then, they had won two and drawn five of the twelve games played. Form was no better than it had been in the most recent seasons. Significantly, with an eye on attendances, a home game had still to be won. Ryan had been more effective at centre but he still wasn't the answer, so Manager Reid decided to take another gamble on an untried centre forward when he paid £2000 to Motherwell for American-born Gerry Baker, brother of Hibs' Joe.

Gerry had been with Chelsea for a short time before moving in December 1956 to Fir Park, where he played a few times for the 'Well first team as a winger, but failed to make the breakthrough. At St. Mirren Park on 22 November, he made a scoring debut in a 2-1 home win over Hibs, and demonstrated an energetic style of play which went down well with the fans. His impact on Paisley was immediate; it would also be lasting.

On 2 December, Saints signed Davie Walker on a month's trial. Walker, formerly Airdrieonians' goalkeeper for five years, had returned to Scotland after a short spell with Oldham Athletic. He didn't have too long to wait for his chance. On 13 December, St. Mirren were beaten 4-2 by Walker's old team, and Forsyth's performance in goal, not for the first time in the season, was rated as less than impressive. The following week Walker played against Third Lanark but was not seen as any improvement on Forsyth, who returned seven days later.

Unlucky Bobby Holmes made his first team comeback at the end of January when he lined up against Clyde in a forward line of Rodger, Bryceland, Baker, Gemmell, and Holmes. The combination of Bryceland and Baker, the "two busy Bs", was beginning to unsettle the best of defences, while Jim Rodger was staking a claim to be the side's right winger for the rest of the season.

By the time the Scottish Cup was due to start, Baker had scored eight goals in ten games, but the team's points-collecting record of six wins and six draws from twenty-two matches was no better than the immediate previous years. The Cup would ignite the season!

The competition itself began as a slow-burner; Saints were given a bye! In round two it was scarcely more demanding. A crowd of 8,085 enjoyed ten goals being hit past little Peebles Rovers, with four from Baker, a hat-trick from Bryceland, two from Holmes, and one from Rodger. Each player earned an extra £5, arising from an agreement to pay a bonus of ten shillings for each goal scored! One of the players was 'keeper Walker, who replaced an unfit Forsyth. Walker didn't have a single shot to save! He would take a few matches to settle into the side, then retain the custodian's position for the rest of the season.

Apart from the score, the Peebles match was noteworthy for two other reasons. It took place on "Friday the 13th", and was the first to be played under floodlights at St. Mirren Park. The lights were still at an experimental stage, and there were some dark patches on the pitch, but fourteen more lights would be added before the next home game in four days, and the facility would continue to be improved.

Saints then regained their appetite for goals. In the following three League games they scored sixteen times! A home League game against Dunfermline was won 6-2 by fielding Walker, Lapsley, Wilson, Neilson, McGugan, Leishman, Rodger, Bryceland, Baker, Gemmell, and Kerrigan. Wilson was back after a nine game absence, having been covered by Ian Riddell, signed from Jordanhill College in September. The team was just one short of one of the Club's most famous elevens.

Tommy Leishman, making his return from injury against the "Pars", played in all but one of the last eighteen first team matches, one less appearance than his predecessor, Tony Gregal. Seventeen year old Donald Kerrigan, signed from Drumchapel Amateurs back in June, was continuing to do well.

Then a visit to Dens produced a further ten goals, with Saints scoring six of them, including four from Baker. Under the Love Street lights, 12,500 spectators saw Motherwell beaten 4-1 in an excellent dress rehearsal for the forthcoming Scottish Cup tie. Neilson was back to his power-house best, and two-goal Baker, whose problems with cramp in his leg muscles had marred his career until then, was benefiting from Trainer Jimmy McGarvey's proper loosening-up exercises. Saints were by this time ninth in the League

The following Saturday the "Steelmen" returned to Paisley on Cup duty. This was a superb Motherwell side carefully created by ex-Saint Bobby Ancell, and many people's favourites for the trophy. The tie, watched by 26,956, turned out to be a thriller. In the twenty-fifth minute Bryceland fell in a tackle and went off the field for attention. Five minutes later Rodger put the ten men 1-0 ahead. Meanwhile, Bryceland had been given a pain-killing injection into the pulled muscle, and a further five minutes later was back on the pitch with no apparent ill-effects.

Baker made it 2-0 for Saints in the sixty-fifth minute, but 'Well scored via Pat Quinn within a minute. In a further sixty seconds it was all-square when Quinn converted a penalty. Eleven minutes later, with the tie still finely balanced, Saints' winner was scored by Bryceland. Teenage exuberance then took him onto the running track, where he was engulfed by his team mates.

The fourth round home tie against Dunfermline Athletic provided less football than the tie against 'Well, but was equally intense. With less than thirty minutes to go, Saints were still trailing to an early goal when Gemmell set up Rodger for the equaliser, then Baker prodded home a late winner to the delight of the majority in the 14,449 crowd. The injured Bryceland had been missed, but the result was good enough to take Saints through to the semi-final, where they would face Celtic. Saints' fans now believed that, if all their top players were available, the Buddies would win the "Semi", and the Final too!

Four weeks after his injury, Bryceland returned for a 3-3 home draw with Airdrie and the line up on 25 March, for the first time as a unit, was Walker, Lapsley, Wilson, Neilson, McGugan, Leishman, Rodger, Bryceland, Baker, Gemmell, and Miller. A week later, for a Renfrewshire Cup tie against the tyre workers of India of Inchinnan, Saints selected a reserve team defence but the same forward line. Saints won 10-0, Baker hitting a double hat-trick. Prior to this match, Jim Rodger had only played fifteen games. Nine appearances by Tommy Flynn, signed from St. Rochs on 24 October 1958, and seven by Ryan showed how problematic the right wing had been.

It was little different on the left. Alistair Miller's ability was never in doubt, but his inconsistency meant he had only played twice since 1 November, despite Willie McCulloch being given a fee transfer on 15 January. Miller forced himself back into contention by scoring hat-tricks in two earlier Reserve games. He replaced the flu-affected Bobby Holmes for the Celtic match on 18 March, played an outstanding game, and scored the only goal of the match!

On 14 April 1959 at a very windy Hampden Park, the side representing St. Mirren and Paisley in the Scottish Cup semi-final against Celtic were the eleven players who had faced Airdrie in the League two weeks earlier. Saints lost the toss, and faced the elements in the first half. They began well, took the initiative, and went ahead in the fifteenth minute. In the middle of the park, outside left Miller gave the ball out to Rodger on the right wing, and then burst forward to take up position in the inside right channel. Three Celtic defenders were left bemused as Miller received the return pass just outside the goal area. Moving forward, he lofted his strong shot high into the top corner from twelve yards.

Seventeen minutes later Saints were two up, the scorer again being Miller. Tommy Gemmell, who would be black and blue by the end of the game from the attention he received, dispossessed Bobby Evans and hit a great pass into the space vacated by Evans. Miller ran on to it, took the ball to the right of Haffey's outstretched arm, skipped by the 'keeper, guided his right foot shot beyond a Celtic defender, then watched it roll slowly into the left hand corner of the net. The lead was thoroughly deserved. Unbelievably, three minutes later Saints were three up! A quickly taken free kick was moved forward to Gerry Baker, who checked to ensure he was on-side, then clinically slammed the ball behind Haffey. Thirty eight minutes gone: St. Mirren 3, Celtic 0!

Saints were scintillating! They looked a quality team from goalkeeper to outside left, and Celtic simply had no answer to their precise pattern of play. 3-0 up at half-time was beyond any Buddie's expectations, but the scoreline in no way flattered Saints: it could easily have been more!

Celtic came out for the second half in determined mood, and Saints were slow to settle. Gradually the Buddies got back into it, but the standard of the game had dropped and scrappy play predominated. Suddenly, halfway through the second half, there was a spontaneous outburst of singing from the South Stand, a cue quickly taken up by Buddies on the terracing. The volume of sound produced by Paisley voices of all ages was unprecedented, their sense of pride and belonging unmistakable:

> Oh, when the Saints
> go marching in
> Oh, when the Saints go marching in
> I want to be in that number
> When the Saints go marching in.

A "battle song" was born! After the game, nineteen year old pivot Jackie McGugan said when he heard the singing he "felt his heart bursting out of his jersey". There were men much older than nineteen who found it difficult to keep their emotions in check. Few had ever seen St. Mirren play better.

The Hampden crowd had been 73,855, but fifteen minutes before the end most of the Celtic fans had seen enough and began to leave. Saints fans, on the other hand, wanted to see much more from their team. Bryceland obliged in the last minute. Standing almost on the goal line, he was perfectly placed when Rodger's shot wasn't gathered by the Celtic 'keeper, swiftly dispatching the loose ball into the right hand corner of the goal.

The final whistle went. On the field, the Saints players couldn't contain their delight. On the terracing, half of Hampden was ecstatic: the other half was empty! Saints had humbled Celtic with just about the finest exhibition of attacking football ever seen from a Paisley side. Much of the credit went to Alistair Miller for his two well-taken early goals, but the whole team had played well; Willie Reid had found a rare blend.

Saints' opponents in the Final were to be Aberdeen, the team which had beaten them in the 1955/56 League Cup Final. Since then their relative merits had greatly altered. In 1955, Aberdeen had been Scotland's champions and overwhelming favourites; in 1959, the "Dons" had just avoided relegation. After Saints' magnificent semi-final triumph, the feeling that it must be Paisley's year was a sentiment held by most Buddies. More importantly, the team also believed they could win!

It is doubtful if any other St. Mirren match has equalled the excitement generated by the build-up to the 1959 Cup Final. Shop windows were decorated in black and white favours, large photographs of the team and replicas of the Cup were proudly displayed; no one in the town could talk about anything else! On 25 April 1959, the biggest-ever exodus of Buddies, perhaps as many as 60,000, left the Paisley district and headed for Hampden.

"Oh, when the Saints" rang round Hampden as Davie Lapsley led out the team. The eleven players who had won the semi-final so convincingly were named again. They were playing together for only

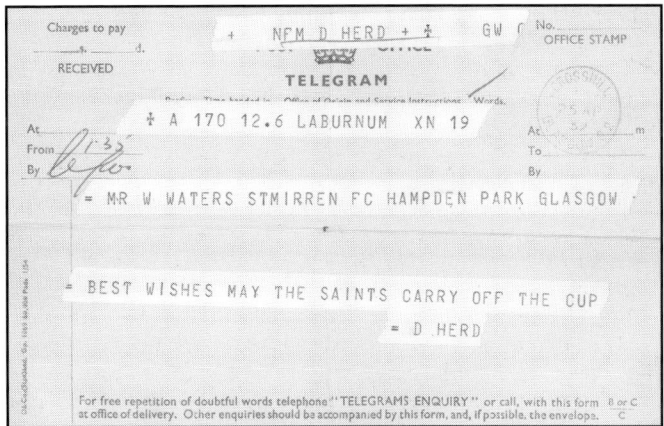

Good luck telegram sent to Saints Director W. Waters at Hampden Park on the day of the final.

I'll have that! Davie lifts the Cup for Paisley.

the third time, but had quickly become the popular choice. Aberdonians had travelled down to Glasgow in good numbers, and a marvellous crowd of 108,591 looked forward to a dramatic ninety minutes. They were not disappointed.

Aberdeen won the toss. They opted to face the Mount Florida end with the wind at their back, but the difficult underfoot conditions caused by earlier showers would prove harder to contend with. The "Dons" settled quickly, although both teams had early chances. Then in the twenty-eighth minute, Dons right back Dave Caldwell pulled a muscle as he stretched to tackle Gerry Baker. After treatment he swopped places with Jackie Hather, and played the rest of the game at outside left.

The game remained finely balanced until the forty-third minute, when Miller beat stand-in full back Hather on the goal line near the eighteen yard box. His cross from the left eluded the jumping Brownlee, and waiting to pounce two yards behind him was Bryceland. Tommy timed his jump to perfection, and, with a twist of his body, his well-directed header flew over the body of Martin, who had slipped while diving to his right. The ball nestled in the back of the net as Bryceland began a jig of joy.

It was the perfect time to score. After the resumption Saints took charge of proceedings, and it was no surprise when they went two-up in the sixty-fifth minute. A searching pass from Bryceland dissected the Aberdeen defence and found Gemmell just ten yards from the goalkeeper. His first time shot squirmed from the hands of the onrushing Martin and fell behind where Dons defenders Hogg and Clunie, standing just one yard from the goal line and under intense pressure from Gemmell, got themselves into a terrible fankle. When the ball broke to Miller all he had to do was side-foot the ball into an empty net.

In the seventy-sixth minute a forward-positioned Lapsley started off the move which led to the third goal. His pass to Bryceland was pushed forward to Baker. A slip by Dons' pivot Clunie put Gerry in the clear, with only the onrushing Martin to beat. This he did with remarkable composure, his chipped shot hitting the net in spectacular fashion.

In the last minute, Dons' centre Hugh Baird gave his team a deserved consolation goal when he struck an excellent shot from fifteen yards. The final whistle sounded, Saints fans spilled onto the field, Davie Lapsley was carried off the pitch shoulder high by his team mates, and the Aberdeen players sportingly congratulated the St. Mirren legend.

The celebrations began immediately after the match, when Saints all-time top scorer, Davie McCrae, appeared on television with Davie Lapsley and Scottish Television's courteous commentator, Arthur Montford, to open a bottle of whisky which had remained unopened since the victorious 1926 Cup Final. Davie McCrae had promised it would only be opened when Saints again won the Cup. The thirty-three year wait was over, and he poured a small drop for the Saints captain and congratulated his successors.

Congratulations of a different magnitude awaited the team. Despite torrential rain, thousands lined the streets leading to the Council Chambers in County Square. The singing crowds in "Jail Square", much bigger than had been anticipated, made it almost impossible for the team to pass from bus to building. It had been easier to beat Aberdeen!

To protect the Cup, the trophy had to be to thrown over the heads of the engulfing crowd. The cheering reached a new volume when the team finally appeared on the balcony waving the Cup. Paisley and St. Mirren were once again synonymous. "I'd like to thank you for your faithful support", proclaimed Davie Lapsley, " and I think the best team won the Scottish Cup!" What more needed to be said?

1959-60

Amidst all the Cup celebrations, it almost passed unnoticed that Saints ended the League programme in a respectable seventh position. They had also won the Second Eleven Cup, and were the first club to win both competitions in the same season since 1929. For good measure, the Cup-winning side completed a 7-5 aggregate win over Morton in the Renfrewshire Cup on 9 May. Later that evening, St. Mirren's players and officials received further public recognition for their achievements when they attended a civic reception.

Leading the Saints' party at the reception was Davie Lapsley, whose retirement had been slightly deferred! He played in the two county cup matches, took part and scored in both Highland tour games, and lined up in the pre-season Paisley Charity Cup match against Manchester City. He would also appear in the first four League Cup ties before dropping down to the Reserves until mid-November, when he finally hung up his boots.

16,000 people attended the charity match on 1 August, an indication of the high hopes for a best-ever season. On show was the Cup-winning team minus an on-holiday Tommy Gemmell. Subsequent injuries and loss of form ensured that this was as close as Willie Reid would ever get to again fielding his most famous eleven, a side that played together on only five occasions yet made 1958-59 such an unforgettable season.

The League Cup started with a casual home display against Third Lanark, which led to a 3-2 defeat, then Gerry Baker was sent off and Gemmell injured in a tousy 3-0 away defeat in Dunfermline. When the third tie was lost, 4-2 away to Clyde, hopes of advancing in the tournament were abandoned. The first League fixture, against Third Lanark, was

Scottish Cup Winners, 1959

Back Row: Trainer McGarvey, Wilson, Baker, Neilson, McGugan, and Leishman.

Front row: Rodger, Bryceland, Lapsley, Gemmell, Miller, and Bell (Physiotherapist).

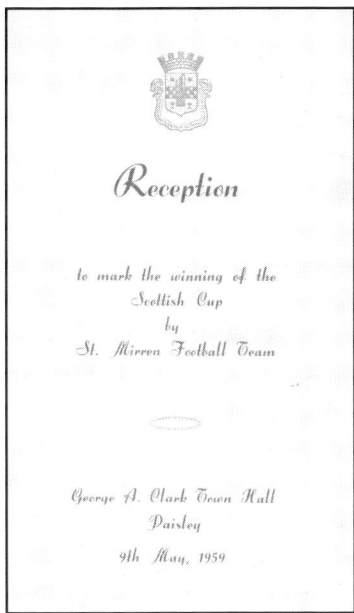

Reception itinerary for the cup winning side.

also lost, as were the next two League Cup ties. Played six, lost six was the depressing start to the season. Gemmell was still injured, and by this time Tommy Leishman had been dropped.

On 29 August, Saints got their elusive first win, a 2-1 home victory over Clyde. It coincided with news that Newcastle United had enquired about pivot Jackie McGugan. Saints' cup success had alerted, other clubs and several players were said to be unsettled. It was an understandable situation. Many had aspirations to go full-time, an opportunity not open to them at St. Mirren Park.

At this time, St. Mirren received £11,017 as their share of the S.F.A.'s semi-final and final income, which easily wiped out the previous year's loss of £683. The cup money put the Club in a healthy financial position, and the upbeat picture continued on 5 September when Saints travelled to Rugby Park, played a brand of football which equalled any of their cup performances, and comprehensively thumped Kilmarnock 5-0.

The next week at St. Mirren Park, newly promoted Arbroath were as outclassed as the 8-1 scoreline would suggest. Motherwell were next! Skill, strength, and speed were all on display at Fir Park as Saints romped to a 4-1 win. Two days earlier, McGugan made what was the first of three transfer requests that season.

Seven days after the 'Well match, Saints needed only the ten opening minutes to score three against Raith Rovers. 14,000 fans then watched the home side rest on its laurels, allowing the Kirkcaldy team to mount a two-goal comeback. It was just enough for a fourth League win in a row, re-kindling hopes of a best-ever season; Saints were top of the League!

Two matches against English Cup winners Nottingham Forest a week apart at the end of September ended in a 5-4 aggregate win for Saints. These games provided a pleasant diversion, but a visit to Pittodrie the following Saturday was an immediate reminder of how tough the League could be. Aberdeen, alive to the dangers of allowing Saints to play football, employed tactics which, if not attractive, were certainly effective, and they ran out 3-1 winners. It was Saints' first defeat in eight matches, in a game which also saw Davie Laird, at inside left since Gemmell was injured in the second League Cup tie, suffering a broken leg.

Hopes were still high! Sixteen thousand people turned up for the next home game, a 2-2 draw with Clyde on 10 October. The following Saturday, with Gemmell back, Saints won 3-1 at Ibrox. This result took Saints to within three points of League leaders Hearts, but there was further cause for celebration; the Ibrox victory was the first there since 1 October 1904!

The Buddies then lost five consecutive League games between 24 October and 21 November. In the midst of this run, Tommy Leishman became the first 1959 cup-winner to leave when he joined Liverpool for £9,000. It was a strange transfer. He had played in only eight of twenty-two competitive matches during the season, and not once had been at his best. At Anfield he would win an English Second Division Championship medal in 1961/62.

Saints improved their twelfth position with a narrow 4-3 away win over Ayr United and a terrific 2-0 win over Hearts at Tynecastle. Prior to the Hearts' match, a band had played "Abide with Me" in tribute to the late Mr. William Woods Waters, former Chairman of St. Mirren, Chairman of the SFA International Selectors, and President of the Scottish Football League, who had passed away on 29 November.

As holder of the latter post on 22 October 1955, the day Saints played Aberdeen in the League Cup Final, it fell to Mr. Waters' wife Caroline to present the trophy at the end of the match. In moments of abandoned neutrality, he had fervently hoped that the recipient would be Willie Telfer! It was not to be, but Mr. Waters brought honour of a different kind to St. Mirren by serving Scottish football with distinction; the Tynecastle tribute was no more than he deserved.

Following the Tynecastle victory, a run of four defeats began on 15 December and ended on 2 January with a truly awful display at Gayfield, where bottom club Arbroath won 6-2. Watching from the stand were Forsyth, Baker, Gemmell, and wing halfs Jim Thomson and Tony Gregal, all dropped following a 3-0 Ne'erday drubbing by Killie. An off-form McGugan was dropped after this match and immediately submitted his third request to be transfer-listed: the demand was met.

The following Wednesday, Tommy Gemmell was restored to the team for the Third Lanark match and made captain. The team drew 2-2 and the captain scored. Three days later, 16,000 saw a 5-1 home win over Motherwell, Baker's first goal in nine games, and a rejuvenated Gemmell. The Buddies then lost 6-1 to Raith Rovers in Kirkcaldy! This pattern of results was driving the fans to distraction.

The Scottish Cup first round draw paired Saints with the students of Glasgow University on 30 January 1960. The University team started well enough but as the game progressed the gap in class became a veritable chasm. The final score was 15-0, St. Mirren's record score in any competition. It might have been more. A clash with the University's goalkeeper in the seventy-eighth minute meant that Gerry Baker missed the remainder of the game. The students breathed a sigh of relief; by then Gerry had scored ten!

Saints stalwarts line up for the camera at Renfrew Airport for the 1959 close season Scottish tour: Jackie McGugan, Director Willie Waters, and Tommy Leishman.

Celtic were Saints' second round visitors on 13 February. Only two goals this time, one for each side. Jim Rodger scored after sixty-two minutes, and straight from the re-start Alex Byrne equalised. Bad weather meant the replay didn't take place for eleven days. At half-time at Celtic Park Saints held a 3-1 lead; by full time it was 3-3. In extra time, Saints regained the lead only for Celtic to peg them back yet again.

A League game at Dens on 27 February was sandwiched between the two Celtic replays, and meant that the part-time Saints were due to play three games in five days. It proved too much. Celtic, 3-0 up at half-time, finally ended Saints' reign as cup-holders by winning 5-2. The three Celtic ties, watched by over 130,000 people, meant that the Cup had again been a money-spinner, but that was little consolation when the team was sixth bottom of the League.

The Cup exit was followed by the worst result of the season, a 7-0 hammering at home by second bottom Stirling Albion! After that, the season retained its unpredictable pattern. Saints, table toppers at the beginning of October, finished fourteenth.

The team was regarded as weak at wing half, on the creative side at least. Additionally, Bryceland, Baker, Gemmell, and Miller all had varying durations of being badly off form. However, there had been glimpses of the heights the side could achieve, which led a growing number of Saints' fans to conclude that such inconsistency was due to the part-time status of the players.

It was a point which had been made by Willie Reid back in October 1954. By 1960, Saints' players were on £16 per week; amongst the best paid part-timers in Scotland. The question of how much more it would cost to introduce full-time football would have to be addressed without delay.

Going, Going, Gone... Then Goals Galore!
1960-61

Football talk during the 1960 close season was dominated by the stunning Real Madrid v Eintracht Frankfurt European Cup Final, played at Hampden in May. The match set new standards, and Manager Willie Reid, always keen to enhance his football knowledge, accompanied Drumchapel Amateurs to West Germany to identify "continental" coaching techniques which could be adopted to the advantage of St. Mirren.

CHAPTER TEN

One player who would not benefit from these new ideas was Bobby Holmes, who had announced his retirement on 7 March. Bobby had never really recovered from the leg break he sustained in May 1958, and had been advised that to continue playing would endanger his health. It was a terrible blow to a player who had been hailed as one of Scotland's brightest prospects in 1957. The original injury had deprived him of an appearance in the 1959 Cup Final and the near-certainty of playing for Scotland, but he would always be held in the highest esteem by all those who saw him wearing the black and white stripes.

Two of the 1959 Cup-winning team would also be missing. Jackie Neilson was one of five players given a free transfer in May 1961, the third member of the team to leave Love Street. Jackie had been a Saint since 1949 and had served the Club with distinction, picking up Scottish League and Scotland "B" representative honours along the way. The fourth player to depart was Jackie McGugan, who finally got his transfer wish on 30 July.

Jackie's oft-stated desire to go full-time was met just one day after the Club's A.G.M. when two major announcements were made. The much-criticised floodlighting system would be greatly improved, and a number of players would become full-time at the end of August. Manager Reid also used the A.G.M to reiterate the Club's policy on transfers: "No one who is wanted by the Club will be allowed to go," he stated.

Despite spelling out its transfer policy, the Club was annoyed when the press suggested that McGugan's move was the prelude to the departure of others. Such uninformed speculation, according to Willie Reid, could only have an unsettling effect at St. Mirren Park. His fears were realised less than a week later when Tommy Bryceland asked for a transfer, which was turned down.

The news about Bryceland coincided with the announcement that Saints had signed centre half Jim Clunie from Aberdeen on 11 August, just in time for the testing League Cup opener against champions Hearts

David Lapsley's Cup Winners medal, won season 1958-59

at Tynecastle. Clunie, who would miss only one competitive match all season, began his Saints' career with the first of countless outstanding displays, as the Buddies left Edinburgh with a confidence-boosting 1-1 draw. Expectations were quickly dashed by back-to-back 4-0 drubbings by Motherwell at home and Clyde at Shawfield.

In the return game against Hearts there was considerable improvement with a 3-1 win which included a vintage performance from Tommy Gemmell and a promising debut by seventeen year old local boy George McLean, signed from Drumchapel Amateurs, who played at centre forward. A 5-2 defeat at Fir Park and a 0-0 home draw against Clyde meant that Saints had collected only four points by the end of the sectional ties, and had also lost their opening League fixture, a 4-2 away defeat to Clyde.

After the Fir Park defeat, press reports suggested that up to four of the goals conceded by Forsyth were preventable, and with Walker dropped after the season's Charity Cup opener and out of contention, it came as no surprise when Saints announced on 1 September that another goalkeeper, 6ft 2" Bobby Williamson, had been signed from Arbroath. Williamson made his debut on 19 September, and was destined to play in the Cup Final the following season. Saints' previous Cup Final keeper, Davie Walker, would be given a free transfer at the end of the season.

At the beginning of September the promised transition to a full-time set-up began. One of the full-timers was Gerry Baker, who was the subject of a late September transfer enquiry from Manchester City. It was turned down flat. "Baker is not for sale," pronounced Willie Reid. This unambiguous statement didn't kill the story, thanks to one newspaper insinuating that the player was unhappy. It was an unwanted development which greatly annoyed Gerry Baker, and forced him to make a detailed public statement which confirmed that he had no intention of asking for a change of club.

Just as Baker's situation was being clarified, the Club let it be known that they were willing to sell Tommy Bryceland, who had repeatedly expressed his desire to leave Paisley. For the match against Celtic on 8 October, Bryceland was dropped, with Birmingham City the latest club to show interest, but he was back in the team a week later for the match against Partick Thistle. At right back that day was the industrious Bobby "Red" Campbell, signed from Drumchapel Amateurs on 1 July 1958, then farmed out to Ardeer Recreation. He would retain his place for the remainder of the season.

Also arriving at the Club was 6ft 1" centre forward Billy Hume, who joined on 29 October from Birmingham City for £3,000, having previously played for Dunfermline Athletic. Hume had made eight appearances and scored twice for the "Blues" during the previous season. In three months he also made eight appearances for Saints, scoring three League goals before being given a free transfer on 3 February 1962.

Four days after Hume was signed, Gerry Baker was transferred to Manchester City for £17,000. By his own admission he had not been playing well during the season, and had only scored four goals in fourteen games, but his departure was not well received by Saints' fans, particularly when he had been so public about his desire to stay at Love Street. Many supporters were not clear as to how the decision to let go a fifth 1959 Cup-winner complied with the Club's stated transfer policy.

Heading to Paisley after nine years at Maine Road was Manchester City's regular choice centre half John McTavish, who had lost his place when Jackie Plenderleith arrived there from Hibs. John played eight consecutive games at right half before the arrival at Love Street of Rab Stewart, Kilmarnock's longest serving player, on Boxing Day 1960. McTavish played a further eleven games at inside left.

Another signing, Bobby Williamson, although playing eleven times in a row for Saints, hadn't satisfactorily solved the goalkeeping position. As a result, thirty-five year old personality player Jimmy Brown was signed from Kilmarnock. Making the opposite journey was Campbell Forsyth, who recorded seven consecutive appearances in the early part of the season and was still rated by many observers as a keeper of considerable potential.

Brown went straight into the team to play St. Johnstone in Perth on 19 November, and was not shy about offering advice to his new team mates! He didn't miss a game for the rest of the season and became captain, but despite the confidence he brought to the defence, League results only slightly improved by the turn of the year. One win per month from September to December and two draws had produced just ten points from seventeen matches; Saints were anchored at the bottom of the League.

The new year started brightly, with four consecutive wins over Kilmarnock, Raith, Third Lanark, and Dunfermline. Then a 1-1 home draw with League leaders Rangers was followed by a home win over Celtic. Much of the credit for the improved form went to Stewart's spirited and constructive wing half play, a previous area of deficiency in the team, and those eleven points from a possible twelve were the best possible preparation for another tilt at the Scottish Cup.

Before the Cup got underway, Johnny Frye, unable to get a regular place in the team and less than a year with Saints, was transferred to Sheffield Wednesday for £3,500. Immediately £2,500 of the Frye fee was given to Dundee F.C. in return for the experienced Albert Henderson. Henderson would play ten times at wing half and inside forward, and make an eighteen-game contribution the following season before being freed at the end of 1961-62.

A bye in the first round was followed by a disappointing tie at Tannadice, where a half-hit shot from Stewart was sufficient to send Saints onwards as 1-0 winners. Then a 3-2 League defeat by Thistle at Firhill ended an eight game unbeaten run just before high-flying, high scoring Third Lanark visited Paisley on 25 February.

This thrilling tie ended in a 3-3 draw thanks to a tremendous first-time shot from Stewart, which flew past Robertson three minutes from time to give Saints a second, if more difficult, chance to progress. The following Tuesday a crowd of 20,893 rolled up to Cathkin Park to see a repeat of the closely fought first tie. No one could have predicted what followed.

A Saints' line-up of Brown, R. Campbell, Wilson, Stewart, Clunie, Riddell, Rodger, Bryceland, Kerrigan, McTavish, and Miller put on a stunning display in which Jim Rodger ran riot on the right and threatened to score every time he got the ball. He hit four past 5ft 5½ins Jocky Robertson, Scotland's smallest goalkeeper, as Saints hit the heights. A double from Bryceland and one each from Kerrigan and former Hi-Hi man Miller completed an 8-0 rout! Only the most rabid of "Thirds" fans thought the score flattered Saints. It had been exhibition stuff!

A 2-1 home win over Hibs and a 2-0 defeat at Dens intervened before Saints made their way to Tynecastle for the quarter-final tie against Hearts on 11 March. A Kerrigan goal was just enough to take Saints through to their second semi-final in three years, where they met Dunfermline, managed by Jock Stein. A dull 0-0 draw was followed four days later by a 1-0 defeat courtesy of a freak own goal from Stewart. It was an extremely disappointing end to a memorable Cup campaign.

The second half of 1960-61 saw Saints add a further nineteen points to their total to finish in fourteenth place, before a four-match tour of Iceland completed the season. Three games against club sides produced two wins and a draw, ten goals scored and none conceded. These positive statistics were severely dented in the last match, when a South West Iceland select team emphatically won 7-1. The star of the Select team and scorer of a hat-trick was their young inside forward, Therolf Beck. His subsequent signing would add at least one "continental" touch to the Paisley scene.

1961-62

In a season where money matters would predominate, enquiries made by Manager Willie Reid revealed that St. Mirren's full-time wages of £20 were the lowest in the First Division. As a result of Mr. Reid's representations, the Board agreed to raise this figure to £24, no doubt increasing Willie Reid's popularity with his players!

On the field, six points gained and no goals conceded was Saints' strong start to the 1961 League Cup, but an early set-back occurred when key man Tommy Bryceland suffered a broken leg in the third tie against Hearts. In the return matches against Killie, Raith, and Hearts, the goals against column jumped to eleven as each game was lost. The Buddies' bright start was not enough to keep them in the tournament.

The first six League outings produced six points, but after a particularly poor 3-1 defeat at Tannadice in mid-October, the Manager confirmed he would look closely at Reserve Team Coach Bobby Flavell's reports on recent second team games and consider some promotions. The following week, young Icelander Therolf 'Tottie' Beck lined up at inside left, the first of twenty appearances during his first season.

1960's collector's card featuring Tommy Bryceland.

Team Group 1961-62 Back Row: Bobby 'Red' Campbell, John 'Cockles' Wilson, Bobby Williamson, Rab Stewart, Jim Clunie, and John McTavish Front Row: Tommy Henderson, George McLean, Therolf 'Tottie' Beck, Willie Fernie, and Don Kerrigan.

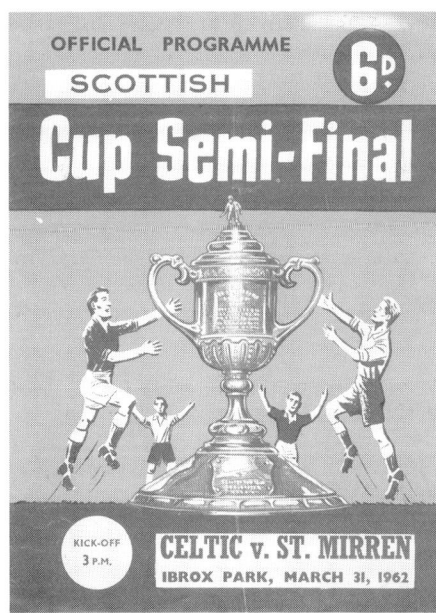

The match programme for the famous semi-final victory over Celtic. A contemporary newsreel of the day described the crowd invasion of the park as being "like a scene from South American politics".

At a Board meeting on 24 October, Willie Reid, who had been in charge of team affairs for over seven years, intimated that he wished to tender his resignation "as he felt his health was being undermined". Although the Board were aware that there was dressing-room discontent with a perceived over-emphasis on defensive play, they were unanimous in asking Mr. Reid to reconsider his desire to resign, a request which he agreed to.

At Celtic Park on 15 November, there was little evidence of an excess of defensive tactics as Celtic won 7-1. St. Mirren by then were in mid-table with ten points from eleven matches. The Manager felt the team needed an inside forward with a style similar to Bryceland, and Celtic's former internationalist Willie Fernie matched his requirements. Thirty-three year old Willie was available for £3,000, and he made a scoring debut in a 3-0 win over St. Johnstone on 25 November. He would prove to be an excellent acquisition. Four days earlier, and after some prolonged discussions, another good deal was struck when "Tottie" Beck signed his first professional contract.

Saints' line-up at Perth had not included Jim Rodger in his usual position. Three days later St. Johnstone asked about buying the right winger, but did not pursue their interest when the disparity in valuation of the player became obvious. Jim had played fifteen times on the right wing up to that point, and would play five times on the left before being transferred to Hearts on 2 February 1962, the sixth 1959 Cup medalist to leave the Club.

St. Mirren's position as one of Scotland's best supported clubs was underlined when it was revealed that the average home "gate" until 12 December was 13,000, but the away average was only 6,000. The pertinent point, under the prevailing system, was that gate income was not matching the Club's expenses, and the current account balance was overdrawn by more than £5,000 and steadily worsening.

Saints' financial problems were by no means unique, as the League asked clubs to submit ideas on how to make the game in Scotland more attractive and competitive. One proposal was the establishment of three divisions of 12, 12, and 13, but it was understood that the Rangers board favoured two leagues of sixteen teams, with the obvious consequence for five existing clubs.

Some clubs, such as Kilmarnock, wanted any set-up which provided more games in a season. The St. Mirren board advocated, amongst other things, that teams be allowed to keep their home gates, or the "guarantee" be raised to £600. In the meantime the Club were attempting to reschedule the payment of certain debts, such as the Fernie fee, investigating ways of increasing income from their Development Club, and considering friendlies against attractive English opposition.

On 13 December the Manager intimated that he had accepted the managership of Norwich City, following the sudden resignation of their manager, Archie MacAulay. Willie Reid had been at St. Mirren Park for nine years as a player and seven as a manager. He would be long remembered as the man who brought the Cup back to Paisley, and he continued his cup success when the "Canaries" won the second English League Cup Final on 1 May 1962. Ultimately, finishing seventeenth out of twenty-two clubs in England's Division Three South was the real measurement of success, and Willie Reid resigned just eight days after his team won the Final.

St. Mirren immediately approached their recently departed Reserve Team Coach Bobby Flavell, who had been Manager of Ayr United for just seventeen days. Mr. Flavell took over the St. Mirren hot seat on 18 December. One of his first actions was to follow up a signing target he had as Ayr's manager. Together with Director Mr. Walker, he travelled through to Edinburgh and signed Hearts' all-action outside right Tommy Henderson for £2,000. On his debut, Henderson helped Saints to a 1-1 draw at home to Dundee, with the Buddies scoring through Fernie.

Although the team had drawn with Dundee, the new Manager "thought that it could be strengthened". He couldn't have been more correct! In the second League game under his charge, Dunfermline administered a 7-0 thrashing at East End Park on 30 December. Just thirteen points had been amassed from seventeen games, and once again the season had "relegation battle" written all over it. The magnitude of the task facing Mr. Flavell could not have been clearer.

It wasn't any easier in the Cup! In the Second Round, Saints were drawn against top of the table Dundee at Dens. It was hardly the usual early Cup diversion from League pressures, but it did provide the opportunity to undertake preparations with a difference, as the players and management team enjoyed a pre-match stroll along the Broughty Ferry seafront. It seemed to work! Against all expectations, Saints defeated the "Dark Blues" by 1-0, thanks to a George McLean goal.

It was hoped that a Cup run would provide some much needed finance. The overdraft was by then over £7,000 and still rising. Just prior to Saints' departure for Aberdeen on 2 February, the Jim Rodger move to Tynecastle was arranged. The fee was £2,000, but Saints received no money as this was the amount still owed for the incoming transfer of Henderson.

In the Third Round of the Cup, Raith Rovers were beaten 4-0 in a February replay, following a 1-1 draw at Stark's Park. First choice 'keeper Jimmy Brown had been injured in the Kirkcaldy match, his place being taken by Bobby Williamson. The former Arbroath 'keeper would retain the berth for the rest of the season, playing seventeen times in all.

Two weeks later, a McLean goal from a Henderson pass was enough to eliminate Dunfermline Athletic at the quarter-final stage of the Cup. Another McLean goal gave Saints full points at Firhill on 17 March, taking them to the twenty-three point mark with seven games to go. The team then proceeded to lose the next six matches. Second Division football and the financial implications of relegation would be a very real prospect when Dunfermline visited Love Street for the last game of the season, but before that Saints had a Scottish Cup semi-final to contest, their third in four seasons!

The Buddies' opponents on 31 March were the talented but inconsistent pre-Stein Celtic, who just five days earlier had visited Paisley and won 5-0. The clever and confident Tommy Bryceland was back after being sidelined for seven months, but the relegation-threatened Saints remained far from being favourites!

Paisley prospects improved when, prior to the kick-off at neutral Ibrox, Celtic made two decisions which turned out to be crucial. Teamwise, John Hughes was selected in preference to Bobby Carroll, who had played a significant role in that 5-0 League game. Tactics-wise, Celtic captain Duncan McKay won the toss and inexplicably opted to play against the considerable wind.

Saints took full advantage of the elements. In the 1959 semi-final it had taken thirty-eight minutes to go three up against Celtic; this time they did it in thirty-five! In the seventh minute, right winger Henderson chipped over a dangerous cross, which Haffey, under pressure from a jumping Bryceland, could only partially palm away. The ball fell to Fernie, and from six yards out he calmly slotted the ball past the Celtic 'keeper.

Seventeen minutes later Beck hit a through pass to Kerrigan, who swiftly dispatched the ball behind Haffey before the Celtic defence knew what had hit them. Sixty seconds later, another accurate chip from Henderson, from just outside the penalty area, landed in between two Celtic players and was accepted by Beck in front of goal. The Icelander half-wheeled to his left before hitting a great shot between the two recovering defenders, and to the right of Haffey.

In the second half the wind dropped, and this helped Saints maintain control of proceedings. The game was heading for a shock result, and one which some Celtic supporters found difficult to tolerate. Fighting broke out on the terracing, bottles began to fly, and eventually, seventeen minutes from time the game had to be stopped when the pitch was invaded by many hundreds of supporters. Action was re-started after eight minutes, but by that time thousands had gone home. Alex Byrne scored a consolation goal for Celtic three minutes from time as the game was played out in a half-empty stadium.

Some of the scenes at Ibrox that day were a disgrace to Scottish football, but nothing could detract from Saints' success. It had been a famous victory, and probably Fernie's finest performance in black and white. The eleven who played – Bobby Williamson, Bobby "Red" Campbell, ever-present Cockles Wilson, Rab Stewart, Jim Clunie, George McLean, Tommy Henderson, Tommy Bryceland, Don Kerrigan, Willie Fernie, and Tottie Beck – would be selected for the Final on 21 April.

This meant that only two players, Wilson and Bryceland, survived from the 1959 Final. The "semi" had been Beck's first game of the season at outside left, a position which had been filled by Alistair Miller on twenty-four occasions during the season. On 10 April it was announced that Cup hero Miller, who had asked for a transfer earlier in the season, had been granted a free transfer at his own request.

Also missing out on the big day was left half John McTavish, who had played forty-one consecutive games in that position up to the semi-final before failing a fitness test. His place in the "semi" and Final was taken by George McLean, but John would be recalled for the last League game of the season against Dunfermline.

Therolf 'Tottie' Beck

127,940 watched the Final, including a number of friends, relatives and fans of Tottie Beck, who had made the journey from Iceland. For forty minutes they saw a well-drilled Saints defence, with Williamson and Clunie outstanding, containing a very attack-minded Rangers side. They also saw a Saints team which carried its own threat, notably from McLean, Fernie, and Beck.

A scrambled effort by Brand five minutes from the interval was the difference between the two sides as the second half commenced. Saints then had a spell where an equaliser looked the most likely outcome. However, a second Rangers goal, from Wilson, put the game beyond Saints. The whole team had put on an admirable display of skill and determination, a battling performance which totally belied the Buddies' League position.

Many of the thousands who had travelled to Hampden repeated at least one aspect of '59 when they re-assembled at "Jail Square". Prior to the match, the Club had been offered a civic reception by the Provost, "win, lose or draw", and the official party were met by what the Club's minutes later described as "a surprisingly large and enthusiastic crowd at County Square". The fans were keen to acknowledge the teams' efforts; the players and officials greatly appreciated the welcome home.

The season though, was far from over! Only four days after the excitement of Hampden, Saints headed for Dens for the penultimate game against Champions-elect Dundee. Like the previous five League matches, it was lost. The effect of the 2-0 reverse, as official minutes summarised, left the Club "in a very precarious position regarding relegation".

On 28 April to the relief of Paisley, Saints thumped Dunfermline by four goals to one. The Buddies were safe, but it couldn't have been closer: goal average meant it was St. Johnstone who were relegated along with Stirling Albion.

Off the field the news was also good. In seven days at the beginning of April the overdraft was reduced from £10,283 to £6,661, thanks to the Cup run. By 1 May, a £7,000 payment from the S.F.A., on account of Saints reaching the Cup Final, meant that the overdraft was reduced to a much more manageable £1,073.

It was a heartening position after months of financial struggle, but football was changing fast. In England and Wales a threatened players' strike in January 1961 had led to the abolition of the maximum wage. St. Mirren and plenty of other clubs would begin to find it harder than ever to hang on to their young players and compete with the big city clubs. Overcoming such difficulties remained the St. Mirren objective.

1962-63

Goalkeeper Jimmy Brown and Tommy Gemmell were amongst those released at the end of 1961-62. For Tommy it was the end of an eleven-year association with the Club, during which he distinguished himself not only as the complete team player, but also as one of most skilful, intelligent, and popular individuals in St. Mirren's history.

Tommy's departure meant that only Cockles Wilson and Tommy Bryceland survived from the famous Cup-winning eleven, but Bryceland's future at St. Mirren Park was yet again in doubt when it emerged during re-signing talks that he was still keen to obtain a transfer. Re-signing was a prerequisite to any development, and he was back in his usual place for the season's opener, a Paisley Charity Cup 1-1 draw against Norwich City.

In the League Cup, three points were taken from the first two ties, against Third Lanark and Hibernian. Making his debut in the Thirds game was Jimmy Robertson, who had played for Cowdenbeath as an amateur before signing for the Buddies on 22 May. Robertson would remain first choice left-winger throughout a season which seemed to promise much when Rangers were beaten 2-1 in Paisley before a 37,000 crowd. Unfortunately, Saints were unable to maintain this excellent start when a draw at Cathkin and a defeat at Easter Road preceded a 4-0 reverse at Ibrox on 1 September.

Three days after the Rangers game the Board considered transfer requests from Bryceland, Kerrigan, and Stewart. The latter had been moved to right back from right half in a straight swop with Red Campbell for the first two games of the season. Campbell retained the right half role, but in the third game young Cameron Murray was selected at right back. His debut was impressive, and his form continued to be so good that the former Drumchapel Amateur, who had joined the Club back in January, played in every game until the season's end. It was agreed to let Rab Stewart go for "the best offer obtainable".

In the third League match, Bryceland scored the only goal against Raith Rovers. It proved to be his last appearance in black and white for some considerable time. The following week Norwich City bid £20,000 for his services, but the player asked for some time to consider the offer. Just before the kick off against Motherwell on 22 September, he verbally agreed to move to East Anglia. By then technically a Norwich player, and with possible injury a consideration, he was withdrawn from the team immediately!

Tommy's position was taken by Don Kerrigan, while Raith's Tommy White arrived for £1,000, he made a winning start scoring both in a 2-1 victory over Aberdeen. He hit two again in a 2-2 draw with Hibs but Saints then collected only three points from eight matches, beginning with a 2-1 defeat to Thistle and a 7-0 home defeat to Celtic. Three days prior to the Celtic game £1,100 took Rab Stewart to Ayr United.

Bouncing back from the 7-0 result, a reshuffled Saints defeated Dunfermline 3-1 at East End Park and then drew 1-1 at home to Airdrieonians. Unfortunately, the relief was merely temporary. Four consecutive defeats followed, in which fifteen goals were conceded and only two scored.

Five of these fifteen goals came in one match away to Hearts on 24 November, when outside left Roy Kemp, a summer signing from Camelon and making only his third first team appearance, unfortunately sustained a broken leg after only nine minutes play. His loss greatly contributed to the defeat, but the Directors also felt that 'keeper Williamson could have saved up to three of the goals. The Manager also concluded that the team needed a new goalkeeper, and soon reported that he had watched Eddie Connachan of Dunfermline Athletic, but "Pars" manager Jock Stein was unwilling to quote a price.

Team Group 1962-63
Back Row (left to right): Rab Stewart, John Wilson, Bobby Williamson, Red Campbell, Jim Clunie, John McTavish, Front row: Tommy Henderson, Tommy Bryceland, Don Kerrigan, George McLean, and Roy Kemp.

The four consecutive defeats up to 15 December marked a turning point as far as the Board were concerned. Three days later they unanimously expressed dissatisfaction with Mr. Flavell and decided to dispense with his services. When informed of their decision, he intimated that it had been his intention to resign at the same meeting. In addition to the severance pay he was due, the Club also awarded Bobby Flavell a substantial bonus for reaching the previous season's Cup Final.

Not surprisingly, there was also growing concern at this time amongst the supporters regarding the direction the Club was taking. So much so that a protest meeting was convened by four travel clubs in the Town Hall two days before Christmas. An estimated five hundred fans attended, and from the meeting came a decision to boycott the home match on 2 January 1963. A deputation would also seek a meeting with the Board.

Thirty-two hopefuls applied for the Manager's post, but none was deemed suitable. However, an application from Mr. Jackie Cox, previously Ayr United's manager, had been re-directed to the home of the Chairman, Mr. W. Walker. The Board felt that the enthusiastic Mr. Cox was the man for the job, and he accepted the post on 28 December.

Jackie Cox's first game in charge was a home match against Rangers, which was lost 2-0 on December 29, followed by 2-1 defeats from Kilmarnock away and Raith Rovers at home. It was the first of only two wins all season by bottom club Raith. It was also the designated "boycott" game, but weather conditions were so miserable that any evaluation of its effect was impossible. The protest ended officially on 11 March.

Following those two New Year games, the Directors and Mr. Cox agreed that "it was essential to sign a goalkeeper". A second unsuccessful attempt was made to sign Dunfermline's Connachan, then Kilmarnock rejected a move to buy back Campbell Forsyth. On 4 January 1963, twenty-six year old former Celtic and Portsmouth 'keeper Dick Beattie was signed for £2,000 from Peterborough United. He went straight into the side, playing in a 1-1 away draw against Motherwell the next day, and would be an ever-present for the rest of the season.

The new Manager's first victory came at Berwick on 26 January in a second round 3-1 Cup win. Missing from the team was George McLean, whose prolonged transfer saga was finally concluded on 23 January when he joined Rangers for £26,000, a Scottish record. George had played mostly at inside left, a position which was filled by Tottie Beck, who would later be named the supporters' Player of the Year.

Ten days after McLean's departure, £7,000 of his fee was spent when Celtic's Bobby Carroll was signed. Bobby immediately slotted into the team at outside right for a visit to Pittodrie on 16 February. Saints won 1-0, and in doing so showed much greater spirit. Carroll would play fourteen times in all, mostly at outside right.

During the first three months of the year adverse weather conditions severely disrupted the fixture card. In an attempt to beat the freeze, Saints travelled to Dublin to meet old friends Drumcondra on 26 February. It proved to be a useful exercise. After the Dublin break, the Buddies returned to competitive football with a 1-1 home draw with Partick Thistle. They then drew 2-2 away to Falkirk, 1-1 at home to Celtic, and beat Dunfermline 3-1 at home to sustain a five match unbeaten run.

The third round of the Cup brought strong-going Partick Thistle to Paisley on 19 March. Saints, 1-0 up with six minutes to go, were pegged back. In the replay 18,200 spectators saw the combination of a White goal and a Beattie penalty save take Saints through to the quarter-finals. In between the two Thistle ties, the unbeaten run came to end with a 4-2 defeat by Airdrieonians at Broomfield.

Five days after the Firhill tie, the Cup campaign continued when Celtic were the visitors. A crowd of 35,644 saw a tie dominated by foul play, and, consequently, the referee's whistle, as six were booked in a poor advert for Cup football. The fans saw only one goal, an early close-range effort from Celts Frank Brogan. Eighty-two minutes later Saints were out.

Five points collected from the next five League games meant that a draw against Dundee United in the second last fixture would be good enough to ensure Division One safety. A 2-1 win saw Saints finish in twelfth place, but only five points ahead of second bottom Clyde. St. Mirren's existence at the bottom end of the League had continued, much to the dissatisfaction of a growing number of Buddies as crowds of 5,000 became commonplace.

1963-64

A crowd of 7,000 watched Saints' opening League Cup tie, in which they secured a 1-1 home draw against Hibs thanks to a Don Kerrigan goal. A much improved display was given in the second tie, when they gained a creditable 2-2 draw at Pittodrie.

The Buddies then failed to defeat a weakened Dundee United side at Love Street in front of 8,000 spectators. Seventy-two hours later, with the influential Jim Clunie out injured but Cockles Wilson back in the team as left back and captain, Saints' morale was lifted when the Tannadice team returned to Paisley on League business and were beaten 2-1.

For the fourth League Cup tie on 24 August, Hibs showed a vitality at Easter Road which Saints couldn't match. The match was lost 3-0, as was the home tie against Aberdeen. The final sectional match at Tannadice was also lost, despite two terrific goals from Kerrigan. Saints had gained just two points from six ties to finish bottom of the section.

It was essential that better form was shown in the League. The second fixture, a difficult visit to Rugby Park on 7 September, ended in a 2-0 defeat by Kilmarnock, but it was followed by a rousing home 2-1 win over Motherwell. Just seconds into the second half and 1-0 down, Dick Beattie was taken off when two bones in his left ankle were broken. With White in goal, a Bobby Carroll double gave the Buddies the points in a victory which owed much to the great backing provided by the 8,000 spectators.

The highly-rated and popular Beattie would be out of action for weeks. In the absence of Bobby Williamson, whose free transfer request had been granted earlier, Beattie's place at Pittodrie the following week was taken by former Airdrieonians goalie Bobby Dempster, who had originally been signed on 12 August on a one month contract. Saints won 2-0, and it could have been more. The disappointments of the League Cup were beginning to recede, a feeling consolidated when Saints beat Celtic 2-1 at home to record their third win in a row.

Enthusiasm amongst the fans was rekindled as forty supporters buses and many private cars headed for Firs Park, Falkirk. Newly promoted East Stirlingshire were most people's favourites to be relegated, but the Saints team made the fundamental error of under-estimating their opponents. The "Shire" won 2-1! Rangers then came to Love Street on 12 October, and won 3-0 as Saints' stand-in 'keeper Dempster was blamed, in part at least, for each of the goals.

A trio of defeats was completed when Falkirk scored two excellent goals in the last three minutes of an otherwise drab game at Brockville. Tommy White was dropped for this match, having scored only one goal in thirteen appearances up till then. Six days later another forward was missing from the line-up to face Third Lanark. Only two hours before the match, Don Kerrigan was exchanged for Aberdeen inside left Willie Allen, with St. Mirren also receiving £7,000.

Jim Clunie

It was, to say the least, a surprising transaction. Kerrigan was the Club's top scorer with seven competitive goals. Allan would play twenty-six times, mostly at inside left, and score four goals. After the sale of Kerrigan, and later White, no-one successfully replaced either at centre. Three of inside forward Beck's forty appearances were at centre and Carroll played there ten times; neither were at their best in the position. Towards the end of the season Wilson was again tried. Cockles was at least as successful as anyone else, but had shown in the past he was not the long-term solution.

Young Gerry Queen looked a more likely proposition. Queen had been signed from Johnstone Burgh in February 1962, making an impressive debut on 6 October 1963, Saints' 86th birthday, and playing eight times during his first season. He would make twelve appearances in his second term, including nine at centre, scoring four League goals.

On 25 October, a crowd of only 5,000 turned up as Saints won two welcome points against a poor Third Lanark side. The only goal of the game was scored by left half Bobby Ross, who had arrived from East Fife as a left winger for £3,300 in December 1962. During the season he would play thirty-one times, mostly at left half. In a rare back-to-back victory, another two points were won at home when Saints saw off Dundee by two goals to one. White was still out of favour, but several clubs, including Hearts expressed an interest in the centre forward. Five days after Saints visited Tynecastle on 9 November, Tommy White was transferred to the "Maroons" for £7,250.

Dempster's uncertain performances in goal prompted Jackie Cox to look for another 'keeper. His search took him to Portadown, where ex-Celt Frank Connor had been voted the best goalkeeper in the Irish League. Connor was signed on 14 November, and was selected for the next match against Partick Thistle at Firhill. A 2-1 defeat ensued, but the new goalie gave a five star performance, so that appeared to be one problem solved.

Next up, a visit to Paisley by Hibs attracted just 6,500 people. It was further evidence that St. Mirren's "hard-core" support – which up until then had usually been assessed as 9,000 – was not irreducible. A 1-1 draw in this thirteenth match produced the thirteenth point, but tellingly only fifteen goals had been scored. Such a goals ratio not only pointed to another relegation struggle, but was unlikely to attract back lapsed supporters.

By the time Queen of the South came to Paisley on 21 December, Saints had lost 5-0 at Dunfermline and 4-2 at home to Airdrieonians. Like his predecessor, Connor had disappointed in goal, so it was a less than completely fit Dick Beattie who returned to first team duty against the "Doonhamers" at a time when the steady number of critical letters sent to the "Paisley Daily Express" showed a marked increase. Only 3,500 fans, a new low, watched Jimmy Robertson score late on for a 3-2 win. The attendance was one third of what the Club needed to break even.

The points return became fifteen from twenty games as results continued to deteriorate. Some improved form was shown on 4 January with a 3-1 home win over the "Dons" before a 5,000 crowd. The problem centre forward position was filled for the first time by Gerry Queen, who scored the third goal. Also brought back were two old favourites. Cockles Wilson replaced Ian Riddell, as the pair again competed against each other for the left back position, and the traditional black and white stripes were worn again for the first time in ages.

Tannadice was the scene of Saints' first round Scottish Cup tie on 11 January. Two weeks earlier a 6-2 League defeat had been suffered at the same venue, but a merited 0-0 draw in Dundee gave Saints a second chance. They grabbed it when goals from Clunie and Jimmy Robertson produced a 2-0 victory. Next round opponents were Second Division Stranraer. A third-minute goal by Queen was not the signal for a subsequent goal rush, and the Galloway team's challenge was only snuffed out nine minutes from time when right winger Tommy Robertson, signed from Petershill during the 1963 close season, hit a second.

With Beattie back at his best and Clunie returned from injury, Saints headed to Ibrox on 8 February in good spirits for a fixture which had seldom added to their points total, but an excellent 3-2 win proved to be the result of the season. Three days later storm clouds gathered when some allegations began to emerge in the Press about activities involving Dick Beattie before he joined St. Mirren. The Club's initial view was that it was entirely a matter for the player.

By mid-February the Board were coming to the conclusion that the immediate solution to the Club's financial problems "would be to sell a player for a considerable sum of money," but Chairman Mr. Alexander Lamb's view prevailed "that no player of quality should be sold at the present time". At the same Board meeting a written transfer request was coincidentally received from Jimmy Robertson.

In the third round of the Cup a strongly disputed goal at Love Street by Falkirk's Sammy Wilson was enough to eliminate Saints. In the next match, on 19 February, the "Bairns" were again the visitors. This time only 2,800 people turned out. The following week a visit to Dens Park produced what would turn out to be Saints' worst result of the twentieth century! Humiliation was on the cards when the "Dark Blues" ran up a four-goal lead by half-time. In the end it was 9-2, with an already under-pressure Beattie attracting most of the post-match flak.

On 13 March, the Manager reported that Tottenham Hotspur wished to buy Jimmy Robertson. In view of the player's persistent requests to be transferred and the transfer deadline being just three days away, Mr. Cox was authorised to discuss the matter with Spurs. He was not in a strong bargaining position. On 14 March for a fee of £23,000, Robertson was transferred to Tottenham, where he would win a cap for Scotland and thereafter enjoy a highly successful career with Arsenal and Stoke City, amongst others.

Seven days on, there was some good news on the park when a 2-1 home win over St. Johnstone ensured that Paisley's Saints retained their Division One status. Relegation had been avoided yet again, but this time the attendances told their own story: the fans' patience had finally snapped. By 21 April it was estimated that a weekly loss of almost £1,000 was being incurred, the equivalent of selling a George McLean and Jimmy Robertson every year.

The team ended the League campaign with an away draw against relegated Queen of the South, a result which gave Saints twenty-nine points from thirty-four games and twelfth place in the table. It was a record which said as much about the number of poor teams in Scotland's top Division as it did about the quality of Saints' play. Something had to be done urgently about the latter if the support was not to continue to haemorrhage.

1964-65

As the 1963-64 season came to an end, press assertions persisted that Dick Beattie and a number of other players had taken bribes to "throw" games in England. By 20 April, the St. Mirren Board concluded that it was in the best interests of the 'keeper and the Club if he was "relieved of his training and playing obligations, pending investigation of the allegations made against him". Beattie continued to receive his normal wages until 27 June, when he was given a free transfer.

Frank Connor, also to be freed at the end of the season, was recalled for the last League game, but the Club urgently needed an experienced goalkeeper as they were committed to taking part in a League Cup-style Summer Cup competition, and were due to face Third Lanark, Partick Thistle, and East Stirlingshire.

Seventy-two hours before the Summer Cup started, Paisley-born goalkeeper and self-confessed Saints' supporter Pat Liney was signed from Dundee. Liney had been in the Dens Parkers' 1961-62 championship-winning team before losing his place to Bert Slater. By the time the summer competition got underway, East Stirlingshire had joined Rangers and Celtic in pulling out; Shire's place was taken by... Morton.

This was a Morton team which had not only reached the 1963 League Cup Final, but had proved almost unbeatable as they sprinted to the Second Division title, watched by crowds of 12,000. Morton were not only in the ascendancy, but their spectacular progress under their colourful Managing Director Hal Stewart was exerting additional pressure on everyone at St. Mirren Park. In the circumstances, there was some relief when Saints took three points from the "Ton", but results against Thirds and Thistle ended Saints involvement in the tournament.

Trainer Ernie Nash

At the beginning of July some re-organisation of the training, coaching, and medical staff began with the full-time appointment of Trainer-Coach Ernie Nash, who for five years had been Assistant Trainer at highly successful Kilmarnock FC. Jimmy McGarvey would concentrate on the treatment of injuries, but from December onwards would perform this role in a part-time capacity. Other support staff would also switch to part-time as cost-cutting measures continued.

Two days prior to the start of the 1964-65 season, Saints signed twenty-three year old centre forward Alastair McIntyre from St. Johnstone for £8,000, with £6,000 of the fee being provided by the expanding Development Club. On the same day, Dick Beattie was charged with "conspiring with others between 1 April and 30 April 1963, to defraud". There was specific mention of the Dundee v St. Mirren match of 13 April 1963 which Dundee won 5-1. This was the first suggestion that any of the bribery accusations may have related to Scottish football.

The League Cup started on 8 August with an unimpressive but welcome 2-1 away victory over St. Johnstone, Tottie Beck scoring both. Meanwhile, one Saints fan who watched the Reserves on the same day was enthused by the play of a seventeen year old who had been signed in the summer from Drumchapel Amateurs. In a letter to the "Paisley Daily Express", the anonymous supporter reckoned the youngster was "a terrier in the tackle, refused to be beaten, was full of energy and drive and had several mazy runs". The newcomer's name was Archie Gemmill.

The second match, a thriller against Rangers in Paisley, finished 0-0, mainly thanks to the heroics of Liney. Saints then picked up a fourth League Cup point when a Tommy Robertson hat-trick helped earn a 3-3 home draw with Aberdeen. It was the "Dons" again for the opening League fixture four days later, when the team tried to defend a 1-0 half time lead, only to lose 2-1.

Two more sectional points were won when the Perth Saints were beaten 2-0, but any hopes about advancing to the knock-out stage of the competition vanished at Ibrox as Saints lost 6-2. The last tie finished in a 2-2 draw at Pittodrie. As the League championship began, some encouragement was drawn from Saints having scored eleven goals in their six League Cup matches. Unfortunately, this scoring rate was not maintained.

The first eleven League outings produced only five points. In the ninth game, Rangers won 7-0 at St. Mirren Park, scoring six in an unhappy second half for Liney. That result was bad enough, but even poor teams were easily beating Saints. On the plus side, the team were looking fitter under the new Nash regime, Liney was generally showing outstanding form in goal, Cammy Murray and Cockles Wilson had few peers at full back, and Jim Clunie's defensive qualities were recognised when he won his first representative honour, a Scottish League cap against the League of Ireland in Dublin on 23 September. The minus was that, once again, some of Saints' other players were simply below the required standard.

Although the team were punchless in attack, a lack of creativity remained the key problem. An attempt was made to improve matters when inside forward Willie Allan, who had only shown spasmodic good form during his eleven months in Paisley, moved to Falkirk on 11 September in exchange for another inside man, Alan Redpath.

On 2 October, Dick Beattie made his first appearance in court. A Sunday newspaper reporter told the court that he had confronted the player with allegations made by one of Beattie's co-accused, which the reporter had secretly taped. "Beattie made a gesture of despair and admitted the allegations against him," stated the reporter, "but denied that he had ever thrown or lost a match while at St. Mirren".

On the day after the court case opened, Saints achieved their only win in the opening eleven League fixtures, a 2-1 home victory over Dundee United. The game included two penalty saves by Liney and a sparkling debut by seventeen year old Gemmill at inside left. The 4,000-strong crowd took to the youngster immediately.

By the end of October, Saints were second bottom of the League, crowds were down to 3,000, and Rangers made a written offer of £14,000 for Therolf Beck. A 3-0 win over bottom club Airdrieonians on 7 November was a boost of sorts, although the crowd of only 2,000 highlighted the alarming extent of disillusionment. One week after the Airdrie victory, fellow strugglers Third Lanark managed two breakaways at Cathkin to secure the points. By this time Beck had joined Rangers.

Part of the fans' disenchantment focused on the perception that many of the incoming players were of inferior quality to the ones being sold. This attitude reached its zenith when Norrie Davidson was signed from Partick Thistle. He made his debut on 28 November in a home match against Dunfermline. When the team was read out his name was booed! Given such a reception, it is perhaps not surprising that Norrie failed to make a favourable initial impression. He played in just one other first team game.

One player who had suffered similar treatment was Bobby Carroll, whose displays had been mostly disappointing. Davidson's arrival coincided with an upswing in Bobby's performances. In four matches between 5 December and the end of 1964, ten goals were scored to win three and draw one. Carroll hit six of them as Saints doubled their points total to fourteen. Mid-way through his four-week purple patch he withdrew his earlier request for a transfer.

The team would add just ten more points in their remaining sixteen fixtures. The Cup, so often a pleasant diversion, ended in the first round when Celtic visited and won as easily as the 3-0 scoreline suggests. Saints were far from being alone in their struggles. Boardroom upheaval at Cathkin Park halfway through the previous season began to have its effect on Third Lanark's on-field performances: they won just seven points all season. Sadly, continuing maladministration would close the Crosshill club within two years. Airdrieonians were little better on the

Team Group 1964-65
Back Row (left to right): Murray, Wilson, Liney, Clark, Clunie, Gray
Front Row: Quinn, Carroll, Ross, Beck, Robertson.

park, with a final points total of fourteen. These two clubs ensured that Saints, for the first time in years, were not unduly threatened with relegation.

That didn't mean the season was any less of an endurance test for the faithful supporters, a fact appreciated by the Directors. At an April Board meeting, concern was expressed regarding the performance of the team. Corrective action was deferred, but it was agreed that, if improvement was not shown during the 1965 Summer Cup competition, then "some drastic action would have to be taken".

Following the second tie, a 2-0 defeat at Cappielow on 3 May, the Board referred to the team's "general lack of ability", and it was reluctantly agreed that a change of Manager was necessary. Jackie Cox was asked to resign with three months salary in lieu of notice. Mr. Cox, who had held the post for two and a half years, agreed to leave on 4 May, but asked for permission to be allowed to release the news to the press.

Four months earlier a side of the Manager's job not seen by supporters came to light in a Nottingham courtroom. On 12 January 1965, Dick Beattie admitted two of the four fraud charges against him and was jailed for nine months. "I was sorry I was caught out," stated Beattie at the time. "I was dreading the day it would happen because I thought I had a wonderful life ahead of me in football. I'm only sorry I was caught when I was at St. Mirren. They thought so much of me, and couldn't do enough to help me. The Manager, Mr. Cox, even fixed up a part-time job for my wife to help me out. I was a fool. I accepted the bribes and did my bit to earn the money. I never thought I would be caught."

The Beattie case was a tragedy, but one beyond the control of anyone at St. Mirren Park. The same could not be said for the team's performances. A sustained improvement was the minimum expected from a new Manager.

1965-66

The unlucky Roy Kemp and mid-season buy Norrie Davidson were the best known players in the 1965 free transfer list, but the number of notable departees was set to increase when the Directors reluctantly concluded that St. Mirren's full-time set-up was "an uneconomic proposition". From 1 July, the Club would revert to part-time status, and the new wage would be £16 per week.

The other big decision facing the Board was the selection of a Manager to replace Jackie Cox. On 7 June, thirty-three year old Doug Millward joined Saints from Southern League Poole Town, having taken the Dorset club to promotion twelve months earlier. He was a fully qualified English FA coach, a player who had won two successive championship medals with Ipswich Town under the managership of Alf Ramsay, and a super-enthusiast who was set to make a favourable early impression on Paisley.

Eight days after Doug Millward's appointment, Mr. H.V. McNaughton, the Paisley Burgh Engineer, succeeded Mr. A Lamb as Chairman. Messrs. Millward and McNaughton were taking over the lead roles at a club in the midst of major transition, as the introduction of a part-time playing staff inevitably accelerated Saints' transfer activities. First to go was the versatile Bobby Ross, who had made twenty-eight appearances the previous season. He joined Grimsby Town on 15 June. A week later, wing half Billy Gray and centre forward Alastair McIntyre made the shorter journey to Cappielow.

Team captain Jim Clunie, who wished to remain full-time, looked as if he was heading for Norwich City after the two clubs had agreed a £7,000 fee. Clunie visited Carrow Road, but after asking for some time to consider the move, decided it wasn't for him. On 29 June, the thirty-two year old centre half was transferred to Bury FC for £4,750. That same day, Red Campbell, who had been a Saint since July 1958, asked for a free transfer. Although he had only made eleven appearances during the previous season, the Club were looking for a fee or a player exchange. On 23 July, Campbell also moved to Morton, with left winger Bobby Adamson and wing half Jim Kiernan coming to Paisley.

Adamson would prove to be a great success. Playing mostly at outside left, he would end the season as the team's top scorer, with eighteen goals and the Supporters' Club Player of the Year. Kiernan, another more than useful acquisition, would begin the season as a left half, take over at centre half for twenty-one games in the middle of the season, then revert to half back for the last quarter.

At centre half for the first ten matches would be Jackie Young, who had been signed on 17 July 1965. Twenty-eight year old Young had been given a free transfer from East Fife, but the Methil club had only let him go because they couldn't afford to pay him a testimonial fee he was due if he had stayed. "Jake" remained in the first team until the end of September, but by then he had become a target of fans' criticism regarding his perceived lack of pace. It transpired he was troubled with his breathing and had to get a nose operation, but he didn't play again for the first team.

Bobby Carroll was the last of the first team regulars to move before the season started when he joined Dundee United on 29 July, having previously turned down the chance to sign for Carlisle United. In the Charity Cup opening match, against English First Division new boys Northampton Town, Saints' lack of firepower was again in evidence as the team lost

Bobby Adamson

2-0. It was much the same four days later in a second pre-season friendly at Darlington, which was lost 2-1.

The new Manager by this time had a much better idea of the problems he faced. This knowledge included the fact that the Club had made a loss of £9,107 in the previous year, despite receiving £7,738 from the Development Club. The result was that player swops, and not direct signings, became the more likely method of recruitment. Mr. Millward's problems worsened during the Northampton match when Archie Gemmill, Saints' most eye-catching performer and Player of the Year in his debut season, was carried off with what turned out to be a hairline fracture of his right tibula. The injury would keep him out of the first team until 30 October.

Despite such set-backs, Doug Millward remained positive. Part of his imaginative approach included the experiment of bringing Brazilian players to St. Mirren, beginning with the arrival in Paisley of Fernando Jose De Azevedo Pakeiras on 31 July. "Nando", as he quickly became known, gave a fantastic demonstration of ball-juggling at half-time in the Charity Cup game, but documentation delays meant that by the time he made his debut on 11 September against Morton he had been joined by fellow Brazilian Roberto Faria, a centre half. A local derby was perhaps not the best fixture to demonstrate South American skills, and Azevedo gave the immediate impression that he was unhappy with the physical aspects of the Scottish game.

Three weeks later both Azevedo and Faria were selected to play in a Renfrewshire Cup tie against Babcock and Wilcox, but neither impressed. On 8 October the Brazilian initiative neared its end when Nando checked out of the Friarshall Hotel. Later he stated that he felt he was unable to cope with the Scottish climate. Faria soon returned to Portugal. The exercise had at least been worth a try.

Jim Thorburn

The League Cup began with a tie against Morton, who had the majority of the game and won 2-1. This was followed by a 1-0 loss at Easter Road and a 1-0 victory over Falkirk at Brockville on 21 August. A day earlier, transfer-seeking right-winger Henry Quinn was signed by Celtic for £2,000.

Saints also won 1-0 at Cappielow, but home defeats from Hibs and Falkirk left them with four points from six League Cup games. It was only a 33% success rate, but it was one they were unable to match during an agonising League programme, which began with a 3-2 away win over Falkirk on 25 August. It was not the shape of things to come. Between 11 September and 9 October the next five games were lost, including a 6-1 home defeat by Rangers.

Saints' second League victory came on 16 October. It was a 1-0 win over Clyde at Shawfield, thanks to an Adamson penalty and some outstanding saves from Pat Liney, who had been a bit shaky in matches immediately prior to this. In the meanwhile, former Raith Rovers 'keeper Jim Thorburn joined from Ipswich Town in mid-September. Thorburn replaced Liney for a Renfrewshire Cup tie against Morton on 3 November, a change coinciding with Pat submitting an unsuccessful transfer request just prior to the tie. Liney would later enjoy a nine-game run at the beginning of 1966, but Thorburn became the preferred choice.

An eight match sequence from 6 November to New Year's Day 1966 began with Saints losing 5-1 away to Dunfermline, and ended with a 7-4 home defeat by Kilmarnock. In between, two games were won and one drawn, crowds again dipped as low as 1500, and Craigmark Bruntonians' highly rated half back Bobby Pinkerton was signed on 17 November. Bobby would play over twenty games before the season ended, mostly at left half.

A couple of weeks after the 7-4 game, Kilmarnock expressed an interest in Saints' hard-working inside forward Gerry Queen, who had earlier been a transfer target of Fulham, Preston North End, and Liverpool. On 21 January, after four years with Saints, Gerry was transferred to Rugby Park in a deal which brought Ronnie Hamilton to Paisley. St. Mirren also received £4,000. The next day, Hamilton's eighteenth minute goal gave Saints two welcome points in a 1-0 home victory over Aberdeen.

Two weeks on, Saints headed for Cowdenbeath's Central Park on Scottish Cup business. Their opponents were a mid-table Second Division side, but Cowden won 1-0, causing further despair for the Saints' support. The fight for First Division survival resumed, and a small step was taken when Clyde were beaten 2-1 at Love Street, with a winning goal from Pinkerton in the dying seconds.

Thereafter, the pattern of results continued to cause concern, but the whole Club was given a boost on 8 March 1966, when Jim Clunie transferred back from Bury; his absence had been so short that Bury hadn't paid the last instalment of the transfer fee! His presence was immediately felt in a 1-0 away win over Stirling Albion four days later. This gave Saints their second win in a row, the only consecutive victories of the season. Four matches were then lost between 19 March and 9 April, as the second relegation place became the preserve of St. Mirren or Morton.

The second last game, on 23 April, was against Hamilton Academical. The "Accies" had been badly adrift all season and were already relegated, their defence having conceded one hundred and twelve goals in thirty two games. Saints were unable to increase that total, whilst Hamilton's twenty-sixth League goal was enough to win a game which beforehand had seemed likely to secure Saints' safety.

The Buddies entered the final game on 30 April level on points with Morton, and a goal average superiority of just 0.019! Only one point was gained against Hearts at Love Street in an extremely tense ninety minutes, but it proved sufficient as Morton lost 2-0 to Celtic at Cappielow. Saints had remained in the First Division by one point, but they were getting nearer the precipice.

1966-67

Throughout the 1966 close season, Doug Millward maintained his high profile in the community and was regularly pictured presenting cups and prizes to sports winners. At the same time his negotiating skills paid off when three prominent first team players, Bobby Adamson, Archie Gemmill, and Cammy Murray, agreed to re-sign.

Adamson, like Gemmill and Murray before him, had enjoyed a very successful first season as a Saint, but had also submitted five transfer requests along the way, citing as his reason that "part-time football doesn't suit me". He wasn't alone in that view. Pat Liney, who had wanted away since November 1965, was transferred to full-time Bradford City on 16 June for £1,000, and twenty-one year old regular winger Tommy Robertson, who was also determined to leave, joined Crystal Palace on 29 October for £6,000 following a three month refusal to re-sign. It was going to be a while before St. Mirren would gather a squad of good players who were also content to be part-time.

In the meantime, Saints created a bit of Scottish football history when Jim Clunie injured his back at a rain-sodden Shawfield Stadium on 13 August 1966. It was the first day of a new rule which allowed a twelfth player to be introduced at any time during the match, irrespective of injuries. After just twenty-three minutes, Clunie became the first player to be substituted in a competitive match in Scotland; at the same time Archie Gemmill gained additional early fame by becoming the first substitute. In an otherwise uneventful match, Saints lost 1-0.

The following tie, against Hearts at St. Mirren Park, featured Saints' longest-serving player, John "Cockles" Wilson, for the first time in twelve months. Cockles had sustained a career-threatening injury in the second tie of the previous season's League Cup, and then damaged bones in his ankle during a mid-December comeback for the Reserves. A second

Bobby Pinkerton

Scottish football's first ever substitute, Archie Gemmill.

comeback for the second team, just as the 1965-66 season ended, showed he would be fit and ready to begin his eleventh term in the colours.

The Hearts' match ended in a 0-0 draw, and Saints' inability to score would become the season's recurring theme. It happened in three more of the League Cup ties and would occur in no less than twenty-one of the thirty-four League games. That draw with Hearts was the only sectional point gained, although Saints did score twice at Celtic Park. Unfortunately, European champions-to-be Celtic scored eight as this third tie proved to be something of a mis-match.

At the September A.G.M., the Chairman clarified the part-time status of the playing staff when he stated that "where conditions justified it, the Club would have some full time players". Accounts for the year ended 31 March 1967 emphasised the extent of the Club's financial difficulties when, despite savings in wages helping to cut costs by £10,000, the loss was £9,806. Such figures suggested the employment of "some full time players" would be on a very limited basis indeed.

Two days after the A.G.M., Saints won their opening League game, but didn't win another until their fifteenth fixture on Christmas Eve, when a Gemmill hat-trick against second bottom Ayr United took the Buddies' points total to six, allowing them to take Ayr's place in the table. This abysmal run included 5-0 home defeats from Dunfermline Athletic and Motherwell within a four week period, and, for the second year in a row, a 6-1 hammering at Love Street by Rangers. Against all the odds, Saints became the first team to take a point from the all-conquering Celtic when they drew 1-1 at Celtic Park on 5 November, thanks mainly to an inspirational performance from debutant 'keeper Denis Connaghan, who had been signed from Renfrew Juniors earlier in the season.

By this time, the Directors were once again looking for a new manager. On 11 October, the Board agreed to Doug Millward's request to be released from his contract, enabling him to take a coaching post in America's new National Professional Soccer League (NPSL). "The opportunity in going to America, "explained Mr. Millward, "is that there is no history, no ghosts from the past." Few people thought he was only talking about the United States.

Doug Millward would quickly prove himself in America by being named the 1967 N.P.S.L. Coach of the Year, but it was agreed he would remain at St. Mirren Park on a week-to-week basis until his successor was found. It was all very amicable, but not the ideal circumstances for a manager to get the best from his players. Within a fortnight, Millward took charge of the Reserve team, retaining this capacity until he left at the end of November, whilst Reserve Coach Willie Paton became interim manager of the first team.

Since news broke of Doug Millward's departure, the Club had made public their thoughts about the next Manager. He would be a well-known, high profile individual, and it was hoped such an appointment would underline the ambitions of everyone at St. Mirren Park. By 11 November, reports linking St. Mirren with former Scotland Manager John Prentice were described as "premature" by the Chairman. Three days later it was announced that Mr. Prentice had turned down the job, with travelling from his Edinburgh home being given as the biggest stumbling block to a deal.

The Board were still keen to get their man, and Prentice, who had built part-time Clyde into a formidable force, was offered the post on a part-time basis on 26 November. He again turned it down because of the travel involved. Two days later it emerged that Partick Thistle's thirty-five year old coach Alex Wright, who in turn had been recommended by Prentice, was the new hot favourite for the job. Such an appointment was something of a gamble, as Wright had no previous managerial experience. It also seemed to be a bit of a let down for those supporters who felt that Wright did not conform to the "well-known, high profile" description. Such doubters would be pleasantly surprised.

Alex Wright's initial two year deal commenced on 3 December when he watched his new side lose 2-0 to Dundee at Dens. They were bottom of the League again. Twelve days later, Wright made his first signing when twenty-three year old centre half Jim Hannah was bought from Airdrieonians for £2,000. Injuries would defer Jim's debut until the end of January, against Cowdenbeath in the Cup, he would then play in only half of the subsequent League games.

This expenditure was made possible when £14,000 was raised by the sale of Club property in Caledonia Street to Shell & BP Ltd., who opened a petrol station on the site. This welcome income was used to temporarily clear the Club's overdraft, but an adjacent site was retained as a possible location for social club premises.

Alex Wright's third game in charge, a 2-2 draw at Tannadice, preceded the season's second win, but the Christmas Eve 3-1 victory over Ayr United was no prelude to a revival. A 1-0 Hogmanay loss to St. Johnstone at Muirton was followed by three straight 3-0 defeats. In the midst of this run, Jim Clunie was given a free transfer at his own request. He had made eight first team appearances at the beginning of the season, but thereafter was not selected. He felt there was no place for him in the future scheme of things, and the new Manager agreed. They were both correct about the immediate future, but Jim Clunie's connection with St. Mirren would of course be restored in the late 1970s.

Five days after Big Jim's mid-January departure, £6,500 was spent to secure the signature of St. Johnstone's excellent wing half Willie Renton at the third attempt. As part of the two and a half year deal, Willie was offered a full-time wage to tide him over until he could get a job in the Paisley area. Renton would not be eligible to play in a re-run of the previous season's Scottish Cup tie against Cowdenbeath. This time the tie was in Paisley, and although Saints gained an early lead – their first goal of 1967 – Cowden's game plan to take the tie back to Fife became apparent after they equalised.

In the replay, an Archie Gemmill thirty-yarder thrust an unconvincing Saints' side into the next round, where they hosted Division Two Hamilton Academical but lost 1-0. A week earlier, on 11 February, Saints had convincingly beaten third bottom Stirling Albion 4-0, to give the Buddies nine points from twenty-two fxtures and a chance to close in on the Annfield club. Much credit for this third win was given to the link play of new centre forward Peter Kane, the leading goalscorer of Crewe Alexandra who had been signed the day before the Albion game. He played in almost every game thereafter, but scored on just three occasions. After the Stirling match, only one more victory was achieved and six more points collected.

Alex Wright packs his bag at Firhill following his appointment as St Mirren Manager. Alex served Thistle for 14 years as 1st team coach and player.

Throughout this gloomy season, right half Jim Kiernan's consistency shone through, and his spirited displays were recognised when he was named the Supporters Club's Player of the Year on 20 March. A week later, a 0-0 draw with Aberdeen at Pittodrie took Saints to within three points of third bottom Stirling Albion. Unfortunately, it was as near as they got.

With three games still to go and relegation a near certainty, it was announced that 'keeper Denis Connaghan was joining Doug Millward in Baltimore. Penalty-save specialist Connaghan's £4000 transfer had in fact been agreed in mid-January with effect from 30 April. Baltimore then intimated that Denis was needed urgently, so his transfer date was brought forward to 13 April, with St. Mirren receiving a further £1000 in compensation. Connaghan's predecessor, Jim Thorburn, returned for the last three games.

At Fir Park the following Saturday, Motherwell were 4-0 up at half-time. The remaining forty-five minutes became an irrelevance; St. Mirren were relegated. Two 0-0 draws completed the season, the last one being a home game against St. Johnstone watched by a crowd estimated to be little more than seven hundred. Now the only way was up!

1967-68

The end of Cockles Wilson's great St. Mirren career coincided with the Club's first relegation since 1935. It was a demotion many had anticipated for years, as Saints had managed no better that seventh bottom in an eighteen-club Division One in any season since Cockles and his team-mates won the 1959 Scottish Cup Final, but the reduction in status didn't become a reality until the fixture list was issued.

The Buddies were set to compete against eighteen teams, Queen's Park excepted, who were drawn from Scotland's smaller towns. The accepted wisdom was that St. Mirren should never be in such company, but the debilitating effect of too many relegation battles meant that few supporters held high hopes of making a speedy exit from the lower division. "It is now a question of doing everything possible to make our stay in the second division as short as possible", was all Chairman Val McNaughton was in a position to say. With more certainty he knew income would drop and further belt-tightening was unavoidable.

The first economy was the abandonment of a Reserve side. This led to the conclusion that only a part-time trainer was required, so the services of Ernie Nash were reluctantly dispensed with on 23 April. He would be

"Big Jim" Blair beats the Alloa defence in the 67/68 championship year at snowy St Mirren Park.

replaced by Bill Cochrane from Benburb FC. On the same day as the Nash announcement, Bobby Adamson, Kenny Aird, Alex Clark, Jim Hannah, and Ronnie Hamilton were each placed on the "open to transfer" list.

One of the five, right winger Aird, a 1965 close season signing from Celtic who had since averaged over twenty games per season, moved to St. Johnstone fifteen days later for £2,000. Kenny would become a prominent member of Willie Ormond's attractive Perth side, but it was another of the Buddies' "tiny tots" who would attain lasting football fame.

Archie Gemmill was one of a number of players unhappy at the prospect of Division Two football and wages. Preston North End began to make enquiries about him on 15 May, and only five days later, for a fee of £13,000, Archie moved to Deepdale. He would go on to enjoy a most successful career in England, creating along the way a moment in Argentina which would long be cherished by Scottish supporters.

New recruits began to be acquired. In mid-June, a small fee was paid to the Scottish League, custodians of the players belonging to the tragically defunct Third Lanark, for the services of twenty-three year old right back Tony Connell, who would soon make his name as a most reliable left back for Saints. Three weeks later, Saints snapped up another former Thirds player from the League when twenty-two year old goal-scoring forward Hugh McLaughlin was secured.

Other summer signings included Frank Brodie from Blantyre Victoria and right winger Johnny Lawson, who had been released by Leeds United. Both would be freed at the end of the season, each having made only five League starts, but right half Willie Fulton, signed from Falkirk, would make that position his own.

Welcome though these newcomers were, there was real concern that not only were the consistent Cammy Murray and Player of the Year Jim Kiernan refusing to re-sign, but the remaining four who were up for transfer had each appealed to the Scottish League regarding the size of their transfer fees, which suggested a determination to leave Paisley.

A week before the Charity Cup opener with some of his best players not available to him, Wright took a characteristically positive view of the forthcoming season: "It will be easier for youngsters in Division Two and it means that if we do get promotion we will be going forward with a promising formation. Promotion is pointless if we just scrape home with a bad team. We must go forward with a pool of players capable of keeping the Club in Division One."

Unsigned players meant that the last-ever Paisley Charity Cup match – against a Preston North End team captained by Archie Gemmill – didn't really give the 2,500 crowd a proper chance to evaluate Saints' prospects but the following day in a step forward, Adamson and Clark re-signed but remained on the open to transfer list. Wing-half Clark, who had joined Saints in 1961 from Stewarton Amateurs, had averaged around twenty appearances in the four previous seasons, but would make just half that number of Division Two starts before being "freed".

The team's evolution continued during the League Cup sectional ties against Ayr United, Berwick Rangers, and Stranraer, where the very real incentive of a much needed money-spinning quarter final match with Celtic was narrowly missed.

During this League Cup campaign, one significant piece of transfer business was completed. At the end of August, nineteen year old six-footer Jim Blair was provisionally signed from Shotts Bon Accord, and made a scoring debut in the 2-2 home draw with Cowdenbeath on 21 October. "Big Jim" would score nine goals in his first nine games, within six months St. Mirren would turn down offers in the region of £50,000 for the new star inside forward. Five days after the Cowden match, Bon Accord agreed to release Blair, who along with Adamson, Hamilton, Kane, and Pinkerton would play at least twenty-five League games to underline Alex Wright's continuity of selection throughout the team.

By this time Saints had completed eleven League fixtures, having won seven and lost none. Three of the victories were by just one goal, but Manager Wright's team was beginning to take shape. At the beginning of October, Bobby Adamson asked to be taken off the open to transfer list, telling the press he was enjoying his football and was happy to stay!

The convivial atmosphere of a winning dressing room must have percolated to Cammy Murray, who had been involved in a somewhat drawn-out player swop with Clyde centre Kenny Knox, which the latter player ultimately rejected. On 12 October, Cammy agreed to re-sign on the understanding that the Club would not stand in his way if another team wanted to sign him. He immediately displaced Bobby Duffy, who had been the regular right back up to that point.

The first six players in the team then became automatic choices for the rest of the season: Thorburn, Murray, Connell, Fulton, McFadden, and Renton. Young pivot Andy McFadden, whose size 12 boots were reputedly the biggest in Scottish football, had been a 1966 close season signing from Port Glasgow Rangers, and had played in the two Division One games after relegation had been confirmed. He would greatly benefit throughout the season from the advice and guidance of his two wing halves, Fulton and Renton.

The consistency of these six and the absence of a reserve team made life difficult for others. At the end of September it was confirmed that centre-half Jim Hannah, restricted to just two appearances, had been transferred to Stranraer. Hannah

Alex Wright's Second Division Championship Medal.

1968-69

Towards the end of March 1968, and with promotion looking a certainty, wing half Willie Renton's ambition to go full-time led him to ask for a transfer. There was an immediate public response from the Manager. "We have worked hard at building up a happy atmosphere in the Club," explained Alex Wright, "and we do not want to keep dissatisfied players. In view of the circumstances we have decided to listen to offers for Renton". Part of "the circumstances" was that St. Mirren would be remaining part-time.

The influential Renton was transferred to Dunfermline Athletic for £7,000 on 15 July. That same day and for the same fee, Kilmarnock's 1965 League Championship-winning team captain Eric Murray was signed as a replacement. Twenty-six year old Murray was to be one of three experienced players signed over the summer, the other two being Dundee United forward Billy Hainey and Celtic defender Ian Young, both picked up on free transfers.

A fourth arrival was Johnstone Burgh's speedy winger Hugh Gilshan, who had been a signing target throughout the promotion season. The Manager's perseverance paid off on 10 February when Gilshan became a Saint, but he was allowed to remain at Keanie Park until the "Burgh" were out of the Junior Cup. His call-up came on 30 April, a few days after a Gilshan goal had helped capture the coveted trophy.

Saints players celebrate winning the 67/68 Championship after the 1-1 draw at home to 2nd place Arbroath.   Back Row (left to right): Ronnie Hamilton, Bobby Pinkerton, Jim Blair, Jackie Copland, Willie Fulton, Bobby Duffy, Willie Renton
Front Row: Tony Connell, Cammy Murray, Andy McFadden

was Manager Wright's first signing nine months earlier, but had played only eight times in his first season. Jim Kiernan, who had re-signed on 13 September, would only play six times before being given a free transfer in mid-March along with Alex Clark.

A 2-1 away defeat from East Fife on 4 November, the thirteenth fixture, ended Saints' unbeaten League sequence. It would be the Buddies' only defeat in thirty-six matches, and no more than a temporary setback. The team then began a Club record sixteen consecutive victories, the cornerstone of the whole campaign. Goals began to flow and few were being conceded. By 26 February, with ten games still to play and Saints eleven points ahead of nearest challengers Arbroath, Alex Wright conceded that not only did he think his side would go up, but they had a good chance of staying up.

This confidence in his team's future prospects looked a bit mis-placed when Saints, with Hamilton and skipper Renton absent, made a very shaky start to their Scottish Cup tie at Tannadice at the end of January. They managed a first half equaliser, but two further United goals in the first six minutes of the second half ended their involvement in the competition, and reminded everyone at St. Mirren Park of the higher standard of football they were aiming to re-join.

The Division Two leaders immediately got back into their stride with a 6-1 home win over Alloa Athletic. By 6 April they had fifty-two points from thirty games, and a win that day at Montrose would clinch promotion. To the frustration of everyone with St. Mirren connections, the game was called off at the last moment. Four days later the return journey to Links Park produced a goal-less draw. Another draw, 2-2 with Albion Rovers at Love Street, was enough to gain the quickest possible return to the top flight.

The following week, Saints celebrated their first Championship title in seventy-seven years of League football when they drew 1-1 with nearest challengers Arbroath in front of over 5,000 fans at St. Mirren Park. With the pressure off, the team then scored seventeen times in the last four matches to take their goal tally to exactly one hundred.

It had been a record-breaking season on a number of fronts as the Club finished nine points ahead of excellent runners-up Arbroath, managed by ex-Saint Albert Henderson. Alex Wright's go-for-goals policy had certainly re-kindled enthusiasm for the Club, but doubts persisted. The team's limitations had been exposed by Division One Dundee United in the Cup, and by Morton in two end-of-season Renfrewshire Cup ties when the Greenock side looked the superior outfit. To widespread amazement, Saints were about to take the top division by storm.

All four newcomers lined up for the opening League Cup tie against Montrose at Links Park. Also in the team was goalkeeper Denis Connaghan, who had re-joined St. Mirren from Baltimore Bays in March, but had been unable to displace Jim Thorburn from the promotion-winning team. The returning Saint had reunited with a Manager who had a clear view of how he wanted his team to play: "Last season we learned that we played better going forward all the time in a bid to win games. Our target now is to score goals. Even if it means losing one or two, we will sacrifice goals as long as we score more than the opposition. Defence in depth is finished at Love Street; our plan is to play open, quick, attractive football".

This admirable statement of intent was not matched by early performances in a League Cup section of Division Two teams. Four points were taken from the first two ties, against Montrose and Hamilton Accies, but a visit to Fir Park to face newly relegated Motherwell ended in a disastrous 6-0 defeat, as Saints played for eighty minutes with only ten men following the dismissal of Hainey. A further four points were collected from the return ties, but the eight point total was insufficient to progress.

This failure to qualify against lower Division opposition was quickly forgotten as Saints made a sensational ten-match unbeaten return to Division One, winning five and drawing five against a cross-section of top teams. One player not involved in this Saints revival was Ronnie Hamilton. Ronnie had played in the opening four League Cup ties, but didn't make a starting appearance thereafter. On 9 October he asked to be allowed to stop playing and training in order to concentrate on obtaining his accountancy qualifications. Despite only having a squad of seventeen players, the Club agreed without hesitation, but reserved the right to have first call on his services if he decided to take up professional football again.

The eleventh fixture, on the eleventh day of November, was a home match with Rangers. Saints were proudly positioned in second place, the only unbeaten team in British senior football. They were a point behind Celtic and one ahead of their visitors. A non-ticket crowd of 43,600

Hugh Gilshan

spectators assembled, intrigued to see how Paisley's promoted side and its recent additions, brought together for less than £10,000, would cope with an Ibrox side boosted by their new scoring sensation from Hibs, Colin Stein, who alone had cost £100,000!

Alex Wright was not intimidated by such comparisons. "We are all confident that we can continue our run of success," he proclaimed to the press. In a special edition of the "Paisley Daily Express" marking the return of big-time football to Paisley, local fans were interviewed about Saints' prospects: the Manager's optimism was overwhelmingly shared by those on the terracing. Paisley pride had returned!

Saints' line-up against Rangers on a foggy afternoon was: Connaghan, C. Murray, Connell, Fulton, McFadden, E. Murray, Adamson, Blair, Kane, Pinkerton, and Gilshan with Hainey as substitute. Up to this point only an occasional injury or suspension had upset this preferred selection in the League campaign, but this was Saints' biggest test yet. Captain Willie Fulton – who had been calmness personified just before kick off when he treated the crowd to a stunning display of his "keepie-uppie" skills – and Denis Connaghan were in inspiring form as Saints not only coped magnificently with considerable Rangers' pressure for much of the first half, but managed to create their own chances, notably a tremendous Peter Kane shot which hit the post.

Cammy Murray

This pattern continued until the sixty-ninth minute when 1967-68 Player of the Year Bobby Pinkerton, following some combined play with Adamson, passed the ball into a space created by Kane. Gilshan, who had run thirty yards off the ball, cut in from the left, latched on to the Pinkerton pass and shot past 'keeper Martin. It was a goal that brought the house down! Thereafter Saints displayed the team-work which had quickly become their hallmark to clinch a famous victory. At the end of the game hundreds of scarf-waving fans poured onto the pitch; the more composed Buddies restricted themselves to giving their team a standing ovation! It was the season's high point.

The following week the unbeaten run ended with a 2-0 defeat by Aberdeen. Seven days later, a Gilshan header earned a 1-1 home draw in a top of the table clash with Dundee United after a particularly impressive first-half performance. In the next two matches the team also played well in the first forty-five minutes, but their visit to Celtic Park on 7 December resulted in a 5-0 defeat, and was followed by a 6-2 reverse at East End Park.

These three losses in four matches proved to be a temporary blip. An excellently taken goal by Kane was enough to beat Clyde 1-0 in late December, a result which started a run of five wins, two draws, and only two goals conceded, which meant that as the Buddies made their preparations for the Scottish Cup against Dumbarton on 25 January, they were back up to third in the League, with thirty points from twenty-two fixtures. It was a position that no one had predicted back in August.

The Buddies' League form prompted high hopes of a great cup run and a large Paisley contingent formed the majority of the 8,860 crowd at Boghead. The "Sons", although struggling in Division Two, made life very difficult for a St. Mirren team displaying their worst form of the season. Saints lacked cohesion and understanding throughout, whereas only magnificent goalkeeping by Connaghan defied Dumbarton's eager forwards. The hosts deserved at least a replay, but a last minute Jim Blair goal took Saints through to the second round.

Incredibly, this Boghead victory was to be the last win of the season! Just two more points, from draws, were gained in the remaining twelve League fixtures. This complete switch in fortunes began with a terrific game against Dundee the following week, when goals in the seventy-third and eighty-third minutes gave Saints a 2-1 lead, but a double in the last five minutes enabled the "Dark Blues" to take the two points and end the Buddies' eighteen month unbeaten home record.

In the Cup, Saints drew with Airdrieonians at Broomfield after dominating the game, but went down 3-1 in the replay on 24 February. By this point injuries had begun to affect team selection. To ease the situation, eighteen year old provisional signing George Urquhart, an inside left, had been called up from Renfrew Juniors on 29 January. He made a promising debut in a League game against Airdrie in February, and would be used frequently during the remainder of the season.

The other players brought in – keeper Jim Thorburn, Bobby Duffy at full back or on the right wing, Hugh McLaughlin at centre or at wing half, and Ian Young at full back or centre half – all did well, but these three outfield players were expected to be able to play in more than one position, underlining the demands of operating with a squad of just seventeen.

The number of injuries sustained in the last third of the season was unfortunate, and such absences were sorely felt by the small squad, but Manager Alex Wright publicly touched on the real problem in mid-March: "I am a little concerned about the failure to score goals and we have now got to the stage of looking for new players".

The end of season statistics supported the Manager's analysis. St. Mirren eventually finished eleventh in the League, equal on points with ninth-place Dundee. In line with that, eight teams bettered the fifty-four goals conceded by the Buddies but their total of forty goals scored was the third worst in the whole Division. Thirty-one goals in twenty-two fixtures up to the Dumbarton cup-tie showed that even their first choice team were finding it difficult to score goals in Division One. Kane, Blair, and Adamson, so prolific in Division Two, scored nine, eight, and seven League goals respectively. After the Boghead match only nine goals were scored in the remaining twelve fixtures.

It was a problem which demanded attention, but the season would long be remembered for Saints' terrific start to the League programme. It was so good that right up to the third last game it was still possible for the Buddies to qualify for the Inter-Cities Fairs Cup. It was not to be, but in every other respect St. Mirren's return to the top Division had exceeded all expectations. For that, the small group of players and their Manager deserved the highest praise.

1969-70

The introduction of stringent economy measures in 1967 had not only transformed a St. Mirren loss of £16,000 into an £8,000 profit twelve months later, but allowed Club Chairman Mr. Val McNaughton to set an expansionist tone as Saints began their first season back in Division One: "We hope that the increased gate receipts will permit us to reach a stage where it will be possible to revert to a substantially full-time playing staff and also run a second team".

By the end of that first year, Manager Alex Wright also saw the revival of a reserve side as a core part of his plans to make St. Mirren one of Scotland's foremost teams of the 1970s. His side had successfully re-crossed the Scottish League's great divide, but the complete collapse in results at the end of 1968-69 merely confirmed to everyone at St. Mirren Park that although only one recognised first-teamer, Billy Hainey, had been released, new players were required, and the restoration of a Second Eleven was agreed.

In May, twenty-five year old centre forward Jim Young, scorer of twenty-two goals for Forfar Athletic during the previous season, was signed for a £2,500 fee. Also arriving in May was twenty-two year old schoolteacher George Cumming, recently freed by Partick Thistle, but a player whose whole attitude to the game was admired by Alex Wright. Cumming would be a virtual ever-present in the team until mid-January, usually on the right of midfield, but was deployed less often in the remainder of the season.

June saw the capture of two players with varying degrees of experience of English football. Eighteen year old forward Gordon "Gus" Eadie, who had briefly been with Bury, was snapped up from Rutherglen Glencairn. Eadie would play a handful of games in the early part of the season without making a great impact or scoring any goals.

At the end of the month experienced left-winger Tommy Knox was signed. He had begun his career with East Stirlingshire before moving to Chelsea, Newcastle, then Mansfield Town. Tommy had joined Northampton Town for a £6,000 fee in 1968, but when the "Cobblers" were relegated he moved back to Scotland on a free transfer. His St. Mirren career was limited to four appearances on the left wing up to 6 September, which led to the offer of a free transfer on 14 January.

Throughout the close season with the longer-term in mind, the Manager fixed up a number of promising youngsters, but in July he regained an experienced player, when Ronnie Hamilton, his accountancy exams behind him, returned to training and made himself available for selection.

In a relatively good start to the League Cup, Saints were still in contention for the quarter-finals on the last day of the sectional ties.

Tony Connell, Player of the Year 1969/70

These aspirations ended at Tannadice, where some shocking finishing from the Paisley forwards meant they went in at half-time just 1-0 up, when it should have been considerably more. Dundee United, with the wind at their backs after the interval, scored twice in a twelve-minute spell to end the Buddies' challenge.

Saints had taken no points from United, who would finish fifth in the League, but three points from both Hearts and Morton, who would finish fourth and tenth respectively. It was a level of points-gathering which they seldom emulated during the League programme. "The team played well but didn't take their chances," summarised Alex Wright after the United match, "but I am confident they will have a good season". Unfortunately, the Manager's point about missed chances not only proved to be the team's recurring weakness, but ensured that his hopes for a good season would fail to materialise.

In the first League fixture, ex-Saint George McLean scored all three Dunfermline goals in a 3-1 home defeat which could have been greater. The following week at Easter Road, Saints began brightly, but the sheer class of Hibernian's Peter Cormack exposed Saints' defensive frailties as they lost 2-0. The next match was also away, at Ibrox, and although Thorburn had something of an off-day in another 2-0 defeat, some encouragement was taken by an improved defensive performance.

Jim Young ended the growing goals drought when he scored his only League goals of the season with a hat-trick in a 4-0 win over a defensive-minded Clyde at Love Street. However, two points from five matches remained the return when the chance-squandering Saints lost 1-0 against Airdrieonians at Broomfield on 20 September. Alex Wright put the sequence of results down to "players lack of confidence in themselves" and noted that they were "dispirited too easily at times".

The players and the fans too had some reason to be dispirited when Kilmarnock visited St. Mirren Park. Another 2-0 defeat ensued, but the gap in ability between the teams was there for all to see. Changes were required for the next match – at home to Hearts on 4 October – and Mr. Wright made no less than eight alterations from the Killie match line-up.

Some of the Club's more experienced players, such as the previous season's Player of the Year, Willie Fulton, and Eric Murray, were reinstated. They returned to some effect, hustling Hearts out of their stride and winning a point in a goal-less draw. Fulton would play in most of the remaining twenty-one fixtures, but Murray became unsettled during November and December when, in swift succession, he was made captain, demoted to substitute, then dropped. He responded with a transfer request, which happily was later withdrawn.

For the October visit to second bottom club Raith Rovers, Bobby Pinkerton, who had been plagued by injuries since August, lined up on the left wing, but it was long-striding striker Jim Blair who captured the headlines with a well-taken hat-trick after the Kirkcaldy club had taken a 1-0 lead. Pinkerton would finish the season strongly, and from the beginning of March onwards was once again the automatic choice for left wing.

There was an undoubted improvement in form at this time, but most observers felt the team still lacked composure. The Manager obviously agreed, and after much delay due to a Dunfermline Athletic injury crisis, the talented Ian Lister signed for Saints for £3,000 on the last day of October. He would remain in the team for the rest of the season, slotting in perfectly either as a link-man or forward.

In his debut game at Fir Park on 1 November, Lister saw at first hand the most obvious reason why his new team were struggling, as Saints missed all their chances and Motherwell converted three. Four days later the Buddies looked to be a different team, as their brand of pacy, attacking football, goals from Gilshan and Blair and a resolute defence proved too good for Aberdeen.

In his second home match, a 2-1 win over Ayr United, twenty-three year old Lister gave an outstanding display in mid-field: "a maestro in a team of triers" was the "Paisley Daily Express" summary. The player admitted after the match that he was "enjoying his more meaningful role at Love Street". It certainly showed.

A Hugh Gilshan goal after three minutes against bottom of the table Partick Thistle was enough to earn Saints three consecutive wins, their best sequence of the season, but the successful mini-run ended on a snow-covered pitch at Dens, where an unlucky bounce beat Connaghan to give Dundee a 1-0 win on 29 November. It was the beginning of a nine-game sequence without a win, crowds dropped below the 5,000 mark, and "relegation" was mentioned in the local press for the first time.

For the ninth game, a 1-0 away defeat to Clyde on 17 January, Jim Thorburn was back in goals after a ten-week absence, while former Drumchapel Amateurs' youngster Iain Munro made his debut. During this dismal period, Saints took just three points from three draws, and only five goals were scored. One of the five, against Kilmarnock on Ne'erday, came from the unlikely source of the team's most consistent player, left back Tony Connell. It was Tony's first-ever goal in Junior or Senior football, and it gained Saints a point.

The first round of the Cup, against Division Two Stirling Albion, saw two goals from Jim Young take St. Mirren through to the next round, but before then Rangers had to be faced in the League. The result was a 4-0 home defeat, sending Saints to third bottom of the table, only two points ahead of Raith and Partick. The heavy defeat certainly wasn't the best preparation for the next round of the Cup, which Division Two Falkirk won 2-1 at Brockville, but the defeat owed more to a combination of ineffective forward play and slack defending.

The combination of the Falkirk result and the widely expected relegation produced a volume of St. Mirren correspondence not seen in the "Paisley Daily Express" for many a year. There was the usual criticism of the Board, but less predictably there was widespread dismay at Manager Alex Wright's perceived adoption of defensive play in seeming preference to the "open, quick, attractive football" he had previously advocated.

More positively, there was almost unanimous praise for his purchase of Ian Lister, but the summer acquisitions of Eadie, Cumming, and Knox were deemed far from satisfactory. Doubts were also expressed about Jim Young's ability to operate at Division One level, whilst many writers expressed regret over the decisions to give free transfers half-way through the season to the industrious Bobby Adamson and versatile Bobby Duffy.

The first League game following the Cup dismissal, at Tynecastle on 21 February, was also lost. Saints then put together a five-match unbeaten run, beginning with a spirited home draw with second bottom Raith Rovers after being three goals down. This run gave the Buddies another seven points, but they were still only two points and the same number of places ahead of the Kirkcaldy club.

Two mistakes by Denis Connaghan in a challenge match against Aberdeen on 3 March and reservations about some of Thorburn's more recent displays prompted Alex Wright to buy East Fife's twenty-four year old 'keeper Billy McGann, who had been at Methil for five years. His debut match on 10 March coincided with an adventurous 2-1 win over Dundee, the first victory of 1970! It was followed four days later by a 3-1 victory over Dundee United, and such was McGann's form that he retained his place for the remainder of the season.

A 1-1 draw at Pittodrie on 18 March thanks to a resolute defence meant that Saints were undefeated for a fifth consecutive game. By the third last fixture, against Partick Thistle, a ten-man Saints side held out for a point which virtually assured them of Division One survival, almost certainly relegated Thistle, and put Saints two points ahead of Raith, who had only one match to play.

By the time Saints played their penultimate match at Perth, which was won 3-2, their continuation as a Division One club had already been verified. It was a welcome outcome, but not one which erased the feeling that it had been a season of continual struggle. It was also the end of a decade which many St. Mirren fans viewed in much the same way. The 1970s would surely be better!

Nadir to Zenith... Thanks to 'Fergie'

1970-71

In the biggest end-of-season clear-out by any club, St. Mirren freed eleven players, most of whom had first team experience. The list included goalkeeper Jim Thorburn and forwards Peter Kane and Jim Young, the latter duo having scored just five League goals between them during 1969-70.

CHAPTER ELEVEN
The 1970's

• • • • • • • • • • • •

This goalscoring deficiency - the prime Paisley problem during the previous season - was not helped when top scorer Jim Blair, who had hit fifteen of Saints' thirty-nine League goals, was sold to Hibernian in June. The move enabled "Big Jim" to achieve his oft-stated wish to become a full-timer, whilst the record £38,000 transfer fee transformed St. Mirren's financial situation by cancelling out the 1969/70 loss of £8,158, and offsetting the reduced income from the Gleniffer Pools. On the downside, the transfer begged the question: where would Saints' goals come from?

The countdown to the new season commenced at Selhurst Park, where English First Division side Crystal Palace effortlessly cruised to a 4-0 victory, but Alex Wright took the opportunity to field the highly-rated forward Alasdair McLeod and emerging centre half Gordon McQueen, in addition to Iain Munro, who had made his first-team breakthrough the previous year. All three had benefited from the reinstatement of a

the future. Just as obvious was Saints need to find a goalscorer. "We were the better side," said Alex Wright, "but our shooting was woeful."

Saints began the League Cup with a rather unlucky 1-0 defeat at Dens, but four more defeats and just four goals scored in the five other sectional ties underlined that the previous season's main problem had not been solved. The defence had also shown its weaknesses, with an average of two goals conceded in each sectional tie. One early-season change was made after the fourth tie, a defeat at Rugby Park, in which Billy McGann was said to have made two mistakes which led to Killie's two goals; Connaghan took over and retained his position as first choice 'keeper for the rest of the season.

By 17 September, to the surprise of most Buddies, Saints' were sitting second equal in the League with five points from their first three fixtures. In the opening no-scoring home draw with Rangers, gallant defending,

Saints line up for the 1970-71 season

Back row:
J. Traynor, E. Reed,
B. Osborne, W. McGann,
D. Connaghan,
D. Prentice, J. Chalmers,
W. Borland

Middle row:
R. Pinkerton, C. Palmer,
H. McLaughlin,
K. Brown, A. McFadden,
G. McQueen, C. Murray,
W. Fulton, E. Murray

Front row:
H. Gilshan, R. Hamilton,
R. McKean, A. MacLeod,
I. Munro, I. Lister,
A. Connell

Reserve side, and personified the Manager's desire to foster a successful youth policy at St. Mirren Park.

McLeod had been a player much in demand when Manager Wright made a midnight car journey on 1 April to sign the nineteen year old from Renfrew Juniors. On the morning of the Palace match, Alex Wright enthused about "Ally": "I think this boy has a great deal of ability and is the type of player who always scores goals. He has obviously proved himself or I would not put him into the team straight away." He was equally keen to test McQueen's abilities: "This is likely to be the chance he has been waiting for and he is certainly not over-awed about playing in the match".

In the second pre-season friendly - a 1-0 home defeat by English Fourth Division Southend United - Iain Munro showed he was a star of

with Andy McFadden to the fore, was the basis of a tremendous fighting performance.

The centre half was again prominent in the first win of the season, when a fifty-third minute goal from Kilmarnock gave Saints a much-needed jolt. Young right winger Bobby McKean, called up from Blantyre Victoria at the beginning of September 1969, began to cause all sorts of bother to the Killie defence, and in the sixty-third minute Saints equalised through Ernie Reed, a summer signing from Arbroath. Two minutes later a goal from Lister was sufficient to clinch two away points. McKean would be a virtual ever-present in the starting line-up right through to New Years' Day, and thereafter was involved in about half of the fixtures.

In the third League match, Saints were 1-0 down and struggling when an incident involving Morton's Stan Rankin and Saints' seventeen year old substitute winger Willie Borland roused the home team and the fans. Late goals from Gilshan and Lister shocked the visitors, but Alex Wright was the first to admit it had been a poor performance. He was content to praise the players for the way they fought back but, with League Cup failures fresh in the memory, wasn't fooled by the lofty League position.

To improve goal-scoring matters, twenty-three year old Archie Knox was signed from Forfar Athletic for a fee of £5000. In his first game - against Dundee at Dens on 19 October - the debutant hit a glorious left-foot angular shot from twenty-five yards to give his new team an unlikely but deserved share of the points, having been 2-0 down after nineteen minutes. Knox would eventually score seven League goals and retain his position as the Club's main striker.

The early League results proved to be as misleading as the Manager suspected. Two draws were followed by a 1-0 home defeat by Clyde on 10 October, when the Buddies failed to show even a semblance of rhythm in their play. The same eleven weren't much better the following week, losing 2-0 to St. Johnstone at Perth.

Five days after the Muirton Park defeat, the shock news broke that Alex Wright had become the £5,000-a-year manager of bottom-of-the-table Dunfermline Athletic. Wright, who resigned from St. Mirren with immediate effect, was moving to East End Park in succession to George Farm, who had been abruptly sacked earlier in October following the full-time "Pars" poor start to the season.

"We're very sorry to lose Mr. Wright," said a Club spokesman, who confirmed that Trainer Willie McLean was to act as temporary Manager. McLean, a former Clyde and Raith winger, was a qualified S. F. A. coach and had arrived at St. Mirren Park from Kilmarnock on 11 February 1970, following the surprise announcement in the wake of a Scottish Cup defeat by Division Two Falkirk that the services of Bill Cochrane were no longer required.

Willie was to be assisted by 1959 Cup hero Alastair Miller, who had re-joined the Club as a coach a few weeks before the new Trainer's arrival, and Willie Paton, who was responsible for the Reserve team. The interim management team were in charge for four matches, but the unsuccessful run continued as only one point was gained.

On 9 November the new St. Mirren Manager was revealed. He was Wilson Humphries, forty-two year old part-time coach at Motherwell FC, full-time English teacher at Dalziel High School in Motherwell, and one-time player with St. Mirren during the 1956/57 season. "I feel great," he enthused. "It's a big challenge to leave the security of the teaching profession to take over a football manager's job but it is something I have always wanted to do." Four days after his appointment, he signed Raith Rovers' twenty-four year old captain and attack-minded wing half Dave Miller for £10,000.

Miller went straight into the team, but unfortunately neither he nor his new manager were able to stop the slide down the League. Humphries' new career began with a 1-0 win over relegation-favourites Cowdenbeath in late November. It was the first, if a less than impressive, victory in over two months, but Saints would play another nine League fixtures before the Scottish Cup commenced on 23 January, and not one of them would be won.

During this period the Manager showed he was not afraid to make difficult decisions, as he dropped ever-present Andy McFadden, an off-form Tony Connell, and Cammy Murray for the first time in his nine-year career. At the same time he gave teenage pivot McQueen, the Club's only full-time player, what proved to be an extended run in the side.

In the first round of the Cup, Saints drew 1-1 with promotion-chasing East Fife at Bayview, when Ronnie Hamilton equalised with only ten minutes to go. Saints were equally indebted to Denis Connaghan, who prevented a real drubbing from a Methil side brilliantly generalled by player-manager Pat Quinn, the ex-Motherwell and Scotland star.

Three days later, a Love Street crowd of 8,075 saw Saints miss a number of first half chances, then lose the initiative to the Fifers in the second half. Extra time couldn't separate the sides, and the game again finished at 1-1 before an Archie Knox hat-trick in a second replay, also in Paisley, finally took the Club through to a money-spinning tie with Rangers.

Between the second and third East Fife ties, Saints put on a welcome fighting performance, with McQueen completely snuffing out the danger of Joe Baker to beat Hibs 3-1 at home on 30 January. One week later, a 2-1 victory at Shawfield gave some hope to the supporters, but two

Wilson Humphries lays down the law, while Archie Knox has a quick drink as extra time beckons against East Fife.

Rangers goals in the first twenty-one minutes not only formed the basis of a 3-1 Cup exit, but also proved to be the prelude to another poor run of League results. In eight fixtures from 20 February onwards, only bottom team Cowdenbeath were beaten.

Spirits were lifted on 26 February, when Jim Blair returned to Paisley as a full-timer for less than £15,000. His second Saints' debut coincided with a determined display at Pittodrie which won a point, the margin which separated the Buddies and second bottom Dunfermline, but there followed a lethargic 2-0 home defeat by Ayr United, later described by Manager Humphries as "rubbishy" and "lack-lustre".

Saints dropped to second bottom and that's where they remained, despite a very late resurgence which saw them draw with Airdrieonians at Broomfield, and deservedly take two points after beating Dundee United at Love Street.

By then, Dunfermline Athletic had completed their programme, were one point ahead, and had a superior goal difference. It meant that a home win over Celtic in the last match was the only outcome which could salvage Saints' top team status. After an hour's play, Saints were 2-1 up, and Ally McLeod, whose first team appearances had been sporadic, had not only grabbed both goals, but was impressing everyone with skills and style reminiscent of Tommy Bryceland.

Celtic got the equaliser all Paisley dreaded, and St. Mirren became the first team to be relegated on the newly introduced "goal difference" rule. The warning signs had been there right from the start of the season, and attempts to address the lack of fire power, such as the genuine attempt in mid-January to sign Joe Baker from Sunderland and the re-signing of Jim Blair, had either failed or come too late to be effective.

Saints had been demoted for only the third time in their history, but, unlike 1936 and 1968, few thought there would be an immediate return to Division One.

1971-72

Wilson Humphries refused to countenance any pessimism about St. Mirren's third-ever season in Division Two, making the customary "promotion is our primary objective" declaration, but also spelling out one consequence of failure to make an immediate return to the top League: "I will pack my bags and go," was the unambiguous message.

He wasn't the only one making a public pledge. The Board decided to switch to a partial full-time set-up, and offers were made, mainly to the younger players, in the belief that it would quicken their rate of progress. It was a financial gamble. Crowds had dropped from a total of 204,000 in 1956-57 to 105,000 in 1970-71, and during the Club's last period in Division Two support went down to 63,000. It also meant there would be no money for new players without selling first.

On the eve of the new season it was announced that Player of the Year Denis Connaghan, who had turned down the full-time offer made to him in mid-May, had agreed to accept part-time terms. The popular Denis and his team-mates would be playing in a League Cup section with three other Division Two sides, a situation which gave Saints every

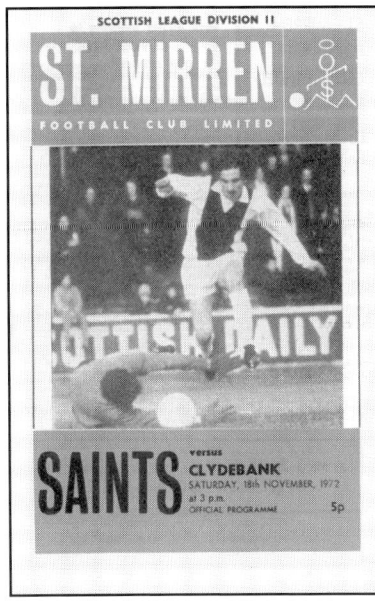

Featuring on the cover of this 1972 programme is John Dickson who was bought from Queen of the South. Saints wore this Ajax style kit at the time.

chance of progressing to the quarter finals for the first time in sixteen years.

It was an opportunity they were to take. The opening team selected by Wilson Humphries included the promising talents of full-timers McQueen and McLeod, and part-timers Munro and McKean, all of whom were by then regulars. For the second time in four seasons, loyal servants Willie Fulton and Cammy Murray were embarking on what they hoped would be another promotion season. The Division's "big team" appeared to be a balanced blend of youth and experience.

In the opening League Cup tie against Montrose, Dave Millar's sixty-second goal was Scotland's quickest. Despite this super start, Saints gave a strangely spiritless performance in a flattering 4-1 home win. The following Wednesday they lost 2-0 to Stranraer due to missed chances and some poor goalkeeping by Connaghan. A narrow and unimpressive victory over Albion Rovers was followed by better wins against Stranraer and Montrose, each without conceding a goal, before the last sectional tie on 1 September was lost at Cliftonhill, where an inability to convert chances was again evident.

Two days earlier, Ian Lister joined Raith, having been injured for the latter part of the previous season before being placed on the open-to-transfer list at his own request. Ian was leaving a side which had done enough to reach the quarter finals, where they met Stirling Albion at the beginning of September. A Munro penalty and an eighty-sixth minute header from winger Billy Lawson, who had been signed on 19 February following his release by Sheffield Wednesday, gave Saints a 2-0 first-leg lead in a rather scrappy affair.

Three weeks later at Annfield, a crowd of 5,000 saw the Buddies take a 3-0 half-time lead with goals from McKean, Blair, and McLeod. Five up on aggregate, Saints eased their way towards a big-money Hampden semi-final against Celtic on 6 October, when a large St. Mirren following in the 29,488 crowd saw a Paisley team in control at the back and looking dangerous up front until Hugh McLaughlin's hotly disputed thirty-fourth minute dismissal. The ordering-off ended the match as a contest, with Celtic's three goals all coming in a five minute spell which began just before the hour mark.

Saints' focus was now solely on their promotion bid. In terms of points gathering, they had made a satisfactory start, winning six of their first seven fixtures but performances were inconsistent. In their first three matches they played well enough in bursts, scoring eleven goals in the process, but had also shown some weaknesses in defence. Such lapses cost them dear in a 2-1 home defeat by East Stirlingshire, in front of 4,200. In the run-up to the League Cup semi-final, they won the next three games, scoring twelve goals. So far. So good.

In the eighth fixture, following immediately after the semi-final, the same eleven played badly and lost 2-0 in Kirkcaldy. They then won their next two games by 2-0, at home to Brechin City and Stranraer, to move into equal first position with Cowdenbeath after ten games. Encouragingly they also had a game in hand, but there was a concern that they had not played well since the Celtic game.

That Hampden defeat didn't quite end Paisley's connection with the 1971 League Cup tournament. Saints' conquerors had faced Partick Thistle in the Final, where, against all predictions, it finished 4-1 for Thistle. Two days after the Final, Celtic manager Jock Stein signed Denis Connaghan for £10,000 in a move designed to provide increased competition for Parkhead 'keeper Evan Williams. This income not only helped to reduce St. Mirren's financial burdens, but fulfilled the agreement made when Connaghan re-signed that he would be released if a reasonable offer was received.

Connaghan's replacement was Danny Stevenson, an ex-Rangers player. Physical Training teacher Stevenson, who would remain first choice 'keeper until 8 March when Ayr United's Jim Gilmour was signed, made a shaky start in a 3-1 defeat against Montrose at Links Park on 30 October, but soon settled into the position as a further ten points were collected from a possible fourteen up to Christmas Day.

The other defeat during these seven games was against League leaders Cowdenbeath in a period when Saints' performances continued to fluctuate, and fluent play became a casualty of the heavier ground conditions. Saints were now three points behind Cowdenbeath with two games in hand, but there were at least four other teams also in contention.

As the Buddies prepared to play four games over the holiday period, news broke that former Saints' star Tommy Bryceland was looking for a move from Oldham Athletic back to Scotland, although press speculation suggested he was unlikely to come to Love Street unless Oldham lowered their fee.

On Christmas Day, a Paisley crowd of 5,500 saw Dumbarton hold a 2-0 lead with just fifteen minutes to go, but late goals from Munro and Borland saved a point. Two days later against Clydebank, another home point was dropped by a St. Mirren team lacking cohesion, particularly in midfield. In the third holiday match, a visit to Annfield provided great entertainment, but a bitterly disappointing result, as promotion rivals Stirling Albion won 3-2. The disastrous festive period ended on 3 January, with a 1-0 home defeat by lowly-placed Stenhousemuir, with the Buddies failing to threaten the Larbert side's goal in any of the ninety minutes.

Concern over diminishing promotion prospects was compounded on 7 January, when a flurry of headlines stunned the Saints support. "Humphries Quits As Miller Takes Over" and "Bryceland Set To Sign - Knox May Go To Tannadice" summed up a turbulent day!

Wilson Humphries had resigned immediately after the Stenhousemuir defeat. A man of integrity, he had every intention of sticking to his "pack my bags" promise if promotion wasn't gained, but with astonishing candour he explained the anguish behind his decision to go in mid-season: "I feel by going now there is still a chance of the team gaining promotion. I have tried everything I know. I switched players, dropped players and finally got to the situation where I did not know who to leave out to get the best results. When it gets to that stage there is only one thing to do, so I dropped myself. I have made too many mistakes in football judgment in too short a time". Within three weeks Wilson returned to the teaching profession, but he would be back in football as Hibernian's coach by July 1972.

Team coach Alastair Miller was placed in temporary charge. One of his first acts was to transfer Archie Knox, who had made twenty-nine starts, mainly in midfield, and had scored once in every three matches. As planned, Knox's £4,000 fee from Dundee United recouped the cost of signing returning hero Bryceland.

The hectic day of changes was followed by another defeat, as Saints lost 3-1 away to East Stirlingshire. Bryceland got the goal, but the team never looked like winning. Meanwhile, there were more off-the-field distractions. By 12 January it emerged that Alastair Miller, after just five days as interim Manager, did not want the job unless he was appointed full-time manager of St. Mirren. The Directors were not prepared to quickly make a permanent appointment, but another crisis appeared to have been avoided when Miller stated he was willing to continue in an interim capacity in the interest of the Club.

However, the change of mind seemed to be too late, and, perplexingly, Miller's offer was turned down. The Board then made it clear that the Club had no intention of advertising the post, and on 18 January Tommy Bryceland was named as Player-Manager. He had been approached after a practice game on 15 January, and took a few days to consider a move which was coming to him earlier than he had planned. Once appointed, he immediately did his best to combat a rising tide of pessimism: "It is ridiculous for anyone to say our promotion chances are gone. There are still fourteen matches left and any of the top six could go up".

Bryceland's managerial career began on 22 January, with a fine 5-1 away victory over Hamilton which took the team back to second top and helped boost confidence, which the new boss admitted was "flagging". Saints ended January with a 2-0 victory, but it was only achieved thanks to the paucity of finishing by Raith Rovers

The Scottish Cup campaign kicked off at the beginning of February with a well-deserved 1-0 away win over Forfar Athletic. Capping a successful week-end, team skipper Willie Fulton, who was nearing the end of a three month injury absence, was voted Player of the Year by the Scottish Professional Players Association at their Annual meeting in Glasgow.

A very unconvincing 2-1 home win over Brechin City on 12 February preceded Saints' fourth round tie with Rangers at Love Street, which remained 0-0 at half-time, with Saints a little unlucky not to have been in the lead. Two goals in two minutes, starting in the fifty-fifth minute, turned the tie Rangers' way, and they eventually won 4-1.

Willie Fulton

Back in the League, March started with a 3-1 home victory over Montrose, but it was a struggle. The following Saturday defensive errors resulted in a 2-1 defeat at Hampden, as Saints slipped down to fourth position. Not for the first time, some players seemed to take the opposition too lightly. A second successive defeat, at home to Alloa Athletic, dealt another blow to Paisley promotion aspirations. The festive season form had returned, and it continued, in part, in a fortunate away win over Berwick Rangers and a 3-2 defeat at Gayfield on 1 April. Saints dropped to seventh.

The last six games were won, including a final day 2-1 away win over champions Dumbarton, but other results ensured that Saints finished in fourth place, two points behind the two promoted clubs. The Buddies undoubtedly had some outstanding young talent in their ranks, but the team had too often lacked the determination needed to win games in Division Two. For the first time in their history, St. Mirren faced a second successive season in Scotland's lower Division.

1972-73

Tommy Bryceland shared his predecessor's targets, but there was a noticeable difference in style and emphasis. "My main objective is to get into Division One as soon as possible," he said in a pre-season interview. "If we do not get promotion it will be disappointing but it will not be the end of the world". The new tone seemed more relaxed; it remained to be seen if it was to be any more successful.

Saints' eighty-four League goals during 1971-72 qualified them for entry to the Drybrough Cup, an eight-club competition for high-scoring teams. Each participating side had been given a minimum £1000 from the sponsors, and in an attempt to see if these teams could increase their scoring rate the normal offside rule was dispensed with up to the eighteen yard line which was extended to the two touchlines.

The competition commenced on 29 July, and 'keeper Jim Gilmour did his best to nullify any benefits of the rule change by thwarting Division One runners-up Aberdeen on countless occasions, including a brilliant penalty save from Dons' scoring star "Joey" Harper, but Aberdeen were clearly the smoother-moving side, and Harper almost inevitably got the goal which eliminated the Buddies.

The team at Pittodrie had been Gilmour, Clelland, Munro, Millar, McQueen, Johnston, O'Neill, Blair, Storrie, McLeod, and Prentice. Playing against his old team was twenty year old Sandy Clelland, a March 1972 signing who had played in a handful of games at the end of the previous season, and would make twenty-eight appearances during 1972-73. Clelland was partnered in defence by twenty-one year old sweeper Billy Johnston, who had been released after four years by Division One Partick Thistle. Johnston joined Saints on 16 May, and would prove to be the most consistent of the new intake, a virtual ever-present and the 1972-73 Player of the Year.

Less successful was twenty-eight midfielder George O'Neill, a former Partick Thistle, Morton, and Dunfermline Athletic player who had been signed on 10 July, having played twenty-five games in the previous season for the relegated "Pars". George would play just six times as a Saint in the early part of the season, and was one of ten players to be freed in April 1973.

Following a similar pattern would be summer signing Jim Storrie, previously with Airdrieonians and Leeds United, who had been given a free transfer by English Second Division side Portsmouth, having played over twenty games for them in the previous season. Centre forward Storrie was named team captain in place of Willie Fulton, who had decided after sixteen distinguished years as a wing half, and latterly sweeper, to take on a new role as Tommy Bryceland's "right-hand man".

Jim Storrie would play in all the League Cup ties and the first seven League fixtures, but after the end of September didn't play again. Just before Christmas he was named Player-Coach with the Reserves as part-of a back-room re-shuffle. Signing experienced players like Storrie was intended to help the development of youngsters like winger Dave Prentice, who had been signed from Queen's Park on 17 July 1970, but had yet to become a regular in the side.

In Dave's case it didn't happen. Sensing greater football opportunities in Australia, he would be released in April because of his proposed emigration.

The policy of signing free transfer men was equally important in keeping costs to a minimum, thus enabling the Club to retain a number of full-time players for a second season in the lower Division. An exception to this prudent approach was made on 3 August, when Saints signed Manchester United's former Scotland centre half Ian Ure, who had been unable to regain his position at Old Trafford. Tommy Bryceland regarded Ure as a significant acquisition: "This signing proves to the supporters that we are having a go at making St. Mirren a top side," he said. "We are not sitting back, but trying to attract the best players available."

League Cup sections were now a mixture of teams from both Divisions, and Saints were grouped with Division One Ayr United and Rangers, and second tier Clydebank. The first game ended in a 2-1 defeat at Ayr's temporary home at Dam Park Sports Stadium, with debutant Ian Ure giving away the penalty that led to the first goal. He appeared to have lost a bit of pace, but most observers felt that in Division Two this could be offset by his experience.

Four days later two defensive errors gave Rangers the initiative, and after that they coasted to a 4-0 win. Saints then got their first sectional points with a 4-2 home win over Clydebank, and although the Manager stated that goalie Jim Gilmour was "not entirely to blame for the two goals," he was subsequently dropped, played once more in a county cup tie, and was given a free transfer at the end of the season!

In the fourth tie, Saints went behind after just four minutes at Ibrox. Another 4-0 defeat looked possible, but the previous season's top scorer Ally McLeod and his mates had different ideas. The team buckled down to the task, and McLeod proceeded to put on a vituoso performance, scoring four stunning goals to give Saints a memorable victory.

In the next game, the side gave a second half performance which the Manager described as a "bit of a shambles", as Ayr United left Paisley with a 3-0 win under their belts, and Saints' last action in the tournament ended with a 3-3 draw at Kilbowie Park.

The League campaign began with two wins and a defeat, a pattern of results which was replicated over the next thirty-three fixtures. There were no poor runs, but nothing bettered the four wins and a draw during late September and October.

By then Saints had lost two prominent players. On 26 September, Jim Blair made an £18,000 move to Norwich City, whose officials had watched "Big Jim" for a number of weeks, having originally been impressed by him during Saints' pre-season friendly at Carrow Road. Three days later, Gordon McQueen finally joined Leeds United after the Elland Road club increased their offer to £35,000, ending a seventeen-month scrutiny of the player.

In just one week Saints collected £53,000 in transfer fees, and spent £6,000 on Cowdenbeath's centre forward John Dickson, a former Leeds and Scottish Youth internationalist. These outgoing transfers looked unavoidable when the Club revealed a loss of £10,000 in the year to 31 March 1972, a predicament which was set to worsen due to reduced attendances, and a need to find £50,000 to meet the cost of statutory ground improvements following the 1971 Ibrox disaster.

Sixteen goals had been scored during Saints' four consecutive wins, and the expected weakening of the team due to the loss of Blair and McQueen hadn't materialised. Speaking on 21 October, the Manager noted that the team had moved up to fourth position, two points behind leaders Stirling Albion, and had the same number of points after eight games as had been accrued in the previous season. Mr. Bryceland felt that the deal to bring Dickson to Love Street had more than cancelled out the loss of Blair, although he did admit "we still have problems in defence but they are gradually being sorted out". He rebuffed claims that the sale of Gordon McQueen had exposed weaknesses of his team, stating that "the defence was shaky when McQueen was playing here".

Some of these defensive frailties were due to the unexpected absence of the injured Ian Ure, which led to the early November signing of twenty-seven year old former Stirling Albion centre half Drew Rogerson, who had been on a month's trial with Ayr United. Rogerson would play until the last few matches when he was freed. His replacement was young John Redburn, who had been signed from Shettleston Juniors in March, but after just three matches he was also given a free transfer, following his sending off for a tackle on Hamilton Academical's Paul Hegarty. By the end of the season Saints had used seven players in the key pivot's role, but the side's deficiencies extended beyond one position.

One player who had done well as stand-in centre half was summer signing Angus McLeod, who had been with Glasgow Perthshire before turning senior with Albion Rovers. The versatile "Gus" was equally at home as a bustling forward, as he proved when he scored five in a 7-1 demolition of Hamilton Accies on 9 December. It was the type of result expected from a promotion-bound team, but it was notable only for its rarity.

By late December, the Buddies had dropped to sixth place, and the festive season matches began with a "must win" home game against second top Clyde two days prior to Christmas. It was lost 1-0. Included in the team was wing half Jim Lumsden, who had been signed three days earlier, having been described by the Manager as a "workmanlike player". Jim, who had been at Leeds United for seven years and had played thirty-five games for Division One Morton during the previous season, would make only twelve starts for Saints, and was one of those freed.

A week after the Clyde game, bottom club Brechin scored a late goal to secure a deserved 3-3 draw. Much improved form was needed, and it was in evidence not only on New Year's Day when League leaders Stirling Albion were convincingly beaten 4-1, but on 6 January, when Saints drew 1-1 with Dunfermline Athletic at East End Park.

In their next League game three weeks later at Central Park, Saints won 2-0 against a ten-man Cowdenbeath, but were in less than sparkling form. Despite this, the Cup visit of Partick Thistle was anticipated with confidence. Unfortunately, the team showed their more typical League form by wasting numerous scoring opportunities. Thistle, on the other hand, scored in the sixtieth minute with their one real chance of the game, and the Buddies were out.

The League programme re-started on 10 February with a dire 0-0 home draw with Forfar Athletic, and the game ended amidst a chorus of Saints fans' boos. It was "the worst of the season," according to Tommy Bryceland, who hinted at notions of superiority which hadn't been completely dispelled despite eighteen months in Division Two: "We had the wrong attitude towards the game. We thought we would win at walking pace. Forfar were given too much scope. It was our own fault and we did not deserve to win".

A 4-1 victory at Montrose one week later offered some temporary hope, but a 1-0 home defeat to Queen's Park and a 1-1 home draw with Stenhousemuir on 24 February meant promotion was by then almost impossible, as the Club began to run out of games. On 24 March, a 1-1 draw with Clydebank at Kilbowie forced the ever-optimistic Manager to concede that, with only four games left, "it certainly looks a little dodgy for us at the moment. Three teams would have to collapse and we would need to win all our matches"

It didn't happen, and the season finished with a sequence of half-hearted displays. Boos greeted the end of the last home game on 21 April, which was won 3-1 by East Stirlingshire, the fourth time 'Shire had beaten St. Mirren in two seasons.

Further confirmation of Saints' continuing decline came in the last game against champions Clyde at Shawfield, where the home side not only scored five, but played a quality of football which exposed St. Mirren's inadequacies. Only three players in black and white who were on view in Rutherglen had also been selected for that Drybrough Cup match nine months earlier. Unfortunately, as the Buddies edged towards an unprecedented and unwelcome third season in Division Two, few people thought the side had improved, and even fewer expected an early change in the Club's downward direction.

1973-74

At the beginning of May 1973, Tommy Bryceland clarified his aims: "My main objective is to get back into Division One. But getting back is not the answer. It is what you do when you get there. I want it to be worthwhile when we do".

In the same interview he again stressed that "it takes time to sort things out". This was entirely in line with the philosophy he had articulated at the 1972 A.G.M: "The future of any provincial club, not just St. Mirren, has got to be based on a youth policy. It is not possible to keep buying players because this only leads to a short-term solution. We have now strengthened our scouting system in order to get boys of school age to the Club quickly."

On 11 May, only two days after these objectives were spelled out, top scorer Alisdair McLeod was transferred to English First Division outfit Southampton for £40,000. Manager Bryceland, aware that the Club was losing £800 per week, still found it difficult to hide his disappointment: "It is obviously a big blow for us because Ally is a difficult type of player to find. It was a hard decision to make to transfer him". McLeod, one of just two full-timers left at St. Mirren Park, had not asked for a transfer, but no doubt St. Mirren's decision to revert to part-time football had a bearing on his decision to move.

At this time the "Paisley Daily Express" invited supporters to comment on the prospects for St. Mirren Football Club. Few correspondents were optimistic, and the fund of goodwill which Tommy Bryceland carried from his dazzling days as a Saints' player no longer guaranteed him immunity from criticism. His lack of success in the transfer market was noted, and some fans reluctantly concluded that perhaps he wasn't the man to shake the Club out of its apparent lethargy.

Restoring the Club's fortunes was the prime aim of newly appointed Chairman Harold Currie and Vice-Chairman William Todd, and it was the latter who confirmed on 28 May that Tommy Bryceland had ceased to be St. Mirren's Manager after "a disagreement over club policy". The Manager's contract had been cancelled by mutual agreement, and although neither party was willing to elaborate on the decision, Mr. Bryceland added one extra comment that he "would like to have done a job for the Club."

St. Mirren were now managerless, but not inactive, as £19,000 was splashed out on two new players the day after Tommy's departure. Montrose centre forward Brian Third, second top scorer in Division Two with thirty-five goals, was signed for £15,000, and a further £4,000 was used to capture wing-half Jim Taylor, who had spent the previous six seasons with Cowdenbeath.

Twenty-four hours later, the books were balanced with the sale of versatile Iain Munro to Hibernian for £20,000. Iain had been placed on the transfer list back in January 1973 at his own request, expressing the need for a fresh start, but there had been no bids for him until Hibs manager Eddie Turnbull, a long-time Munro admirer, made his approach.

With so much activity on the player front, there was an urgent need to appoint a new Manager. Former St. Mirren player Willie Cunningham was the clear favourite, and it was no surprise when he was unveiled as the new boss on 20 June. Previously manager of Dunfermline Athletic and Falkirk, Cunningham was joined by new trainer Dunky McGill, who had been Saints' inside right for eight years in the 1950s. Mr. Cunningham declared he was "a Buddy at heart" and enthused about the challenge of putting Paisley back on the football map.

A team of experienced players appeared to be the new Managers' preferred method of achieving the quickest possible promotion. In mid-July he signed ex-Birmingham City and Scotland goalkeeper Jim Herriot, who had been surprisingly freed by Hibs, and also captured former Cowdenbeath and Blackpool full back Henry Mowbray from Bolton Wanderers. Ayr United's centre half Stan Quinn, who had been at Somerset Park for eight years, was appointed captain in succession to Billy Johnston, and former Airdrieonians full back George Caldwell completed a quartet of acquisitions which the Manager believed would "add solidity and depth to our pool".

There was plenty of Paisley enterprise as well as solidity on display at Easter Road as the season opened, with a 2-1 Drybrough Cup defeat from star-studded holders Hibernian, for whom Iain Munro scored the opener. Lining up for Saints on the right wing was highly-rated seventeen year old Tony Fitzpatrick, a product of Possil YMCA and a member of St. Mirren's ground staff before being signed on the eve of the season.

An inept showing six days later in a pre-season friendly against Crewe Alexandra was attributed to the new team's bedding-in process, and this seemed to also apply in the first League Cup tie, where Saints dominated the first half before succumbing to incessant second-half pressure from Berwick Rangers, who grabbed an equaliser five minutes from time. A much more convincing display, albeit against a weak Stenhousemuir side, produced a 2-0 win, but a controversial first goal by Dunfermline Athletic in the third tie set the tone for a match which ended in a flattering 5-1 win for the "Pars".

In the return ties, a much-improved Stenhousemuir were overcome thanks to a superb double from John Dickson, Dunfermline were beaten 2-1 in Paisley after Saints had gone behind, and, in a difficult section-winning decider, two late goals meant Berwick Rangers were beaten 2-1. Saints had collected nine points from twelve, and were through to the quarter finals!

It was hoped that the League Cup success would provide the impetus for a promotion push, but plenty of other clubs had similar ambitions, none more so than Airdrieonians and Kilmarnock, who were seen by most people as the leading contenders. The first fixture took place on 1 September, and six more matches were played in the following twenty-eight days. It proved to be the most successful month by far, with six victories and a season's high point of fourth top.

The one defeat in this opening batch of fixtures came from a very strong-looking Kilmarnock side, who provided Willie Cunningham and his players with an early benchmark. Saints, by comparison, were taking unsteady steps towards the top of the League, although they did at least show the determined approach the Manager was looking for, when each of the last three September matches was won after the Buddies had gone a goal down.

Saints were also a goal down after a tough first leg quarter final tie at Shawfield on 12 September. Already without injured pivot Stan Quinn, Jim Herriot was carried off with a cartilage injury after thirty-nine minutes, and Sandy Clelland took over in goal. It became a containment exercise, and there was some relief that the deficit with Division One Clyde was limited to just one goal. In the second leg on 10 October, Clyde scored after just twenty seconds to put them 2-0 up on aggregate. It was a gap Saints could not close, despite scoring four goals in the second half, including two in the last six minutes, as Clyde won 6-4 over the two legs.

The League Cup exit had come just four days after Queen's Park won much more easily at St. Mirren Park than the final 4-3 scoreline suggests. Herriot was being missed, and Danny Stevenson was also injured, so seventeen year old 'keeper Gordon Knowles was signed from Dundee just hours before he made his debut in the Clyde tie. Quinn's continued absence at centre half had also weakened the defence, and this was addressed the morning after the Clyde defeat when Motherwell's pivot for the previous thirteen years, Willie McCallum, was signed.

Between 6 October and 17 November, none of the six League fixtures played were won, only two points were gained, and the team slipped to tenth in the table. At the beginning of the season, Mr. Cunningham had made known his standards: "I am not interested in players whose entire mental as well as physical purpose is not directed towards playing Division One football". Half-way through this six-match run, the Manager was publicly expressing his concern about players "lack of dedication".

The mediocre team performances continued to the end of the year. Along the way, a 5-3 win in Paisley by Airdrieonians on 10 November showed that the "Waysiders" were far more likely to gain promotion, as they continually created gaps in the Paisley defence. A home point was dropped to Cowdenbeath on 22 December, and seven days later a 2-0 home defeat by Stranraer prompted a demonstration by a small band of supporters outside the main stand.

A brighter note was struck on Ne'erday, when a point was taken in a 1-1 draw with "Killie" at Rugby Park, but four days later a 0-0 home draw with Raith Rovers showed up the team's deficiencies. They were unimaginative and pedestrian, and had it not been for the Kirkcaldy side's inability to take chances, it could very easily have been St. Mirren's biggest defeat for many years.

A mid-season clear-out followed, confirming to everyone that all hopes of promotion had been abandoned, with half the fixtures still to play. Defenders George Caldwell, Henry Mowbray, and Stan Quinn, plus goalkeepers Gordon Knowles and Ian Dick were offered free transfers, and the Club announced it would consider offers for Gus McLeod, John Dickson, and Jim Taylor. Meanwhile, Kilwinning Rangers' young centre half Bobby Reid was immediately called up, and others, like eighteen year old winger Davie McFall, would follow him. The Club were reverting to the youth policy approach, which Tommy Bryceland had advocated was the only option for St. Mirren to adopt, although some questioned whether, for financial reasons, the policy change should have been deferred until after Saints' Scottish Cup interest ended.

The results didn't get any better in the second half of the season, with lack of experience being a predictable reason for some defeats. However, the team should have been good enough to eliminate Stranraer from the Cup. The first two attempts to separate the sides ended in 1-1 draws, and in the third match on 4 February at neutral Somerset Park, it was Stranraer who eventually progressed, winning 3-2.

St. Mirren ended the season in what would transpire to be the worst League position in the Club's first one hundred and twenty-five years. They had won thirty-four points to finish in eleventh place, and there were now twenty-eight teams above them in the rankings. The Club had completely changed its strategy halfway through the season, and the new approach, whilst laudable, needed time which Saints didn't appear to have, as their hard-core support dropped to less than 1,000 and continued to dissipate.

The end of the following season would see the creation of a new League set-up, and unless St. Mirren's seemingly inexorable deterioration was arrested, they were on track to begin 1975-76 in the oblivion of Scotland's third division. Thankfully, it was not to be. The arrival of one man ensured that 1973-74 would turn out to be the nadir of The St. Mirren Football Club. The years of demoralising decline would give way to recaptured pride and unprecedented enthusiasm. It was no more than the people of Paisley deserved.

1974-75

The challenge could not have been clearer in 1974-75. St. Mirren had to finish in the top six if they were to gain a place in the new First Division, and the team had to be strengthened if this was to be achieved.

Manager Willie Cunningham made his first move on 10 May, when he used his knowledge of Falkirk FC's playing staff to capture two young defenders who had tasted first team experience before being freed by the newly relegated Brockville club. Twenty-two year old John Young, who had previously been with Hibs, and twenty year old Alex Beckett would quickly establish themselves, John starting all but one of Saints' forty-five League and cup matches, and Alex beginning twenty-nine.

There were three more signings. Ian Reid of Partick Thistle, equally effective at full back or midfield, and forward Bobby Laurie of Falkirk were added to the playing staff on 15 July. They were joined eleven days later by twenty-six year old former Morton utility man Walter Borthwick, who had been transfer-listed by East Fife. "Walter will give us a bit more depth and his experience in a team whose average age is about 21 will be invaluable," stated the Manager. Borthwick would only be missing from three starting line-ups all season.

One player leaving Love Street was twenty-six year old inside forward John Dickson, St. Mirren's only full-time player during the previous season, but one whose inconsistent form had led him to be placed on the transfer list the previous January. He signed for Division One Ayr United on 8 July.

Also missing was experienced goalkeeper Jim Herriot, who failed to report for training on 8 August, having been a notable absentee in each of the four pre-season games. It transpired that the former Scotland 'keeper had walked out of the Club, his place for the opening League Cup sectional tie at home to Stirling Albion on 10 August being taken by Alex Morrison, signed from Larkhall Thistle.

The game was won 3-2, with the young Saints side outshining Stirling more convincingly than the scoreline indicates, but the same starting eleven disappointed against Clydebank four days later in a 2-0 defeat. Then, to Paisley delight, the previous season's Division Two champions Airdrieonians were beaten 1-0 at Broomfield.

In the return ties a single strike by Brian Third was enough to defeat the "Bankies," but the fifth tie provided a real set-back when Division One Airdrieonians, looking the better side throughout, left Paisley with a 6-0 victory. The gloom which descended after this drubbing from the 'Diamonds' was alleviated when Stirling Albion were beaten 4-0 in the final game, but it was not enough to stop the Broomfielders winning the section on goal difference.

The first three League games resulted in two wins and a draw, including an outstanding performance by right winger Bobby McKean in a easy 5-1 away win over Berwick Rangers on 4 September. Five days later, Player of the Year McKean asked for a transfer, citing his desire to play full-time football. His request was turned down on 11 September, with Willie Cunningham stating that "the status of the Club is the first priority at the moment and there will be no transfer of players."

The undefeated run continued with a comfortable 4-0 home win over Stranraer, but the fifth fixture ended in a mid-week 4-0 defeat by League Cup semi-finalists Falkirk at Brockville. Less than forty-eight hours later, twenty-two year old Bobby McKean, after six years at Love Street, was transferred to Rangers for £50,000. Saints supporters were well used to such deals, but there was widespread dismay that the Board had sanctioned the McKean move just nine days after the Manager stated that no such transfers would occur.

Saints showed no ill-effects from Bobby McKean's departure when they came away from Glebe Park with a fine 6-2 win over a injury-weakened Brechin City, with centre Brian Third in particularly impressive form. Saints had nine points from a possible twelve, and were sitting in second top position, two points behind Montrose, with a game in hand.

An unconvincing 1-0 home win over Berwick Rangers was the prelude to three very disappointing results. On 28 September, Saints lost 5-0 at home to a much superior Queen of the South side. After the match, Willie Cunningham admitted to being disappointed by the lack of character which had been apparent in previous matches and acknowledged that it had given him "food for thought," whilst adding, "I still have faith in the staff I have at Love Street".

That loyalty was severely tested the following Saturday, as his team, leading Stenhousemuir at Ochilview by four goals to two with just thirteen minutes to go, allowed the "Warriors" to grab two goals in the last five minutes. The team had conceded nine goals in two games; it was hardly top six form.

In a bid to strengthen the defence, Manager Cunningham moved quickly to sign Alloa Athletic defender George Brown. Twenty-six year old Brown, who had been at Recreation Park for seven years, was set to replace the promising but out-of-form young pivot Bobby Reid.

Brown's debut was the home match against third top East Fife on 12 October, but defensive weaknesses were again easily exposed in a 3-0 defeat which left Saints in eighth place after ten fixtures. Two days later the Club announced that Willie Cunningham had resigned. It was an unfortunate sequence of events for Brown, who would play only four more times before being transfer-listed on 18 December and freed at the end of the season by the new Manager.

The Club stated that Mr. Cunningham was leaving "for personal reasons," and added that his resignation had been accepted "with great reluctance". Underlining the amicable nature of the parting, the Board confirmed that Mr. Cunningham had agreed to carry on until a successor could be appointed. It was later revealed that the outgoing Manager even recommended the name of his eventual successor!

Within three days, applications to replace Willie Cunningham came pouring into St. Mirren Park, but the thirty-four year old recently-appointed manager of East Stirlingshire, Alex Ferguson, was favourite to be selected. By Monday 21 October, he was outlining his aims for St. Mirren:

"I want to see St. Mirren finish in the top six this season and once we have achieved that objective I will then strive to make the Club comparable with the best in the country". It was stirring stuff from the country's youngest manager, but he quickly brought Saints fans back to reality: "Until then, we must fight, and fight hard to succeed. With patience, we will achieve that".

Alex Ferguson

Mr. Ferguson did make one promise. "I never played defensive football at East Stirlingshire for it would have broken my heart to sit and watch it from the dug-out. Supporters are not interested in teams which are going to defend. They want to see exciting football."

Managerless Saints had won 4-2 in their first-ever visit to face Scotland's newest League club, Meadowbank Thistle, on 19 October and although this win took them back into sixth place they had been less than impressive.

The Alex Ferguson era began a week later when the same eleven drew 0-0 at Kilbowie Park against struggling Clydebank. Saints lacked penetration up front and were lucky to gain a point. "I was disappointed in the lack of football in my side," Ferguson confessed. "I now know what I have to work on, although the effort, discipline and professionalism of the side pleased me." Saints were fifth, with two other clubs also on the fifteen point mark. It was an erratic rate of progress but one which was set to continue.

Greater creativity was shown on 2 November, but lack of penetration persisted in a 1-0 home defeat from mid-table Hamilton Academical, whose negative tactics drew scathing criticism from the new boss. A week later, Saints were deservedly beaten 3-1 at Alloa and slumped to twelfth in the table. The players' confidence had dropped, but the same could not be said of Alex Ferguson, who felt there would be many twists and turns in such a competitive League, but he expected to see St. Mirren back in the top six.

To achieve that, it was becoming increasingly likely that the Manager would have to undertake some external recruitment, as he acknowledged that the Club lacked "natural strikers", a situation not helped by the various injuries which would keep top scorer Brian Third out from the beginning of November until the end of February. On 12 November, winger Bert Ferguson was signed from Ayr United, and thereafter only illness or injury kept him out of the team.

Behind the scenes, Mr. Ferguson's plans to consolidate the Club's youth policy were moving apace, and meetings with local club secretaries were lined up. "The future of this Club," he explained, "is based on the players now playing in youth and juvenile football".

In truth there wasn't an alternative. The Board were about to announce that the Club had made a loss of £14,430 to 31 March 1974. The coming of speedway to St. Mirren Park in February 1975 was expected to provide much needed extra income, but money would remain tight.

The Manager was well aware of this, but he believed that two more players would make a real difference to the present side, and when Saints hosted the visit of Cowdenbeath on 23 November, the team included a pair of debutants. Former Clydebank and Partick Thistle striker Allan Munro joined from Dundee United, where the outstanding ability of the precocious Andy Gray had severely limited his opportunities. Donny McDowell had been signed from Partick Thistle, and would prove to be a significant acquisition.

Both new players impressed in a greatly improved performance, but only one point was gained when it really should have been two. This progress continued the following week when a vociferous visiting support watched a brilliant first-half display provide the basis of a 4-2 win over Albion Rovers at Cliftonhill, Saints' first win since 19 October. Replacing Alex Morrison in goals for this match was Jim Herriot, who had asked to return to the Club immediately after Alex Ferguson's appointment.

Only twenty-two points had been gathered from twenty-one games, but many supporters believed that Saints were now playing their best football for years. They were lying in twelfth place, but it was the potential of his team that convinced the Manager that a top six finish was achievable, and his faith seemed well placed when Saints led 1-0 against League leaders Montrose on 7 December with just twenty minutes to go. However, two errors by Jim Herriot let the Angus side off the hook.

The same eleven could only draw 1-1 the following week at Station Park against a defensive Forfar side, as a winning run continued to prove elusive. The year was rounded off with a standard-setting 2-0 home win over bogey side East Stirlingshire, and a 1-1 away draw with Stirling Albion. A half-time substitute at Annfield was Jackie McGillivray, who had been signed from the Ayrshire Junior side Annbank United on 13 November. He would be the first choice left winger from mid-January onwards.

Saints' inconsistencies were carried into the New Year. Another two errors by Jim Herriot and a questionable attitude adopted by the players contributed to a disastrous 3-0 home defeat from a superior Queen's Park side, as the team slipped to eleventh. Three days later, and with Alex Morrison reinstated as keeper, a lethargic, shot-shy Saints side were eliminated from the potentially lucrative Scottish Cup as East Stirlingshire extended their fine early 1970s record against Saints with a 2-1 win at Firs Park.

The 'top six' target got back on track when Donny McDowell inspired Saints to a very one-sided 6-1 home win over Brechin City, which also featured a hat-trick from fellow new man Allan Munro, and the beginning of a regular run in the side for a young midfielder by the name of Tony Fitzpatrick. A twenty-third minute goal from McDowell turned the next game - against Queen of the South at Palmerston - in Saints' favour. It was enough to capture both points, but three wins in a row continued to be beyond them as lack of concentration led to a 2-1 defeat at a muddy Stair Park, Stranraer on Burns Night.

Outwardly confident, Alex Ferguson felt that the underlying trend showed that his team had turned the corner, but the hard-working new Manager was not slow to acknowledge when his team played badly. However, between 1 February and 29 March this was seldom an issue, as a McDowell-influenced Saints hit a purple patch, scoring twenty-four and conceding just five goals as eight fixtures in a row were won, and fourth place in the table was attained.

Tony Fitzpatrick

There were five games left. In typical fashion, Alex Ferguson set the target of winning all five to finish as champions! A 1-1 draw with a very defensive-minded Albion Rovers, who had four booked and were reduced to ten men in the second half, immediately ended such lofty aspirations, then the fourth-last fixture was lost 2-1 to a skillful Montrose side at Links Park.

Success! A 2-0 home victory over bottom team Forfar Athletic on 19 April meant that Saints were promoted with two League games to spare. Then a trophy was won in the penultimate match of the season. Already 2 0 up from the first leg in Paisley, Saints captured the Renfrewshire Cup at rain-swept Cappielow as their attacking style, and an eighteenth minute Allan Munro goal, proved good enough to beat Morton 1-0.

That result rounded off a season of accomplishment, but one which could so easily have led to Second Division obscurity and financial disaster. Alex Ferguson's belief in attacking football and his flair for publicity had revitalised St. Mirren. After years of stagnation, Buddies were talking optimistically about Paisley's team again.

1975-76

The Ferguson factor and the new spirit he brought to the Club had been just enough to gain entry to the new middle Division, but playing at a higher level meant the squad had to be re-modelled; the Manager began this task with the release of nine players on 25 April.

Prominent names in the freed list were centre half George Brown, full back Ricky McLachlan, right winger Bobby Laurie, and inside forward Bobby Biggar. McLachlan had been signed by Tommy Bryceland, and the three others were Willie Cunningham recruits, but each one had progressively dropped out of the first team picture under the new management team.

In addition to these planned changes, Alex Ferguson learned on 5 May that centre forward Brian Third, and wing half Billy Johnston had refused the Club's terms for 1975-76. Billy eventually re-signed and would start thirteen League games, mostly in the second half of the season, but twenty-eight year old Brian expressed a desire to move back north after the Club had turned down his request for better terms.

The centre, whose twelve goals in twenty-six League games as a Saint fell some way short of his Montrose goal-scoring prowess, signed for Highland League Peterhead at the end of July.

The improving young talent at the Club and the continued presence of players such as extremely influential forward Donny McDowell and pacy left winger Jack McGillivray increased the Manager's confidence that his team, which would remain part-time, would finish in the top half of the fourteen-team First Division. To prepare for their most testing season for five years, Saints took part in five pre-season friendlies that began with an easy 3-0 away win at Selkirk on 26 July.

Playing against his former and home town team was new first choice 'keeper Dave McConnell, who had replaced Alex Morrison after the latter had walked out of the Club at the beginning of July, insisting that he wished to give up the game. Alex would return to Love Street on 5 August, but would play on only three occasions before being put on the transfer list in November at his own request.

The line up at Selkirk also included a trialist from Anniesland Waverley who did so well that Alex Ferguson signed him immediately after the game. Billy Stark would feature in all but five of the forthcoming League fixtures, and would add authority to his cultured midfield play as the season progressed.

The following Monday, Saints relinquished a 2-0 half-time lead when a vastly more experienced visiting Hereford United side earned a well-deserved draw. One of the Saints' forwards on the night was seventeen year old Derek Hyslop, who had been picked up on a free transfer from Hibernian on 10 May and would be on the fringes of the first team throughout the season.

In the third pre-season match, Saints displayed skill and confidence in the first half at home to champions Rangers before eventually losing 2-0, but they were punchless in Paisley against a Bury side that should have been beaten. This inability to convert pressure into goals would be a recurring problem all season, but it wasn't evident in the final friendly when Icelandic visitors Reykjavik KR were beaten 5-3 by a very young Saints eleven. Four of the goals came from Frank McGarvey, who had been called up from Kilsyth Rangers during the summer. Despite his frail appearance, young Frank combined energy and courage with an awkward, highly effective style, and would quickly become a fans' favourite.

The League Cup began with a deserved 2-1 home win over East Fife which was played in sweltering heat, and featured notable contributions from second half substitutes Frank McGarvey and seventeen year old centre forward Peter Leonard, a product of local side Johnstone United. A generation of St. Mirren players set to become "household names" was emerging.

After the East Fife fixture, the Manager declared that he thought St. Mirren had "the nucleus of a really good side" but the rest of the League Cup results seemed at odds with that assessment, as only two more points, from draws away to Montrose and at home to Raith, were realised. "The players know themselves that they threw the Section away," the Manager asserted. "I hope they have learned from that. They have got to play for ninety minutes, take chances and stop giving goals away."

Mr. Ferguson stated that he was confident that he had the players necessary for a successful season in the First Division, and repeated his basic aims: he wanted a team that was prepared to play football, provide entertainment for the supporters, and attract more people through the Love Street turnstiles.

By the end of November, Saints would be attracting crowds of more than 4,000, a doubling of attendances but still short of an estimated break-even figure of 4,500. The Manager could barely comprehend why more Paisley fans were not taking the opportunity to see his team: "They should be falling over themselves to see the McGarveys, Fitzpatricks,

Frank McGarvey

and Starks because there have not been so many young players of that calibre at Love Street for years."

Early League results were little better than the League Cup, with only one win in the first six fixtures. It meant Saints were in ninth place at the beginning of October, but it was encouraging to note that they were trying to play good football in all circumstances.

A fine home performance against East Fife marked the beginning of a three-match winning run, and they climbed to fourth after nine fixtures, three points behind the top two, Kilmarnock and Partick Thistle. A week later the Manager was expressing the view that "the mistakes that were made early on in the season have been invaluable in the sense that they have learned by them. They are still making mistakes but they are sorting them out quicker".

Saints moved up to third place after they drew 2-2 at home to Airdrieonians, then showed more than a hint of complacency in a disastrous 4-1 defeat to a very experienced Arbroath side up at Gayfield. A further two points were dropped on 22 November against the League leaders at Firhill, but the narrow 2-1 defeat indicated that fighting qualities had now been added to youthful skills!

There was a growing sense in the town that Alex Ferguson's team were going places, and a confidence-boosting 2-0 home win over Dunfermline Athletic on 29 November was followed by an entertaining 0-0 home draw with Kilmarnock and a 2-0 win over East Fife at Bayview. A mini-slump then occurred at the turn of the year as a home draw with Hamilton was sandwiched between lost matches at Dumbarton and Greenock. Promotion, never really expected anyway, was now unlikely.

A return to winning ways came with an easy 3-0 home victory over relegation-threatened Clyde on 3 January. Champions-elect Partick Thistle were the next visitors in a match surrounded by massive publicity, generated almost single-handedly by Alex Ferguson, who seldom missed an opportunity to declare the merits of his team in the local and national media. A crowd of over 9,000 saw the team lose 3-2 in a game that underlined that although they were certainly no less skillful than Thistle, they still had a bit to learn before a sustained promotion bid could be mounted.

One week later another three goals were conceded, this time to Second Division Cowdenbeath, as the first hurdle of the Scottish Cup proved insurmountable. It was certainly the poorest Paisley performance of the season, notably by 'keeper McConnell and the defence.

As January closed, a 2-1 defeat at Montrose prompted Alex Ferguson to admit that his young team had "gone off the boil". He did not dwell on that, but instead praised his players for what had been achieved to that point. The back four had improved, thanks to the partnership of Bobby Reid and Brian Kinnear, and the consistent, tenacious play of full back Alex Beckett.

Bobby Reid

Bobby Reid, often faced with the opposition's most troublesome player, had made the vital centre half position his own, showing a growing composure which was complemented by the calm and unobtrusive Brian Kinnear, a summer signing from Fernhill Amateurs.

The education of the young Paisley players was extended when the technically gifted and tactically aware Polish side Legia Warsaw arrived in town for a challenge match on 4 February, but to Alex Ferguson's dismay, fewer than 4,000 turned up to watch a highly entertaining game which Saints won 1-0; an excellent result by any standards.

Sadly, only one of the last four fixtures were won, as the team finished in sixth place with twenty six points from the same number of games, and thirty-seven goals both scored and conceded. There was always the likelihood that such a young side could quickly return to their early season form, and the commencement of the Spring Cup at the beginning of March offered such an opportunity.

Run on the same lines as the League Cup, Saints first opponents were Second Division bottom club Meadowbank Thistle, who were easily beaten 4-0. Third bottom Forfar Athletic fared no better, as the experienced and versatile Walter Borthwick unusually captured all the headlines with a hat-trick in a 5-0 win, and a young Billy Abercromby, destined to lift the Scottish Cup in 1987, made a quiet debut as a half-time substitute.

The next match saw a visit from League champions Partick Thistle, a side whose style of play didn't over-impress Alex Ferguson one bit! "Nobody is going to tell me that Partick Thistle are a better side than St. Mirren," he proclaimed. "I will never be convinced of that. As far as I am concerned they cannot hold a candle to us". The match was an extremely ill-tempered affair in which Thistle were responsible for thirty-seven of the game's forty-nine fouls, but the visitors dominated the midfield and Saints lost 2-1.

In the return ties, Forfar were easily beaten 1-0, and Meadowbank were again defeated 4-0, with another new signing, Lex Richardson, making a confident debut. Twenty year old Richardson, just signed from Arthurlie, would add some much-needed aggression to Saints midfield in each of the remaining Spring Cup games. In the last tie, a fourth match against Partick Thistle, victory was finally achieved on 10 April when two goals from danger man McGarvey and one from the remarkably mature Tony Fitzpatrick, youngest captain of a Scottish senior side, produced a very satisfying 3-1 win.

The Buddies faced a superior Second Division side, Alloa Athletic, in the quarter finals, but attacking football at home and away produced two three-goal winning margins in a 7-1 aggregate. They were then duly installed as favourites to lift the new trophy, and a semi-final clash with Morton beckoned.

In the first leg at Cappielow on 21 April, a pass-back mix-up between 'keeper McConnell and Junior Supporters Association Player of the Year award-winner, the versatile and industrious John Young, gave the defensive-minded home team a scarcely deserved 1-0 lead. Three days later, Saints spent eighty-nine minutes trying to open up the Greenock defence to secure an equaliser. Then in the ninetieth minute Morton scored again.

Alex Ferguson was not down-hearted. He acknowledged that if further improvement was to be achieved the team needed a goalscorer to cash in on the skillful play of McGarvey, McDowell and Stark, but he had produced a team of exciting, talented young players capable of competing in the new First Division: "I am delighted with the performance of the team this year. We have now got to look for the same progress next season". It was an expectation which would be met, and surpassed!

1976-77

The 1976 free transfer list spoke volumes about the Club's ambitions. In releasing six players, Alex Ferguson explained that he had considered whether they were of a standard required to play in the Premier Division, and reluctantly concluded that they were not.

Forwards Bert Ferguson and Allan Munro were publicly praised by the Manager for their services to the Club, and he sympathised with full back Ian Reid, who had been restricted to just twelve first team appearances due to injury. Midfielders John Hughes and Joe Plommer had failed to realise their potential, whilst young keeper John Hunt was similarly regarded, having offered insufficient challenge to Dave McConnell for the goalkeeper's jersey. Two days after Hunt's release, Dave McConnell told the Club he wasn't coming back, thus leaving the Buddies without a keeper.

The promising McConnell had just completed his first season at St. Mirren Park, but had continued to be domiciled in Selkirk. The Manager wanted the big keeper to move to the Paisley area to enable McConnell to train more often with the rest of his team mates and work on aspects of his play. However the player was not prepared to leave his home town, and would eventually sign for Berwick Rangers in late October 1976.

The goalkeeping problem was resolved on 3 June, on the eve of the Club's Caribbean tour, when Rangers reserve keeper Donald Hunter was signed on a two year loan basis. He would not only prove to be a safe, confident custodian, but would play in every one of Saints' League and cup matches.

Donald joined a travelling party comprising defenders Billy Johnston, Brian Kinnear, John Mowat, Bobby Reid, and John Young, midfielders Billy Abercromby, Walter Borthwick, Tony Fitzpatrick, Lex Richardson,

Billy Stark

and Billy Stark, and forwards Peter Leonard, Donny McDowell, Frank McGarvey, Jackie McGillivray, and Robert Torrance. The only notable absentee was full back Alex Beckett, who was to be married during the tour period. As a precaution, Manager Alex Ferguson and his Assistant Davie Provan were also registered as players.

The ambitious tour began on 10 June in Barbados, and continued through Trinidad, Guyana, and Surinam before returning to Barbados for the eighth and final match on 27 June. Retrospectively, eight games were considered too many, but in every other aspect the tour was considered a huge success.

Six of the high-standard matches were won, and the players returned oozing with confidence, in no doubt that they were going to win everything! The Manager would make no such predictions, and although he wanted to acquire another experienced player "with character", he expected his team to do well: "St. Mirren have the best young players in the country but we have no money to buy experienced players. It is the team spirit, like that built up on the tour, which will be of the greatest assistance to us".

Six weeks after the tour's end, Saints started their one hundredth season at Ayr United's Somerset Park, the first in a series of testing League Cup ties against three Premier Division teams. "We will raise our game for these matches," promised the Manager, but he added that "anything we get from the League Cup will be a bonus. Our main objective this season is promotion to the Premier Division."

As it turned out, they didn't get very much. An opening day 2-1 defeat owed much to that weakness in front of goal, and this reluctance to shoot was repeated in the second tie, a 3-2 home defeat from Aberdeen.

Without displaying the quality play of the opening two games, Saints won their first point in a 1-1 draw at Kilmarnock. Up to this half way point, goalscoring apart, Saints had shown they could match their higher division opponents, but that changed when Aberdeen striker Joe Harper hit a hat-trick in a 4-0 win which didn't flatter the Dons.

The fifth tie secured their first victory, a narrow, unimpressive 1-0 home win over Kilmarnock, the section was then completed with a 2-2 home draw with Ayr United, Saints having been 2-0 up after seventeen minutes and then missing a penalty at 2-2.

Alex Ferguson felt that the side's "carelessness" throughout the League Cup had been "unbelievable". The giving away of "silly goals" meant that games were lost and drawn which should have been won, and the section was lost as a result.

Now the "main objective" commenced. After just one season, the Spring Cup had been scrapped, which meant that First and Second Division clubs would play thirty-nine fixtures and oppose each other three times. Saints were widely regarded as major promotion contenders, along with the relegated but experienced St. Johnstone and Dundee, the Dens Parkers having the added advantage of being full-time. No one mentioned newly promoted Clydebank's excellent side.

The campaign didn't get off to the best of starts. A combination of negative tactics by visitors East Fife, who would not be alone in this approach, an outstanding display from Fifers' goalie Ernie McGarr, and the curious sight of two own goals resulted in a 1-1 draw on 4 September. It was an unexpected point to drop.

At Brockville the following week, Saints' classy, entertaining football was again on show, but chances, simple chances, were missed as the "Bairns" won 2-0. The Manager's post-match verdict included the rebuke that his team would remain "the prettiest losers in the League" unless they started to be "hungry in the penalty box". It was a refrain he would not be forced to repeat too often.

Saints outfield superiority was finally converted into goals in a 5-2 hammering of hard-working Hamilton at Love Street on 14 September. It was the start of an incredible twenty-eight match undefeated run in the League which did not end until 12 March, the only other championship defeat.

The eighth fixture, on 2 October, was a home match against undefeated Dundee, which was seen as the Buddies first big test. Fans who braved the wet and windy conditions watched a compelling match which Saints won 4-0, and in so doing replaced Dundee in third place. There was more wind at Links Park on 6 October 1977, but the winning run continued with an excellent 4-2 win over Montrose. As if predetermined, St. Mirren moved to the top of the league on the hundredth anniversary of their first-ever match!

The next three fixtures, also away from home, produced two draws and a win, but Clydebank were matching Saints step by step. By the time they met on 23 October, the "Bankies" had drawn level with St. Mirren at the top of the league, and had a game in hand. Four days before the Love Street clash of the joint leaders, Manager Ferguson challenged the Paisley public to attend in large numbers and he was strongly supported by the "Paisley Daily Express": "Time to support your local team. Don't let Saints down" exclaimed the double headline.

Alerted by the pre-match publicity and enticed by the prospect of seeing two attack-minded teams, 10,515 turned up on a dismal October day to watch a thrilling match which had everything but goals. It was the best attendance in many a long year. The message was finally getting through; Paisley did have a team worth supporting.

A 0-0 draw had been a fair result, although either side could have won. The following Saturday, on 30 October, another 10,000 plus crowd assembled at St. Mirren Park to witness a 5-1 thrashing of Morton. Although young Jim Liddell in the Morton goal was said to be at fault with three of the goals, the margin of victory was not misleading, and was certainly satisfying.

November began with Saints conceding three avoidable goals in a 3-3 away draw with bottom club East Fife in front of a voluble visiting support. It was the second point dropped to the Fifers, and the match again underlined the need for more composure at the back.

Three days after the Methil match, Alex Ferguson clinched a deal to bring back to Love Street twenty-nine year old, highly experienced Dundee United sweeper Jackie Copland, who had played as a teenage forward in two League games for St. Mirren during the 1967-68 Championship-winning season. It was revealed that the £25,000 transfer had only been made possible thanks to the Manager's ability to persuade the St. Mirren Supporters' Social Club to give the football club a loan.

As Jackie Copland arrived, Saints agreed to transfer the versatile and popular Walter Borthwick to St. Johnstone for a nominal fee. Walter, who had been signed from East Fife by Willie Cunningham in July 1974, was still featuring in most League games, but increasingly from the bench.

There were two more wins before the transfer of Jackie Copland was completed on 22 November. Jackie began phase two of his St. Mirren career five days later, in a 3-0 home win over Arbroath. The new signing's organisational skills were apparent from the start, and the defence looked more secure as a consequence. He would play in the next fourteen League and Cup matches before a cartilage injury sustained on 5 March against Clydebank put him out of the team for the rest of the season.

Commerative joint programme produced by both clubs for the Christmas Day "Battle of the Gladiators of the First Division". The programme was distributed at the turnstiles "on the house".

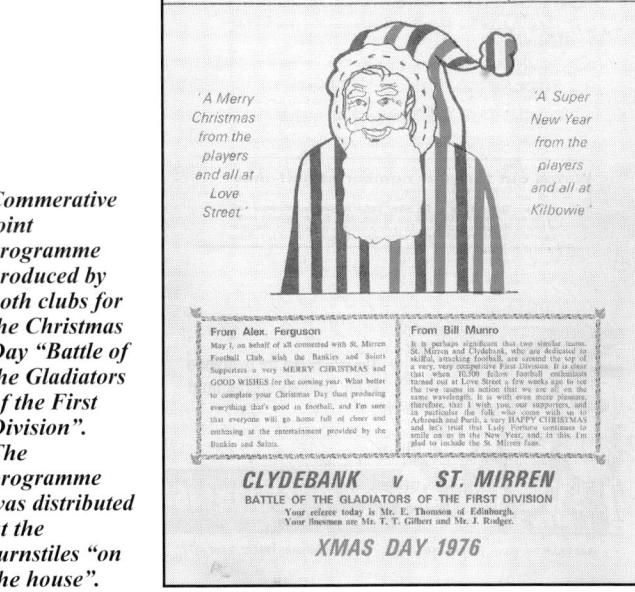

After a three week break caused by adverse weather conditions, the successful run re-started on 18 December, when two goals from Derek Hyslop produced a 2-1 home win over rather physical Queen of the South on a tricky, snow-covered surface.

In the middle of this enforced break, the Club confirmed that, although average home gates had increased from 2,500 to 4,100 to bring in additional revenues of £90,000, a loss of £13,463 had been made in the year to 31 March 1976, due to "the reduction in transfer fees", "We have made strides but we have not yet bridged the gap between income and expenditure," explained Chairman William Todd, but he added encouragingly that "we still have quite a considerable way to go without selling players".

On Christmas Day the 10,000 all-ticket crowd who assembled at Clydebank's Kilbowie Park created an electric atmosphere for Britain's only senior game of the day, as they watched the two best teams in the League draw again in a fast and furious, winner-takes-all encounter. This time it was 2-2, Saints having been 2-0 down.

The centenary year started in the best possible way, with an extraordinary 6-3 win over Morton at Cappielow, having again been 2-0 down after only seven minutes. The game turned on a twenty-seventh minute incident when Donny McDowell and Morton keeper Liddell clashed and were sent off.

Three more points were collected from two away games, before January ended with one of the most memorable matches in St. Mirren's history.

Drawn in the Scottish Cup at home against the Premier Division's fourth top team, Dundee United, Alex Ferguson immediately claimed that thousands of cheering Paisley supporters "could just be the spur to ensure victory for us."

That's exactly what happened as 16,357 spectators saw two goals from the talented Bobby Torrance, a summer signing from Eastwood High School, and one each from Stark and McGarvey overtake Paul Sturrock's early opener. A missed penalty was just one indication that the winning margin could have been even wider. Veteran reporter Hugh Taylor dubbed them "Fergie's Furies," and wrote in glowing terms about the young team's "infectious enthusiasm". His report was part of unanimous praise which emanated from the press; it was no more than the team deserved. It had been a sensational performance.

With St. Mirren euphoria at its height, the whole Club was given a boost on 1 February, when Alex Ferguson announced that he was to become the full-time manager of St. Mirren. Four days later, the other Dundee club came to town for one of the season's most crucial games, a match won by Saints much more emphatically than the 3-1 scoreline suggests.

After the Dens men were defeated, the team won another three on the trot, scoring twelve goals and conceding just two in the process. Then came the reward for beating Dundee United in the Cup, a fourth round tie away to Premier Division Motherwell on 26 February.

It was a match which caught the public's imagination, an interest not harmed by some publicly-stated, pre-match differences of opinion between the respective managers about the playing strengths and drawing powers of each team! An astonishing 26,709 people packed into Fir Park, with Paisley fans perilously positioned on top of refreshment huts, in the floodlight pylons and even up trees! Outside, an estimated 2,000 Saints supporters failed to gain entry when the gates were closed.

The kick off had to be delayed for fifteen minutes, but the tone of the match was set right from the first whistle, when some shocking tackling by the home side escaped censure from the referee. The physical nature of the game seemed to unsettle some in the young Saints team, causing the side's play to be far less cohesive than usual. The match ended in a bitterly disappointing 2-1 defeat, Saints first reverse in twenty-seven matches.

Back in the League, a 2-0 win over East Fife at Bayview preceded the last of the season's "big" games. Throughout the season, Saints' unbeaten run had not allowed them to pull away from the equally consistent Clydebank, but crunch-time came on 5 March when 15,000 saw Saints triumph after another closely-fought contest, a result which greatly increased the likelihood of the Championship coming to Paisley.

A point was dropped in the home match against St. Johnstone on 8 March, then Saints suffered their second League defeat, a comprehensive 3-0 thumping by Morton at Cappielow, which ended a magnificent run of twenty-eight fixtures without loss.

There was no denying that since the tough Cup encounter with Motherwell the team had hit a bad patch. Some of the younger players' confidence seemed to have been affected by the Fir Park experience, but lack of continuity in selection, a hallmark of the season up till then, was proving equally upsetting. Alex Beckett was still recovering from injuries received in the Cup match, and, able though his young deputy John Mowat was, the loss of the much improved Beckett, the disturbance of his partnership with experienced ex-skipper Billy Johnston, and the continuing absence of Copland, were all disruptions the defence could have done without.

The stuttering form continued at the end of March in two back-to-back games against Hamilton, when one goal was scored and three points gained. One public announcement could perhaps be added to that equation, because Derek Hyslop's eighty-ninth minute strike in the home game against the Accies looked an unlikely occurrence until the atmosphere in the ground was transformed by a helpful announcer who informed the crowd, and the two teams, that Clydebank had just been beaten!

Windy conditions at Love Street on 2 April made good football difficult, but a Frank McGarvey double over relegation-threatened Raith Rovers was enough to secure the two points. When the two sides met again the following week, Saints knew another victory would ensure a precious place in the Premier Division. In a competent if not spectacular display, goals from McGarvey, Mowat, and Hyslop saw off the Rovers - the season's main objective was achieved!

Everyone at the Club was delighted, but with four games still to play the target was now the Championship. Suddenly, the post-Motherwell depression lifted on 16 April, with a back-to-their-best first half display which produced a 3-0 win over Airdrieonians. The team needed just one point at Dens the following Tuesday to become champions, and a large contingent of Buddies made the journey to Dundee. They were rewarded with what Chairman William Todd described afterwards as "the best St. Mirren performance in fifty years."

1976/77 First Division Championship medal won by Jack Copland.

Clydebank had claimed promotion at Dens the previous week, but Dundee remained highly-competitive opponents. In fact, the "Dark Blues" had the edge until Billy Stark scored in the thirty-ninth minute. A minute later top scorer Frank McGarvey made it two, and after that there was only going to be one winner. McGarvey scored another two in the second half, as the team gave a brilliant display of attacking, entertaining football which epitomised the season.

The players, who had predicted they would win everything, were ecstatic, and reportedly sang all the way home from Dundee! Saints drew 2-2 with Airdrieonians at Broomfield the following Saturday, but the real celebrations were reserved for the thirty-ninth and final fixture, a home match against Montrose when 10,000 Saints fans saw the team parade with the coveted trophy.

The game ended in another 2-2 draw, but the season wasn't quite over. A near 10,000 crowd turned up at Love Street on Sunday May 8th to see if Saints could overcome a 1-0 deficit and capture a second piece of silverware, the Renfrewshire Cup. They were not disappointed, as a Bobby Torrance hat-trick and goals from Lex Richardson and Peter Leonard helped Saints demoralise Morton in a 5-2 victory to end one of Saints' most memorable seasons.

John Young runs towards the Main Stand, Renfrewshire Cup in hand, pursued by Tony Fitzpatrick, Bobby Torrance, and Bobby Reid.

County supremacy was always satisfying but, Saints were now officially one of Scotland's top ten teams. It had taken the invigorating presence of one very motivated individual to get Saints to the top level of Scottish football. On the field, Alex Ferguson had insisted on playing good football at all times. Off the field, he had done much to re-organise the structure of the club. Not since the successful John Cochrane era of the 1920s had the Club been in such optimistic mood!

1977-78

On 7 June, Alex Ferguson signed a four year contract and hoped the move would end his name being linked with managerial vacancies at other clubs. He expected his team to show an improvement on the previous season's outstanding form, but recognised that having a two-to-one ratio of part-timers to full-timers was going to be a handicap in the Premier Division.

By the end of July, the Manager abandoned his attempts to strengthen his squad because of what he called the "astronomical" fees being demanded by other clubs. Although he felt the squad was vulnerable if hit by too many injuries or suspensions, he was well aware that Saints' finances were already stretched by overdue and unavoidable ground improvements; Scottish football's highest level would have to be tackled by the existing playing staff.

The first team would in fact be little changed from the previous season, although popular former captain Billy Johnston would make only two early-season League appearances before being freed in April, whilst the industrious Billy Abercromby would establish himself in midfield. Also making a contribution with twelve League starts would be seventeen year old Barrhead boy Brian Docherty, who had been signed from Arthurlie the previous summer.

Competitive football began on 3 August with a comfortable enough 4-1 away win over Stirling Albion in the Anglo-Scottish Cup, but it was participation in the prestigious Tennent Caledonian Cup at Ibrox alongside Rangers, West Bromwich Albion, and Southampton which would be a better gauge of the team's continuing progress.

In the game against West Brom, it was 3-3 until a special goal by Albion's Bryan Robson settled the match in the seventy-seventh minute. The next day's play-off for third and fourth place was also lost, 2-1, but it was less of a spectacle, as Southampton unfortunately adopted a more physical approach, and had one man sent off and three booked.

The following week-end a crowd of 9,000 watched as the black and white "First Division Champions 1976-77 Centenary" flag was unfurled prior to Saints first-ever Premier match, against old friends Clydebank. Otherwise, it was not a particularly memorable match, but the 1-1 draw ensured that Saints were at least off the mark.

The second Premier fixture away to Dundee United, by contrast, was a superbly entertaining affair, and although the game was lost 2-1, the Buddies had shown up well against one of the Division's better teams. Three days later, on 23 August, a 1-0 second leg win over Stirling Albion was enough to continue Saints' presence in the Anglo-Scottish Cup.

The third League match produced the first victory, a well-merited 2-0 home win over Ayr United, before the League Cup intervened for the first time. On 31 August, the Buddies faced a Kilmarnock side which included their summer signing from Saints, Jack McGillivray, but neither team was able to take their chances and the tie finished goal-less.

The return leg, three days later in Paisley, produced a late 2-1 winner for St. Mirren, but it was a fortunate outcome, as Killie had missed a number of first half chances and Saints were far from their free-flowing best. Six days after the second tie, Killie addressed their apparent goalscoring weakness by spending £10,000 on popular Saint Donny McDowell, who had been unable to gain a regular place in the Paisley first team since the season started.

The next League game, on 10 September, would turn out to be one of Saints' best all-round displays of the season, as old adversaries Motherwell were beaten 3-0 at Fir Park, a confidence-booster for the visit to Craven Cottage to face Fulham in the "Anglo-Scottish".

In London, the Buddies went behind after just three minutes in an opening period of intense Fulham pressure, but a minute after the interval Lex Richardson deservedly equalised with a brilliant twenty-yard free kick, and thereafter the visitors enjoyed the bulk of the attacking play,

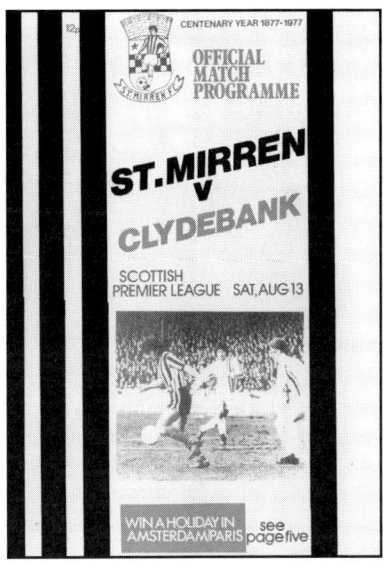

Programme for Saints' first ever Premier Division match, versus Clydebank, featuring Derek Hyslop (above) in First Division action from the previous season.

before an eighty-ninth minute penalty from Tony Fitzpatrick was saved to set up an intriguing second leg.

Two weeks later, a crowd of nearly 10,000 braved the rain to witness one of the finest cupties seen at St. Mirren Park for many a year, as eight goals were shared. Saints moved into a 3-1 lead and looked to be in control, but Fulham fought back to draw level. With two minutes to go Saints went 4-3 ahead, courtesy of an own goal, then Brian Docherty made sure with a last minute strike.

In between the two Fulham ties, a crowd of 25,000 watched Saints draw with Rangers on 17 September, in a match which was full of attacking football, six goals, and an outstanding performance from two-goal Frank McGarvey. They were less impressive in the next game at Easter Road, where a poor Hibs team won 2-0 as the team failed to convert numerous chances.

Saints got back on the winning trail on the first day of October with a 2-1 home win over Partick Thistle, before switching to League Cup business, an uninspiring 2-0 first leg win away to Hamilton Accies. It was not the form needed to face a visiting Aberdeen team whose technical and tactical superiority was not exaggerated by their 4-0 league win.

The next assignment was at Celtic Park to face a home side trying to cope with the transfer of Kenny Dalglish. After an entertaining but goalless first half, an own goal gave Saints an early second half lead, and although Celtic equalised ten minutes later, a mazy run past three defenders and an eighteen yard shot from Billy Stark meant Saints became the sixth of the Division's other nine clubs to beat Celtic, who slumped to second bottom.

The kaleidoscope of competitions continued. In the Anglo-Scottish Cup, a goal-less draw against Notts County seemed likely until the seventy-fifth minute, when the "Magpies" went ahead and stayed on top for the remainder of the game. The second quarter of League fixtures began with a 2-2 draw with Clydebank at Kilbowie in a game of fluctuating fortunes, then it was back to the League Cup for the visit of Hamilton. Two up from the first leg, the home tie was lost 2-1, but Saints went through to a money-spinning quarter final against Celtic, albeit in a most disappointing manner.

Play was immeasurably better against Dundee United in a marvelous match at St. Mirren Park, with an abundance of quality football. In the end, only a thirty-fourth minute United goal separated the teams; a pity as a win would have moved Saints into third place.

On the last day of the month, former Scottish international 'keeper Alastair Hunter joined Saints from Motherwell on a month's trial, and would eventually play in seven League games before being released at the end of the season. However, it was his namesake Donald who retained the jersey for the return semi-final tie with Notts County on 1 November. One player who did make his debut was versatile and experienced twenty-six year ex-Saint Iain Munro, signed from Rangers for £25,000 on the morning of the tie.

Iain's new team needed to score two more goals than their visitors, and that's exactly what

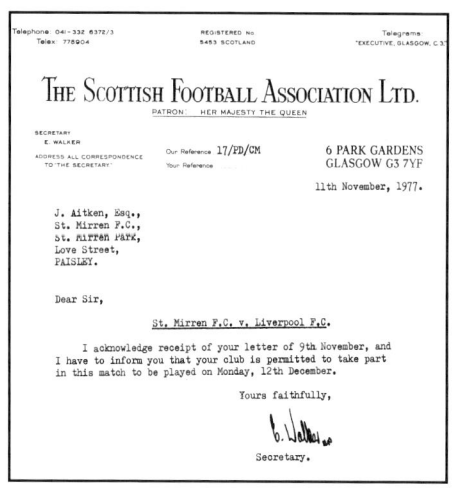

Letter from Scottish Football Association granting permission to play centenary match versus Liverpool.

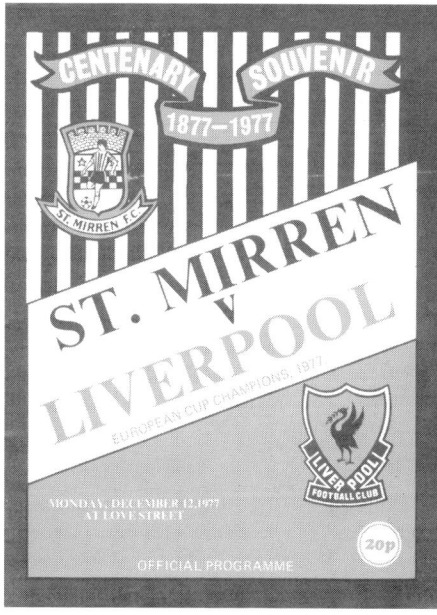

Centenary Match Programme.

Jersey worn by Jack Copland in the St. Mirren Centenary match versus Liverpool at St. Mirren Park. Final score St. Mirren 1 Liverpool 1 (Liverpool won on penalties).

9,000 very enthusiastic Saints fans saw them achieve, but it was not until the ninety-third minute that Frank McGarvey scored the extra time winner to give Saints the chance to become the first Scottish winners of the tournament.

Saints headed for Ayr on 5 November, and were leading 2-1 with twenty minutes to go when second bottom United staged a great fightback to win by the odd goal in five as Saints slipped to sixth in the table. Four days later the competition changed again when Celtic came calling in the League Cup. The Celts' recent record showed an ability to score goals and an even greater propensity to lose them. At Love Street on a miserably wet night their positive side was on show, as they hit three goals in less than an hour before Saints finally got the better of 'keeper Peter Latchford and pulled one back through the ever-dangerous Bobby Reid.

Seven days later, Saints travelled to Parkhead in the hope of overturning Celtic's two goal lead, but a further two goals were conceded to make the aggregate score a disappointing 5-1. Much better was the performance against Rangers at Ibrox on 19 November, despite the loss of pivot Bobby Reid, sent off just before half-time with Rangers Tommy McLean. The home team went ahead just after the interval, but a Billy Stark special from twenty yards levelled the scores after sixty-two minutes, before Rangers scored the winner from a soft penalty award.

Although the team had won just one of the previous five fixtures, that decent Ibrox display set Saints up for the Anglo-Scottish Cup Final, where they were due to meet the formidable Bristol City, who had played well in a draw with Liverpool at Anfield the previous Saturday. A crowd of more than 20,000 was expected for the first leg at St. Mirren Park, but unfortunately torrential rain before the match on 23 November not only restricted the attendance to only 8,000, but turned the pitch into a quagmire. The more experienced Bristol City players quickly adapted their play to the terrible conditions, and it was no surprise when they went one up through Kevin Mabbutt after twenty minutes.

The goal increased City's composure, and when former Scotland internationalist Peter Cormack extended the visitors lead to two in the seventy-third minute, the task of retrieving the situation looked extremely difficult, such was the Bristol team's superiority. However, a goal four minutes from time from Billy Abercromby, one of Saints' few stars on the night, improved Saints prospects for the second leg.

Back in the League, a 3-0 home win on an icy pitch over a struggling Hibs team was a more convincing victory than the scoreline suggests, and gave hope to the hundreds of Saints fans who journeyed to Ashton Gate on 5 December. Those who travelled gave the team terrific backing, and although not rewarded with a cup win, they did see a great performance by Donald Hunter in goal and a spectacular overhead kick from centre half Bobby Reid which levelled the aggregate score in the sixty-eight minute.

Two minutes later, Saints were again a goal behind when Kevin Mabbutt scored his second goal of the Final, but a further two minutes after that Frank McGarvey looked to have scored a second equaliser when he met a corner from the right, and as he headed in, collided with the City keeper. To the utter disbelief of the Saints support, the goal was disallowed, McGarvey being adjudged to have made contact with the goalie before he headed the ball. It was an infringement seen only by the referee, but it meant the Mabbut goal proved to be the winner.

With midweek distractions coming to an end the League became the sole focal point, and in early December, Saints travelled to Pittodrie to face the Dons. The match produced a 3-1 win for the home side, who again showed they were at the top end of the League on merit.

Opposition of an even higher quality beckoned on 12 December 1977, when European Champions Liverpool came to Paisley for a challenge match which was the highlight of the Club's centenary celebrations. An 18,000 crowd saw Kenny Dalglish open the scoring for the assured-looking Anfielders in fifty-seven minutes, but an eighty-seventh minute equaliser from Billy Abercromby took the game to penalties. It was 4-4 after Frank McGarvey and Jimmy Case had each missed one. Then Bobby Reid missed the sixth, but David Johnston scored to take the Centenary Silver Salver to Liverpool.

Saints returned to a League campaign nearing its halfway mark with a 3-3 home draw with Celtic, followed on Christmas Eve by a Premier Division victory over relegation-placed Clydebank at the third attempt. This 2-0 win proved to be the only two points gained from a possible eight over the festive period. At Tannadice on Hogmanay, they held a thoroughly deserved 1-0 half-time lead, but defensive lapses gave United a very fortunate 2-1 win.

That defeat in Dundee could not spoil any review of a wonderful centenary year which had seen promotion gained, a championship won, and a cup final reached. The calibre of the playing staff at St. Mirren Park had seldom been higher, as indicated by the capping of seven young players at Scotland Under 21 and Under 18 levels.

The holiday matches continued in the New Year with an inept home performance against second bottom Ayr United which produced a shock 3-2 reverse, and left Saints just one point ahead of the "Honest Men". The result was an undeniable set-back, and the Manager's dissatisfaction with the two goalkeeping Hunters became obvious when two days later he made an unsuccessful bid for Jim Stewart or his reserve Alan McCulloch from Kilmarnock.

Despite another over-physical encounter with Motherwell at Fir Park on 7 January, some much improved play was on show, but the conceding of a fluke goal meant it was now three defeats in a row. Consolation was taken from the fact that a similar run of victories in a tight ten-team league could transform the picture, but sentences containing "St. Mirren" and "relegation" began to appear in the press.

Following the Fir Park defeat, top-of-the-league Rangers came to Paisley and left with a 2-0 win, thanks to the two team's contrasting ability to take and squander scoring chances. Saints' play looked as attractive as ever but they were now equal second bottom with Ayr United.

Alex Ferguson's search for new players was rewarded when twenty-eight year old striker Jimmy Bone arrived from Arbroath on 2 February for a fee of £30,000, and much was expected of the new Bone-McGarvey partnership, which had its first outing two days later against Jimmy's first club, Partick Thistle. A crowd of 8,893 saw Saints more than match third-placed Thistle, and Bone's strength proved telling on a very muddy pitch as he laid on Bobby Reid's equaliser to move a point ahead of Ayr United and, thankfully, end a four-match losing sequence.

Two days later, the Scottish Cup campaign kicked off with a third round home tie against First Division Kilmarnock, knowing the possibility of a lucrative fourth round tie against Celtic awaited the winners. Saints, with Jimmy Bone missing from the ranks, failed to cope with the power play of Killie and lost 2-1, with the Ayrshire side's eighty-eighth minute winner coming, ironically, from Donny McDowell.

Arctic-like weather then made League fixtures impossible in mid-February, as three challenge matches were played in four days against First Division Morton, Arbroath, and Dundee. Real action resumed at a playable Parkhead on 25 February, and Saints showed the 22,000 crowd both style and substance in beating Celtic 2-1, with many fine saves from Donald Hunter, who in previous weeks had been criticised by sections of the crowd. Saints were now one point ahead of Hibs and two in front of Celtic and Ayr United.

Seven days later the same eleven players could only draw 2-2 against bottom club Clydebank at compact Kilbowie. Worse was to follow as a hitherto struggling Hibs team deservedly won 5-1 at Easter Road, despite Billy Abercromby grabbing an early lead! Saints and Hibs were now both on the twenty-two point mark, two ahead of second bottom Ayr.

There were plenty of failures at Easter Road, and absent pivot Bobby Reid was badly missed, but goalkeeper Donald Hunter followed up a poor performance at Kilbowie with another disappointing display in Edinburgh, and was said by some to be responsible for up to three of the Hibs goals. Three days later, Alex Ferguson re-approached Kilmarnock regarding their Barrhead-born reserve keeper Alan McCulloch, who was signed on a loan basis.

McCulloch's first match was against high-flying Dundee United at St. Mirren Park on 15 March, but his new team seemed to lack confidence against a United side whose control of the game was much greater than their narrow 2-1 victory indicates. McCulloch remained first choice until the end of the season whilst Donald Hunter would end his loan period from Rangers and return to them at the end of the season.

Saints - and a large contingent of Paisley fans - then visited Ayr for the second time. With just four minutes left and a draw looking the likely outcome, Frank McGarvey reacted quickly to a mistake by the Ayr keeper and hooked the ball high into the net for the only goal of the game. It had been a much more disciplined, cautious performance than usual from Saints, but the importance of the result validated the more defensive approach. St. Mirren were now five points ahead of second bottom Ayr with eight games to go, but wins were still needed.

A well-worked four-man move produced the goal which gained another point in a hard-fought 1-1 home draw with Motherwell, whilst Ayr lost the same day at Pittodrie, increasing the safety margin to six points with seven games left. Ayr appeared to have the more difficult run-in, but it wasn't going to be that easy for Saints either, as Aberdeen proved with a 2-1 win under the new £42,000 Love Street lights which had been funded by the efforts of the Centenary Development Committee. However, Saints' Premier Division class was evident the following week at Ibrox, where only a Peter McCloy penalty save from Iain Munro stopped both points coming to Paisley after each side had scored just before half-time.

The Manager concluded that the "bad spell" was at an end, and an impressive 3-0 home win over Hibs on 8 April seemed to confirm this. By then, second bottom Ayr United were nine points behind, with only ten points to play for. The likelihood of relegation was ended, but a season-long lack of consistency remained in Saints' last four matches.

Deservedly one up against Thistle at Firhill, they let the home side back into the game, and midway through the second half conceded two goals in six minutes to lose 2-1. Against title-chasing Aberdeen, they took a two-goal lead within the first ten minutes, but eventually lost 4-2. Four days later they returned to Firhill, and although the team's top three players, Reid, McGarvey, and Fitzpatrick, were missing that was no excuse for the worst performance of the season, as Thistle ran out easy 5-0 winners.

The last game of a roller-coaster season was at home to Celtic on 29 April, and finished with a well-earned 3-1 victory. The win was made certain in the eighty-sixth minute thanks to a brilliant goal by Dougie Bell, signed from Cumbernauld United after making his debut as a substitute three days earlier. The promoted team finished in a respectable eighth place, a comfortable six points above the relegation zone.

Six days after the Celtic match it emerged that Alex Ferguson had rejected a lucrative three year offer from a top United States club. "I am delighted to be staying with the Club," he said at the time, and he was soon repeating his aspirations about taking St. Mirren into Europe following his return from the European Cup Final between Liverpool and Bruges. During the rest of the month he was pictured taking part in various PR photo opportunities for the Club, he approved a tough new training plan, and spoke about the importance of the new Saints lottery, which was to be run on behalf of the Club by a subsidiary of Littlewoods Pools.

On Tuesday 30 May 1978, the "Paisley Daily Express" reported that St. Mirren's Under 18, Under 16, and Under 15 sides had all triumphed in major competitions in the previous seven days. "That's some going,"

Chairman William Todd

enthused Alex Ferguson, "there is no other club in Scotland with that youth record".

It was typical "Fergie"; talking up every aspect of St. Mirren's achievements. It would also be his last public quote as St. Mirren Manager. The following day the Board issued a short statement that shocked every St. Mirren supporter and shook Scottish football: "It was agreed that because of the serious rift which had occurred between the Board and the Manager, and the breaches of contract on the Manager's part, that it would be in the interests of both parties that the Manager's contact be terminated from 31 May 1978".

These forty-seven words ended a highly successful Paisley partnership which had lasted for three years and two hundred and twenty-two days. The Board's decision was unanimous. A short statement was added by Chairman William Todd later that day. "Moves will begin immediately to find a replacement for Mr. Ferguson."

Two days later, on 2 June, the press correctly predicted that Southampton coach and ex-Saint Jim Clunie was odds-on to be appointed Manager "next week". On the same day, Alex Ferguson was named as the new boss of Aberdeen in succession to Billy McNeill, who had taken over from Jock Stein at Celtic Park.

The speed of events was bewildering. Six months later Alex Ferguson took the Club to an industrial tribunal, claiming unfair dismissal. The tribunal unanimously upheld St. Mirren's decision to dismiss Mr. Ferguson, and supported the Club's contention that the Manager had become "unwilling to work under the supervision and direction of the Board".

One of the conclusions by the three-man tribunal was that Alex Ferguson had "neither by experience nor talent any managerial ability at all". It was a verdict many found difficult to reconcile, at least when considering his record as a football manager.

Alex Ferguson's sheer enthusiasm to get the whole Club moving, combined with the absence of a precise job description, had undoubtedly taken him into areas of non-football administration for which he had no training, and this had clearly led to a deterioration in relationships, but no one could deny that "Fergie" had completely revitalised St. Mirren. It was a desperately sad turn of events for all concerned but the benefits of Alex Ferguson's tenure at St. Mirren Park would be long-lasting.

1978-79

Coinciding with Jim Clunie's formal appointment as St. Mirren Manager on 5 June 1978, Chairman William Todd underscored the collective objective to take St. Mirren to the top of Scottish football: "Our policy remains the same. No players are for sale. So Bobby Reid, Tony Fitzpatrick and Frank McGarvey will be at Love Street at the start of the season".

Manager Jim Clunie

The Club were given another boost when their highly respected trainer/physio Rikki McFarlane announced on 10 June that he had turned down a tempting offer to join Alex Ferguson as Assistant Manager of Aberdeen FC. Saints supporters felt even more positive about Paisley prospects two days later, when the new Manager expressed the hope that "this year we will win a piece of silverware and get into Europe."

Saints' former centre half wanted his team "to be a bit more solid in defence. It is every manager's dream to have a team with a good defence and one that scores goals at the other end". Seven fewer League goals scored during 1978-79 would ensure that this vision wasn't to be wholly fulfilled, but the other half of the new boss's aspiration would be very successful, as the number of goals conceded reduced by a third.

One of Jim Clunie's first tasks was to recruit an experienced goalie, following his predecessor's decision to give free transfers to Donald Hunter, Ally Hunter, and Fred Jackson. Goalkeepers Campbell Money of Dailly Amateurs, who had played in some Reserve games the previous season, and Andy Stevenson of Kilsyth Rangers, had both been called up, but neither were deemed ready for first team action.

The problem was partially solved when Aberdeen free transfer man Ally McLean, who had also played Premier Division football with Ayr United, was signed for a two month trial period. Meantime, Tony Fitzpatrick and Frank McGarvey had nothing to prove as far as Motherwell FC were concerned, the Fir Park club having offered £400,000 for the Saints pair at the beginning of July. It was a bid which, encouragingly, had been immediately and unanimously rejected by the St. Mirren board.

The competitive season began with an unlucky 1-0 Anglo-Scottish Cup defeat by Motherwell on 6 August, but the situation was rectified in the return three days later when the Buddies ran out convincing 3-0 winners in Paisley.

The League opener at Ibrox saw Saints cope confidently with everything the new champions threw at them, and "super-sub" Robert Torrance continued his great start to the season with a goal which deservedly captured both points. Keeper McLean also played well, but his long-term future as a Saint seemed questionable when William Todd announced in mid-August that the Club were willing to pay up to £50,000 for a keeper. "We have a great team and no keeper", opined the Chairman.

In the second League fixture, a third meeting with Motherwell in thirteen days, the team lacked the vitality of the previous week's Ibrox victory and lost 1-0. Two days after this reverse, Scotland Under 21 keeper Billy Thomson was signed from Partick Thistle for a Club record £40,000. He made a quiet debut in a surprisingly hard-fought 2-0 home win over Dumbarton in the League Cup, his new team having played out a tedious 0-0 draw a week earlier at Boghead.

Another Scotland Under 21 star, Bobby Reid, had made just one appearance, for the Reserves, since being injured playing for a Scottish League Select against a Highland League representative team towards the end of season 1977-78. The injury had not properly responded to treatment, and he would go into hospital to have a cartilage removed at the end of August. There was much better news about Barrhead-based young midfielder Peter Weir, who had agreed to become a full-timer following his promising appearance against Rangers at Ibrox, when he deputised for the injured Billy Stark.

The Premier Division programme resumed with a sparkling 3-1 away win over an excellent Morton side in front of 12,000. Afterwards, Jim Clunie was quick to highlight the role played by Billy Thomson: "He's magic isn't he? He's settled down the whole defence with his confidence". During the following five days, Saints played Berwick Rangers twice in the League Cup and emerged as 8-2 aggregate winners, but there was disappointment on 9 September when an evenly balanced, entertaining encounter ended in a 1-0 defeat at Easter Road.

The busy start continued with a 2-1 away win over old rivals Bristol City in the Anglo-Scottish Cup. Both Paisley goals were superbly executed by the recalled Ricky Sharp, but it was Frank McGarvey who caught the eye with his constantly threatening work on the left wing.

The talent in the team was again obvious, when, despite prevailing gale-force winds, Saints' superior skills culminated in a classic move which produced the game's only goal against a more than competent Partick Thistle side. Then a third defeat in six games was sustained when table toppers Dundee United left Paisley with a 3-1 win, a result that delighted manager Jim McLean because he reckoned Saints had "the best midfield in Scotland".

That midfield was to be severely tested when Bristol City came north on 26 September with the aim of pulling back a one goal deficit from the first leg. A crowd of 7,181 saw a great advert for the Anglo-Scottish Cup as the "Robins" twice took the lead, before a brilliant Derek Hyslop goal five minutes from time levelled the tie at 2-2 to allow the team to move into the semi-finals on a 4-3 aggregate.

Saints slipped to seventh place four days after the Bristol tie when they displayed only sporadic good form at Celtic Park and lost 2-1, but

This picture features four St. Mirren managers – Jim Clunie, Rikki McFarlane, Jimmy Bone, and Tony Fitzpatrick (Five if you count Iain Munro who accepted the post only to turn it down 24 hours later).

Season 1978/79
Back row:
I. Munro,
M. Fulton,
A. Dunlop,
C. Money,
D. Walker,
J. McEachran,
R. Bell.

Middle row:
E. McDonald,
R. McFarlane,
J. Mowat,
R. Sharp,
R. McAveety,
R. Reid,
B. Stevenson,
B. Stark,
J. Copland,
R. Torrance,
D. Bell,
J. Clunie.

Front row:
P. Weir,
A. Beckett,
D. Hyslop,
J. Bone,
A. Fitzpatrick,
W. Abercromby,
A. Richardson,
J. Young,
R. Pattison,
R. McAllister.

there was nothing insipid about their next performance, a League Cup tie against Rangers at Ibrox on 4 October. Superior Saints deservedly took a two goal lead, both from Tony Fitzpatrick, before a Davie Cooper goal gave the Govan side some hope. It proved decisive, Rangers going on to win the first leg 3-2. "We threw it away," concluded Jim Clunie. "We have got to hold teams up when we get ahead."

There was some evidence of an Ibrox hangover the following week at Tynecastle as Saints struggled to contain an aggressive Hearts team in the first half, but it was a different story in the second period. "I don't know how we survived," was Hearts manager Willie Ormond's typically honest verdict, after the points had been shared.

In the League Cup return leg, Rangers' publicised decision to defend their one goal lead adversely affected the game as a spectacle and the resultant no-scoring draw ended the Buddies first chance of the season to win silverware. However, there was still plenty of Paisley optimism around, and three days later 11,000 turned up at Love Street to see Saints grab a two-goal lead after Aberdeen had looked the more threatening side. The "Dons" pulled one back with seven minutes to go but a home victory was the appropriate outcome.

The first leg of the Anglo-Scottish Cup semi-final was next. Unfortunately, for the 6,000 crowd at Oldham Athletic's Boundary Park there was little to get excited about in a poor first half, apart from an early penalty goal for the home side. Billy Stark grabbed an equaliser for an unconvincing visiting eleven, but the draw was enough to encourage thoughts of a second consecutive appearance in the final.

Back in the League, Saints failed to convert their superiority into goals when Rangers left Paisley on 21 October with a 1-0 win, then a second defeat was sustained at Fir Park when Motherwell deservedly took both points. On Halloween, another 1-1 draw with Oldham Athletic meant there was no hat-trick of defeats, but a combination of poor St. Mirren finishing and in-depth defending by Oldham led to elimination from the Anglo-Scottish Cup after the Lancashire side went through on penalties after extra time.

November began with an unusually flat, goal-less home derby match with Morton in which both keepers hardly touched the ball, and there was more defensive play from visitors Hibernian as Saints squeezed a narrow 1-0 Remembrance Day win. The best of Premier football was back on display the following week in a thrilling match at Firhill, where 11,000 saw Partick Thistle take a 2-0 lead before John Young pulled one back just before half-time. Although the attack-minded Buddies failed to take a point from the game and slipped to third bottom, it was their best away performance to date.

A 1-1 draw at Tannadice on 25 November meant that after fifteen matches, fifteen points had been amassed, fifteen goals scored, and fifteen conceded. It was a satisfactory situation, and one which no doubt would have gratified former trainer and physiotherapist Bobby Bell, a hugely popular Club servant for twenty-three years, whose sudden passing at the age of sixty-one had occurred on 15 November as he was preparing to leave his Glasgow home for his administration job at Love Street.

Bad weather at the beginning of December caused matches against Celtic and Hibs to be postponed, but the action continued off the field. There was some good news when accounts showed that a loss of £31,813 for the fourteen months to 31 May 1977 had been turned into a profit of £1,797 for the year to 31 May 1978. Less welcome was the announcement on 7 December that Frank McGarvey had asked for a transfer. "I am not very happy at Love Street," stated Frank. "A move can only benefit the Club and myself". The Club didn't agree and made it clear that everything possible would be done to keep the player.

McGarvey was dropped for the visit of Hearts on 9 December, a match played in appalling first-half conditions and one much closer than the 4-0 scoreline suggests. In the end, the 6,000 crowd who braved the elements saw a game of goal-mouth thrills from both sides and a St. Mirren team at the top of their form in the second half.

Aberdeen was the venue for the seventeenth League fixture, and Saints returned with a rather fortunate point from a 1-1 draw. The Buddies were back at their attractive best a week later at Ibrox, but still lost 1-0. Jim Clunie, who had failed to sign Aberdeen striker Ian Fleming on St. Andrew's Day, afterwards expressed his continued concern about the team's lack of a goalscoring threat.

The Manager felt that defensive capabilities had been enhanced since his arrival, but he promised that this improvement would not be at the expense of the side's natural attacking spirit. This pledge was made more deliverable on 27 December when Frank McGarvey, valued at £300,000 by the Club but attracting no takers at that price, withdrew his transfer request: "I am not really unhappy about not getting a move. I enjoy playing with St. Mirren and I am looking forward to the Motherwell game and hope we get both points."

That Motherwell game was postponed. In fact, Saints didn't play again until 20 January, when they had a marvellously entertaining 2-1 victory over League leaders Dundee United to move to fifth top. The

Jack Copland

chance to do a double over United failed to materialise when the Scottish Cup tie at Tannadice was postponed one week later, the first in a series of such deferments.

Another League match, away to Celtic, was cancelled on 4 February. Saints hurriedly swopped Parkhead for Firs Park to take part in a much needed challenge match with East Stirlingshire, before League business resumed the following week at Tynecastle with a battling 2-1 victory on a liberally sanded but rock-hard pitch. The Buddies were now in third place, just two points off the lead.

One player making a real contribution to the improved defensive record was centre half Andy Dunlop, signed from Dalry Boys Club in 1975 and playing well during Bobby Reid's prolonged absence. By 13 February and four months after his cartilage operation, Bobby's knee had slightly swollen up after a Reserve game against Partick Thistle. At the beginning of March this recurring post-match swelling would be examined by a London specialist

Frank McGarvey and Motherwell were finally re-acquainted on 17 February when, after ninety minutes of almost incessant Saints pressure and the visitors' oft-operated offside trap, his tenth minute goal was enough to give Saints twenty-four points from twenty-one fixtures and joint leadership of the Premier Division.

They scored two more in a sensational home draw with Alex Ferguson's Aberdeen the following week, when the fired-up Dons had five players shown yellow cards and two sent off. This welcome point after being 2-0 down meant that Paisley's talented team were table toppers, one point ahead of second top Rangers but a game more played than the Ibrox men. The month finished in fine style when the much-postponed Scottish Cup tie at Tannadice ended in a 2-0 win, a victory built on Billy Thomson's first-half save from a Dave Narey penalty and an exceptional defensive display throughout.

Frank McGarvey presents a £1,000 cheque on behalf of The St. Mirren Lottery. Saints' Lottery operation was one of the largest in Scotland or England.

The up-beat atmosphere at St. Mirren Park was boosted by the news on 2 March that the Saints Lottery was selling 40,000 tickets each week, the maximum legally permitted. A second lottery was planned by thirty-four year old Richard Kernick, a former Assistant Commercial Manager of Leeds United, who had been appointed St. Mirren's commercial boss in mid-October, the first holder of such a post in Scotland.

Three days after the Tannadice tie, a confident Paisley party returned to Tayside on Scottish Cup business, this time to face First Division leaders Dundee. Wild and windy weather greeted both teams, but the home side, with the wind behind them, adjusted to the conditions more quickly, never letting their more elegant opponents settle and scored twice. It was much the same story in the second half, as Saints, from goalkeeper Thomson outwards, failed to adjust their game, and in the end Dundee fully deserved their 4-1 win. For St. Mirren the result was a disaster, and afterwards the Manager accused his team of complacency.

In the League there was still much to play for. Three goals from Frank McGarvey produced two easily won points over a very inexperienced, bottom-of-the-League Motherwell team at Fir Park, as Saints remained top equal with Dundee United. That proud position was retained after a hard-fought 3-1 win over Morton on 17 March, and the "Daily Record" noted that "the St. Mirren babes who stormed into the Premier Division two seasons ago can win the title in the next couple of months".

Other press coverage was in similar vein. That Saints would eventually finish sixth, collecting just seven of the remaining twenty-four points available was inconceivable at this stage.

Two days after the Morton game, the Club announced that striker Ricky Sharp, who had failed to gain a regular first team place following his move from Kilmarnock in 1977, had been released. Two remaining strikers, McGarvey and Bone, were both on target in the first quarter of the home game against Hibernian, but Hibs scored two late goals in four minutes to deservedly win the match 3-2. On the same day, Dundee United lost at Cappielow and Saints lost the chance to top the League; it was a turning point.

The last two March matches were also lost. Rangers visited, survived two justifiable St. Mirren penalty claims, won 2-1, and moved above Saints into second place. The Buddies then failed to match the competitive spirit shown by Partick Thistle and were beaten 3-1 at Firhill. The mini-slump ended at Easter Road, when, after numerous chances were missed by the home side, brilliant goals from Frank McGarvey and Billy Stark earned a hard-fought victory.

Following this twenty-eighth fixture, Saints had thirty-one points, one more point than the previous season's finishing total. Europe was still a possibility, even after a 2-0 defeat at Tannadice on 7 April which kept the Club in third place, but looked less likely when a brilliant Andy Ritchie winning goal, five minutes from half-time, settled a typically close fought derby at Cappielow.

The Morton result was the fifth defeat in six games, which became six from seven when Celtic left Paisley with a 1-0 win as the team slipped to fifth. On the morning of the Celtic match, Frank McGarvey's named was linked with a transfer to Liverpool.

Saints remained in fifth place after a 2-1 home win over the soon-to-be-relegated Hearts, and Paisley hopes were still on the rise when the Buddies held a 1-0 half-time lead at Celtic Park on 25 April. Then a second half onslaught from the fast-improving home team produced two Celtic goals in the last fifteen minutes to deprive the team of any points.

European dreams were again revived when a McGarvey-inspired side gradually overcame a sixteenth minute Aberdeen goal at Pittodrie, and goals from Bobby Torrance and Billy Stark sealed a spirited comeback, but the door to continental competition finally closed on 2 May, when a late Partick Thistle goal made the final score 1-1.

Two days after the Thistle match, Frank McGarvey joined European Champions Liverpool in a record £300,000 transfer deal for the Club; the experienced and powerful Partick Thistle striker Doug Somner was immediately earmarked as McGarvey's replacement.

The Club had reluctantly agreed to the Frank McGarvey transfer, explained the Chairman. "We are extremely disappointed at losing

Jimmy Bone

McGarvey but we could not just stand in his way and deny him the opportunity of joining Liverpool. The player was not sold because we needed the cash but simply because we could not stand in his way. All the money from the transfer will be ploughed back into buying talented players," promised William Todd.

The season's second last game was the Renfrewshire Cup Final on 5 May. It finished 1-1, but the more determined Morton triumphed 3-2 in the penalty shoot-out. Earlier in the day it had been announced that Derek Hyslop and John Mowat had been included in the list of free transfers. Neither had been first team regulars under Jim Clunie. In five seasons as a Saint, defender John Mowat had made thirty League appearances, whilst more than half of Derek Hyslop's seventy-seven games were during Saints promotion season.

Playing surface work at St. Mirren Park meant that the final game of the season was switched to nearby Ibrox, where two second half goals gave Celtic their fourth League win over Saints during 1978-79. In a period of a few weeks, Saints had gone from realistic championship contenders and at the very least European participants to mere mid-table Premier respectability. Disappointment with such an outcome merely underlined how far the Club had come in a short time. There was indeed life after Alex Ferguson, and the capture of a trophy would prove it.

1979-80

There was further recognition for Paisley's revitalised football club on 2 June, when Iain Munro's consistent and influential play led to him being selected to play for Scotland against World Champions Argentina, the first Saint to win a full cap since Tommy Gemmell in 1955.

Iain's achievement apart, the 1979 close season was dominated by big-money deals and transfer speculation, initially involving Tony Fitzpatrick, who was reportedly attracting Bristol City's interest. Regarded by many Saints supporters as the backbone of the team, the thought of "Fitz" following Frank McGarvey into English football was not a welcome development. These fears heightened when Director John Corson admitted that Tony, like Frank McGarvey, had a clause in his contract which allowed him to leave if a suitable offer came along.

On 5 June, a Bristol bid for Fitzpatrick wasn't deemed acceptable, but a fortnight later the player publicly confirmed that he had refused a new deal and hoped a club would make an offer which matched the Buddies valuation. Such moves don't always happen overnight, as Doug Somner could verify. On 20 June, six weeks after Frank McGarvey's departure, the Partick Thistle striker was signed for £100,000. Seven days later, another proven striker was purchased when Clydebank's Frank McDougall signed in a record £180,000 Scottish deal.

In capturing the Bankies' leading marksman, the Board had increased their original bid of £100,000, beaten off the challenge of Celtic for his signature, and kept their word

Doug Somner

about using all the McGarvey fee to strengthen the team. Additionally, Jimmy Bone would soon be returning from his summer stint with Toronto Blizzard, whilst Bobby Torrance was a more than useful member of a greatly strengthened strike force.

By 24 July, two significant figures had left the Club. After careful consideration, Tony Fitzpatrick joined Bristol City in a £250,000 deal. Four days later it was announced that Richard Kernick, the architect of the three successful St. Mirren lotteries, was to take up a similar post with Hearts. One obvious result of Mr. Kernick's efforts was the partial financing of the first major ground alteration since the 1920s. During the close season, the terracing at the "Love Street end" had been re-built, "squared off", and moved to within ten metres of the goal.

Competitive football started on 28 July, when visitors Hibernian left it late to grab a 3-3 draw in the Anglo-Scottish Cup. In the second leg, a Billy Stark goal fifteen minutes from the end gave Saints a fortunate lead. It was one they held, despite Edinburgh efforts to squeeze through on the away goals rule.

The League campaign got underway fourteen days later with a lacklustre 2-2 draw against newly-promoted Kilmarnock. Unfortunately there was more of the same the following week at Dens, as First Division champions Dundee made the best possible Premier return with a 4-1 win. A 3-0 home defeat by Morton then meant that Saints had conceded nine goals in three matches and were bottom of the League, amidst much muttering about McGarvey and Fitzpatrick being missed.

The rapidly descending early-season gloom was then partially lifted in a hard-fought 4-1 victory over Stenhousemuir in a League Cup second round tie. At least the team appeared to be working for each other, but there was another unconvincing performance in the return leg, despite a 4-2 win and a hat-trick of magnificent Somner headers.

In the fourth fixture at Ibrox on 8 September, a more spirited Saints were drawing 1-1 with ten minutes to go when a dithering defence allowed the home side to regain the lead, then Rangers converted an eighty-sixth minute penalty. Despite this defeat, there were encouraging signs of improved passing and a greater desire to win the ball. It was a recovery of form which gathered pace the following week, when visitors Dundee United were beaten 3-2, with Doug Somner hitting another brace, and Frank McDougall completing the scoring.

The ex-Bankie continued his gradual settling-in process when he also hit a double as Saints took an incredible 4-0 lead in the first twenty-five minutes of the Anglo-Scottish Cup tie against Bolton Wanderers, who had taken five points from five First Division games by 19 September but would eventually finish bottom. At 4-0 down and with an hour still to play, the visitors then had midfielder Len Cantello dismissed, but still managed to score twice to ensure a competitive second leg.

The climb up the league table continued with a stylish 2-0 win over Hibs at Easter Road, and League Cup progress looked likely when the third round first leg was won 3-1 at Douglas Park against a resilient Hamilton Accies side who had been two behind inside the first ten minutes.

Jimmy Bone's return was seen as an important factor in Saints improved results, playing just behind the two main strikers. However, September ended with a 3-1 set-back at Celtic Park, in a tense match marred by stoppages and a sending-off for both teams. Two down at half-time, the Buddies regained some composure after Billy Stark scored, but hopes of a point were dashed when a last minute goal was conceded.

The second leg of the Anglo Scottish Cup in Bolton on 2 October saw Wanderers dominate proceedings without looking overly dangerous, apart from set pieces when they relied on the up-field presence of a couple of big defenders. One of them, Sam Allardyce, scored twice to make it a 4-4 aggregate score after ninety minutes. Twenty-nine minutes later, a Jimmy Bone goal from a perfect Lex Richardson cross clinched a tie in which skipper Jackie Copland had been outstanding.

The pattern of inconsistent performances continued the following Saturday at Pittodrie, where a last minute Frank McDougall goal gave an inept Saints side a 2-2 draw and a sixth League point they scarcely deserved. After eight fixtures they remained third bottom; after losing to Hamilton Academical in the League Cup on 10 October, the season's low point was reached.

At the end of ninety minutes, two goals from Accies' Assistant Manager Bobby Graham had levelled the aggregate score at 2-2 before

Billy Abercromby meets young fans at a local shop. Billy went on to captain Saints to victory in the 1987 cup final.

the ten-man visitors survived the goal-less extra period to win 4-2 on penalties. It was a humiliating result, and a section of the crowd demanded the Manager's resignation. "Big Jim" was not slow to hit back at his critics: "All the people shouting 'Clunie must go' will have to put up with it because I am under contract for two years". Then he added, "I think the confidence is gone from the players and I don't think the supporters helped them".

The Manager adopted a more conciliatory tone after the next match, a 2-1 defeat from a well-in-command Partick Thistle side, when he talked about the great encouragement provided by the supporters, who had certainly witnessed a much more enthusiastic Paisley performance. The fans were again in good voice at Kilmarnock seven days later, the first match since Jimmy Bone took over the captaincy. Despite losing a very unfortunate goal, the team played well throughout, equalised through Billy Stark, and should have taken both points. They played less well in October's penultimate match, but did enough to defeat Dundee 4-2.

Anglo-Scottish Cup action resumed at Sheffield United's Bramall Lane on 30 October, when Billy Thomson was acknowledged to be the main reason for the goal-less outcome against one of the English Third Division's in-form teams. Four days later a Thomson penalty save at Cappielow contributed to another no-scoring draw, giving Saints four points in their three most recent matches. "We have picked up a bit," was the cautious Clunie claim, but that seemed something of an understatement after Rangers were beaten 2-1 at rain-swept Love Street, a winning margin which greatly understated the Buddies' superiority.

There was yet another 0-0 draw - at Tannadice in mid-November - but this time the team played attractive, entertaining football, with Richardson, Stark, and Abercromby absolutely outstanding in the middle of the park. Saints should have won, a fact freely acknowledged by United manager Jim McLean: "St. Mirren were far and away the better side. I have nothing but respect for them".

The Board of Hibernian FC were also due a bit of respect when they audaciously obtained the registration of George Best from Fulham. The legendary player made his Premier Division debut for Hibs at St. Mirren Park on 24 November, but the hullabaloo over the new Hi-bee seemed to affect both teams, who produced a hard-fought but unattractive spectacle for the 13,670 crowd. The industrious Doug Somner scored two opportunist goals and, although George Best grabbed a great goal just before the final whistle, it ended in a 2-1 home win. Saints were now joint third top with fifteen points from fifteen games.

Four days later, a considerably reduced media presence at Love Street saw Morton beaten 4-1 in the first leg of the Renfrewshire Cup Final, the good form continuing into December with a 2-1 home win over Celtic. This was followed by a convincing 4-0 win over Sheffield United in the return leg of the Anglo-Scottish Cup, with goals from Stark, Munro, and a double from Somner. Saints' cup goals then increased from four to ten on 8 December, when Morton were hit for six in the return leg of the county cup, a scoring rate which owed much to the growing partnership of Somner and McDougall.

The run of success was halted one week on at Pittodrie where the loss of two "silly goals" meant the points stayed in Aberdeen. Adverse weather conditions then delayed the action until New Year's Day, when Saints and Morton shared four goals in a derby draw in Paisley. Two days before the resumption, the fans learned that Scotland Under 21 cap Billy Abercromby had broken his leg in training and would be out of action until late March.

The first away trip of 1980 was to Ibrox, where spectators saw slick-moving Saints win 2-1; it should have been more. The good results kept coming. Another two decisive goals from Doug Somner gave the Buddies a hard-earned 2-1 triumph over Dundee United to ease the team into third place.

If Saints looked like European qualifiers against United, they played embarrassingly badly in the first half against Scottish Cup opponents Brechin City on 26 January. A Brian Docherty goal in the forty-eighth minute changed the game's direction, then he added a second on the seventy-five minute mark. It was an infrequent first team appearance for Brian, who would find himself freed at the end of the season. The impressive Peter Weir added a third, but the tie finished 3-1 when valiant City immediately got one back.

A fortnight after the Brechin cup tie, Saints were back to their very best when they drew 1-1 with Aberdeen in an exciting encounter at Love Street, a result which bolstered the team's confidence for the Scottish Cup trip to Celtic Park on 16 February. A McDougall header in the thirty-eighth minute gained a merited lead, but Celtic's much improved play in the second half earned them an equaliser two minutes from time.

The non-ticket replay four days later caught the imagination of both sets of fans, the kick off being delayed for fifteen minutes to allow the official attendance of 27,166 to take their places, as an estimated 10,000 were locked out. Those inside saw Saints take the lead twice before the game was settled at 3-2 by John Doyle of Celtic in the first minute of extra time, a goal which seemed palpably off-side to Paisley eyes.

The visitors had played much of the oft-times tousy game with ten men, and appeared to have a far greater will-to-win than the home team. "We just did not rise to the occasion," said Jim Clunie afterwards. "All credit to Celtic because they gave total commitment".

The Buddies' chances of winning were not helped when Frank McDougall, who had endured a series of

Frank McDougall signed for a Scottish record transfer fee, suffered a leg break in a tousy cup tie against Celtic.

heavy challenges, suffered a leg break from what was felt by many to be an extremely reckless tackle by Danny McGrain. McDougall would be out for the rest of the season, while Saints suffered several other injuries during the match. In a controversial aftermath, the Club were asked by the S.F.A. to explain comments attributed to Frank McDougall which were published in the 'Star' newspaper.

Back in the League, 8,000 saw McDougall's replacement, Alan Logan, score a goal after just two minutes at Firhill and impress throughout his debut. Partick's Donald Park was sent off seconds before the interval, but by then Saints, through Somner, were two up. A fifty-ninth minute goal from Billy Stark tied things up, although Thistle had enough chances to change the outcome of what was a poor quality match.

Much of the next fixture - at Rugby Park on 1 March - was equally disappointing. Two evenly-matched sides cancelled each other out for the first seventy minutes until young Alan Logan hit his second goal in two games. Six minutes later, Killie drew level to continue an incident-packed final twenty minutes which were in stark contrast to the earlier proceedings.

In the following game, at home to Dundee, there was no such period of sustained excellence. The team won 2-1 and moved up to second in the table, yet put on a poor display. Both goals again came from Doug Somner, but the win owed as much to Billy Thomson's abilities, a reflection of the contribution made by the struggling Dens Parkers.

The underlying trend remained good, as the 1980 unbeaten League run continued at Celtic Park. Man-of-the-moment was Celtic's new signing Frank McGarvey, who had ended an unsuccessful ten month spell with Liverpool, but it was Doug Somner's magnificent two-goal performance which rightly grabbed the headlines as Saints drew 2-2 after being two down.

Three days later, the number of points dropped to Morton increased to six in a fiercely competitive derby in Greenock. In the thirty-ninth minute, and 1-0 ahead, Saints had a stonewall penalty claim turned down. Two minutes later, Billy Thomson brought down Morton's Ally Scott, and Andy Ritchie converted the penalty. The scoring ended in the fifty-fourth minute when John Young unfortunately conceded an own goal.

That Cappielow reverse did not deter around 1,000 fans from making the journey to Bristol City's Ashton Gate on 25 March for the first leg of the Anglo-Scottish Cup Final. It was an eagerly awaited clash from Saints' point of view, but less so for the relegation-haunted Robins, who were a shadow of the Bristol finalists Saints had faced two years earlier.

Remarkably, Bristol City would be relegated for the next three seasons, but they were still an English First Division team when Saints faced them, and had beaten Morton at the semi-final stage. Ex-Saint Tony Fitzpatrick, who had missed only one game up to this point, was in the City line up, but, like his colleagues, failed to shine as two goals from Billy Stark gave the Buddies a promising first leg lead.

The following Saturday the venue was a wind-swept Tannadice, when a make-shift side thwarted Dundee United in an uninspiring 0-0 draw. However, the travelling support were delighted to see that the re-arranged team included Bobby Reid, returning to first team duty after nearly two years of injury and close monitoring of his fitness. He performed with credit.

Four days later, it was back to Tayside to face a Dundee side fighting for Premier Division survival. The Buddies' 2-0 first half lead didn't discourage the "Dark Blues," who got a goal back in the seventy-first minute, but a typically spectacular Stark strike secured the points for Paisley. The Championship challenge was then maintained, as shot-shy Hibs were swept aside more convincingly than the 2-0 scoreline indicates.

It was a much harder test at Firhill, where Saints and difficult-to-beat Partick Thistle shared the points in a very entertaining 1-1 draw, but a defensive Kilmarnock side were much less enterprising when they came to Paisley. The Rugby Parkers' unimaginative approach was consolidated after taking a surprise lead, but their game plan was spoiled when Lex Richardson hit a twenty-five yarder in the fifty-fifth minute; it proved to be the springboard for a worthy 3-1 triumph.

It was thus a confident Saints side, and one holding a 2-0 first leg advantage, which took the field on 16 April for the second leg of the 1979-80 Anglo Scottish Cup Final. A disappointingly drab first half ended goal-less, but everything changed when Doug Somner scored in the forty-

St Mirren, the first ever Scottish winners of the Anglo-Scottish Cup. Left to right back row, Billy Abercromby, John Young, Billy Thomson, Mark Fulton, Jimmy Bone (Captain), Jackie Copland, Jeff Curran, and Campbell Money. Left to right front row, Billy Stark, Alan Logan, Doug Somner, Iain Munro, and Peter Weir.

ninth minute to take the aggregate score to 3-0; the Cup was almost certainly coming to Paisley and the large crowd responded accordingly.

Twenty minutes later Doug made it 2-0 on the night, and the margin stretched to three when Alan Logan scored with sixteen minutes to go. An eighty-second minute goal by defender Paul Stevens pulled one back for City, but it was Paisley's night as St. Mirren became the first Scottish club to win the trophy, and by a convincing 5-1 aggregate.

This was not a fluke cup win in the midst of mediocre League performances. This was a trophy triumph which had been predicted for years, by a team who were more than capable of competing with the best. Now it had finally happened, and thirteen thousand Buddies were nothing less than euphoric!

Scotland's first-ever winners of the trophy had five more fixtures and another trophy to play for. Jim Clunie regarded clinching the title as an "outside probability", but one which would be chased. A good start was made at Firhill with a 2-1 win three days later.

By then both Celtic and Saints had played thirty-two fixtures, with Celtic holding an increasingly fragile three-point lead. In second place, a point ahead of Saints and with a game less played, were Aberdeen, who provided the next challenge. A 2-0 Pittodrie defeat ensued, as Saints failed to show the form they were capable of and slipped five points behind the "Dons" with three games left.

The third last fixture was also lost, by 2-1 to already relegated Hibernian, the winning goal being scored by ex-Saint Bobby Torrance, who had been transferred to Hibs a few weeks earlier for £30,000. This shock defeat meant that Saints had to take something from the home games against Celtic and Rangers to finish third.

On 3 May, a crowd of 20,166 watched Scotland's second and third-placed teams play out a 0-0 draw, but results elsewhere guaranteed Saints the coveted third place in the table. "This year we have been a more consistent and better team than last year," was the Manager's summary. "If it had not been for our bad start we would have been challenging with Aberdeen for the title". Four days later, the season finished on a high as an understrength Rangers were comprehensively defeated 4-1, with Doug Somner ending a superb season with a hat-trick, the League's top scorer with twenty-five goals.

Rangers team selection caused the St. Mirren Board to protest on behalf of supporters who had paid their ticket money two months earlier to see a competitive match, but throughout the season there had been very little else to complain about. The Renfrewshire and Anglo-Scottish Cups were emphatically won, a never-bettered League placing had been achieved, and, to top it all, Paisley would host competitive European football for the first time in the Club's history.

Late 1970s promise had blossomed into 1980s reality: St. Mirren were once again a much-respected force in Scottish football.

Triumphs... and Trophies at Last!

1980-81

The summer of 1980 underlined St. Mirren's progress on a number of fronts, as tours to Brazil and Finland were undertaken, a red brick extension to the rear of the "North Bank" terracing was completed and two more Saints became Scottish internationalists.

CHAPTER TWELVE
The 1980's

Billy Thomson and Peter Weir made their Scotland debuts against Northern Ireland on 16 May, a double honour which meant St. Mirren had three full Scotland internationalists on their books for the first time since 1933, although Iain Munro's continuation as a Saint was beginning to look doubtful as contract talks failed to make progress.

On 24 May, a week before his contract expired, Iain tore a thigh muscle whilst playing for Scotland against England, his seventh cap in the space of twelve months. It meant Bobby Reid would replace him for the ambitious three-match Brazilian tour, a personal boost for Bobby after all his own injury problems. Also travelling was new pivot and central midfielder John McCormack, a £55,000 signing from Clydebank.

The tour began with a 2-0 defeat against Bangw on 5 June, as the Scots struggled on a poor pitch and in very warm conditions, but some satisfaction was drawn from Bobby Reid's excellent performance in defence. Twenty-four hours later Saints endured a tough encounter with Victoria Santos to win 1-0 and collect a trophy, which had been donated by a local businessman.

In the third match, four days later against Cortiba, Saints had to settle for a 1-1 draw, with Alan Logan scoring a magnificent second half goal. It was the best performance of a highly successful trip but a shadow was cast over the touring party with the sudden death of kit man Jackie Goff, a St. Mirren servant for fifteen years, on the return flight.

Six weeks later, St. Mirren headed for Finland to play challenge matches against SJK Helsinki and Lahti Reifas. The first match, on 20 July, ended in a 2-2 draw and the following day Lahti were beaten 2-0. Ten days later Jim Clunie informed the Board that he believed the Finnish trip "had helped to iron out several problems".

Some on-field problems still remained, judging by the indifferent play on show in the Drybrough Cup, a competition for the previous season's top-scoring sides. Despite this, Saints recorded successive 2-1 home wins over Falkirk and Ayr United to set up a Final appearance against Aberdeen at Hampden on 2 August. Paisley play was again not especially good and this time it was the Dons' turn to win 2-1. A week later Aberdeen also provided the opposition in the opening League fixture, a much better match that was lost 1-0 but could have been won if outfield pressure had been converted into goals.

In the second fixture, at Cappielow, the match kicked off a minute early, and before those sixty seconds elapsed Saints had taken the lead through a Somner penalty! Doug eventually hit a hat-trick but Lex Richardson was deemed equally instrumental in the impressive dismantlement of Morton. After their Greenock display, Saints were strongly fancied to beat promoted Hearts at home but more missed chances and the loss of Copland and Weir during the match combined to produce a 3-1 defeat. Still missing from the team was Jimmy Bone, who would not be back from Canada until 28 August, but two defeats in the first three League fixtures was certainly not a Championship-winning pattern.

In fact, it was form barely good enough to beat Second Division Albion Rovers 2-1 at Cliftonhill in the League Cup but there was a much more competent performance in the second leg, which was won 5-0. That same day Iain Munro played for the Reserves, having ended a two month period in limbo by signing a twenty-eight day contract which would, at the very least, remind other clubs of his qualities.

There wasn't much quality and even less application about Saints' play in the third round League Cup tie at Firhill on 3 September. They deservedly lost 2-0 to Thistle. Three days later, lack of concentration was again on show when a late 2-1 lead over promoted Airdrieonians was thrown away less than sixty seconds later. A crowd of 5,220 had seen the first home point of the season gained but it should have been two.

No points were taken on 13 September from the season's second visit to Maryhill, which ended in a 1-0 defeat. It was however a considerable improvement on the League Cup display with a number of chances created. This patchy form was a far-from-perfect prelude to Saints' UEFA Cup debut, where the Club, known as "Paisley St. Mirren" for European purposes, had been drawn against Idrottsforeningen (IF) Elfsborg, Sweden's third best-supported club.

Three well respected Saints Managers attend a Club function together. From left, Jim Clunie, Alex Wright and Rikki McFarlane.

Continual rain during the day of the first leg meant that the pitch at the 20,000 capacity Eyavallen Stadium was slippery and unpredictable, conditions that played their part in the fifteenth minute when a long kick from home 'keeper Svensson caused confusion in the Saints rearguard and Nilsson was able to stroke the ball home from about ten yards.

The Buddies quickly recovered and got into their stride after a shaky first twenty minutes. Two minutes before half-time Doug Somner latched on to a superb long ball from John McCormack, raced between two Elfsborg defenders, drew the 'keeper and slotted the ball home. With twenty minutes to go, Saints attacking policy produced a deserved 2-1 lead when Billy Stark twisted and turned before crossing to Billy Abercromby whose powerful drive from ten yards was touched in off the post by the diving Svensson. It was a pleasing European start for the four hundred travelling Buddies in the 3,800 crowd.

On the following Saturday, Scotland's two UEFA Cup representatives attracted a disappointing crowd of just 5,700 to St. Mirren Park. Those in attendance saw an impressive first half display from the home team, good defensive work in the second and a Billy Stark goal two minutes from time which clinched a 2-0 win over Dundee United; it was Saints' first home League victory of the season!

Two more goals were required on 24 September if Thistle's first leg lead in the League Cup was to be overturned but the Manager remained cautious. "We must go out and attack Thistle but remain tight at the back," he previewed. "We must not let them steal another one from us". Thistle didn't, but disappointing Saints also failed to score and were out. The team then looked more impressive than Rangers in everything but chance taking at Ibrox on 27 September as the League leaders took two of their scoring opportunities without reply.

The part-timers of Elfsborg, 2-1 down from the first leg, were the next opponents. Surely Saints would get a confidence-boosting big win over the four-times Swedish champions. Unfortunately not, but progress was made. On the night traditional Scottish weather, namely a gale force wind and driving rain, certainly provided testing conditions but they could not fully excuse ninety minutes almost devoid of goalmouth incidents and shots on target. The homesters dominated the opening half without looking like scoring, then Elfsborg were reduced to ten men in the seventy-second minute when their 'keeper suffered a leg-break in a clash with Peter Weir. Thereafter, the Swedes seemed content with a respectable 2-1 aggregate defeat.

It was an approach that made life difficult for St. Mirren and was not appreciated by a section of the 8,200 crowd, that began voicing their disapproval of the containing nature of Saints' play, some no doubt aware of Mr. Clunie's pre-match statement that Saints "didn't have to score to go through".

As a result the morning newspapers carried some controversial post-match comments by Jim Clunie. "The attitude of the supporters towards the team was the saddest thing which has happened to me since I came to Love Street. I felt very disappointed by their reaction". In typically plain-speaking style, he also mentioned his disappointment at the size of the crowd and suggested that St. Mirren might attract bigger crowds in another town!

Admittedly attendance figures at St. Mirren Park to the end of September were certainly causing alarm, running at half the previous season's average of 10,000. The general reaction, though, of Paisley Daily Express readers to Jim Clunie's remarks about the size of the crowd centred on the cautious tactics adopted by the Manager.

Big Jim's team answered such criticism in the best possible way, albeit against troubled Kilmarnock, by winning 6-1 at Rugby Park on 4 October. Four goals up after thirty-two minutes, the side included Iain Munro, who had impressed the Love Street backroom staff by his professional attitude in Reserve games despite the disappointment of unsuccessful trials with Aston Villa and Alicante during September.

Three days after Munro's first team recall came news of renewed interest from Stoke City whose previous bid of £205,000 failed when no agreement could be reached with the player. Finally, on 8 October Iain Munro, whose playing time for Scotland exceeds any other player in St. Mirren's first one hundred and twenty-five years, joined Stoke City for £160,000. That night Saints defeated Tampa Bay Rowdies 4-2 in a challenge match watched by a respectable crowd of 7,016.

Ten goals in two matches was a very welcome trend but one which ended when Celtic came to Paisley three days later and won 2-0, courtesy of two first half own goals! On the eve of the Celtic match Jim Clunie apologised to the fans for his post-Elfsborg comments, which he said were uttered in the heat of the moment.

Saints' fluctuating form continued at Pittodrie with a struggling performance in a 3-2 defeat from a below par Aberdeen side. There would need to be an improvement for the visit on 22 October of former European Cup finalists St. Etienne, whose side contained some world-class talent.

Another European night; another traditional Scottish downpour. In torrential rain 11,471 spectators witnessed a second 0-0 draw but this time they saw a much more entertaining encounter in which a spirited home side, with Peter Weir in outstanding form, gained control of the game in the second half but found themselves unable to break down a composed French defence. "I'm disappointed in the result not the performance," was the Manager's verdict.

He was certainly disappointed with both after drawing 1-1 with Morton the following Saturday. The Renfrewshire rivals contrived to put on a truly dreadful show for the 7,000 fans, with Saints' counter coming from an own goal in a game littered with fundamental errors. "Without introducing new faces, what do you do?" was the post-match question posed by a seemingly perplexed Jim Clunie. It had been a real off-day, but not for the first time comments were made regarding an apparent lack of effort from some in the team.

Star midfielders Billy Stark and Lex Richardson were dropped for the visit to Tynecastle as November opened, when a Doug Somner strike earned a point against struggling Hearts. "We should have had the match sewn up. We missed chances again. Our football was not as good as it should have been but the concentration and effort were reasonably good".

Unfortunately, "reasonably good" was not going to be good enough to beat a St. Etienne side that would include Michel Platini this time. So it proved on 5 November. A thirteenth minute goal allowed "Les Verts" to take command and a second confirmed the predicted outcome. St. Mirren's first European foray was over.

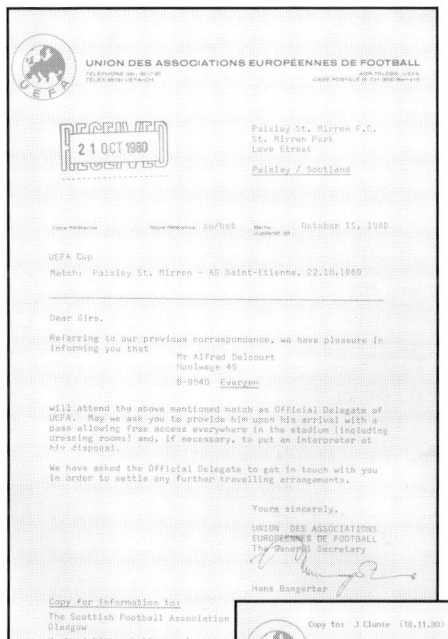

European Correspondence... UEFA write to inform the Club of the arrival of their official delegate for the home tie with St. Etienne (left)...

...while (right) they intimate the cautions picked up by Doug Somner and Billy Abercromby in the return leg.

Back in the Premier Division, Saints and Rangers shared the points in an over-physical clash at Love Street in which six players were booked. At least Saints looked "competitive" again, which was not the case against Dundee United at Tannadice on 15 November when only the heroics of Billy Thomson kept the score down to 2-0. The Buddies' two attempts at goal over the ninety minutes told its own miserable story.

In the next match Saints proved that they can always conjure up surprises. The travelling support watched two poor teams at Celtic Park cancel each other out for the first eighty minutes. With the final whistle looming, and the match seemingly heading for a 1-1 draw, right back

Alex Beckett hit a wonderful twenty-five yarder past the Celtic 'keeper to clinch an unexpected two points. "My team have played a dozen times better that that and still got beaten," was Big Jim's typically honest assessment.

In truth, given the quality of performance, talk of a turning point was perhaps premature. That victory meant that Saints had amassed twelve points from fifteen fixtures but they still remained fourth from bottom, fourteen points behind leaders Aberdeen.

Two days after the Celtic match a meeting of the Directors was called at which only one topic was up for discussion: "Position of Manager". It was not a subject that had been raised at any of the season's previous board meetings, although the minutes made reference to "an earlier meeting with the Manager" which "highlighted a general lack of confidence in Mr. Clunie to the extent of allowing him funds to acquire players".

It was suggested by one Director that Mr. Clunie's devotion and ambition was not seen to match that of the new Board. The upshot of the meeting was a decision to terminate Mr. Clunie's contract. It was not a unanimous decision, an opposing motion having been defeated by five votes to two.

On Wednesday 26 November Mr. Clunie was invited to attend a meeting with the Chairman and Vice-Chairman at the offices of car dealers A&M Pottie Ltd. That afternoon's Paisley Daily Express broke the news: "Jim Clunie Is Sacked". The Club's statement was the epitome of brevity. "The Board of Directors of St. Mirren and Mr. Clunie have mutually agreed on the termination of his contract with immediate effect. The Board would like to express their appreciation of his services". Mr. Corson added that Assistant Manager Rikki McFarlane, who during the summer had given up his job as physiotherapist to go full-time, would take charge until a new appointment was made.

Mr. Clunie spoke of his shock at the turn of events the following day. He felt, and many agreed, that he had done a good job. "I don't want to blow my own trumpet," he said, "but they won the Anglo-Scottish Cup and played in Europe". He also pointed out that in his two years as Manager, St. Mirren's points total had increased each year from thirty to thirty-six to forty-two. "The Directors felt in the long term I was not the man for the job," he correctly summarised.

The initial reaction of some fans centred on Mr. Clunie's at times constrained approach, contrasting this with his predecessor's emphasis on attack. Others felt the dismissal had been badly handled. Crucially, this latter view would gather support amongst thirty-seven leading shareholders. St. Mirren's weeklong domination of the sports pages continued on Saturday 29 November when Chairman John Corson declared that he thought his own position was under threat.

Alongside Mr. Corson's remarks, the papers recorded that caretaker Manager Rikki McFarlane had made a call for all-out attack and entertaining football. That's exactly what the 5,200 crowd witnessed. On an icy, bone-hard pitch Saints greater mobility and skill overcame a Killie side anchored at the bottom of the League. It was only the Buddies' second League win at home. After the match Mr. McFarlane confirmed that he would not be putting himself forward as a candidate for the Manager's job!

Rikki McFarlane then oversaw a second victory on 6 December, a 2-1 win at Broomfield, when goals by a back-to-his-best Billy Stark and John McCormack put Saints two up in twenty-eight minutes. The interim Manager felt that his team were then sidetracked by Airdrie who got one back. "They started to get involved and forgot about playing football," he noted.

Chairman John Corson's prediction that he would be next to lose his position became a reality on 12 December when the Board voted, again on five to two lines, to replace him with Mr. Gordon Foulds, although Mr. Corson would continue as a Director. A day later, and back on the field, it was three wins out of three for Rikki's regime when a Jimmy Bone goal was just enough to defeat Partick Thistle in a hard-fought match played in atrocious weather. Saints were now up to fourth with eighteen points from eighteen fixtures.

Rikki McFarlane and the players were achieving a string of successful results against a most difficult backdrop. Club politics then erupted again on 16 December when former Chairman William Todd called for the new Chairman Mr. Foulds to be replaced! Mr. Todd claimed the Boardroom antics had made St. Mirren "the laughing stock of Scottish football". Three days later, Rikki McFarlane lent slightly towards that view when he told shareholders at the AGM that he believed that "the Club's image has been seriously tarnished" and hoped things would now settle down.

Saints "settled" approach allowed them to take part in the season's best game so far when they shared six quality goals with Dundee United in a thrilling 3-3 home draw. The visitors were deservedly 2-0 up at half-time; it would have been more but for Billy Thomson. United then lost the services of the influential Dave Narey as a rejuvenated Saints side came roaring back in the second half, earning a deserved standing ovation at the final whistle.

In spite of the much-publicised Boardroom manoeuvres, six leading names in Scottish football regarded the St. Mirren post highly enough to attend for interview during the fourth week in December. However, the Board felt that none had more suitable qualities than their "caretaker" and so, on Boxing Day, it was announced that Rikki McFarlane, the players' choice right from the beginning, was St. Mirren's new Manager.

The New Year opened in splendid fashion as Saints took Morton apart with a devastating first half display that yielded three goals in an eventual 3-1 victory. Two days later the points were shared with Aberdeen in a 1-1 draw but the unbeaten run came to an end on 10 January when a hard working but lacklustre Paisley eleven lost 2-0 to Kilmarnock.

Halfway through the following week, a virtual Reserve side travelled to Cappielow for a County Cup tie. Two down at half-time, the youngsters staged a remarkable comeback to make the final score 2-2, with Saints' equaliser coming from twenty year old midfielder Frank McAvennie, a late-October signing from Johnstone Burgh. Five days later, a crowd of 1,800 watched Saints demolish Morton 4-0 to win the 1980 Renfrewshire Cup. In the process, Frank McDougall scored one, laid on the other three and in doing so put himself firmly back into first team contention.

Success since the Parkhead victory in November encouraged many Buddies to think that a long run in the Cup was achievable but First Division mid-table Dumbarton came to St. Mirren Park on 24 January with other ideas. Saints missed chance after chance before the very young Sons side scored twice from their own few scoring opportunities, leaving the majority of the 7,000 crowd to trudge home bitterly disappointed. "We did not start with the right attitude. It was only after Dumbarton scored their second goal that we began to show any urgency," said the Manager afterwards.

There was a much grittier performance in a 0-0 draw at Firhill a week later but missed chances were again a key feature, a situation not helped by Jimmy Bone's ordering-off and the absence of out-of-form Doug Somner and internationalist Peter Weir.

After back-to-back challenge matches against Hamilton Accies and Arsenal, League football resumed on 21 February when Saints and First Division-bound Hearts put on an abysmal show for the 3,400 spectators. The team won 2-1 but Rikki McFarlane did not hide his feelings afterwards. "The performance disappointed me very much. I am not interested in winning in that fashion. I want to give people their money's worth. And hopefully get results at the same time".

They won 2-1 again the following week at Pittodrie, in what was a much-improved display against one of the League's top teams, with Frank McDougall gaining confidence from his headed winner. A hat-trick of 2-1 wins came seven days later against a very determined Airdrieonians side.

Our glorious weather continued to play its part when the mud bath conditions in the next match, at home to Kilmarnock, were so bad that Manager McFarlane actually hoped the game would be abandoned. His fears were justified. With players slipping and sliding in all directions, a last minute mistake by Billy Thomson gave Killie a point they scarcely deserved.

Saints were still determinedly chasing the remaining UEFA Cup spot, Dundee United having claimed the other one by retaining the League Cup. The next three fixtures were away to Celtic and United, and a home match with Rangers. Saints headed for Parkhead in mid-March in confident mood, with attack very much part of the Manager's thinking. The game, though, turned out to be a disaster. A heavy 7-0 defeat could have been worse but for Billy Thomson's outstanding display.

The extent of that reverse was completely unexpected, a freak result, as St. Mirren finished the season with seven victories from their last eight matches, the only loss being a narrow 1-0 defeat at Ibrox. They finished fourth, losing their head-to-head battle with Rangers for a UEFA place only on goal difference. Under Rikki McFarlane's stewardship, twenty-nine points had been gained from twenty-four matches. It was a record to be proud of.

Halfway through these twenty-four fixtures, an Extraordinary General Meeting was called by a Shareholders Action Group; unhappy about Jim Clunie's dismissal, John Corson's removal as Chairman and the manner in which both actions had been implemented. On 26 March, the E.G.M. decided to remove the five Directors responsible for these decisions. However, John Corson remained on the Board and a few days later the other surviving Director, Yule Craig, became the Club's fifth Chairman in four years.

The Boardroom upheaval had been regrettable, it was to be hoped that St. Mirren's future headline-making would be restricted solely to on-field achievements.

1981-82

The 1981 League Cup competition reverted to a "first round" sectional set-up, with Celtic, Hibernian and St. Johnstone providing the opposition. It was a group that Rikki McFarlane would later describe as "financially profitable". The same could be said for his close season transfer dealings.

In a series of significant moves on 28 May, internationalist Peter Weir was sold to Aberdeen for a Scottish record £220,000 while the services of Dons winger Ian Scanlon were secured. Also arriving, for a fee of £150,000, was ex-Saint Tony Fitzpatrick, whose return from Bristol City was widely acclaimed. With nothing coming of Lex Richardson's verbal transfer request of ten days earlier, supporters could look forward to the restoration of the formidable Fitzpatrick, Richardson and Stark midfield combination.

The first League Cup tie was at Celtic Park, where a Frank McGarvey first-half header put the Glasgow side ahead, with Saints looking ill at ease. Celtic pivot Willie Garner then became a Paisley goal hero when firstly he deflected an innocuous Frank McDougall effort into the roof of the net then, in the sixty-second minute, headed spectacularly past his own 'keeper! Late in the game, a John McCormack header gave Saints a flattering 3-1 win.

Four days later Saints failed to capitalise on their chances in a goal-less home draw with Hibs, but full points were collected with 3-2 and 1-0 away wins at Muirton Park and Easter Road respectively. As a result, only one point was needed to qualify but the team failed spectacularly, losing 5-1 at home to Celtic.

A win over St. Johnstone in the final game then became a must. A twenty-third minute missed penalty by Billy Stark didn't diminish the great vocal support from the 7,000 home fans, but it took two Ian Scanlon goals in the last ten minutes to secure a 2-0 victory and continuation in the competition.

The left-winger followed up this brace with another two goals in a closely fought 2-0 home win over Morton in the opening League fixture. Disappointingly, only 5,069 attended the derby.

The growing level of unemployment in the Paisley area was undoubtedly affecting the size of Saints' attendances, while reducing gate money was a threat to their status as a leading Premier team. Indeed, it had been the main reason for the unwanted transfer of Peter Weir. Thankfully, at the end of August, Club funds received another much needed boost when pivot Andy Dunlop, who had featured in only ten League games since the end of the 1978-79 season, was sold to Partick Thistle for £35,000.

Figures released on 19 September would show a loss of £50,254 for the year ending 31 May 1981. Without lottery income and a transfer fee surplus of £99,661 it was stressed that the deficit would have been £395,890, double the amount of only twelve months earlier.

The season's second League game, a thrilling 4-3 win at Broomfield, saw the birth of a star! The first half and early part of the second were dominated by Airdrieonians but two goals from Billy Stark and another two from young midfielder Frank McAvennie, making his League debut as a late replacement for the injured Tony Fitzpatrick, was just enough to finish off the home team who were leading 3-2 with only three minutes to play! The Manager reckoned that Billy Stark was the difference between the sides, but Saints fans left the ground talking about midfielder McAvennie.

A 1-1 home draw with Rangers followed. "We were the better side. I don't think anyone would dispute that," asserted Manager McFarlane afterwards. Saints certainly weren't the better side in the first leg of the League Cup Quarter-Final on 16 September, when it took a twenty-five yarder from Frank McAvennie and some great goalkeeping from Billy Thomson to earn a 1-1 draw at Forfar. By contrast, the "Loons" were over-run a week later in the return leg at a wet Love Street. It finished 6-0, the highlight being a curling thirty yarder from Frank McDougall, the equal of any goal seen at the ground for years.

A win, a draw and a defeat became the opening League sequence as Dundee matched Saints' industry and crucially made much more of their few chances to win 3-0 at Dens. The month drew to a close with a dreary 1-0 win over an unimaginative Hibs team. On the positive side, Saints remained second top, three points behind Celtic, but doubts about whether they could remain in such a lofty position re-surfaced after a Frank McDougall goal, three minutes from time, rescued an undeserved point in a 1-1 draw at Firhill.

Next came the Semi-Final of the League Cup, never Saints' favourite tournament. There wasn't much improvement in the first half of a poor match. One down to Rangers at half-time, the Buddies equalised in the forty-ninth minute when Tony Fitzpatrick's replacement Frank McAvennie beat three defenders and scored a stunning goal. Now the 14,000 crowd at last had a tie worth watching!

McAvennie also featured in the game's biggest talking point when he appeared to be fouled by Rangers' Bett in the penalty area but play was allowed to continue. The loose ball was hit upfield by winger Willie Johnston to a suspiciously offside-looking John McDonald. The freak nature of the sequence then continued when McDonald's shot was intercepted by Jackie Copland, whose effort to clear resulted in him sending the ball into his own net off keeper Billy Thomson.

To their credit, Saints' players did not capitulate, and three minutes later they were awarded a late penalty, which was converted by Ian Scanlon. The first leg finished 2-2, and although Frank McDougall injured his cartilage and would be out for the following two months, the belief remained strong that a place in the Final was achievable.

League hostilities resumed on 10 October with a visit from Celtic. A crowd of 16,441, three times Saints' average, saw the League leaders win 2-1 but Celtic's victory, albeit against an injury-hit home side, was more authoritative than the score-line indicates. The following week, 6,840 fans witnessed their favourites lose a second successive match by the odd goal when Aberdeen also left Paisley with a 2-1 win. The team had been without key players Fitzpatrick, Richardson and McDougall as they dropped to fourth. This lack of strength in depth was to hinder Paisley prospects all season.

The same three players, plus Alex Beckett, were also missing for the match at Tannadice on 24 October. This allowed young winger John McEachran, formerly with Greenock Juniors, to make his debut but it was veteran Jimmy Bone's two goals that saw off Dundee United. It was a timely triumph with the second leg of the League Cup due to be played the following Wednesday. Saints were ready.

In the return leg at Ibrox, a Jimmy Bone "goal" was disallowed when offside was given against Lex Richardson but the Buddies went ahead from an Ian Scanlon spot-kick on the half hour mark after Jim Stewart had blatantly fouled Frank McAvennie. The converted penalty gave Saints, with Tony Fitzpatrick still missing, a merited first half lead but they lost much of their composure after the break as a more aggressive Rangers applied constant pressure which produced two second half goals.

Rikki McFarlane admitted afterwards that Rangers had been the better side, but the Paisley cause was not helped by two highly controversial refereeing decisions.

The first came early in the second half when a raw Jackson tackle from behind felled Lex Richardson in the box as he bore down on the 'keeper. "Penalty" roared the Saints' fans behind the goal. No penalty was given. The second controversy related to the award of a penalty-kick to Rangers, when McDonald went down in the box following a tackle by John McCormack, who later claimed he hadn't touched the Ranger. Jim Bett equalised with the resultant kick and despite chances falling to Bone, Stark and Logan late on, Buddies' hopes of League Cup glory were shattered by John McDonald's well-taken winning goal five minutes from the end of an incident-packed cup tie. The League Cup ... never a favourite!

John McCormack

So it was back to League business on the last day of October with a deserved if late 2-0 victory over Morton. Less impressive was the following Saturday's display at Love Street where, despite almost incessant if uninventive home pressure, it took until the eighty-first minute to score. Sixty seconds later, visitors Airdrieonians equalised, and a point was lost.

On 14 November there came another match with Rangers, and another clash between McDonald and McCormack. The argument this time centred on whether the tackle occurred in or near the Saints' penalty area. The decision proved crucial. Although leading 2-1, Rangers had been under increasing pressure until Bett netted from the spot. Three minutes later they scored a fourth. In truth, Saints had only two shots on goal and generally lacked conviction and creativity. They were now fifth.

Billy Stark and Ian Scanlon found themselves dropped as the team was given a bit of shake-up for the visit of bottom team Dundee on 21 November. Two Frank McAvennie goals and one from Tony Fitzpatrick produced a 3-0 lead after twenty-five minutes, an opening spell greatly appreciated by the 3,500 die-hards who had ventured to a wet and windy Love Street.

The heroics of Dundee goalkeeper Bobby Geddes ensured that only one more was added in a game that marked the beginning of a nine-match unbeaten League run. It continued at Easter Road on 28 November, where supporters were given less return for their admission money as Saints scrambled a point in a boring goal-less draw.

Adverse weather conditions then restricted the Club to just one match in December, a spirited if fortunate 2-1 home win over Partick Thistle, having been one down until the eighty-second minute. Late goals from Jimmy Bone and Billy Stark enabled Saints to end the year in joint second place, as news came through that talented and popular centre-half Bobby Reid, eight years a Saint, had finally been forced to give up the game due to injury.

The weather eased somewhat and fixtures restarted on Sunday 3 January, with a closely fought 3-1 home win over Morton. The match was watched by 7,000, an attendance boosted by the Club's joint initiative with the Paisley Daily Express in which 2,670 of those present used vouchers which entitled the bearer to a fifty pence discount on the admission charge. It was an idea that was expected to be repeated.

Frank McAvennie had given Saints the lead with a marvellous goal in the twenty ninth minute but his effort was eclipsed early in the second half when winger Ian Scanlon's swerving run was rounded off with an explosive right foot shot. It was a goal to remember, but the Morton challenge was only finally extinguished when McAvennie produced a delicate lob in the last minute to move Saints into second place.

The derby match had actually been played on a Sunday due to policing costs. The following day it was revealed that during the 1980-81 season, as attendances dropped by 11%, police charges had accounted for an astonishing 23% of the Club's share of the gate money!

Twenty days later it was Morton at home again, but this time in the Cup. One down at half time, after what the Manager described as a "disastrous" first forty-five minutes, Saints' play improved considerably with the half-time introduction of Jimmy Bone, who scored in the seventieth minute. The consistent Billy Abercromby completed the comeback seven minutes later with a twenty-five yard cracker that gave "Ton" keeper Baines no chance. Saints marched on and Morton were out.

The second League fixture of 1982 ended in a deserved, if hard-won, 2-0 success at Dens and was followed by a 1-0 win over Dundee's near neighbours from Tannadice. "In the first half-hour the team were different class," proclaimed Rikki McFarlane, "although they did not have the same fluency in the second half". The game was settled by a rather fortuitous Lex Richardson close range goal, scored eight minutes from time. Saints now had twenty points from eighteen matches and remained in second place. Sadly, only 5,000 were at Love Street to see the team complete their Dundee double.

Attendances would continue to drop if there were more games like the dreadful 0-0 Firhill draw in early February, although Mark Fulton impressed at centre half. The defence needed to be good, because there were only ten Buddies for the last twenty-nine minutes following Billy Abercromby's dismissal for two bookable offences.

Progress in the Scottish Cup continued seven days later at Kilbowie Park in Clydebank, where goals from Ian Scanlon and Frank McAvennie in the first twenty-five minutes proved decisive, although the home side squandered their best chance to score when Saints' debutant defender Davie Walker, who had been a regular in the Reserves since 1978, gave away a first half penalty which was brilliantly saved by Billy Thomson,

The big 'keeper, Scotland understudy to Alan Rough, was far from his international best against a surprisingly attack-minded Hibernian side, when two disastrous goalkeeping mistakes gifted the visitors a point. It was a match Saints should have won, the same could be said of the next 1-1 League draw at Tannadice. Frank McDougall opened the scoring whilst the other Frank, McAvennie, showed the outstanding form that had won him his first Scotland Under 21 cap three days earlier, scoring the goal in a 1-0 victory against Italy.

McAvennie's meteoric rise then received a slight setback. On 6 March, almost 10,000 saw an absorbing home Quarter-Final tie which was ultimately settled by a twenty-yard rocket shot from Tony Fitzpatrick, who had pounced on a McAlpine punched clearance. Saints had reached their second cup semi-final of the season, despite all Dundee United's strenuous efforts to gain an equaliser. It was a task not made any easier when a hairline skull fracture prevented Frank McAvennie from appearing after the interval.

Four days after the United tie, Saints held a 2-1 half-time lead over Rangers, courtesy of two goals in two minutes from Richardson and Scanlon. The scoreline barely reflected the home team's superiority or their tenacity in overcoming the elements. It was a different story in the second half, when a complete collapse allowed Rangers to take over the match, score two, and leave Paisley with both points. The Buddies slipped to third after a match that at one point featured a blizzard, Tony Fitzpatrick being sent off, two bookings and two penalties!

On 12 March, two months after there had been some exaggerated press speculation that The St. Mirren Football Club was "in crisis" and estimated to be £200,000 in the red, spokesman David Murdoch provided

St. Mirren F. C. 1981/82 Season
F. Campbell, L. Richardson, R. Bell, J. Young, C. Money, D. Somner, S. Sorbie, T. Fitzpatrick, R. Doig, A. Logan, G. Speirs
J. Teirney, I. Scanlon, S. Munro, B. Stark, J. Mallin, B. Thomson, P. McAveety, M. Fulton, J. Curran, B. Abercromby, E. McDonald
E. Sorenson, F. McDougall, F. McAvennie, A. Beckett, R. Reid, J. Copland, A. Dunlop, J. Bone, D. Walker, J. McCormack, R. McFarlane.

a synopsis of the Club's position. "St. Mirren are not in a critical situation. There is no way we are going to close down. But we possibly need to sell one player a season to keep viable and in a totally healthy situation. The Club is not in any danger but our situation isn't as healthy as we would like it to be".

Back on the field, Celtic were next to leave Love Street with two points but there was no dispute about the outcome as the Parkhead men went four ahead by half-time. The injury absence of fourteen-goal Frank McAvennie and the suspension of Tony Fitzpatrick were undoubtedly felt but the real problem lay in a defence that contributed to three of the first half goals. The match finished 5-2 for Celtic and this second successive defeat killed off any Paisley talk about taking the championship. However, a place in Europe and a cup final appearance remained legitimate and encouraging targets.

By mid March, McAvennie was back for the Reserves, just two weeks after sustaining his head injury. He was missed by the first team at Cappielow that same day, as Lex Richardson hit a stunning seventy-ninth minute winning goal, to the utter disbelief of Morton Manager Benny Rooney, who had watched his side fail to take numerous chances.

Indifferent form continued in a dismal match against Airdrieonians. Although Billy Stark had opened the scoring in forty-three minutes, passing was generally poor, defensive frailties again evident, and finishing so woeful that Airdrie's John Martin seldom had a save to make. Late goals from the two Franks produced a 3-0 scoreline that was scarcely deserved but welcome nonetheless.

Rikki McFarlane admitted as much, but felt the lack of atmosphere generated by the 4,389 fans was a factor. It was an attendance many found perplexing, just a week before a Scottish Cup semi-final appearance. "It was certainly a disappointing crowd," admitted the Manager but it was not any less disappointing than the meagre 16,782 who attended the Semi-Final against Aberdeen at Celtic Park.

The game itself was nervously balanced until the sixty-first minute, when the Buddies, minus Tony Fitzpatrick because of his son's illness, went ahead in controversial circumstances. A corner was awarded to Saints after Frank McDougall had barged into Dons keeper Jim Leighton, with the loose ball narrowly missing the goal. From Lex Richardson's corner kick, John McCormack smartly passed it on for Frank McDougall to score.

The Aberdeen players, understandably fired up by this apparent injustice, responded with wave after wave of pressure and within six minutes their efforts paid off when Gordon Strachan converted a penalty after Mark McGhee was adjudged to have been pulled down by Billy Thomson, who until then had magnificently denied the Dons, notably McGhee, on numerous occasions.

The penalty decision left the Paisley players, Manager Rikki McFarlane and the noisy Buddies' support seething with anger but more detached observers felt that Billy Thomson had in fact tripped McGhee. Two minutes after the Dons equaliser, Billy Abercromby was ordered off for a second bookable offence, a bad tackle on Dons danger man Strachan. This far-from-classic encounter ended 1-1. A better playing surface could have enhanced the game's quality but both sides left the Glasgow ground content that they were still in the Cup.

The team for the replay at a drenched Dens Park showed some changes from the first game. John McCormack was moved to full back to replace the suspended Abercromby with Mark Fulton taking over the centre half role. Up front Doug Somner was preferred to Jimmy Bone.

With just seven minutes on the clock, Dons' skilful midfielder Gordon Strachan made his presence felt when he pushed the ball out to the right, from where Mark McGhee made a jinking run towards goal, a move which appeared to have ended with a weak left foot shot. To the dismay of the 3,000 Buddies in the 15,000 crowd the wet, muddy, ball squirmed through the arms of Billy Thomson and into the net, giving Aberdeen the early boost they were looking for.

Their lead lasted only eleven minutes, when Frank McAvennie took advantage of some indecision between Miller and Leighton to prod the ball home for a close range equaliser. The downpour continued but now it was Saints who had the upper hand, but in the thirty-sixth minute an excellent Aberdeen cross-field move reached Neil Simpson, whose low twenty-five yard shot skidded and skimmed along the greasy surface, just beyond the reach of a diving Billy Thomson.

Back came Saints but it remained 2-1 until the fifty-seventh minute, when Alex Beckett's well-flighted cross from the right glanced off the head of Miller, eluded Leighton's grasp and allowed Doug Somner the chance to slot in Saints' second equaliser from eight yards.

It was now anyone's game but with only quarter of an hour to go, Gordon Strachan gained possession on the right, waiting patiently before releasing the ball to the overlapping Doug Rougvie. The big Fifer's floated cross, intended for McGhee, found its way to the feet of ex-Saint Peter Weir, whose indifferent shot agonisingly slipped through Billy Thomson's legs.

"St. Mirren were unlucky," said Peter Weir after the game. That was no compensation for those in the St. Mirren dressing room where tears were openly shed at the disappointment of not reaching the Final. Manager Rikki McFarlane tried his best to sound upbeat: "We did not disgrace ourselves. It was a good game and I'm full of praise for the way the team came back twice. At the end of the day it could have gone either way."

Some supporters were bitterly disappointed by the Scottish Cup exit, as they would demonstrate at the next League match, but the season still held one more target, qualification for Europe. This objective hit a setback as Saints slipped to fifth place following Dundee's 1-0 win in Paisley on 10 April. Again Billy Thomson looked at fault when he failed to stop a twenty-five yarder from Albert Kidd. Throughout the remaining sixty-five minutes, the team continued to dominate but were subjected to some barracking as they failed to break down the relegation-threatened visitors' defence.

The next fixture was against Cup finalists Aberdeen, but Frank McDougall did not take part, his Manager being of the opinion that he had not "given enough" in the shock defeat by Dundee. At Pittodrie, the only shock was the obvious gap between the two sides as Aberdeen gave St. Mirren a goal of a start and still finished 4-1 winners. Saints were now four points behind Dundee United in the race for the remaining UEFA Cup place.

Afterwards Rikki McFarlane kept the players in the Pittodrie dressing room long after the crowd had dispersed. It seemed the exclusion of Frank McDougall was unlikely to be the last dropping of a star player if results and performances didn't improve.

A workmanlike 2-0 win over visitors Partick Thistle followed, with Alan Logan making a significant contribution to the victory. Four days later at Broomfield, another 2-0 win was recorded as Frank McAvennie scored a magnificent second half double in an otherwise disappointing match. Saints were now only one point behind fourth placed Dundee United.

There was more featureless football on view, especially in the first half, in a 2-1 defeat by Hibs at Easter Road on 24 April. Despite Saints still chasing for that UEFA slot Billy Stark's late penalty goal was the team's only major attempt at scoring and many supporters felt the team didn't look sufficiently interested. This semi-detached approach seemed to be captured in the Manager's summary: "Hibs deserved to win because they put more effort into the game".

Six difficult fixtures remained. In the first, the team was drawing with three minutes to go when Dundee United took a fortunate 2-1 lead. It looked to be all over until an innocuous, last-minute Billy Stark corner was met by United's John Holt who, while attempting to clear, lost his footing, fell, handled the ball, then grabbed it like a goalkeeper! The small crowd of 3,400 saw Stark blast the ball home for the equaliser. Saints were now level on points with United and had two games in hand!

Two days later a point was gained in a creditable 0-0 draw at Celtic Park. St. Mirren were now one point ahead of United but forfeited this advantage when they deservedly lost 3-0 to Rangers at Ibrox and then 5-1 at Pittodrie. That man Strachan once again dominated proceedings.

More of the same emerged in the return fixture at Love Street on 12 May as 3,942 watched the clearly more gifted Dons win convincingly again. Despite these three consecutive defeats, a UEFA place was still possible until the last day of the season but a 3-0 defeat at Celtic Park on 15 May meant Dundee United finished three points ahead.

For Saints there was no title, or cup triumphs, but the big breakthrough to major domestic honours had been tantalisingly close. They had reached two semi-finals and for the third season in a row had finished in Scotland's top five. At their best, they were capable of matching any side in the land but a lack of strength in depth was their biggest problem and, for financial reasons, was one that would be most difficult to resolve.

1982-83

Fans favourites Jimmy Bone and Alex Beckett were the two big name players given free transfers at the end of the 1981-82 season. The much-travelled Jimmy had been a St. Mirren player for five seasons, three less than Alex, who had been a first team regular since joining the Club from Falkirk. Also leaving was Jeff Curran, who had made eight starts and four appearances in League fixtures over a three-year period.

Concern was expressed about losing Jimmy Bone's experience, particularly his coaching potential, but the decision had been dictated by the Club's financial predicament, as had the scrapping of the Under-18 Professional Youth side and the post of General Manager. This series of regrettable measures was aimed at reducing annual running costs by £100,000, thus guaranteeing the continuation of full-time football in Paisley and endeavouring to maintain St. Mirren's position as a challenging force in the Premier Division.

Notable close season arrivals were Stephen Clarke, who joined Saints from Beith Juniors and fellow full back Tommy Wilson who had transferred from Queen's Park on 13 July. Both newcomers, who would prove to be prominent players in their first season, were joining a club with a new disciplinary code. Players would be fined £5 for lateness, £20 for a caution for dissent and £40 for a second such caution. Players were also advised that anyone seen in or near licensed premises, after a Wednesday before a Saturday game, would be liable for a fine of up to one week's wages.

Pre-season exertions began on the Isle of Man where an island select team were beaten 5-0 on 2 August and shared a 1-1 draw two days later. In the final game, Saints played well against Sunderland of the English First Division, winning 2-1 in front of 600 holiday-makers and locals. Unfortunately, Gardner Speirs injured his knee ligaments and would miss virtually the whole season. The season's preparations were rounded off at Love Street with a 3-1 win over English Second Division Leeds United.

Billy Thomson, who featured on the programme cover for the opening League Cup match against First Division Ayr United, had experienced an indifferent 1981-82 season by his own high standards. His optimism had returned by July. "Last year we came close, very close. Our confidence is high again and we are determined to do well."

The Ayr game was won 3-1 with Lex Richardson, transfer-listed ten months earlier, hitting his first-ever hat-trick. "Each goal was a gem," said the Manager who felt it was a good result considering that Copland, McAvennie, McDougall and Abercromby were suspended and of course Speirs was injured.

A totally unacceptable display against Second Division Queen of the South at Palmerston nearly provided a shock result until Frank McDougall scored in the sixty-sixth minute to take both points. Thankfully, the approach was much more professional at Annfield where Frank McAvennie, in his first outing in the striker's role, scored two goals and made the other in a comfortable 3-0 victory over Second Division Stirling Albion.

A 6-0 home win over Queen of the South on 26 August, watched by just 2,200 spectators, meant the last two ties were academic. It was a situation not lost on the players, most of whom showed neither the purpose nor passion of Ayr United, who were well worth their 2-1 win. Rikki McFarlane made his displeasure public. "Supporters come in to see players giving their best. They don't want to see players posing about at various stages of the game."

This criticism had only limited motivational effect, as his players failed to overcome a lively Stirling Albion side in a goalless draw. Some of the Love Street lethargy could be attributed to the uncompetitive nature of their League Cup section but after just six competitive games, the supporters' pre-season optimism had quickly vanished as jeers replaced cheers.

So to the League programme, which opened in Leith with another 0-0 draw, but this game remained goal-less only because back-at-his-best Billy Thomson defied Hibs with a catalogue of amazing saves. Four days later in the League Cup Quarter Final, Hearts' Henry Smith experienced the other side of goalkeeping when he let a harmless-looking Alan Logan header slip through his hands in the closing minutes. A draw hadn't looked possible after a first half in which the 5,500 Paisley crowd witnessed the home team's complete inability to disturb First Division Hearts. Things improved in the second half but 1-1 remained a favourable result for out-of-form Saints.

The supporters expected more!

They got it, in part at least, the following Saturday at home to Celtic, with much more fighting spirit on show, increased teamwork and no little skill either. Ultimately, two second-half penalties were sufficient to give the visitors a fortunate 2-1 victory after a stunning twenty-yarder from Lex Richardson had put Saints ahead in the eighteenth minute. Had Frank McAvennie taken any of three clear-cut chances that came his way, the game may well have had a different outcome.

It was a frustrating time. The display against Celtic confirmed the view of many Love Street regulars; their team had the ability to be a more than decent side.

In the next fixture, the efforts of Aberdeen and Saints cancelled each other out at St. Mirren Park, the game ending in a 1-1 draw. It was a creditable point to gain from the more competent Dons side but the same level of commitment would surely be needed in the League Cup second leg against hard-working Hearts at Tynecastle if Saints were to succeed.

Unfortunately, such application was absent, the game being lost 2-1. It would have been more but for Billy Thomson. Another money-spinning semi with Rangers had been lost; more crucially, Saints had managed just two shots on goal all night. "There was a lack of conviction about the things we did," said a furious Rikki McFarlane afterwards.

This lack of penetration was again on show for all to see at Tannadice where Dundee United convincingly won 3-0. Lack of cohesion in defence was also recurring but things improved somewhat in early October with a 3-2 home win over Kilmarnock, an attractive match settled by a gracefully chipped third goal from star man McAvennie.

Surprisingly, it was in-form Billy Thomson who attracted the blame on 9 October when he let the ball squirm out of his hands and over the line in the seventy-sixth minute. This was all a rejuvenated Motherwell needed. Seven minutes later they got a second to win 2-0, an unimaginable scoreline before half-time, such was Saints' superiority at Fir Park.

There was a better outcome the following week as the team drew 2-2 in an evenly contested home match with Rangers. Two-one up after sixty-two minutes, the Buddies were forced to share the points when three minutes later a shot was fortunate to be deflected off two defenders into the net. Overall, it had been a display that confounded those who had written off St. Mirren.

Despite dominating for long periods, another point was dropped at Dens on 23 October, when the absence of a killer touch in front of goal was again obvious. It became three draws in a row on 30 October and only one win in the first nine, when a poor derby crowd of 3,400 watched a passionless St. Mirren side hold their much more committed Greenock visitors to a 1-1 scoreline, thanks to a goalkeeping mistake by Morton's Roy Baines who palmed a weak Tony Fitzpatrick cross into his own net.

Hibs' Jackie McNamara always competed, but his dramatic sending off on 6 November permitted Saints to display some fast, aggressive skilful play in a 3-0 win. Two up in the first twenty-two minutes, McNamara's eventful departure from the field signalled the end of the game as a contest; sixty seconds later Doug Somner scored a third.

It was not so easy the following week at Celtic Park, where all Saints' weaknesses were exposed in seven shambolic first half minutes as four goals were conceded. A Roy Aitken goal, two minutes from the end, completed the 5-0 rout. Rikki McFarlane didn't appear for the post-match press conference.

On 16 November it was announced that veteran full back John Young had left St. Mirren to join Hong Kong Rangers. A first team regular since arriving from Falkirk FC in 1974, John had played in two hundred and seventeen games, a total which would have been greater had it not been for a double fracture of the leg sustained in a Reserve match against Ayr United in November 1981, sidelining him for nine months. As John departed, it was also confirmed that the Club had won the race to sign eighteen year-old James Charnley from Rutherglen Glencairn on a part-time contract; "Chic" would play once for the first team during his debut season.

After Celtic Park, four goals were then conceded at Pittodrie without reply and the slump continued on 27 November when Dundee United came to town and easily won 2-0. It was now eleven goals lost, none scored, in three games. Saints remained seventh, only two points ahead of bottom club Hibernian, amid repeated accusations in the Paisley Daily Express correspondence pages concerning lack of teamwork.

Kilmarnock were also struggling, indicated not least by the pitiful 2,200 crowd for Saints' visit, four days into December, to a windy and rainy Rugby Park. What proved to be a sometimes towsy tussle ended in a 2-2 draw with the Paisley visitors coming back twice. They also demonstrated the worst possible combination; a needless concession of goals and a recurring scorning of scoring opportunities. Afterwards, the attitude of some unnamed players was called into doubt by the Manager.

It was a much more composed performance, despite the conditions, at home to an insipid Motherwell one week later, when two goals in the last ten minutes gave the battling Buddies a welcome 3-0 win.

A week before Christmas, Saints remained three points ahead of bottom club Kilmarnock, following a 1-0 defeat at Ibrox. The Paisley cause was not helped when Jackie Copland was sent off following two cautions but it took some world-class saves by Billy Thomson, for whom Rangers would make an unsuccessful bid in early January, to keep the deficit to one. Rikki McFarlane later commented that in the first half his players looked as if they had not met each other before!

The year ended with a fortunate 0-0 home draw against Dundee on 27 December. It proved to be an endurance test for the 4,412 crowd in more ways than one. The match was played in torrential rain but even taking such conditions into account, both sides' finishing was lamentable, with Saints creating only one clear-cut chance.

Off the field, it was decided that ground improvement plans would need to wait until the Club's financial position was more stable. There wasn't much choice. Throughout the season, Rikki McFarlane would make several attempts to strengthen the side but insufficient cash to meet signing-on fee demands put paid to most of his potential acquisitions, particularly a much needed striker.

That looked a priority at the beginning of 1983. In the Ne'er day derby, Morton's new signing Ian Gibson put his team ahead after just three minutes. Thereafter, despite the efforts of 'keeper Thomson who heroically saved two penalties, the outcome was never in doubt. Saints failed to match Morton's method and confidence, as the home team ended the Cappielow clash as 2-0 winners. Rikki McFarlane called the display an "absolute disgrace". Forty-eight hours later there was a distinct improvement in a deserved 1-1 draw at Easter Road, although the equaliser was achieved courtesy of an own goal.

The run of poor performances and results hadn't gone unnoticed in the Boardroom. On 6 January the Board held a long discussion on the subject and considered whether "Board action" was required. It was agreed that the Manager's by then expired two-year contract would be extended on a month-to-month basis, whilst soundings were made about a possible replacement.

The improvement in play continued at home against Celtic and Aberdeen. Against the former, Saints put on a never-say-die performance and only a Murdo MacLeod screamer in the fifteenth minute deprived them of a deserved point. In the Aberdeen game, a magnificent goal by Ian Scanlon secured a 1-1 draw but it should have been more as goalscoring problems continued.

After twenty-one fixtures, the Buddies held seventh place with fifteen points, but other emerging statistics were concentrating Directors' minds. Only 4,350 had attended the match against championship contenders Aberdeen amid news that Saints' poor form was being blamed for supporters club membership dropping, in one case from fifty-five to just eight members, as branches struggled to fill buses for away games.

Those who travelled the road and the miles to Dundee on 22 January saw United take a 3-0 lead within the first nineteen minutes, although the Buddies came back well and, at 3-2, just failed to save the game. The conviction shown by the players failed to dispel the feeling at Board level that perhaps a managerial change was required; on 24 January it was decided that a second possible replacement was to be approached.

Five days later, Dundee United travelled the same miles to St. Mirren Park on Cup business. In a match surprisingly devoid of skill but not lacking in determination, a close range scrambled shot from Doug Somner in the twenty-seventh minute gave the more energetic Saints the right to move into the fourth round.

It was a welcome first win of 1983, a possible turning point, and the majority of the 7,020 in attendance made clear their enjoyment in watching their team show renewed pride and fighting spirit. Making a superb comeback against United, after a prolonged knee injury absence, was wholehearted defender John McCormack. It was perhaps no coincidence that his return marked an upturn in the team's results.

A stunning Billy Stark volley and a thirty-yarder from Frank McDougall were enough to overcome struggling Kilmarnock, but the Manager wasn't entirely pleased. "One or two players disappointed me a little bit in terms of application, particularly in the first half", pointedly adding that professional footballers didn't have "any real excuse" for not giving their all for ninety minutes.

The next League game, at Fir Park, was called off, allowing Saints a good break before facing bitter rivals Morton in the Cup. During this period Rikki McFarlane finally added to his squad with his mid-February signing of Sunderland's Barrie Wardrobe on a temporary contract. Barrie would eventually play in five league games before returning to England at the end of the season.

In the Cup, the supporters expected a derby victory, and they got it. The tie turned out to be one of the displays of the season, with Frank McDougall's two cracking goals merely emphasising Saints' superiority from first to last. Three days later, the Board were advised that informal approaches regarding a new Manager had been turned down. There was recognition that the team's performances had improved, but the situation would continue to be monitored.

The Cappielow success appeared to have spilled over into the League fixtures when visitors Rangers were beaten 1-0 in an incident-packed match settled by a Tony Fitzpatrick goal in the seventh minute. Next came the re-scheduled match at Fir Park, but the goalless draw was as bad as such scorelines often suggest, with an unattractive fight for Premier points far outweighing any entertainment for the paying customers.

Back to Dundee in early March, the next match at Dens could not have been more different with seven goals scored, five by the Buddies. Saints' composed control in the first half was the platform for the first away win of the season, as they moved into sixth place and prepared for the next round of the Cup.

First Division Airdrieonians were their opponents, but in the words of their manager, Bill Munro, it turned out to be "no contest" as Billy Stark hit a first-ever hat-trick in a 5-0 demolition of the "Diamonds". Saints were two goals up after only seven minutes and proceeded to demonstrate a standard of finishing at Broomfield that had been missing before March.

Two more were scored at home against relegation-threatened Morton but the visitors took both points, despite only "scoring" twice! In the eighty-first minute, and with the game locked at 2-2, Morton's Bobby Houston fired in a shot which was apparently cleared off the line but the referee, badly positioned and without consulting his linesman, decided that the ball had gone in! Afterwards Houston admitted it hadn't!

Saints scored three legitimate goals at home to Hibs on 19 March, all in the last thirty-four minutes, to do much to erase the memory of an almost incident-free first half that had drawn jeers at half-time. Billy Stark was continuing to show an excellent run of form and his skills were expected to be a much-needed commodity as Saints travelled to Celtic Park the following week.

Surprisingly, it turned out to be a poor match; scrappy in the first half, not much improved in the second. Mark Fulton put Saints ahead in the sixty-eighth minute but Provan scored a late equaliser. Two more excellent points were taken from an equally unusual location with a spirited 1-0 triumph in the snow against the league leaders at Pittodrie. Saints were now edging nearer the always respectable point-per-game return as they moved up to fifth.

In almost customary fashion, that ratio deteriorated again the following week after Saints lost 2-1 at home to an almost totally dominant but far-from-brilliant Dundee United. The Manager admitted that the best team won "by a mile" but added: "I thought we were shocking, but I can't put my finger on why we were as bad as we were".

Perhaps the players' thoughts were on their next game, a Cup semi-final with Rangers at Celtic Park. It turned out to be extremely poor fare for the 31,000 rain-soaked supporters. Centre forward Sandy Clark had scored what appeared to be the winner for the Glasgow team in the seventy-second minute before Craig Paterson kept Saints' hopes alive with an own goal seven minutes from time.

It was a piece of luck the team were scarcely worthy of. "You don't deserve to win if you don't play, "said Rikki McFarlane afterwards, adding that he felt his players "froze". Two days later at Hampden they did much better and took the tie to extra time.

With two minutes to go, a cross from the right reached Saints' penalty box and was twice headed on to reach Sandy Clark, who flicked it goalwards. There was a scramble on the line before the ball was cleared by Lex Richardson but the referee pointed to the centre spot, indicating it had crossed the line. Saints' players protested, but "the goal that never was" went into the record books. "The players all felt no way was it near over. I am just sick," was the candid McFarlane summary.

It was a decision equally hard to take for the Saints fans on the East Terracing. They may have been further from the action than the players but they unanimously came to the same conclusion; the ball hadn't crossed the line!

To their credit, the team responded in the best possible way, by winning convincingly. A loyal band of 3,257 supporters saw Saints go one up a minute before half-time against a Motherwell side who had missed several chances, then Frank McDougall made it 2-0 a minute after the re-start. It was the beginning of a brilliant second half performance in which Frank McAvennie scored two more for his hat-trick.

Next up at Rugby Park, the two Franks scored one each in the first twenty-five minutes against bottom-of-the-league Kilmarnock but in the second half, a complete slump allowed Killie's Brian Gallacher to hit two goals in the last twenty-two minutes to give the Ayrshire men a merited point.

The third last match of the season, away to Rangers, was lost 4-0. The scoreline barely reflected the chasm between the two sides and the match exposed a tired Paisley team. Prospects of qualifying for Europe seemed to have lengthened but a 2-1 win over sixth-placed Dundee at St. Mirren Park on 7 May, thanks to a last minute Frank McDougall header, kept Saints in the hunt. When third top Aberdeen magnificently defeated Real Madrid in the Cup Winners' Cup Final it meant the Dons would defend their title in that competition and Saints' UEFA Cup fate would be decided on 14 May, the final Saturday.

Already relegated Morton were Saints opponents but the 2,000 Saints' supporters at Cappielow simultaneously took an unusual interest in a Tayside derby. Goals from Frank McDougall in the fortieth and fiftieth minutes put Saints in the best possible position, then the result from Dens Park came through before the Morton game had finished; Dundee United had won the Championship, Saints had qualified for Europe for the second time in their history!

It was an achievement that didn't look possible for half the season, amid recurring questions about players' commitment and behind-the-scenes doubts about the Manager's tenure of office. Saints had finished in the top five for the fourth consecutive season and had again reached the Scottish Cup semi-final; they remained, against the odds, a recognised power in the land.

1983-84

The statement of a year previously, that "it might be necessary to sell one player a season", seemed to become a reality with the £70,000 transfer of Billy Stark to new European Cup-Winners' Cup holders, Aberdeen. To be fair to the Club, however, Stark's contract had expired and he was keen to move on.

Rikki McFarlane reiterated the difficult situation faced by St. Mirren; "We have got to try to maintain full-time football at Love Street as well as a youth structure, so the Club has got to get money from somewhere. Given our current small gates, we can only get money in by selling players like Billy Stark". Fortunately, the Board were thereafter able to turn down a second six-figure bid from Luton Town for Frank McAvennie, and discourage Liverpool's interest in Billy Thomson.

Doug Somner moved to Hamilton Academical on a free-transfer, Jack Copland retired to the position of Lottery Manager, and, while it was made clear that most of Stark's transfer fee would be used to offset some of Saints' considerable debt, twenty-two year-old Rowan Alexander was purchased from Queen of the South for £27,000.

Alexander had played with the "Doonhamers" for five seasons and twice netted over twenty goals in the Second Division, although McFarlane warned that he was not yet "the finished article". Interest in Jim Tolmie of Lokeren ended when the player signed for Manchester City, and Norwich City forward Ross Jack turned down the chance to sign for family reasons.

A financial boost arrived in the shape of a one-year £20,000 sponsorship deal with local bus operator Graham's Bus Service brokered by the Club's new commercial consultant and BBC radio commentator David Francey. The Graham's "G" became the very first sponsor's logo to appear on the team jerseys, the company was also promoted on track and programme advertising, and there would be luxury coach travel provided for all the Club's away matches. Nevertheless, the cash injection was not enough to stop season ticket prices being increased by ten-percent, the first rise in four seasons, and general admission charges rising by twenty-percent.

Andrew Graham (left) of Graham's Bus Service signs the first ever Shirt Sponsorship deal St. Mirren secured.

Looking on are Chairman Yuill Craig (seated), Allan Marshall (left) and legendary BBC Scotland commentator David Francey.

Initially only the Graham's Logo appeared on the shirts, however, this was later changed to the words "Grahams Buses".

The deal ran out just prior to the 1987 Cup Final. Saints wore the name of rival bus operators Clydeside Buses on the Cup Final jerseys.

On the playing front, Mark Fulton was confirmed as the Club captain for the new season and Stevie Clarke helped Scotland reach the quarter-finals of the Under-19 World Cup in Mexico. There was the excitement of being drawn to face Feyenoord in the opening round of the UEFA Cup, but disappointment when Manchester City pulled out of the proposed testimonial game for Jack Copland.

After a relaxing break in Magaluf courtesy of the Club, the squad travelled to the Isle of Man again to start the pre-season build-up. Rowan Alexander, who had looked sharp in netting three goals in bounce games against Partick and Arbroath prior to the trip, was stretchered off after only ten minutes of the first match with a bad knee injury. The team defeated the local select 3-0 but went down by a single-goal to English sides Sunderland and Burnley.

Much better was the 3-2 win against Queen's Park Rangers at St. Mirren Park. The Londoners (and their plastic pitch) would end the season only seven points behind champions Liverpool in the English First Division. Young John McEachran made his mark with two goals in the victory. The third was netted by sixteen year-old debutant Danny Diver, four minutes from time. Two days later, Lex Richardson led a mostly inexperienced team to a 2-1 victory against full-strength Morton in the Renfrewshire Cup Final at Cappielow. John McCormack and Gardner Speirs both played in the match to complete their preparations for the new season after lengthy lay-offs through injury.

The good result against QPR was followed-up seven days later by a 1-1 draw at Ibrox to get the season-proper off to a promising start. In an incident-packed match, Frank McAvennie scored a magnificent individual goal, Ian Scanlon was red-carded for disputing Rangers' controversial second-half penalty, and Tommy Wilson was carried off with serious knee ligament damage in the closing minutes.

Nevertheless, the opening eight Premier Division games would pass without a single win, leaving the team languishing at the foot of the table; the fact that twenty-one players were used in these games tells its own story. In addition to Wilson and Alexander's injuries, Fitzpatrick and Logan were both carried off in League Cup ties, and McDougall missed games through suspension and injury. The absence of senior players meant brief recalls for Phil McAveety, Fraser Campbell and David Walker, and full debuts for Robert Cousar and sixteen year-old Ian Cameron.

During September, Lex Richardson got his desired move in a straight swap for Dundee forward Eric Sinclair. This transfer looked to be a good one for Saints as Sinclair had played over two hundred games for Dundee and had scored seventy-six league goals. However, whilst Richardson made over fifty appearances for the Dens Parkers before moving on to Morton in 1985, Sinclair turned out in only three League matches after arriving at Love Street before being moved on to Airdrieonians for income of only £7,000. To the fans it was almost as if Richardson had been given away for nothing.

To add to the problems of an unsettled team struggling in the League there was also the distraction of cup-ties filling virtually every midweek through to the end of October. Moreover, these games were not completed with any greater degree of success than the League encounters.

The League Cup format had been altered once again, this time requiring two qualifying rounds before the remaining teams were set into four sections of four. Immediately after the League draw with Rangers, Saints faced home-and-away meetings with Forfar on August 24th and 27th in the second qualifying round.

The Loons had been making steady progress and were an altogether tougher proposition than they had been in the same competition two years earlier. The 1-0 home victory in midweek was just enough to help Saints negotiate a 2-2 draw at Station Park. St. Mirren were never behind on aggregate, but losing a second-leg equaliser with only five minutes remaining created a nervy ending to the tie. Gardner Speirs continued his return to action with two of the three goals.

All ten Premier teams reached the sectional split and Saints were drawn together with Rangers, Hearts and First Division Clydebank. As with Forfar, Saints had a recent history of cup meetings with each of these three sides.

The opening group tie on 31 August meant the third League Cup game in a week and resulted in a thrilling 2-2 home draw with Hearts, all four goals coming in the first half. However, by the time the final two group matches were played in November, Saints' interest in the competition had long since evaporated. The only other point gained came in another home draw, 3-3 against Clydebank in front of a mere 1,440 fans on 26 October, and the team ended the six matches bottom of the section.

The other midweek distraction at this time was the Club's second foray into Europe, when former World Club Champions Feyenoord visited Paisley on 14 September. The Dutchmen had signed 36 year-old Johan Cruyff in the summer, and had a young Ruud Gullit in their squad together with a further six full internationalists. Cruyff, in particular, would be a formidable opponent given all his experience with Ajax and Barcelona.

Billy Abercromby was ineligible for the first-leg due to his carried-over suspension from 1980 and a crowd of 10,211 watched Feyenoord leave with a 1-0 advantage courtesy of a deflected goal; Ruud Gullit's shot spinning into the net off John McCormack. Saints fielded Thomson, Clarke, McAveety (D Walker), Fitzpatrick (McDougall), Fulton, McCormack, Richardson, McAvennie, Alexander, Speirs and Scanlon.

Clarke, McAveety, Fulton, McAvennie, Alexander, Speirs and Walker were still very inexperienced, even at a domestic level, and McAveety, Fitzpatrick, Alexander and McDougall were all well short of full fitness. In any other circumstances these four wouldn't have played. In fact, Fitzpatrick and Alexander aggravated their injuries and missed the return match. "It would be stupid and naive to suggest that we should have won," McFarlane admitted, "but, all things considered, we held our heads up and took credit out of the game".

In the rematch a fortnight later John McCormack was played in midfield to counter the threat of Cruyff, David Walker was at right back, McAveety moved into the centre, Abercromby returned in place of the departed Richardson, and McDougall started despite missing the last three League games. Another youngster, John McEachran, came off the bench in the second half for Gardner Speirs. The home side advanced safely into the next round with a 2-0 win in front of 18,858 at Een Kuip, sending St. Mirren home beaten but not disgraced.

The only black spot was the late sending-off of Frank McDougall together with Michel van der Korput for violent conduct. McDougall had also been booked earlier in the game and received a four-match ban from UEFA. In time that would become the concern of another Scottish side, but McDougall's indiscipline as a St. Mirren player was troubling the Club.

The Feyenoord meetings would be the only time that St. Mirren suffered home and away defeats in seven European pairings, and Feyenoord confirmed their pedigree by going on to win the Dutch League and Cup double that season for the first time since their World Club Championship winning side had done so in 1969.

Manager Rikki McFarlane decided that he could do no more, however, and his resignation was announced on the Club's return from Holland. McFarlane had been popular with his players and respected by the support, but admitted to having lost his enthusiasm for the job. He sought a return to working as a physiotherapist and looked forward to spending more time with his family.

Now managerless, Saints' exit from Europe was followed by a run of four away matches. With assistant Eddie McDonald also resigning, Erik Sorensen was in charge for the first of these games. A 1-1 draw at Celtic Park, which robbed the home side of its one hundred per-cent League record, was of little consolation as it preceded 5-0 defeats at both Ibrox (in the League Cup) and Pittodrie. Possibly even harder to take was the 3-2 reverse at bottom-of-the-table St. Johnstone.

Morton's player-manager, 34 year-old Alex Miller was appointed to the Manager's chair on 2 October 1983 prior to that heavy League Cup defeat at Ibrox, which resulted in the incredible situation of Miller conducting a pre-match pep talk with his new charges before rushing off to Cappielow for his final match with Morton! Alex Ferguson's brother Martin came to St. Mirren Park as first-team coach while Drew Jarvie was brought from Airdrieonians as reserve team player-coach at a cost of £2,500.

Alex Miller

The general feeling among fans and the media was that Alex Miller was too young and lacked the necessary experience for such a job. Although Alex Ferguson had been only thirty-two at the time of his arrival at St. Mirren Park, and with less managerial experience, Saints were now a top-five Premier Division side and not the disjointed team of 1974, languishing in the League's lower reaches. The fact that Miller was ex-Rangers, and worse ex-Morton, didn't help the supporters' attitude towards him either.

In fact, one of Alex Miller's first tasks was to face up to disgruntled fans; whether it was the couple of dozen youths that protested loudly outside the Main Stand after the League Cup draw with Clydebank, or the three hundred that turned up at Knox Street for a "meet-the-manager" night a week later. Another of Miller's first acts was to dispose of Eric Sinclair. "I didn't sign him. He wouldn't have been in my long-term plans." Sinclair had been at St. Mirren Park less than a month!

There had now been sixteen competitive matches played, with the only victory being over Forfar back in the second game of the season, and St. Mirren were a mere matter of goal-difference off the bottom of the Premier Division table. However, if results in the first three matches following the Manager's appointment were hardly encouraging then that was soon to change.

On 29 October, Rangers made the short trip along the M8 to Paisley for the teams' second league meeting. They too were in "crisis", sitting in the lower half of the table and, on the day after their manager had resigned, Saints trounced them 3-0 with the goals coming from Frank McDougall, Drew Jarvie, and Ian Scanlon.

That result sparked an excellent run of form. Seven League matches were played without loss through to the beginning of December. Seventeen goals were scored and only seven lost. The away fixtures at Motherwell, Hearts and Dundee were drawn, and there were wins in each of the other three home matches, against Hibs, Celtic and Dundee United.

The most exciting of these were the back-to-back victories in four days over League leaders Celtic and reigning champions Dundee United. On Saturday 19 November, Celtic raced to a 2-0 lead in twenty minutes, but by the interval Saints had hit back with goals from Stevie Clarke, John McCormack and Frank McDougall. In the final minute Ian Scanlon added a truly memorable fourth goal, returning a clearance on the volley from thirty-five yards high into the net. £12,000 signing from Grimsby Town, Neil Cooper, made his debut in this match. He must have been impressed by his new teammates!

On the Tuesday evening Dundee United arrived to play the game postponed from 15 October. Saints were two up by half-time and it would have been three had Stevie Clarke's thirty-yard shot been hit seconds earlier, but the referee had blown for half-time moments before the ball hit the net. Frank McAvennie was the evening's hero with a hat-trick in the 4-0 rout.

During this run of success Derek Hamilton was also added to the squad, costing £4,000 from Aberdeen. Hamilton and Cooper would go on to play major roles in the Scottish Cup win three years hence. The side was now much more settled, with only fourteen players being used in these seven games compared to the twenty-one in the opening eight.

The Manager's decision to play Drew Jarvie a dozen-or-so times in the first team led to unforeseen problems. Firstly, the Club was severely censured for fielding him in a League Cup match, as he was already cup-tied with Airdrie. Then, his former club demanded compensation as they had agreed to release him only on the understanding that his appearances would be limited to reserve fixtures. Saints were forced to cough up an additional £1,500.

The good spell of League form was not to last, and the four victories in seven was followed by only another five wins in the remaining twenty-one fixtures. The tide turned abruptly with two successive home defeats, 2-1 to struggling St. Johnstone on 10 December, and 3-0 on Christmas Eve to an Aberdeen side that had won the European Super Cup four days earlier and was on the way to regaining the Premier Division crown.

St. Johnstone, ironically en-route to relegation in two successive seasons, were one of only two sides that St. Mirren failed to defeat in the League during 1983-84, the other being Hearts. Despite the two earlier League Cup defeats, Rangers were the one team that Saints remained unbeaten against in League matches.

The five remaining League wins were memorable nonetheless. A 2-1 New Year holiday success over Motherwell at St. Mirren Park, two high-scoring victories against Dundee, 4-0 in Paisley and 5-2 at Dens (for the second year running), and two other home wins, 3-1 against Hibs and 3-2 on the closing day over the season's champions Aberdeen. There was also a standing ovation for a fight-back from 2-0 down against Dundee United in the "Tangerines" return visit to Paisley, with second-half goals from Abercromby and McAvennie levelling the score.

In January, Phil McAveety left to join Morton, in a deal compensating the Greenock side for the loss of its manager, and Chic Charnley joined Ayr United for £1,500 after an initial month's loan. We'd see him again! Sadly, physiotherapist Bobby McCrae died following a short illness. He was replaced by Fifties legend Bobby Holmes. Club Chairman from 1965-71, Val McNaughtan, also passed away at this time, as did the last surviving member of the 1926 Cup winning side, Willie McDonald.

Before the end of the season, goalkeeper Campbell Money and former St. Aelred's High School pupil, David Winnie, would break through into the first team, and Frank McAvennie signed a new contract until June 1986. John McGregor was signed on loan from Liverpool and made five appearances before suffering an unfortunate injury and returning to the English side.

The League campaign closed with Saints sixth, a drop of one place from the previous year. The team had managed only nine wins, exactly half the number managed three seasons earlier. Turning some of the fourteen draws into victories would be a target for the coming season.

The real story of the second half of 1983-84, however, was the team's run to a third successive Scottish Cup Semi-Final. Following the traumatic exits in the previous two semi-finals Saints' fans had every confidence that the team would make it "third-time-lucky"!

The Third Round draw produced a meeting with First Division Meadowbank Thistle, but any thoughts of easy progress were soon dispelled, as it took 300 minutes of football before Saints squeezed through 2-1 after a second replay. Perhaps good fortune would indeed play its part this season; "We were lucky to survive," a relieved Manager admitted.

Meadowbank were twice ahead in the matches, one of their goalscorers being a certain Tom Hendrie, later to become St. Mirren Manager. Hamilton Academical, similarly placed in the First Division to Meadowbank, were the Fourth Round opponents. The result was another hard-fought 2-1 win, although thankfully this time without the need for replays!

A Quarter-Final pairing with neighbours Morton was greeted with the usual anticipation. Amazingly, it was the County rivals' third Scottish Cup meeting in consecutive seasons, and the Greenock outfit's fortunes were reviving with their surge towards the First Division title. More significantly, both clubs saw themselves a single step away from a Hampden semi-final.

The game was scrappy, but a cup-classic! Following an early opener from McAvennie, Dom Sullivan could have put Morton 3-1 ahead in the first-half, but hit the post with a penalty before Tony Fitzpatrick made it 2-2 on the stroke of half-time. Bearded Ian Scanlon netted twice in two minutes for St. Mirren midway through the second-half and, although Willie Pettigrew scored in the last minute for the home team, Saints held out to win by the odd goal in seven. Another frantic Renfrewshire derby!

With Aberdeen facing Dundee in the other Semi-Final tie at Tynecastle, Saints lined up against Celtic at the national stadium. The Celts were forced to play a rearranged fixture against Motherwell on the Tuesday leading up to the semi-final, whereas Saints had the whole week to prepare after the timely boost of the 5-2 win at Dundee the previous Saturday. St. Mirren had, of course, beaten Celtic at the semi-final stage in 1959 and 1962. Could they do it again?

The dry pitch and swirling high-wind did not make it a day for quality football. In the first-half Frank McDougall equalised a Brian McClair goal, cleverly wrong-footing a defender before firing the ball into the corner past Bonner. However, Saints lost the match to as disappointing a goal as any of those conceded in the previous two years' semi-finals. After a Burns' shot eluded Thomson and hit the post Stevie Clarke moved quickly to block Paul McStay's attempt from the rebound, but the ball spun high into the air off Clarke's boot and drifted wind-assisted under the crossbar as Billy Thomson failed to reach it. Another fluke!

Celtic rubbed salt in the wound with a 4-2 league win at rainswept St. Mirren Park four days later, despite a Scanlon double in the opening half-hour, and the season stumbled to a close with only that win over new champions Aberdeen, in front of a mere 3,450 on 12 May, to lift the despondency.

Billy Thomson was left out of the side for the final fixture as the Manager took a "strong line" over his refusal to accept the Club's re-signing terms. "This club is needing a real shake-up," Miller exclaimed, and the threat of large fines was made to the squad in general if on-field discipline failed to improve during the following season. However, even during the closed season, it was disciplinary matters that held the attention.

1984-85

Given his remarks at the end of the previous season, there was no surprise to learn of the Manager's unhappiness at reading negative comments in the summer's newspapers attributed to Frank McDougall, Billy Thomson and Mark Fulton. Miller was given permission by the Board to fine each player £200 for being in breach of contract and, shortly afterwards, Thomson was sold to Dundee United for £82,500 while McDougall left for Aberdeen for £106,000.

A £50,000 bid for Fulton from an un-named English club was rejected. Nevertheless, together with Tony Fitzpatrick, Fulton was now only prepared to sign month-to-month contracts in the hope of leaving for another club and he was stripped of the club captaincy.

The Club's overdraft was around £180,000 prior to these sales. With funds now available, Miller purchased Jim Rooney from Morton for £47,000, and Brian Gallagher from Kilmarnock for £43,500 with John McEachran moving to Rugby Park in part exchange. A straight player-swap moved John McCormack to Dundee and Peter Mackie to Paisley, and Alex Miller agreed new one-year deals with Ian Scanlon and Billy Abercromby, while Stevie Clarke signed a three-year full-time contract.

"One of our main aims this season is to improve on our away performances as results were very dismal to say the least," admitted the Manager as he anticipated his first full season in charge at St. Mirren Park. An amended bonus structure for the first team set out his priorities; £150 for a win, £50 for a draw, and £70 for a draw at Pittodrie, Parkhead, Tannadice or Ibrox.

A new Adidas playing kit was unveiled before the start of the season and Graham's Bus Service continued its sponsorship of the Club. Following bounce games with Clyde, Hamilton and Kilmarnock, St. Mirren travelled across to the Isle of Man for the third year running to compete for the Gore Cup. The team failed to overcome either of the English sides played, this time Blackburn Rovers and Carlisle United, and for the first time failed to defeat the local select.

There was no "glamour" friendly arranged for St Mirren Park but, in a novel move, the Buddies played both promoted Forfar Athletic and Brechin City on the evening of 7 August. "I'll be taking the full squad of thirty players with me," explained Alex Miller. "Fifteen of them will go one way and fifteen the other."

The League campaign opened with a draw at Ibrox for the second successive season as Rooney, Gallagher and Mackie made their competitive debuts. It would have been the perfect introduction for Brian Gallagher had his 87th minute "goal" not been disallowed for offside. Then Aberdeen were the first visitors to Paisley and the defending champions returned home with full points following their 2-0 victory.

The League Cup kicked-off in the midweek following the Aberdeen defeat. Three years on from the conclusion of its previous sponsorship, the competition was now named the Skol Cup and there was yet another new format, although finally one that hit the right note with both clubs and fans. Sections were a thing of the past, and every tie was played as a single match, concluded by extra-time and penalties if necessary.

Premier teams entered the competition at Round Two, and St Mirren defeated First Division Clyde 1-0 in Paisley with an extra-time Ian Cameron goal. A week later, on 29 August, and on a high from Saturday's 4-0 league drubbing of neighbours Morton in Greenock, the team travelled to Fife to face Cowdenbeath. The Second Division side won 2-0, Frank McAvennie missed a penalty, and the humiliation was heightened by the news that seven players were fined for partying in a local nightclub.

With interest in the League Cup over for another season and no European ties to contemplate, the Club could turn its full attention to the business of gathering League points. Happily, the first quarter of the fixture list was completed with four wins from the six remaining games. Dundee United were beaten 1-0 at home and Hearts 2-1 away, despite falling behind to a John Robertson penalty in fifty minutes.

Indeed, the result at Tynecastle lifted Saints into third place, however by a fortnight later the team had slipped back to fifth. Two goals conceded in the opening seven minutes at Dens Park could not be overturned and Celtic won at St. Mirren Park on 22 September with two goals in the closing fifteen minutes.

That game was marred by fans of both sides spilling out of the "North Bank" and onto the pitch. It appeared that the problem had been caused by Celtic fans "mysteriously" finding their way in amongst the home support. "How some Celtic supporters got into the St. Mirren end I just don't know," the confused police Match Commander admitted. Saints' Chairman appeared equally mystified. "Normally there is segregation. As far as I am concerned there was no difference on Saturday."

This was only one of a number of crowd disturbances to affect St. Mirren Park throughout the season. To make matters worse, local residents in adjoining Albion Street signed a petition calling for action to stop "vandals" using their gardens as a short cut to the Ground and damaging their property!

Meanwhile, Rowan Alexander, who this season had made only a single substitute appearance, left to join Brentford for £25,000. In his place, Kenny McDowall signed from Partick Thistle at a cost of £32,500 plus Alan Logan, and made his debut in the Celtic match. Clean sheets against Dumbarton and Hibs contributed to Saints' other two victories.

The visiting fans from Edinburgh created a stir towards the end of that Hibs' match in October when, having left the Ground some ten minutes early, they began throwing missiles into the St. Mirren support and onto the North Bank roof from Springbank Road. This represented a totally new depth of football hooliganism, yet even that action paled into insignificance when the teams met for a second time in Paisley after the New Year.

On the field, it had been an encouraging start to the season but for that result at Cowdenbeath. Already the side had won more matches "on the road" than in the whole of the previous League campaign! Jim Rooney opened his scoring account with the fourth goal against his former club at Cappielow, and Brian Gallagher's first goal for St. Mirren cancelled out Hearts' penalty at Tynecastle.

Frank McAvennie, especially, was in tremendous form, scoring seven of the team's eleven league goals in the first quarter. However, his off-field behaviour was beginning to raise concerns within the Club and he was twice fined for missing training.

The second round of nine League fixtures proved to be much more difficult than the first. In fact, the outcome of the games was exactly reversed; three wins, five defeats, one draw. The first visit of Rangers to Paisley on 13 October seemed to be heading for another 0-0 until the Gers netted twice in the last three minutes to take full points.

Former international goalkeeper Jim Stewart then arrived on loan from the Ibrox club during the following week to cover for the injured Campbell Money, but his debut on the Saturday was not a happy one. Ex-Saints Frank McDougall scored twice and Billy Stark once as Aberdeen won comfortably by four goals to nil. As well as Money, St. Mirren had been without Derek Hamilton, Mark Fulton, Brian Gallagher and Ian Scanlon at Pittodrie. When Morton arrived seven days later, the midfield duo of Jim Rooney and Billy Abercromby were also missing. It was equally disappointing to have only 3,627 attend the County derby. Drew Jarvie made his one appearance of the season and helped the injury-hit Saints to a 2-1 success. Fortunately, Airdrieonians saw no need to seek further compensation for Jarvie's inclusion!

Peter Mackie scored his first St. Mirren goal in a see-saw battle at Tannadice on 3 November, a game in which Mark Fulton was red-carded. Kenny McDowall netted his and St. Mirren's opener a week later in another thriller against Hearts. Unfortunately, Saints went down 3-2 in both games. Attendances were still poor, as was highlighted when a mere 2,877 turned up at Love Street on 17 November for the 2-1 victory over Dundee. Defender Neil Cooper suffered a serious knee injury in this match and missed the remainder of the season.

Campbell Money and Derek Hamilton made a welcome return in the last fixture of November and, with neither Fulton nor Cooper available to partner Clarke in defence, Billy Abercromby moved back as the team took the lead at Celtic Park with Brian Gallagher's eleventh minute shot. Seventy-nine minutes later the referee's whistle brought the match to an end. Celtic 7 St. Mirren 1.

Twenty-three goals had been conceded in nine matches. As a result, Mark Fulton was returned to central defence as Preston North End thereafter enquired about his availability but did not follow up their interest. The feeling of unrest then continued with Peter Mackie submitting a written transfer request.

Another poor crowd of 2,490 watched St. Mirren contribute little to a dull goalless home draw with Dumbarton, but the inclusion of Gardner Speirs for his first League appearance of the season inspired the side to a 3-2 win at Easter Road. McDowall, Speirs and Abercromby were the scorers and Hibs were becoming favourites for relegation along with Morton.

Apart from the first two fixtures back in August, Saints had been unable to field the same eleven players in two successive games. As the festive period arrived it was the turn of Winnie, Scanlon and McDowall to sit in the stand, and the following players faced up to Aberdeen at St. Mirren Park on 29 December; Money, Wilson, Hamilton, Rooney, Fulton, Clarke, Fitzpatrick, McAvennie, Gallagher, Abercromby and Speirs.

Gallagher and McAvennie countered an early McDougall strike to put Saints ahead at half-time. Although the Dons hit an equaliser to end the match at 2-2, this was a much-improved home performance from the Buddies and one which inspired them to win their next three matches. The first of which was a 2-0 Ne'erday triumph away to Morton with the goals again coming from McAvennie and Gallagher.

Despite the improvement in results, Alex Miller wanted a more commanding presence in the heart of the defence, and he got just that when Peter Godfrey was brought in from Meadowbank Thistle in the first week of the New Year at a cost of £32,000. Big Peter made his debut in place of Fulton in the 1-0 victory over Dundee United.

This was the only change to the team that had performed so well against Aberdeen, and the Manager seemed happy with the formation. The same players picked up full points on a heavily sanded Tynecastle pitch a week later, with Gardner Speirs netting the winner when his thirty-yard free-kick bounced badly off the surface and deceived Henry Smith. Frank McAvennie's gesture of celebration to the home support earned him his second yellow card and an early bath.

The winter weather then took its toll and, in an effort to fix any kind of a bounce match during this period of poor ground conditions, Alex Miller even tried unsuccessfully to arrange a game against The Navy at Rosyth where Hearts had played a week previously on a near perfect pitch.

Kenny McDowall replaced the suspended McAvennie for the following visit of Celtic, prior to which Director Alan Marshall made a public appeal for fans to turn up early. Thankfully, there was no repeat of the crowd trouble from the sides' earlier meeting. The Glasgow side won by two goals, but the team returned to full strength for Monday 4 February's Scottish Cup Third Round tie in which the "ghost of Cowdenbeath" was well-and-truly exorcised. The League Cup defeat was forgotten as Saints recorded a comfortable 4-0 victory at Central Park with goals from Rooney, McAvennie, Gallagher and Speirs.

Kenny McDowall

A Board Meeting was hurriedly convened for 4pm on 9 January to discuss yet another offer from Luton Town for McAvennie. The offer was firmly rejected and the player responded by submitting a formal transfer request, which was also rejected with equal firmness!

All hopes of maintaining a settled side through to the end of the season were destroyed by injuries to Hamilton and Fitzpatrick at Dumbarton on 9 February, a situation compounded by the home side's second-half equaliser. A week later, Scottish Cup business saw David Winnie return at left-back, as young Fraser Campbell celebrated his own comeback with the only goal in the Fourth Round tie at Ayr.

A special train was organised to transport Paisley Buddies to the coast for the cup-tie, at a cost of £2 return per adult and £1 per child, helping to add considerably to the Somerset Park crowd.

Campbell then kept his place for the 1-0 defeat that followed at Dundee, but Peter Mackie was then asked to take over Tony Fitzpatrick's role for the following week's game against Hibs. This match was preceded by a minute's silence, and the players wore black armbands, to mark the passing of 1959 Cup hero John "Cockles" Wilson. The team did its bit to honour his memory by winning thanks to a Speirs penalty and a goal from substitute McDowall.

The visiting fans once again departed the terracings early and the anxious home fans were happy not to suffer the previous encounter's barrage of masonry. However, the Edinburgh "casuals" surprised everyone by boldly marching in through the open Love Street gates and squaring up to the home-bound Paisley support on the exit slope. Fortunately there were no serious injuries, but football violence was becoming an ever-increasing problem for the authorities to handle.

Happier news came with another success in the County Cup. Retaining the new format of a one-off meeting, which was introduced during the previous season, the trophy was lifted yet again. Morton 2 St Mirren 3. Local pride satisfied, always welcome!

Saints were holding on to fifth spot in the Division but would need a strong finishing quarter to fight off Dundee and Hearts for the final UEFA Cup place. March opened with a trip to Aberdeen where a 3-0 defeat moved Saints one position in the wrong direction. Perhaps the best chance of playing in Europe would come through the Scottish Cup.

The Quarter-Final draw brought Dundee United to Paisley on 9 March and, as Saints had defeated Jim McLean's side twice already at home in the League and also twice in recent years in the Scottish Cup, the omens appeared positive for reaching a fourth successive semi-final. Well, mostly positive, because the Club expressed its amazement at the appointment of a Dundee-based referee, Mr. Valentine, to officiate the tie!

1959 Cup-winning legends Tommy Bryceland and Alistair Miller were present as guests of the Club and how the Saints' fans must have wished for their talents on the field as Dundee United eventually ran out comfortable 4-1 victors.

As well as missing the suspended McAvennie, Saints lost Campbell Money for a period of the match after he suffered a nasty facial injury clashing with Paul Sturrock in the move that led to United's second goal. Mark Fulton took over between the sticks until the brave 'keeper returned and, as the match degenerated into ill-temper, Paul Sturrock was sent off for clashing with a grounded Billy Abercromby. Both Alex Miller and Campbell Money were later severely censured by the SFA for remarks made following the match.

Out of the Cup, St. Mirren could now focus all energies on the final eight League fixtures in the quest for Europe. Injuries to Clarke and Rooney further disrupted selections, but the team certainly "had a go" and won five of the eight games.

Cameron and Scanlon (twice), scored to see off Rangers on 16 March, and Winnie, Speirs (twice), and Gallagher took Saints through in a thriller against Dundee. Four wins in the four meetings with Hibs was achieved in style; Winnie, McAvennie (twice) and Gallagher firing the goals past Alan Rough for a 4-0 trouncing in Edinburgh, and Peter Godfrey scored his first goal for the Club in a keenly fought match against Dumbarton.

Amongst the victories were a 3-1 defeat at Tannadice and a 3-0 reverse at Celtic Park. These were not altogether unexpected, though.

May 11 arrived with the UEFA place a straight battle between St Mirren and Dundee. Had it not been for a surprise 3-2 home defeat to already relegated Morton on 2 April, Saints would by now have made sure of Europe. That was a rare 1980s defeat to the Buddies County rivals who sped to a two goal lead within the opening three minutes and then stole both points in the dying seconds after Campbell Money dropped a simple free-kick.

So, instead of facing the final day of the season almost certain of finishing fourth ahead of Rangers, St. Mirren needed a win against Hearts to stay clear of Dundee in fifth place and gain the last UEFA spot. Those fans with a particularly positive outlook noted that a victory over Hearts together with a heavy Rangers defeat at Easter Road could still see St Mirren sneak into fourth place. As there was a goal-difference of eighteen in Rangers' favour it was an unlikely outcome!

By half-time at least the results were going in the right direction. St. Mirren 2 Hearts 1 (two Brian Gallagher goals against a Kenny Black penalty) and Hibs 1 Rangers 0. Only sixteen goals to make up now! The less optimistic chose to focus on the interval score from Dens Park, although that was an unnecessary precaution as Speirs, Mackie and McAvennie added to Saints' total in the second period. Had Stevie Clarke scored in the Hearts net rather than his own it might have inspired even more. 5-2 was a great win, nonetheless. Europe again awaited the Saints!

Campbell Money later received a letter of commendation from the SFA for his actions in helping prevent possible violence after the final whistle of the Hearts' game. Rival fans had begun to spill over from the terracing and "Dibble's" Tulliallan training came in handy to help "police" Saints' fans back over the wall.

Fourth equal on points. Fifth on goal difference. Frank McAvennie topped the goal-scoring list with sixteen League goals. Brian Gallagher netted nine in his first season. The total of seventeen wins and four draws was a big improvement. As was seven away wins. The enhanced bonus scheme for results at Ibrox, Parkhead, Pittodrie and Tannadice was not a success, however. Saints managed just that opening day draw at Ibrox. In the other seven trips, four goals were scored and twenty-five conceded. The Manager would have to devise a different plan for improving the team's performance away to the League's top clubs. All-in-all, though, it had been a reasonably successful campaign.

1985-86

A new season dawned which was to be one of sharp contrasts, a fact no better illustrated than by the Club's experiences in the UEFA Cup from mid-September through to early November.

A more than decent performance wearing a specially ordered all-blue strip behind the "Iron Curtain" in Prague against European competition regulars Slavia was followed up by a magnificent night in Paisley on 17 September. A 42nd minute attempted clearance that deflected in off Brian Gallagher levelled the tie and took the teams into thirty minutes of extra-time, during which Frank McGarvey, who had re-joined St. Mirren at a cost of £94,000 from Celtic during the close-season, added two more in front of an estimated 18,000.

It was later learned that the visitors' boots had been lost in transit and that replacements had to be hurriedly sought from a branch of "Army and Navy Stores" in the town's Piazza shopping centre! Nevertheless, a notable scalp had been taken.

Brian Gallagher then became the first Scottish player to score an away hat-trick in the UEFA Cup when Saints drew 3-3 in Sweden against Hammarby. Each goal was a gem and the score could easily have been 5-1 in St. Mirren's favour as two other goals were questionably ruled-out and the hosts were gifted two goals of their own.

However, these two exceptional results counted for nothing when defeat was snatched from the jaws of victory in the home leg with Hammarby on 6 November. The visitors scored twice in the final three minutes to win 2-1 on the night and 5-4 on aggregate. Many fans had actually left for home with the score 1-0, thinking that the tie was safely won. Inexperience on the pitch cost the team and the Club dearly. To say that emotions were "contrasted" after these two home ties would be a massive understatement.

During the closed season, Mark Fulton, who had fallen out of favour during the previous campaign, left to join Hibernian for £52,000 and the Frank McAvennie transfer saga eventually ended, with a final Luton bid outdone by West Ham United at the eleventh hour. The "Hammers" paid St. Mirren £350,000. This was the highest transfer fee received by the Club to date and it was more than welcome because, despite the sales of the previous summer, Saints' bank overdraft had again crept up to just below £200,000.

The commercial side of football was on the increase. St. Mirren's Lottery continued to make a significant contribution to the Club's income through the 50,000-plus tickets sold weekly in and around Paisley, Saints' home matches were open to sponsorship by local companies, and "Graham's Buses" would once again appear on the team jerseys.

On a wider perspective The Scottish Football League was to be sponsored for the first time, something that would benefit each team in the Premier Division of the "Fine Fare League" to the tune of £10,000. For the fan, however, admission prices would again rise, the third increase in successive seasons.

Crowd safety was also becoming of increasing concern to footballing authorities; and not only due to hooliganism. Stringent safety checks were demanded in the aftermath of the 11 May disaster at Bradford City's Valley Parade ground, and the Club declared itself "very pleased" that the Main Stand was given the "all-clear". Being predominantly formed of wood within a steel framework, Saints' stand was similar to the Bradford construction that had caught fire, resulting in fifty-six deaths and hundreds more injured.

This was the first of a trio of stadium disasters that would have an impact on St. Mirren, and football in general, before the decade came to a close.

Jim Stewart's move to St. Mirren from Rangers was made permanent and defender Graeme Sinclair joined his hometown team after being released by Celtic. Unfortunately, Sinclair's chronic injury problems would not ease and he retired at the end of the season without making an appearance.

Tony Fitzpatrick at last agreed to commit himself to the Club for more than a month at a time by signing a one-year contract with an option for another. Billy Abercromby, however, preferred to continue playing on a month-to-month basis. The injured Neil Cooper's request for a transfer was accepted by Alex Miller, and notice of his availability was circulated to the leading clubs in Scotland and England. "If he wants to leave St. Mirren that's up to him," the Manager insisted. Youngsters Stevie Clarke and David Winnie were signed up until June 1989.

Wins over Waterford, Portadown and Kilkenny during a tour of Ireland helped prepare the players for the season ahead, and a good season it promised to be if the first couple of months were anything to go by. In addition to the Slavia Prague success, First Division Kilmarnock and Morton were comprehensively beaten during August in the Skol League

The only returns had come from a 3-2 win against Hibs on 24 August and a 1-1 draw at Pittodrie on 21 September. One positive, Neil Cooper made his return to action at Pittodrie, settling into a mid-field role in preference to Peter Mackie.

Something that became apparent in the first half of the season was that St. Mirren no longer had a potent strike threat from any individual player. Goals were being spread around the team. Gallagher (8), Speirs (7), McGarvey (7), Fitzpatrick (4), Rooney (3), Mackie (2), Godfrey (2), and a single each from McDowall and Clarke accounted for the thirty-five goals scored in the twenty-one competitive matches until the 1-1 draw with Clydebank at New Kilbowie on 13 November.

Derek Hamilton missed this Clydebank outing due to another injury and it was not until April that he was fit enough to be selected again on a regular basis. This allowed David Winnie to make a re-appearance in the side and Billy Abercromby also pushed himself back into contention. The defensive structure was further affected by injuries to Tommy Wilson and Stevie Clarke around the turn of the year.

Most specifically, the side struggled in the absence of a settled back-line and a recognised goalscorer in the five months through the winter from 13 November until 12 April. During eighteen League fixtures (half the full calendar) thirty-two goals were conceded and fifteen scored,

St. Mirren F. C. 1986/87 1st Team Squad
Back (left to right): Holmes (Physio), Godfrey, Lambert, Cooper, Winnie, Duffy, Money, Gallagher, Rooney, Clarke, B. Hamilton, Jarvie (Coach) Front (left to right): Ferguson (Asst Manager), Cameron, Speirs, McDowall, Wilson, Fitzpatrick, D. Hamilton, McGarvey, Abercromby, Miller (Manager).

Cup, 3-1 and 4-1 respectively, and Saints were extremely unfortunate to go out 2-1 on 4 September to Dundee United after dominating most of the second-half in the Quarter-Final at Tannadice.

In the Premier Division, the first home fixture on 17 August almost brought a repeat of the result in 1984-85's final match. In fact, it was even better. This time, Hearts were hammered by six goals to two and it was encouraging also to have an attendance in excess of six thousand. Keeping to the theme, six different players netted for Saints; Speirs, Godfrey, McGarvey, Fitzpatrick, Clarke and Rooney!

Neil Cooper was not yet fully fit and the Manager showed consistency of selection until his return in late September, fielding Money, Wilson, Hamilton, Rooney, Godfrey, Clarke, Fitzpatrick, Mackie, McGarvey, Gallagher and Speirs.

Home form, in particular, was impressive. Five of the opening six League fixtures in Paisley were won. The 6-2 victory versus Hearts; 4-1 against Motherwell; 1-0 against Dundee United; 1-0 versus Dundee; and 2-1 over Rangers, a game in which the Saints' supporting Paisley Daily Express reporter, Bill Leckie, counted fourteen good chances created by the Buddies! Another positive: home attendances were definitely on the rise.

The single defeat during these six fixtures was to bottom-of-the-table Clydebank on 31 August. A result that may have been another example of the effects of over-confidence at work.

Away from home, by contrast, the deficiencies of 1983-84 were much in evidence. There had been defeats to Dundee, Rangers, Celtic, Hearts and Motherwell by the time Saints made their exit from the UEFA Cup.

and the team netted more than one goal in only two League fixtures, both against Clydebank. As a consequence, victories were difficult to come by. Indeed, only four matches were won, three drawn, and the remaining eleven were lost during these five months.

The effect on away form was even more dramatic. The 2-0 win at Clydebank on 22 March was the first on-the-road since defeating Hibs 3-2 on 24 August; a run of eleven away fixtures without a victory. Significantly, Saints' goal difference would drop from negative five in 1984-85 to negative twenty-one in 1985-86.

During January, a squad of players was taken to the Ingliston indoor arena on the outskirts of Edinburgh to play in the third annual "Tennent's Sixes" competition. Following four victories out of five the team reached the final but lost 3-0 to Aberdeen. The Club awarded each player a £200 bonus for their efforts.

Despite the downturn in League form, St. Mirren managed once again to reach the Quarter-Final of the Scottish Cup. An away draw in the Third Round sent the side to Methil on 25 January to face East Fife who were performing well in the First Division. The Fifers' determined display and a rock-hard pitch made for a nervy ninety minutes that ended in a 1-1 draw. Saints remained confident, though, and goals from Clarke, Gallagher and Speirs saw them safely through the replay ten days later with a 3-1 scoreline.

Promotion chasing Falkirk presented Saints' next Cup challenge. The tie was postponed on no fewer than five occasions due to the inclement weather before finally being played on Monday 4 March at St. Mirren Park. The "Bairns" equalised Frank McGarvey's opener with a penalty and a replay was required. The Quarter-Final ties were by now due to be played at the end of the week, so it was off to muddy Brockville twenty-four hours later for the second instalment of Round Four. The pitch was barely playable, however Saints comfortably progressed 3-0 with goals from Rooney, Gallagher and Speirs.

Disappointingly, the Quarter-Final provided another cup anti-climax for Saints' fans. Playing in Edinburgh on Sunday 9 March, Hearts opened the scoring and Campbell Money was carried off with concussion all within ten minutes of the start. Neil Cooper took over the goalkeeper's gloves but could do little to halt the maroon tide as Hearts, aiming for a League and Cup double, powered to a 4-1 victory.

Out of the Scottish Cup and with little prospect of achieving a UEFA place, Alex Miller gave teenager Brian Hamilton his debut in the 1-1 home draw with Aberdeen on 15 March in place of the injured Tony Fitzpatrick. The youngster went on to play in eight of the closing ten fixtures and Paul Lambert was also given his first taste of Premier Division action when he came on as substitute for Jim Rooney at Fir Park on 12 April. Drew Jarvie and Brian Gallagher scored the goals in a 2-1 victory.

That Motherwell match broke a run of four straight defeats in which only one goal had been scored and twelve lost, the worst being a 5-0 drubbing at Tannadice on 8 April, and heralded three 2-1 successes in a row. In the second of these, on 19 April, McGarvey and Abercromby put Saints 2-0 ahead against Rangers at St. Mirren Park before Ally Dawson pulled one back in the second-half. In the third, two Brian Gallagher goals nullified Ian Redford's opener for Dundee United and gave St. Mirren ample revenge for the previous visit to Tannadice three weeks earlier.

A brief interruption to League business came on 1 May in the shape of the annual Renfrewshire Cup tussle with Morton. In the 1986 Final, a single Paul Lambert goal enabled a mix of first-team and reserve players to retain the trophy for yet another year as well as continue the team's current winning streak.

The run of success heartened the supporters into believing that the final game of the season on 3 May could also bring a reversal of Celtic's 2-1 win at Love Street five weeks previously on 5 April. The visiting fans had their own agenda. Trailing Hearts in the title race for the majority of the campaign they knew that a victory in Paisley, coupled with a defeat for Hearts at Dens Park, would leave the two sides level on points. In fact, a 3-0 win would be sufficient to take the championship if Hearts were to lose. By half-time Celtic were four up. Their fifth goal was the 5000th lost by St. Mirren in the Scottish League.

What a contrast to Saints' first home league fixture back on 17 August! It was a bad end to the season, especially as St. Mirren's supporters were confident going into the match, and their favourites had started brightly against the Celts.

Many followers of the Tynecastle club blamed St. Mirren for Hearts' failure to secure the title. Certainly, taking St. Mirren's 5-0 defeat to Celtic together with that 6-2 victory over Hearts at Love Street back in August meant that Saints had contributed heavily to the goals differential against Hearts. The truth is that Hearts held their fate firmly in their own hands before going down 2-0 at Dens!

As for St. Mirren's supporters, many retained their own particular bitterness for season 1985-86, as the Hammarby defeat in November would come to represent a turning point in the Club's fortunes. Thirty-one points and seventh place was the poorest end to a season since the thirty points and eighth place back in 1977-78, the Club's first Premier Division season.

There were, however, still at least a couple of glorious occasions to celebrate before reaching the Club's 125th birthday, and one of them would arrive as quickly as the following season!

1986-87

The "St Mirren" name was introduced to the African continent when an eight-day, two-game tour of Nigeria was undertaken during July. On return from their African safari the team then travelled to Ireland for a second successive year. Among four victories in the Emerald Isle, Saints' defeated Eire's European Cup representatives Shamrock Rovers 1-0, before returning home to face West Ham United on Saturday 2 August.

The "Hammers" included a certain Frank McAvennie in their line-up but his performance was outshone by that of Frank McGarvey who netted twice in Saints' comfortable 3-0 win. Meanwhile, a proposed testimonial match for Tony Fitzpatrick against English outfit Watford failed to materialise.

This hectic schedule involved playing nine matches in less than four weeks and in three different countries. Unlike the previous two close-seasons, however, the summer of 1986 was relatively quiet on the transfer front. Free-transfers were given to Jim Stewart and Peter Mackie while Ian Scanlon, a favourite with the supporters, was forced to retire following his long struggle to overcome injury, having managed just a single substitute appearance during 1985-86.

Speirs, Rooney and Derek Hamilton extended their contracts to the end of the forthcoming season, but Cooper and Wilson would only agree to sign on a month-to-month basis. Bids for Rangers' trio Robert Fleck, Bobby Williamson and Robert Russell were unsuccessful so the list of players joining the Club was restricted to five teenagers; Lambert, McWhirter, Butler, Shaw and Kerr each of whom signed for one year under the Government's new Youth Training Scheme.

St. Mirren were the first club in Scotland to take advantage of the new initiative, perhaps not surprisingly, as the Manpower Services Commission officer helping the Club complete the necessary paperwork was none other than former top-goalscorer Doug Somner!

Manager Alex Miller was offered a new two-year contract that contained a clause indicating that the agreement was terminable in the event of relegation. This was the first reference to any possibility of demotion since the Club had consolidated its top tier status and, as the Premier Division had been enlarged by the addition of two clubs for the forthcoming season, it was an inclusion that may have aroused criticism at the time had it been made public.

Fortunately, there was no relegation, however a change of Manager would take place before the season had reached its halfway point and, on the field of play, the widely contrasting fortunes of the previous season would continue. An early humiliation left Saints' fans in turmoil, yet the season was to end on such a "high" as had not been experienced by the "Buddies" of Paisley for twenty-eight years!

Competitive play commenced with a run of three matches in the new twelve-team Fine Fare League Premier Division and, in a major irony given the events of the final Saturday of 1985-86, the first-day fixtures saw St. Mirren play host to Hearts, while Dundee would visit Celtic Park!

Alex Miller's first selection of the season was Money, Clarke, Abercromby, Fitzpatrick, Godfrey, Cooper, Lambert, Winnie, McGarvey, Speirs, and Gallagher, with Wilson and McDowall on the bench. The Love Street match on 9 August attracted a healthy attendance of 8,869 but, perhaps mercifully, it finished in a fairly uneventful no-scoring draw.

A midweek trip to Dens Park resulted in a 2-1 defeat, following which Tony Fitzpatrick suffered a double fracture of his jaw on 16 August in the 1-1 draw at Motherwell, an injury that was to keep him out of the side for two months. As cover for Fitzpatrick, former Saint Dougie Bell was signed on a month's loan from Rangers and he made his second debut four days later as St. Mirren entered the season's Skol Cup with an away tie at Dunfermline.

Progress into the Third Round was earned thanks to a Frank McGarvey double, however the following three matches through to the end of August left the fans in despair and the team in apparent disarray.

Firstly, Clydebank took both points from St. Mirren Park in a game that saw Saints' fan Stuart Gordon net the only goal, Speirs miss a penalty, and Winnie carried off. As a result Winnie's services were lost to the team until the following Spring.

Drew Jarvie then departed Paisley to become assistant manager of Dundee a few days before Saints made a third trip of the decade to Station Park, Forfar in the League Cup. This game on Wednesday 27 August resulted in St. Mirren's first ever defeat to the Angus club; although the emphatic 5-1 scoreline wasn't so much a defeat as a stunning blow to all associated with St. Mirren. Scarves were thrown to the ground as the travelling fans directed their anger at Manager Miller and the Directors.

Three Supporters' Clubs voted to boycott the next match and, for those who did head back along many of those same miles to reach Tayside for a League fixture with Dundee United on the Saturday, the journey could not have been pleasant. Returning home after another loss, this time by three goals to nil, would have been even less so.

Frank McGarvey indicated his dissatisfaction at recent events by tabling a transfer request and Alex Miller moved quickly to add new faces to his squad and hopefully new spirit to the dressing room.

The first addition was Paul Chalmers, signed from Celtic for £15,000. The twenty-two year-old had been unable to establish himself in the Parkhead first-team and made his St. Mirren debut in an entertaining 1-1 draw with Aberdeen on 6 September. Paul Lambert scored his first-ever senior goal, netting within sixty seconds of Billy Stark's 40th minute opener, and it was only the brilliance of the visitors' international 'keeper that denied Saints' victory in the closing stages. Another piece of good news was the return from injury of Derek Hamilton.

During the following week a second signing was made, that of Ian Ferguson for £64,000 from Clyde. Miller had been pursuing the nineteen year-old's signature since the summer and fought off strong interest from Liverpool to convince the youngster that his immediate future lay in Paisley. It was to prove a significant signing indeed!

Ferguson took over the number "8" jersey from Brian Hamilton and made his debut on 13 September, scoring the only goal with a superb volley following an Abercromby corner, in a victory against Hibs at Easter Road that lifted the team two places from second-bottom of the Division. Dougie Bell was then unexpectedly recalled by Rangers and sold to Hibs, despite having been loaned to Saints' until the end of the season.

Spirit within the side had undoubtedly revived. Frank McGarvey netted the only goal against Falkirk on 20 September, and a week later the team fought back from being behind at the interval to defeat Hamilton Academical 2-1 with a Cameron penalty and a McGarvey strike. These successive home wins at the end of September saw Saints climb to seventh place, a position the team would retain until the end of the season.

Although home attendances had been disappointing, the defeat at Forfar had certainly done nothing to encourage stay-at-home fans to venture down to Love Street. Meagre crowds of 3,070 and 2,640 paid to see these two home victories against the two promoted clubs. St. Mirren had assumed a relatively healthy financial state following the big-money transfers of the recent past, however the current level of weekly income was far from sufficient to cover expenditure. It was a concern.

Despite this situation the Club was able to reject a substantial bid from Celtic for young captain Stevie Clarke who was currently out of the side following an injury picked up in the recent win at Easter Road. Saints also agreed a new three-year contract with seventeen year-old Paul Lambert, a first-team regular since the start of the season.

Yet another injury, this time to new signing Paul Chalmers, resulted in the Manager trying unsuccessfully to swap Jim Rooney for Kilmarnock striker Sam McGivern, before handing out-of-favour Brian Gallagher the chance to regain his place in the side.

October saw Peter Cormack join St. Mirren as Alex Miller's assistant just in time for back-to-back meetings with the Old Firm. Unfortunately, Stevie Clarke broke down in an attempted comeback at Celtic Park as the side lost 2-0, and a single goal gave Rangers both points seven days later in Paisley.

These two defeats were quickly swept aside though as the team played a further four games without loss to re-assert its improved form. With Stevie Clarke's return the team line-up had a settled look. Alex Miller regularly fielded Money, Clarke, D. Hamilton, Ferguson, Godfrey, Cooper, Gallagher, Speirs, McGarvey, Abercromby and Cameron, with Paul Lambert enjoying a "rest" on the bench together with fit-again Tony Fitzpatrick. A further boost came when news was received of Ian Ferguson's first inclusion in the Scotland Under-21 squad.

Away draws against Hearts and Clydebank were interspersed with home victories over Dundee (which included a McGarvey hat-trick) and Motherwell. However, that midweek 1-0 win over the Fir Parkers on 29 October was achieved at a cost. A confrontation between Billy Abercromby and Motherwell's Steve Kirk, following the award of a 24th minute penalty to Saints, resulted in both players being ordered-off for "violent conduct".

Yet, so incensed was Saints' midfielder that, as a result of his repeated remonstrations, he was reported twice more for "foul and abusive language". In total, Abercromby had committed no fewer than three red-card offences and the incident resulted in a distinctly undesirable "world-record" being accredited to the Club's playing captain. He then received a hefty twelve-match ban from the SFA and, furthermore, was fined £500 by the Club and placed on the open-to-transfer list. For the record, Gardner Speirs missed the penalty kick!

Tony Fitzpatrick stepped in to replace Abercromby but even so the team slumped to a run of nine games with only a single victory, 3-1 at home to Hibs on 15 November. Meantime, Jim Rooney was sold to Dumbarton for £8,500 having made only a single appearance as substitute during the trying start to the season.

On Friday 5 December, two days after a 2-0 defeat at Ibrox, Alex Miller ended speculation linking him with the vacant posts at Aberdeen and Hibs by announcing that he was leaving St. Mirren to become manager of Hibernian. Peter Cormack took control of the first team for the no-scoring home draw with Hearts and the 6-3 defeat away to Dundee, a game in which Saints were 5-0 behind at one point; to make matters worse 'keeper Campbell Money was sent off. Cormack then left together with Martin Ferguson to join Alex Miller in Edinburgh.

A group of Saints fans at Shawlands Cross en-route for the '87 winning Final.
Note: The wee boy sipping his drink is a young Steven McGarry – later to win a First Division medal with 'his team'.

The St. Mirren Board considered that the crop of young talent at the Club would be best served by the appointment of a recognised, established coach, and decided to interview two men for the managerial vacancy; long-time Stirling Albion boss and Scotland Youth Coach Alex Smith, and former St. Mirren player and Scottish internationalist Archie Gemmill. Shortly thereafter, Gemmill advised the Board that he was no longer able to attend and so, following a successful interview, Alex Smith became St. Mirren's twenty-third Team Manager. Another two appointments quickly followed. Former Saints' player Jimmy Bone arrived as Assistant Manager and Archie Rose as Reserve Team Manager.

In common with a growing trend towards compensating clubs for the loss of staff, St. Mirren were paid £25,000 by Hibs and, in turn, wrote Arbroath a cheque for £9,000 to cover the termination of Jimmy Bone's contract as player-manager at Gayfield.

Alex Smith's first game in charge came on Saturday 20 December at home to Clydebank in front of a disappointing crowd of 2,601. The team sheet read; Barney Duffy, Clarke, Derek Hamilton, Fitzpatrick, Godfrey, Cooper, Cameron, Brian Hamilton, McGarvey, Chalmers and Speirs, with Lambert and Gallagher on the bench. Money, Ferguson and Abercromby were missing through suspension.

The fixture was won 3-1 and young Lambert made a successful return following a cracked shoulder bone, but Gallagher suffered a leg-break that would effectively end his St. Mirren career. Victory at Motherwell a week later brought the curtain down on 1986 and gave Saints two wins in a row for the first time since September. However, three straight defeats in the first games of the New Year robbed the team and its new manager of any further impetus, and only four more League matches were won from the eighteen remaining fixtures.

Heightening interest in Stevie Clarke resulted in an Emergency Board Meeting being called on Thursday 15 January. There had been "firm" enquiries from Celtic, Rangers, West Ham United and Chelsea, and the resolution of the Meeting was that these clubs should be informed of St. Mirren's position that "while we were not concerned if the player were not to be sold, we would be willing to accept an offer of not less than £400,000".

As it transpired, Clarke had played his last match in a St. Mirren jersey and was sold to Chelsea within days for a fee of £422,000. Scotland Youth international goalkeeper Les Fridge moved in the other direction at a cost of £54,000.

Following Clarke's departure as few as 1,965 paid to watch Ian Ferguson's pile-driver clinch a midweek home win over Falkirk on 27 January. Already missing half a team through injury, the Falkirk game ended with the new Manager short of another player as Tony Fitzpatrick was taken off with ligament damage, he would play in only two more full games to the end of the season.

On that same evening, Alex Smith reported to the monthly Board Meeting his view that "it should be possible to sign players from the lower Divisions in Scotland for relatively modest fees - up to about £50,000, who he felt could do a good job for us as full-time players in the Premier League". As Smith had one or two players in mind he was authorised to open negotiations.

Frank McGarvey made a welcome return to the team for the Third Round Scottish Cup tie against Highland League Inverness Caledonian, played at St. Mirren Park on Saturday 31 January. High-scoring Caley were already in an almost unassailable position at the top of their League and they gave an excellent account of themselves for an hour in Paisley despite the treacherous underfoot conditions.

The Highlanders could actually have been ahead by half-time, and even after Kenny McDowall headed St. Mirren in front five minutes after the break it took a great save by Money to stop Caley from equalising. Two quick goals finally settled the tie in Saints' favour. Firstly, McDowall set up McGarvey in the 68th minute then, five minutes later, Ferguson netted an explosive thirty-five yard free-kick to allow Saints to eventually make comfortable progress into Round Four.

Gary Peebles took over the right-back berth in a 3-0 defeat the following Saturday at Celtic Park, and David Winnie suffered a recurrence of the ligament damage which had already kept him out of action for four months. It was only his third game back in the team and meant at least another month on the sidelines. Due to injuries and suspensions, Smith had been forced to field no fewer than twenty players in his first eight matches in charge. Hardly an ideal baptism for the new boss!

Visitors Rangers then inflicted Saints' eighth defeat in twelve League games since mid-November, winning 3-1 on St. Valentine's Day. One week later it was back to Cup business; serious Cup business in the shape of an away Renfrewshire Derby on 21 February. Quite incredibly it was now the fifth time in six years that the County rivals had been drawn together in the two major cup competitions, and the appearance of ex-Saints Lex Richardson and Rowan Alexander in the First Division pace-setters' line-up added extra spice (if any were needed) to what turned out to be an electric and controversial tie.

Paul Chalmers put St. Mirren ahead with an early goal after intercepting a pass-back. Before the break Morton scored and it was all-square at half-time. Action swung from end to end as the respective sets of supporters roared on their favourites. The home side then grabbed the lead with a penalty after Cooper had handled but within sixty seconds referee Duncan awarded a spot kick to Saints when Derek Hamilton went down under a clumsy challenge. Ian Ferguson's driven kick was blocked but he reacted quickest and forced home the equaliser!

Then, with only six minutes remaining Chalmers netted his second with a real opportunist goal. The St. Mirren supporters nearly raised the roof off the Cappielow cover. It was a good hard-fought win over a confident Morton side that would go on to win promotion as First Division champions. Victory was sweet, and the Saints were on the march!

The Quarter-Final line-up paired St. Mirren with a confident Raith Rovers, the Second Division leaders, yet injured skipper Tony Fitzpatrick's cry that "we can win the Cup!" left many still to be convinced. Perhaps for the first time since the beginning of the decade, there was actually little feeling of optimism amongst the support that a Cup win was "on-the-cards".

Back on League duty four days after the scintillating success over Morton, St. Mirren ended Aberdeen's fifteen match unbeaten run by winning 1-0 at Love Street with another Ian Ferguson rocket. The attendance; 3,553.

Alex Smith's transfer negotiations resulted in a down payment of £25,000 being made for one of his former players at Stirling Albion, Keith Walker, who would remain with the Second Division side until the end of the season. On the commercial front a second local bus operator, Clydeside Scottish Omnibuses, agreed to become the Club's new shirt sponsor from 21 March. The previous four-year deal with Graham's Bus Service had been the longest lasting among Premier Division clubs.

Scottish Cup Winners Medal won by David Winnie.

Two disappointing 1-0 League defeats then preceded the Cup trip to Kirkcaldy, the first being a fixture at Tynecastle that was described by Alex Smith as "a rugby game played with a football". Nevertheless, Saturday 14 March summoned up a sunny day on the Fife coast, and the presence of a large Saints' support amongst the 8,392 crowd caused the start to be delayed for fifteen minutes.

The more experienced Tommy Wilson, who was still signing on a monthly basis, took over from Gary Peebles in defence, Peter Godfrey headed St Mirren in front after seventeen minutes, and Paul Chalmers put a better reflection on the scoreline with a last-minute goal. Cup bonuses of £170, £275 and £450 had now been paid out to the players. In stark contrast to expectations created by the team's performances in the Skol Cup and the Premier Division, St. Mirren had reached another Scottish Cup Semi-Final and fans were now believing that this could indeed be Saints' year.

Alex Smith certainly thought so. He described his side as a "big occasion team" and Saints' weekly League form supported the manager's judgement. The Cup victory against Raith was followed by a scrappy 1-1 draw at Love Street with Motherwell and a 2-1 defeat away to relegation bound Clydebank. Yet, the team travelled to Aberdeen and repeated the 1-0 home scoreline of a month previously with a rare Tommy Wilson goal, gaining a first win in the Granite City for four years.

Seven days later, on 4 April, Cooper and Cameron netted the team's first goals in four meetings with Dundee United and halted the run of three successive losses to the "Terrors". The 2-1 win over United was played a week before St. Mirren would journey to Hampden Park to play Hearts for a place in the Cup Final, yet the 2,538 attendance at Love Street that day was among the lowest of the season.

In keeping with tradition, Saints took off to Seamill for the week in preparation for the Semi-Final. On the coast the financial rewards for winning the next two ties were revealed; £1000 for the semi, £1500 for the final! Unfortunately, due to injury neither of the Fourth Round goalscorers, Peter Godfrey and Paul Chalmers, would play any further part in the competition.

The Hampden Semi-Final on 11 April was a tense affair played in front of 32,390, approximately 15,000 of whom favoured black and white. Both teams were missing key players, and David Winnie replaced

"Buddies Bathtime" - Cup celebrations in the Hampden tub!

Manager Alex Smith, Assistant Manager Jimmy Bone, Archie Rose and Bobby Holmes atop the bus as Saints return to Paisley in triumph following the 1-0 extra time victory over Dundee United.

"finals", his university degree examinations.

These five fixtures passed winless with only two goals scored, but Alex Smith's concern remained focussed on Cup Final Day and how many of his injured quartet, Fitzpatrick, Godfrey, Chalmers and Gallagher, could be nursed to fitness.

Following the week at Seamill, Smith decided that only Tony Fitzpatrick could be risked and even then "Fitz" would start the match on the substitutes' bench.

St. Mirren's opponents at Hampden would be UEFA Cup Finalists Dundee United. The Tannadice team were formidable opponents but perhaps had their attentions divided between two crucial matches, as they also had to face IFK Gothenburg in the second-leg of their UEFA Cup Final on 20 May. Quite properly, St. Mirren were deemed Hampden underdogs, however, as so often happens it was a determined Saints' side that responded better to the pressures of the day.

On 16 May 1987, an estimated 35,000 St. Mirren supporters took their places among the 51,782 on the Hampden Park slopes for an encounter billed by the media as "The People's Final". In truth, it was a disappointing match. A cautious, nervy, ninety minutes proved uneventful. The outcome then hinged on a five-minute spell during the second period of extra-time.

United had a "goal" controversially disallowed for offside ... 35,000 Buddies breathed an audible sigh of relief. Then, taking strength from this good fortune, cheered on "the famous stripes" with renewed enthusiasm. Saints responded quickly while United could only watch as Ian Ferguson ran on to a flicked pass from Brian Hamilton, held off the challenge of a defender, and hammered a left-foot shot past ex-Saint Billy Thomson in the United goal.

Cue bedlam among 35,000 Buddies, then jangling nerves as the minutes passed until Kenny Hope blew the final whistle. Saints had won the Cup for the first time since 1959, and deservedly so. Being St. Mirren's 110th year it felt fitting to learn that the timing of the winning goal was recorded as the 110th minute!

The victorious line-up was Money, Wilson, Derek Hamilton, Abercromby, Winnie, Cooper, McGarvey, Ferguson, McDowall, Brian Hamilton and Lambert, with Fitzpatrick and Cameron (who had actually completed his university exams on the very morning of the Final) coming off the bench late in the match. Spare a thought, also, for physiotherapist Bobby Holmes, now able to savour a Cup triumph after missing out as a player in 1959.

On the day Tony Fitzpatrick, Frank McGarvey and Billy Abercromby gained the unique distinction of being the only players in the Club's first 125 Years to have played in both a League title winning season and a Scottish Cup winning year. Team Captain Abercromby led his players up the South Stand steps to receive the Cup, the oldest trophy in world football, before turning towards the massed fans on the West Terracing and thrusting it triumphantly into the air, just as David Lapsley had done twenty-eight years previously.

The St. Mirren party returned to Paisley in an open-top bus (appropriately provided by new sponsors Clydeside Scottish) for a brief reception in the Town Hall, and were greeted by thousands of fans in and around the town centre. Pubs charged 1959 prices, streets were closed

Godfrey in the centre of the defence, while Brian Hamilton made his first appearance of the Cup run allowing Ian Ferguson to be pushed forward to lead the attack.

Ferguson's speed and strength caused the Hearts' rearguard no end of problems and it was fitting that he should open the scoring, beating Henry Smith to a through pass before cutting the ball into the net from an acute angle. With fifteen minutes remaining the Edinburgh team equalised, but Frank McGarvey settled the issue with a clever shot on the turn seven minutes from time. The Buddies had reached their first Final since 1962.

In a season liberally sprinkled with disappointments, the remaining five Premier Division fixtures were played cautiously. The Manager rested Billy Abercromby for fear of further suspension and brought young Norrie McWhirter into the first team squad. Frank McGarvey was played sparingly and Ian Cameron was given time off to prepare for other to traffic, Robert Tannahill's statue sported a black-and-white scarf, and Paisley partied. Oh, how it partied! Afterwards, a celebratory Club dinner-dance was held in the Excelsior Hotel.

Next day, Sunday 17 May, Saints did it all again. Another open-top parade took the management and players through streets lined with flag-waving families before arriving at St. Mirren Park and the welcome of the 12,000 ecstatic supporters inside the famous old stadium.

Neither the season nor the trophy collecting was over, however. Immediately following Cup Final weekend, Alex Smith and his players jetted off to Singapore to take part in the Epson Invitational Tournament. In the group were new signings Keith Walker (£53,000) and Robert Dawson (£34,000) both from Stirling, and Mark McWalter (£53,000 from Arbroath).

The Buddies overcame the challenge of Perth Azzuri from Australia, English side Southampton, and the Mexicans Universidad Autonoma de Neza, to return home with the Epson Cup and complete a spectacular ending to what had been, on the League front at least, a largely frustrating season but an unforgettable one for all in the black-and-white end of Renfrewshire!

1987-88

Twenty-seven full-time players and seven YTS teenagers reported for training following the short summer break which had included a formal Civic Reception on 24 July in recognition of Saints' Hampden success. A Supporters' Rally organised by the Friends Of St Mirren Association (FOSMA) allowed fans the unique opportunity of being photographed with their chosen players and the famous old trophy itself.

There would be no closed season additions to the squad, but an eye-catching new strip was unveiled. The new look had equal numbers of black and white one-inch stripes distributed around the top, and sported a white "bib" effect on the chest that could display the Clydeside Scottish logo to best effect. The top was almost universally detested from the outset!

Alex Smith kept the pre-season programme deliberately light, a single high-profile friendly following a series of "exhibition" matches in the Western Isles and Galloway. Southampton provided the "real" opposition at Love Street and, with memories of the clubs' recent meeting in Singapore still fresh, the play degenerated into a physical battle that the English team eventually won 1-0.

That result aside, there was an understandable, renewed optimism around both the Club and the Town as, for the first time in many years, St. Mirren had a credit balance in the bank and silverware on display. Indeed, the Cup win had encouraged a welcome increase in season-ticket sales. Noticeably improved August attendances saw new signings Robert Dawson and Keith Walker make their home competitive debuts against Hearts and newly promoted local rivals Morton respectively.

Throughout 1986-87 there had been as many as fifteen League matches out of the twenty-two played at St. Mirren Park with an attendance below 4,000. During the new season that figure would drop to only four of the twenty-two, a real improvement! In fact, even setting aside the four Old Firm matches, St. Mirren's average home League gate during 1987-88 rose to 5,065, a healthy thirty percent increase compared to the previous season.

Unfortunately, this improvement in attendances was not mirrored by an improvement in the number of points gained or matches won, and hopes that the Cup triumph would act as a springboard to bounce Saints back into the League's top-five proved to be unfounded as the season progressed.

Neither was the team able to rise to the occasion in the annual cup competitions. Even given home advantage against lower division opponents, the Buddies were unable to survive the first hurdle in either of the major domestic tournaments.

On Tuesday 18 August, Saints' League Cup campaign opened and closed when St. Johnstone of the Second Division left Paisley with a thoroughly merited 1-0 win. The Club fared no better in its defence of the Scottish Cup when, in the Third Round opener on 30 January, the holders made an even more ignominious exit, 3-0 at the hands of a First Division Clydebank team that also missed a penalty!

St. Mirren and their supporters did, however, fare better in what was to be the last taste of European competition during the 1980s. First Round European Cup Winners' Cup opponents were Tromso, from the town of the same name lying three hundred and fifty miles inside the Norwegian Arctic Circle. Having watched Tromso play, Manager Alex Smith commented that the draw "could have been a lot worse" and reckoned that St. Mirren should be able to win the tie.

The Manager's major concern remained that of being able to field a team well enough equipped to do the job. Mark McWalter had not yet played due to a troublesome groin injury suffered in pre-season and Derek Hamilton was out injured once again. Brian Gallagher, Paul Chalmers, and the ever-popular Peter Godfrey all appeared to have recovered from their long-term injuries; although none of the three had yet re-established themselves in the team. There were also niggling doubts over the fitness of youngsters Lambert, Speirs, Cameron and Brian Hamilton to contend with.

Of equal concern was the need to keep Cup Final hero Ian Ferguson match-fit. The twenty year-old was in the middle of a five-game domestic suspension, so Smith arranged closed-door bounce matches to give Ferguson and the injury doubtfuls much needed practise. By matchday, Ferguson, Godfrey, Chalmers, Lambert and Cameron had proved themselves ready for selection but the Manager warned the support not to expect a team firing on all cylinders given the recent history of injuries and suspensions. He also stressed the importance of not conceding a home goal.

Quick-fire Saints made the best possible start to the home-leg on 16 September by scoring in the second minute when McDowall nudged the ball home with his knee from close range. Thereafter, the visitors seemed the more determined outfit, and McGarvey and Lambert were replaced by Chalmers and McWhirter as the Manager tried to alter the flow of play. There were one or two near things at either end before the Belgian referee brought proceedings to a close with the scoreline remaining 1-0 in Saints' favour. Many in the 7,729 crowd were far from impressed and made their feelings clear by booing the team from the field.

The bibs have it. The Cup yes, Style... No!

Back in the dressing room, frustrations also surfaced and Assistant Manager Jimmy Bone and senior player Frank McGarvey traded angry words, and possibly worse if the following days' tabloids were to be believed. Later, Bone and McGarvey were severely censured by the Board but the immediate effect of the confrontation saw McGarvey walk out on the Club and demand a transfer. Worse, his action meant that the experienced striker was missing from the team line-up for the second-leg in Norway a fortnight later.

Billy Abercromby then sustained an achilles injury in the League clash with Celtic prior to travelling to Norway and, as a precaution, Alex Smith returned Tony Fitzpatrick to the squad for the first time since 11 August. Saints' captain had argued himself out of the Manager's plans following the second League fixture of the season. The dispute centred on Fitzpatrick's desire for regular first-team football, something that the Manager had told the Directors was "not at present guaranteed for him".

In the event, the inclusion of Fitzpatrick as substitute on 30 September proved to be a wise decision as Abercromby's leg seized up after only sixteen first-half minutes. Fitzpatrick took over and proceeded to run the show with one hundred percent commitment, including one particularly over zealous challenge that led to a yellow card.

The match ended in a no scoring draw. Smith was quick to lay abundant praise at the feet of his first-half substitute, "Money can't buy Fitzpatrick's type of experience. He was magnificent". That said it all.

Opponents in the Second Round were another unknown quantity, namely Mechelen of Belgium, and it was a draw that brought with it its own special problem; since the riot at the 1985 Champions' Cup Final in Brussels that had resulted in thirty-nine deaths and four hundred injured, not only had English clubs been banned from European competition by UEFA, but the Belgian Government had banned British teams from the country!

Now, two years later, St. Mirren became the first club to test the Belgian Government's resolve, pointing out that Scottish supporters had an immaculate record in Europe during recent years. Delicate negotiations took place before the way was cleared for several busloads of supporters to travel by ferry across the North Sea for the first-leg.

The potential seriousness of the situation resulted in SFA Security Chief David McLaren accompanying the Saints' party and a British Embassy official meeting the team in Brussels. Immediate talks were then held to confirm the security arrangements for the game, which saw the two hundred and fifty or so St. Mirren fans being chaperoned to and from the stadium by an escort of armed officers and dogs!

Apparently, much of the concern focussed on how some locals might react on the night, but the evening of 21 October passed without incident. In fact, probably the biggest shock awaiting the St. Mirren fans was the unexpected sight of seeing their opponents take to the pitch wearing "Partick Thistle" strips!

Following his earlier spying mission to the continent, Alex Smith reported back to his players, "Mechelen are well organised at the back with at least eight men behind the ball in their half of the field, but they break very quickly from defensive positions. Mechelen have very good players, they will be difficult to break down".

New signing Billy Davies, acquired for a £6,000 signing-on fee after being released by St Mirren's former European opponents Elfsborg, was not eligible to play so Alex Smith fielded Money, Wilson, Winnie, Fitzpatrick, Godfrey, Cooper, Lambert, Ferguson, Chalmers and Cameron. Saints were confident and the players' composure throughout the first-leg earned plaudits from Belgian sportswriters as the team returned to Scotland with a creditable 0-0 draw. The bad news was that Ian Ferguson would miss the return leg following his second yellow card of the tournament.

The two weeks' wait for Mechelen's visit to Paisley passed quickly as events at home overflowed beyond the daily sports' pages. Off-the-field news was all very positive: a telex arrived from the Belgian Government applauding the behaviour of the St. Mirren fans; there was confirmation that Tony Fitzpatrick and Neil Cooper had finally agreed to sign new contracts after months of uncertainty; and Alex Smith was quoted as believing there to be a "fairly realistic" possibility of Oleg Blokhin and other top Soviet thirty-somethings coming to join St. Mirren.

On the other hand, articles relating to on-field incidents proved less encouraging: David Winnie and Campbell Money were both classed as "very doubtful" for the European tie following nasty injuries in League matches against Hibs (2-2) and Dundee United (3-2) respectively; and Ian Ferguson's impending absence was clearly emphasised as he netted four of the five goals scored in these two games.

Robert Dawson and Kenny McDowall were drafted into the team to replace Winnie and Ferguson, and Campbell Money was declared "fit" at the eleventh hour, meanwhile Mechelen's Dutch coach, Aad de Mos, admitted that he had underestimated St. Mirren in the first leg and declared that he would be content to win the tie with a 1-1 draw in Paisley.

There were just short of 15,000 in St. Mirren Park on 4 November as the Buddies began strongly and put Mechelen under pressure. True to Alex Smith's assessment, however, the visitors sat in numbers behind the ball and soaked up the pressure. Then, in the thirty-third minute, speedy Israeli winger Ohana side-stepped Peter Godfrey and drilled a low shot past Money. Four minutes after the restart he scored again when a Sanders shot rebounded from a post straight into his path.

After the game, Alex Smith bemoaned the loss of Ferguson, Winnie and Abercromby. "Until the first goal we were every bit as good as Mechelen." To be honest, however, the Belgians had played the game exactly as it suited them and St. Mirren lacked the cutting-edge necessary to break them down. Saints, along with their fans, drew some consolation later when Mechelen defeated Ajax 1-0 in the Final to win the trophy, and then beat PSV Eindhoven 3-1 to lift the European Super Cup.

At the time of St. Mirren's elimination from the Cup Winners' Cup in early November the team was placed a reasonably healthy fifth in the League with six wins and five defeats from the opening sixteen fixtures. Disappointingly, over the following twenty-five League games under Alex Smith's management the fans would only celebrate a further two victories.

The first of these was by 4-1 on 12 December at home to Dunfermline Athletic. Mike Conroy, a £76,000 signing from Clydebank, scored on his debut and then his second-half replacement, Frank McGarvey, also netted in his first appearance since resuming training on 30 October. Another serious injury suffered by Neil Cooper took any gloss off the victory.

The second win was 2-0 away to bottom-of-the-table neighbours Morton on 19 March, in which Cameron and Chalmers were the scorers. Between these two victories, eleven League fixtures had been completed with only three goals scored but twenty-one different players used!

To be fair, the Club was still suffering from the injury blight that had dominated so much of the previous season. Abercromby was in plaster, Fitzpatrick had a broken bone in his foot, Speirs was found to require a cartilage operation, Walker had severe bruising on his shin, Gallagher played only three full matches all season following his leg break, McWalter had still to recover from his pre-season groin problem, and even Campbell Money sustained a leg injury that kept him out of the side for three weeks allowing Les Fridge to make his debut.

Moreover, injuries to key central defenders were causing Alex Smith particular problems. Godfrey was making slow progress from his ankle injury, Cooper only recovered in time for the final three games of the season, McWhirter suffered the first of his many joint problems, and Winnie had broken down again following another attempted comeback. In an effort to strengthen the defence, an offer was made to sign defender Dave Beaumont from Dundee United at a cost of £75,000. United rejected Saints' bid.

Unfortunately, a second vital factor influencing team selection throughout the dark winter months was continuing behind-the-scenes unrest. Frank McGarvey was still not considered for a starting place until mid February, despite a run of five substitute appearances in December. The Directors had actually agreed in principle at their meeting on 14 January to sell McGarvey to Dunfermline for £40,000 providing the team could widen the gap between themselves and the "Pars" over the forthcoming few fixtures. The following three matches resulted in 3-0, 6-0 and 4-0 defeats to Falkirk, Hearts and Rangers respectively, and McGarvey stayed.

Mounting speculation over Ian Ferguson's future led to the midfielder also being left out of the team. Ferguson made both verbal and written transfer requests as Rangers' repeated enquiries since Saints' European exit became public. Having the tabloid press openly support Ferguson's desired move to Ibrox was clearly unhelpful to St. Mirren, but the Directors held firm and the Manager "rested" the player for a month from the end of November. Saints were not going to be dictated to.

Then, during the scheduled Board Meeting on 11 February, Alex Smith reported that Manchester United were prepared to pay close to Saints' asking price for Ferguson. The meeting was interrupted as telephone negotiations were held with both United's manager and chairman before the Board agreed to accept an offer of £700,000 plus a further £100,000 when the player received his first full international cap. Alex Smith met up with Ferguson and his agent later that evening and travelled to Manchester with the purpose of completing the deal.

There is some irony in the fact that the 4-0 defeat at Ibrox two days later on 13 February became Ferguson's last, and McGarvey's first, ninety minutes for St. Mirren following both their lengthy off-field distractions.

Ferguson had been unwilling to accept the move to England and St. Mirren eventually agreed to accept Rangers' offer of £775,000. An additional payment of £125,000 became payable once Ferguson had gained five full international caps. On the deal being completed £46,000 was forwarded to Clyde in dues agreed on Ferguson's arrival at St. Mirren.

At a specially convened Board Meeting on 19 February to consider how the Club might best deal with such a large amount of income, the question of the team Management was raised. Following deep discussion of all aspects of recent events a split vote carried the motion to dismiss all coaching staff with the exception of the Team Manager himself. Following further consideration this was later amended to the effect of dismissing only the Assistant Manager, Jimmy Bone.

On 27 February, Saints faced their next League fixture, hosting Motherwell at Love Street. A reduced admission charge tempted 5,419 spectators along to watch what was a fairly scrappy 0-0 draw. £97,000 signing from Hamilton Academical, Brian Martin, made his debut at right-back, while Keith Walker and Peter Godfrey both returned from injury. However, Conroy and Derek Hamilton were now out of the side and Billy Davies would play only one further match before the season's end. It was remaining impossible to field a settled side; as one player returned to action, another was lost to injury.

At the time of Alex Smith's appointment in December 1986 there was no reference to a "relegation clause" in his contract as there had been with Alex Miller. Now, as the team neared the end of 1987-88, the dismal run of results since the start of November had plunged the Club into a critical situation.

To allow the Fine Fare League to reorganise itself back to a 10-14-14 arrangement three clubs were to be relegated and only one promoted. St. Mirren had spent many weeks as the fifth-bottom team but had been drawn closer and closer to those sides beneath them. Now, with a mere four fixtures remaining, the threat of relegation had become a very real one as Saints sat only four points above third-bottom Falkirk.

1987 Cup Final Programme featuring Saints Frank McGarvey and Paul Sturrock of Dundee United.

On 16 April, Brian Martin scored his first goal for the Club when he headed home an Ian Cameron cross after thirty minutes of the match against second-bottom side Dunfermline Athletic at East End Park, but two second-half goals by the Pars denied St. Mirren any return from the game. Ominously, Saints dropped below Motherwell into ninth position.

Thankfully, Falkirk also lost, 4-2 at Dundee, but the "Bairns" next two games were against the bottom two, Dunfermline and Morton, and they also had a game in hand at home to Dundee United. By contrast, St. Mirren's next two matches were against third-placed Rangers in Paisley and away to a Hearts team that was two points ahead of the Glasgow side. There was every possibility that Saints could then face the final match of the season in one of the relegation places. The pressure was on.

On Tuesday 19 April, the seven Directors met away from the Ground in the Excelsior Hotel at Glasgow Airport, to discuss "the precarious position of the Club". Three of the seven preferred that no action be taken meantime. The remaining four voted that Alex Smith be asked to resign.

Some months earlier it had been agreed that Yule Craig would stand down as Chairman in favour of Lewis Kane at a convenient point before

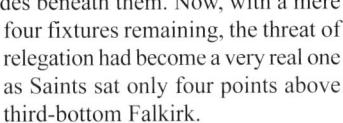

Brian Martin

the end of the season. Having voted against the motion to replace Alex Smith, Mr. Craig decided that this would be an appropriate time at which to pass the Chair to Mr. Kane.

The new Chairman's first tasks were to communicate the Board's decision to Alex Smith and invite senior players Tony Fitzpatrick and Frank McGarvey to take interim control of team affairs. With the remainder of the coaching staff also departing, Jack Copland, Graeme Sinclair and Kenny McDowall were each given roles helping run the playing side of the Club.

On 23 April, the caretaker Manager and his Assistant fielded the following players against visitors Rangers; Money, Wilson, Derek Hamilton, Fitzpatrick (McWhirter), Winnie, Cooper, Martin, Chalmers, McGarvey, Conroy (Gallagher) and Cameron. The selection meant returns to action for long-term absentees Hamilton, Cooper, Conroy and Gallagher but there was no glorious beginning. The game ended in defeat by three goals to nil, and the news from Brockville that Falkirk had beaten Morton 4-1 to close the gap to two points was met with deep concern.

Seven days later, on the last day of April, Keith Walker returned from a four-week absence to replace Mike Conroy in the starting line-up. The majority of the 9,626 Tynecastle crowd were expecting another home victory but St. Mirren took the game to Hearts straight from the kick-off. The team was certainly not prepared to entertain thoughts of relegation and, backed by a vociferous support at the Gorgie Road end, they set about securing the two vital points.

Twice within the opening forty-five minutes home 'keeper Henry Smith defied Paul Chalmers with brilliant saves, but one goal was to be enough to decide the outcome and it came to the visitors with a little over fifteen minutes remaining. Paul Chalmers was again at the heart of the action, feeding the ball out to Frank McGarvey on the right, the Assistant Manager's cross was met on the run by Chalmers again and headed high into the goal from around the penalty spot.

Campbell Money broke sweat for the only time in the match with his forty-yard jig-of-joy. The fans on the terracing celebrated wildly, too. Such was the elation that it seemed like "Hampden" all over again. It was the only match lost at home by Hearts all season, and Saints' first victory in seven weeks!

Falkirk also won on 30 April to remain two points adrift and now their all-important game-in-hand was due to be played during the following midweek. That night the ten o'clock evening news reported; Falkirk 1 Dundee United 2. St. Mirren were almost safe. A two-point and five-goal advantage in Saints' favour going into the last match would surely be enough.

On 7 May, Peter Godfrey replaced David Winnie in an otherwise unchanged team for the visit of Dundee. Prices were reduced to all parts of the ground, and 5,798 gave Saints a warm welcome in acknowledgement of the previous week's victory. By half-time the fans were celebrating the side's survival. Keith Walker's third St. Mirren goal put the Buddies ahead while the full-time news from Falkirk was equally satisfying. The record books show the day's results as St. Mirren 1 Dundee 0 and Falkirk 0 Rangers 5, and a final safety margin for Saints of four points.

Just two months beyond his thirtieth birthday, Tony Fitzpatrick was confirmed as the new Manager, with thirty-one year-old Frank McGarvey his Assistant at the Board Meeting on 9 May. The pair then celebrated in style on the evening of their appointment as the team won back the Renfrewshire Cup from relegated Morton. A season of ups-and-downs had closed in satisfactory fashion.

1988-89

There was a million pounds in the bank and a renewed sense of purpose when St. Mirren kicked off the new season on 13 August, in what was now the B&Q Scottish Football League. The strain of those final few weeks of 1987-88 had subsided and Saints' supporters were confident that the two Club legends controlling team affairs could continue their positive start.

That belief was only slightly tempered by a Dundee United goal, scored two minutes into the second-half at Love Street, that denied Saints any reward for their first ninety-minutes' effort. Following the match, however, the new Management team received a first taste of the type of news that had plagued their predecessor.

The two players substituted during the match, Derek Hamilton and Kenny McDowall, would play little part in the remainder of the season. Indeed, Hamilton's St Mirren career was all but finished due to his chronic injury problems, and he managed only one further appearance before being released at his own request in October. McDowall had not enjoyed the best of luck with injuries either since his arrival. In nine League appearances during the new season, he would complete only a single match.

On Tuesday 16 August Saints travelled across the Erskine Bridge to take on Dumbarton at Boghead in Round Two of the Skol Cup. The "Sons", relegated to the Second Division at the end of 1987-88, made their Premier Division opponents fight all the way and extra-time was required before St. Mirren won through thanks to goals from Brian Hamilton, Paul Chalmers and Assistant Manager Frank McGarvey.

Four days later it was back to League business, and the long trip north to the "Granite City". The journey was made worthwhile when Peter Godfrey's 77th minute equaliser gained Saints their first point of the new campaign. Big "Basil" had a second effort ruled out for handball, but the 1-1 scoreline was gratefully accepted considering the Dons missed a penalty and Brian Hamilton was sent-off ten minutes into the second-half.

Another four days passed, heralding another League Cup tie with Dundee United who would be visiting Paisley for the second time in a fortnight. This time the visitors were on top form and convincingly won their passage into the Quarter-Final thanks to a 3-1 scoreline. A busy couple of weeks was then brought to a conclusion when United's city neighbours, Dundee, defended in depth at St. Mirren Park in the last game of August, departing with both a clean-sheet and a League point. Saints had only a Norrie McWhirter shot worthy of mention throughout the ninety minutes.

Three League matches, two points, one goal, and out of the League Cup. It was neither the start that the fans nor the new Management Team had been hoping for. Saints were sitting seventh in the re-established ten-team top Division and, although there was a long way to go before the end of the season, no-one wanted to consider a repeat of last term's brush with relegation.

After all, the pre-season preparations had been completed with a sense of optimism. There was prestige in the appointment of Director Yule Craig as Vice President of the Scottish Football League, and results had also been encouraging, both during the pre-season tour of Ireland and in the showpiece friendly at Love Street.

Standing at 1-1 following the first leg in England, the expected re-match with 1987 English Cup winners Coventry City to complete the "British Cup Winners' Cup" two-leg challenge match did not take place, and so Aston Villa agreed to fill the void. Paul Chalmers' early goal unsettled the English First Division newcomers, and the visitors' frustrations culminated in an ordering-off for a dreadful challenge on David Winnie. Fortunately, the big defender survived the incident without any recurrence of his injury problems.

"We made a lot of chances in all of the pre-season games, but just didn't take them." Tony Fitzpatrick's assessment of his side's potential suggested the need for a new goalscoring forward, it was a quest that would occupy him for the duration of the season.

The Club received a cheque for £20,000 as its share of the League's new sponsorship, and a further £20,000 was deposited in the bank following young John Butler's move to Airdrieonians while, on the "décor" side, some of the previous season's significant transfer income was spent on freshening up the stadium.

There was now a 500-seat enclosure in front of the Main Stand, which itself was given a face-lift by being re-seated and having the Directors Box extended. A seated Family Enclosure was created at Cairter's Corner, a perspex cover was added to the players' tunnel, the car park at the corner of Love Street and Albion Street was fenced-off and lined to allow for income through the sale of permits, and some £30,000 was spent to erect a crowd segregation barrier between the north and east terracings following police advice after trouble at the Celtic fixture in January.

The Directors were also determined that the Club's healthy financial state would not be eroded by poor "housekeeping". At the Board Meeting on 18 August Tony Fitzpatrick announced that he wished to place the injured McDowall, together with Billy Davies, on the open-to-transfer list as part of a plan to reduce the playing staff and its burdensome wage bill.

"I've got to try and sell some of my players because we have a squad of forty full-timers here," the Manager explained to the Media. "That's the largest squad of any club in the country, so I intend to offload."

Mike Conroy left for England, joining Rotherham on loan; Derek Hamilton, Brian Gallagher, Robert Dawson, and Gary Peebles were each offered a deal to cancel their contracts; and medical reports were sought on the long-term injured Billy Abercromby and Gardner Speirs before a decision would be taken regarding their futures at the Club.

Conroy was eventually sold to Reading in October for £40,000; Gallagher and Abercromby left to join Partick Thistle in November; Peebles followed in January; and Speirs spent short unsuccessful spells on loan to Kilmarnock and Dunfermline later in the season before being released on a free-transfer. Dawson preferred Paisley and remained a St. Mirren player.

The Club was not solely interested in "offloading", however. An unsuccessful offer of £400,000 for Dundee forward Tommy Coyne was followed by an abortive £325,000 bid for his strike partner Keith Wright. Luton Town's Brian Stein turned down Paisley in preference to France and a further fruitless approach was made to attract Chelsea's Kevin McAllister to St. Mirren for £150,000. Despite Saints' money, either clubs wouldn't sell or players wouldn't move.

Another Anglo-Scot, Aston Villa's Alan McInally, did agree to return north for £300,000, but his club then decided that they needed him and put the deal "on ice". Although unsuccessful, these attempts to attract top class forwards to Love Street were without doubt the actions of an ambitious club.

The first League win was earned away from St. Mirren Park, on 3 September to be exact, in a repeat of April's crucial victory at Tynecastle. Paul Chalmers and Brian Hamilton put Saints two-up in the first-half and Campbell Money saved his second penalty of the season before Hearts pulled a goal back. New skipper Neil Cooper was given his marching orders in what was a towsy match, with eight players booked, but St. Mirren deservedly held on for full points.

One week later the League programme was suspended due to Scotland's World Cup qualification programme, so the Club arranged a challenge match for the evening of Monday 12 September against a touring team from the U.S.A., Orlando Lions. Saints fielded virtually a first-choice side to start the game but also took the opportunity to make half-a-dozen changes during play. Two goals in a minute shortly before half-time were enough to win the match.

After losing Derek Hamilton and Kenny McDowall on the opening Saturday, Tony Fitzpatrick had been able to maintain a settled eleven of Money, Wilson, Winnie, Brian Hamilton, Godfrey, Cooper, Cameron, Martin, McGarvey, Davies and Chalmers, with Lambert, McWhirter and McWalter as substitutes. These players, with McWhirter in the starting line-up for the suspended Cooper, added to the Club's points total with a 1-0 home victory against Motherwell on 17 September but young

McWhirter was injured again. One month later, the unlucky youngster would suffer a broken leg playing in a reserve match and be ruled out for the remainder of the season.

The Motherwell result lifted St. Mirren into fourth place but one worrying aspect of this fixture remained the team's inability to make more of almost total domination of the play, and it was no real surprise that it took a midfielder to break the deadlock. Brian Martin heading home the only goal from a McGarvey cross.

It was another midfielder who netted the team's goal twelve minutes into the next fixture, on the following Saturday at Ibrox Park. Billy Davies' first goal in the stripes was an absolute cracker, enjoyed by the Buddies in the 35,523 crowd and the millions of viewers tuning in to television later that evening. Following a driving run in off the left wing, Ian Cameron slipped the ball into Billy's path, in full flight he hit it first time high into the Rangers' net from twenty-five yards.

Brian Hamilton, who was only eligible to play due to a postal strike delaying notification of his suspension for exceeding the disciplinary points threshold, was red-carded again and Campbell Money saved yet another penalty as Saints held onto their 1-0 advantage until the break. Disappointingly, Rangers netted from a second spot-kick in the 61st minute, and six minutes later hit a second to complete the 2-1 score.

On the following Wednesday evening, 5,384 watched Saints lose a first-half goal, the Manager's sympathy, and both points to Hibs at Love Street. Tony Fitzpatrick blasted that insipid performance as "criminal" but the side returned to winning ways by defeating Hamilton 2-0 three days later at the same venue. Billy Davies, with another spectacular drive, and Paul Chalmers were the players who returned the smile to Fitz's face as the team cemented itself in fifth spot with eight points from eight games, seven goals scored and only six conceded.

The team line-up remained settled, the only change coming as far back as that Hamilton game when Mark McWalter began his first extended run in the side since signing in May 1987. This allowed Frank McGarvey to step back into a substitute role and a place in the dugout beside his managerial partner.

£16,000 was spent to replace the old television gantry above the players' tunnel with a new construction below the North Bank roof. It was also proposed to erect a roof over the new Family Enclosure, however both this task and a proposed stadium clock were sidelined when the Club began discussions with Kelvin Homes regarding the wholesale redevelopment of the Ground.

Despite the reasonable start to the League campaign any thoughts of holding Celtic to a tight game at Parkhead on 8 October were quickly dispelled. The Celts were two points and two places behind Saints in the table before kick-off but raced into a two goal lead within fifteen minutes; Paul Chalmers did pull one back, but by half-time it was 4-1, and by full-time 7-1.

Yet again, St. Mirren had suffered a heavy defeat to Celtic against all expectations and the Manager's frustration turned to anger when three players, Money, Lambert and McDowall, submitted written transfer requests. Fitzpatrick agreed to listen to offers for the latter pair. None were forthcoming and all three transfer demands were eventually withdrawn.

The freak nature of the Celtic result was further emphasised by the team immediately embarking on a seven-match unbeaten run. Three testing home fixtures were drawn 1-1 beginning against Aberdeen on 12 October. However, the relief felt at Brian Martin's 89th minute equaliser against the Dons was soon snuffed out in the other two games, as first Rangers cancelled out Saints' opener in the 87th minute, and then an own-goal by Peter Godfrey two minutes into stoppage time presented Hearts with a point.

Manager Fitzpatrick was fined £100 by the SFA for remarks directed towards the referee following the Hearts' game, but it must have been pleasing for him to see Mark McWalter find the net for the third time in four matches. In fact, twenty year-old Mark had scored his first St. Mirren goal at Tannadice on 22 October, in the game following the Aberdeen draw, with a powerful thirty-yard run and shot which gained Saints their fourth victory of the campaign.

Saints' fans at Tannadice unfurled a large "Spend Our Money" banner and their wishes were at least partially granted at the same time as the team continued towards a run of four successive away wins. On the first day of November, Davies and McGarvey efforts resulted in a midweek 2-1 win at Motherwell and during the following week £135,000 was spent to bring Peter Weir back to Paisley from Leicester City. The popular winger replaced Ian Cameron to make his debut in that home draw against Hearts on 5 November.

Fireworks came a week later when Saints won 1-0 at Dundee, courtesy of a first-half Paul Chalmers rocket shot, and another seven days down the line St. Mirren came from behind to win 4-2 at Douglas Park, Hamilton, with Peter Weir opening his scoring account through a 37th minute equaliser. Billy Davies and Paul Chalmers helped put Saints 4-1 ahead before Accies snatched a late consolation goal.

Peter Weir's contribution at Hamilton brought praise from his Manager, "He was different class. His display was superb".

This was the first time since being promoted in 1977 that Saints had put together a run of four consecutive away League wins. Next opponents were Celtic at Love Street. Surely this time St. Mirren would give a better account of themselves. The visitors opened the scoring a minute before the break, but Saints replied quickly after the restart when Peter Weir converted a 50th minute penalty-kick after Chalmers had been floored in the box. Celtic regained the lead five minutes later and ex-Saint Frank McAvennie then put them further ahead with a simple tap-in seven minutes from time. Mark McWalter's 87th minute reply gave Saints' some late hope but they couldn't find another goal to level the score.

Although producing a much-improved performance against the reigning champions, St. Mirren's second loss to Celtic marked a major turning point in the season's fortunes. Having fallen to seventh position following the heavy defeat at Celtic Park back in October, Saints had succeeded in fighting their way back into fifth place thanks to their seven-match unbeaten run, and were as few as six points off the pace with nineteen fixtures played. Yet, the side would now win only four more games from December through to the season's end and, in particular, would struggle to recapture their away form, losing nine of the remaining ten League fixtures on-the-road.

In the first of these, the defence was given a torrid afternoon by Hibs at Easter Road on 3 December and it was thanks to Campbell Money's heroics, especially in saving yet another penalty, that the score was kept to 2-0. Six-feet-plus striker Steve Galloway, a £20,000 on-loan signing from Djurgardens of Sweden, made his debut in Edinburgh and kept his place a week later against Motherwell at St. Mirren Park, when nineteen year-old George Shaw also made his first starting appearance, having previously appeared twice as a substitute for the first-team. Cameron and Chalmers netted in the closing quarter-of-an-hour to defeat a "Well" team that had led since the thirtieth minute.

Other than Peter Weir's inclusion, these had been the only two changes to a starting line-up that had remained comparatively consistent since the start of the season. Improvements were continually sought, nevertheless, as the Manager travelled Europe to watch potential signings in action. Nearer to home he opened negotiations with Dunfermline Athletic for their available midfield player Craig Robertson. The Pars were willing to take Robert Dawson in part-exchange together with Saints' £100,000 cash, but the deal still fell through.

On the park, the 3-1 defeat at Pittodrie on 17 December, saw Fitzpatrick field Money, Wilson, Winnie, Brian Hamilton, Godfrey, Cooper, McGarvey, Martin, McWalter, Chalmers and Weir. Unfortunately, Ian Cameron was unhappy at being left out since Peter Weir's arrival and asked for a transfer. Worse, Money and Cooper were both injured against Aberdeen (Money ironically in a collision with the Dons' new signing Craig Robertson) and the Manager would soon have another quartet of players become unavailable to him.

Les Fridge took over in goal and Billy Davies returned following a couple of week's absence for the Hogmanay visit of Dundee United. Although United took the points with a 1-0 win, Saints put on a superb second-half show and were unlucky to find former 'keeper Billy Thomson in such inspired form for the visitors.

Innovations at the Club continued when a "Club Call" phone-line began on a trial basis from New Year's Day with hopes of raising £1,200 per month, but when Dundee "called" at Love Street for the 3 January meeting they stole a point in a 1-1 draw. The "Club Call" expectations failed to ring true and it was discontinued at the end of March with a £520 loss over the three-month trial!

That Dundee game in January was Steve Galloway's last outing for

St. Mirren as, following two starts and two substitute appearances, he returned to Sweden without having completed his contract, leaving St. Mirren to seek compensation from Djurgardens.

On the plus side, there was a welcome return to first-team action for Keith Walker who appeared in his first game of the season four days later at Tynecastle. In a poor performance, the Buddies went down 2-0. The Manager was further disappointed by the loss of Brian Hamilton with an injury that would keep him out until mid April.

A 2-1 away defeat at Parkhead preceded a 1-0 home win over bottom-club Hamilton, which was secured thanks to a Peter Weir penalty on the stroke of half-time. Now, just a week before the Scottish Cup Third Round, St. Mirren also lost the services of Tommy Wilson, Mark McWalter and Billy Davies to lengthy absences. Suddenly the team was without five first-team regulars.

Partick Thistle on 28 January was the Cup hurdle facing the Buddies. The First Division side had four former Saints in their squad as Gary Peebles, Brian Gallagher and Billy Abercromby had been joined by recent signing Chic Charnley. Only the latter two featured in a Firhill encounter that saw a reshuffled Saints fail to convert chance after chance in a no-scoring draw.

The Paisley replay provided the home fans in the 9,000 crowd with another Cup disappointment, as the team failed to get to grips with an energetic "Jags" attack prompted from midfield by Charnley, the same player who had also orchestrated Clydebank's Cup win twelve months earlier. To real disappointment the match was lost 3-1 after extra-time.

The Cup defeat sparked a lengthy "talk-in" between the Manager and his players. Honest as ever, Tony Fitzpatrick acknowledged the gravity of the result; "I couldn't have argued if I'd been sacked".

Following this setback, bad weather resulted in an enforced three-week break, the only action coming in the Tennent's Sixes indoor tournament at the S.E.C.C. in Glasgow. The players didn't moan too much, each securing a £250 bonus for their efforts in reaching the Semi-Final.

It wasn't until 21 February that St. Mirren returned to the real stuff again. Hibs were the visitors and with Robert Dawson at right-back in place of Wilson, Frank McGarvey in for McWalter, and Paul Lambert for Davies, a 3-1 win gained the Club three valuable points in the race for a UEFA Cup place at the expense of one of their closest rivals.

A 3-1 defeat at Ibrox four days later marked the debut of £90,000 signing from Motherwell, twenty-two year-old Paul Kinnaird, when he replaced Paul Lambert in the second-half. Unfortunately the injury problems were made worse as that match also robbed the team of Peter Godfrey for all but two of the remaining games.

Les Fridge

The highlight and performance of the season was yet to come. Saturday 11 March saw Saints travel through to Tayside to face Dundee United. A relatively young and inexperienced line-up of Fridge, Dawson, Winnie, Walker, Martin, Cooper, Shaw, Lambert (Kinnaird), McGarvey (McWalter), Chalmers and Cameron, contrived to hit the League challengers for four, United only managing one in reply.

Playing in front of 8,320 and the BBC "Sportscene" cameras at Tannadice, a first-minute Hegarty own goal helped Saints make a perfect start and, although Malpas equalised, excellent second-half goals from Shaw, Chalmers and Walker completed a rare away double over Dundee United. It was an inspired performance.

In spite of this four-goal success, all hopes of another season in Europe evaporated thereafter when no more than four goals were scored in total during the closing eight matches, seven of which were lost! Twenty players were fielded in these remaining fixtures as the Manager now struggled to field a settled side. McDowall and McWhirter remained unavailable and only Keith Walker and Paul Chalmers appeared in all eight fixtures. This situation allowed yet another promising youngster, central defender Martin McIntosh, to make his full debut in the season's closing fixture, against Celtic at home on 13 May, having appeared as substitute in the previous Saturday's 2-1 defeat away to the one relegated club, Hamilton Academical.

Saints ended the League campaign in seventh position, fifteen points clear of Hamilton's points total. Nevertheless, although thoughts had generally been focussed on a possible UEFA Cup place until late in the season, the poor finish and final total of twenty-nine points left the side a mere two points above second-bottom position.

Tragic events preceding April's English Cup Semi-Final in Sheffield, when ninety-five supporters were crushed to death and hundreds more injured in an overcrowded enclosure, stunned the football world and St. Mirren's Directors recorded their condolences as well as forwarding a £1,500 donation to the Hillsborough Disaster Fund.

Welcome reward for St. Mirren's youth development efforts, came when the Club gained recognition in an Under-19 invitational tournament in Deventer, Holland, finishing third against high-class opposition. A trophy was received for being voted the "most promising team" on show.

As far as the first team was concerned, however, great goals and great wins were becoming fewer and farther between. The supporters expected improvement. Now, if the Club could only get rid of that awful strip ...

1989-90

Saints got off to a winning start, even before a ball was kicked ... the "bib" had disappeared and the famous stripes were back; not only on the jersey but also on the North Bank roof! The dramatic backdrop would leave visiting supporters in no doubt as to where they were. There was also a new sponsor's name emblazoned on the strip as Kelvin Homes made their mark as the Club's major backers.

Tony Fitzpatrick reminded supporters of his disappointment at the previous season's late slump that had dashed hopes of a UEFA Cup place, and set his sights on Europe for the campaign ahead. "There is a certain magic on European competition nights and it must be our aim to return to that arena this season," the Manager enthused.

The Directors agreed, and a bonus payment of £10,000 per man was set for European qualification.

Ten of the first team squad were made available for transfer as Fitzpatrick continued his plan to restructure the playing squad. Ian Cameron and Brian Hamilton departed for Aberdeen and Hibernian respectively. Cameron for a fee of £215,000; Hamilton for £285,000. Neil Cooper also travelled east, joining Hibernian for £30,000. Of the other transfer-listed players, Wilson, Walker and Chalmers would leave during the course of the season, while Money, Dawson, Davies and McDowall surprisingly attracted no offers.

Gudmundur Torfason

Utilising this new injection of cash Fitzpatrick signed Icelandic international forward Gudmundur Torfason from Rapid Vienna for £160,000 following a week's trial. Torfason's father was a close friend of 1960s Saint Thoroll Beck, a connection that helped pave the way for "Gunni" to come to Scotland. Central defender Roddy Manley arrived from Falkirk for a Club record £250,000, and the Manager also brought Fraser Wishart from Motherwell and Tom Black from Airdrieonians. The fees for these two full-backs were set by transfer tribunal at £70,000 for Black and a new, increased Club record £285,000 for the highly regarded Wishart.

In addition to the net financial "loss" from these deals the Board remained conscious of the Club's monthly shortfall and "the need for financial prudence" was once again emphasised.

Former Saint, and ex-Airdrieonians boss Gordon McQueen, re-joined the Club as Reserve Team Manager and twenty-two year-old David Winnie was appointed team captain for the forthcoming season. Pre-season friendlies against English opposition in the shape of Queen's Park Rangers and Middlesbrough both ended in narrow victories. As Torfason's work permit had not yet arrived the fans missed out on the chance of an early glimpse of the twenty-seven year-old in action. Fraser Wishart wasn't quite match fit and also sat-out the pre-season games, but while

Manley and Black played they both incurred injuries which delayed their competitive debuts.

The opening competitive match was played in front of 39,951 sun-drenched fans at Ibrox Park on 12 August when Saints spoiled the new champions' flag-raising party thanks to a Kenny McDowall goal in the 28th minute. Hailed as the "Mad Monk" by fans, McDowall outjumped Rangers' 'keeper and then stroked the loose ball home. The opening day line-up was Money, Dawson, Wilson, Walker, Godfrey, Winnie, McDowall, Martin, Torfason (Lambert), Davies (Chalmers), and Weir.

The Skol Cup kicked-off on 15 August with a successful trip to Berwick in which Wishart made his debut and Torfason immediately impressed the travelling fans by opening his scoring account with a curling free-kick from the edge of the box. During the following mid-week Saints took ample revenge over Motherwell for the 2-1 defeat in the summer's Final of the Isle of Man Tournament to the Lanarkshire side, winning 1-0 thanks to Paul Kinnaird's first-ever senior goal.

The Quarter-Final draw sent St. Mirren to Aberdeen on 30 August where a George Shaw goal wasn't quite enough to stop the home side progressing into the semis. There was some encouragement to be taken from the League Cup performances, however, especially at Pittodrie where home 'keeper Snelders defied Saints' efforts with a breathtaking display.

Much of the off-field activity at the Club continued to centre on ground improvements and a seventy-seat restaurant and further sponsors' lounge had been opened within the Main Stand. The ever-improving relationship with new sponsors Kelvin Homes was leading St. Mirren towards major redevelopment of the Love Street site. Club Secretary, George Pratt announced that feasibility studies and long term plans were "at an advanced stage" and that the objective was "an all-seated stadium combined with leisure and recreational facilities available to the community as a whole".

Such forward planning helped put the Club in a positive position with regard to the recommendations of The Taylor Report, set up to consider stadium safety following the Hillsborough Disaster. Yet, St. Mirren fell into disagreement with the then responsible authority, "Strathclyde Regional Council", over the crowd safety limit for the new season. The Club wanted an agreed capacity of 24,000, but the Council insisted on 20,000 and threatened to prohibit the admission of any spectators to St. Mirren Park should steps not be taken to comply with their wishes.

So, on 9 September, a near "capacity" 19,813 saw St. Mirren complete an early-season Old Firm double by defeating Celtic 1-0; Keith Walker netting the winner with a flashing header from Kinnaird's cross. It was a fiery encounter and Kinnaird was later one of three players sent-off.

This win had been a long time coming as it was Saints' first over the Celts since the 4-2 game at St. Mirren Park back on 19 November 1983, a gap of twenty-two meetings and twenty losses! Not since a similar lack of success against Rangers between 1912 and 1922 had St. Mirren gone such a number of League games against an individual club without victory.

Tom Black and Roddy Manley finally made their debuts in the Celtic game and Norrie McWhirter returned to the first-team following his own lengthy absence. The complete line-up was Money, Wilson, Black, Walker, Manley, Winnie, Kinnaird, Martin, Torfason (McGarvey), Davies and McWhirter. The unlucky Peter Godfrey had been injured yet again and would be on the sidelines for a further eight weeks.

Despite enjoying victories over both halves of the Old Firm, St. Mirren propped up the Premier Division table at the end of September. Four of the other five League games had been lost, the only other point gained in a 0-0 draw at Tannadice on the last day of September. Gunni Torfason, destined to become a firm fans' favourite, netted his first League goal at Motherwell on 26 August as he and his "Buddies" went down by 3-1. Tom Black scored his first goal in another defeat by the same score at Easter Road in mid-September.

The Saints' supporters began to leave the Easter Road terracing as long as twenty minutes before the end such was the inadequacy of the team's performance and the Manager demanded a Sunday morning training session from his players. "I cannot allow a performance like that," he complained.

The search for new players continued. An agreement was reached between the clubs for Saints to sign Brian Rice from Nottingham Forest, but the player refused even to talk to St. Mirren. Interest then switched back to Chelsea's Kevin McAllister who was now prepared to return to Scotland, but on this occasion the Londoners' asking price was considered too high. Fellow Scot, Ian Redford of Ipswich Town, was another who "might" have moved to Love Street at this time.

Frustrated by his failure to land any of these signing targets, Tony Fitzpatrick decided to focus his efforts on continental players and, over the following couple of months, a succession of potential imports arrived in Paisley as he invited internationalists from Poland, Belgium, Iceland and Paraguay for trials.

The frustrations continued, however. If the player proved to be good enough, he departed homesick; if he wasn't homesick, he proved not to be good enough! And so the search continued.

St. Mirren finally notched up a third League win at the start of October at home against Dundee and moved up one place to ninth. The "Dark Blues" took a 2-0 lead after half-an-hour but the Buddies fought back to win 3-2. Les Fridge was in goal for the injured Money, Geordie Shaw was back in the side and Mark McWalter played in attack alongside Torfason who scored an excellent double in the fight-back.

Gunni netted again in the following League match at Dunfermline, but later missed a penalty as the side crumbled to a dreadful 5-1 defeat. The supporters were disappointed especially given the quality of the close-season signings. The team were underperforming, a fact borne out by their next victory not coming until 13 December.

Between times they lost heavily to Hearts (4-0) and Aberdeen (5-0), but managed scoring draws against Celtic (1-1), Dundee (3-3) and Motherwell (2-2). Manager Fitzpatrick agreed that there was need for real improvement and three of the transfer-listed players, Wilson, Walker and Chalmers, eventually moved on. He was complimented on a good piece of business by the Board as a combined sum of £246,000 was banked from these transfers.

Peter Godfrey's header at Dundee on 9 December made him joint second-top scorer with Walker and Lambert, each with a mere two goals after sixteen League fixtures. Torfason was undoubtedly the man in form, though. He then netted himself a present as his seven League goals became eight on his twenty-eighth birthday in an excellent 1-0 victory at home to Dundee United.

With Paisley in the grip of a 'flu epidemic Saints home match against Dundee United was postponed from 2 until 13 December as the playing staff battled against the bug. Although home attendances had remained in excess of 4,000 throughout most of the season, only 2,800 managed to watch this midweek win.

Injured yet again, Peter Godfrey missed the following four games during which Hearts were beaten 2-0 at home while New Year holiday matches against Motherwell and Celtic were both lost by the same score. "Basil" was sorely missed. When the big central defender returned, the team put together its best run of the campaign.

Torfason and McDowall shared the goals between them as first Dunfermline were beaten by two first-half efforts at Love Street, then it was "unlucky" Hibs at Easter Road on 13 January, beaten by another first-half strike, this time a spectacular overhead kick from Torfason who also saw another two efforts hit the woodwork. This win was the first away from Paisley since the two opening games of the season, a gap of ten away matches!

Indeed, an away victory was more than welcome as St. Mirren were drawn to face First Division Ayr United at Somerset Park in the Third Round of the Scottish Cup. They survived the trip, returning with a 0-0 draw and defeated the "Honest Men" 2-1 in the replay on Wednesday 24 January, thanks to a blistering twenty-five yard drive from Davies and a clever shot from McDowall.

Gudmundur Torfason was ordered off on the stroke of half-time for gesturing to the Ayr fans and was suspended for the visit of Aberdeen as January closed, allowing Mark McWalter back into the starting eleven. Saints pulled off a fine 1-0 victory fielding Money, Wishart, Black, Davies, Godfrey, Manley, Martin, Lambert, McWalter, McDowall, and Kinnaird. Kenny McDowall scored the goal with a well-taken looping header.

The side had risen to the occasion against the Dons and stretched its unbeaten run to five matches, however, there then followed seven fixtures without scoring. In terms of results it could have been worse as single

Peter Godfrey

Paul Lambert

points were taken from four 0-0 draws, but it was the longest goal-less run in Saints' entire League history and one that left the side in a precarious League position for the second time in three years.

In a break from the hurly-burly of Premier Division action, St. Mirren reached the final of the Tennent's Sixes Indoor Tournament for the second time, and lost for the second time, this time going down to Hibs by 2-0.

Back to outdoor action, it was now almost certain that the only chance of earning a place in Europe was by reaching the Cup Final. Hopes were high when the Fourth Round paired St. Mirren with their fourth First Division opponents since lifting the trophy in 1987. A home tie against Clydebank not only provided the opportunity to progress to the last eight but also to gain revenge for that humbling 3-0 home defeat of two years earlier.

The tie was delayed until Wednesday 28 February when the "Bankies" denied Saints victory by equalising with a last-minute deflected shot. The 1-1 draw meant a replay at New Kilbowie that was not played until Monday 12 March, again due to adverse weather conditions, by which time it was known that the winners' Quarter-Final opponents would be Second Division Stirling Albion at home.

This was a real opportunity for St. Mirren to reach another Scottish Cup "semi", but Clydebank had other ideas. They quickly sped to a 2-0 lead that Saints succeeded in clawing back through goals from Shaw and Davies, but a late third goal for the homesters by Paisley-born Ken Eadie dumped St. Mirren out of the Cup. The defeat was hard to take for the disappointed travelling support.

Despite this difficult spell Saints still managed to field new talent. Youngster Kevin McGowne was given an introduction in defence while an unknown foreign trialist made an exciting debut in attack. Twenty-four year-old Tomas Stickroth from Bayer Uerdingen came on for Mark McWalter in a no-scoring home draw against Rangers on the Saturday following the Scottish Cup exit.

He immediately fired the crowd's imagination with his skill and searing pace, the fans didn't need a second look - "Sign him! Sign him!" cried the North Bank.

Stickroth's first three appearances may have failed to ignite the attack as much as it had done the support, but it was noted that the German had yet to feature in the same line-up as Torfason, so when they were paired together at Celtic Park on 7 April there was a buzz of anticipation among the travelling contingent of Saints' fans in the 18,481 crowd.

With looks reminiscent of 1980s pop-stars George Michael and Jon Bon Jovi the duo were certainly "on-song" that day. As Saints outclassed their Glasgow opponents, Stickroth shimmied past a defender and whipped over a great cross for Torfason to head home Saints' first goal in almost seven hundred minutes of play. Geordie Shaw then intercepted a pass back, rounded the 'keeper and slotted home the second... whereupon he was booked

Tomas Stickroth

for over-celebrating behind the goal. Half-time; Celtic 0 St. Mirren 2. What a way to end a scoring drought!

In the second period Paul Lambert strolled through the home defence and struck a third past Bonner in the Celtic goal to secure a brilliant win. It could easily have been six!

With four games remaining that precious result pushed St. Mirren six points ahead of bottom club Dundee; with the following week's match due at Dens Park it would be a proverbial four-pointer.

The players were placed on a win bonus of £500 per man and the Club also financed almost forty supporters' buses to transport the large travelling support. 7,415 spectators were inside Dens Park for a match crucial to both sides; almost 3,500 more than watched the corresponding fixture in December. Tony Fitzpatrick fielded exactly the same team as at Celtic Park and the players responded with a victory that thankfully secured Premier Division status.

The two points certainly hadn't seemed likely when the home side snatched a first minute lead and were then awarded a penalty kick fifteen minutes later. Billy Dodds rattled his shot off an upright and the Buddies' huge sigh of relief turned to unmitigated joy only minutes later when George Shaw smacked home the equaliser. After the interval, Brian Martin headed home a Paul Kinnaird corner for the all-important winning goal. Dundee were down, Saints stayed up! And the 2-1 success meant that the final three fixtures could now be faced in some comfort.

Following away defeats to Dunfermline and Aberdeen, the last game produced a no-scoring draw at home to Dundee United on 5 May. Young Danny McGill made his first start for the team and came closest to scoring with an effort that rebounded off a post. Incredibly, and not to be outdone, George Shaw hit the rebound off the other post!

The Manager's final selection of the season was Money, Wishart, McGowne, Lambert, McWhirter, Manley, Shaw, Martin, Stickroth, McGill, and Kinnaird. Surprisingly, only three of these players had taken part in the opening day win at Ibrox ... even allowing for the heavy injury burden which continued to haunt the Club, the team was definitely beginning to take a new shape under Tony Fitzpatrick and, as the season closed, the Club transfer record was broken for the third time in twelve months as Stickroth signed for £400,000. Shortly thereafter Peter Weir left for the coast, moving to Ayr United for £40,000.

In keeping with events elsewhere in the League, transfer activity had increased markedly in the second-half of the decade. From the summer of 1985 Saints' spending more than quadrupled compared to the previous five seasons, rising 417% from £403,000 to £1.68 million. Over the same period, the net profit from players moving to and from St. Mirren Park was £389,000 a rise of 269% on the first half of the decade.

In particular, Tony Fitzpatrick had spent over £1.1million and recouped £810,000 in sales since April 1988. But then, close to a further £300,000 was required during the summer of 1990 to finance re-signing fees, and the related tax costs, simply to hold on to a dozen of the existing squad. The financial revolution that had hit Scottish football was certainly making itself felt in Paisley.

On the playing front, the team had frustrated both Management and fans during the closing seasons of the decade. There appeared to be a lack of urgency and consistency about the play, however there was a great deal of credit to be taken from the 1980s as a whole: a Scottish Cup triumph; four European campaigns; and remaining one of only five clubs to have played the entire ten seasons of the decade in the Premier Division.

Nevertheless, some irony existed in the fact that, during the three seasons following the Cup win, home matches had been better attended than throughout an earlier six years that provided superior League performances. In fact, 1989-90 saw the least number of home crowds beneath four thousand of the entire decade; only two matches compared to fifteen in 1986-87 and nine in both 1982-83 and 1983-84.

Clearly the support was behind Tony Fitzpatrick and his players, yet the 1980s ended with the Club looking ominously over its shoulder at the First Division. It remained to be seen whether the big-money signings could turn St. Mirren's recent fortunes around and re-establish the Club among the country's top-five.

On the other hand, perhaps the Club's long-term future would lie in the hands of homegrown talent as, for the first time, St. Mirren had entered an Under-18 team in the Scottish Amateur Youth League alongside teams from other Premier Division sides ... and won the title at the very first attempt!

Struggles and Champagne...

1990-91

Manchester United 1 St. Mirren 5. No, it wasn't a dream, but in terms of the season (and even the decade) ahead it might as well have been. On 5 August, Tony Fitzpatrick took his first team squad to Manchester United's Cliff Training Ground for a closed-door bounce-match against a team of United fringe players.

CHAPTER THIRTEEN
The 1990's

Saints went 3-0 ahead before half-time with a scintillating display, and continued to dominate throughout the second period with Gunni Torfason in sparkling form. The big Icelander eventually netted a hat-trick for a Buddies' line-up of Money, Wishart, Black, Godfrey, Lambert, McDowall (McWalter), Shaw, Martin, Stickroth, Torfason, McGowne (van der Gyip ... a Dutchman, and one of several foreign trialists at the Club during the closed season).

This was Saints third pre-season practice match in six days. On the first of August the team travelled to Dumfries to face Frank McGarvey's new charges, Queen of the South. The former St. Mirren Assistant Manager had become full-time Player-Manager of the "Doonhamers" during the summer and he netted a consolation goal for his new side as Saints triumphed by four goals to two.

Two days later St. Mirren won again, this time 3-1 at Carlisle's Brunton Park, and the short pre-season programme ended with a 3-2 win over Ayr United. Hopefully fifteen goals in four matches was a sign that the team's scoring problems were finally over. Tony Fitzpatrick clearly thought so; "In recent seasons we have had problems killing-off sides that we have outplayed simply because of an inability to find the net. This term I believe we have a much more potent strike-force and I want to see that pay-off in terms of goals scored."

As a further incentive towards "killing-off sides", a radical review of bonus payments was put in place for the new season. Rewards would now emphasise the importance of taking points from the "lesser" teams ... a marked change indeed!

Off the field a new St. Mirren "Club Call" service was in place for the beginning of July, allowing fans to call direct and hear daily news updates and interviews from the Club. One piece of unwelcome news transmitted by the service was that admission prices were to be raised by £1 per match for the third successive season. It would now cost £5 to stand on the North Bank.

The Club's chronic injury troubles were also targeted during the summer as a new physiotherapist was sought. Bob Pender, formerly employed at the National Sports Injuries Clinic, became the man in charge of "magic sponge" duties.

As a £70,000 bid from Kilmarnock for Kenny McDowall was rejected a former Killie player, Gordon Smith, arrived as Assistant Manager to replace Frank McGarvey. Interestingly, Smith had turned out as a trialist in a reserve match for the Club during the previous season.

Unsettled pair Billy Davies and David Winnic continued to seek a move to pastures new. Davies was first to depart, leaving for Leicester City in June. As the clubs had failed to reach agreement on a fee it appeared that the matter would be resolved by the "Transfer Tribunal". Eventually a compromise fee of £160,000 plus further conditional payments was agreed with Leicester to avoid a tribunal decision.

Allan Marshall was subsequently appointed to lead the Club following these transfer negotiations and, prior to the turn of the New Year, Jack Gilmour retired from the Board. Mr. Gilmour's decision ended a personal association with St. Mirren that stretched back to the 1950s when he joined as a scout; his father had served as Club Chairman in the 1930s.

Billy Davies made a quick return to St. Mirren Park on 15 August when his new club played Saints in a challenge match. Two days later, it was Middlesbrough's turn to make the trip to Paisley to help complete Saints' pre-season preparations. This was the second successive year that the English Second Division side had played at Love Street, and Saints recorded another 1-0 win.

There was, however, one final curtain-raiser to the new season of interest to St. Mirren fans. On Saturday 18 August, a commemorative match was played at Hampden Park between a Scottish League Select and a Scotland XI to celebrate the one hundredth anniversary of the Scottish Football League's formation. St. Mirren, one of only five original members still participating in the competition, was represented in the Centenary Match by Paul Lambert, playing for The League side, and Campbell Money, who received an unofficial "cap" as substitute goalkeeper for the Scotland eleven.

Saints' competitive season began at home to Arbroath in the Skol League Cup and the 2,536 crowd looked forward to a positive start. Tony Fitzpatrick fielded a side showing only two changes from that which had performed so well in Manchester; newly appointed team captain Roddy Manley returned to the defence and Paul Kinnaird took his normal position on the left wing.

For Fraser Wishart it was a welcome return to competitive action following a season plagued by injury and the tie was won 1-0; Tomas Stickroth netting his first St. Mirren goal with a thirty-yard "belter". Nevertheless, the overall performance was very disappointing, as was the loss of Gunni Torfason after only a few minutes with a knee ligament injury. Having already broken his nose during the closed season, this new injury robbed the side of Torfason's influence until the beginning of October.

In the opening League fixture Paul Kinnaird's counter was enough to earn a good point at Tynecastle, and the winger netted again in narrow and unlucky defeats to both Aberdeen and Celtic. Tony Fitzpatrick then gave a chance to yet another foreign trialist, Gunther Tiele, who appeared as substitute when the team suffered a further narrow 1-0 defeat at Tannadice. In the meantime, Mark McWalter seized his opportunity as Torfason's replacement by scoring twice in three games, one of these helping the team to a 2-2 home draw with newly promoted St. Johnstone.

Following this pattern of narrow defeats, the team was unluckily eliminated from the Skol Cup at St. Mirren Park on 29 August. Saints went down to Hearts 1-0 following extra-time after Peter Godfrey had been sent-off in an engrossing contest played before a satellite television audience.

Tomas Stickroth then netted his second goal for the Club soon after the half-time break to finally lift both points in a deserved 1-0 League win over Motherwell. That Arbroath cup-tie aside, the new season had begun with some spirited play and Manager Fitzpatrick reported to the monthly Board Meeting on Thursday 4 October that he did not believe that results gave a true reflection of the team's performances.

Nonetheless, by the time Torfason returned to the side at rain-drenched Easter Road on the first Saturday of October, St. Mirren had lost half of their opening six league fixtures. The number of losses doubled over the next three fixtures as the team failed to score away to Hibs 0-1 and Rangers 0-5, and then at home on 22 October to fellow-strugglers Dunfermline 0-1.

Saints were now bottom of the table and the Manager's attitude was changing; "Whilst the defenders have been conceding goals, our strikers have not been doing their job in attack, and therefore the whole team must shoulder responsibility and show something more in terms of fighting spirit." Despite this analysis, the Manager was continuing contract negotiations behind the scenes in which the "going-rate" for a re-signing fee had now risen as high as £60,000, with an additional £25,000 being paid over one particular three-year deal as a "loyalty bonus". St. Mirren would not shrink from competing in a financially demanding market.

There was clearly not a bottomless pot of cash, however, as interest in Borussia Dortmund's Scot, Murdo McLeod cooled after personal terms were discussed. Nevertheless, Tony Fitzpatrick was intent on adding to his squad and even aired the idea of "renting" a player from another Bundesliga club until the end of the season.

On 27 October, Saints faced their second consecutive home match and their second consecutive bottom-of-the-table clash. It was also the season's third meeting with Hearts. The first choice central-defensive pairing of Roddy Manley and Norrie McWhirter was absent through suspension, resulting in a return for Peter Godfrey and a first game of the campaign for last season's captain David Winnie, who had been signing monthly contracts and turning out for the Reserves.

The opening goal came in eight minutes courtesy of a bizarre foul conceded by Hearts' Henry Smith. The 'keeper dithered over clearing a punt upfield by Tom Black and was eventually forced to handle outside his area. Black's free-kick struck the post before Paul Lambert fired home the rebound into the opposite corner. The visitors levelled the scores in the fifty-fifth minute but with twenty minutes remaining Torfason put Saints back in front, netting his first goal since returning from injury, powerfully heading a Stickroth cross into the postage-stamp corner.

This was a big win for Saints and over the next week optimism increased when the Club signed free-agent Steve Archibald from RCD Espanyol and paid Japanese side Mazda £20,000 for former Falkirk and Liverpool striker, twenty-seven year-old Allan Irvine. A successful eight days was then completed on the Saturday when Saints moved clear of Hearts at the foot of the table courtesy of a 25-yard Torfason "rocket" against high-flying St Johnstone at McDiarmid Park. Had the Club's fortunes finally turned?

For the following home game against Aberdeen on 10 November, Steve Archibald made his debut as Fridge, Dawson, Black, Lambert, Godfrey, McWhirter, Martin, Archibald, Stickroth, Torfason, and Kinnaird took to the field, with Shaw and McDowall on the bench. The Dons' emphatic 4-0 win brought the team back down to earth and a 4-1 defeat at Celtic Park, a week later, added the "thud" ... "it could have been seven or eight," lamented an ever-forthright Fitzpatrick.

Steve Archibald

Although the team was once again propping up the Premier Division, another new signing made his debut at Celtic Park and fuelled the feeling that a charge up the table was imminent. He was the world-renowned Spaniard, Victor Munoz!

Thirty-four year-old Archibald had encouraged his former FC Barcelona team-mate to join him in Paisley and Tony Fitzpatrick looked to the wide experience of these two

Victor Munoz

star players to help St. Mirren play themselves out of trouble. "Archibald is a proven goalscorer," the Manager enthused, "and Victor is a player of the highest class." Although available at only £30,000 from top Italian club Sampdoria, the thirty-three year-old former Spanish international captain would not come cheap. Yet it would prove to be a snip if he helped save the Club from relegation.

By the time title-challenging Dundee United arrived to play at Love Street on the first day of December, David Winnie had been sold to Aberdeen for £265,000 and Reserve Team Manager Gordon McQueen had left to pursue a broadcasting career. The running of the Reserves was taken over by former Celtic and Ayr United player Brian McLaughlin.

Having replaced both full-backs following the poor performance at Celtic Park, the Manager retained an unchanged line-up for the next two fixtures and the team responded with two successive 1-1 draws.

St. Mirren now sat level with Dunfermline and Motherwell on ten points, with Hibs just two points better off in seventh position. A couple of wins could see the side jump into mid-table. Unfortunately, the team formation was disrupted by further injuries to both Torfason and Stickroth, although Allan Irvine finally made his debut in the 3-0 home loss to Rangers on 15 December. In a commendable gesture, the Club invited recently released former Iraqi hostage, Saints' supporting Dougie Ferguson, to attend the Rangers game.

A 1-0 victory on the following Saturday at home to Hibs improved the team's chances of pulling away from the relegation zone. Saints were now off the foot of the table and within four points of Celtic in sixth place.

Fellow strugglers Motherwell were the Club's "first foots" of the New Year and Steve Archibald finally opened his account in the stripes as the two teams fought out a 2-2 draw in front of 6,653 spectators. He scored again only three days later at Tannadice, but this time the team went down 3-2 in a controversial match against third-place Dundee United.

With the Club continuing to invest in an attempt to secure safety, a £40,000 signing from Plymouth Argyle, twenty-six year-old Julian Broddle, made his debut in that Tannadice match; but in almost tragic circumstances. Goalkeeper Les Fridge suffered serious internal injuries in a challenge for the ball with United's Darren Jackson. Fridge was rushed to hospital where he spent four days recovering. In all, the young 'keeper lost four pints of blood and required three operations to repair the severe groin injury he sustained.

Having already netted Saints' opener in the game, Kenny McDowall took over between the sticks and Broddle slotted into midfield. The stand-in 'keeper sensationally saved a Paatelainen penalty-kick late in the game. After the match, the Club lodged an official complaint against the referee. One week later, in less dramatic circumstances, a second formal protest was registered after Manager Fitzpatrick declared that the team had been "cheated" in a 2-0 defeat at Tynecastle.

The issue of possible League re-organisation had reared its head again earlier in the season and Saints' Directors had originally proposed to support the status quo of a ten-team top division. However, the appetite for change among the country's clubs would be as ravenous throughout the 1990s as it had been one hundred years earlier and, at a Special General Meeting of The League held in January, a motion was passed by fifty-five votes to twenty-seven to revert to a twelve-team Premier Division in 1991-92. St. Mirren was now one of the clubs voting in favour of the change ... and relegation would now be suspended for the current season!

With a Premier Division place secured, Saints turned their attention to the Cup. On the morning of Friday 25 January the squad breakfasted at St. Mirren Park before travelling down to Stranraer to complete their preparations for the next day's Tennent's Scottish Cup clash. Neither side was in the best of form. Stranraer had managed only a single win in their last eight Second Division fixtures and Saints similarly had only a single win to show from their past twelve.

If there was any real concern at the possible outcome, those anxieties would not have been helped by the need to make wholesale changes. Steve Archibald was missing with a kidney infection, Brian Martin was suspended, Roddy Manley was about to undergo a knee operation, and new Scotland U-21 skipper Paul Lambert was not risked as he continued to make his recovery from a cartilage operation. However, Gunni Torfason was welcomed back after recovering from a fractured cheekbone to a

Ex-Barcelona star Victor Munoz in action versus Hearts at Tynecastle in January 1991.

line-up which read Money, Wishart, Black, McWhirter, Victor, Godfrey, Shaw, McDowall, Broddle (McWalter), Torfason (Stickroth), and Kinnaird.

Saints' huge travelling support swelled the crowd to threaten Stair Park's modest capacity. The teams took the field before a packed ground with spectators climbing the perimeter walls and choosing to view proceedings from the branches of surrounding trees.

After a nervy opening spell, Saints hit Stranraer twice in three minutes mid-way through the opening forty-five minutes. First, Torfason fired home from close range following a corner, then Kinnaird netted from a Shaw pass. Any lingering threat from the homesters was killed-off a mere eight seconds into the second period when Kenny McDowall ran the ball into an empty goal following a defensive blunder straight from the kick-off!

Saints added a further two goals through another Torfason effort and a sensational thirty-yard "blaster" from Victor. In between times the home side netted a single consolation goal. It had been a comfortable 5-1 victory.

A narrow 1-0 league defeat at Ibrox preceded the Fourth Round tie away to Celtic, played at 8pm on a Tuesday evening to accommodate live television coverage. There was to be no Cup glory, however. Celtic went 3-0 ahead within twenty-five minutes and, although Saints passed up three excellent chances before the interval, the homesters coasted to victory in the second half.

League re-organisation meant that the following two fixtures against fellow-strugglers Dunfermline and Hibs were no longer crucial to St. Mirren's survival in the Premier Division. As a result, a mere 2,589 watched the Buddies fight out a 2-2 draw at Love Street with the "Pars", a game in which Victor scored his first League goal.

A week later Saints' fans travelled through to Easter Road and watched as their favourites took a deserved 3-1 lead, and appeared to be "strolling" to victory, before conceding three late goals. "We were comfortably ahead and knocking it about like Real Madrid," the Manager seethed, "then we finished the game like Real Madrid Boys' Club!"

Two days after that 4-3 defeat Tony Fitzpatrick's resignation was announced. "I just feel the time is right," he explained. "It gives someone else ten games to sort things out." Tony was his own fiercest critic and his undoubted love for the Club retained him the loyalty of the fans even when results were poor. It could not be denied, however, that his investment in big-name players had failed to bring the required improvements.

Assistant Manager Gordon Smith took temporary control of the team when Dundee United came to town on 9 March. The caretaker boss recalled Dawson to replace Wishart, brought in McGowne for the suspended Victor, and preferred Shaw to Stickroth. Despite these adjustments the side went down rather unluckily 1-0 to the visitors.

Following further defeats to Celtic 3-0 and Motherwell 3-1, Paisley-born David Hay was appointed Manager. The former Motherwell and Celtic boss was making no rash promises for the future of a side three points adrift at the foot of the table, but he did indicate that there would be changes made to the playing staff in time for the following season.

In the first of these, popular Peter Godfrey was given a free transfer and moved to Falkirk. Gordon Smith, on the other hand, was retained as Assistant Manager. Hay's first selection; Money, Dawson, McGowne, McWhirter, Victor, Martin, Stickroth, Lambert, Torfason, Archibald, and Kinnaird; pulled off a creditable no-scoring home draw against Hearts on 30 March.

Victor Munoz ended his St. Mirren career and returned to Spain following a 2-1 defeat at Perth the next Saturday. The gamble had failed as far as the Spaniard was concerned ... in his eighteen league appearances Saints won only a single match. The supporters did, however, appreciate Victor's skill and efforts in a St. Mirren jersey.

Three further single-goal defeats and a 2-2 draw followed to leave the side on a mere seventeen points from thirty-five matches. The team had now fallen eight points adrift of second-bottom Hibernian, visitors to St. Mirren Park on the final day of the season.

Saints' last league victory had been a distant eighteen games previously, ironically on Hibs' last visit to Love Street, and season 1990-91 ended with another 1-0 victory over the "Hibees". Youngster Alex McEwan made a scoring League debut in what was Steve Archibald's final game.

St. Mirren had been saved from relegation only by the restructuring of the Scottish Football League set-up and Chairman Allan Marshall encapsulated everyone's thoughts in the final Matchday Programme; "There can be little doubt that in terms of results, the season just ending has been a traumatic one for St. Mirren Football Club".

The statistics certainly supported the Chairman's words. Three players shared the "high-scoring" honours, but with a mere four league goals apiece; away from home, Saints' most expensive ever squad had won only a single League match and there was a run of seven away defeats in-a-row; at St. Mirren Park the team managed only four League wins and there had been a sequence of eight games without a victory, and another of five without a goal, prior to that last-day success over Hibs; the seventeen-game winless run between the two Hibernian matches remained the longest spell without a League victory in Saints' first 125 years; and, possibly worst of all, a side sprinkled with first-team experience had gone down 1-0 to ten-man Greenock outfit Belleaire Amateurs in the Renfrewshire Cup Semi-Final!

What could David Hay do to improve this sad state of affairs?

1991-92

During the previous season, it had been suggested that St. Mirren might move from the "Love Street Grounds" to a new £200 million National "Super Stadium" complex proposed for the outskirts of Paisley near St. James Interchange. However, with Renfrew District Council losing out to a planned re-vamp of Hampden Park, Saints continued with ground improvements on the Love Street site.

Therefore, supporters returned to a new-look St. Mirren Park with the covered North Bank terracing converted into a colourful 4,200-seat "North Stand". The change had reduced the ground capacity to just under twelve-and-a-half thousand with almost half of that number now seated and, on the pitch, the new first-choice kit would mirror the two stands' black, white and red seating pattern. The time-honoured stripes on the top were joined by a red band running the length of both sleeves and the white shorts sported black and red flashes.

While traditionalists might have been concerned that Saints' stripes were no longer purely "black and white" there was a deep sense of satisfaction among the support at the new "change" kit. Not only did the outfit gain widespread approval because of its ground-breaking all-black design, the change from the previous season's all-white also symbolised the type of stark contrast that Saints' diehards were hoping for in the team's results.

Campbell Money's Testimonial Match against Rangers was the highlight of pre-season activity that had also included home friendlies against Oxford United and Charlton Athletic, a game during which new physio Andrew Binning found the increasingly injury-prone Torfason to have suffered another broken jaw.

The League campaign kicked-off with two away fixtures ... and two 4-1 defeats. At Easter Road on 10 August, David Hay fielded four new signings. The Manager had brought Lex Baillie from Celtic and former Celt Mark Reid from Charlton Athletic and, in addition, he acquired David Elliot and one-time Saint Chic Charnley from Partick Thistle in a deal that saw George Shaw and Mark McWalter move to Firhill.

The starting line-up for the new League campaign read Money, Wishart, Reid, McWhirter, Baillie, Martin, McIntyre, Lambert, Kinnaird, Charnley, and Elliot. Alan Irvine scored Saints' consolation goal after replacing Paul Kinnaird in the second half. Three days later, at Tannadice Park, another debutant, young Tony McDonald from Arthurlie, made his first appearance as substitute for Irvine.

The next two fixtures were both at home, the visitors being Airdrieonians and Falkirk, the two sides promoted in the re-organisation of the divisions. Manager Hay rang the changes, bringing in Fridge, Dawson, Black and McDowall but the team was able to respond by winning only a single point. Saints were already being quoted as relegation favourites. Something drastic had to be done!

Tom Black

Scotland's former international captain, Roy Aitken, arrived from Newcastle United for £150,000 and made his debut at the heart of Saints' defence in the 0-0 draw against Falkirk. The defence had definitely benefited from Aitken's experience. So much so that, on 7 September at Celtic Park, the back-line led the team to its second point in another no-scoring draw. Perhaps the intimidating black "away" kit, making its League debut, also played its part.

With the Manager's £350,000 transfer budget having now been exceeded the seriousness of the financial situation once again became an issue. The Directors decided that Paul Lambert could be allowed to leave if the price was right. That price would be £1 million. Efforts were also made to realise the value of other players throughout the season.

The fixture pattern of "two away, two home" continued with League-leaders Hearts and second-placed Rangers visiting Paisley in the middle of September. There were welcome returns to action for Manley, Torfason and Broddle and signs of continued improvement as the side took the lead in both matches. Sadly, both were eventually lost by the odd goal.

The team's first victory was finally gained in the ninth League fixture, away to fellow-strugglers Dunfermline Athletic on 28 September, and a fine win it was. Irvine, Charnley, Lambert and Broddle were the goalscorers as Saints fought back from conceding an early opening goal to run out comfortable 4-1 winners. Saints fielded Fridge, McGowne, Reid, Aitken, Martin, Manley (McDowall), Lambert, Torfason, Irvine (McGill), Charnley and Broddle.

Unfortunately, the pleasure of victory was short-lived as Saints then suffered ten games without victory, scoring only four goals, and picking up a mere two points. Trips to Airdrie and Falkirk resulted in 4-1 and 3-0 defeats as the side became anchored in one of the relegation places.

Minus the suspended Aitken, the defence conceded nine goals in two matches and the barren spell was noteworthy only for the following four reasons: (1) the filming of scenes from the St. Johnstone match on 9 October to become part of the official video history of the Club; (2) Roy Aitken's international appearance in Bucharest during his domestic suspension, making him Saints' twenty-eighth and last full Scottish Cap of their 125 years; (3) the inclusion of teenagers Jamie Fullarton and Barry Lavety as substitutes for the home fixture against Celtic on 26 October, a game lost by five goals to nil; and (4) the transfers of Brian Martin and Tom Black, respectively to Motherwell and Kilmarnock for a combined income of £240,000.

David Hay's perspective on his side's performances was blunt; "the team has an ingrained relegation attitude and too many players have believed this when we go out to face the opposition." Hay also bemoaned the fact that he had found no youth policy to speak of when he arrived at the Club. Ironically, his predecessor, Tony Fitzpatrick, was now working as a Community Coach at St. Mirren Park in a post jointly funded by the Club and the SFA with a remit of developing youth football within the area.

At the November Board Meeting the Chairman was direct in acknowledging that the Club was at a low ebb both on and off the pitch. The borrowing limit had been reached and additional security had been signed in favour of the bank. The financial situation was described as "bleak" and £80,000 was required for essential safety work on the Main Stand exits ... unfortunately, the selling of a player remained the best escape route for the Club.

The six-mile trip along the M8 to play in front of 40,000 at Ibrox Park on 23 November would hardly have been seen as the perfect escape route from such a form slump, but in recent seasons Saints had made a habit of contriving victories in similar situations against all the odds. Straight from the kick-off they showed that they felt in no way inferior and almost took the lead. Charnley rolled the ball back to Money who launched a huge kick-out into the Rangers half. A stretching Richard Gough could only glance it into the path of Danny McGill, who ran on and drilled the ball off the underside of the crossbar and back into play. Time, twenty-six seconds.

Saints' winning goal came in the final minute of the first half. Julian Broddle swept a pass out to the left, setting Alan Irvine free. The big man's fierce shot cannoned off a defender before being met first-time by Kevin McGowne some 35 yards out. According to Rangers' 'keeper the shot rose, dipped and bent before flashing past him and into the top right hand corner of the net.

In his first game back after a four-match suspension following a red-card in the 4-1 defeat at Airdrie, Chic Charnley was enjoying the chance to indulge in some "showboating". A 64th minute booking, however, led David Hay to believe that Chic would be better watching the remaining minutes from the sidelines.

During Saints' run of 10 winless games leading up to Ibrox, Manager Hay had accused the squad of slacking, cut bonuses, and even threatened to dock their pay. Now with a famous win to savour, the Club presented the players with £500 per man for the victory! The team that day was Money, McGowne, Beattie, Aitken, Charnley (McDowall), Manley,

Kinnaird, McIntyre, Irvine, McGill (Elliot) and Broddle. St. Mirren now sat three points ahead of bottom-of-the-table Dunfermline Athletic but five below Airdrieonians; it was time for the players to repay the Club with more than just a single high-profile victory.

David Elliot netted his first League goal in the home fixture with Dundee United that followed while only the width of a goalpost stopped Alan Irvine doubling the lead before United snatched a late equaliser. Unfortunately, instead of confirming a period of success, this result marked the beginning of another winless run, this time lasting nine matches. Most worryingly, with Irvine and Torfason struggling to find form and Stickroth still short of match fitness, the side found goal-scoring increasingly difficult. The supporters were now becoming more than a little concerned.

On 11 January, around two hundred of them gathered at the rear of the Main Stand calling for Manager Hay's head following a heavy home defeat to St Johnstone. Even scoring first, the team's first goal since that one-all draw against Dundee United on 30 November (thus equalling the Club record drought of seven matches), proved only a momentary lift for players and supporters alike. Four goals conceded before half-time, and another in the second-half, stretched patience and tolerance beyond the point of no return and left some fans baying for blood.

Perhaps unsurprisingly, several forwards were being linked with a move to Paisley. The Club refused to give credence to rumours surrounding Sam McGivern of Falkirk, ex-Saint Danny Diver of East Stirlingshire, or Raith Rovers' pair Peter Hetherston and Gordon Dalziel. Meantime, interest in two players was admitted. Sheffield United's Peter Duffield was training at St Mirren Park and a signing offer had been made to ex-Don John Hewitt recently released by Celtic.

There would be no new additions to the squad in time for the following Saturday's return trip to Tannadice, but the Manager removed some of the metaphorical heat from himself and his players by arranging a five-day trip to the heat of the sun in the Costa del Sol. "We'll train morning and afternoon and get a chance to talk over a few things," explained assistant boss Gordon Smith. "The weather conditions will be much better and the players will get a lift," added the under-pressure Manager.

The Saints' supporters that travelled through to Dundee on 18 January might have missed out on the Spanish sun but were nevertheless soon in holiday mood as Saints grabbed the lead after quarter-of-an-hour. Gunni Torfason won the jump for a David Elliot corner and his delicate looping header floated into the net.

Twenty minutes later, it was 2-0. Another corner, this time from Tomas Stickroth, was again hooked goalwards by the big Icelander before being handled on the line by a United defender who was red-carded. Gunni whacked home the spot-kick! After the interval ten-man United put the Saints' goal under siege and might have pulled a goal back when Jackson missed a sitter.

Then, in a rare sortie upfield, Saints went three ahead. David Elliot was fouled some thirty-five yards out from the home goal and Chic Charnley hit a vicious low free-kick through the wall and into the net. United did finally pull a goal back minutes later but Saints held out for the closing ten minutes. The victory brought back memories of the dramatic 4-1 triumph at Tannadice in 1989.

It might have been only the third win of the season, but the result was the perfect fillip for the visit of Hearts in the Scottish Cup third round seven days later. Despite two earlier losses to the Capital outfit at St. Mirren Park in the League, Saints earned a replay with a hard-fought no scoring draw. It was their third draw in the season's three cup matches to date, having tied in August with both Brechin City and Dunfermline Athletic away from home in the Skol League Cup.

These earlier draws had been resolved by penalty shoot-outs (one favourable, the other not) but there was no need for such a finish at Tynecastle as Hearts comfortably won the replay by three goals to nil.

Saints' season-ticket holders were finally treated to a home triumph at the sixteenth attempt when Gunni Torfason hit a hat-trick, and new-signing John Hewitt netted on his debut, in a 4-1 demolition of Airdrieonians. Torfason then hit his sixth goal in three league games on 8 February against Rangers but the visitors held on to their 2-1 interval lead and returned to Ibrox with full points.

At the monthly Board Meeting on 13 February, John Corson retired as a Director and three newcomers were co-opted onto the Board; Robert Earlie of Club sponsor Kelvin Homes, George Storrie, and 1970s player Charlie Palmer. One of Mr. Earlie's first tasks was to accompany Chairman Allan Marshall to a meeting with the bankers and his impressions were not good. There had been a huge turnaround in the Club's financial fortunes in a relatively short period of time and the £900,000 overdraft limit was proving insufficient. There was already a commitment to pay £165,000 in signing-on fees at the end of the season, something that had "horrendous implications" according to Mr. Earlie; "the Club is in serious bother and will not be able to meet its commitments if money is not gained fairly urgently."

Bob Earlie

Over the following four months the Board convened fortnightly as the seven men in control of the Club pursued every available avenue in an effort to release the financial pressure that had built up around them.

By 28 March the bank's position was made clear; if the Board were unable to "turn the Club around" in three to five years then the sanction of selling the ground would be exercised. Fortunately it was also reported that the bank was not in the business of foreclosing on the Club and use of the ground would be permitted on a lease-back basis. In the interim, the bank sought a £300,000 reduction in the overdraft limit, and they wanted it immediately! Saints had to react.

The suspended Charnley was sent on trial to Bolton Wanderers and Port Vale's interest in Wishart was pursued. Dundee United expressed an interest in Lambert and Stickroth travelled to Germany for a medical in advance of a possible move back to his homeland. Nevertheless, all four remained St. Mirren players and a £50,000 bid from St. Johnstone for Kevin McGowne was rejected. It wasn't enough.

Other fund-raising options had to be considered and the Directors discussed selling the ground, a public flotation, and asking the shareholders for help. Finally, it was agreed that the £300,000 would be realised by the Directors themselves in personal cash injections before the end of April. This alone would not satisfy the bank, however, and it would be necessary to prepare a budget that showed staffing costs cut by at least half for the next year.

The existing wage bill for players was in excess of £100,000 per week and the new Directors pointed to the "naivety" of the contract system that had been in place. Mr. Earlie, in particular, was of the very definite view that the Club should be run on a substantially more business-like footing and his opinion was validated in a critical report written by business management consultants KPMG.

Two long-standing Directors took on non-executive roles as Mr. Earlie was appointed Chief Executive in charge of running the "Company's affairs" on a daily basis but, by the beginning of April, an already bad situation took a further turn for the worse. With the Club about to exceed its overdraft, one of the new Directors considered that he no longer wished to be part of the organisation and resigned.

A replacement was urgently sought and two potential candidates were approached; neither was deemed suitable. The Board was left to face up to its commitments with four executive and two non-executive members.

Throughout this difficult period the team continued its fight against the ever-increasing threat of relegation. Paul Lambert was now captain of Scotland's Under-21s and Jim Beattie, signed in November from Celtic, had also earned an Under-21 cap, but with a dozen games to play St. Mirren were still nine points adrift of Airdrieonians who also held a game in hand.

On 22 February the trip to Dunfermline was taken in the hope of repeating that September victory at East End Park. Steve Kinsey, a former Manchester City forward who had been training at Love Street since returning from a spell in the USA, scored four goals in three reserve team outings and was given his first chance as substitute alongside David Elliot. Manager Hay fielded the following selection for what was undoubtedly a crucial match; Money, Dawson, Beattie, Aitken, McIntyre, McGowne, Stickroth, Lambert, Torfason, Hewitt and Broddle.

Disappointingly, the game was spoiled by a fierce wind and finished goal-less. A great save by Campbell Money from ex-Saint Billy Davies went a long way to denying the Pars both points. Mid-table St. Johnstone were then defeated in Perth on the first Saturday in March but once again Paisley's Saints were unable to consolidate the victory. Single-goal losses to Falkirk, Motherwell and Hibs meant that no points were earned over the following three weeks.

By the time Celtic visited Paisley on Wednesday 8 April St. Mirren were two points from relegation. To make matters worse, Saints were without Roy Aitken, suspended for the third time since his arrival at Love Street, but hopes were raised by John Hewitt's 16th minute goal. The slim survival hopes remained despite the visitor's second-half equaliser. The inevitable was delayed by no more than three days, however. A 0-0 draw at Tynecastle meant relegation after fifteen consecutive seasons in the Premier Division.

By a strange quirk of fate, relegation had once again occurred despite the side including players who would later become Scottish internationalists. In 1934-35 it had been Bobby Ancell; 1967-68, Archie Gemmill; and 1970-71 had seen Iain Munro, Gordon McQueen and Bobby McKean as regulars. Following 1991-92, Brian Martin and, more notably, Paul Lambert would develop into full internationalists after moving to other clubs. Yet, it was perhaps even more ironic that on this occasion the team had also contained two current internationalists; Scotland's Roy Aitken and Icelander Gunni Torfason.

David Hay admitted that the season had been poor and that his signings "had performed below expectations", nevertheless he was given the chance of a new contract if he could halve his management costs. Instead, Hay decided to take advantage of a job offer in the USA. In the final match programme of the season he wrote that "the Club will have the chance to rebuild in the First Division without the rigorous pressures of the top league. It will allow some breathing space in order to develop and bring through vital homegrown new talent."

Some of that talent was on show in the final match of the season at home to Dunfermline on 2 May. Martin Baker made his debut in a team that read Money, McGowne, Baker, Aitken, McWhirter, Lambert, Stickroth, Hewitt, Torfason, Lavety, Broddle. Despite the huge amount of money spent in transfer fees in recent years six of the side were "homegrown". One of them, Barry Lavety, scored his first two St. Mirren goals in only his third start, and Tomas Stickroth netted the third in his final game for the Club. It was also the last time that Roy Aitken would wear Saints' stripes.

On 26 May the new Manager arrived. It would be the third spell at St. Mirren Park for an old favourite; one who had shared in some of the Club's best recent memories. Hopefully he could rebuild the team to achieve similar success.

1992-93

Jimmy Bone strode through the doors of St. Mirren Park prepared to embark on a five-year plan aimed at re-establishing the team in the Premier Division.

On the opening day of August, the new Manager sent out an experienced line-up for his first competitive match in charge. The opposition was Raith Rovers, a mid-table First Division side during the five seasons since their promotion from the "Second" in 1987. The venue; Stark's Park.

It is unlikely that anyone could have predicted the outcome on that sunny Saturday; neither the most ardent home fan nor the most pessimistic visitor. Rovers went in three ahead at half time, and the situation deteriorated for Saints as a further four goals were lost after the interval as well as the services of Chic Charnley for the next seven fixtures due to another red card.

This was only the first of many disciplinary problems for both player and Club throughout the season. Regarding the match result; few, if any, of Saints' fans following that day would have taken consolation from the fact that Raith would eventually win the title at a canter.

During the summer months, it had been necessary for business to proceed as normal despite the loss of Premier Division status. Negotiations continued towards developing both ends of St. Mirren Park and Renfrew District Council agreed to convey certain areas of land within the boundary that had been discovered not to actually belong to the Club. It was estimated that the entire redevelopment would cost around £5 million, and that the first phase could be funded by St. Mirren's successful lottery.

To supplement the Club's commercial income another new weekly prize draw was unveiled and by October the "Gold Bond Scheme" had attracted almost three thousand members paying £1 per week. The Club's main sponsor for the season would be The Ingram Motoring Group, a

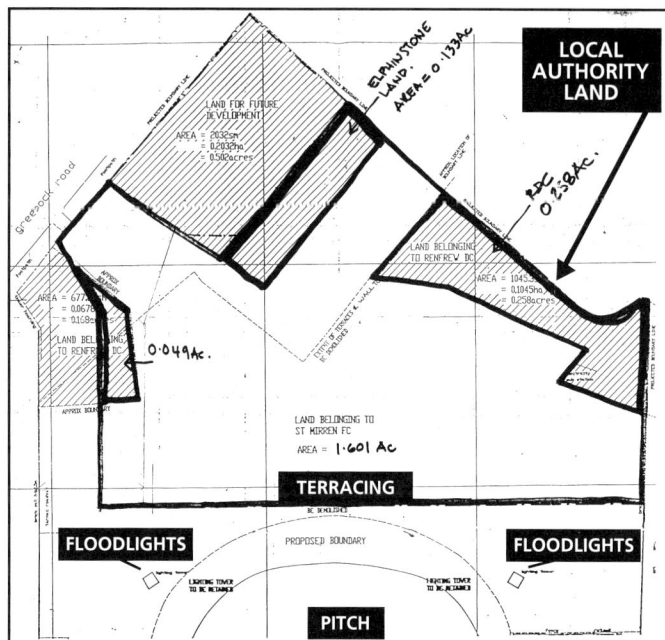

The Caledonia End of St. Mirren Park, showing land 'inside' the Stadium's boundary belonging to the local authority.

Volkswagen dealership with a showroom in Paisley's Rowan Street. "Ingram" became the fourth company name to appear on the famous stripes. Also during the non-playing break a substantial sum in the form of transfer revenue was finally received when Bundesliga side FC Saarbrucken paid 350,000DM for the transfer of Tomas Stickroth.

The Club's overdraft was now considerably reduced, and the Board's aim was to further lower it to around £300,000. Thereafter, the budget would be reviewed monthly to keep spending in check. During the season Commercial Manager Bill Campbell would set up a Business Club that would act at once as a fund-raiser and also as a way of fostering positive relations between the Club and the local business community.

The heavy defeat at Stark's Park did help simplify one difficult decision for the Club; an £80,000 bid from St. Johnstone for Gunni Torfason was thereafter accepted. Other than the suspended Charnley, however, Manager Bone kept faith with the remainder of his first-day selection over the following weeks. Money, Dawson, Reid, Manley, Baillie, Elliot, Lambert, McGill, Broddle, McIntyre and Lavety all remained in the thirteen-man squad, with young Barry McLaughlin leading the attack in his league debut at Hamilton on 5 August.

McIntyre then dropped out to allow Kenny McDowall's return and yet another youngster, ex-Falkirk player Roland Fabiani appeared days after his signing as a substitute in the 1-0 win at Cappielow. That match signalled Mark Reid's final appearance for Saints before his release. Teenager Martin Baker took over to establish himself in the Number "3" jersey.

The seventh match, on 5 September away to Meadowbank Thistle, saw the somewhat controversial return of forward John Hewitt to the team. Jimmy Bone re-signed him from Highland League club Deveronvale only three months after his release from Saints on a free transfer. The Scottish League ruled that the normal time stipulation over re-signings did not apply and manager Bone hoped that Hewitt's experience would help progress the talents of the Club's youngsters.

A "crowd" of 1,337 did little to provide any atmosphere at Edinburgh's Meadowbank Stadium, but Saints took the points with their sixth consecutive league shut-out, equalling the club record set back in 1967/68. In the victory, Barry Lavety netted his third and fourth League goals of the season and Saints climbed up to fourth position with a playing record which now read; won three, drawn three, lost one, goals scored seven, goals lost seven!

That Meadowbank game was the first in a run of five successive victories that continued the rise up the table and Saints sat in second place at the end of the first quarter, raising hopes that an immediate return to the top division could be achieved. The next match, on 10 October, was a top-of-the-table clash against Raith Rovers, providing the opportunity to gain revenge for that opening day drubbing, although now only five of Saints' opening-day eleven were still in place.

As it was it took an own goal four minutes from time to present Saints with a share of the points in front of 6,194, the largest home league gate outwith an Old Firm match since the New Year holiday fixture against Motherwell eighteen months previously. With two promotion places up for grabs, a share of the points against the league leaders was not a bad result but, without the injured Hewitt over the next five weeks, the team dropped points to strugglers Dumbarton and Meadowbank as well as losing the home derby meeting with Morton by three goals to two.

Roddy Manley was dropped, as was Kenny McDowall, while Barry Lavety was relegated to the bench. It was, however, good to see Norrie McWhirter return to action and young Jamie Fullarton breaking into the side.

On Sunday 13 December, St. Mirren Park hosted the third final of the League's new "Challenge Cup" competition. Known by its sponsor's name, the "B&Q Cup" was competed for by First and Second Division clubs. Saints' first attempt had ended ... at the first attempt, when Ayr United won the sides' First Round clash 2-1 at the end of September. The Final was between Hamilton Academical and Morton. The Lanarkshire club ensured that Saints' County neighbours could not boast of winning a national final at Love Street.

By the 2-0 home defeat to Hamilton on 19 December, Saints had won a mere three games out of twelve since that home match against Raith two months earlier. The most noteworthy of these being a 5-0 home success over Cowdenbeath on 2 December in which Ricky Gillies joined his elder brother Kenny in the line-up. He made a scoring debut at the tender age of sixteen years and one hundred days to become Saints' youngest player of the first 125 years. Campbell Money also made his mark on the game by showing his outfield colleagues how to take a penalty kick after a recent sequence of misses.

The result was less convincing than the score-line suggests as the opener came on the stroke of half time, in an incident that lost the visitors their goalkeeper. An eccentric display between the sticks by Cowdenbeath's left back eventually contributed to the size of his side's downfall.

Three days later a 2-0 defeat at Ayr brought Saints back down to earth and led to a parting of the ways with Chic Charnley. The volatile midfielder was one of THREE Saints dismissed at Somerset Park but, while the club felt Lavety and Lambert to have been harshly dealt with, Charnley's conduct was "not to be condoned" and his contract was terminated due to "persistent serious misconduct".

Boxing Day provided St. Mirren with the welcome present of maximum points when Clydebank came calling. Money, again, netted a spot-kick and new signing Eddie Gallagher from Dundee opened his account with the winner. Gallagher had been signed on the basis that a fee of £10,000 would only be payable if St Mirren were promoted in 1993 or 1994.

Bone continued to shape his side while dealing with the ever-present financial constraints. Youngsters Baker, Taylor, Cummings, and the Gillies brothers were tied up on two-year deals, while former first team regulars Jim Beattie and Danny McGill were offered free transfers in an effort to further cut the wage bill.

Gallagher struck again to open the scoring at Cappielow in the 2 January Renfrewshire derby but the Buddies' County rivals equalised in the second period to keep Saints stuck in mid-table. It was now apparent that only a concentrated effort would set the promotion challenge back on track and it would have to be done without the team's second top scorer over the past five matches ... Campbell Money!

Les Fridge returned to goal; in front of him former Stoke City youngster Steve Farrell and Paul McIntyre contested possession of the number "2" shirt; Norrie McWhirter and Lex Baillie formed the central defensive partnership and Martin Baker played at left-back when fit; Eddie Gallagher and David Elliot were now the favoured combination up front.

There was a brief reminder of what it was like to travel to a Premier Division ground when Saints were drawn to face Hibernian in the Third Round of the Scottish Cup. It was also a reminder of what travelling to a Premier ground had become prior to relegation; the hosts enjoying a fairly comfortable 5-2 win to repeat Dundee United's three-goal margin that had knocked St. Mirren out of the League Cup at Love Street on a midweek evening back in August.

On 14 January it was announced that local businessman George Campbell had been co-opted onto the Board and that St. Mirren was now operating on an "even financial keel on a day-to-day basis". This

Amongst the players going through their paces in pre-season training are Paul McIntyre (16), David Elliot (6), Barry McLaughlin (17), Barry Lavety (15) and Manager Jimmy Bone.

positive news was qualified by the information that the Company nevertheless remained in the position of having to cope with accumulated debts built up over recent years and that the Club was again operating close to its overdraft limit.

The need to cut back on spending freed Julian Broddle to move to Partick Thistle for no fee and Mark Reid accepted a severance payment to end his contract with the Club. The cut-backs then stretched to the position of Assistant Manager when Gordon Smith's resignation was reluctantly accepted early in February and the post was not continued. Campbell Money and Kenny McDowall were both promoted to player-coach roles in support of the Manager on a daily basis. This move was viewed positively by the supporters.

An undefeated start to the New Year in league fixtures was maintained with five wins and a draw up to the end of February but, such was the lapse in form between October and the end of December, that the undefeated run only pushed Saints up one place to fourth position. However, if further good results could be gained over the next three games then the team would be boosted at the expense of their closest challengers; Kilmarnock, Dunfermline and Raith Rovers.

Robert Dawson returned at right-back but more significant was the loss, through injury, of John Hewitt. The side went down 1-0 in both of the first two games but managed to win a point from Raith Rovers.

All was not lost, but Saints could afford few slip-ups through to the forty-fourth game if they were to win a coveted promotion place. Unfortunately, slip-ups were exactly what the fans got, as convincing wins over Morton and Clydebank were bounded by defeats to the bottom three clubs; Dumbarton, Stirling Albion and Meadowbank Thistle.

The introduction of fresh faces in the form of Alex Bone, the Manager's nephew, and James Peacock, a youngster released by Queen's Park Rangers, failed to provide the desired effect and the team slipped to sixth. With five games remaining, there was now absolutely no margin for error.

A 2-1 win at second-placed Dunfermline Athletic on 17 April raised some hope, and John Hewitt's return a week later for the visit of Kilmarnock set the Club up for a barnstorming finish. 8,432 watched as Hewitt curled in a wonderful free-kick winner against Killie and, seven days later, Eddie Gallagher struck twice to send Hamilton Accies home pointless. A sizeable support followed the team to Ayr for the penultimate game, another that just had to be won.

It turned out to be a topsy-turvy roller-coaster of a match, which in many ways mirrored Saints entire season. 1-0 down after the first half, Saints threw caution to the wind in an effort to gain the only result that mattered. At the end of a pulsating ninety minutes, six goals had been shared; the team had given everything, but it wasn't enough.

The home match against Cowdenbeath on 15 May was now meaningless in terms of the promotion race, so the Manager chose to test the abilities of several of the youngsters on whom the Club's future would have to depend. Promotion had floundered on those defeats to the bottom three, just over a month earlier, and Saints ended the season a mere three points behind Kilmarnock who were promoted in second-place. No fewer than thirty-five players had appeared for the Club in League matches throughout a season of rapid transition.

With the failure to return to financially advantageous Premier Division football, and having been unable to make significant income from the sale of players, the Chief Executive now referred to the financial situation as "dire". Legal action was being threatened by seven individual creditors and the bank was regarded as being "not particularly flexible" in supporting the Club's position. The Chief Executive made the situation clear, "in short we do not have enough money to meet our debts."

Mr. Earlie recommended to the Board that John Paton, a man with considerable experience in both the banking and footballing worlds, be appointed as financial consultant with immediate effect. Within months Mr. Paton would become a Director of the Club.

Sunderland became the latest club to show interest in Paul Lambert but there was still no concrete offer forthcoming. Most of the older players were now out of contract, allowing the club to re-negotiate deals with the aim of slashing the wage bill for the forthcoming year; £400,000 was the target for the season, a sum that was equivalent to what was fairly recently being paid out every four WEEKS.

The Knox Street Supporters' Association was able to lend the Club £100,000 following an EGM of its members, allowing for a significant easing of the situation with regard to the most pressing creditors and further good news arrived in the form of planning permission for the redevelopment of the Caledonia Street end of the ground. Good news for the fans, also ... there would be no increase in admission charges.

However, one worrying development had appeared on the horizon of Scottish Football ... the idea of a breakaway "Super League". There was a very real fear that such an occurrence would have potentially catastrophic financial repercussions for the clubs currently outside the top division.

1993-94

The repercussions of the threatened "Super League" were immediate. Given such a backdrop of uncertainty the Scottish Football League could find no sponsor for its two major competitions, the League Cup and the League itself. This in turn meant reduced revenue for all the member clubs during the new season; a situation St. Mirren could ill-afford.

It was a particularly difficult time for Saints' long-serving Director Yule Craig who, as President of the Scottish Football League, found himself facing the troubles from two separate perspectives.

Earlier in the year, the Board had discussed its preference for a 16-12-10 League set up, but by now the favoured compromise across the country appeared to be for four divisions each containing 10 teams. The Directors put their vote behind this attempt to keep the earning power of the self-proclaimed "Big Boys" within the Scottish League structure, whilst continuing to focus the Club's attention on its aim of rising back to play amongst them.

An Executive Committee was formed to take control of the day-to-day running of the Club. This was a significant development towards regarding St Mirren as a "business operation" rather than simply a football club. The Committee would be chaired by Mr. Earlie, the Chief Executive, and consist of two other directors, Messrs. Palmer and Campbell, together with General Manager Jack Copland and Commercial Manager Bill Campbell. Also included was newly appointed financial consultant John Paton.

The six men would convene on a fortnightly basis, and report to the monthly meeting of the full Board of Directors. At this time former Chairman, Willie Todd, decided to retire and was awarded the position of Honorary President in recognition of his stalwart service to the Club. His place on the Board was taken by John Paton, who had now ended his previous association with Montrose FC.

Whilst the new Executive Committee worked to ensure that the Club was operating "to budget", only a major reduction in borrowing seemed likely to convince the bank to assist in the financing of the proposed ground developments. However, that situation would not be resolved for several more months.

In the meantime, the sweeping terracing at the Caledonia Street end was cleared and a ten-feet high advertising hoarding temporarily spanned the width of the pitch to conceal the area behind. Bob Earlie explained the next steps in the process: "We are currently awaiting bids from contractors for the construction of the new stand. Only as and when these become available will we be able to apply to the various grant authorities for financial assistance for the project."

Nevertheless, the problem of financing the likely balance of the new stand project was high on the Executive Committee's agenda, as was simultaneously finding ways and means of satisfying the bank manager's demands for reduced borrowing and the remaining creditors' demands for repayment. Fortunately, sponsorship deals had not been halted at a local level and the Commercial Manager "traded-in" Volkswagen for Ford as Clanford Motors became the Club's latest major backer.

One particularly disappointing cutback that had to be implemented was the closure of the Club Shop in the town's Piazza Shopping Centre. It was estimated that approximately one-quarter of the Club's current losses were tied up in the shop, a situation highlighted during the month of May when one week's takings amounted to a mere £54. The selling of the new replica strips and souvenirs would now be handled in the Main Stand office on weekdays but would be located rent-free on match days at 63 Love Street, the site of Campbell Money's former sports shop.

This proved much more successful, and when these premises were first used on a Saturday for the visit of Dunfermline Athletic on 16 October, £350 was taken on the single day. Later in the season a portakabin at the Love Street end of the ground would be converted to provide matchday sales.

Summer 1993 - with the West terracing cleared and the North Bank now seated, the stadium awaits construction of the Caledonia Stand.

A timely financial boost came thanks to a clause in Ian Ferguson's transfer contract, activated when he gained his fifth Scottish Cap, and the closed season also saw Paul Lambert in the transfer spotlight, as brothers Jim and Tommy McLean expressed interest in the Scotland Under-21 captain's services for their respective clubs, Dundee United and Motherwell. Lambert's contract had ended and it was certain that he would go to the highest bidder as a way of easing Saints' financial worries.

After appearing in three of St. Mirren's first four fixtures Lambert finally moved to Motherwell for £100,000 cash, plus £65,000 rated left-winger Jim Gardner and other possible payments depending on his progress. The well-publicised external pressure to raise money had encouraged the bidding clubs to offer well below Lambert's worth, a situation further compounded when the Club's bankers refused to discharge any of the funds received ... all went towards reducing the overdraft.

Seven of the thirteen players that featured in the 7-0 defeat at Kirkcaldy twelve months earlier were no longer on the playing staff. Neither were a further seven that had made appearances later in the season. This latter group included goalkeeper Les Fridge (now with Clyde) and Kenny McDowall whose injury problems forced him to concentrate on his coaching role.

Despite everything, hopes were high for a good year ahead. In particular, the anticipation was that lessons had been learned from the previous season, and that promotion would now be won at the second attempt. The process of League re-organisation had reduced the odds, however, as only one club would step up to the Premier Division. As it transpired, Saints reached a cup final before Christmas, but the main prize of promotion would once again elude Paisley's finest.

The Manager's first selection included two new signings; one from either end of the experience scale. A new goalkeeper, nineteen year-old Alan Combe, arrived at a cost of £24,000 from Cowdenbeath while veteran defender Neil Orr was snapped up after his release from Hibernian during the summer. Unfortunately, opening-day visitors Airdrieonians were not impressed and headed back to Lanarkshire with full points after their 1-0 victory.

In retrospect, the opening to the League campaign may appear less traumatic than twelve months earlier: nonetheless it would eventually develop into something significantly less successful. Two goals and two draws, from six matches included three home defeats, was far from promotion form. Indeed, following Gardner's debut, in a 3-0 home loss to Dumbarton on 11 September, Saints sat firmly at the bottom of the First Division.

Four days later the team set off on a trip to Fife and a meeting with a Dunfermline Athletic side that appeared similarly troubled following their own failure to win promotion at the first attempt. Saints won a midweek thriller by the odd-goal-in-seven with Gardner scoring his first for the Club. On Saturday next the number of victories was doubled courtesy of a 2-1 win against Clyde in Paisley.

By 23 October, Saints had taken ten of a possible twenty-six points, winning three of the thirteen fixtures, and had only just climbed above the two relegation places. Win number four seemed certain when an Eddie Gallagher hat-trick had them coasting 3-0 ahead at Boghead against Dumbarton with under fifteen minutes remaining. It wasn't to be, as the loss of a goal resulted in inexplicable panic, and the team were eventually fortunate indeed to escape with a 3-3 draw.

At least that point was enough to lift the team one place, and an excellent 2-1 victory at Cappielow over deadly rivals Morton raised the team another spot to eighth by the end of the month and provided a much-needed boost for the fans

The improved run of league results coincided with Saints' advance into the semi-finals of the Scottish League's only sponsored competition; the B&Q Cup. Clyde, Morton and Airdrieonians had all been defeated on their own grounds and now Jimmy Bone had another trip to prepare his players for as the draw paired Ayr United with St. Mirren, and Falkirk with Meadowbank Thistle.

Two goals from Eddie Gallagher cancelled out the home side's opener and carried the Buddies into the final where their opponents would be a Falkirk side that already appeared destined for the Premier Division.

Having been an ever-present since his signing, Jim Gardner would hereafter start only another five games with David Elliot returning to favour on the left wing. Another player brought back into the fray was Barry McLaughlin, whose best position had now been established as being in central defence. Jamie Fullarton (very soon to replace Lambert as Scotland's Under-21 captain), Paul McIntyre, Alex Bone, and newcomer Jim Dick from Airdrieonians, had also established themselves as regulars in the Manager's plans. The continually evolving side strung together a run of five league wins in the lead up to its biggest day of the season so far.

Now sitting on the fringe of the promotion race, a confident Saints faced up to table-toppers Falkirk on Sunday 12 December in the B&Q Cup Final at a sodden, freezing Fir Park, Motherwell, where almost 14,000 fans braved the driving wind, rain and sleet to urge on their respective favourites. Much of the St. Mirren support was open to the elements behind the town-end goal, in the only uncovered part of the stadium, suffering in the biting cold. Children cried and shivered in shocking conditions while some present thought that the match might be abandoned ... it wasn't.

St Mirren dominated early proceedings and were unfortunate not to be ahead by half-time ... if only injured top-scorer Eddie Gallagher had been available. In what turned out to be the proverbial game of two halves, the Bairns' aerial dominance was used to good effect. Two unchallenged jumps from set-pieces led to goals that literally turned the game on its head, and they eventually won the trophy by a 3-0 scoreline. Saints' team at Fir Park was Money, Dawson, Baker, McWhirter, McLaughlin, Orr, Bone (R. Gillies), Dick, Lavety, Hewitt (McIntyre), and Elliot. Despite his coaching responsibilities, Campbell Money still played over thirty times for the first team during the season.

Although defeated, St. Mirren had given a good account of themselves, gaining £10,000 as the competition's runner-up as well as the unique distinction of becoming Scotland's one and only club to have played in the final of a national knockout tournament in every decade of the twentieth century!

Back to League business; and there was a lot of work ahead if the recent good form was to translate into a charge up the table. A 3-1 win over Falkirk on 3 January at St. Mirren Park was enjoyed both as revenge for the Challenge Cup defeat, and as a promise of improved fortune in the New Year.

This optimism failed to be totally justified and the following eleven victories and seven defeats left the team in sixth position, fifteen points shy of promotion at the end of "hostilities". The team was never in contention for the sole promotion slot and, for the most part, was clear of any real danger of ending in one of the five relegation places.

The Manager's assessment of the season was that "the quality of experience in all departments is not good enough", a statement perhaps explaining the increasingly less frequent selections of Orr, Hewitt and Gallagher; the last of whom played his final game for Saints on 19 March in a 2-0 home defeat to Dunfermline Athletic.

Jimmy Bone was happier at the progress of his younger players. At the end of March he wrote in his match programme column; "Against Airdrie we had six teenagers in our pool of 14 and that did not include Barry Lavety and Martin Baker who were given a rest ... We will get there to give all St. Mirren fans a side to be proud of but it will take time."

Much of the praise for Saints' youthful complexion was due to the efforts of Joe Hughes, who was appointed by David Hay to develop a youth structure within the Club. His aptitude for the role was only highlighted when the Scotland Under-21 team, captained by Jamie Fullarton against Austria on 19 April, included no fewer than three Saints; the others being Martin Baker and Barry Lavety.

The real successes of the year were definitely in the financial aspects of the game. Although the season had seen a continual struggle to remain within the agreed borrowing limit, and almost constant liaison with the bank, the Chairman's Report at the Club AGM later in the year contained some positive detail. Allan Marshall confirmed with some satisfaction that income from commercial activities had risen by twenty-percent despite a difficult economic climate and that the net deficit in the Statement of Income and Expenditure had been reduced by fifty-percent compared to the previous year despite a significant drop in transfer income.

1994-95 would represent a new era for Scottish football with the reconciliation of the disputing parties and a restructuring of the League. Saints' fans could only hope that it would also herald a new era for their famous Club!

1994-95

Construction of the West Stand finally got under way. Barr Construction, an Ayrshire firm at the forefront of stadium development, had been awarded the contract and, as the steel superstructure began to take shape, the scale of the new enterprise became apparent; the new stand would be a marvellous addition to the Club's famous old ground. Almost exactly one hundred years on from the opening match at the "Love Street Grounds" in September 1894, the shape of St. Mirren Park was undergoing another major change.

Significant moves were agreed behind the scenes at a monthly meeting of the Board of Directors that coincidentally took place on the occasion of the Club's 117th birthday. Robert Earlie added the position of Club Chairman to that of Chief Executive as Allan Marshall's business commitments led to him assuming a non-executive position. Furthermore, Stewart Gilmour, a local businessman with a strong family association to the Club, was co-opted onto the Board and Executive Committee.

At that same 6 October meeting, former player Jack Copland became temporary Company Secretary in addition to his post of General Manager

Groundsman Tommy Docherty 'cuts a dash' on his hallowed turf.

and it was noted that, with the new stand fifty-percent complete, discussions were ongoing regarding funding possibilities. A sizeable grant had been received from the "Football Trust" and the excess land behind the new stand was being sold for a housing development.

Nonetheless, there remained a substantial funding balance to be met, a situation not helped by additional costs of approximately £100,000 required to purchase four parcels of land from Renfrew District Council, the related legal fees, and a "title indemnity policy" in favour of Woolwich Homes to cover the "defect" in the 1905 title deeds that had led to the confusion over land ownership.

The final decision over whether or not to proceed with the planned sports and leisure complex within the new stand was delayed until the last possible moment as the Directors weighed up all the financial implications and funding options available to them. On 10 December, the Executive Committee agreed to recommend that the Club should proceed with the project in its entirety; there would be further grant aid available to help finance the additional work and the estimated annual income of around £140,000 from letting the facilities would be welcomed.

Back in 1921 the Club's Directors had opted to minimise financial risk by reducing the size of the planned grandstand that was the focal point of the "Greater Love Street Grounds". In later years that decision had appeared short sighted to many observers of the Club. The current Directors were anxious to avoid a similar error of judgement and were prepared to expend the considerable efforts required to provide a long-term addition to the Club's earning power.

On the playing front noteworthy additions to St. Mirren, "the team", during the new season were Steven Watson, a former Rangers youth player who made twenty-nine appearances, and another of the Club's prodigal sons, Frank McAvennie, who played seven matches between October and December. McAvennie showed that he still had a few touches of class, but he ultimately left without scoring a goal and only having helped the side to a single victory.

That win, 1-0 at home to Ayr United on 5 November, courtesy of a Robert Dawson spot-kick, was only the second victory of a campaign that had included four defeats and six draws up to fireworks night.

The new Bell's League had introduced more than simply a different arrangement of the country's clubs. Teams were now competing to earn three points for every victory and one point for every draw, thus giving an increased advantage to sides capable of fielding a winning combination. Remaining undefeated might still provide some psychological benefit but, in terms of progress, a run of two losses and two wins was now as profitable as two draws and two wins had been previously.

Such innovations had temporarily satisfied the League's disaffected clubs but the new divisional-split would last only four seasons.

Unfortunately St. Mirren remained one of the clubs that found fielding a winning combination most elusive. Only two of Saints' First Division opponents won fewer matches; and only a further two teams throughout all four divisions. Not until 11 March did Jimmy Bone's men win their fourth League fixture; a 3-1 southern success away to Stranraer in front of an audience of only 935. That result finally, and thankfully, lifted Saints out of the dreaded second relegation place.

A higher-than-average five wins in the closing ten games secured First Division status for another year, but it was extremely worrying that Saints had spent twenty-four of the thirty-six weeks of the campaign in a bottom-three position and were as close as four points off second-bottom with only five games remaining.

The cup competitions failed to offer any respite for players, Club or supporters. In what was now the Coca-Cola League Cup, Dundee United proved to be Saints' nemesis for the third successive season, winning 1-0 in Paisley, and any thoughts of another run of success in the B&Q Cup were halted in Round One when a penalty shoot-out was lost at Stranraer's tidy Stair Park after 120 minutes of struggle had ended in a 1-1 deadlock.

Memories of another era were certainly rekindled by a Scottish Cup draw which sent the team to the national stadium, Hampden Park, to face temporary residents Celtic on 28 January in Round Three. The team's form leading up to the tie was far from ideal. They had tasted victory only once in the previous twelve First Division games that began with a 2-2 home draw against St. Johnstone in November and ended seven days prior to the Hampden trip with a 5-1 away drubbing from the same side.

A superb travelling support of approximately 5,000 Buddies travelled in good heart to Glasgow and cheered the team from start to finish. The players responded by giving their best performance of the season to date. Given that twenty goals had been conceded and only seven scored during the recent poor run of League form, the 2-0 defeat to Celtic was not achieved without some merit. Nevertheless, consecutive defeats to Hamilton, Raith and Airdrie followed before results in those final ten matches dragged the team seven points clear of relegation.

Football was taking a back seat to financial matters and possible transfer activity remained close to the surface of Club business throughout the season. Liverpool expressed an interest in Gillies, while Dundee United and Bolton Wanderers did likewise with Lavety, but neither were followed through. There were also discussions with Airdrieonians regarding a possible swap deal involving Eddie Gallagher but, despite protracted efforts on both sides, the deal failed to materialise.

Three seasons into Jimmy Bone's five-year plan, the portents appeared increasingly less favourable. The Club's direction, however, was crystal clear; of thirty-one players used in League matches, only a dozen had played for other senior clubs and only six of these could have been considered first-team regulars. Saints were rearing their own again.

Campbell Money's appearances were reduced to fifteen as he focused more and more on coaching, and Alan Combe took over as number-one choice keeper. Robert Dawson was the Club's third-longest serving player behind Money and Norrie McWhirter and he continued to be an essential member of the team, missing only six games, Martin Baker and Steven Watson alternating as his full-back partner; John Boyd, a £35,000 December signing from Dumbarton (financed personally by the Executive Committee Directors), filled in on the left side of midfield and Barry McLaughlin had now become a fixture in the centre of defence alongside Norrie McWhirter; in attack, Alex Bone became Barry Lavety's most regular partner but the pairing managed only nine goals between them.

Ricky Gillies' career development continued with twenty-four League appearances and he had now become captain of Scotland's Under-17s, giving the Club two international captains on its books. Teenage 'keeper Derek Scrimgour made his debut on the final-day victory at home to relegated Ayr United, a game in which diminutive crowd pleaser Gary McGrotty scored the winner.

These last two players were regular members of a Saints' Reserve side that consisted throughout the season almost entirely of the Club's youth players. The boys performed exceptionally well, finishing runners-up to Rangers in the Reserve League West. The youthful approach was further emphasised when an under-19 team was selected to represent St. Mirren in an international tournament in the Netherlands ... eleven of the squad chosen had already featured in the first-team! The young Scots finished third in typically Scottish style; undefeated. Barry Lavety captained the team and ended as the competition's top scorer. Another player that caught the eye of the organisers was fifteen year-old Hugh Murray.

There definitely was hope on the horizon but, as Jimmy Bone had stated a year previously, "it will take time".

1995-96

With the new stand now towering over the Caledonia Street goal, and its funding package close to being finalised, discussions were opened regarding possible redevelopment of the Love Street end of the ground.

One decision that was quickly made concerned the uncovered family enclosure at "Cairter's Corner". A number of brave souls had still been prepared to suffer whatever conditions mother nature chose to throw their way on the prevailing westerly wind and watch proceedings from this famous part of the stadium. With the new 3,000-seat stand now available for opposition supporters, the visitors' previous accommodation in the west section of the North Stand was put to use for children and accompanying adults.

The Club's financial concerns remained pre-eminent and there was considerable commercial activity in advance of the new season. An estimated 3,000 fans were tempted along to the Club's first open-day on Sunday 6 August to view the facilities and watch Jimmy Bone put his players through a rigorous training session. The day was a great success.

Another winning idea (certainly as far as the fans were concerned) saw the "Blackburn Rovers" style, black-and-white halved strip of the previous campaign consigned to the bin, and the traditional vertical stripes re-instated.

A new shirt sponsor, Phoenix Honda, was confirmed following an innovative "Main Sponsors' Dinner". The gala-event was packed with companies each donating a flat-rate sum that allowed them entry into a lucky-draw, the winner of which would have the firm's shirts profiled on the jerseys. It was a winning idea that would be repeated, with one hundred and fifty companies signing up for the 1996 Dinner.

The Commercial Manager was happy to report that sales of lottery scratch-cards had evened out following an initial decline due to the introduction of a National Lottery in November 1994; in fact, the Club introduced a new incentive for members to commit to its new Gold Bond Scheme. "SaintsClub" was launched, offering a free monthly magazine and local retail discounts together with an entry into the Gold Bond prize draw, all for advance payment of Gold Bond subscriptions.

By the end of the season SaintsClub would account for one-third of all Gold Bond income; the hope was to increase this further. A new member of staff was employed to oversee this aspect of commercial operations; his name, Campbell Kennedy.

On weekdays, the Club Shop was now located in the foyer of the Sports' Complex, whose membership had already risen to an encouraging seven hundred. The facilities were further enhanced when an entertainment licence was granted to allow a members' bar to be opened in the foyer, and its use was extended on matchdays to season-ticket holders joining the new "Lapsley Club".

These were just some of the developments that the Board felt it necessary to introduce in an effort to become more pro-active with regard to the Company's financial operations. Another initiative was the introduction of the Club's own team of stewards run by its own Security

Adviser, Peter Copland, thus reducing matchday costs and increasing the level of professionalism and care for spectators. Against this innovative backdrop, transfer income still remained the most likely route to reducing the Club's debt and a closed season offer of £150,000 from Dundee United for Jamie Fullarton was accepted. Fullarton chose to reject the move.

Five separate loan-securities now existed with a combined value of £1.85million and, although a repayment structure was in place, the Club was pressed into creating a holding structure incorporating two companies (St. Mirren Football Club Limited and St. Mirren Sport and Leisure Complex Limited) and capitalising a proportion of the Directors' near £500,000 loans through a share issue to "improve the Club's underlying financial stability and the position of its secured creditors".

An EGM, held on 4 February, accepted the motion to increase the authorised share capital from £10,000 to £370,000. Unfortunately the final income generated fell well short of target and, by June 1996, John Paton reported that the bank was now seeking cashflow projections for the following two seasons; and these had to show that the Club could "at least break even".

If St. Mirren's financial future remained potentially perilous, then its immediate footballing future would provide the fans with a boost right at the outset of the campaign. In anticipation of the 1995-96 playing season, the new "Caledonia" Stand was formally opened on 4 April 1995 by Tom "Tiny" Wharton, Deputy Chairman of the Football Trust and a former first-class referee, and then officially "christened" on 14 August when Rangers provided the opposition in a challenge match.

The Club's main sponsor donated a superb cut-crystal vase, to be presented to the winning team in celebration of the occasion. After the match Saints' captain Robert Dawson stood proudly holding aloft the Phoenix Honda Trophy; Saints had beaten Rangers by one goal to nil. The delighted home supporters now looked forward to a much-improved autumn compared to the previous two seasons' abysmal openings.

It wouldn't be an easy task. The line-up of teams was about as hard as it could be in the First Division ... both Dundee sides; Dunfermline and St Johnstone; Lanarkshire rivals, Airdrieonians and Hamilton; near neighbours Dumbarton and Clydebank; and finally Morton, always guaranteed to raise their game for a derby clash with St. Mirren. Each of these clubs, like Saints, had a Premier Division history to look back upon and an unquenchable thirst to relive it.

There was some promise shown in an opening three games that produced two draws and a 2-1 away win against Airdrieonians on the first Saturday in September in which front-pair Bone and Lavety both netted. Disappointingly, the promise was not "kept" and Saints, once again, found themselves in the second relegation spot, having taken only a single point from the following five matches up to the beginning of October.

During this dip in performance the Club moved swiftly to support young striker Barry Lavety who was suffering high-profile personal problems. In the face of intense media attention, the Chairman wrote in the match programme, "The Board of Directors, the Management team and the players are fully committed to assisting Barry regain his former stature within the Club." The message was unequivocal; irrespective of its own monetary and performance problems, St. Mirren would stand by their young players and offer them every support in coping with the pressures of modern living.

Deputy Chairman of the Football Trust and former Referee Tom "Tiny" Wharton opens The St. Mirren Caledonia Stand on 4th April 1995.

However, it wasn't until the somewhat unexpected back-to-back away wins at Airdrie and Dens Park in mid January, that the team finally climbed out of the bottom three. A further six victories from their remaining fourteen games pushed the Club into mid-table respectability.

In addition to poor league form, there was a distinct lack of excitement generated by any of the three national cups. Aberdeen knocked Saints out of the League Cup in the opening round and Dunfermline Athletic did likewise in the Scottish Cup. The single win came by defeating East Stirlingshire in Round One of the League Challenge Cup, but Livingston ensured that Saints made no further progress.

Not one of these four cup-ties was played with the advantage of a home draw; a situation that was beginning to grate on the minds of St. Mirren followers. Amazingly in twenty-six cup draws since the beginning of the decade, Saints had been handed nineteen away ties!

Stuart Taylor battles against St. Johnstone.

On 2 March, Campbell Money played his last-ever match between-the-sticks before accepting the post of full-time Manager with Stranraer. From his first match in an August 1978 pre-season friendly against Southampton, "Dibble" played over four hundred matches in a superb Saints' career spanning close to eighteen years, saving more than his fair-share of penalty kicks ... and scoring a few as well. A true St. Mirren legend!

The other significant changes in playing staff were the departures of Orr, Dawson, Elliot, Gardner, Hewitt, McIntyre and Bone and the signings of combatant midfielder Robert Law from Partick Thistle, Canadian international defender Paul Fenwick from Dunfermline, and Mark Yardley from Third Division Cowdenbeath.

Yardley, in particular, would endear himself to the support throughout a stay of seven seasons with the Club. Signed for £25,000 thanks to what the Chairman described as "a benefactor who preferred to remain anonymous", big "Yards" netted within a minute of his debut against Hamilton on 23 September, and ended the season with eight goals. By the end of his time at St. Mirren Park, he would have become the Club's fourth highest post-war goal scorer with seventy-one goals.

As well as his scoring prowess, Yardley provided a physical presence in attack, an adept aerial ability and an awareness that helped to bring the best out in young Barry Lavety alongside him. This was no better demonstrated than in the derby victory over Morton on 18 November. The strike pairing ripped Saints' rivals apart with quick inter-passing and clinical finishing. Yardley hit a brace and fit-again Lavety netted a sensational hitch kick in the 3-0 win at Cappielow. Perhaps this was a combination that would point St Mirren in the direction of glory in the years to come.

1996-97

The anticipated Yardley/Lavety assault on First Division defences would not materialise ... not for a few more seasons at least. Barry Lavety was transferred to Hibernian on 13 August for £250,000 in one of many changes to life around St. Mirren Park both on and off the pitch.

Jamie Fullarton left for France at the end of his contract and, the day after Lavety's departure, further need to reduce expenditure resulted in a redundancy notice being handed to Coach Kenny McDowall. On learning of the decision Jimmy Bone sought urgent talks with the Directors. Unable to weaken the Board's resolve, the Manager resigned.

The Club looked to a committed St. Mirren man for help, in the familiar guise of Tony Fitzpatrick, who stepped back into the breach immediately. Taking extended leave from his SFA Community Coach post he accepted the role of "caretaker" until a new Manager was found.

The position appeared to have been filled just short of a month later when, at 6pm on 9 September, former player Iain Munro was named as Jimmy Bone's successor. Munro spent most of the next day discussing his remit with Bob Earlie and all seemed well ... he would begin his duties the following morning. Then, an early evening telephone call was received from his lawyer; Iain Munro would not be accepting the post, there were other opportunities available to him that he wished to pursue!

Having been appointed, Munro became the shortest-ever serving Manager in Saints' long history. Many supporters thought the snub unforgivable. The Board acted quickly to resolve the situation and Tony Fitzpatrick was quickly appointed Manager for a second term. It was a popular decision amongst the fans.

As Fitzpatrick worked tirelessly to maintain a focus on playing matters, there was soon further disruption behind the scenes when first Charlie Palmer and then Bob Earlie resigned from the Board.

Mr. Palmer had overseen the Club's vital youth development work since his appointment. The under-19 team had again travelled to Holland early in the summer and finished third out of twelve teams from across Europe, this time returning with three trophies; "Top Scorer" won by Chris Iwelumo, "Player of the Tournament" won by Brian Hetherston, and "The Most Promising Team of the Future". Such had been the success of the youth structure at St. Mirren that Mr. Palmer felt compelled to resign out of concern over the proposed direction of financial cutbacks.

Mr. Earlie, on the other hand, had cited his intention during the summer to stand down due to business pressures. Throughout his relatively short tenure he had driven a complete restructuring of the Company's business management and guided the major redevelopment process at the ground. His influence would not be quickly forgotten.

In the interim it was decided to operate without a Chairman, so the Club's Financial Director, John Paton, led the Board in the role of "Managing Director". The depleted Board of Directors had some hard facts to face. It was now almost certain that the Lavety transfer would be the last income of its type for the Club. The implications of a ruling passed in the European Court (the "Bosman" case) had recently been ratified by UEFA and meant that players had the right to move freely to another club at the end of their contract, as indeed Barry Lavety and Fullarton had been.

Whilst a transfer fee would remain necessary to move a player under contract, interested clubs could choose to wait until such times as the player was available for nothing. It was as if the plug had been pulled on St. Mirren's principal escape route from possible financial ruin.

All thoughts of further ground re-development were set aside and the focus turned to one issue; survival. Peter Dallas was appointed new Commercial Manager and the success of the Club's commercial activity was now more vital than ever. "Phoenix Honda" would remain on the team jerseys but there was a new kit supplier, a new strip ... and a new badge.

Following unexpected correspondence from The Court of the Lord Lyon, official heraldic authority for Scotland with responsibility for prosecuting as a criminal offence anyone unauthorised to use a Coats of Arms, the Club would no longer be permitted to display elements of the Paisley crest on its badge. A new design was required and, following several attempts at satisfying the Lord Lyon King of Arms, a stylised version created by graphic designer and St. Mirren shareholder Jack Paterson was deemed acceptable.

During the summer of 1996, the Friends of St. Mirren Association (FOSMA) was reformed with the expressed aim of "promoting the Club in the community, increasing revenue through fundraising ideas, and giving the club back to its supporters". One of the group's first acts was to resurrect "The Saint" newspaper. Other tasks included instigating a general maintenance programme of work around St. Mirren Park, thus ensuring safety certificates were obtained that allowed all parts of the stadium to remain open.

FOSMA even persuaded one local fast-food chain to instigate a free match-tickets scheme for primary school children. This resulted in more than seven hundred paying adults accompanying the ticketed youngsters at one particular home match; much needed income for the Club and an idea that would be often repeated.

In spite of the turmoil "upstairs", the playing side of the Club actually enjoyed its most successful season since relegation five years earlier. As in 1993, the team finished in fourth place, but this time a mere two points away from the chance to face Premier League club Hibernian in a "play-off" to settle the second promotion/relegation issue.

League business commenced on 17 August with a heartening result: East Fife 0, St Mirren 4. At the seventh attempt, Saints had finally succeeded in beginning a First Division campaign with a victory! It was Tony Fitzpatrick's first game as Caretaker Manager and he received a rapturous welcome from the large travelling support at the Fifers' Bayview home.

The players who set the Club off to a winning start were Combe, Dick, Baker, McWhirter (McLaughlin), Fenwick, Watson, Hetherston, Taylor, Gillies, Mendes, and Yardley. The only newcomer was nineteen year-old Londoner, Junior Mendes, who had been released by Chelsea.

Helping Tony Fitzpatrick on the touchline was Youth Coach Matt Kerr, but Matt also made a telling contribution on the park. Ricky Gillies, who had taken over Lavety's main striking role, revealed after the game that he had taken a liking to Kerr's boots and secretly "borrowed" them for the day! Matt's reaction at half-time was to promise Ricky he could keep them if he scored another goal in the second-half; he duly obliged. The lucky boots also helped Saints' new rising star earn his first Under-21 call-up a few days after the match. He was later joined in the international squad by Brian "Bubbles" Hetherston.

Pride preceded a fall, and four defeats in the following five games plunged the team back into a familiar eighth-place at the same stage of the fourth successive season. Fitzpatrick took action; Jim Dick was moved into midfield and another of the youth squad, Brian Smith, took over at right back. Stuart Munro, a former youth player from the 1980s, was signed on monthly contracts from the end of September to add some much needed experience to the midfield.

St. Mirren utilised the services of an 'Advan' in the mid-nineties, to advertise forthcoming matches. Paisley Panda liked the idea too!

The response was immediate. On 28 September Junior Mendes opened the scoring, and his own personal account, in the ninth minute of yet another win at Cappielow. By the time Saints beat Morton again on 16 November, the team had climbed to second in the table!

The tightness of the division was illustrated when the following reverse to Airdrieonians dropped the team back down to sixth. However, this turned out to be one of only two defeats in sixteen games through to the end of January; a run that raised thirty-four points.

It appeared that the team had lost a third fixture during this run of success by going down 1-0 at Falkirk, but the result was declared void when it was discovered that the home side had illegally fielded a trialist. Re-played on 8 January, Saints returned from Brockville with a one-all draw and rubbed salt in the wound just six days later, defeating the "Bairns" 1-0 in the scheduled fixture in Paisley.

Another experienced midfielder, Johnstone born Tommy Turner, was signed on a short-term contract after being released by Partick Thistle and scored his first goal in the 3-2 win over Dundee on 28 January. Paul Fenwick had an influential game, laying on Turner's goal and scoring the other two himself.

As had happened so often in the past, however, the team's staying power was open to question; first in a 3-1 home defeat to struggling Stirling Albion, and then by picking up only a single point from visits to Cappielow and Firhill.

The Scottish Cup draw sent St. Mirren on the road again with a trip to face Second Division Clyde; the Buddies' third cup-tie of the season against a team from the lower division. On 8 August, in the first competitive match of the season, recently relegated Hamilton Academical eliminated Saints from the League Challenge Cup with a 2-1 win. Five days later Berwick Rangers had made the long trek to Paisley and were comprehensively beaten 4-0 in Round Two of the Coca-Cola League Cup.

St. Mirren's continuation in the Coca-Cola competition lasted no further than the next stage at which Dunfermline Athletic, newly promoted to the Premier Division, defeated them 3-1 at East End Park. Any hopes of a longer run in "the Scottish" were ill-founded and Clyde repeated the Pars victory margin at their new home of Broadwood Stadium in Cumbernauld. In ten years since famously lifting the Cup in 1987, Saints had now won a mere three Scottish Cup ties.

St. Mirren continued to disappoint their followers in cup competitions, however the loss of Lavety had not proved to be the major blow anticipated and there were a couple of new goal scoring talents on the horizon. Chris Iwelumo, who had made a scoring debut against Dumbarton twelve months earlier when he replaced Lavety in a 5-0 win, was now pushing for a regular starting place.

The second striker to make a mark in the wake of Lavety's departure was local boy, and Saints' supporter, Steven McGarry. Young Steven went straight into the first team for the third game of the season, at Firhill on 31 August. Fittingly for a "Saints man", his first goal for the Club was scored against County rivals Morton at St. Mirren Park in March, with a Yardley brace completing the 3-1 victory.

Commendably, given the traumatic start to the season, spring arrived with Saints retaining an outside chance of promotion. Experienced forward, Wayne Foster, became the third short-term signing when he was brought in to play the final ten matches. Hopefully he would provide the cutting edge Saints sought to carry the team into the play-offs.

Foster netted on his debut against St. Johnstone on 22 February as the team won 2-1, but the Englishman managed only one other goal, and Saints fell just short of their target. Ultimately, the number of suspensions incurred by having the worst disciplinary record in the four divisions conspired against the promotion bid; important players sat in the stand as the team faced up to vital matches.

Of the four games lost in the closing straight, three were against the teams destined to finish above the Club in the league - St. Johnstone, Airdrieonians and Dundee. The fourth, however, was a 1-0 loss away to fourth-bottom Stirling Albion.

The two recent results against the "Binos" had ensured that Saints' would spend another season in the First Division. Twelve months on, in somewhat different circumstances, there would be cause to celebrate a result against the Stirling outfit that, thankfully, ensured another season in the First Division.

For everyone connected with the Club, 1996-97 had appeared to mark a turnaround in playing fortunes. Now, if it could only be built on.

1997-98

"This is the Year." Supporters were sure of it and a Mendes hat-trick on the opening day at New Broomfield added to the optimism; especially as the 3-1 victory on 2 August had been achieved without the services of several experienced players.

Stuart Munro and Wayne Foster had left at the end of the season and Ricky Gillies was transferred to Aberdeen with a year of his contract remaining. This meant Dons' boss Roy Aitken spending a reported £350,000 to secure the signing. Gillies had been a youth player during Aitken's time at St. Mirren Park.

Martin Baker was also on the move, leaving for Rugby Park with Kilmarnock player Tom Brown arriving at Love Street in exchange. "I tried to sign Tom Brown last year," the Manager admitted. "I have a great admiration for him and I'm certain he'll score goals for us."

With an early season injury list that included Yardley, Watson, Turner

Tommy Turner who captained Saints to the First Division Championship 1999/2000

and Fenwick, Saints' first line-up of the new season marked the promotion of a further four recruits from the youth system. Also included was former Northern Ireland Under-18 internationalist Russell Kelly who was at Love Street on a month's trial. The team was Combe, Smith, Galloway, McWhirter, McLaughlin, Archdeacon, Murray, Dick (Milne), McGarry (Iwelumo), Mendes, and Kelly.

Tom Brown made a scoring debut in the disappointing 2-2 home draw against Stirling Albion a fortnight later, but away defeats at Dundee, Raith and Falkirk created minimal concern as Mendes' sixth goal in seven games was enough to defeat Partick Thistle in Paisley on 27 September and secure third place in the Division.

Fans were pleased to see the "big-guns" returning from injury over the past few weeks and even happier to welcome back another prodigal son. 1987 Cup winner David Winnie, returned after spells at Aberdeen, Hearts, Dundee, and Middlesbrough to wear the number "3" shirt. With a full squad now available the feeling was that St. Mirren would soon be leading the table.

A run of four defeats and three draws provided a reality check, however, and ended with the team sitting ... eighth in the middle of November again!

There had been similarly no improvement in the Club's recent cup performances. The seemingly annual late-summer away trip in the Challenge Cup resulted in the seemingly annual late-summer exit from the Challenge Cup; this time a 1-0 defeat to last season's relegated East Fife. The League Cup followed the same pattern as the previous season; a clean sheet in a home victory over a Second Division club, then defeat away to Dunfermline Athletic by two goals.

Another experienced player, Andy Roddie, was signed from Motherwell as the Club's focus appeared to take a further turn away from youth. Roddie made his debut on 18 October at home to Ayr United in a line-up of Combe, McLaughlin, Winnie, McWhirter, Fenwick, Watson, Murray, Turner, Brown (McGarry), Mendes, and Roddie (Hetherston). Disappointingly much the same formation failed to find the net over the next three weeks.

A return to scoring form coincided with the inclusion of Stuart Taylor in midfield. In fact, five successive two-goal performances helped Saints win ten points from a possible fifteen to the middle of December. The team rose only two places, but at least it was a move in the right direction.

The Scottish Cup ended at the first hurdle yet again when Dundee took a 4-0 lead at Dens Park. The Buddies did pull back two late goals and Tony Fitzpatrick saw further hopeful signs. "The desire to win seemed to have returned," he wrote in the following match programme, "but when you are reduced to nine men the numbers game definitely tells against you."

Whether or not the Club itself was about to move in the right direction was quite another matter. A solution was offered to end the continually worsening financial plight. However, not everyone saw it as an opportunity; more a threat!

At the beginning of February, St Mirren remained a relatively secure sixth in the First Division table. It was already clear that there was too much ground to make up on the four-horse race at the top between Dundee, Falkirk, Raith and Airdrie so another mid-table finish seemed on the cards. Then, on 5 February, the front page of the Paisley Daily Express broke the news that an English businessman wanted to buy a controlling interest in St. Mirren. The man in question was Reg Brealey.

Since 8 September, when the "Super League" scenario had re-surfaced, Managing Director John Paton had been controlling efforts to minimise its effects on the Club. On that day a press release had announced the proposed resignation from the Scottish Football League of all ten Premier Division clubs. Their intention was to form a distinct Scottish Premier League. As well as assuming a leading role in negotiations on behalf of all First Division clubs, Mr. Paton also had the financial future of St. Mirren to secure.

The Board of Directors called an Extraordinary General Meeting of the shareholders, scheduled for 15 March, with the purpose of creating an additional 120,000 shares in the Company. This was not intended as an issue for existing small investors as had occurred in 1996. Rather, as the Managing Director pointed out, "the problem is to create a vehicle which would allow an investor or group of investors to gain 75% control of the Club." In other words, the move was designed to facilitate a take-over.

Mr. Paton continued, "the take-over investment will be channelled towards reducing debt, settling creditors and strengthening the playing squad"; with an aim of being able to sustain life in the new Premier League. Reg Brealey was identified as the only potential investor and it was made clear that he had the support of the existing Board of Directors.

In a highly charged atmosphere the meeting took place in the sports' hall on the top floor of the Caledonia Stand. Most of those present wanted to believe in the proposed investment, however a few prominent supporters and major shareholders harboured serious doubts. After hearing Mr. Brealey's vision for the future of the Club, the majority voted to accept the Board's proposals; in effect, agreeing to Mr. Brealey becoming the new owner of St. Mirren Football Club. The vote and decision was not quite cut-and-dried, however.

Despite the severe pressure of the situation, and the willingness of the Board of Directors to proceed with Mr. Brealey's plans, those key major shareholders together with a few others voted against the proposal. Their voting power was sufficient to temporarily halt the plan.

Indeed, in the run-up to this crucial meeting the major shareholders had, in effect, become the joint guardians of the Club's survival. Over the weeks, worrying details had begun to emerge regarding Mr. Brealey's suitability as the man to lead St. Mirren into the new Millennium. Club Director Stewart Gilmour tendered his resignation and set about creating a consortium of local businessmen that could challenge for the position of "preferred investor". Fellow Director and supporter of the cause, George Campbell, remained on the Board in order to keep the new consortium fully appraised of developments.

The extent of the concerns regarding Mr. Brealey became clear on Tuesday 14 April when BBC Television broadcast a half-hour "Frontline Scotland Special". The programme was scathing in its characterisation of the English businessman. As well as reporting that a warrant for his arrest had been issued in India; former employees and even his own brother urged St. Mirren to have nothing to do with him.

However, perhaps the most damning evidence was detailed by the programme's presenter Shelley Jofre: attempting to trace the company, "Antrac Investments Limited", that was being used by Mr. Brealey to close the deal, Jofre found that the address in England at which they were supposedly based was unoccupied and had been up for sale for

Team Manager Tony Fitzpatrick deep in thought...

seven months; that the telephone and fax numbers did not exist; and that telephone "Directory Enquiries" had no record of such a company's listing anywhere in the UK.

On the evening before broadcast, Mr. Brealey's offer was sensationally withdrawn, leaving the local business consortium as the sole bidder. The aims of the initial take-over plan would not be entirely met; there would still be debt and there would not be scope for much in the way of strengthening the playing squad. However, the Club's bankers, the principal creditor, were satisfied. St. Mirren's new Board of Directors took over with immediate effect.

The men now in charge were Stewart Gilmour, George Campbell, Bryan McAusland, Ken McGeoch and Dr. Roger Lucas. Former Chairman Allan Marshall returned as Company Secretary and, with a post of General Manager no longer tenable, Jack Copland took over the running of the Sports and Leisure Complex.

Many supporters, including the small band that had voted against the proposals, at that vital highly charged meeting, regarded the whole affair as a near miss with disaster.

This was an especially harrowing time in the life of the Club because, with one storm averted, another was already looming on the horizon; and heading towards Paisley at breakneck speed. If anything could unhinge the business plan of the new Board it would be relegation to the Second Division. Following the 11 April 2-0 defeat in Greenock, a mere seventy-two hours prior to the Brealey bid being withdrawn, that was precisely the possibility, or perhaps even probability, that had to be faced.

There were only four matches remaining. The team was fourth bottom of the division and two of these bottom four teams would be relegated ... St. Mirren, Ayr United, Partick Thistle and Stirling Albion. A mere six points, the value of two victories, was all that separated the sides.

St. Mirren's remaining fixtures were against title-challenging trio Raith Rovers, Airdrieonians and Dundee in Paisley; and fellow-strugglers Stirling Albion "away" at Forthbank Stadium. Each one of Saints' opponents had as much to play for as St. Mirren. The new Directors, management team, and supporters alike crossed their fingers and said their prayers ... the Club's fate lay at the feet of the team.

Saturday 18 April; St. Mirren lose 2-0 to Raith Rovers, Partick Thistle win 1-0 at Stirling, and Ayr United draw at Dundee. Saints remain in seventh place, now one point ahead of Ayr, three ahead of Thistle, and four ahead of Stirling.

Saturday 25 April; St. Mirren lose 1-0 to Airdrieonians. Ayr win at Morton. Partick draw at Hamilton. Stirling win at Raith! Saints drop a place to third-bottom, one point ahead of Stirling and two ahead of Thistle.

Saturday 2 May; St. Mirren travel to Stirling. Back into the side come Alan Combe after missing five games, Steven McGarry for his first start in six, and Junior Mendes after only three appearances as sub in the last eight weeks. Out go Scrimgour, Iwelumo and Yardley.

A large travelling support packed Albion's recently built stadium in an atmosphere heavy with concern. As might be imagined, the game itself was a deeply tense affair. The first half ended all-square but not without its moments of high anxiety. Thankfully no goals had been lost.

If anything the atmosphere intensified after the interval and it was not until Hugh Murray's 63rd minute goal that fraught emotions were released by 1,500 Saints. A gate was thrust open and supporters spilled onto the trackside to join the players' celebrations.

At the sound of the final whistle Buddies' supporters rejoiced in style, cheering the team off the park, and the party mood continued in the long queues of buses and cars heading home from Stirling. Horns blaring, black and white flags flying from the windows, drivers and passengers singing in unison; seldom could a sense of relief have been so enjoyed.

It was the team's first win over Stirling in seven recent meetings and its first ever win at Forthbank. Most importantly, it was enough to retain a place in the First Division. Although generally accepted that defeat at Forthbank would have automatically relegated St. Mirren, that belief is not entirely accurate.

Certainly, if St. Mirren had lost at Stirling, the team would have dropped to the foot of the table, a point behind Partick Thistle and two behind both Stirling and Ayr. The following Saturday would then have borne comparison to 1939, 1962 and 1971, and Saints' last-game battles against threatened relegation. A home win over champions Dundee would have offered the only possible route of escape. Even then, if Stirling were to win at Greenock, only a share of the points at Firhill between Thistle and Ayr could have saved St. Mirren.

Thankfully, Tony Fitzpatrick was instead able to give last-day debuts to teenagers David McNamee, Chris Kerr, Alan Prentice and Paul Rudden, as well as a rare start to David Milne, and bring on Burton O'Brien as sub for only the fourth time. The 1-0 win over Dundee was a bonus that enabled the final league position to look a lot more comfortable than had actually been the case.

Four days after the final league fixture a Saints team, formed principally of Reserve players, lifted the Renfrewshire Cup at Cappielow after Morton had missed three penalties in the shoot-out that followed a 1-1 draw.

1997-98 goes down in history as one of the most traumatic seasons in the history of St. Mirren FC. 1998-99 would mark the beginning of a new era.

1998-99

The men now charged with leading the Club into another new era faced up to their first full season. Financial survival remained the overriding priority, with First Division survival a very close second. Campbell Kennedy who had now held the Commercial Manager post for twelve months following Peter Dallas' departure was delighted to welcome Arriva Scotland West Ltd. as the new season's shirt sponsor following the now traditional Sponsors' Dinner.

Conversely, marketing staff at the Scottish Football League had been unable to attract sponsorship for any of its three competitions, something that would hit the remaining member clubs hard following on the heels of the breakaway Scottish Premier League. St. Mirren responded to the new circumstances by reducing the number of players to twenty-four. The new Chairman had already expressed the opinion that a squad of sixteen full-timers, six part-timers and a small group of YTS signings was his optimum size of squad.

It was accepted, however, that a new Coach was needed to help the Team Manager. In September former Dynamo Kiev, Ipswich Town and St. Johnstone defender, Ukrainian Sergei Baltacha was appointed to the position. There was an added bonus; nineteen year-old Sergei Jnr. would also be joining the Club on a trial basis.

Seventeen of the previous season's squad had been out of contract at the end of the season and three of them chose to leave St. Mirren on "Bosman" deals; Alan Combe joined Dundee United, Paul Fenwick crossed the line and signed for Morton in a move that went down like the proverbial "lead balloon" amongst the fans, while Chris Iwelumo decided to try his luck playing in Denmark. Among the players "freed" by the Club were Winnie, Watson, Roddie, Taylor, Smith, Galloway and Archdeacon. Most disappointingly, the talented Brian Hetherston developed health problems that led to his release.

Of the League's traditional early season cup competitions, only one would take place in 1998. The Challenge Cup was discarded as it had now failed to attract a sponsor for the third successive season. In the League Cup, Ayr United, who had finished a point behind St. Mirren in securing their own escape from relegation, were the Buddies' Paisley Fair opponents at St. Mirren Park on 8 August.

For only the second time in the decade the Club would be drawn home ties in both major cup tournaments; it didn't improve results. Ayr left Love Street 3-1 victors but the Scottish Cup exit in February would prove far more distressing.

The League programme got under way. For the opening at Stair Park Stranraer on the first Saturday of August, the thirteen players selected included David McNamee, Paul Rudden, and another three youngsters with only a handful of appearances between them; Derek Scrimgour, Colin Drew and Alan Prentice. The squad was completed by regulars McLaughlin, McGarry, Mendes, Brown and Yardley, together with new signings Iain Nicolson and Ronnie McQuilter, and the fans new hero Hugh Murray.

Stranraer were defeated 1-0 and Raith 2-1 to give Saints a double winning start for the first time in seventeen years! Iain Nicolson hit the winning goal in both matches, coincidently both in the fiftieth minute. St. Mirren were top of the table with only thirty-four matches to play!

No-one was expecting miracles, yet the Directors hoped that the sense of realism off the playing pitch would stretch to a similar realism

A real Saints fan and player, Norrie McWhirter (left) follows Hugh Murray. Norrie retired from the game shortly after his testimonial season in 2000.

on it. Progress was being made and the next pair of victories, following on a month after the first, brought real satisfaction as first League leaders Hibs and then neighbours Morton were put to the sword without the loss of a goal.

Disappointingly, another month passed before the next victories with results appearing to take on a regular pattern; two wins, three winless. Consequently, the team's League position bobbed up and down like a buoy on rough seas and, after ten games, there were only three teams below St. Mirren in the table.

Contact between Youth Development Officer Joe Hughes and Manchester City's Gerry Creaney led to the out-of-favour former £1 million player arriving at Love Street on a two-month loan. The former Celt hit two on his debut, as St. Mirren fought back from a 2-0 half time deficit at home to Hamilton on 24 October and lifted all three points. Taken together with the previous week's 1-0 home win over Stranraer, Creaney's debut had continued the two-win element of the results' pattern and lifted the team back up into fourth place.

The now "expected" run of three winless games was broken thanks to a 1-0 home victory over Morton at the beginning of November but the pattern was immediately re-established due to draws with Clydebank and Ayr, and a comprehensive midweek 4-1 loss at Easter Road towards the end of the month.

This Hibernian match was re-scheduled from 14 November because of highly unusual circumstances. Having departed St. Mirren Park for the Capital at 11.30am that morning, the team bus was caught up in a five-mile tailback of traffic caused by an accident on the Kingston Bridge through Glasgow's city centre. Even the eventual assistance of a police escort could do no better than help get the team to the east end of Glasgow by 2.30pm by which time the match referee in Edinburgh had decided to postpone the game.

A further two successive wins in the first two games of December might have returned Saints to a top four position. Instead, a 2-1 win at Stranraer was followed by a home defeat. Losing 5-1 to Airdrieonians on 12 December not only broke the results' sequence but also the Manager's heart. For the second time in his career Tony Fitzpatrick left St. Mirren by "mutual consent" in the belief that the Club and its support deserved better.

"We took an in-depth look at the way St. Mirren were proceeding," commented Chairman Stewart Gilmour, "and in conjunction with Tony decided to seek a new management structure. It was felt to be a decision that was best not only for the Club but also from the point of view of Tony's future career."

Tony's replacement was full-time schoolteacher and part-time football manager Tom Hendrie, who had led his two previous clubs, Berwick Rangers and Alloa Athletic, to promotion at the end of his first full season in charge at each. Hendrie gave up the job security of school life to commit himself to St. Mirren on a two-and-a-half year contract. He was joined by his assistant at Alloa and Berwick, John Coughlin.

The Chairman admitted that the pair had been head-hunted; "We had the usual galaxy of applicants but felt it was time for someone to come in with fresh ideas. So, we looked at who was performing well in the lower leagues." Sergei Baltacha Snr. left in the wake of the two new appointments, however his son signed a two-year contract as a full-time player.

The task facing the relatively unknown Managerial partnership was simple: ensure at least First Division status over the next few years whilst the Chairman worked at stabilising the financial situation; "We are not losing money the way we used to and we are repaying creditors all the time. The gap between our expenditure and income is ever closing." Good news ... but Mr. Gilmour remained cautious, "a good Cup run would give us some financial breathing space."

The new Manager quickly assessed the options available to him and threw a regular starting place in the direction of sixteen-year-old Burton O'Brien. Former French Under-18 internationalist Ludovic Roy, signed in the closed season following Alan Combe's departure, also immediately took over as goalkeeper. Junior Mendes was re-called from loan at Carlisle United and Tommy Turner was similarly brought back into the fold from a loan spell at Queen of the South. Hendrie's decision to field Turner as a defensive "sweeper" was an inspired move that would eventually act as a catalyst, transforming the team into a winning combination.

With Chris Innes brought on-loan from Kilmarnock to cover for the injured Barry McLaughlin, Hendrie's preferred line up began to take shape; Roy, Nicolson, McNamee, Turner, McQuilter, Innes, Murray, O'Brien, McGarry, Mendes and Yardley; with a choice of substitutes from teenagers Rudden and Prentice, and "squaddie" David Cameron. Cameron was an Argyll & Sutherland Highlander who was working in the regiment's Paisley recruitment office. Known to the new Manager, he was given a contract until the end of the season.

The team was handed a chance of earning the "good Cup run" that Stewart Gilmour was looking for when a home draw in Round Three sent St. Mirren to meet fellow First Division side Hamilton Academical on 23 January. The season's three earlier league meetings had resulted in two 0-0 draws at Firhill, Hamilton's temporary home, and a 3-2 home win for St. Mirren.

The Buddies got off to the best possible start, scoring as early as the fifth minute. Yardley and Brown combined to set up Mendes, and the pacy forward rounded the 'keeper before picking his spot in the net. Despite constant pressure Saints were unable to find a second goal and suffered the consequences in the dying seconds when the visitors equalised. The referee's final whistle was timed to have sounded sixteen seconds later!

The Fourth Round draw announced that the winner of the replay had "hit the jackpot" with a home tie against Rangers; exactly what the Club was hoping for. Hope was lost, in a replay that was lost, 1-0 on 2 February. The massive travelling support that evening made up at least seventy percent of the 3,050 Firhill attendance. The very real frustration was later compounded by the fact that Hamilton ended the season relegated.

Having lost out on vital Cup cash, and with ever increasing interest in teenagers O'Brien and McNamee from major clubs in Scotland and England, the Club decided that it could no longer hold onto the youngsters. Blackburn Rovers paid £600,000 up-front, with the promise of an additional £2.2 million when the pair completed twenty first-team games; something that they had barely achieved in their short time at St. Mirren Park! It was a good deal; even more so, it seemed, when Blackburn agreed to allow the players to stay at St. Mirren until the end of the season.

Another good deal appeared to have been secured when a "mystery" Malaysian company agreed a five-year shirt sponsorship deal. Colloid Environmental Technologies Company (CETCO) had a St. Mirren supporting Managing Director, Robert Bell, but the agreement was destined to last only a single year before LDV Vans Ltd became main sponsor for 2000-01 season.

Form continued in a topsy-turvy vein; a sequence of four consecutive victories was bounded on both sides by longer, unsuccessful runs. The season ended on a positive note with convincing home victories over Stranraer 5-1 and Airdrie 3-0, and a 1-1 draw in Kirkcaldy. Saints finished in fifth place with Mark Yardley and Steven McGarry sharing nineteen of the forty-two goals.

The team's league position had remained unchanged from the time of Tony Fitzpatrick's departure, and those sympathetic to the former Manager would point to the 5-1 home defeat at the hands of Morton on 10 April as being at least as calamitous as the Airdrie result that led to his leaving. Tom Hendrie despaired over statistics that showed St. Mirren to have had "more shots at goal, more shots on target and won more corners than Morton on the day". Whatever the Manager's feelings about the performance it would take something special for the supporters to forgive such a defeat.

Perhaps wisely in the circumstances, Tom Hendrie was more than complimentary of the St. Mirren support in his closing programme notes of the season. "Even when things haven't been going well or we have been enduring some considerable pressure, your verbal encouragement has been tremendous - my sincere thanks to every one of you."

A potentially difficult season had been negotiated without a repeat of the team's recent flirtings with relegation. That in itself was grounds for optimism, now could the new manager gain the fans' forgiveness and repeat the promotion feat of his two earlier jobs?

1999-2000

Neither press nor bookmakers tipped much for Saints' prospects other than another relegation fight. In fact, St. Mirren were regarded as second favourites for the drop. Despite these pessimistic predictions, many fans felt a quiet optimism about the season to come.

With a mere £40,000 transfer budget available there were few close season changes to personnel. Scott Walker arrived from East Stirlingshire and was joined by Ian Ross following his release by Motherwell. Ross, in particular, was an addition that pleased the Manager as he had tracked the player's career since coaching him years before in a West Lothian schools' select team.

Tom Hendrie introduced a new pre-season training programme that included golf and swimming in addition to a more traditional fitness regime. One thing that was out, however, was a trip to the Gleniffer Braes; "We won't be running up and down hills. Football isn't played on hills," commented the Manager.

A testing sequence of pre-season challenge matches began with Rangers visiting St. Mirren Park in July. Two goals in the closing six minutes from Steven McGarry overturned an earlier Rangers goal and alerted the 6,000 crowd to Saints' potential, justifying the confidence held by sections of the support. Oxford United were the next visitors but their heavy-handed approach was not appreciated by Hendrie. The Club were so disgusted by the English tourists' tactics that they publicly stated they would never play them again.

A much less physical encounter was enjoyed in celebration of Norrie McWhirter's Testimonial Year. Kilmarnock provided the opposition and Tom Brown enjoyed scoring the winner against his former team-mates.

The antics of Paisley Panda and Junior P received extensive coverage in the national press. Famous for sailing a wee bit close to the wind, the twosome always pointed out to officialdom that they were a 'protected' species!

The "birth" of a son to popular Club mascot "Paisley Panda" was celebrated at the testimonial match; the antics of "Junior P" and his "Pan-dad" would be a feature of the season. More importantly, the victories over two Premier League teams had sent out the signal that a successful side was also born.

In an indication of the commercial age that was now dominating sport, Saints took to their famous surface at Love Street for the opening League fixture on 7 August sporting the ninth different black-and-white kit-design of the 1990s. A tame one-all draw followed against an Ayr United side that had provided many difficulties during the previous twelve months. One week later in Kirkcaldy, the countdown to a memorable season began with a result that went a long way to repaying the Manager's "debt" to the supporters.

The "ghost" of 1992 was also well and truly exorcised by a 6-0 victory over Raith Rovers in which Walker and Ross opened their scoring

After yet another goal on the way to the Championship, Barry Lavety wheels away, Scott Walker jumps for joy and the Saints fans in the Caledonia Stand go wild!

accounts. The crowd's cheers swung between "We want seven!" (a reference to that 1992 result) and "There's only one Barry Lavety!" (in honour of the former Saint who had returned on what was initially a short-term loan spell from Hibs). The day's triple strike-force of Lavety, Yardley and McGarry each netted in the six-goal whitewash. It could have been ten!

Following a season devoid of sponsorship, The Scottish Football League was back in favour with the commercial world. Whisky brand "Bell's" put its name to both the League competition and the Challenge Cup, while The Co-operative Insurance Services Ltd backed the League Cup. The luck of the (cup) draw once again seemed against Saints. It was determined that St. Mirren would face newly promoted Inverness Caledonian Thistle once in each of the three tournaments during an eleven-day period from 10 August, including two long midweek treks north.

These would be St. Mirren's first competitive meetings with the club born from an amalgamation of the town's Caledonian and Thistle clubs in 1994 to accept a place in the re-structured Scottish Football League. Saints' twelfth successive Challenge Cup tie away from Paisley ended with "Caley-Thistle" winning thanks to an 88th minute goal. Then, the attempt to add to St. Mirren's two victories gained in the seven previous away League Cup ties of the decade also failed when the northern club hit the Buddies with two extra-time strikes. The season would include four treks up the A9 to Inverness, the best return being a 1-1 draw in December.

Fortunately, the Highlanders proved a slightly easier proposition at St. Mirren Park. On 21 August Inverness were beaten by the odd-goal-in-five in a game that Saints dominated despite falling behind to a controversial penalty award and losing young defender Chris Kerr to an horrific injury. A quite shocking tackle resulted in a Caley-Thistle player being red-carded and the unfortunate Kerr suffering knee ligament damage that would keep him out of the first team for seventeen months. Versatile left-sided player Gary Bowman was subsequently signed from Clydebank as a replacement.

Playing on a Sunday eight days later, because of Clydebank's ground-sharing arrangement at Cappielow, Saints again won by a 3-2 scoreline and now led the League. Yet, it was the results of the following three weeks that did most to convince onlookers of the team's pedigree.

Airdrieonians had generally proved to be difficult opponents, especially in Paisley, so to be 3-0 ahead within half-an-hour had the home fans ecstatic, even more so given the quality of goals scored. A further two classy counters during the second period took the final score to 5-0.

In the weeks prior to this match, Hugh Murray had been selected to travel with the Scotland Under-21 squad that weekend, but Tom Hendrie had convinced the International Team Management to release him. "Shuggie" scored a fantastic goal in each half to justify Hendrie's decision. Murray would gain further Under-21 opportunities later in the season, as would Sergei Baltacha. Indeed both featured when Scotland met Bosnia Herzogovina at St. Mirren Park in early October, Baltacha becoming the first-ever capped "Scot" to have neither blood nor birth ties to the country.

The trip to face nearest promotion challengers Dunfermline on 11 September enabled St. Mirren to impress on the 6,128 crowd that they were more than worthy of their place at the head of the division. Saints bettered the Pars in everything but goal-scoring in a match that ended in a 1-1 draw. The corner-count was fourteen to one in St. Mirren's favour!

Morton were the next victims as goals from Yardley, Lavety and McLaughlin secured another 3-2 win in front of almost 7,000 highly-charged spectators. Played seven, won five, drawn two ... the Club's third-best start to a League campaign in the first 125 years!

The Press said it wouldn't last, and briefly it didn't. On 25 September, Falkirk showed how dangerous they could be by racing into an early 3-0 lead at Brockville. Hugh Murray's solitary reply had no effect on the outcome. A week later Saints had to fight tooth-and-nail to claw back a point from the other promoted side Livingston, after the visitors had taken a first-half lead. Such fighting qualities became a trademark of the season.

The run of eight successive wins that followed suggested that "the bubble" would not burst. Twenty-one goals were scored and only seven conceded ... in fact, the team struck a scoring average of almost three goals per game throughout the entire first half of the season. Their explosive start to the campaign received recognition from the League's sponsor when a selection of Manager and Player-of-the-Month awards found their way to Paisley during each of the first four months of the season.

Barry Lavety's move from Hibernian was first extended to three-months and then became "permanent" until the end of the season when his existing contract with Hibs would expire. He celebrated with twelve goals in eighteen outings. Even better was the effect on Mark Yardley; reunited with his old strike partner, "Yards" had the net bulging on thirteen occasions.

Defender Chris Kerr and right the medal he received on winning the First Division League Championship.

At home to Falkirk and Steven McGarry is on the attack. The Falkirk player to the right is Scott McKenzie who moved to Saints in time for their 2000/2001 Premier League campaign.

There had been a consistency of selection that tends to follow all successful sides. A total of only sixteen players had been required to fill the fourteen matchday places through to November. What made this figure all the more amazing was the fact that two players, Paul Rudden and Chris Kerr, shared just five appearances between them.

With half the fixtures completed, St. Mirren had amassed forty-three points from a possible fifty-four. The Buddies were five ahead of Dunfermline and looking good. 1999-2000 offered one of the best opportunities for promotion as the SPL was to be increased to twelve teams for the following season. In spite of this decision, there remained an element of uncertainty over exactly how the promotion places would be decided.

If the top three First Division sides met the "breakaway" clubs' stadium criteria then only the champions would gain automatic promotion. The second and third placed teams would then enter into a round robin play-off along with the bottom SPL outfit, with two from three being placed in the top tier. On the other hand, if one of the top-three First Division clubs failed the "stadium test" then the other two would receive guaranteed promotion.

The long-and-short of the situation was that only the highest placed club with 10,000 covered seats would be guaranteed a place in the Premier League; Saints were in pole position and could do no better than continue their winning ways.

Plans were already in the pipeline for a new stand to replace the Love Street end terracing and, as early as 19 October, planning permission had been granted. The SPL deadline for stadium compliance was 31 March 2000. An EGM vote on 26 October authorised the release of 100,000 additional shares with the purpose of funding the new stand. At the same EGM local businessman Jim Purves was co-opted onto the Board.

Additional funding for the stand came later in the season, in the shape of a "Making A Stand" raffle, organised by a grouping of interested supporters to allow non-shareholders the opportunity of contributing to the building costs.

On the field, match nineteen produced Saints' first major setback since that Falkirk defeat in September. One week before Christmas Day, Ayr United reminded the rest of the division of their capabilities by winning 2-1 at St. Mirren Park. The defeat served to put into sharp focus how much could be lost, because it marked the beginning of the one spell during the season when it appeared that Saints might not earn promotion after all.

Only three victories were achieved in a ten-game spell through until early March. Second-half goals from Mendes and McGarry transformed a 1-1 interval scoreline into a 3-1 result in St. Mirren's favour when Airdrieonians played at Love Street on 8 January; Gary Bowman's first goal tied up the points in Paisley on 12 February after Mark Yardley had put the Buddies ahead against Inverness midway through the first half; and an incredible ending in the return visit to Kirkcaldy on 26 February saw both Mendes and Yardley score after Raith Rovers had taken the lead, and seemingly won the match, with a mere four minutes remaining.

These victories aside, such a dip in performance did not provide the perfect backdrop for a Scottish Cup clash; especially one against an SPL team. Needless to say the draw created a great deal of interest, especially as the club in question, Aberdeen, were bottom of the Premier League and the most likely candidate for the possible end-of-season play-offs. Despite their league position the Dons would be formidable opponents.

Given the unaccustomed advantage of a home draw, Saints attacked the visitors from the off on 29 January, with a well-honed 3-4-3 formation stretching the Dons' defence. When Steven McGarry put the Buddies into the lead it looked as if a victory was on the cards, but an audacious free-kick scored by the Dons' Moroccan winger Zerouali forced a replay. Manager Hendrie was philosophical, "while we didn't outplay Aberdeen, I thought we were the better side over the piece. We took our goal well but there is little or no legislation in the coaching manuals when you are subjected to an equaliser in the style of the one they scored." Turning to the replay on 8 February the Manager gave a bold prediction. "We won't be subdued and to make an impact on the result we must take the game to them."

That is exactly what St. Mirren did. With Tommy Turner on the bench and Barry McLaughlin captain for the night Saints gave their travelling support plenty of encouragement during the opening forty-five minutes. Among several other near things, the closest to a goal being a Lavety header that glanced off an upright.

Aberdeen approached the second period in much more determined mood and scored a controversial opener in the 53rd minute from a suspiciously offside position. That setback spurred St. Mirren into renewed territorial advantage but their pressure could not be converted into something more tangible. In the very last minute Aberdeen broke away to score a second. The Dons were undoubtedly flattered by the scoreline.

The Cup performance built-up hopes of a successful return to the elite level of Scottish football. Yet, promotion was not yet guaranteed.

A black and white (what else) clad policewoman joins in the good humour in Old Sneddon Street after Saints clinched the title against Raith Rovers.

A famous Buddie celebrates amongst his own. Robert Tannahill sports the colours as the supporters gather in Abbey Close to watch the victorious team show off the First Division Championship Trophy from the Town Hall balcony.

During the winter form slump, only one point had been taken from a possible twelve in the meetings with promotion challengers Dunfermline Athletic, Falkirk and Livingston. Saints dropped into second place.

With the new East Stand nearing completion, the team got back on the rails in the best possible way; a Club record-equalling eight goal winning margin over Clydebank on 11 March returned St. Mirren to the top of the table. Lavety (3), Murray (2), McGarry, Ross and Walker were the scorers. The last goal was netted with twenty minutes yet remaining ... for the second time in the season "it could have been ten".

There was certainly no opportunity to hit double figures when the sides met again fourteen days later at the Bankies' temporary lodgings; Cappielow Park, Greenock. Despite the travelling fans' expectations there were no goals scored and there was also the alarming experience of seeing their embarrassed favourites taking the field wearing Morton change tops!

The explanation given was that the referee was unhappy at the lack of contrast between the sides' strips and wouldn't delay the kick-off to allow the St. Mirren kitman to drive to Paisley for an acceptable outfit.

Disbelief spawned initial hesitation and silence among the Saints' support. That was not long in changing. It must have been one of the very few occasions in St. Mirren's history that the team was "booed" even before a ball was kicked! Many supporters felt that these circumstances adversely affected the performance. The Saints' supporting players in particular were desperately unhappy at the situation and wore a St. Mirren jersey under the Morton top. It was a truly bizarre day.

The latest unexpected slip-up precipitated a flurry of transfer activity as Tom Hendrie added Joe McLaughlin of Clydebank, Jens Paeslack on loan from German side Karlsruhe, and Rangers' Paul McKnight to the squad with half-a-dozen games to play. Former Saint Ricky Gillies also returned on loan from Aberdeen in an effort to secure that all-important first place.

The new players helped steady any frayed nerves and played their part in the eventual League triumph. None more so than McKnight who weighed in with stunning late goals against Falkirk, at St. Mirren Park on 8 April, and Ayr United, at Somerset Park two weeks later, gaining an extra four points for the team during the run-in.

St. Mirren, Falkirk and Dunfermline Athletic had broken away from the "pack" to contest the end-of-season honours, however the promotion issue was already decided. The Bairns received notification that Brockville was not an acceptable venue for SPL fixtures and would not be promoted. St. Mirren and Dunfermline would go up; but who would be champions?

That issue was finally settled on 29 April, the second last Saturday of the season, when Saints defeated Raith Rovers 3-0 at Love Street. Five points ahead with one game to play the title-flag would fly in Paisley.

Needless to say, it was an emotional day. There were balloons, bands and banners; as the flag-waving, all-ticket 9,000 crowd also witnessed the official opening of the new "Paisley Daily Express East Stand" without which entry to the SPL would have been refused. Lord Macfarlane, Chairman of Bell's, cut the tape to officially open the 2,000-seat construction that had been used unexpectedly two weeks earlier to ease congestion at the Falkirk match.

When the day's real action started, Raith threatened to spoil the party. However, after the interval, Saints hit them with three goals in seven minutes. The game, and the championship, was won.

After the victory, players and Management circled the pitch with the First Division Championship Trophy, wearing specially printed t-shirts that pointed out to all the doubters ... "THE BUBBLE DIDNAE BURST" and "THE SAINTS ARE BACK". A 5-0 defeat at Inverness on the final Saturday failed to dampen spirits and it was "enjoyed" in party-mood by the travelling fans, even to the extent of cheering each Inverness goal!

There was a friendly pitch invasion from all four sides of the ground at the end of the match as the singing, flag-waving Buddies demanded a "curtain call" from their heroes. Eventually the Manager appeared in the stand and addressed the fans to thank them for their magnificent support throughout the triumphant season.

Hendrie and Coughlin had done it again; another team and another promotion at the first time of asking. Their transformation of St. Mirren earned them extended five-year contracts. Now, it only remained to be seen if they could carry the club onwards and upwards.

The New Millennium, Still Marching On...

2000-01

Another new season for the fans. Another new century for the Club. Another new millennium for the World. St. Mirren were in the SPL and the supporters sat back to enjoy their football. Hopefully, increased revenue from larger crowds and improved sponsorship arrangements would benefit the Club; deals such as that which moved the Club Shop back into the town centre with local retailer Provan Sports now having sole rights to sell St. Mirren merchandise.

CHAPTER FOURTEEN
The 2000's

Chairman Stewart Gilmour shows the strain of being at Saints helm, and this was only a pre-season friendly against Johnstone Burgh.

As far as fans were concerned, however, Saints' finances could take a back seat for once. The focus was firmly on football! Tom Hendrie would also be taking a back seat ... at least for the first seven games of the new season. That was the length of a touchline ban following his trackside indiscretions during the promotion campaign.

The pre-season highlight was a visit from County neighbours Morton. Saints' Greenock rivals had resigned from the Renfrewshire Football Association meaning that recent meetings had been restricted to League fixtures. In the interim St. Mirren's Renfrewshire Cup wins had been gained at the expense of local Amateur teams such as Viewfield Rovers, Carlton YMCA and, in 2001, IBM of Greenock.

A meeting away from the pressures of points-gathering, attracted a healthy crowd to St. Mirren Park and was sure to provide a high-tempo conclusion to the team's preparations. The 1-1 draw was everything expected from a Renfrewshire derby.

Having lost Junior Mendes to fellow SPL new-boys Dunfermline Athletic during the closed season, Tom Hendrie moved fast to sign Morton's goalscoring trialist. Mercurial Angolan, Jose Quitongo, was a player who had provided St. Mirren defenders with more than a fair share of problems over the years. Now he would wear the famous black and white stripes.

During the summer, Ricky Gillies and Jens Paeslack signed new deals while the Manager also picked up former Motherwell defender Jamie McGowan, and Falkirk midfielder Scott McKenzie. Disappointingly, the talisman of the previous campaign, Barry Lavety, was lost to "freedom of contract". Saints would struggle all season to find a regular goalscorer to replace him.

The real competitive action got underway with three narrow defeats. On 29 July the First Division flag was unfurled. It was a perfect sunny Saturday, St. Mirren had the lion's share of possession and style, but Kilmarnock spoiled the return to "big-time" football when they scored fifteen minutes from time to win 1-0.

A trip to the Granite City seven days later improved on the previous season's Cup score but unfortunately not the result. After losing an early goal Saints once again had their hosts pinned back for long periods. Gillies equalised, Ross and Quitongo both hit woodwork as the Buddies went all out for a winner but Aberdeen landed a late sucker punch exactly as they had done in the Cup six months earlier.

The campaign's first Sunday fixture to suit live television coverage saw Rangers make the short trip to Paisley. This was also the first in a series of all-ticket games throughout the season as the new 10,800 ground capacity became operational. In actuality, no attendance over the year came within a thousand of the limit and the previous season's home average rose only by six hundred to 5,600. The Paisley public was as likely to watch a successful First Division side as a struggling Premier League one.

Rangers returned to Glasgow with a 3-1 victory but again St. Mirren showed up well for most of the match. Goals were lost to a penalty, a free-kick, and a defensive error. "Perhaps we need to be more street-wise," commented Manager Hendrie. The start to life in the SPL had been disappointing only in respect of the results.

Chairman Stewart Gilmour looks on as Lord McFarlane unfurls the First Division Championship flag prior to the first Premier League match versus Kilmarnock at St. Mirren Park.

Buddies' spirits were soon raised by the first victory. Gillies and McGarry scored as Dundee were defeated 2-1 at Love Street on 19 August and the Buddies jumped two places from the bottom of the table. The men who earned St. Mirren's first SPL points were Roy, Nicolson, Ross, Turner, McLaughlin, McGowan, Murray, Gillies, McGarry, Paeslack (Yardley), and Quitongo; without the injured Walker it was a line-up as close as possible to last season's winning combination.

The joy was short-lived. Five consecutive matches without a goal had fans dreaming of a re-united Yardley/Lavety partnership. Motherwell and St. Johnstone came to town and both repeated Kilmarnock's opening-day 1-0 victory. Mark Yardley missed a last-minute chance from close range on 23 September to level the scores against the Perth Saints who had been in the lead for eighty minutes. The team's top scorer for three of the past four seasons would find life a lot tougher against the country's top defences.

On the road, two trips to Edinburgh resulted in 2-0 scorelines in favour of both Hibs and Hearts. The Easter Road defeat was particularly galling as St. Mirren lost a goal on the stroke of half-time and another in the 92nd minute, despite constant second-half pressure. Only the 16 September trek to Tayside provided any tangible reward. Saints picked up a point in a no-scoring draw after dominating play against ten-man Dundee United; it was to be the only point earned away from St. Mirren Park for seven months.

Having failed in repeated attempts to sign former Scottish international forward Gordon Durie, two other strikers arrived to bolster the attack. Former £1 million player, Englishman Graham Fenton, previously with Aston Villa and Blackburn Rovers, was signed after being released by Leicester City. He went straight into the team for the visit of Dunfermline Athletic on the last day of September. Alongside Paeslack and Quitongo on the bench that day was Maikel Renfurm, formerly of Dutch sides Sparta Rotterdam and NEC Nijmegen, who had been recommended to St. Mirren by David Winnie following his spell in Icelandic football. Surinam-born Renfurm replaced Steven McGarry in the second-half.

This attack-minded selection added three points to Saints' League tally with McGowan and Yardley scoring in a 2-1 victory over the Pars. So far, Saints pickings had all come at the expense of other struggling sides ... the aim had to be at least to continue that pattern.

World Cup qualification matches provided the Premier League and the English Premiership with a blank weekend in early October. St. Mirren took advantage by arranging a challenge match against old friends Middlesbrough. On Saints' 123rd birthday the two teams met at St. Mirren Park, playing for the LDV Trophy. Young Derek Scrimgour gave an excellent performance in goal but was unable to prevent the visitors eventually winning 3-2.

Away losses four and five, 2-0 at Celtic Park and 2-1 at Kilmarnock, preceded the team's third League victory. On 28 October, Aberdeen were the victims in a second successive home success. However, for the first time since the start of the season, Saints had to admit they were fortunate. Derek Scrimgour, on in the second half for injured "Ludo" Roy, again made a series of fine saves to keep the Dons at bay. For all said and done, it was a good result.

On the last day of October the Buddies also gained their third win in one of the season's other competitions, the CIS League Cup. Back on 22 August, a first-ever meeting with Scottish League new-boys Ross County had been successfully negotiated with a 3-1 win after extra-time at Victoria Park, Dingwall. A fortnight later Dundee returned to Paisley for the third round tie and were soundly beaten 3-0, although the Dens Parkers certainly left their mark on the game. Saints' Paul Rudden was carried off and the Dark Blues were reduced to nine men as they allowed their frustrations to get the better of them.

Dunfermline Athletic provided the next League Cup opposition on 31 October and Saints' fans felt fortunate to have a second home draw against a side already beaten in Paisley. In another physical encounter described by Hendrie as "a bone crunching good old-fashioned cup tie", the score of a month earlier was repeated, this time with goals from McGarry and Gillies, and Saints had won themselves a place in the League Cup Semi-Final. It was only the fourth occasion that St. Mirren had reached this stage of the competition, and the first time in twenty years. Indeed, the Club would have to wait a little longer to actually tread the Hampden turf ... the match was not due until February.

While anticipation was understandably high for a semi-final, the first League fixture following the Dunfermline cup game was one of those matches where the words "down", "earth", and "thud" come most readily to mind. Saints had as many as nine players doubtful for the match due to flu-like symptoms and, although there were eventually only three changes in the starting line-up from the midweek CIS Cup win, illness and the efforts expended in winning twice at home in four days had obviously taken their toll; Rangers 7 St. Mirren 1. The large St. Mirren support cheered and encouraged their team from start to finish.

Despite the heavy defeat, Saints remained eight points ahead of

Saints management team, Tom Hendrie and John Coughlin keep an eye on the action with Hibernian's Alex McLeish.

bottom side Dundee United and only two behind Aberdeen. Worryingly, however, the Rangers' match signalled the start of the team's worst run of the season. They struggled through the next twelve games; able to pick up only two points, scoring seven goals but conceding thirty-three. A succession of injuries and illness was hampering the Club and there were seven consecutive defeats. Even both goalkeepers, Roy and Scrimgour, were unfit at the same time. Livingston 'keeper Ian McCaldon was drafted in on loan to see the Club through a difficult few weeks. The Manager was not having his problems to seek.

Three successive home matches over the festive period only served to highlight the problems. Not only were goals hard to come by; the normally reliable defence was losing simple goals; ideal for the opposition. Possession cheaply conceded in defensive areas of the pitch helped Celtic win 2-0 on 23 December. Then, following the efforts of Club officials and supporters to clear tons of snow from the park on the morning of the match, similar defensive errors contributed to Rangers' 3-1 win on 2 January. "We put so much effort into the games and got nothing to show for it," complained the Manager.

Sandwiched between these two defeats, it looked as if the points were there for the taking on Boxing Day in a "pea-souper" against Kilmarnock. With Graham Fenton's first goal having fired the Buddies 1-0 ahead, the visiting fans spent the entire interval calling for the game to be abandoned because of the thick fog. After due consideration and

Ricky Gillies, Saints youngest player of the first 125 years.

much discussion the referee decided to allow play to continue. Through the second period Saints let slip control of the game and Killie eventually ran out 3-1 victors.

The Premier League clubs then enjoyed a three-week winter break between the New Year holiday fixtures and the first matches in the Scottish Cup. St. Mirren headed to Marbella and set about shaking off the winter blues with twice-daily training sessions and bounce matches against former European adversary, KV Mechelen of Belgium, and Dutch club NEC Nijmegen.

Back then from the winter sunshine, and a tough match awaited against Motherwell in the Scottish Cup at St. Mirren Park. Unlike the autumn CIS competition, there was to be no advantage found in having a home draw against a fellow Premier League outfit. The Fir Parkers put paid to any hopes of further cup progress.

Before the match there was a minute's silence in memory of 1950s hero Davie Lapsley whose ashes had been scattered on the pitch earlier in the day. Hoping to honour the memory of a Cup-winning legend, Saints were denied in the early stages by some excellent goalkeeping but Motherwell eventually took control, scoring either side of the break.

By the time substitute Jose Quitongo pulled a goal back 'Well had been reduced to nine men and Tom Hendrie had also thrown Yardley and McGarry into the fray in an effort to salvage at least a replay. There ensued a frantic, but ultimately unsuccessful, finish to the tie. Despite the visitors reduced numbers, and an abundance of forward players on the pitch, Saints failed to create any clear-cut chances. In the aftermath Jens Paeslack was released, having failed to live up to expectations since the summer.

With the League Cup Semi-Final fast approaching St. Mirren were in dire need of a positive result to restore belief in their ability. As so often happens, it came in a timely fashion. Three days before the trip to Hampden to face Kilmarnock, Saints won their third meeting of the season against Dundee in Paisley. Debutant Moussa Dagnogo came off the substitutes' bench to grab the winner four minutes later! St. Mirren 2 Dundee 1. Dagnogo was another forward whose time at Love Street would be much shorter than initially hoped.

And so to the National Stadium. The Semi-Final was originally scheduled for Fir Park, Motherwell but the SFA relented to protests and switched the tie. The original venue may well have been more appropriate on two counts. Firstly, the match attendance of 9,213 was lost on Hampden's vast slopes. Secondly, Saints' 1993 B&Q Cup Final had been played at Fir Park and the current semi-final stirred memories of that earlier match.

Tuesday 6 February 2000 turned out to be an evening not dissimilar to the Sunday in December '93 when the Challenge Cup was decided ... the weather was absolutely foul, and St. Mirren lost 3-0. The downpour and February chill surely discouraged more fans of both clubs from attending. On this occasion, however, the team's performance did little to warm the St. Mirren support. At least this time the fans had a seat and were under cover!

The remainder of the season would be spent in search of points to secure a Premier League place for a second season ... and players to help achieve this aim. Tom Hendrie's desire for a big name goalscorer continued as he worked his way through an ever-growing mountain of agents' faxed recommendations.

It was believed that a deal had been struck with West Ham's Paul Kitson but the player changed his mind. Former Brazil World Cup star Bebeto was another player made available to the Manager, but Hendrie's preference was for another Brazilian.

The Manager liked what he read about a youngster who had lifted an Under-17 World Cup medal in 1997 and a Copa America medal with the full Brazilian squad in 1999. Twenty year-old Ronaldinho arrived in Europe having signed to play for Paris Saint Germain during the following season. There were three months available before he was due to join "PSG" and his agent was hoping to fix up a short-term deal.

Agreement was reached and international clearance sought from the Brazilian FA. Inexplicably, the paperwork was delayed and the transfer deadline missed by a frustratingly small margin. Hendrie would have to continue his search.

With twelve games still to be played St. Mirren were now only a single point ahead of Dundee United who had taken seven points from their last three games. There was, of course, the possibility that there would be no relegation at all; only one of the three teams challenging at the top of the First Division had a compliant stadium.

The new, re-sized, SPL had introduced a novel ending to the season. After the thirty-third game, following completion of three rounds of fixtures, the teams would "split" into two groups of six; a championship pool and a relegation pool. The concluding five fixtures would then be played exclusively within the particular pool in which a club found itself. In St. Mirren's case that was already destined to be the "relegation pool".

As luck would have it, during the seven matches leading up to the "split", Saints faced each of the other five sides that would eventually join them in the lower half of the League. Back-to-back away losses were suffered at Aberdeen 3-0 and Motherwell 1-0, before the "crunch" game with Dundee United at Tannadice on 3 March. "We were beaten by the better side," Tom Hendrie declared afterwards; the 4-0 scoreline seemed to support his assessment.

United were now three points ahead and held a game-in-hand. The situation was at least tempered by a fifth win of the campaign, 1-0 at home to St. Johnstone on 17 March, a game in which Steven McGarry gloriously bent the ball home following a slick passing move involving McKenzie, Kerr and Fenton.

Tom Hendrie finally secured the services of a new forward in time for the next League match, at home to Dunfermline Athletic. During his time as a youth player the Manager had been a contemporary of Gordon Strachan, now in charge of Coventry City. Strachan offered Scottish youngster Stephen McPhee to Saints until the end of the season.

McPhee watched from the bench as Jamie McGowan's goal earned the side a 1-1 draw, but he was in the starting line-up for the final fixture before the "split", a match at Celtic Park that would secure the title for the home side were they to win. St. Mirren put up a tremendous show both on and off the park. 3,000 Buddies consistently out-sang a Celtic support almost twenty times greater in number and the players gave Celts as difficult a match as they had endured all season. Celtic finally scored the only goal of the game. The only issue now to be resolved was relegation.

Regenerated by their efforts in the east end of Glasgow, St. Mirren ironically went on to enjoy their best form of the season and remained undefeated during the five "pool" matches. Each match was crucial, but perhaps none more so than the first, in which Dundee United visited Paisley enjoying a four-point advantage. The situation was reminiscent of the relegation battle three years before;

English striker Graham Fenton is helped from the pitch by physio Colin Brow in the last home match of the 2000/01 Premier campaign. A 2-1 victory over Aberdeen.

Monday 23 April; Almost 7,000 watch as, following an earlier United counter scored by Saints' supporting striker Stephen Thompson, two goals from Ricky Gillies keep survival hopes alive in a deserved 2-1 victory broadcast live on satellite television. The gap reduces to a single point in United's favour. St. Mirren now face two games away from Paisley.

Saturday 28 April; Undeterred by their previously abysmal away record, the Buddies stride into a 2-0 lead and hold on to win 2-1 in Dunfermline. Dundee United win 1-0 at home to Motherwell. The gap remains the same, however news is received that Livingston have secured the First Division title. As they have satisfied the SPL entry criteria ... it is now confirmed that a club will be relegated.

Saturday 5 May; Missing Turner, McLaughlin and Fenton, Saints again race to a 2-0 lead. Agonisingly, St. Johnstone claw back two goals following the dismissal of Ricky Gillies. The match ends all square. Dundee United beat Dunfermline 1-0 at Tannadice. Those two dropped points in Perth could prove to be vital but there's still everything to play for. Three points behind, two games remaining.

Saturday 12 May; Aberdeen are visitors to Love Street and two goals in a minute just before half-time give St. Mirren the perfect boost. St. Mirren 2 Aberdeen 0, and St. Johnstone 2 Dundee United 0; if the interval scores remain unchanged then the drama will extend all the way to the final day. Despite Aberdeen's second-half efforts that bring them a goal, Saints hold out for a stunning win. Ears strain to radio sets listening for the score from Tannadice. Rumour has it that United have equalised. When the final score is confirmed the news could not be worse; St. Johnstone 2 Dundee United 3. Three points behind but with only one game remaining, and a goal difference of fourteen in United's favour; St. Mirren are effectively relegated.

In spite of the devastating anti-climax, players and supporters alike carried the momentum from the closing weeks of the season into the final game at Motherwell on 20 May. As they had done in the three previous matches, Saints again surged into an early two-goal lead; and, as had happened against St. Johnstone two weeks previously, the lead was lost and the match ended all-square. Motherwell 3 St. Mirren 3. So closed a Premier League campaign of the utmost effort.

The season had provided moments of real satisfaction amidst the struggle. Most especially, performances during the closing month encouraged a belief throughout the support that St. Mirren were at least capable of holding their own in the lower half of the Premier League, a situation the team could build on. That belief would be carried optimistically into the following season; together with the accolade that St. Mirren had the best travelling support in Scotland ... they stuck by their team.

2001-02

Given the high levels of expectation, this turned out to be a campaign of great disappointment and frustration for all associated with St. Mirren. By the time the last ball was kicked in May 2002 there was no doubting that the mood, and the "bubble", had definitely burst!

Yet, it all began so positively. Season ticket sales held steady, not far short of the previous season's record number at 3,000-plus. A series of pre-season friendlies against English League opposition had been generally satisfactory in performance if not results. Home opposition in the shape of Premier League St. Johnstone were then defeated 3-2 in Paisley with goals from Quitongo, McGarry and Turner.

Most of the previous season's imports continued to leave Love Street; only McGowan, McKenzie and Quitongo remained. Tom Hendrie's efforts to retain Stephen McPhee were disappointingly rejected when he signed for Port Vale. Irishman Paul McKnight also appeared to have chosen to continue his career elsewhere when he headed for Saints' former Cup-Winners' Cup opponents Tromso. Unable to settle in Norway he returned to Scotland and re-signed for Saints.

The single new signing of the summer was man-of-many-clubs Alex Burns, most recently of Raith Rovers. Another signing target scored for Saints as a trialist in a pre-season friendly against Wigan Athletic. Despite his goal, Hendrie decided he wasn't what was wanted. That decision would return to haunt the Manager.

The season began on 4 August with a trip to Glasgow to face Second Division champions Partick Thistle. An excellent crowd of close to 7,000, fifty percent of which hailed from Paisley, enjoyed the sunshine and the goal-fest in varying degrees. St. Mirren gained the lead three times and lost the lead three times, Thistle's third equaliser being scored in the 86th minute.

The season would eventually be remembered for the high number of "late" goals conceded by the defence. Early in the campaign, when confidence and expectation were high, these late losses were denying points as the team continued to chase further goals. Later, as the effects of unfulfilled expectations began to take hold, fading confidence saw the side concede late counters when attempting to hold an advantage. A free attacking style gave way to nervous defending ... and Saints continued to be vulnerable.

Typical of Saints' performances was the 18 August meeting with Falkirk at Brockville. The Buddies took the lead twice but eventually lost all three points. Falkirk's second and third goals were both scored in the closing eight minutes. A month later, on 15 September, ironically the feast day of St. Mirin, further late counters contributed to Ayr United's 4-2 win at Somerset Park.

Later in the season, it was the Buddies that fought back from an early 2-0 deficit at home to Arbroath on 2 February to tie the scores in the second half. However, rather than continuing to press their rattled opponents, the players by now preferred to retreat into their own penalty area and play out time content with a single point. Having handed possession and territorial advantage back to the visitors, Saints thereafter lost a goal and all three points in a panic-laden last few minutes.

The defence conceded fifty-three League goals over the course of the season, equalling the amount in 1997-98 when the Club was almost relegated. Promotion was never likely with such a poor defensive record.

Ayr United added another three to the "goals against" total in a Bell's Challenge Cup tie at Love Street on 7 August. It might have been St. Mirren's first-ever home tie in the tournament but it was not destined to be a successful one. Neither did the other national competitions prove any more successful. Stirling Albion gained some revenge for being relegated in 1998 by eliminating Saints from the League Cup in their opening round match on 25 September, the CIS competition having kicked-off later than normal. Yet, even allowing for Saints' semi-final appearance earlier in the year, the first-match exit was as early as many supporters had come to expect.

It was the same story in the "Scottish". The attempt on the coveted silverware ended at Broadwood on 8 January; Clyde's second Cup win over St. Mirren at their new home in six years. It was also the eighth successive season that the Buddies had failed to progress beyond the opening round. Three cups. Three games. Three defeats.

Tom Hendrie was quoted at the season's outset warning of "complacency". Indeed his page in the opening match programme cited the word in capital letters! Despite the Manager's alert, many supporters believed complacency to have been a significant factor in the early season results. Injuries also played their part. Physio Colin Brow was kept busy throughout the autumn attending to Ian Ross, Iain Nicolson, Jamie McGowan, and Tom Brown for lengthy spells. Each player was badly missed. Unfortunately for Brown, his injury ultimately led to him being released in the spring.

League form at no time reached the heights necessary for a title challenge, although the team did spend ten weeks of the season sitting in third position behind pace-setters Partick Thistle and Airdrieonians. At one stage, however, this meant being a distant seventeen points behind the leaders and only twelve above bottom side Raith Rovers!

The best spell of results, ironically fell between the CIS and Scottish Cup defeats. Equally ironic was the fact that the heaviest, and most embarrassing, defeat of the whole campaign occurred during this same period. On 8 December Falkirk, sitting well down the table and re-building their side with youngsters, came to Paisley and gave Saints a lesson in finishing, winning the match comfortably by 5-1. The Manager claimed that, taking the goals out of the match, St. Mirren was the better side. Few fans agreed.

Yet, the same St. Mirren took eight points from Airdrieonians and in doing so probably denied them the title. If complacency was one problem then inconsistency was certainly another; undefeated against the team from Airdrie but only one win out of eight meetings with bottom pair Falkirk and Raith Rovers.

There was excitement at the end of September when it was announced the Club had signed Liberian internationalist and former Arsenal striker Christopher Wreh on an initial one-year deal. The growing frustration in the stands increased as Wreh spent most of his time playing for the under-21s or sitting on the substitutes' bench. The Manager criticised his attitude but supporters couldn't understand why he wasn't even given a chance in the first team.

Wreh was released four months after his arrival, having been fielded only five times from eleven selections as substitute. Four of these appearances were away from St. Mirren Park while the fifth was during that 5-1 defeat to Falkirk. The home support had seen only twenty-minutes of a player whose signing had created so much initial anticipation. It was just another disappointment for the fans.

Neither could the support understand the team's total lack of consistency. Saints failed to win any of the opening six away fixtures yet, when away form did begin to pick up, the team's home results then somersaulted in the opposite direction. The opening five undefeated games at St. Mirren Park were inexplicably followed by six home fixtures without victory between 27 October and 12 January, meaning that commendable wins in Inverness, Dingwall, Arbroath and Airdrie were not capitalised upon. Fresh blood was needed. It arrived in the form of new signing Brian McGinty who joined Saints in time to make his debut in the 2-1 win at Caledonian Stadium on 3 November. He then scored his first goals, a double, to secure the 3-2 victory in Airdrie.

With expectations of regaining a Premier League slot clearly misplaced, financial considerations returned to the fore. It became necessary to reconsider the budgeting strategy especially as eleven players would be out of contract come the season's end. Several players left for loan spells at other clubs in a move at least partly designed to cut back on wages for the last few months of the season. Mark Yardley moved to Forfar Athletic, Steven McGarry went to English Conference side Boston United, Chris Kerr was loaned to Alloa Athletic, "Ludo" Roy travelled north to St. Johnstone, and Alex Burns was allowed to sign for Partick Thistle.

Chairman Gilmour expressed a pragmatic view on the proceedings. "We're pruning our finances before they get the better of us," he admitted.

Defender Scott Walker recovers from a heavy landing.

Mark Yardley torments the Clyde defence in their first St. Mirren Park League fixture of the season when Saints won 4-1.

St. Mirren have a proud record of community involvement - disabled youngsters play in front of the East Stand at the half-time interval.

"If we had been challenging for promotion we would have required twenty-four or twenty-five players. We are not, so we only need eighteen."

The Chairman's analysis was accurate; the team was certainly not challenging for promotion. Instead, it was involved in yet another relegation battle. From the 3-2 defeat to Arbroath on 2 February until the end of the season, there were a mere three victories in thirteen outings. To make matters worse, defeats were also becoming heavier. Four goals were lost again at Ayr on 26 February, at Inverness on 2 March, and away to Ross County on 16 March; Clyde then hit three past the defence at Broadwood on 20 April.

Unsigned pre-season trialist, Paul Ritchie, hit a hat-trick for Caley-Thistle against Saints and was well into double figures for the season. Amongst other things, many fans were angry that he hadn't been fixed up in the summer and were not slow to express their collective view. The new Club website had taken over a half-million "hits" in its short existence and many were to vent anger and frustration on the members' "forum". Tom Hendrie would only offer in reply, "there is nobody more frustrated than myself and John Coughlin at the way we have tended to surrender the initiative in matches."

As the fans voiced their impatience so the team displayed even greater fragility.

Former St. Mirren youth goalkeeper, John Hillcoat, returned to Love Street as a replacement for Ludo Roy and Mark Yardley was brought back from loan to provide presence in attack; a move popular with supporters. Saints dropped to eighth place with five Saturday's of the season remaining... the bottom four places of the league table read: Raith Rovers P 31 Pts 32; Falkirk P 31 Pts 36; St. Mirren P 30 Pts 37; Clyde P 30 Pts 38.

The next fixture produced a fierce battle at St. Mirren Park against Raith Rovers in which John Hillcoat rescued Saints with fine stops on several occasions before Jamie McGowan headed the winning goal. Saints' game-in-hand was then played four days later in Paisley. The opponents, Ayr United, had already beaten St. Mirren on four occasions since August scoring twelve goals in the process. Ricky Gillies earned the Buddies a vital point by netting in the 1-1 draw.

On Saturday 6 April, the Buddies then travelled up the east coast to Arbroath still requiring points to ensure safety. A Barry McLaughlin double and another from Iain Nicolson brought a hard-fought victory and a vital three points. The week had produced seven points from a possible nine, effectively removing the relegation threat.

A week later the Paisley fans endured the sight of Partick Thistle winning the title at Love Street with ex-Saint Alex Burns in their line-up. The "Jags" celebrated in front of a packed Caledonia Stand; ironically it was the third title-winning game that Saints' support had witnessed in successive years. The season ended with a no-scoring home draw with Falkirk.

There had been some recent criticism that fewer youngsters were breaking through the ranks since the departure of Joe Hughes to Leeds United. Kris Robertson, Graham Guy, Simon Lappin, and Linwood lad David Lowing made their first-team debuts during the 2001-02 ... they would soon be joined by several more players from the youth set-up.

The season had been a bitter letdown. As ever the Club and its supporters hoped for better things to come.

2002-03

Cash was still king as the new season approached. In making severe financial cutbacks, fourteen players departed the Club during the summer. Among them were defenders Barry McLaughlin and Scott Walker who moved to SPL clubs Kilmarnock and Dunfermline respectively, and Hugh Murray who decided to try a move to England. In their place Tom Hendrie added a mixture of youth and experience.

Three teenagers preferred joining St. Mirren to staying with SPL clubs; Kirk Broadfoot and Billy Bauld arrived from Hibernian, together with Ricky Robb from Rangers. Twenty-four year-old striker Martin Cameron re-joined his former manager from their time at Alloa Athletic, ex-Falkirk captain Greig Denham was added to the defence and, at the other end of the experience scale, twenty-nine year-old former Aberdeen midfield player Andy Dow joined after being released by Motherwell. In a surprise move, Junior Mendes also returned to Love Street following a two-year absence.

The curtain opened on a new season with an "all saints" clash against relegated St. Johnstone on a drizzly 3 August at St. Mirren Park. It was a poor start as the visitors scored twice and hit the frame of the goal twice more. The Buddies had plenty possession but remained vulnerable. Wearing the stripes were Roy, Rudden (Guy), Kerr, McGowan, Robb, Dow (Lappin), Gillies,

Flanked by youngsters, Simon Lappin and Graham Guy, temporary signing, 'keeper John Hillcoat leaves the park after the last game of the season, a 0-0 home draw with Falkirk.

Brian McGinty at his place of work.

McKenzie, McGinty, Cameron (Yardley), and Ross. Under-18 player Graham Guy made his debut in the 70th minute; by that time Saints were already two behind. The fans had expected better from their favourites.

Away to Falkirk for the second League fixture, that score was repeated as was the number of leather scuffs on the St. Mirren posts. The Bairns were actually only in the division because Airdrieonians' bankruptcy resulted in one, rather than two, clubs being relegated from the First Division. Nevertheless, they would take seven points from Saints, feature in the season's most exciting match, and win the division by nine points.

No goals. No wins. No points. "That wasn't the script we had written for the start of the season," Hendrie dismayed. Within another two weeks the situation had improved to the extent that the Manager was moved to write "a wee smile is now back on the Hendrie countenance."

Back-to-back League wins, 3-1 at home to promoted Alloa Athletic and 3-2 away to Clyde, both included late winners, this time FOR St. Mirren! Wearing the number "4" shirt at Broadwood, in a somewhat unexpected move, was Hugh Murray re-signed after failing to tie up a deal in the English League. In the same week Scott McKenzie returned to Falkirk having made eighty-three appearances in Saints' colours.

Not only had league form picked up, but the team had also progressed to the semi-final of the Challenge Cup. A home draw in the opening round brought a youthful East Stirlingshire side to Paisley. The Third Division outfit proved no match for St. Mirren as Martin Cameron rattled in four goals in a 7-0 rout.

Round Two then paired Saints with Clyde at Broadwood where it was definitely a case of third time lucky as goals from Baltacha and Gillies made amends for two recent cup exits in Cumbernauld. On then to Ross-shire where a battling performance on 20 August saw St. Mirren into the last-four after Saints and County tied at one-all over the ninety minutes. A penalty shoot-out was won 6-5.

Last season's Second Division champions, Queen of the South, were the semi-final opponents one week later. With the match being played in Paisley, hopes were high for a final place and Hendrie handed the following players the task of also stretching the team's unbeaten run to five matches; Roy, McGowan, Kerr, Murray, Fellner, Dow, Gillies, Mendes, McGinty, Cameron and Ross.

Austrian defender Gerhard Fellner was playing his third game on a short-term contract and scored the last of the Buddies' three goals in the 80th minute. Unfortunately, the Doonhamers netted five of their own ... helped by some truly dreadful defending late in the game when the scores were level at 3-3. "Queens" scored twice in the final two minutes to leave the home fans feeling shell-shocked and St. Mirren out of the competition.

August had already been chock-full of incident, but "finals" still had another part to play. There was one final game to be played, on the final day of the month, and it marked Tom Hendrie's final game in charge. Only four days on from the despair of defeat in the Challenge Cup, four more home goals were conceded in a desperately poor performance against Inverness Caledonian Thistle.

With young Kris Robertson in goal and another Austrian trialist at the heart of the defence, Saints could offer nothing in reply. Inverness were three ahead in twenty-five minutes, and once again Caley-Thistle's Paul Ritchie played his part, continuing to reek revenge on the Club that had rejected him thirteen months previously.

A statistical record of August 2002 does not actually make particularly distressing reading; played nine, won four, drawn one, lost four, nineteen goals for, eighteen goals against. However, the almost balanced set of figures disguises a highly erratic level of performance. The team was as unsettled as the figure of twenty-one different players fielded in nine matches suggests.

On the touchline the Manager's increasingly agitated demeanour was the clear sign of a problem. He had lost the confidence of the support and, it was rumoured, he had lost the confidence of the players. It was shortly to be confirmed that he had also lost the confidence of the Board.

A dignified press release on Thursday 5 September outlined the Club's solution to what had now become a very public problem; "The Board of The St. Mirren Football Club Limited following concern at recent team performances have requested Tom Hendrie to take leave from his duties meantime while the situation is re-assessed. John Coughlin, the Assistant Manager, will take charge of the team for the very important cup fixture against our Renfrewshire rivals Morton at Cappielow on Saturday."

The relationship between Manager and Club quickly soured as an uncomfortable situation dragged on for several months. Despite the Club's statement, Hendrie sought to claim for constructive dismissal and an out-of-court settlement was eventually reached.

John Coughlin immediately won the fans' favour with a thrilling CIS League Cup victory in Greenock. Greig Denham finally made his debut, in the cauldron of a derby, after sitting out the first month of the season due to injury problems. A sensational match did not start well for St. Mirren. Having fallen 2-0 behind as early as the 29th minute, they eventually took the tie into extra-time thanks to second-half goals from Martin Cameron and Simon Lappin.

Cameron was then replaced by Mark Yardley, and "Yards" became the day's hero five minutes from the end when he scored his last and possibly most stunning goal for the Club. Time seemed to stand still as he dribbled passed defender after defender en route to unleashing a powerful left-foot shot into the net.

The wildly joyous scenes were worthy of an occasion more significant than the first round of the League Cup. However, it was certainly a significant day in the life of the new Caretaker Manager; and there will

French goalkeeper Ludovic 'Ludo' Roy applauds the support.

seldom be an occasion more significant in the life of a St. Mirren supporter than a win against Morton in Greenock. Especially so in this, the most dramatic of come-back circumstances.

John Coughlin made his mark on the team as he began to introduce more of the Club's youngsters into his line-ups. Graham Guy, Simon Lappin, David Lowing and Jamie Dunbar were all handed starting places as fortunes changed for the better under the caretaker boss. Away points were picked up in Arbroath and Ayr, and Queen of the South's return to Paisley for a League encounter on 21 September produced quite a different outcome from their previous visit. Although the "Doonhamers" took an 8th minute lead they were not afforded the amount of time or space they enjoyed in the Challenge Cup. Saints harried and hassled their way to an excellent 2-1 win.

On 5 October 2002, St. Mirren celebrated the 125th Anniversary of the Club's first-ever match, minus one day! The surviving players from the 1959 Cup winning team were invited guests on a suitably sunny Saturday. On the field Ross County were the visitors; one of the original

The last word ... Saints 3000 strong Scottish Cup support outsung the opposition.

members of the Scottish Football League playing against one of the newest. Saints lined-up Roy, Dunbar, Lappin, Rudden, Broadfoot, Lowing, Gillies, Ross, Cameron, Mendes, and McGinty, while the famous striped jerseys displayed a specially embroidered commemorative inscription. An interesting aside was the inclusion of Saints' supporting Steven McGarry in the visitors' line-up.

The match ended in a satisfactory share of the points, the two goals being scored within three minutes late in the first period. During the game's closing ten minutes Yardley replaced Mendes and Guy substituted for Gillies as John Coughlin pushed his team forward in an attempt to end a special day with a special result. It was not to be. The three unused substitutes who shared in the historic occasion were Kris Robertson, Chris Kerr and Andy Dow.

It was back to more mundane fayre one week later when two goals during one minute in Perth ended the team's encouraging run of results. Nonetheless, the best match of the season was only another week away. High flying Falkirk came to St. Mirren Park six points clear at the top of the table, having won eight of their ten league matches to date.

They certainly looked potential champions when they powered their way to a 2-0 lead in seventeen minutes and added another shortly before the interval. St. Mirren 0 Falkirk 3. Within twenty minutes of the second period the scores were tied at three apiece! Cameron and Mendes were menacing the heart of a Bairns' defence that was found wanting. Not only was the defence troubled; the visitors' Manager appeared to be having palpitations on the touchline!

Ricky Robb scored the first in fifty-three minutes. Cameron added the second five minutes later, and the third another eight minutes into the match. There were almost twenty-five minutes yet to be played and the final outcome was anyone's guess; although the initiative had swung firmly in the Buddies' favour. Saints' front two continued to create havoc and close-calls for the Falkirk rearguard before the Bairns suddenly broke away and scored a fourth.

The excitement level was such that more goals were sure to follow and in the 85th minute Junior Mendes drove into the Falkirk box and attempted to force his way between two defenders. He was hauled down. Penalty! Referee Rowbotham was in no doubt and pointed to the spot. Martin Cameron stepped forward and planted the ball firmly beyond the 'keeper to complete his hat-trick and the day's scoring. St. Mirren 4 Falkirk 4. The Saints' fans roared their approval as the North Bank roof struggled to stay in place. This was more like a true fighting St. Mirren side.

That fixture was both the highlight and the high-point of the season. Thereafter form settled into a familiar pattern. Saints' League position moved from seventh to eighth, to seventh, to sixth, and back to seventh where the team ended the season on thirty-seven points. However, as the Chairman admitted, "the injury list had been prodigious." Almost forty players had been required to see the Club through a rollercoaster season. It was heartening that eleven of them were teenagers, almost all of whom featured in an unimportant closing day defeat at Alloa. The Manager, in experimental mood, gave youth its chance.

The passing of former Club Chairman and President of the Scottish Football League, Yule Craig, was noted with sadness prior to Christmas. He had been associated with St. Mirren since the early 1960s, when he became Club Secretary, through until 1998 when he held a non-executive directorship.

On a lighter note, 3,000 supporters enjoyed a Scottish Cup day-out at Celtic Park on 25 January. Once again the fans excelled in difficult circumstances. Saints' main attacking threat, Martin Cameron, was withdrawn injured due to a hamstring injury with the scores tied at 0-0. With him went any slim chance that the team had of contriving a result. Celtic were comfortable 3-0 winners. In the battle of the fans, however, the "Celts" never stood a chance!

Playing on the left side of defence at Parkhead was returning ex-player Martin Baker. He was one of ten changes in personnel that had occurred during the League's first application of a "transfer window". During the month of January, Sergei Baltacha, Ian Ross, Andy Dow, the iconic Mark Yardley and Junior Mendes left. In addition to Baker the incomers were Hibs' defender Mark Dempsie, forwards Ally Mitchell from Kilmarnock, Mark Roberts from Irish side Shelbourne, Scott McLean from Partick Thistle, and finally midfielder Paul McHale from Rangers. Only one of the five would remain after the season's end.

Although finishing a mere two points above relegated Alloa Athletic, the threat of demotion had not been as real as during the previous season. Saints were twelve points ahead of the relegation places with five matches remaining to be played, and it was only the battle between Alloa and Ross County to avoid finishing second bottom that pushed both clubs closer to St. Mirren over the closing weeks.

A new organisation, the St. Mirren Independent Supporters Association (SMISA), was now in its second year supporting the cause, but the cause remained unchanged. The St. Mirren Football Club ended its 125th season as it had ended its very first; owned by its followers, financed by its followers, protected by its followers.

With Alloa eventually demoted, the final game of the campaign, at the "Wasps" Recreation Park, was insignificant other than to note the extremely inexperienced team fielded by St. Mirren. The match was lost 4-0, leaving John Coughlin to think hard about his plans for the season ahead just as previous Managers and Committee Members had done throughout the past one hundred and twenty-five years.

The season was over and with it the completion of a century and a quarter of history. Paisley's finest looked forward to the future in much the same manner as they always did ... with hope and determination, to carry the famous black and white stripes onto the fields of Scotland, to give of their best.

The townspeople and supporters remain firmly behind them; after all, Paisley is St. Mirren and St. Mirren is Paisley, and that's exactly as it should be ...

We are the Buddies!

To be continued ...

Please note, the following dedications were received at the outset of this publication's production. They were 'time accurate' on their submission.

DEDICATIONS & *Memories*

GRAEME AITKEN
ROMFORD
Herrie are, herr arr ra MACAROONS

GRAHAM AITKEN
COATBRIDGE
To my unborn baby and future Saint!

KIRSTY E AITKEN
ROMFORD
Mum, Dad & St Mirren. Life's Greatest

NICHOLAS ATKINSON
STOCKTON-ON-TEES
A Buddie for life due to Tony Fitzpatrick

ROBERT BARCLAY
RENFREW
Lifetime Supporter

GRAEME BARR
BRIDGE OF WEIR
I hate Hammarby!

CRAIG BELL
DERBY
Always proud to be a Buddie

CHRIS BUCKHAM
PAISLEY
Here's to another 125 years

ALAN BUSBY
NEW YORK
Alan, Craig & Ryan Busby - Proud Buddies

THE BYRNE FAMILY
DALRY, AYRSHIRE
Black and White Forever!

JOHN BYRNE
BARRHEAD
Come on the Saints

DUNKY CAMPBELL
PAISLEY
Was a true Buddie all his life 1937-2001

IONA CAMPBELL
EDINBURGH
A Saint forever

GORDON CANAVAN
THURSO
For Frank Canavan & Charlie Duffin

GAVIN CHITTICK
BARNES, LONDON
Still Black & White after all these years

GORDON CLARKE
PORTSMOUTH
Proud to be a Buddie. 125 not out

DAVID COCHRAN
JOHNSTONE
Proud to be a Buddie

SEAMUS CONNOLLY
OMAGH
Lifelong supporter

DAVID CORRIGAN
AUSTRALIA
Thanks Saints from 3 generations of fans

JIM CRAWFORD
PAISLEY
St Mirren - in my heart and in my soul

S & A CRAWFORD
PAISLEY
We're St. Mirren 'til we die!!

AL CUNNINGHAM
PAISLEY
St. Mirren 'til I die!!

FRAZ CUNNINGHAM
RAF LEUCHARS
A Saint... for my sins! FTOF SMTID

JACK DEANS
STROOD, KENT
At one with Saints - JJD1S

EDDIE DEVINE
PAISLEY
A family of Saints

JOHN C DOCHERTY
CORBY
Paisley Buddie, St. Mirren now & always

SCOTT DOCHERTY
ARMY NOMAD
Black & White, Buddie & proud, SMFC 'til I die

IAIN DONALDSON
ERSKINE
St. Mirren 'til I die

TONY DORRIS
PAISLEY
For Joe McGill, a real Buddie

EUAN & CALUM
BEARSDEN
Saints' supporters and honourary Buddies

ANDREW FAIRLIE
ELDERSLIE
Always a Saint

REECE & DAD FARMER
FOXBAR
Forever a BUDDIE with my team & MUM

THOMAS FERGUSON
PAISLEY
Buddie watcher since 1957, still watching

JIMMY FORDE
RENFREW
A Saints' fan

JIMMY FORDE
RENFREW
A Buddies' fan

SHONA FORSYTH
BEARSDEN
Saints' supporter and honorary Buddie

ALAN GALLACHER
RENFREW
Hope, Dream, Believe

ALLAN D. GALLACHER
GLASGOW
Forever a Buddie, St. Mirren 'til I die

JOHN GIBB
PAISLEY
Here's to the next 125 years

STUART GIBB
ARDROSSAN
Go St. Mirren

ALISTAIR GILBERT
UPLAWMOOR
St. Mirren 'til I die

STEWART G. GILMOUR
PAISLEY
Addicted to Saints

PETER GORDON
NUNEATON
Feed the Blair

DAVID GRIER
GLASGOW
St. Mirren - the best club in the world

LORRAINE GRONAN
GLASGOW
Nothing beats being a Buddie

PAUL GRONAN AND SON
GLASGOW
St. Mirren 'til I die

IAIN HAMPSEY
PAISLEY
May the Saints be with you

PETER HAYBURN
IRVINE
Loyal supporter & shareholder

JACK HEATHWOOD
PAISLEY
I'm St. Mirren's youngest fan!

ROBERT HOWE
PAISLEY
Forever a Buddie even on 'nae guid' days

MARTYN HUNTER
PAISLEY
Proud to be a Buddie

IRVINE FAMILY
RENFREW
Buddies for ever

KARIN IRVINE
PAISLEY
St. Mirren: The stars in stripes!

STEVIE IRVINE
NEW ZEALAND
The Paisley Buddies always in my heart

NORRIE JAMIESON
PAISLEY
Always & forever a Buddie

JULEIGH
SCOTLAND
Thank you for all the good times and may they last ...

CAMPBELL KENNEDY
BARRHEAD
Proud to be a Saint

EILEEN KENNEDY
BARRHEAD
Keep the faith

FIONA KENNEDY
BARRHEAD
Thanks Dad

CHARLES C KIPPEN
KILWINNING
First family Buddie

JIM LEYDEN
CYPRUS
For my dad Alan a fan for 70 yrs

RONNIE MACAULAY
MANCHESTER
Always a Saint

BRYAN McAUSLAND
PAISLEY
From ballboy to boardroom

MARC & JILL McAUSLAND
PAISLEY
Proud to be a Buddie

ANGUS McCALLUM
BARRHEAD
Supporting the Saints - win or lose

STUART McCALLUM
ELDERSLIE
St. Mirren - it's a family thing

THE MACFARLANES
PAISLEY
Forever Black & White

KIMBERLAY McGINLAY
JOHNSTONE
Brought up a Saint

LEE J McGINLAY
JOHNSTONE
Born to be a Saint

FRASER McGUIRE
PAISLEY
Dad - thank you for keeping me from the dark side!

OLIVE McILROY
RENFREW
Still walking down Love Street. Happy 25 to Tommy – Happy 125 to Saints

THOMAS McILROY
RENFREW
Happy Birthday Saints!

GREGOR McINTOSH
EASINGTON
Not 2 yrs old and already a buddie 4 life

STUART McINTOSH
EASINGTON
Proud to be a buddie

PAUL McKAY
MELBOURNE, AUSTRALIA
Very proud to be a buddie & my son Kyle

BRIAN McKEOWN
PAISLEY
'Mon The Buddies!!! SMTID, FTOF

McLAREN FAMILY
ARRAN
Generations of Buds

EUAN McLEOD
GLASGOW
In loving memory of my Dad Graham

JAKE McMULKIN
PAISLEY
Here's to another 125 years

JAMES McVEIGH
JOHNSTONE
This Black & White will never fade!

JAMES MANSON
SHETLAND ISLES
The Shetland Saint. Always be a buddy

CAMERON, LISA & GARY MARSH
LOCHWINNOCH
Proud to be Buddies are we three

GRAEME MARTIN
LICHFIELD, STAFFS.
St. Mirren, the greatest team in the world

GREIG MARTIN
ELDERSLIE
I love Saints with all my heart & I always will!

HUGH MATHESON
STENHOUSEMUIR
Proud to be a Buddie

MENZIES FAMILY
PAISLEY
Stick with Paisley

GEORGE MITCHELL
AYR
Dedicated to THE Tommy Gemmell-artist

THE MONEY FAMILY
PAISLEY AREA
Four generations of Saints supporters

STEVEN MORRISON
HOUSTON
I want to be in that number

GORDIAN MOTHERSOLE
BRIDGE OF WEIR
Thanks for all the great moments

GORDIAN MOTHERSOLE
PAISLEY
1987 gubbing Hearts, then Utd - the Cup was ours

GRAEME MOTHERSOLE
BRIDGE OF WEIR
Wrong end, wrong seats, right score, 3-0 Champions...

ALASDAIR NISBET
MELBOURNE
Black and White Down Under

ELAINE PATERSON
LOCHWINNOCH
A real football widow!

JACK PATERSON
LOCHWINNOCH
Brought up a Buddie - always a Buddie

KIRSTEEN PATERSON
LOCHWINNOCH
This is for my Dad: I support him too!

ROSS PATERSON
LOCHWINNOCH
St. Mirren FC: a love that will never die

KENNY POINTON
PAISLEY
To another 125 years in the limelight...

KEN POLLOCK
JERSEY CITY NJ
Still a fan

Q51 & Q52
PRESTWICK
Thanks for the memories

COLIN REID
INCHINNAN
Millennium Champions - never forget ...

BRIAN ROBERTSON
LONDON
Saint Mirren 'til I die

L. J. ROBERTSON
BEITH
I just can't help falling in love with u

DAVID ROBIN
BRIDGE OF ALLAN
Faithful supporter all his short life (34 years)

JOE ROBINSON
PAISLEY
1977 : 1987 : 2000 : Saints fan forever

JONATHAN RODGERS
TAIN
Saint Mirren 'til I die

JOSHUA RODGERS
TAIN
Forever Black and White

TABITHA EMILY RODGERS
TAIN
Forever Black and White

JOHN ROSS
PAISLEY
A Buddie for Paisley to be proud of

WILLIAM 'WILLY' ROSS
PAISLEY
Loyal Buddie, much missed friend. Saints forever

SCOTT & TRINA
LEEDS
Scott 'n Trina Donnell forever Saints !!!

SEPHIROTH
PAISLEY
When you're sWo, you're sWo 4 Life!

ALISTAIR SHARP
LIVERPOOL
Thanks for your support...

STEVE SPARKE
HULL
A Buddie, and proud of it!

A. S. C. & S. A. STAFFORD
CARDONALD
Murphy will smile on us again

JULIE STEEL
JOHNSTONE
A Saint forever. Keep the faith

HAMISH STEVENSON
BO'NESS
Proud to be a Buddie

JODI STRATHEARN
NEUCHATEL
Saints fan all my life (all my 3 years)

JOHN STRATHEARN
NEUCHATEL
Born to be Bud

THOMAS STRATHEARN
NEUCHATEL
Born to be a Buddie

GARETH TOOP
KINGS PARK
Some people say we're crazy... SMTID

SIMON VARNEY
WELSH BUDDIES
Buddies go marching on forever

JIM WALKER
STRATHAVEN
75 years a Saint

BILL WILDE
EAGLESHAM
To the next "125"

ADAM WILSON
GLASGOW
Here's to a Black And White future

ALEX WILSON
GLASGOW
St Mirren 'til I die

DOUGLAS WILSON
PAISLEY
Supporter since 1936 and proud of it

JIM YOUNG
PAISLEY
Experience the highs & lows of life as a Saints' fan

The authors extend their thanks to all who have helped their cause during the production of 'Marching On'...

Acknowledgements

The management and staff of The St. Mirren Football Club, particularly Campbell Kennedy and Jim Crawford.

Alan Lapsley (Son of David) and the Lapsley family, Falkirk

Gordian Mothersole, Bridge of Weir

Alex Jenkins, Johnstone

George Pratt (former Club Secretary), Largs

Bill Waters (former Director), Houston

Bob Earlie (former Chairman), Paisley

Tony Connell (former player), Glasgow

Jack Copland (former player), Paisley

David Winnie (former player), Bridge of Weir

David Weir, Paisley Central Library

Tricia Burke, Paisley Central Library

Claire Baxter, Paisley Central Library

Michelle Evans, Journalist, Paisley

Fulton Crawford, Paisley

Bill McLeod, Bridge of Weir

Albi Mackay, Doncaster

Jennifer Gregory, Coatbridge

Andrew O'Connell, Barrhead

Ross Paterson, Lochwinnoch

Kirsteen Paterson, Lochwinnoch

Thomas Paterson, Paisley

David Cochran, Johnstone

David Roberts, Renfrewshire Council, (Paisley Museum) photographs pages 13 and 26

Jim Stewart, Official Historian, East Fife Football Club

Jennifer Carlile, Johnstone

John Swinburne, Motherwell Football Club

Willie Hunter, Saints Centenary Brochure

Morag Redford, Scottish Place-Name Society

Neil Leitch, Scottish Cricket Union

Elaine Fuller, Paisley

Les Fridge, Inverness ('87 Cup Final Reserve Keeper')

Peter and Marion Copland, Largs

Norrie Jamieson, Official St. Mirren Website

Kenny Pointon, Official St. Mirren Website

Karin Irvine, Official St. Mirren Website

All at Saltire Graphics/Print, Glasgow, in particular Marlene Thomson, Jacqueline Robertson, and David Brotchie

... and not forgetting Ann McPherson, Elaine Paterson and Cheryl Wright all of whom have suffered the production of this book over the course of 2002/05. Thanks girls, you can have your dining rooms back now!

Sponsored by:

Contents

1	Harappa and Mohenjo-Daro	4
2	The Indo-Europeans in Asia	8
3	The Persian Empire	12
4	Buddhism and the Mauryan Empire	16
5	The Indian Subcontinent	20
6	China from Shang to Zhou	24
7	China's Classical Age	28
8	The Empires of Qin and Han	32
9	Ancient Japan	36
10	Indochina and Malaysia	40
11	Peoples of the Steppes	44
12	Sailors of the Indian Ocean	48
13	Links with Iron Age Africa	52
14	The Contribution of Asia	56
	Glossary	60
	Index	62

1 Harappa and Mohenjo-Daro

The map shows central Asia in the 3rd millennium BC with its valley civilizations and other Indian cultures.

This statuette of a bearded man from Mohenjo-Daro is known as the 'great priest'. It is made of soapstone and is thought to show a god or priest-king.

The soapstone seal (inset on map) is one of many found at Mohenjo-Daro. A great number of these seals are carved with religious pictures or animals, like this elephant. Some have inscriptions, which as yet cannot be read. The seals may have been used to identify goods packed ready for transport.

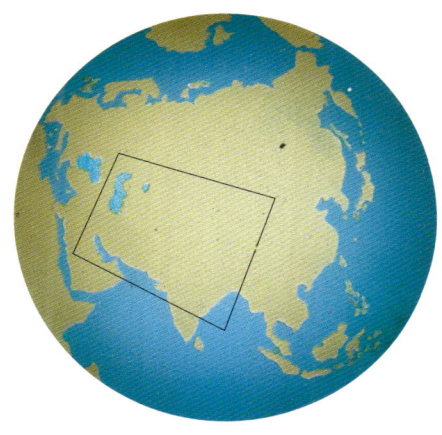

The map (below) shows the spread of farming and town life from the beginning of the 3rd millennium BC. Towns were closely concentrated in the dark red areas and more scattered in light red areas. Rural life flourished in the green areas.

1 Harappa and Mohenjo-Daro

Around the first half of the 3rd millennium BC, farmers and herders living on the plains of Iran began to move towards the Indus Valley (in present-day Pakistan), possibly because of the area's favourable climate. The Indus river and its tributaries formed a vast basin of fertile land from the mud left behind by their floodwaters, similar to the lands around the Nile in Egypt and the Tigris–Euphrates in Mesopotamia. An ample water supply, as well as rich natural vegetation and wildlife, encouraged more newcomers.

In time, a great civilization arose, called Harappa from the name of the first site discovered on the Ravi river, a tributary of the Chenab. We know little about this civilization, and must use guesswork to reconstruct a picture of how these ancient people led their lives.

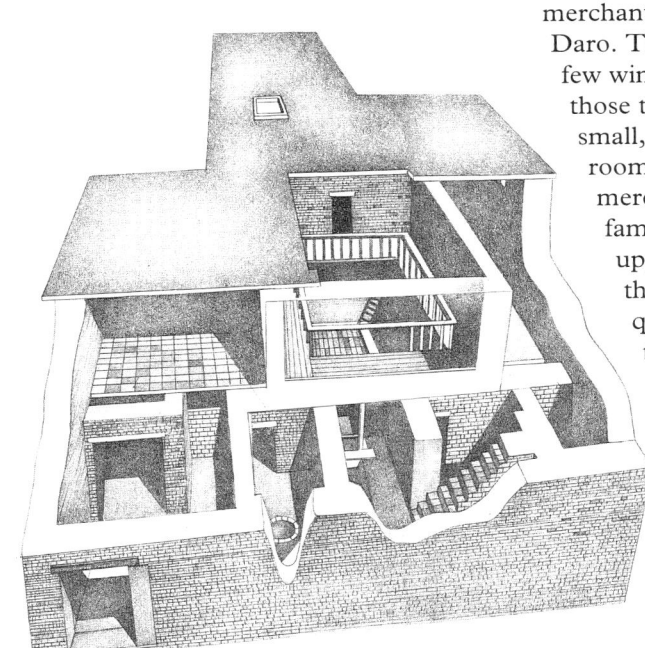

This model is of the inside of a typical house belonging to a wealthy merchant in Mohenjo-Daro. The house has few windows, and those that it has are small, to keep the rooms cool. The merchant and his family lived on the upper floor, while the servants' quarters were on the ground floor, near to the kitchens.

A number of settlements

Archaeologists have shown by their excavations in this region that people did not settle only in the Indus Valley, as was once thought, but in other places too. Settlements that share the same characteristics have been found in the Ganges river valley and on the coast of Gujarat, in northern Rajasthan (Bikaner) and in the easternmost areas of Uttar Pradesh (Alamgirpur).

It is hard to date the beginnings of Harappan civilization, but it seems to have lasted for about a thousand years, from around 2500 to 1500 BC. The oldest traces seem to be from the beginning of the 3rd millennium BC, and the period of greatest development was around 2000 BC.

Two powerful city-states

It is not clear how this great civilization was governed. It may have been one immense empire, as suggested by the similarities of archaeological finds discovered over the region, or it may have been ruled by two great neighbouring states. Two important cities have been discovered: Harappa to the north and Mohenjo-Daro to the south. They are 600 km (373 miles) apart, yet identical in foundation and character.

The existence of cities like Harappa and Mohenjo-Daro suggest that they belonged to an established civilization based on trade, although we can only guess at the type of economy. Evidence of flourishing trade comes from the remains of large stores and granaries found by archaeologists at the city sites. Trade goods moved along the network of rivers formed by the Indus and its tributaries to cities sited along the route, where they could be collected and stored. Remains of small model wagons, made from clay and metal, suggest that goods were also carried overland. The important centre of Lothal on the Gulf of Khambhat shows that there was also a route to the sea. Seals and weights from Harappa and Mohenjo-Daro have been found in Egypt, Mesopotamia and the Gulf, showing that trade

The picture below (which appears in colour on pages 4/5) shows daily life in a city of the Indus Valley civilization. The size and detail of buildings in the city of Harappa reflect its various social classes, among which were probably a priestly class, a rich merchant class and the less well-to-do.

The city grew according to strict town planning rules, with wide, straight roads laid out around a fortified citadel (shown in the background). Inside, and protected by solid walls, lay the centres of government and religion.

In the lower area of the town were flat-roofed houses, most of them built on one floor. Large residences made of brick, such as those on the left, belonged to rich merchants. They were clearly more elegant than the humble dwellings of the poorer citizens, some of whom are shown putting a roof onto a new house.

The roads of the city were paved with brick, as were the drainage canals that carried away rain and floodwaters from the Indus. A drain is shown beneath the brick pathway (far left). Nearly all the houses were well equipped for water supply and drainage. The people also made pots, from clay.

Wheeled carts were pulled by oxen, a form of transport that can still be seen in the Indian sub-continent today.

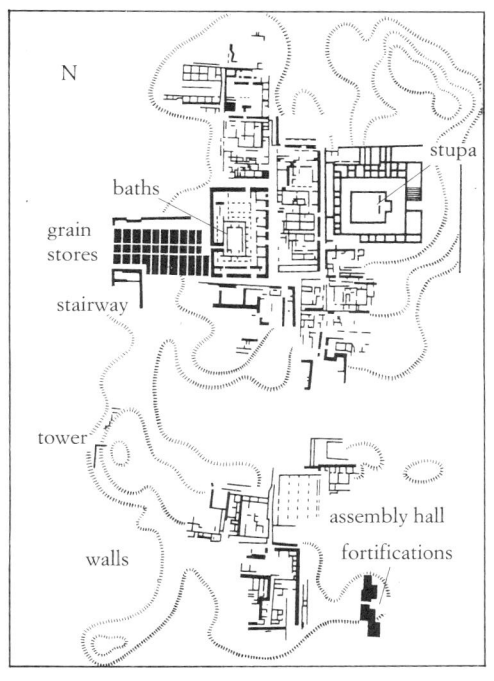

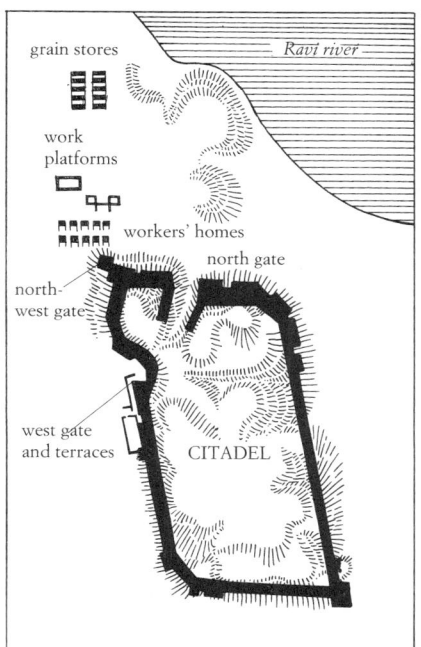

The plan (far left) shows the fortified citadel of Mohenjo-Daro, at the heart of the city.

This street in Mohenjo-Daro (left) shows the drainage canals that ran throughout the city. The system was extremely efficient, carrying away waste water from almost every house.

The plan of Harappa (right) shows its fortified citadel. Although smaller than that of Mohenjo-Daro, it overlooked a city of considerable size.

from the Indian subcontinent reached these areas.

What we know, and what is mystery

Farming was well developed, particularly the cultivation of corn and barley, and animal-rearing. Few weapons have been found, which seems to confirm that the wealth of the civilization was based on trade, and not military might. The richness and variety of the cities' buildings perhaps suggest that the society was divided into classes, as in the earlier Sumerian civilization. This may be evidence of a common origin of the two cultures. Finds from areas on the city boundaries suggest a quite large group of less wealthy people living there. Some experts think that government was in the hands of priests, although no buildings that can definitely be identified as temples have been found. Given the people's trading economy, it is perhaps more likely that power was held by a group of merchants or traders.

Although people in Harappa and Mohenjo-Daro were able to write, nobody has yet been able to read the cuneiform inscriptions found on numerous seals and amulets. This has made it difficult to discover much about the people's religion or culture.

A sudden disappearance

Around 1500 BC, the Indus Valley civilization disappeared suddenly. Many possible causes have been suggested, such as decay from within, or destruction by terrible flooding from the Indus river, particularly of the most important cities such as Lothal. Invasion by Aryans is another possibility.

The Sanskrit word Arya means 'noble'. This may mean a higher social class, as well as a known group of people with a common language, like the people of Iran. The Aryans may be considered as an eastern branch of the Indo-Europeans (a large group of people with related languages). Their arrival in the Indus Valley may have been a bloody and ferocious invasion, to which the people of Harappa and Mohenjo-Daro could offer little resistance.

This small terracotta statue (right) comes from Mohenjo-Daro, and is of a male figure. Such statues are less common than female figures, and their significance is not known.

The female terracotta statue (below) is also from Mohenjo-Daro. Women are often shown wearing many ornate necklaces and bracelets.

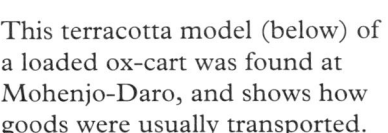
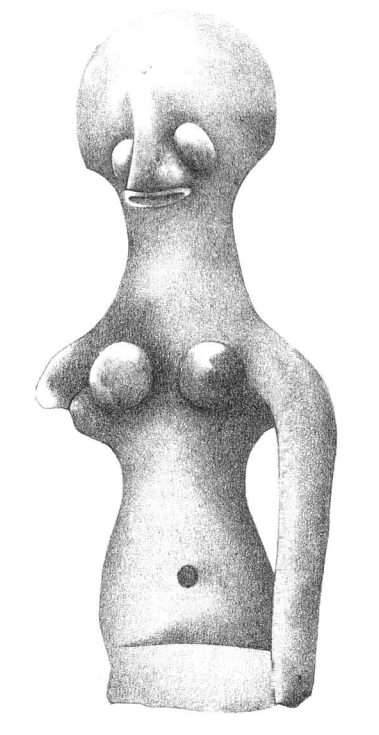

This terracotta model (below) of a loaded ox-cart was found at Mohenjo-Daro, and shows how goods were usually transported.

2 The Indo-Europeans in Asia

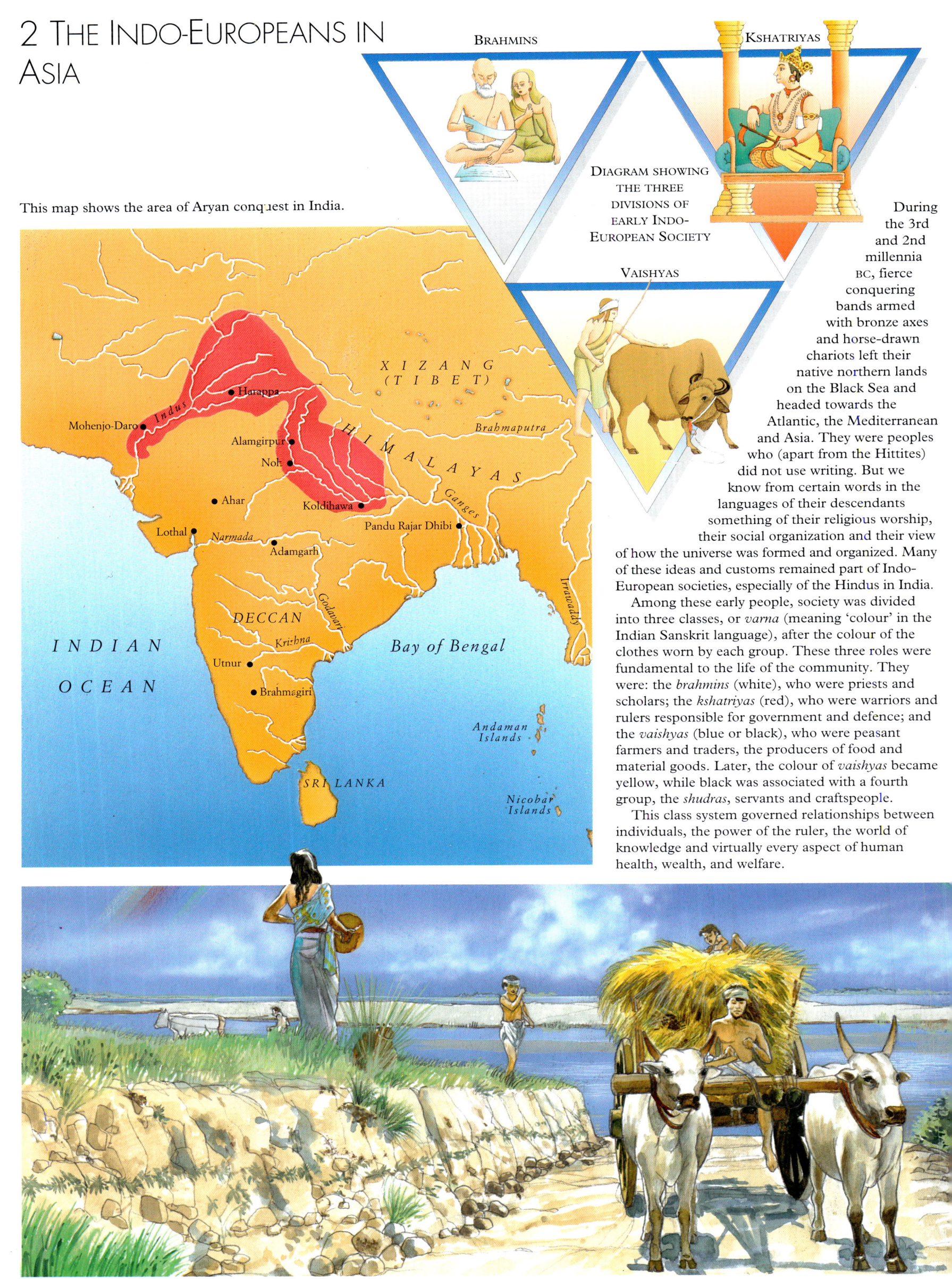

This map shows the area of Aryan conquest in India.

Diagram showing the three divisions of early Indo-European society: Brahmins, Kshatriyas, Vaishyas.

During the 3rd and 2nd millennia BC, fierce conquering bands armed with bronze axes and horse-drawn chariots left their native northern lands on the Black Sea and headed towards the Atlantic, the Mediterranean and Asia. They were peoples who (apart from the Hittites) did not use writing. But we know from certain words in the languages of their descendants something of their religious worship, their social organization and their view of how the universe was formed and organized. Many of these ideas and customs remained part of Indo-European societies, especially of the Hindus in India.

Among these early people, society was divided into three classes, or *varna* (meaning 'colour' in the Indian Sanskrit language), after the colour of the clothes worn by each group. These three roles were fundamental to the life of the community. They were: the *brahmins* (white), who were priests and scholars; the *kshatriyas* (red), who were warriors and rulers responsible for government and defence; and the *vaishyas* (blue or black), who were peasant farmers and traders, the producers of food and material goods. Later, the colour of *vaishyas* became yellow, while black was associated with a fourth group, the *shudras*, servants and craftspeople.

This class system governed relationships between individuals, the power of the ruler, the world of knowledge and virtually every aspect of human health, wealth, and welfare.

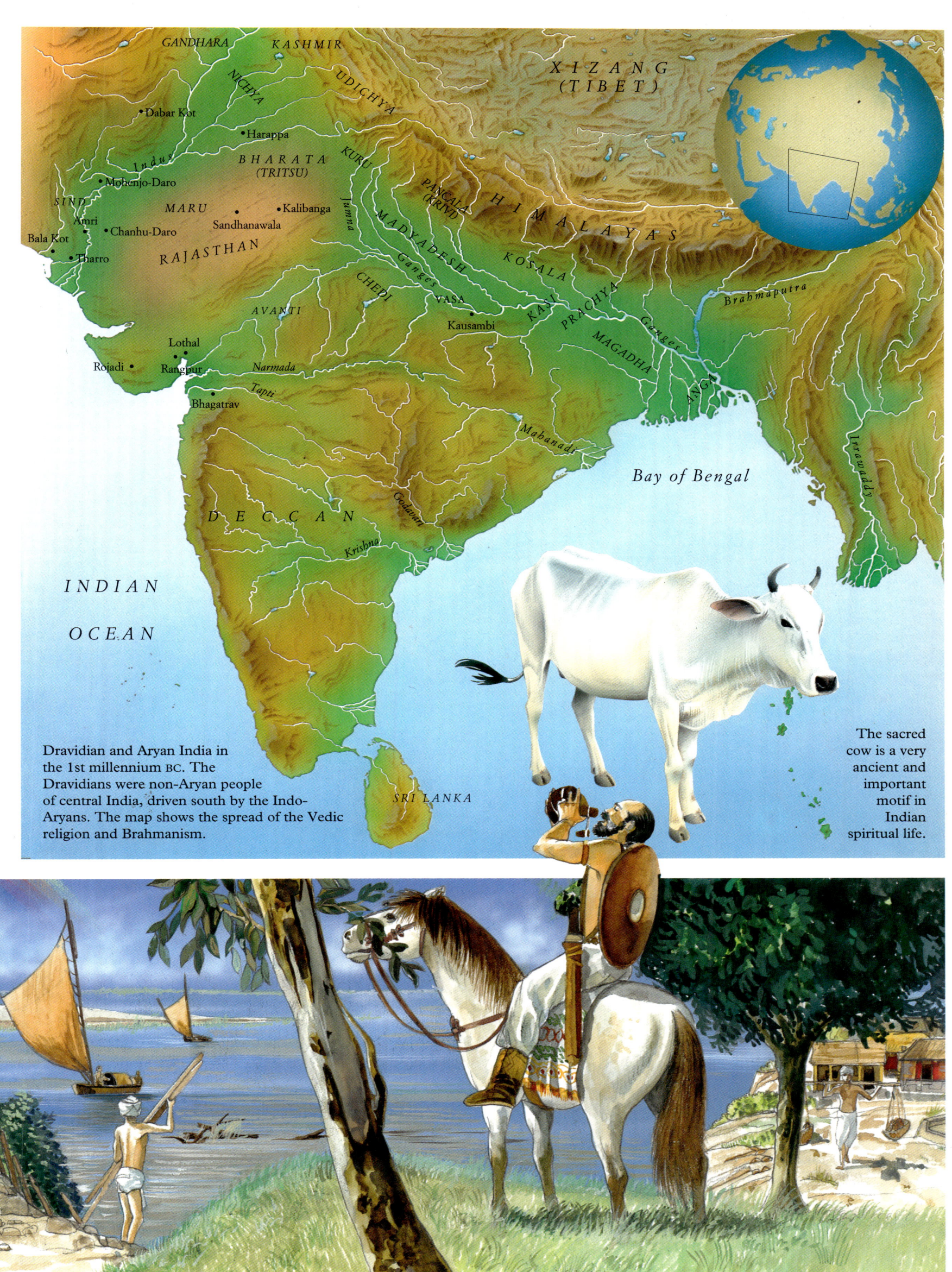

Dravidian and Aryan India in the 1st millennium BC. The Dravidians were non-Aryan people of central India, driven south by the Indo-Aryans. The map shows the spread of the Vedic religion and Brahmanism.

The sacred cow is a very ancient and important motif in Indian spiritual life.

2 THE INDO-EUROPEANS IN ASIA

The bull-headed god Yama (below) was associated with death.

Agni, the god of fire and light (left), was shown with a crown of flames. This figure comes from southern India.

The arrival of the Indo-Europeans in Asia was an important event in history, the effect of which is still apparent today. In large parts of India, people speak languages very similar to those of Iran, Afghanistan and Armenia. Even more surprising is the fact that these languages have strong associations with numerous European languages. Common characteristics between cultures so far apart geographically seem to be explained by the existence of one ancient language family, Indo-European, common to many different peoples.

Origin of the Indo-Europeans

Indo-European civilization has its origins between the 5th and 4th millennia BC, in southern Russia or western Siberia. In spite of later divisions and migrations, it is thought that the Indo-European peoples stayed in this particular area for a long time. Around 3000 BC, one group moved to western Europe, while another migrated south towards the Iranian plains, Afghanistan and Kashmir. In the centuries that followed, this second group split again. Some people moved to Persia (now Iran) and conquered it. Others, the Aryans, headed east around 2000 BC or perhaps later, around 1500 BC. This group entered the Indus Valley and destroyed the civilization of Harappa and Mohenjo-Daro.

The Aryans in India

Towards the end of the 2nd millennium BC, the Aryans had already occupied part of the Ganges basin in India and the land between it and the Jumna river. Here, other peoples began to form alliances, particularly those of the Kuru, or Kaurava, with the Pancala. A king of the Kuru called Parikshita may have founded Asandivate, the first great city of the time. His son Janamejaya is known to history as a conqueror, and the establishment of a strong state between the Ganges and the Indus is attributed to him or to one of his immediate descendants. This was the first area of truly stable government, where the growth of town life took place along the lines of Harappa and Mohenjo-Daro.

The first Aryan kingdoms

The newcomers gradually moved further east and south. Their numerous and scattered settlements became larger and better organized, so that around 400 BC there is evidence of at least 16 proper states. Of these, Magadha is the most important in the history of northern India at this

The scene below (pictured in colour on pages 8/9) shows the Ganges river valley. The warrior on the right, drinking from a flask, is a typical Aryan cavalryman. He has a round shield and a sword. Horses were seldom used in war by other peoples, so the Aryan cavalry inspired fear and gave their army great prestige.

The Aryans settled along the Ganges and other rivers, and made the most of the farmland, which was very fertile because the soil was regularly enriched by river floods.

Sailing craft can be seen on the river, and men and women are at work in the fields. In the background (right) is a house, and a man carrying baskets on a yoke across his shoulders.

The bullock cart was, and still is, a common form of transport. Cattle were considered to be sacred animals, and were not killed for meat. Modern Hindus still do not eat beef. The philosophy of non-violence and respect for all forms of life is a very ancient one in the Indian subcontinent, despite its frequent wars and invasions.

Varuna (below) was the creator of the universe. In the Vedas he was also god of the night and sky. In modern Hinduism he is the god of water.

Indra (above) was god of thunder, rain and lightning. He was also the god of war.

period. Others include Anga, in western Bengal, the outer limit of Aryan expansion to the east; Pancala, between the Ganges and Jumna rivers; Gandhara in the middle Indus; and the kingdom of Avanti at the southernmost point of occupation.

Wherever they went, in Asia or Europe, the Indo-Europeans took their own distinct culture, based on a clear division of society into three parts: priests for religion; warriors, whose use of horses made them almost invincible; and the farmers and herders.

The Aryan caste system

With no archaeological evidence from the first centuries of their rule, what we know of Aryan society comes from the sacred writings or *Vedas* (from the Sanskrit *vid* meaning 'to know'), which gathered together the collective wisdom and religious ideas of these people. The most ancient of these writings may date from before 1500 BC, and show that the people had a society with three castes, corresponding to the three main roles in society: the priests, or brahmins; the kshatriyas, or military caste; the vaishyas – farmers, shepherds and merchants. People were born into a caste and remained within it. Marrying outside one's caste was just one of a number of banned activities, but the ban was not always observed, at least in early times. To the three main castes can be added a fourth, regarded as inferior and impure, made up from the native peoples of conquered territories.

Religion and tradition played a central role in Vedic society, and the male head of the family, or patriarch, was supreme. The view of the spiritual world was based on numerous gods. Mitra and Varuna were rulers of the universe, and corresponded to sovereigns on earth in their powers of creation and justice. Indra, god of war, was often associated with Agni, god of fire, light and intelligence.

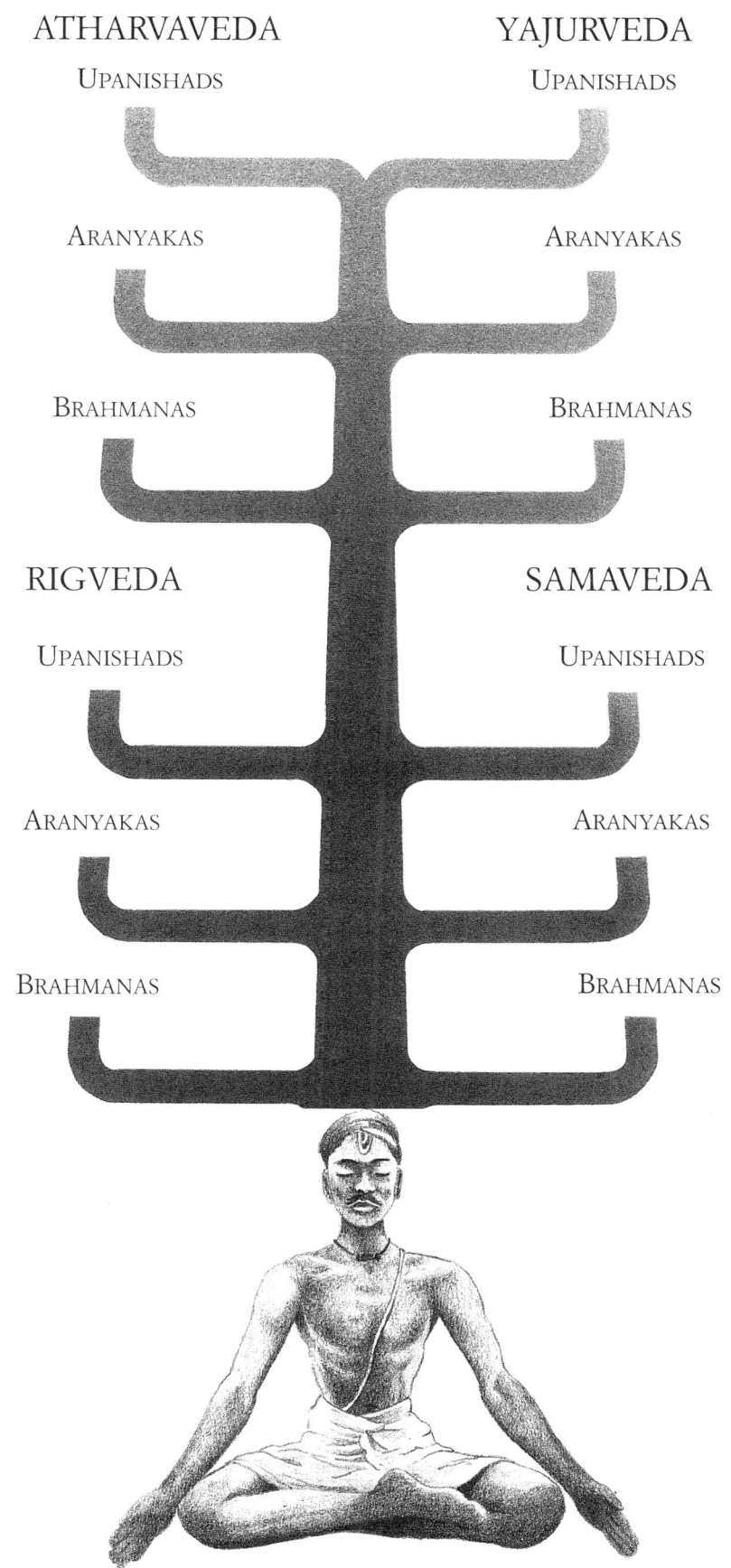

The diagram (top) shows the structure of the Vedas. *Veda* means knowledge. There are four Vedas, each divided into parts. The four ancient texts were the Atharvaveda, Yajurveda, Rigveda (the oldest) and Samaveda. In book form, the pages were usually rectangular and richly decorated, sometimes in gold ink. The figure (above) is of a Brahmin meditating.
The statue (right) is of the god Surya.

3 The Persian Empire

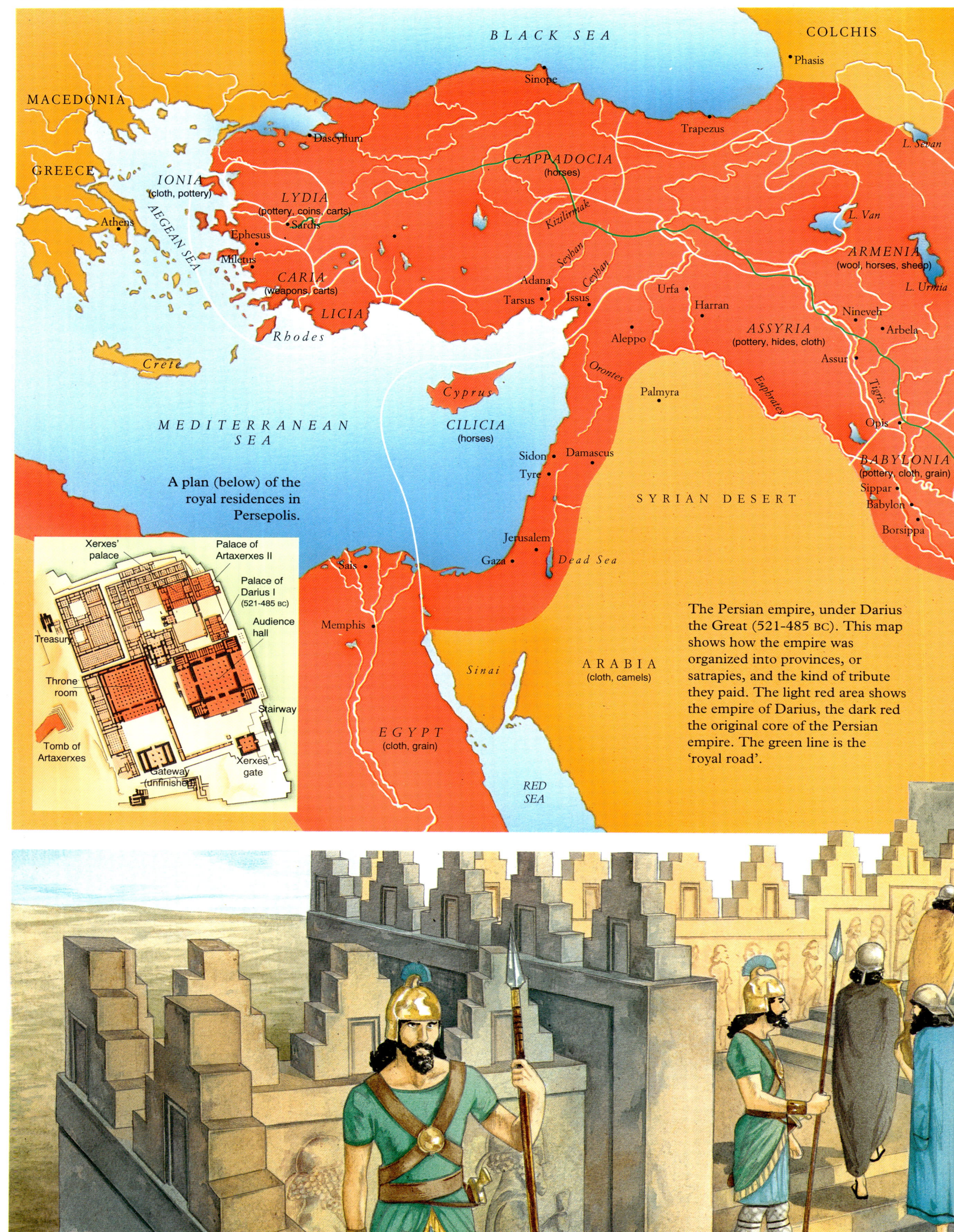

A plan (below) of the royal residences in Persepolis.

The Persian empire, under Darius the Great (521-485 BC). This map shows how the empire was organized into provinces, or satrapies, and the kind of tribute they paid. The light red area shows the empire of Darius, the dark red the original core of the Persian empire. The green line is the 'royal road'.

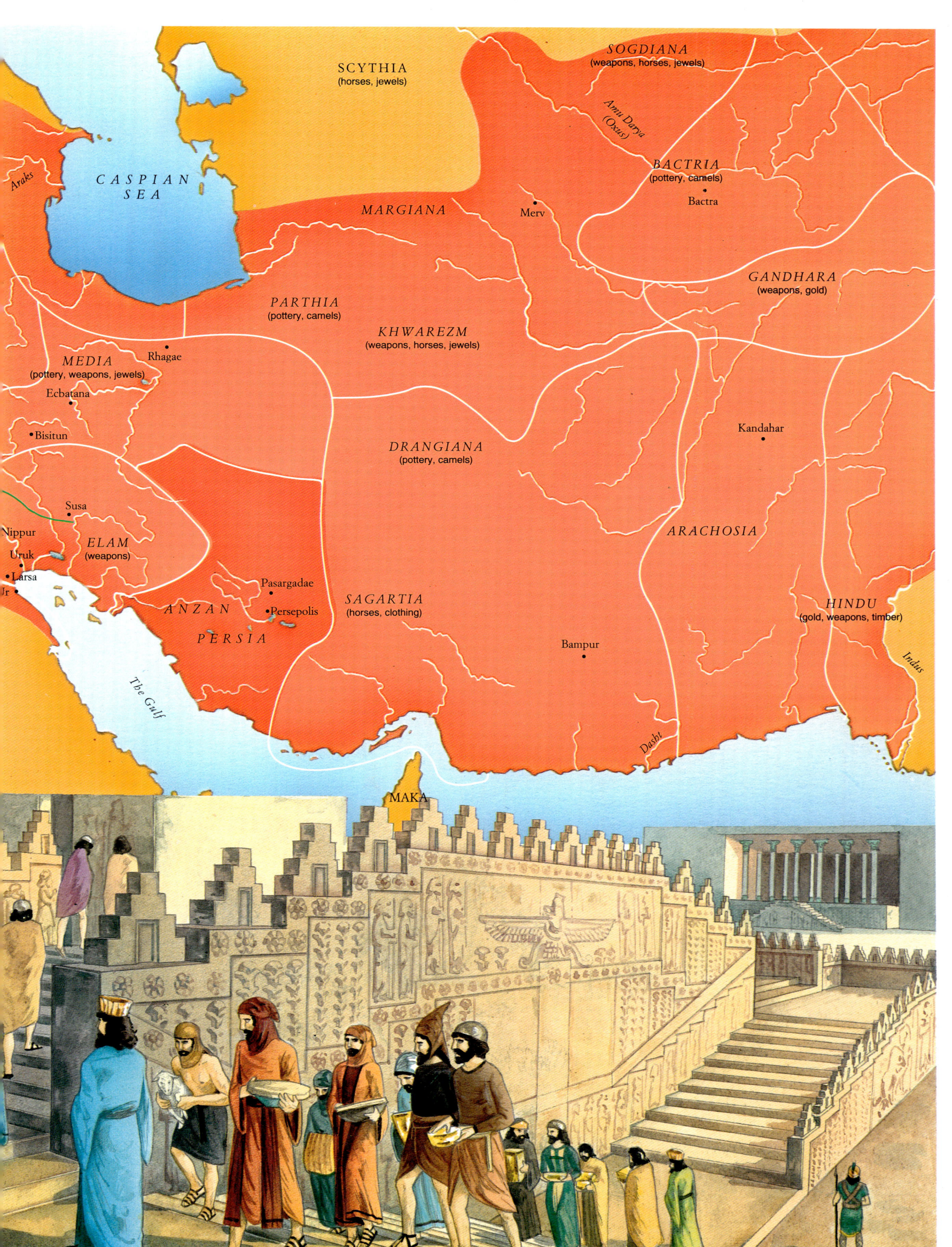

3 THE PERSIAN EMPIRE

The migrations of Indo-Europeans took two related peoples, the Medes and Persians, both Iranian in type, into the lands between the Caspian Sea and the Gulf, close to the borders of Mesopotamia.

The Medes and Cyrus of Persia

The Medes had been subjects of the Assyrian empire from the 9th to 7th centuries BC. But, under their leader Cyaxares, they defeated Assyria and destroyed Nineveh in 612 BC. Their empire then stretched from Lydia to the Iranian plateau. However, in 550 BC the Medes surrendered to the greater power of Persia and Cyrus the Great, then king of Anshan. He conquered Lydia and in 539 BC defeated mighty Babylonia, leaving to his heirs a Persian state that was rich and strong. To this empire, his son Cambyses added Egypt in 525 BC.

A new emperor

When Cambyses died in 522 BC, a new leader emerged: Darius. He was the son of the governor of Parthia, and not a direct heir to the throne. How Darius came to power is unclear. An inscription carved in stone at Bisitun in cuneiform writing and in the languages of Persia, Elam and Babylon, seems to have been an attempt to legitimize his accession. Similar declarations of his right to rule were probably circulated around the empire.

Darius swiftly crushed the revolts that were threatening Persian rule in Persia itself, and in Elam, Media, Assyria, Egypt, Parthia and Scythia. He set out to subjugate all the conquered peoples afresh, and conquered new lands in Thrace, Scythia, Macedonia, and as far east as the Indus Valley. Cyrenaica in northern Africa became a vassal state, though still self-governing. Only once was Darius checked, by the Greeks who defeated the Persian army at the battle of Marathon in 490 BC, thus saving Athens from conquest.

The government of Darius

Darius reorganized his vast empire. Unlike Cyrus, who had left local rulers to run their own governments, Darius created a centralized government of which he was the sole head. The empire was divided into provinces called satrapies. Each satrap (the leader of a satrapy) was a trusted relative or loyal follower of Darius, who kept hold of military and judicial power. To keep in touch with his territories, the emperor set up an efficient communications system of messengers and beacon signals.

At court and for inscriptions, the Persian language was used. But the language of government was Aramaic. The

The scene below (pictured in colour on pages 12/13) shows Persian provincial governors at the sumptuous imperial palace at Persepolis. Each satrap came to present his region's tribute to the emperor, in symbolic form. The real goods were carried in by wagon and caravan.

The satraps climb a long staircase, passing rich relief decorations on the walls and the stern figures of the imperial guards, with their long spears and swords. In the audience hall, the emperor awaits.

Tribute was paid either as gold and silver, or in goods. From Anatolia and Media came silver and iron. From Gandhara came gold, from Egypt and Mesopotamia grain, from the Indus Valley timber. Bactria and Armenia supplied wool. One of the satraps is holding a lamb, as a symbol of his territory's contribution.

The emperor was at the centre of this inward flow of wealth. He stored it in the royal treasury, controlling the entire economy of the Persian Empire.

The small tablet (opposite page) comes from Persepolis. On it are two pictures, made by seals pressed into the clay. One shows a cavalryman defeating an enemy, the other a soldier raising his arms in fear or supplication. The inscription attributes this seal to Cyrus of Anshan.

The map (right) shows how goods flowed in from the territories of the Persian empire. To build the great palaces at Susa and Persepolis required huge resources of workers and materials.

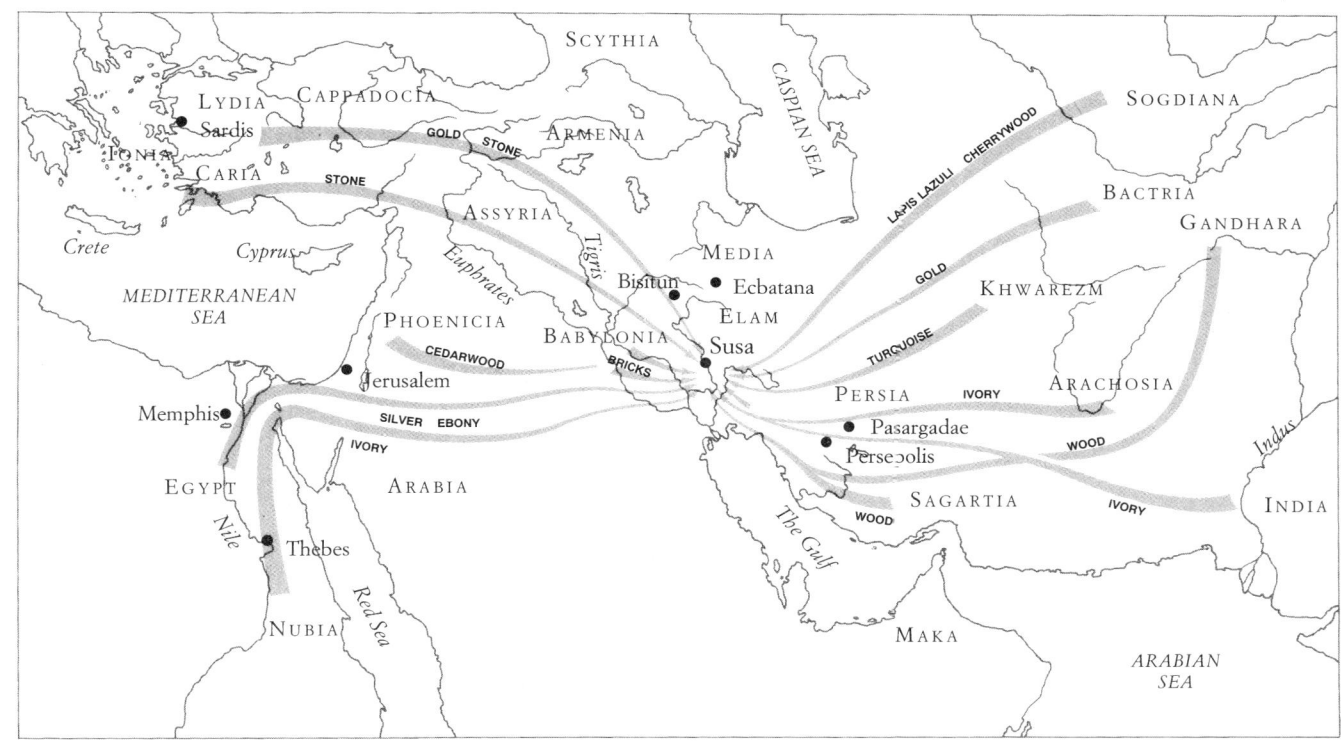

empire was further held together by a common imperial gold currency, by a new and well-run tax system, and by a huge army, with a strong cavalry.

Divine authority, regal splendour

The Persian empire was larger than any in the world before, and was more than simply an assortment of states won by conquest. Darius was determined to make his empire thoroughly 'Persian'. An inscription on his tomb declares that the great ruler received absolute power from the god Ahura Mazda, creator of the universe. According to the teachings of Zoroaster, Ahura Mazda was wholly wise and good. A divinely ordained ruler must therefore be morally virtuous too, and oppose evil. This religious ethic had the effect of making rebellion against Darius and his heirs a sin.

The capital of the empire was moved from Pasargadae, the city favoured by Cyrus, to Susa in Elam, where Darius built a magnificent palace combining the architectural styles of Mesopotamia, Media, Egypt and Greece. Some 40 kilometres (25 miles) away from Pasargadae, work began on a new royal palace, at Persepolis.

The empire extended as far east as India. An inscription at Persepolis, dating from about 513 BC, lists one of the satrapies as Hindu, from the Persian word Sindhu – the region around the river Indus. The Greeks called it 'Indoi', and this name came in time to be used for the whole sub-continent of India. Persian influence on the Indus region continued to be felt for centuries, and the first Indian empire, that of Asoka, was much like Persia's in structure and conventions.

Ahura Mazda (above) was, according to Persian belief, the creator of the universe. He is shown inside a winged disc. The emperor was associated with this god, as his chosen ruler on earth.

This gold relief (right) shows a priest wearing clothing of the kind worn in Media, Armenia and Cappadocia. It comes from a mass of treasure found near the Oxus river.

This female figure (left) appears on a relief decorating a gate at Pasargadae. The artist has included stylistic touches from around the empire. The background shows wings (typically Assyrian), the woman wears Elam-style clothes, and an Egyptian headdress.

4 BUDDHISM AND THE MAURYAN EMPIRE

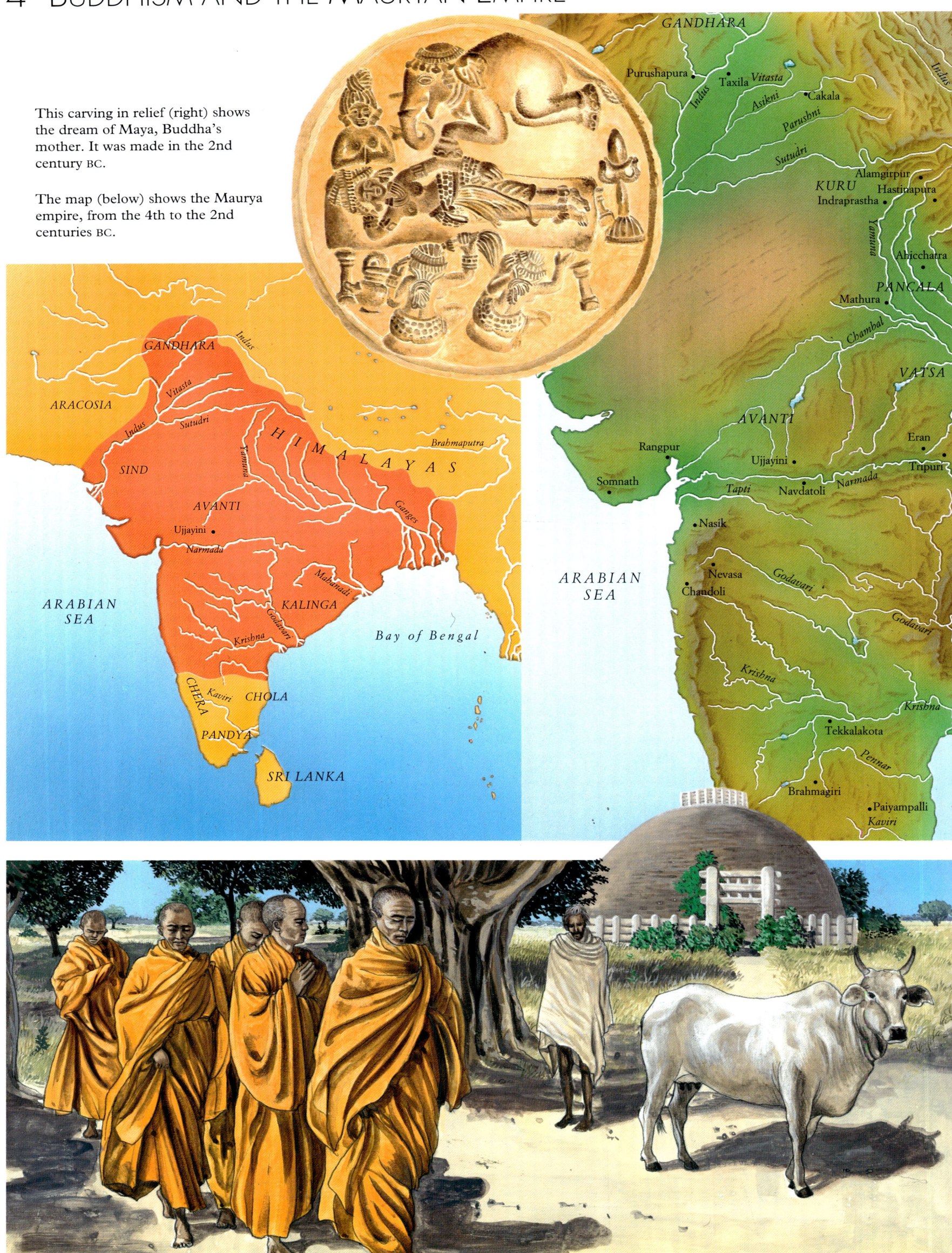

This carving in relief (right) shows the dream of Maya, Buddha's mother. It was made in the 2nd century BC.

The map (below) shows the Maurya empire, from the 4th to the 2nd centuries BC.

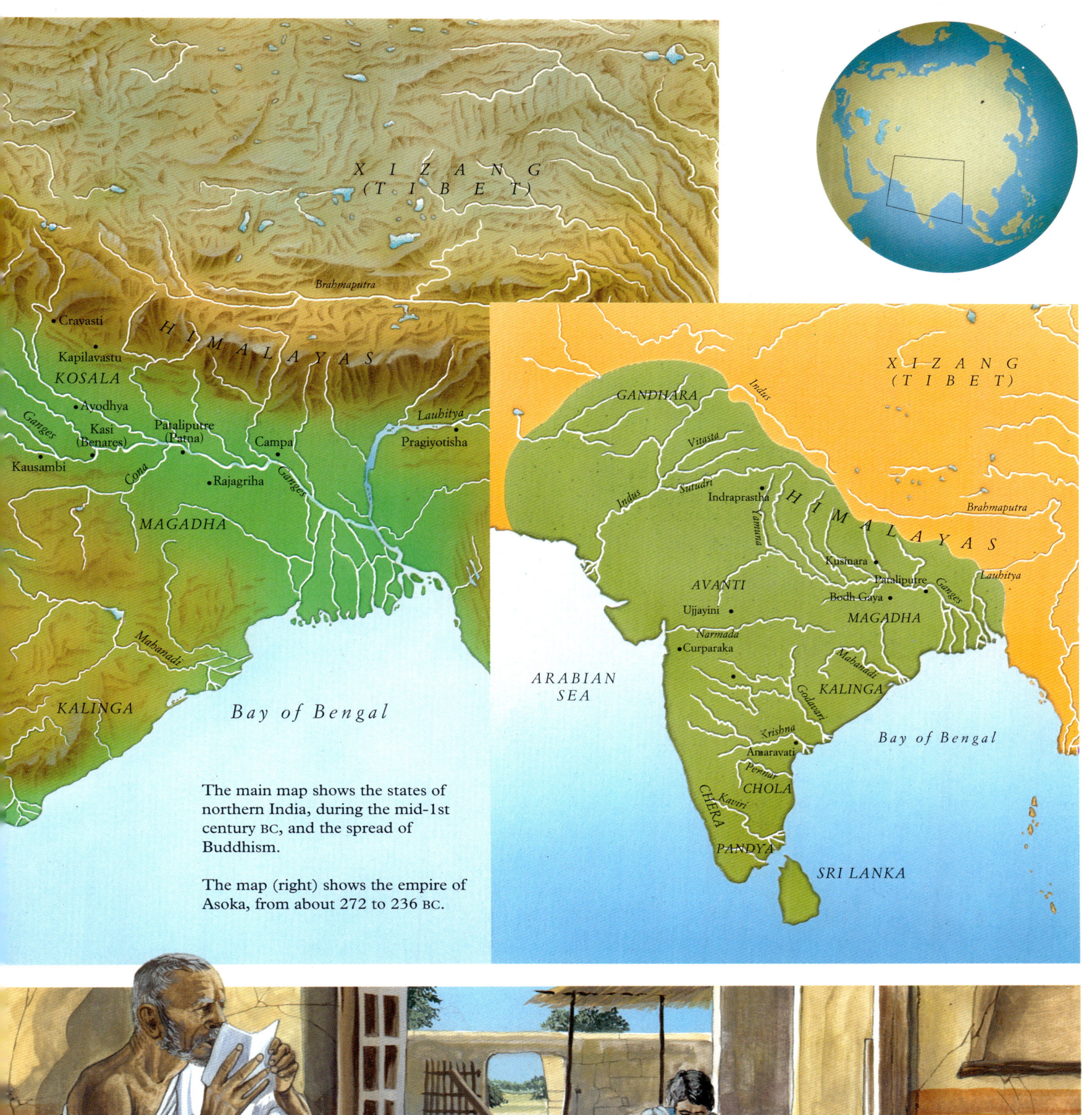

The main map shows the states of northern India, during the mid-1st century BC, and the spread of Buddhism.

The map (right) shows the empire of Asoka, from about 272 to 236 BC.

4 Buddhism and the Mauryan Empire

The Aryans in India formed several states. In the north, the most important was Magadha, in the centre of Bihar. This became the heart of the first Indian empire, and the birthplace of a new religious movement destined to spread far beyond India. The older Vedic beliefs had become rather sterile rites, followed only by the Brahmins, and the time was ripe for a resurgence of religious thought.

Buddha

Many legends surround the life of the founder of Buddhism. His name was Siddharta Gautama, and he was born in Kapilavastu (in what is now Nepal) around 560 BC. He was the son of the king of a small northern kingdom, and was brought up in comfort, protected from commonplace worries and hardships. At the age of 29, this young man experienced a moral crisis when he came face to face with the reality of human suffering. He left his home and family, and began a long, difficult search for truth. He studied meditation and became an ascetic, spurning all luxuries, but this did not satisfy his needs. It is said that one day he was sitting under a tree outside a village, and in a state of long and deep meditation, he found what he was seeking – enlightenment. The place of his enlightenment, in Bihar, came to be called Bodh Gaya. From then on, he was called Buddha, from a Sanskrit word meaning 'enlightened', and taught others what he had experienced himself. He travelled around northern India, and died at Kusinara, aged about 80.

Teachings of Buddhism

The basic ideas of Buddhism can be summarized from Buddha's first public teaching, which he gave at Benares. There were Four Noble Truths – as revealed by his meditation. First, all life is suffering. Second, the origin of suffering is attachment to material things, not knowing that they are illusions. Third, it is possible to escape suffering by becoming aware of it. Fourth, the means of doing so is meditation, to reach a state called *nirvana* (a more than worldly happiness and peace). The path to nirvana involved morality, meditation and wisdom.

Buddhist teachings were spread by monks. There were two schools of Buddhist thought. One, called Hinayana, (later Theravada) or 'Small Vehicle', spread to southern India, Burma, Thailand, Cambodia and Laos. Another, called Mahayana, or 'Great Vehicle', spread to Tibet, China, Korea and Japan.

Jainism

Another important creed in India at this time was Jainism. This was a centuries-old philosophy, which was revived by the teachings of a contemporary of Buddha named

The scene (shown in colour on pages 16-17) shows a group of Buddhist monks in their bright saffron robes. They walk along a dusty road in the cool shade of overhanging trees. Buddhist monks led a wandering life. They lived by begging as they moved across India, spreading the teachings of the Buddha.

This group of monks passes by a *stupa*, one of the many domed mounds put up in memory of the Buddha wherever his followers lived. Some stupas contained holy relics. Surrounding the building is a railing with a gateway. A poor peasant watches the small procession pass.

Jains (shown right) gathered together to pray in their homes. They believed in a simple way of life, free of worldly goods. The old man has in his lap a brush to flick away any insects that might cross his path as he walks. Jains tried to preserve all forms of life and feared they might accidentally kill small creatures.

The carving (opposite page) is from a stupa in Sanchi. It shows an imperial procession leaving a fortified city, typical of a Mauryan settlement. Behind the emperor's carriage, drawn by two horses, are many soldiers and an elephant. The faces of the watching crowd gaze down from the walls of the city.

A stopping place (far left) afforded travellers and imperial messengers on the highway refreshment and overnight rest. At such places, Asoka had pillars erected, inscribed with the teachings of Buddha, and with edicts and sayings of the emperor. In this way, Asoka's message was spread throughout his realm. The pillars, with their handsome mounts (enlarged centre), could be seen from afar. A fragment of script on a pillar at Girnar (left) is the oldest example of writing from India.

Mahavira (540-469 BC), who lived in Magadha. The name Jain comes from *Jina*, meaning victor, and was given to a number of religious teachers who lived before Mahavira. He was the last and his name means 'Great Hero'.

Followers of Jainism believed in moral behaviour, not owning property or acquiring material things. Devout Jains were required to reject all worldly things, even clothing. They respected all forms of life, and were vegetarians. Rich Jains gave away their wealth to help others.

Rulers of northern India

While these religions were developing and spreading, different dynasties ruled Magadha. The Haranka dynasty (546-414 BC) had its capital at Patna, and was followed by the Shishunaga (414-346 BC), which annexed the kingdom of Avanti. Vast regions in central India were conquered by the Nanda (346-313 BC), preparing the ground for the Maurya empire, the first large empire centred in India.

Alexander and Asoka

Alexander the Great invaded India in 326 BC, but eventually turned back westward. Chandragupta Maurya, a northern prince, led the Nanda kingdom to its greatest power in the wake of Alexander's wars. The Mauryan dynasty was able to extend its rule to southern India.

The emperor Asoka came to the Mauryan throne some time after 272 BC. He converted to Buddhism, and followed the Persian ideal of imperial rule – tolerance accompanied by moral vigour. He was a firm governor, and to spread his edicts across his empire he had them inscribed on stone pillars set up for all to see.

Little is known about the Mauryan kings who followed Asoka. The last one was murdered about 195 BC, and by then the empire had shrunk to more or less its original size.

This is a figure of Buddha, made in the Maurya period. It is far less stylized than representations made in 1st-century India.

5 The Indian Subcontinent

The map (right) shows the main peoples and kingdoms of India in the 2nd-1st centuries BC.

This stone statue of Brahma (left) comes from Chapagaon in India, and is from the 5th-6th centuries. Brahmanism is one of the main elements in India's ancient religion, Hinduism. Brahman is the supreme spirit behind the universe, and has three main forms: Brahma the creator, Vishnu the preserver, and Shiva the destroyer.

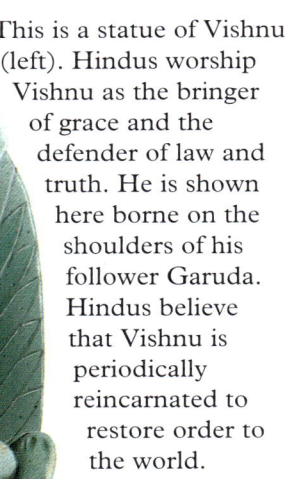

This is a statue of Vishnu (left). Hindus worship Vishnu as the bringer of grace and the defender of law and truth. He is shown here borne on the shoulders of his follower Garuda. Hindus believe that Vishnu is periodically reincarnated to restore order to the world.

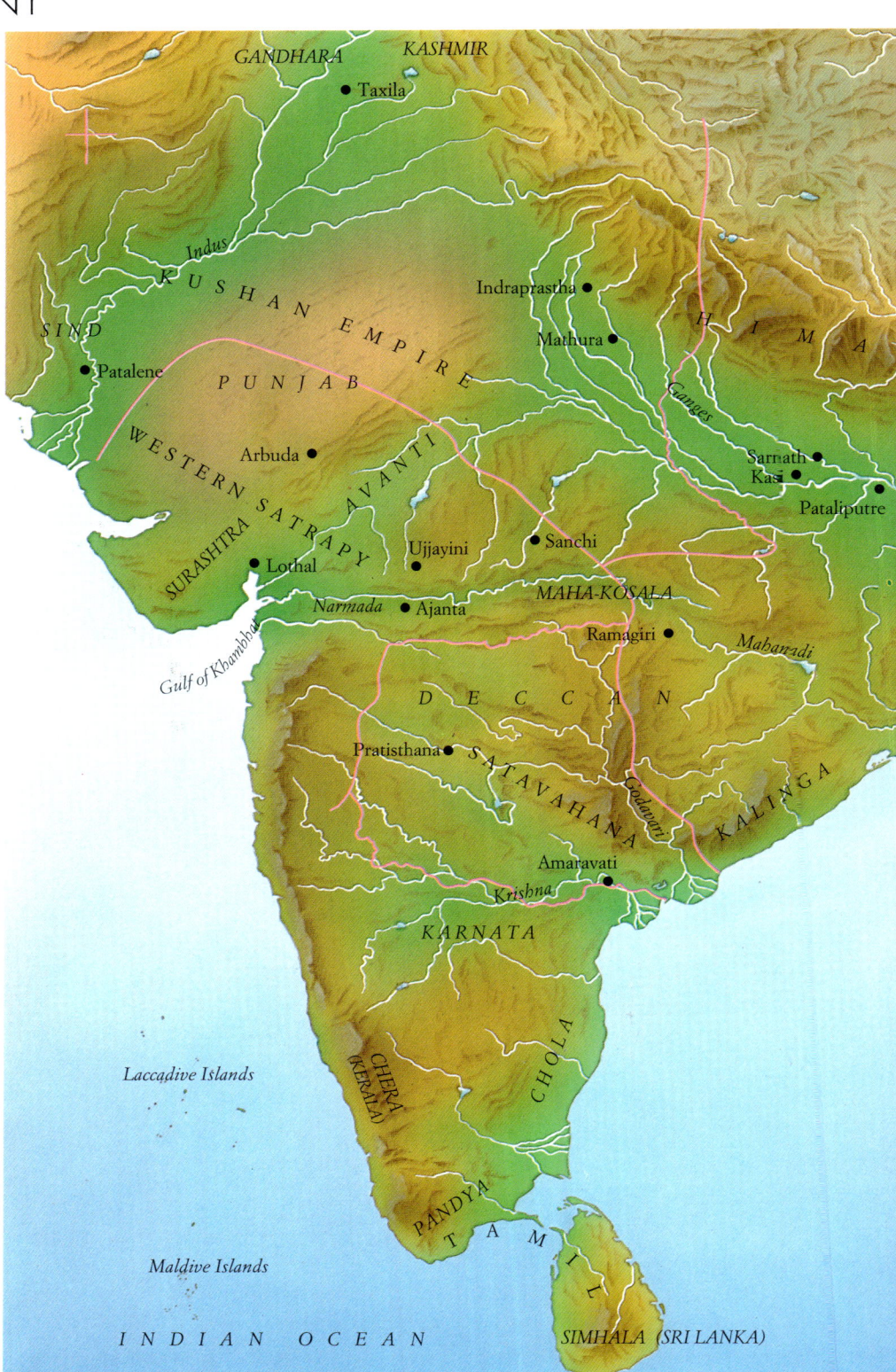

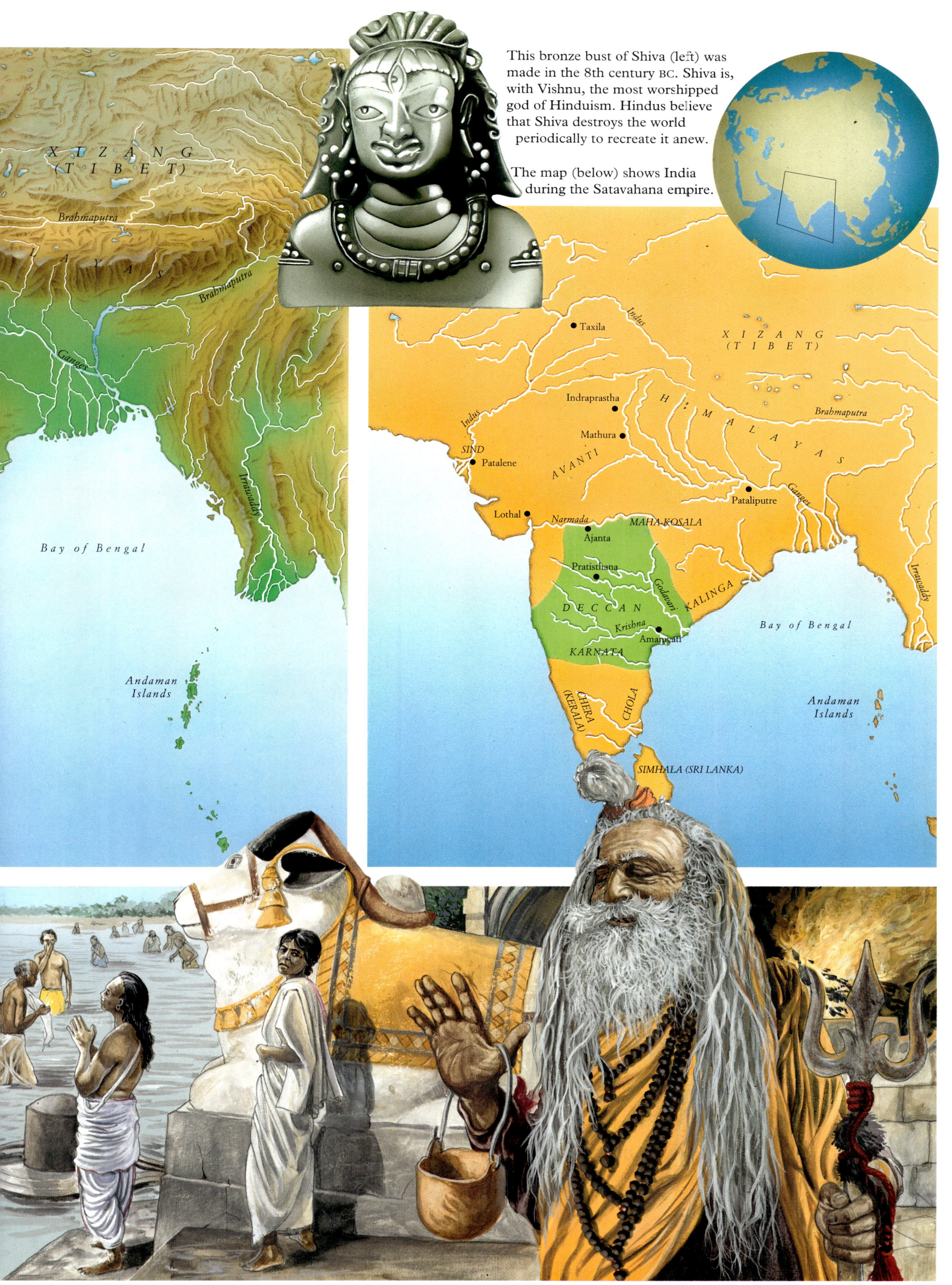

This bronze bust of Shiva (left) was made in the 8th century BC. Shiva is, with Vishnu, the most worshipped god of Hinduism. Hindus believe that Shiva destroys the world periodically to recreate it anew.

The map (below) shows India during the Satavahana empire.

5 THE INDIAN SUBCONTINENT

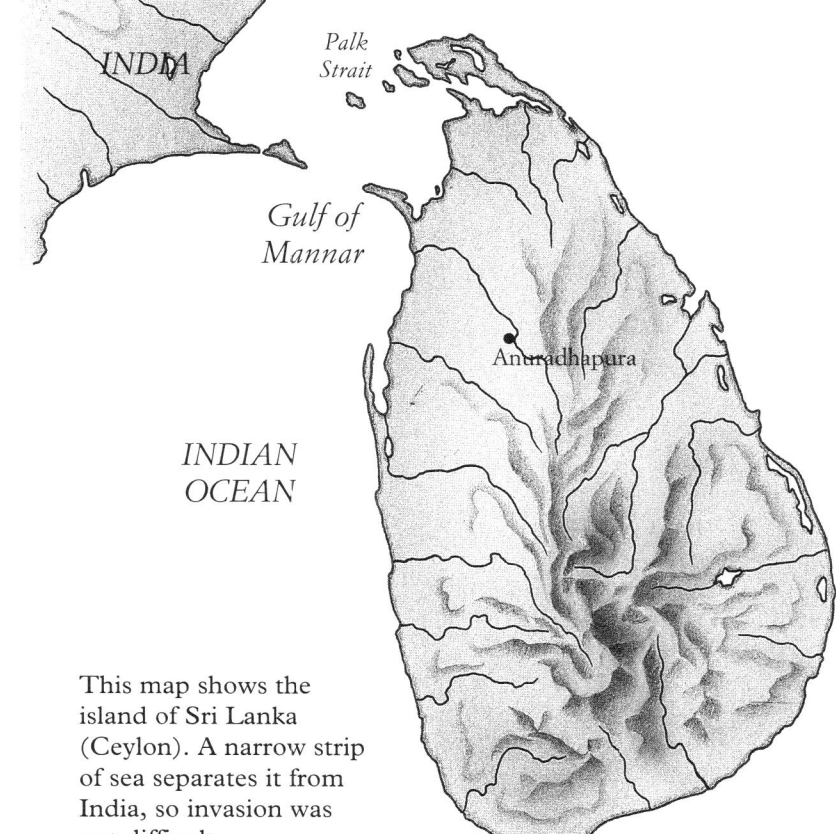

This map shows the island of Sri Lanka (Ceylon). A narrow strip of sea separates it from India, so invasion was not difficult.

The Indo-Europeans reached as far south as India and the island of Sri Lanka. Midway through the 1st millennium BC, the island was occupied by Aryan people who came (it is thought) from near the Gulf of Khambhat. These invaders brought their own Indo-European language, which became Sinhalese. They also introduced social division into castes and their own religious ideas.

Later, the teachings of Buddha reached Sri Lanka, through missionaries led by the son of the Indian emperor Asoka. Buddhism was soon well established, and influenced the art of the island.

The Tamils

In the first century AD, Sri Lanka was repeatedly invaded by new peoples, Dravidians, and they too left their mark on language and culture. The Tamils, who were not part of the Indo-European language group, took over the extreme south of India and proved too strong even for Asoka to dislodge. There were three southern kingdoms, named Chola, Pandya and Chera, but very little is known about them.

The Tamils had a strong historical and cultural identity, but nevertheless took on some aspects of the Indian-Aryan world, and some became Hindus.

The Satavahana dynasty

Further north there were important developments. In the Deccan, the central region of India, a new ruling family emerged. The Maurya empire collapsed, throwing much of India into confusion and from this turmoil the powerful Satavahana dynasty came to power. The time-scale of their rule is not clear. Most historians now think that the Satavahanas were in power from about 50 BC to AD 230.

The Satavahanas reacted against the Buddhist ideas of Asoka and his heirs, and encouraged the old Vedic beliefs of Hinduism. This created a kind of Aryan outpost in southern India, for the seventh emperor Hala conquered Sri Lanka in AD 78. A later emperor named Gautamiputra (2nd century) was an empire-enlarger, and was said to be lord of an empire 'whose subjects drank from the waters of three oceans' – suggesting that his lands touched on the Arabian Sea (west), the Indian Ocean (south) and the Bay of Bengal (east). The successors of this powerful ruler, however, degenerated into decadence, and the empire broke up into many small states of little importance.

Invasions in the north

In the northwest of India, the era after the Maurya empire

The scene below (pictured in colour on pages 20/21) shows Hindu pilgrims bathing in the river Ganges. This is still a supreme moment of religious observance, a time of prayer and purification for devout Hindus. Hindus have been coming to the holy river for many centuries, to take part in ritual bathing. Even the lowest caste of Hindu society, the so-called 'untouchables', share the experience. They are recognizable by their rough, undyed clothes. Men and women bathe and pray together.

A holy man, or *sadhu*, walks into the water for his daily ritual washing. He has a long beard and long hair. In one hand he is holding a begging bowl, to collect offerings. In the other he holds a staff; this is the pitchfork of Shiva, a sign that he is a follower of this powerful Hindu god.

Behind the holy man is a statue of Nandi, the sacred bull. The bull is a frequent representation of the creative force of Shiva. Floating on the water is another fertility symbol, known as a *lingam*, which represents male sexuality. Combined with the female *yoni*, this symbolizes creativity and the continuity of life. The Hindu religion continues to be a powerful shaper of Indian culture, after many centuries.

was troubled. On the borders, which were constantly invaded and changing, were the Greeks. Some of Alexander's Greeks became 'Indianized', but overall Greek influence on India was not large.

Two dynasties, the Shuga and Kauva, rose and fell by 90 BC, when the Indus Valley and the Punjab were invaded by new Iranian tribes, known as the Shaka, and by Scythians from the north. They broke into Afghanistan, but were stopped by rival Indo-Europeans, equally warlike, such as the Parthians (known as Pallava to the Indians), Macedonians, and the 'Indian-Greeks'. By 70 BC they had destroyed the kingdom of Taxila, broken up the surrounding territories, and established a tribal confederation.

The Kushan Empire
Then invaders from China arrived to overrun most of northern India, Afghanistan and parts of central Asia. These were the Yueh-chih, who conquered Bactria in the 1st century BC. They divided the country into five chiefdoms, one of which became the kingdom of Kushan. The Kushan king Kanishka (144-168) began a new dynasty, ruling a centralized empire that stretched from west Afghanistan to the Punjab, covering much of the Ganges river plain.

The Kushan empire was one of the four 'great powers' of the world at this time. (The others were Parthia, Rome and China.) It controlled trade between India and the west (the Persian-Greek world) and the north (central Asia). Along the routes travelled by caravans loaded with trade goods, Buddhism went north and east, and was to alter the histories of China, Korea and Japan.

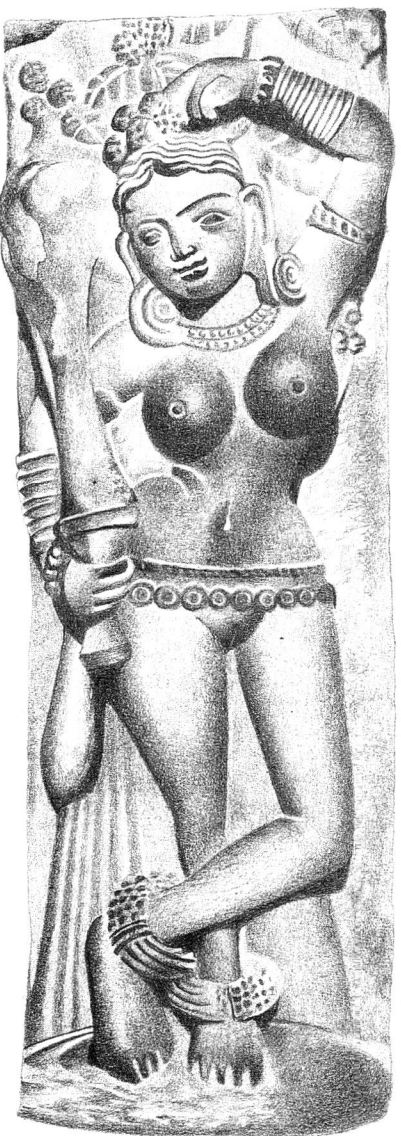

Three Indian coins (top). At the left is a silver tetradrachma, with a picture of Demetrius, a Greek-Bactrian king who made conquests in India around 190 BC. The elephant-shaped helmet is a reference to these triumphs. In the centre is a silver drachma (mid-1st century BC) with a Greek inscription from the Shaka dynasty. On the right is a Kushan coin. The money of the Kushans was made from gold, and was the first coinage to be made of gold on a large scale. The king shown is Vima Kadphises (early 2nd century). He wears Persian-style clothing, and the flames on his shoulders symbolize divine grace bestowed on the ruler.

The carving (above) comes from Mathura and shows a lively street scene. There are travellers of all kinds – on foot, in carriages, on horseback and riding on an elephant.

The dancer (left) appears in relief on a stone pillar dating from the 1st century.

6 China from Shang to Zhou

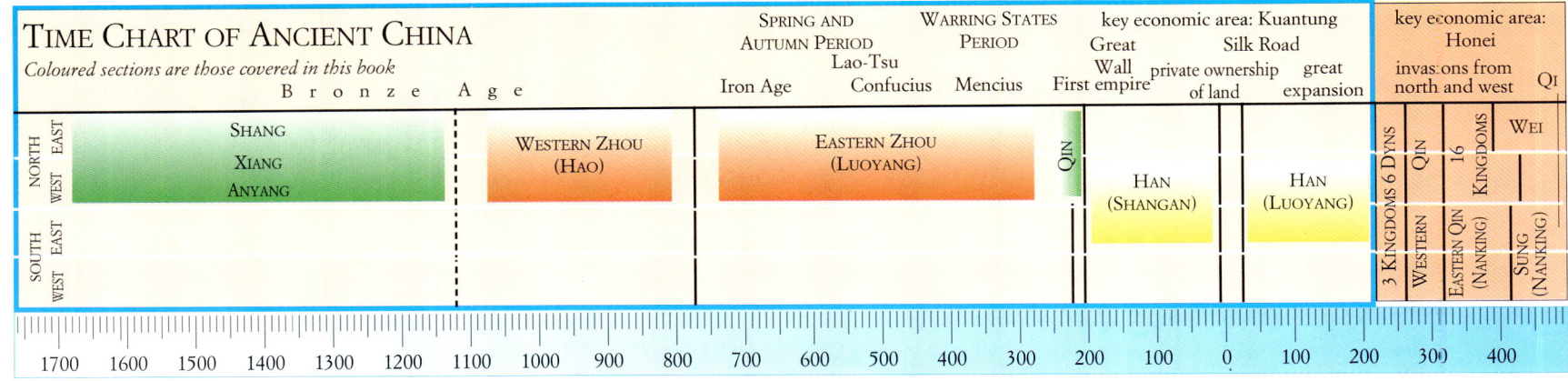

The time chart (above) shows the main periods of ancient China's history, with the kingdoms and dynasties, important events and influences, and most important economic regions. The cities in brackets were capitals at various periods. The blue colour indicates the time-period covered by this book. The scale shows chronology from 1765 BC to the present day.

The map (right) shows the main archaeological sites in China, from the Shang period (about 1400 BC). We can reconstruct ancient China mainly from the evidence of archaeological excavations (such as tombs), historical chronicles, and the oracle bones of the Shang soothsayers (which have writing on them). The names of the cities on the smaller map (far right) were all found written on oracle bones. Most are around the Huang He, or Yellow river.

				key economic area: Chang Jiang (Yangtze)										
				great expansion		Tangut and Mongol invasions	Genghis Khan conquers China			Manchu invasions		Opium Wars and Western interference		
Northern Qi														
Wei	Chu	Sui	Po-Hai	Liao	Hsi-Hsia		Mongols	Mongols			Qin (Manchu)		People's Republic	
			Tang (Shangan)	iron dynasty (Beijing)	Qin		Yuan (Beijing)	Ming (Nanking, Beijing)			(Beijing)			
Liang	Ch'en			5 Dyns 10 Kdms	Northern Sung	Southern Sung							Republic	

600 700 800 900 1000 1100 1200 1300 1400 1500 1600 1700 1800 1900

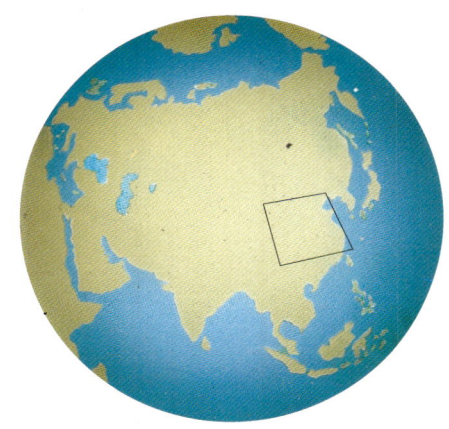

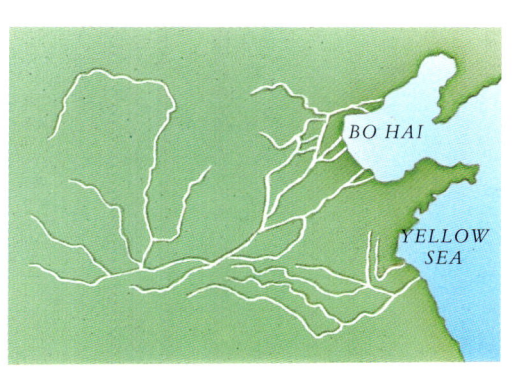

These pictures (left) show changes in the course of the Huang He: 10th century BC (top); 14th century BC (centre); and as it is today. The river has changed course 26 times in the past 3,000 years. It is subject to terrible floods, which have caused many thousands of deaths and much damage. The mud washed down has lifted the riverbed as much as 10 metres (33 feet) above the surrounding flood plain.

The Zhou empire (right). Towards the end of Western Zhou rule (8th century BC), there were more fortified cities. Feuding princes were more powerful and better prepared for war. This led to the break-up of the city-states in the Warring States Period.

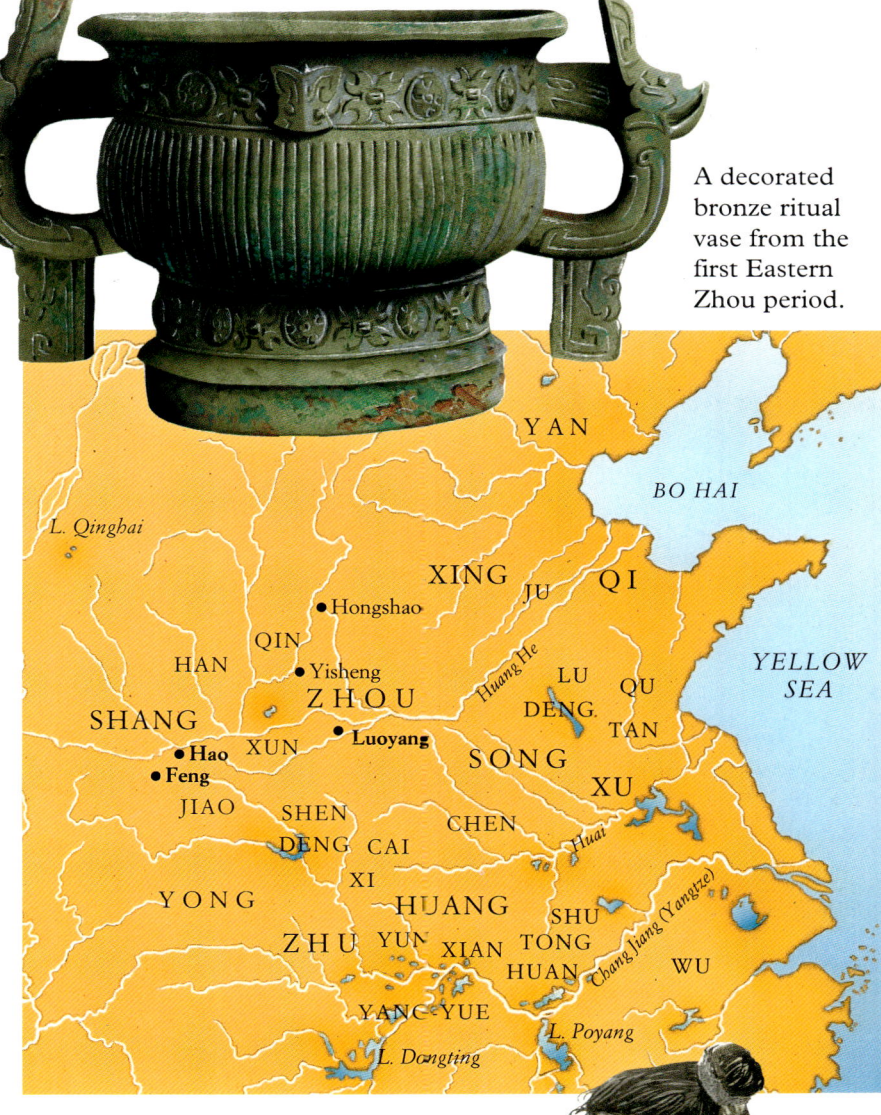

A decorated bronze ritual vase from the first Eastern Zhou period.

25

6 China from Shang to Zhou

This bronze axe was made during the Shang period. It may have been used for ritual executions of sacrificial victims. The grimacing face was no doubt meant to inspire awe and fear.

The wide, fertile plain of the Huang He (Yellow river) provided a settling place for China's first Stone Age farmers, and was the cradle for China's first civilization. The river gets its name from the colour of its waters, rich in yellow silt (mud) called loess, carried down from the Tibetan plateau by the river's many tributaries. The huge area of water forms a basin of over a million square kilometres. The regular, periodic flooding of the river was able to alter the landscape and the history of the human settlements along its shifting course.

The Shang kings

According to tradition, the history of China began with the Xia dynasty about 2207 BC. Historians know that this kingdom existed, but it may not have been the first in China. In 1500 BC the Shang dynasty was founded by a king named Tang. After him there were thirty Shang kings, the last being Di Xin (1154-1122 BC).

China's Bronze Age began in the Shang period, and many bronze objects have been found in tombs by archaeologists. These finds throw light on the social and political life of Shang China. The king was both a warrior-leader and a priest. He had total power over his people. Society was made up of nobles and peasants. Farming was advanced, with irrigation, and wheat, rice and millet were grown.

Consulting the oracles

The Shang believed that ancestors guided their actions. They also worshipped a supreme god of heaven, Shang Di. Before making a decision, the king consulted oracles to find out the will of the gods. An oracle is a person, place or thing, through which people believed that the gods spoke. Usually a priest interpreted the god's reply to questions.

The Shang oracles were bones or tortoise shells. The questions were asked aloud, and the soothsayer placed a heated point against the bone or shell. He then interpreted the cracks made by the heat. To keep track of questions, the soothsayers wrote them down on the bones, and these inscriptions prove that the Shang had a form of writing, with almost two thousand characters. This was probably the basis of modern Chinese writing.

The scene below (shown in colour on pages 24/25) of an army on the march indicates the problems that Chinese soldiers faced. Crossing the country's great rivers was never easy. Here the soldiers have built a bridge of boats, a technique still used occasionally by modern army engineers.

By laying a road (made from bamboo) across the boats, the soldiers are able to cross swiftly, with their supplies loaded in carts pulled by oxen. Small sailing craft keep watch on either side of the bridge for any surprise enemy attack aimed at destroying the bridge. Foot patrols secure the ground around the bridgehead, also as a precaution against an enemy raid. Only the nobles used horses and horse-drawn chariots. Ordinary soldiers fought on foot, with spears and long halberds.

The Shang and Zhou rulers relied on their soldiers to conquer weaker neighbours, and fight off enemies. In the end, the Zhou dynasty collapsed as a result of long wars between the strongest of its subject states.

These characters (right) are early examples of Chinese writing, from the Shang period.

The inscription (below) was made on the bottom of the vessel shown on page 25. The characters are from the Zhou period.

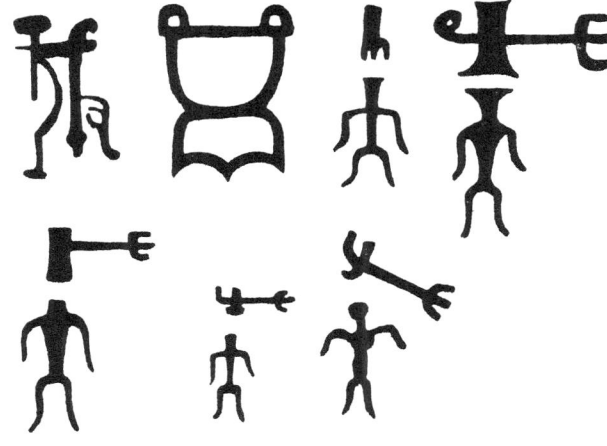

Tortoise shells like this one (top right) were used as oracles, to divine the future. Many shells covered in inscriptions have been found.

The map (right) shows the tribute (tax-gifts) that the Shang kings received from subject lords.

The Shang capital Anyang (right below) was the hub of an economic zone. Its wealth came from mines up to 350 km (220 miles) away.

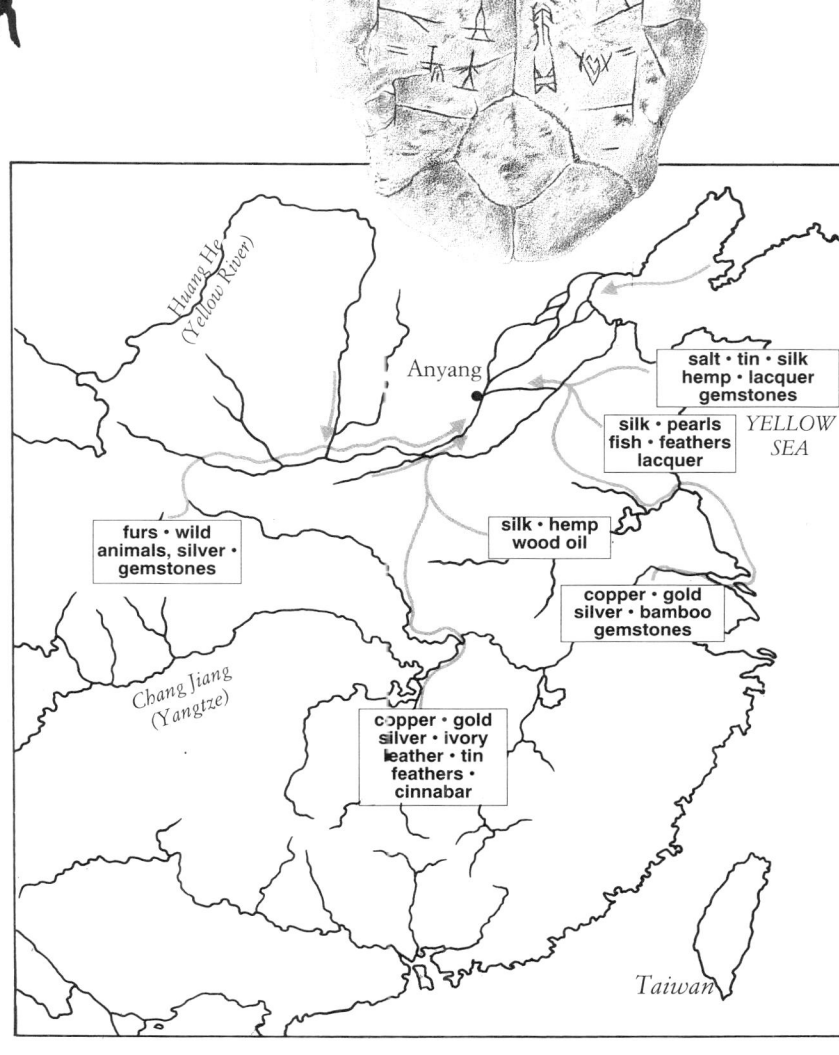

The Shang practised human sacrifice as part of royal burial rites. The last Shang ruler was cruel, and his excesses alienated him from his people. Chinese historians record that a vassal prince, named Wu Wang (or 'powerful warrior'), marched against the king and overthrew him. Wu became the first ruler of a new dynasty, the Zhou (or Chou). This dynasty was the longest in Chinese history, lasting from 1121 BC to 222 BC, though not without long periods of instability.

Rivalries and wars

Under the Zhou kings, the government of China became better organized. The Zhou made their capital in the west, at Hao, south of the river Wei. But in 770 BC, invading nomads forced them to move hundreds of kilometres eastward, to Luoyang in the region of Henan. The two phases of Zhou rule are known as Western Zhou (1121-771 BC) and Eastern Zhou (770-222 BC).

From 722 BC, there was a period that historians call the Spring and Autumn Period. This sounds tranquil, but was not. Powerful lords fought their neighbours, and this led to the even more violent Warring States Period (453-222 BC), when there were continual wars between the seven strongest princely states. These states included Wei in the north, Song in the east, and Han in the bend of the Huang He. All three became self-governing. They were followed by Yan in the north, Qin (Ch'in) in the west, Zhu in the south, and Qi in the northeast. From the power struggle, the well-organized and efficient Qin emerged victorious to form a new ruling dynasty in 221 BC.

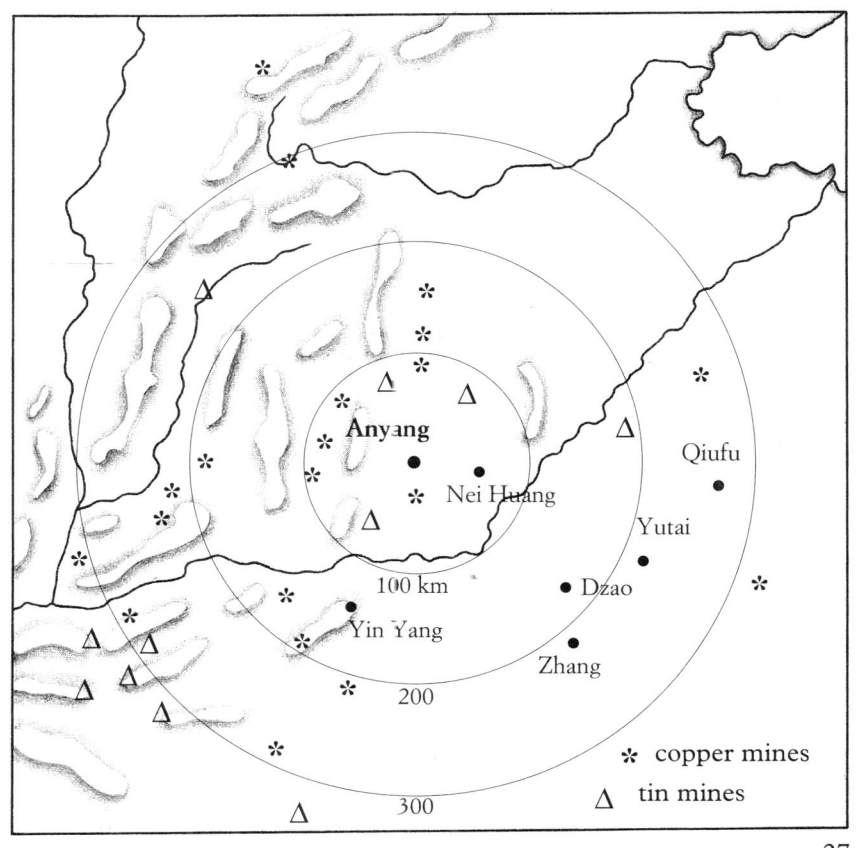

7 China's Classical Age

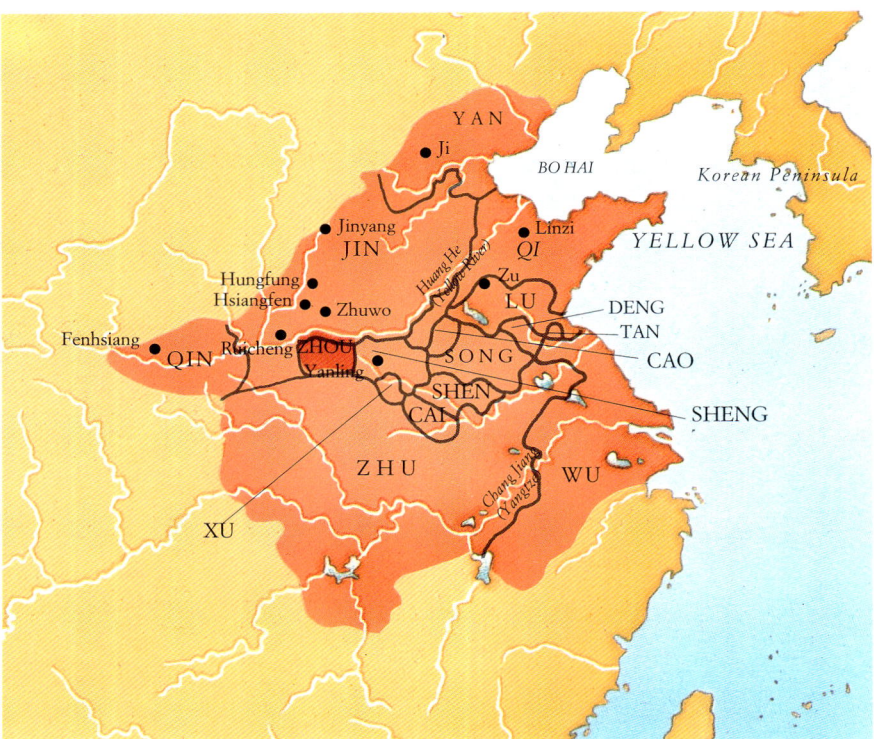

The map (left) shows China at the end of the Spring and Autumn Period, in the mid-6th century BC. The Zhou lost control of China after 770 BC, and for three hundred years there were wars between their former vassals. By the end of the 5th century BC, the number of princely states had shrunk from over 100 to about 20. Despite all this turmoil, China was undergoing remarkable cultural and technological development, with new political and philosophical ideas.

- ■ original Qin territory
- ■ Qin expansion up to 300 BC
- ■ states conquered by Qin
- ■ regions conquered after unification

The map (left) shows China in the Warring States Period. Over twenty years (328 to 308 BC), the state of Qin grew in power in the western region of the old Zhou kingdom. It was then ready to fight the eastern states, conquering them in the course of the next century.

The disc with a hole in its centre (above) is known as a *pi*. Discs like this date from long before Zhou times. Many have been found, but their purpose is not clearly understood. This one is made from jade, with elaborate decoration. It may have been a symbol of the sun or heaven, or have been used to observe the stars. The blue colour represented not only heaven, but also the king's power.

The unification of the vast Chinese territory by the Qin was made possible by the reforms of Shang Yang (about 390-338 BC). As chief minister, he increased the king's power over government and army. The Qin had a strong economy and an efficient canal system. They controlled the important river valleys.

The Great Wall of China (left) is bigger than anything else built in the ancient world, or since. It was constructed on the orders of the first emperor, Shi Huang-di. There were older walls already, built for defence against nomad raids and by the warring lords for defence against rivals. The emperor's new wall linked up these old walls, and added new sections made from stone with watchtowers at intervals. Thousands of workers and their families were deported to the wild frontier, much of it mountainous and semi-desert, to carry out the construction. The Wall was supposed to keep out the steppe nomads, such as the Xiongnu or Huns, but in the long term it proved less than successful. Today it is China's most impressive landmark.

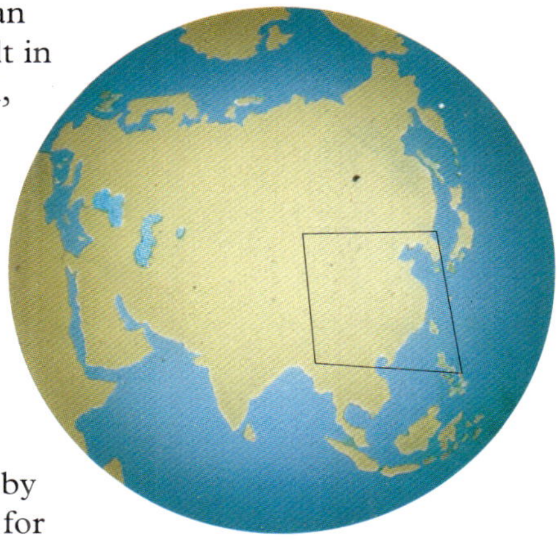

Characters from Chinese writing (above). Those in the left-hand column are from the period when Chinese writing was beginning, over 3,000 years ago. The ones on the right are the modern versions.

7 China's Classical Age

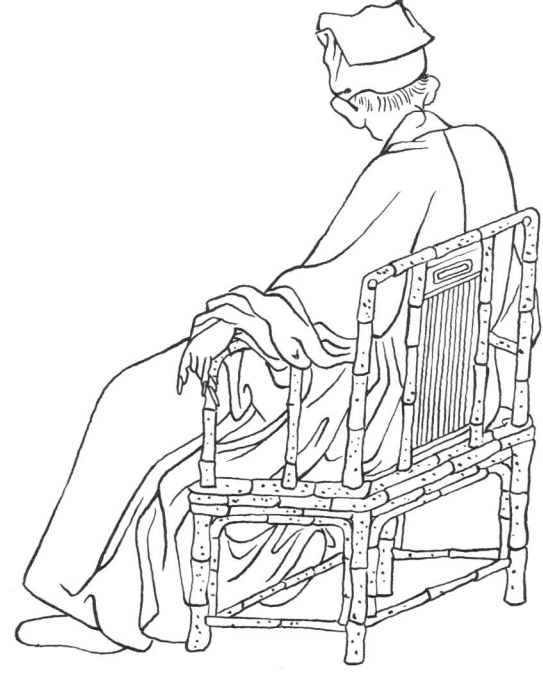

Religion was less important in Chinese life than scholarship and philosophy. The Chinese scholar (shown here, turning his back on the busy world) was an influential figure in society.

During the period from the 5th to the 2nd century BC, China's most important philosophical and ethical ideas were expressed. Confucianism and Taoism stand out, for they have influenced Chinese thought and life to the present day.

Confucius

Confucius (K'ung Fu-tzu or Master K'ung) was born in 551 BC (not long after Buddha, whose teachings would also influence China). He died in 479 BC, shortly before the birth of the famous Greek philosopher Socrates.

Confucius was a man of reason, who believed that society could be rescued from disorder if people behaved morally in their personal and public lives. A person should be sincere, and show respect to his father and his ruler. He should live by rules of good conduct, and be an example to those beneath him in the social order. Rulers, therefore, should be especially virtuous, since their example would be followed by their subjects.

Confucius taught that if a person widened his knowledge completely, he was transformed. That person would then influence his family, and through his family, the state in which he lived. With the state well governed, it followed that the whole empire would be peaceful and happy.

Mencius

The ideas of Confucius had little influence in his lifetime, but his followers spread them. Two important followers of Confucius were Mencius (about 390-305 BC) and Xunzi (mid-200s BC). Mencius wrote that all human nature is essentially good, and that people are drawn to goodness, even without education. The great virtues that should rule a person's life were compassion, hatred of evil, modesty and self-denial, and knowing right from wrong. Xunzi disagreed with this. He believed people were by nature evil, and needed education and clear rules of behaviour to guide them.

Together, the ideas of Confucius and his followers influenced Chinese life enormously. The central idea was social organization, in which everyone observed the proper rules of behaviour, in order to have an ordered and peaceful society. This made it attractive to China's rulers.

The picture below (shown in colour on pages 28/29) shows Chinese junks on a river. Chinese ships were unlike any others in the ancient world. Possibly developed from rafts, they had a flat, wide bottom. Their sails were made from sections of cloth (woven from plant fibres) sewn on to lengths of bamboo. This meant that the sail could be rolled up like a window blind.

The Chinese junk was also the first craft to be steered by a stern rudder, an invention made in China long before rudders first appeared in the West (in the Middle Ages). The junk was a stable, tough craft, ideal for use as a river transport. The crew lived on board, in small hutlike shelters.

The largest junks were far bigger than any sailing ships made in Europe at this time. Below decks, the big junks were divided into watertight compartments by bulkheads.

Riverside towns, like the one shown on the far bank, were centres for trade and anchorages for craft carrying everything from farm produce to ivory and precious stones. Chinese sailors traded as far as Indonesia, India and Arabia. Fleets of junks were sent on expeditions to demand tribute from foreign rulers. By the AD 1400s, the Chinese had explored as far as the east coast of Africa.

Lao-tzu, riding a buffalo, and followed by a disciple (below). This picture is a watercolour of 1700, now in the Bibliothèque Nationale in Paris. Lao-tzu was the author of the key Taoist book, *The Way of Virtue*. The text was taught in all Chinese schools from the 1st century BC, a sign of the philosopher's moral authority.

This picture of Confucius (left) shows him wearing court costume, and is from an 18th-century print in the Bibliothèque Nationale in Paris. His teachings were collected by his followers into a book called the *Lun yu*, or *Conversations*, and became the basic 'scripture' for followers of Confucianism, and for the education of children.

The chart (below) shows the structure of Qin government

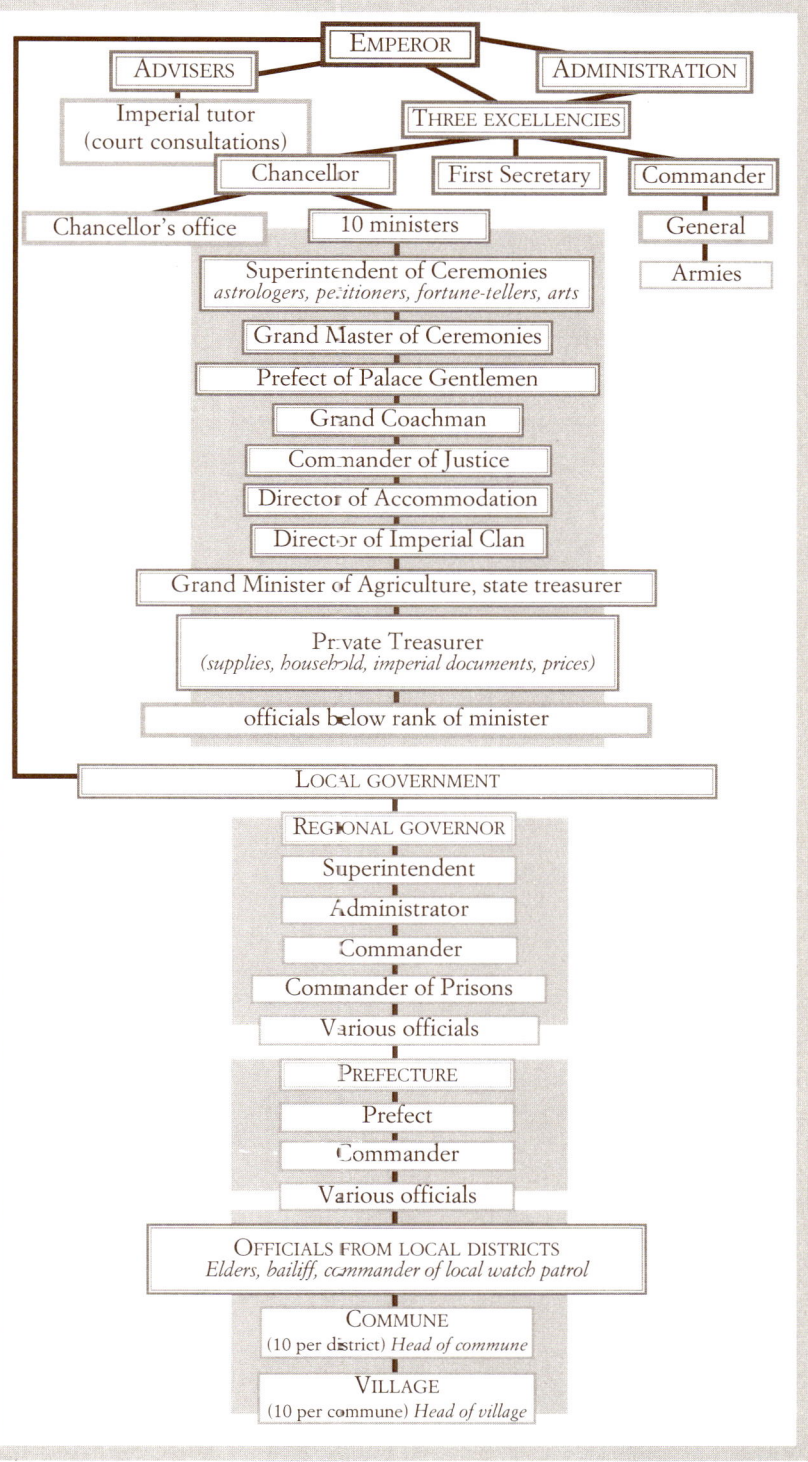

Taoism

The philosophy called Taoism was taught by Lao-tzu (who was born about 600 BC) and Zhuang-zi (4th century BC). Little is known about Lao-tzu, except that he was a 'wise man' and wrote a book about the proper way to live. The book was the *Tao Teh Ching*, or *The Way of Virtue*. Lao-tzu believed that people were rooted in Nature, and that wisdom was self-known. No matter what disasters befell a person (wars, floods, invasions), a person could 'yield and then come back again' – in other words, survive.

Taoism had little time for the order and rituals of Confucianism. People should be spontaneous and natural, trusting to intuitive knowledge. Nor did Taoists want to alter society through education and reforms. They believed that Tao is 'The Way', the natural cycle of living throughout the universe. Taoists thought that government was needed, but should not be so strong that it interfered with the natural way of living. The Taoists were also interested in alchemy, and did experiments. This may have made them the first real scientists in China.

8 THE EMPIRES OF QIN AND HAN

The map (right) shows the Han empire. Areas of Han influence are shown in orange. The blue lines represent trade routes.

The plan (inset) is of Shangan (modern Xian). In AD 50, it was the biggest city in the world.

The population density map (below) is based on China's census of the year AD 2. The empire had 59 million people. The Han people lived along the river valleys. In the mountains, hills and high plains lived non-Han peoples.

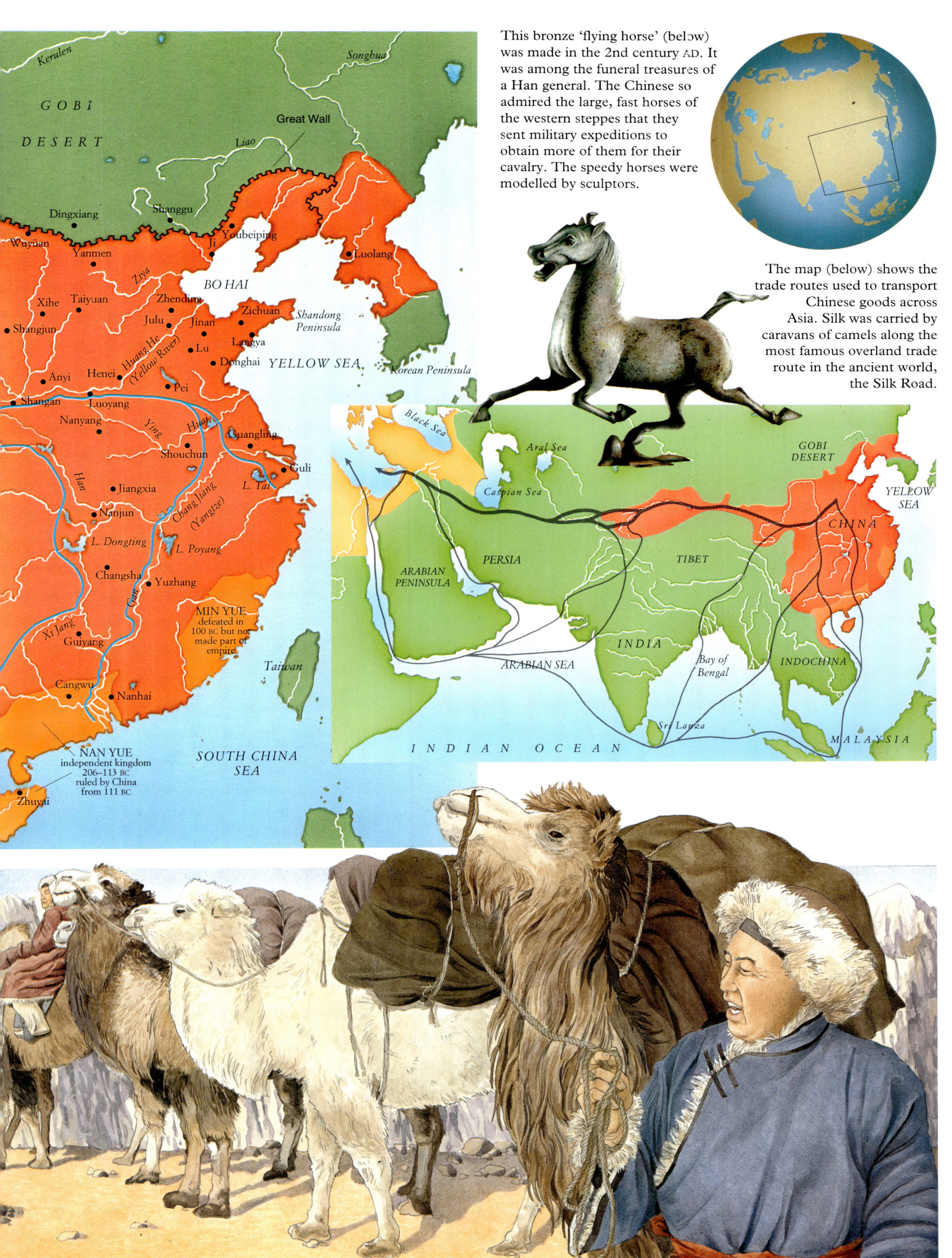

This bronze 'flying horse' (below) was made in the 2nd century AD. It was among the funeral treasures of a Han general. The Chinese so admired the large, fast horses of the western steppes that they sent military expeditions to obtain more of them for their cavalry. The speedy horses were modelled by sculptors.

The map (below) shows the trade routes used to transport Chinese goods across Asia. Silk was carried by caravans of camels along the most famous overland trade route in the ancient world, the Silk Road.

8 The Empires of Qin and Han

This terracotta cavalryman (below) with his horse comes from the tomb of the emperor Shi Huang-di. The Qin emperor ordered the tomb to be started when he was only 13. Inside it was buried an army of 6,000 life-sized model soldiers, to accompany the emperor into the next world. It is one of the most amazing burial finds ever discovered.

The warrior king Zheng, leader of the Qin, led his armies to victory in 221 BC. Master of all China, he took the name Shi Huang-di, or First Emperor. The empire he founded was to last more than two thousand years.

All must obey the emperor

The emperor was divine, sent from heaven. This was the belief which the new dynasty fostered. From the name of the Qin, or Ch'in, dynasty comes the name 'China', which was used by the peoples of India and Iran. The ancient Greeks called the faraway land 'Thinai'.

The Qin emperor ruled strictly. Everyone had to obey the law, and there were severe penalties for those who defied it. The basis of Qin government was the so-called Legalist doctrine worked out by capable ministers such as Shang Yan and Han Fei (280-233 BC), and this became the government code for all China. The individual was subordinate to the state, which had might and divine power to reinforce it.

Central power, little freedom

The vast empire was governed by officials serving the emperor. This centralization of power brought an end to the old feudal system, weakening the powers of the provincial lords. China was now governed as one country, with one system of writing, one money system, one system of weights and measures, and even a standard gauge (width) for wagon wheels.

To keep out barbarian invaders, the Great Wall was built. To keep the people inside China in order, the emperor tried to enforce a strict moral code. Farming and technology were good, and to be encouraged. Trade and the arts were vain and useless, and to be discouraged. This discouragement took the form of punishing any protesters, and burning ancient books containing out-of-date or 'vain and useless' information. Scientific books (such as works on medicine, drugs, agriculture and divinity) were spared.

The Han come to power

In 208 Liu Bang led a rebellion against Qin rule. Within two years he was himself emperor, with the new name of Han Gaozu. Thus the Han dynasty began. It can be

This picture (shown in colour on pages 32/33) shows a merchants' caravan in the mountains of central Asia. The journey overland from China to the Middle East and Mediterranean coast was long and difficult. The Silk Road was more than 7,000 kilometres (4,350 miles) long. It was a track, crossing deserts and plains, and winding through dangerous mountain passes.

For protection against natural hazards and bandits, merchants travelled in groups, resting at safe halts along the way. They also traded as they went, and goods changed hands many times during the journey from China to the West.

The animals used to carry the trade goods were two-humped Bactrian camels. They were strong, sure-footed and able to endure heat or cold. Among the goods carried from China, silk was the most valuable, but iron, bronze, lacquered wares and jade were also highly prized by foreigners.

These drawings (right) are of soldiers of the Han army, dressed for battle. Bows, swords and shields were standard equipment. The pictures were printed by carved woodblocks, inked and then pressed onto paper.

Tambourine players, like this one (right), along with ballad singers and acrobats, were popular entertainers in Han China.

This hunting chariot (below), with banners streaming and bowmen at the ready, is being driven into battle. Chinese chariots were drawn by either two or four horses.

divided into two periods: the Former Han (206 BC to AD 8), which had its capital at Shangan, and Later Han (AD 25-220), with its capital at Luoyang in the eastern province of Henan. In between these two periods was the short reign of a usurper named Wang Mang.

The Han were less repressive rulers than the Qin, but retained their bureaucracy. The civil service now began to dominate Chinese government. From 124 BC the emperor Wu made it compulsory for those seeking high office to pass examinations. Inspectors were appointed to oversee and judge the work of all government officials.

China's economy flourished through trade, especially trade in silk. China also extended its diplomatic links, sending gifts to foreign rulers, and making contacts with the civilizations of Indians, Iranians, Greeks and Scythians. The fame of China and its luxury goods reached as far west as Europe. The Silk Road, a caravan trail across mountains and plains, linked China to the Mediterranean.

Great books recreated

Under the Han, China's culture was developed by the Scholars, learned people who with their assistants founded schools, of various grades, throughout the empire. They rewrote many of the classic books which had been destroyed, but were preserved in memory and oral tradition. Among the most famous and important texts of ancient Chinese literature are the *I Ching* (*The Book of Changes*), the *Shu Ching* (*Book of Documents*), the *Shih Ching* (*Book of Songs*), the *Li Chi* (*Record of Rites*), the *Ch'un Ch'iu* (*Spring and Autumn Annals*) and the *Tso Chuan* (a history of China's states from 722 to 468 BC).

The map (above) shows the various capital cities of imperial China, from Anyang to Beijing (Peking).

This clay model (right) of a Han house was found in a tomb. It is a peasant's home, with the family living on the first floor above the animals' stable.

9 Ancient Japan

This terracotta sculpture, or *haniwa* (right), shows a horse harnessed with saddle, saddlecloth, and bells. There are many models of horses made in the 5th century AD. This suggests that horse-riding invaders came to Japan.

The map shows Japan in the period from the 3rd to the 7th centuries. This age is known as the time of burial mounds, or *kofun*.

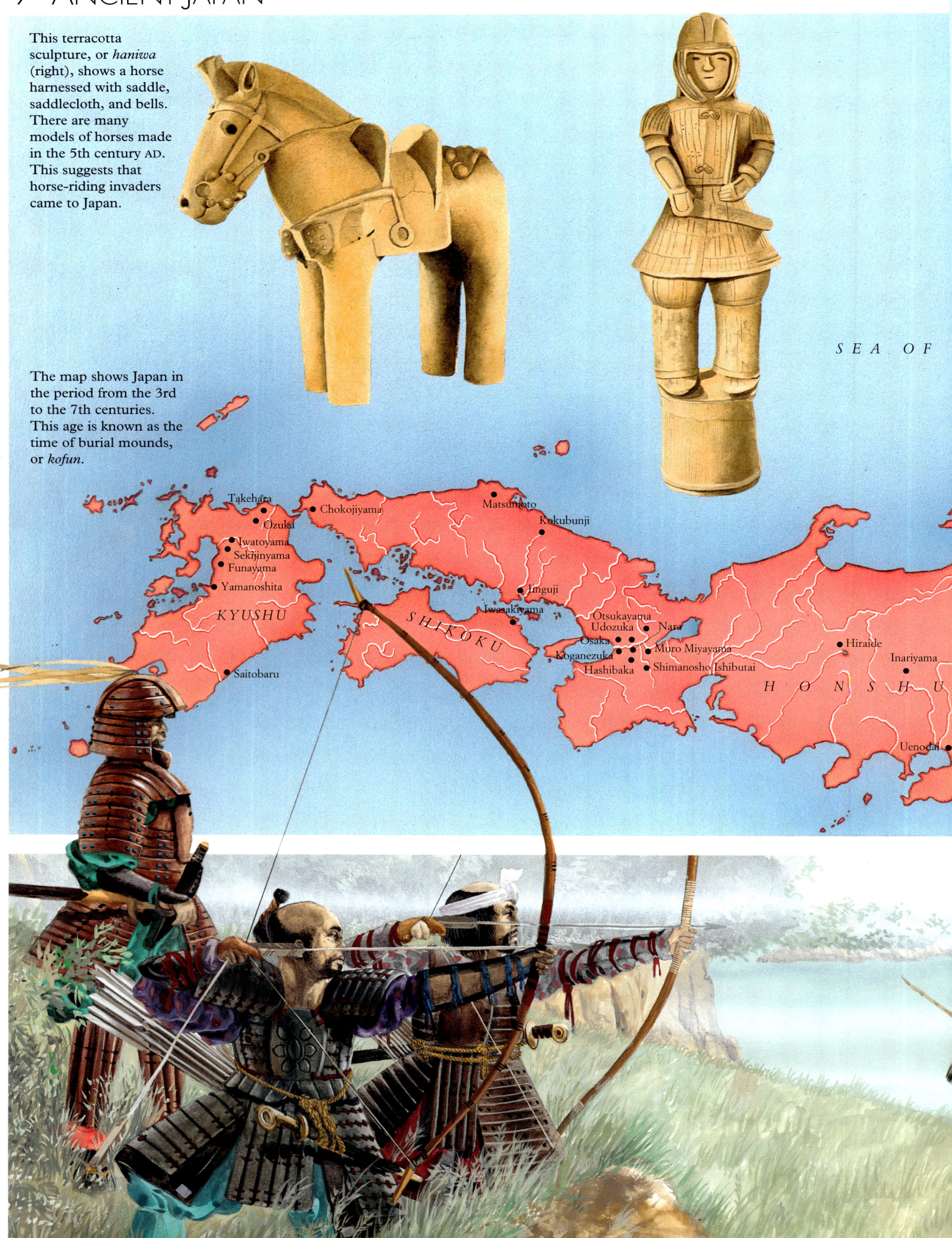

The clay soldier (left) comes from Ota, in the Kanto region of Japan. The word *haniwa* in Japanese means 'circle of clay'. The first haniwa were cylindrical models of objects, animals or people. They were placed inside large burial mounds. A single tomb might have thousands of haniwa in and around it. The models were intended to care for and guard the dead person in the afterlife. Most are about a metre (three feet) tall, but some are larger.

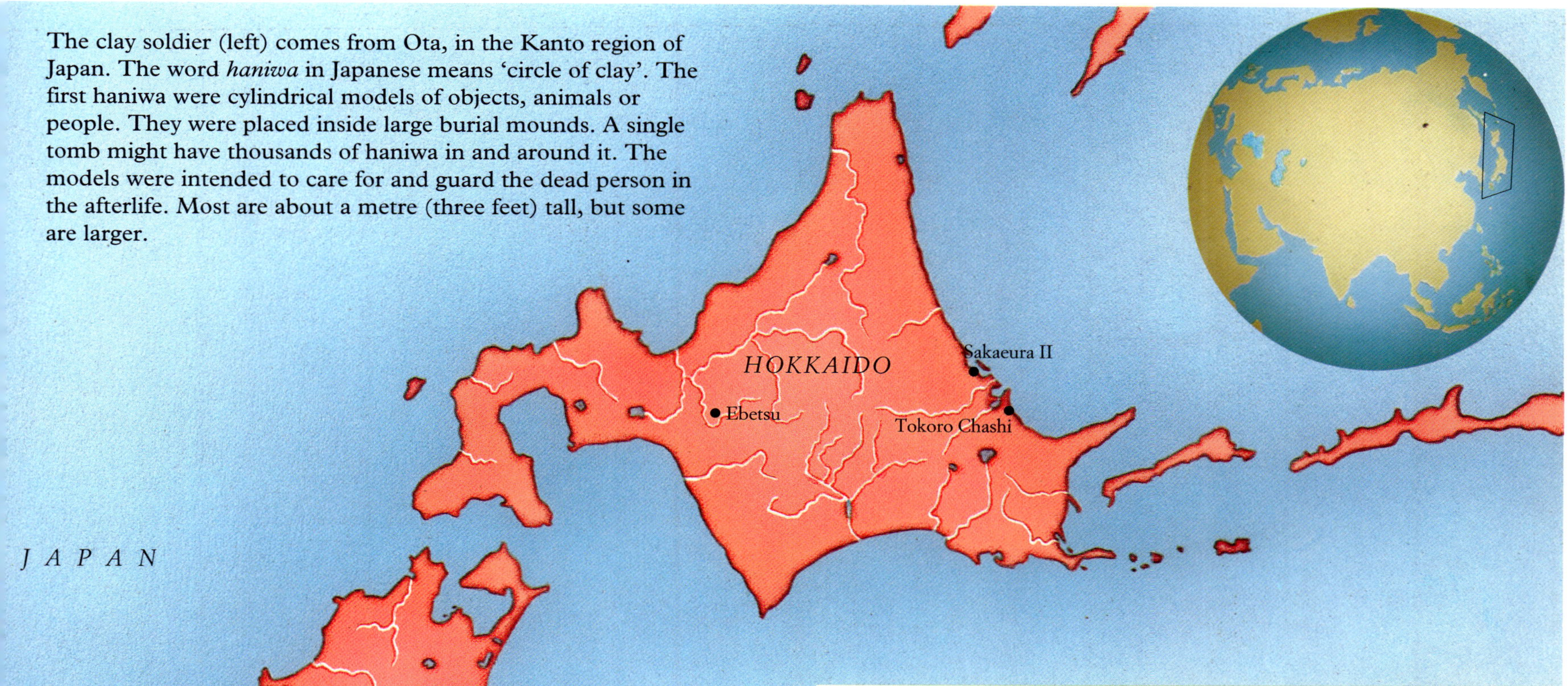

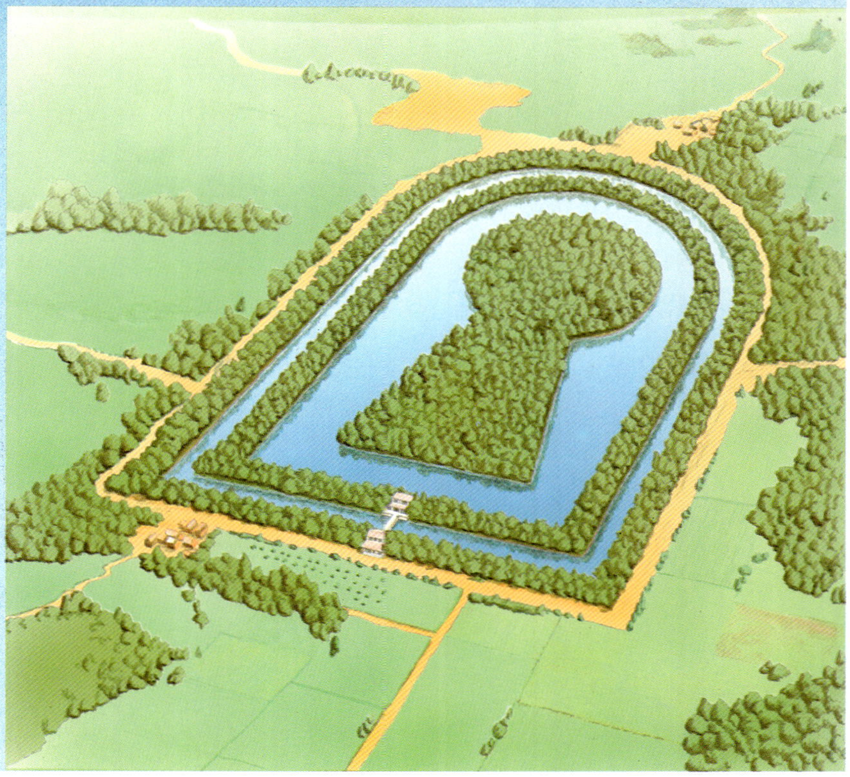

An artist's impression (right) of a large *kofun*, or burial mound. The largest tomb, shaped like a keyhole, on the plains of Osaka is almost 500 metres (1,640 feet) long and was made for the emperor Nintoku. Historians think he was one of the 'Five Kings of Wa', named by Chinese writers from the 5th century.

9 Ancient Japan

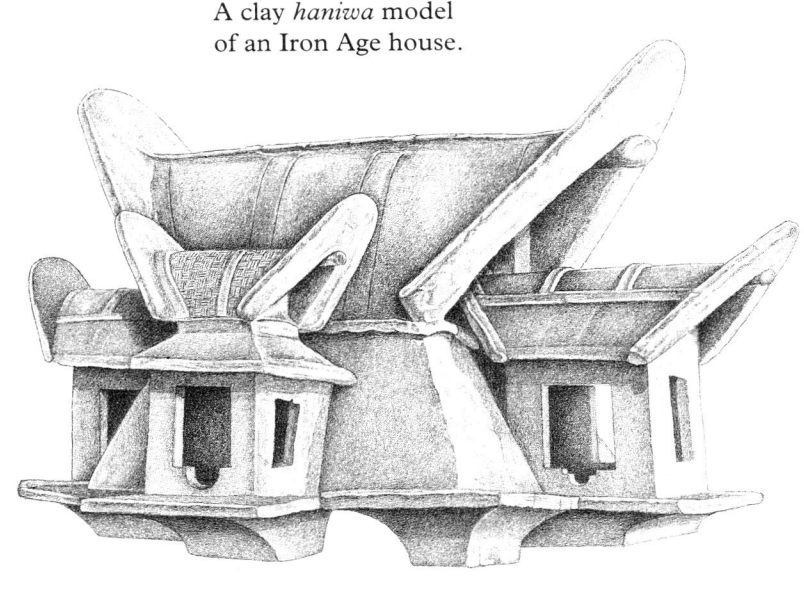

A clay *haniwa* model of an Iron Age house.

Japan's history has been shaped by its geography. It is on the edge of the Asian landmass, almost touching China and Korea. Yet the Japanese islands were isolated from the major cultural movements of the mainland, and developed a culture of their own. For periods in its history, Japan was almost wholly cut off from other Asian civilizations.

Japan's neighbours, China and Korea, were both more advanced in ancient times, and from time to time the Japanese borrowed from the cultures of these countries. Ancient Japan swung between its own native traditions and island character, and the powerful influences that were so close by.

Iron Age Japan

Japan entered the Iron Age late, about the 3rd century AD. It seems likely that the peaceful farmers of earlier times, known to historians as the Yayoi period, were invaded by warlike peoples from the mainland. These invaders had superior metal weapons, and possibly brought with them horses – hitherto unknown in Japan. It is probable that there was a succession of landings by the newcomers, who took over the land and set up a military overlordship. In these warriors lies the legendary origin of the famous *samurai* warriors, who so dominated medieval Japan.

The Japanese then became invaders themselves, for around AD 370 they colonized part of Korea, and founded a small state called Mimana, which lasted for about two hundred years. From Korea, they exported crafts and skills back to Japan.

The Kofun burials

This period of Japanese history is called the *Kofun* period, because of the many burial mounds which were made for important people – kings and warrior nobles. These mounds resemble the barrow-mounds of Europe. Some were hundreds of metres long, surrounded by one or more ditches. Some were square, others round or keyhole-shaped. The walls of the mound were packed with cylinders, made of clay, on top of which were figures of animals (such as horses), servants, warriors and everyday objects. The clay models, called *haniwa*, were put into the tomb to accompany the dead person into the next life.

The greatest concentration of kofun tombs is in the Yamato region, where the huge tomb of the emperor Nintoku (a ruler of the 5th century) is found. It is one of the largest ancient monuments in the world.

Yamato society was organized into a federation of clans, the leaders of which controlled government, the army, and religious rituals. This Yamato region was the core of the emerging Japanese nation, which began to form in the 4th and 5th centuries AD.

Religious ideas

The ancient Japanese believed in a world animated by

The picture below (shown in colour on pages 36/37) shows a fight during the invasions of Japan by mainland warriors. The natives of Japan were farmers, and though not so heavily armed as their enemies, they put up a stiff resistance. Here a party of men with spears tries to fight off armoured archers and swordsmen.

The armour of the invaders resembles that later worn by the *samurai*, who looked on the invaders as their ancestors. The invaders had to form closely-knit bands to succeed in their conquest. Each warrior swore loyalty to his lord, whom he served by combat.

The lightly armed farmers had little chance of driving out such well-armed and dedicated invaders. The newcomers took over Japan.

This map of ancient Japan is based on Chinese accounts, such as the *Wei Zhi*, or 'Tales of the Barbarians from the East'. This book describes a land called Yamatai, and a people governed by a shaman, or witch-queen. There are also instructions on how to reach Yamatai (Japan) from Daifang, but the directions are so vague that which Japanese island is meant is not known – it could be Kyushu or Honshu. The Kingdom of Wa is also referred to by Chinese historians, who evidently regarded Japan as a wild, uncivilized country.

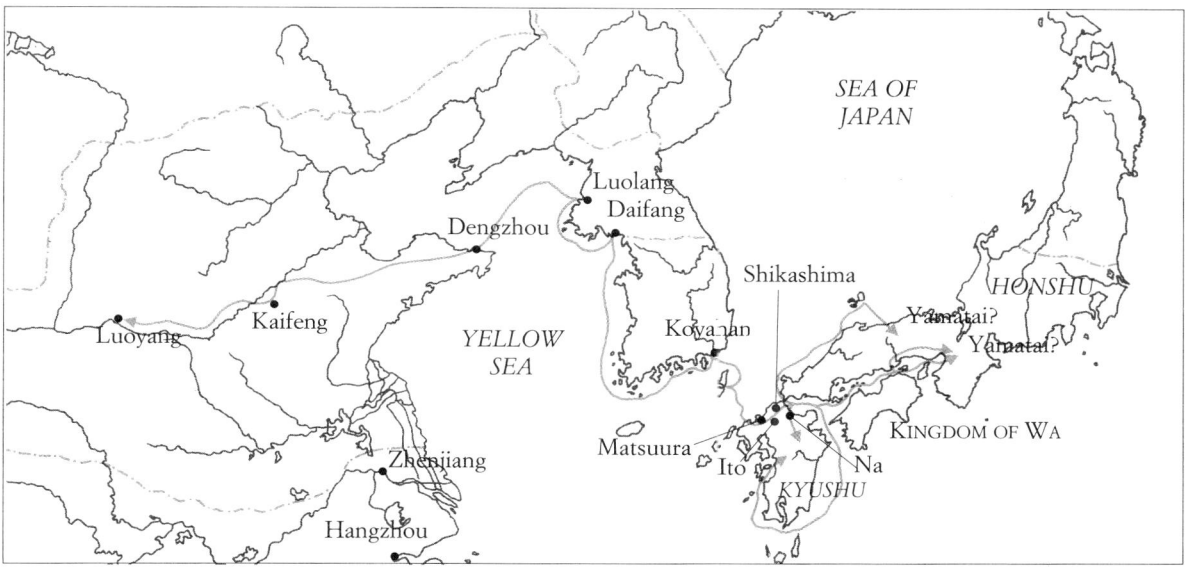

spirits or divine forces called *kami*. These resided in particular places such as waterfalls, springs, rocks, trees, islands, sacred animals or even in some people and cult objects. These 'receptacles for the spirits' were known as *shintai*.

It was not necessary therefore to build temples as part of their religious belief – the cult objects themselves were shrines. An important part of this belief was the cult of ancestors: family ancestors, clan ancestors and state ancestors – the founders of Japan.

Buddhism comes to Japan

The very different tradition of Buddhism came to Japan from mainland Asia around AD 500, after it had reached China and Korea. Korean missionaries may have brought Buddhism to Japan. The more conservative clans were unwilling to accept a foreign religion, and opposed Buddhism until AD 587, when they gave in. The main upholder of the new creed was Prince Shotoku (572-622), an enlightened ruler, who declared Buddhism to be Japan's state religion in 594.

The new religion influenced Japanese art and architecture, as well as morality and political thought. At this time the old spirit-cult was known as *Shinto*, meaning 'way of the kami', to distinguish it from 'the way of the Buddha'. The two beliefs co-existed peacefully, so much so that some *kami* were asked to protect Buddhist temples.

Shotoku's reforms

Shotoku took as his model for governing Japan the example of imperial China. He favoured the Confucian ideal of good government, with a new system of twelve court ranks (marked by the wearing of different coloured hats). This gave the court a dignified organization, in which people of ability were encouraged. In AD 604 a new constitution of Seventeen Articles or basic laws was introduced, setting out the duties and responsibilities of ruler, ministers and people. These changes helped to create a more unified state, with a strong central government.

The characters used in Japanese writing were also imported from China, and have remained little changed to this day. A new calendar was introduced and in 608 Shotoku sent the first Japanese embassy to China, to open permanent trade relations with Japan's powerful neighbour.

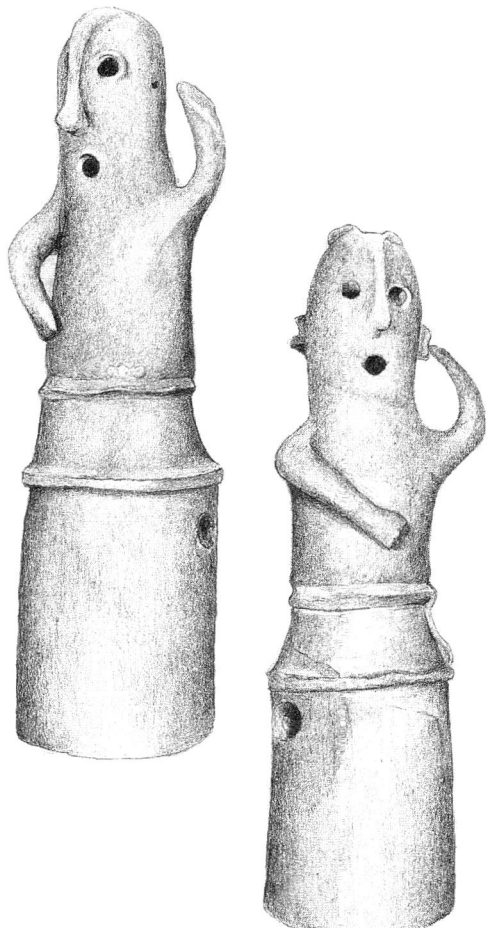

These two *haniwa* models (left) are from Nohara. They show dancers, posed on top of hollow cylinders.

The wooden statuette (below) shows Prince Shotoku at prayer. He was venerated as an ideal ruler in life, and after his death Shotoku-worship became a cult of Japanese Buddhism.

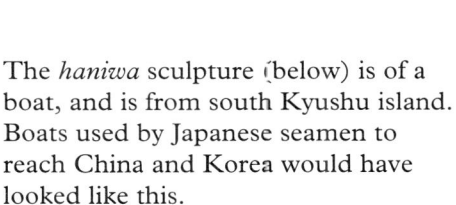

The *haniwa* sculpture (below) is of a boat, and is from south Kyushu island. Boats used by Japanese seamen to reach China and Korea would have looked like this.

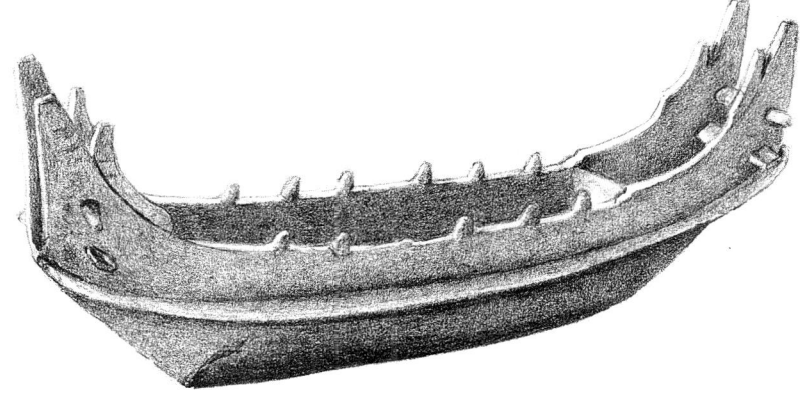

10 Indochina and Malaysia

Bronze Age sites in Southeast Asia.

 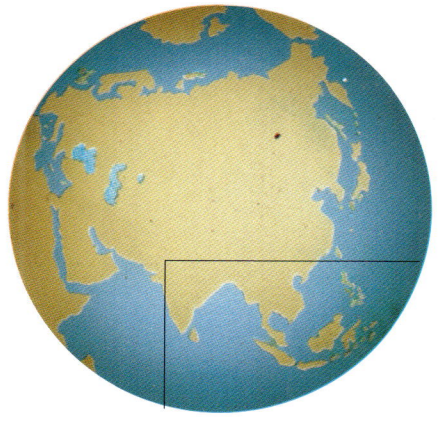

This picture of a canoe (above) carrying the dead to the 'Blessed Kingdom' appears on the bronze drum of Ngoc Linh. The drum was beaten during ceremonies to bring good hunting and fertile farmland. These beliefs spread from the Dong Son culture of Annam throughout Southeast Asia.

This bronze drum (below) comes from Bali, and is known as the 'Moon of Bali'.

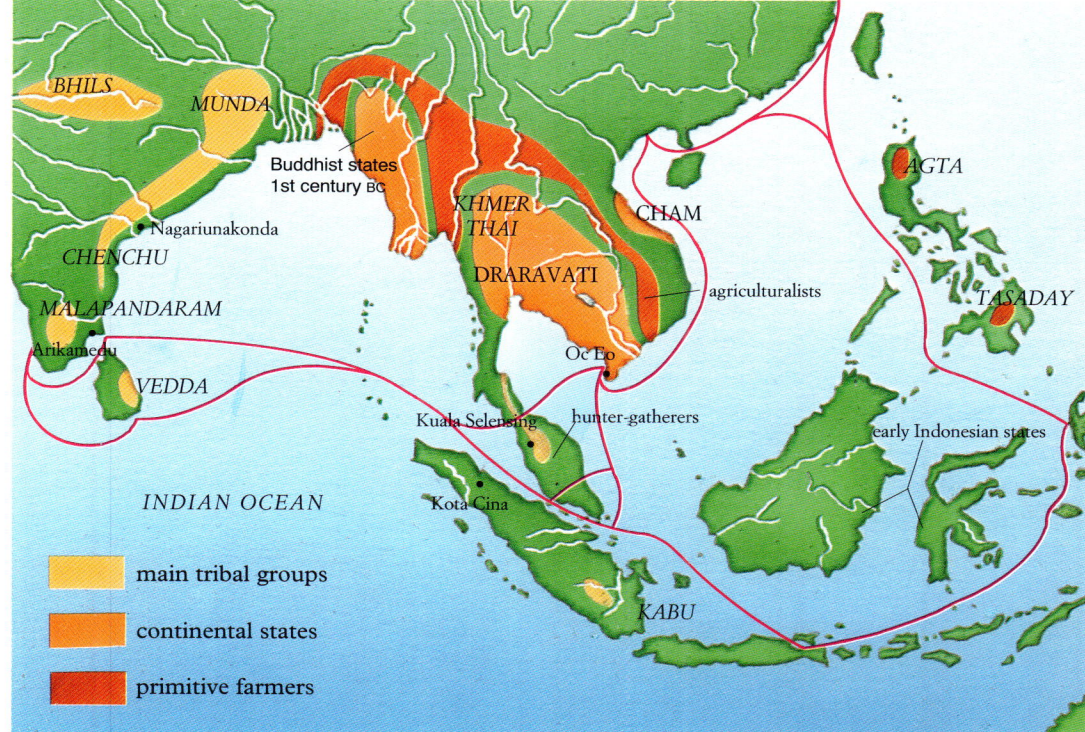

The map (below) shows prehistoric forest cultures in Southeast Asia and trading routes.

10 Indochina and Malaysia

We know little about the prehistoric age in Southeast Asia. There are a number of human remains, dating from almost 40,000 years ago, including evidence of Neanderthal people. The Hoa-Binh site in Vietnam is particularly important because numerous stone tools were found there. The tools had been shaped by striking techniques, and had various uses. People using similar tools lived elsewhere in Southeast Asia. They were hunters and gatherers.

First farmers of Indochina
Another settlement site studied by modern scientists is Spirit Cave in Thailand. This seems to have been inhabited from the 8th to the 5th millennia BC, and finds there show us how these early Southeast Asian peoples lived. They gathered wild plants such as water chestnuts, and may have grown crops of others such as beans and peas. Some experts believe they may have planted rice, and that rice-cultivation spread from this region north into China. But the evidence for rice-growing is not clear. Nor, if these people did know how to grow rice, is it clear why they did not go on to develop a more advanced culture.

The first farmers continued to gather plants and hunt. They hunted deer and other animals, including prey as big as the rhinoceros, and also ate fish and shellfish.

Metalworking and drumming
Bronze tools began to appear in Thailand from the 5th millennium BC. It is likely that the people learned farming and metalworking techniques from their more advanced neighbours. There was evidently quite well-developed trade between the different regions, for bronzes from Burma (Myanmar) and Malaysia are found in India and China. A large quantity of bronze objects was discovered close to the Chinese border in the village of Dong Son in Annam (Vietnam). The people who lived in this region were farmers, but were also well used to the sea and fishing. They were capable of making trading voyages into, and perhaps beyond, the China Sea.

Bronze objects found there are finely decorated, and include monumental drums. How these drums were used is not known, but they were probably beaten during rituals, first to call the people together, and then to arouse a mood of intense excitement.

Outside influences
The peoples of Southeast Asia were influenced most by the cultures of India and China. China was especially powerful during the Qin and Han empires, conquering the Red river

This is a detail from a mask engraved on a ceremonial drum from Pedjeng, Bali. The mask probably represented an ancestral spirit.

The scene below (pictured in colour on pages 40/41) shows a forest village in Southeast Asia. Life for many people here changed little in the thousand years from 500 BC to AD 500. Most people lived by gathering plants, including spices and tree resins, from the jungle. Gradually trade with the outside world developed, as forest products became more sought-after. Goods were taken to the river and loaded into boats, which took them to coastal villages where foreign traders waited.

The village houses are built on stilts, and the distinctive horn-shaped roofs can still be seen on traditional buildings today. The resins gathered from the forest were skilfully worked to make varnishes, sealing wax, and beads for necklaces. They were also used as medicines and in ceremonies. On a raised platform a man beats a set of gongs, perhaps to summon the villagers for a meeting. Others continue their work.

The forest dwellers of Sumatra were expert hunters of elephants, wild boar and monkeys. Men wore only loin-cloths, and pursued their prey with spears and poison-tipped darts. Forest people turned to farming when they began planting roots and tubers in forest clearings.

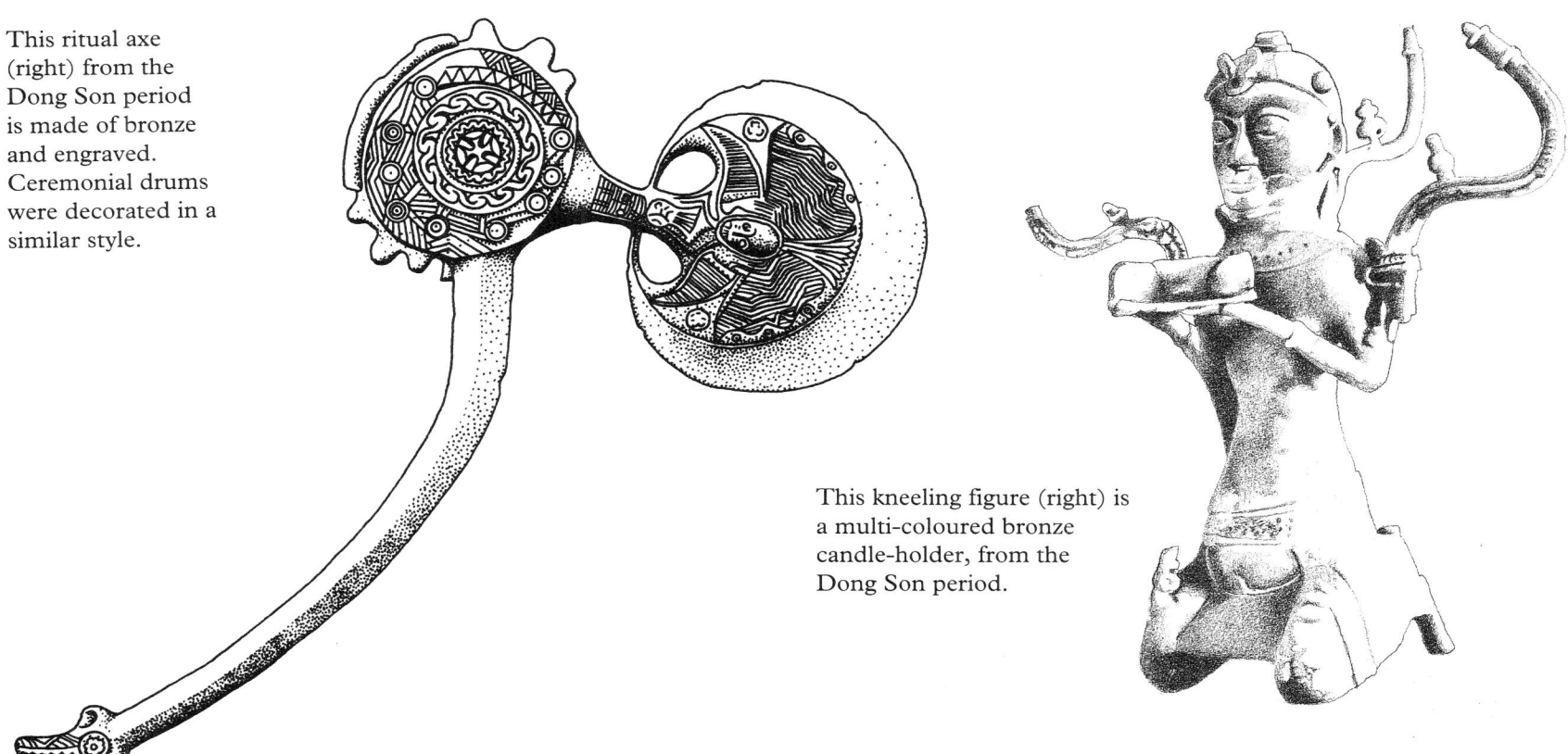

This ritual axe (right) from the Dong Son period is made of bronze and engraved. Ceremonial drums were decorated in a similar style.

This kneeling figure (right) is a multi-coloured bronze candle-holder, from the Dong Son period.

basin and the lands around the Gulf of Tonkin by 111 BC. Most of northern Vietnam was Chinese-ruled until the AD 900s, under the name of Annam. The Chinese imposed their government system, language and writing system on the Vietnamese people.

Indian influence was also great. It came mainly through trade, for Indian seamen had learned to navigate with the seasonal monsoon winds, and made regular visits to Southeast Asia. Indian writing arrived in this way, and is still evident in modern Burma, Thailand, Cambodia and Laos. Sanskrit became the language of the educated and of government. The teachings of Buddhism and Hinduism were also brought, along with Indian ideas in mathematics and astronomy. The concept of the ruler as an absolute and divine authority also came from these powerful neighbours.

Funan and the Khmers

The kingdom of Funan was one of two in southern Vietnam (the other was Champa on the coast) which had developed by AD 100. Here too there was Indian influence. Funan rule extended into southern Cambodia, Burma and Indonesia. At the end of the 6th century, Funan was absorbed by one of its own vassal-states, Chenla. The Khmer people then became dominant throughout the Mekong river valley, Thailand and southern Laos. The Khmer empire remained powerful for hundreds of years.

Thailand and Indonesia

In Thailand, people whose origins were in Yunnan (China) set up small states, like those in India. They were farmers, like most Southeast Asian peoples.

In the East Indies, however, people also lived through sea trade. The straits of Malacca and Sunda were the two key passages for ships trading between the west (the Middle East and India) and the Far East. This made the islands of what is now called Indonesia a focus for Asian communications, and one of the great trading centres of the ancient world.

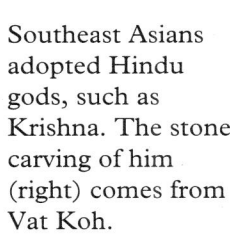

Harihara was a god who combined the characteristics of the Hindu gods Shiva and Vishnu. This stone figure (left) is from Phnom Da.

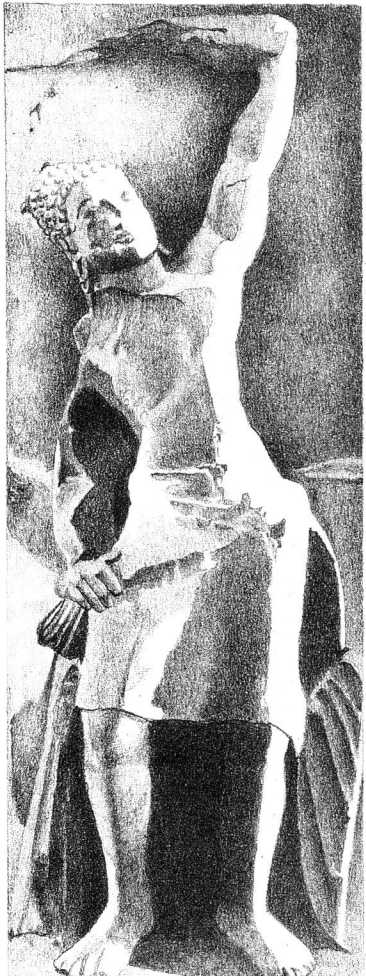

Southeast Asians adopted Hindu gods, such as Krishna. The stone carving of him (right) comes from Vat Koh.

11 Peoples of the Steppes

The map shows movements of peoples from Central Asia in the 1st and 2nd millennia BC.

- → Nomad movements in the Bronze Age
- → Migrations of Huns
- → Migrations of Scythians and Sarmatians

This saddle cover (below) comes from Pazyry in Siberia. Made in the 5th century, from felt and animal skins, it is embroidered in gold thread and trimmed with fur.

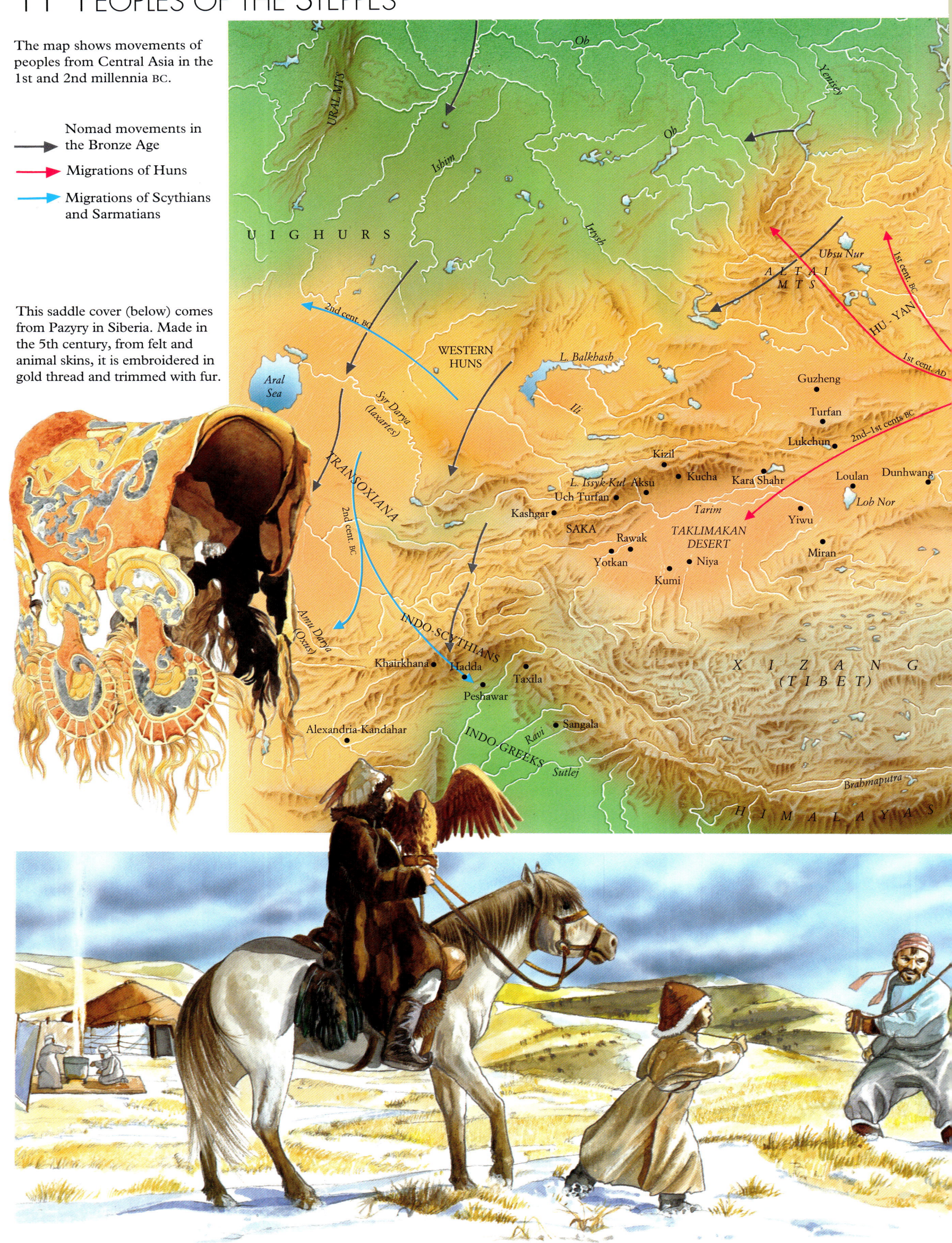

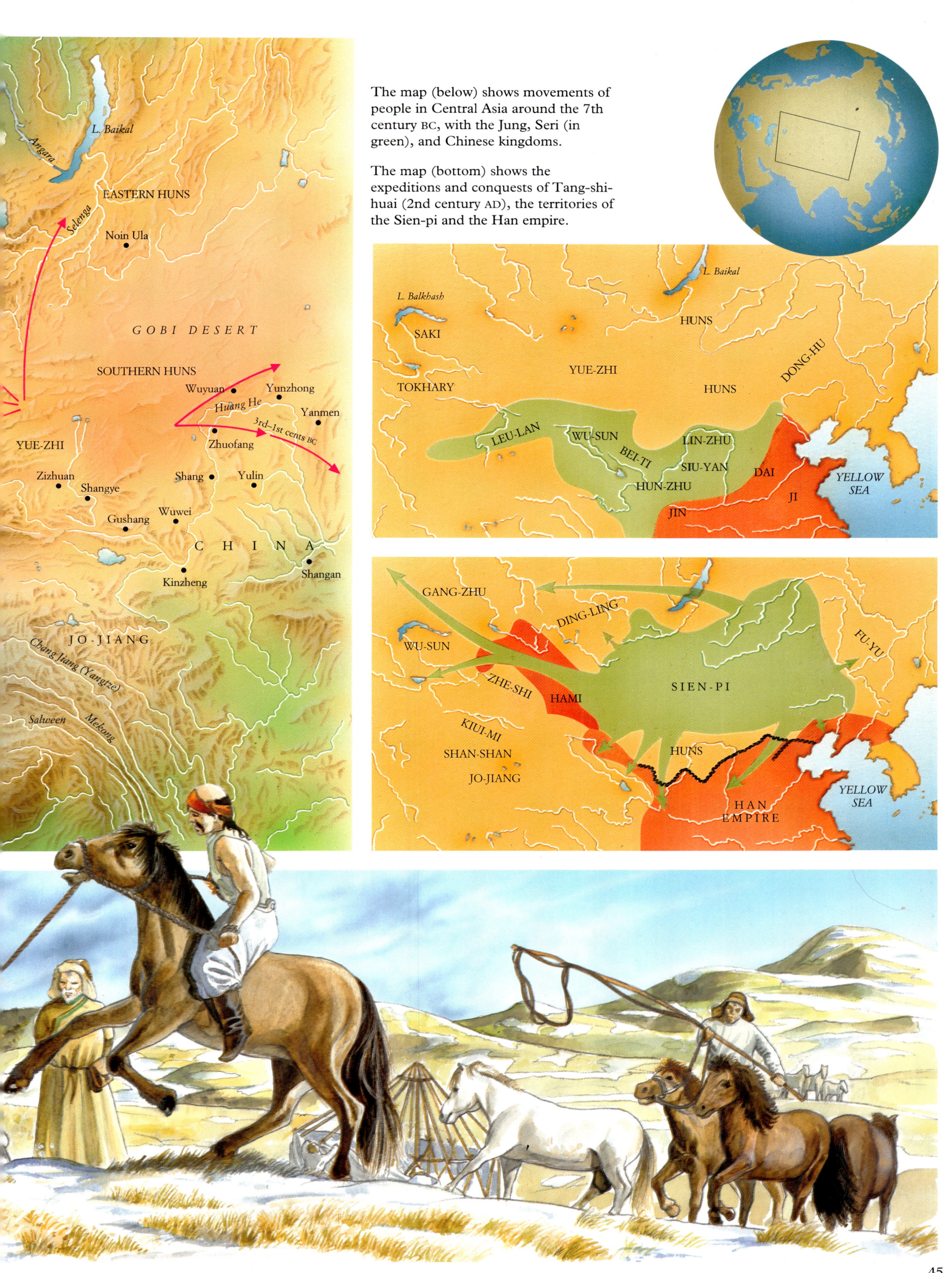

11 Peoples of the Steppes

The steppe nomads lived in yurts, like this one (below). It had a trellis-like framework of easily bent tree branches (willow perhaps). This was covered with a layer of skins. A hole in the centre of the roof allowed smoke from the fire inside to escape. The entrance always faced south. Inside, the northern part of the living space was for the head of the family. Women lived in the eastern part, other men in the western part.

The huge plain extending from the heart of Asia through Central Asia is known as the Eurasian Steppe. This 'sea' of grassland was crossed by many groups of migrating peoples, from Palaeolithic times onwards. In the Neolithic (New Stone Age), the northern steppe was the home of nomad peoples who were hunters and fishers, and gatherers of shellfish, living close to rivers and lakes. Further south, people were farmers, from about the 4th millennium BC, and also rearers of animals such as sheep and goats.

Nomads on the move

In the 3rd millennium BC there came the first great change. There were too many herds for the available pasture, and drought forced the herdsmen to move in search of new grassland. They now had tame horses, and could move further and faster. There also appeared at this time the first wheeled carts, and the custom of burying the dead beneath mounds, or tumuli, known as *kurgan*. The camel was another new animal, used from the 2nd millennium both as a pack animal and for riding.

Their animals were the source of the nomads' wealth. Milk and dairy foods were an important part of their diet. At the head of their groups were male leaders, who owned the largest herds of animals. However, among some peoples, such as the Sarmatians, women were regarded as men's equals, and the bodies of women leaders, complete with weapons, have been found in tombs.

These steppe peoples were a mixture. Some were Indo-Europeans, like those who had invaded India. There were also the Xiongnu, or Huns, as they were later known in the West. Their ancestors were probably people from Inner Mongolia called the Hu, who had cultural links dating back into Stone Age times with the northern Chinese.

About 1200 BC the Hu crossed the Gobi Desert, moving away from the new Zhou dynasty in China. They sought new pastures in Siberia, which was becoming greener as a result of a warming climate. The Huns too were on the move, through southern Siberia, central Mongolia and towards Lake Baikal, and so were other groups of nomads, each seeking control of new grazing lands.

One of the most feared groups was the Yueh-chih (see page 23). By the 4th century BC they were moving west, and by the 1st century BC had arrived in Bactria (an ancient country now within Afghanistan, Uzbekistan and Tajikistan). Their arrival set off changes in surrounding regions, leading to the emergence of the Indian empire of Kushan, for example.

The scene below (pictured in colour on pages 44/45) shows steppe nomads with their horses. The horse was a nomad's most prized possession. These people lived on horseback from childhood, and rode for herding, hunting and war.

In the picture, a man is 'breaking', or taming, a young horse, riding bareback. Another (right of picture) has a lasso on a long pole, for catching horses from the herd. The rider on the left carries on his wrist a falcon, used for hunting.

The people's clothes are made from thick woollen cloth, to keep out the cold winds. As soon as they made camp, they set up their portable homes, tent-like dwellings called yurts. These were made from a framework of poles covered with animal skins, and were taken down when the party moved off.

Small children quickly learned the arts of steppe survival – how to ride, withstand heat and cold, travel far, and fight. Despite the hardships, the Huns enjoyed lively entertainments, feasting and dancing.

The picture (right) shows a nomads' camp, with their flocks. The camels carry the baggage, including the yurts. The horses are kept mainly for hunting and war.

The nomads also used oxen (below) as pack animals, when it was time to move on. A leader's yurt was often too large to be dismantled, and was instead loaded onto a large cart pulled by a team of oxen.

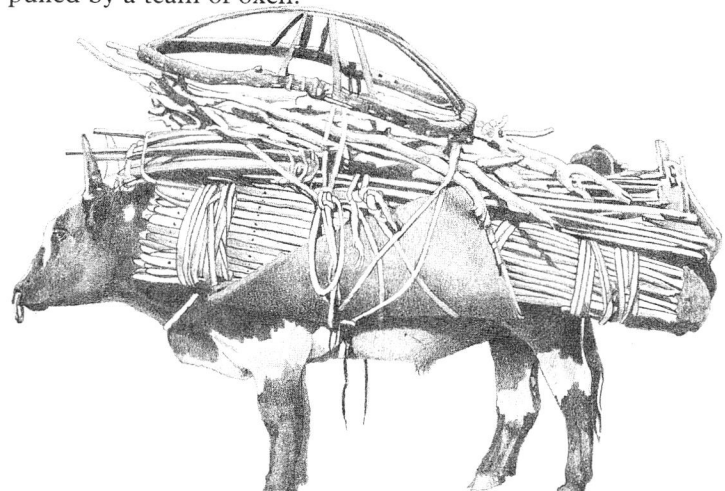

The steppe peoples at war

As they moved west, the nomads met people living at oases and trading settlements. Sometimes there was peaceful trade, sometimes there was war. The steppe people were expert at fighting on horseback, their main weapon being the bow and arrow. Their lightning-fast charges and retreats often bemused and defeated much bigger armies.

This movement of peoples occasionally built up into vast migratory waves, such as the 'barbarian' invasions that attacked the Roman empire in the AD 400s. To fight off the nomads, the great civilizations attempted defence or diplomacy. The Chinese built their Great Wall to keep out the nomads, but instead suffered continual attacks. The Han emperors lavished gifts on their warlike neighbours, and gave their princesses in marriage to Hun leaders to buy peace. But peace treaties were usually violated.

The Huns

The Hun kingdoms were founded on the rule of clans, under a leader known as the *Shan Yu*. His authority was based on his own prestige, backed up by a council of elders and the warriors. All Huns were warriors as well as herdsmen. They wore out their enemies by ambushes and skirmishes, seldom risking frontal attacks. Booty became private property. Pasture belonged to everyone.

In the 1st century BC the eastern Huns were weakened by quarrels between their own leaders, and defeated by the Chinese. Civil wars in China after the end of the Han dynasty encouraged them to make new attacks, but again the Huns fell out among themselves. The northern Huns became a kind of warrior-democracy, while those in the south kept the old tribal traditions, and Chinese influence.

The Sien-pi empire

Towards the end of the 1st century AD the Sien-pi rose to prominence, attacking the northern Huns. China took advantage of the Huns' weakness to push against the nomads westward. The Sien-pi became the third party in this Central Asian conflict. The Sien-pi found a great leader in Tang-shi-huai, who brought a number of tribes under his command in the mid-2nd century AD. In less than ten years, he conquered the Hun territory, more than 6,500 kilometres (4,000 miles) from east to west. His empire, based on a warrior horde, was the model for later Central Asian conquerors.

Assimilation and westward movement

When Tang-shi-huai died, his empire broke up, and war between the Chinese, Huns and Sien-pi began again. From AD 142 to 225 the Huns began to regain lost ground. Those outside Chinese influence assimilated with other peoples, including the Sien-pi, a mingling that was to produce the Turkic and Mongol peoples of the Middle Ages. The Huns living within China were assimilated into the Chinese empire. Huns escaping the victories of the Sien-pi empire mingled with the Uighurs of the Ural Mountains, and thereafter looked west (towards Europe) for booty rather than towards China. It was these 'Huns' who so alarmed Greek and Roman historians, and whose attacks eventually helped to bring down the Roman empire.

12 Sailors of the Indian Ocean

The map shows the Indian Ocean, with coastal sea routes and the direction of the monsoon winds (shown by the grey arrows). Also shown are the main trade goods, and the chief trading ports – at about AD 500.

12 Sailors of the Indian Ocean

The oceans have changed little in millions of years, compared with the constantly shifting continents. But for those first travellers who ventured upon it, the sea was always unpredictable. The oceans were completely unknown to primitive people, who could think of them only as infinite vastnesses. It was not by chance that one of the Titans in ancient Greek mythology was called Oceanus – the great world river, an unknown space too vast to explore.

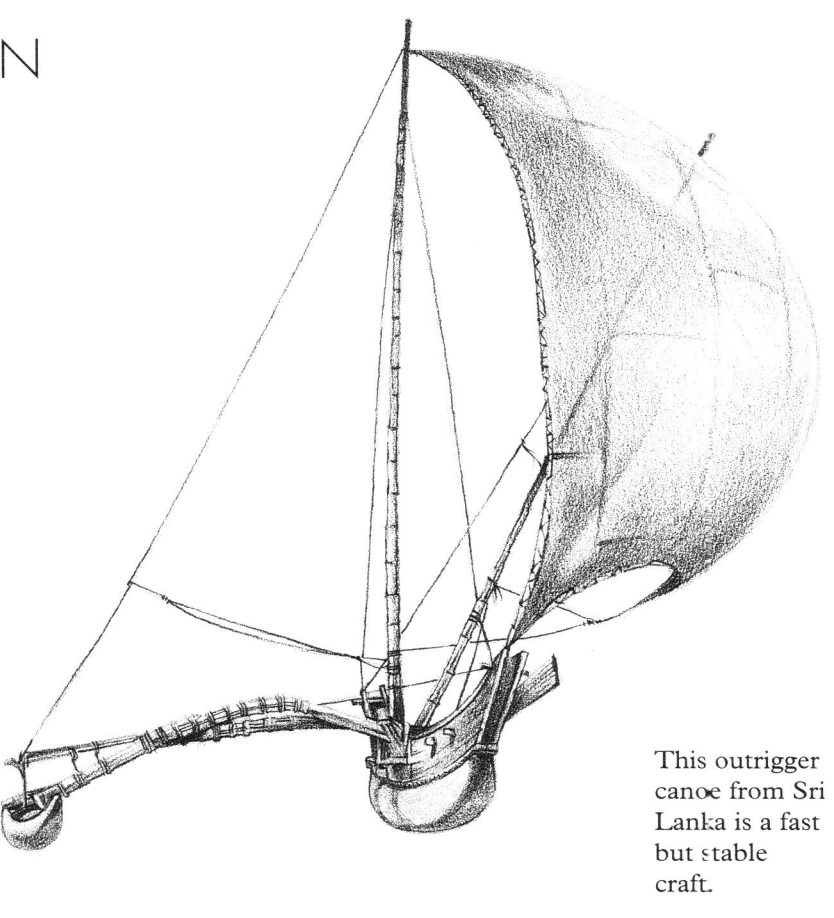

This outrigger canoe from Sri Lanka is a fast but stable craft.

First sailors of the Pacific

The first seas to be sailed upon by people, in Stone Age times, were small, landlocked waters. The best example is the Mediterranean, which had several advanced civilizations growing up around its shores. The Atlantic Ocean remained largely uncharted until the AD 1000s, but sailors did venture out into the much larger Pacific Ocean in earlier times. Certainly people were on the move across the Pacific between 2500 and 500 BC, when the settlement of the Polynesian islands was under way.

Exploring the Indian Ocean

It is difficult to date the beginnings of systematic navigation of the Indian Ocean. The only evidence comes from money, used by traders between one country and another, and from written records of voyages by geographers and explorers. These accounts are seldom precise and sometimes full of fantastic exaggerations.

One of the oldest histories, and perhaps the most reliable, is the *Circumnavigation of the Eritrean Sea*, written (sometime between the 1st and 3rd centuries AD) by an unknown Greek merchant living in Egypt. It describes the busy trade between East Africa and the Far East, and refers to contacts between these regions and India.

Asians sail to Madagascar

To work out when the Indian Ocean voyages began, we can look at the history of Madagascar. This large island is close to Africa, and its people include both Africans and Asians. Archaeologists have discovered evidence of the arrival in Madagascar around the 5th century AD of a large number of people from the East Indies. This means that they had voyaged for some 6,000 kilometres (3,700 miles) from, say, Java. Perhaps they followed the coastline of India and Sri Lanka, with stops, but even so, such voyages could have been made only by people who were familiar with the Indian Ocean.

The picture below (shown in colour on pages 48/49) shows two Phoenician trading ships on an Indian Ocean island. Ships of many lands sailed the Indian Ocean, and among them were some that made the long voyage through the Red Sea (or just conceivably around the Cape of Good Hope) from the Mediterranean.

The Indian Ocean offered sailors many islands to visit, some inhabited, others home only to lush tropical vegetation. Here sailors could seek shelter and rest during a long voyage.

These visitors are welcomed by the villagers, whose beehive-huts line the shore. Outrigger canoes come out to begin the trade.

The Moluccas were known as the Spice Islands, because of the cloves and nutmeg they produced. Cinnamon came from Sri Lanka, gathered in the forest from trees. Cardamom came from the forests of southern India. These spices, and pepper, were sought after in both East and West as food flavourings and preservatives.

The forests of the Molucca Islands were rich in spices. Shown (left) are:
1. cloves
2. nutmeg, with leaves and dried seeds
3. cinnamon
4. cardamom
5. pepper

The map (above) shows the fabled Spice Islands (modern Indonesia).

A small Chinese junk (below). Craft like this, originally from south China, were used throughout Southeast Asia.

Blow the winds regularly

Two factors make the Indian Ocean favourable for navigation. Clear skies most of the time enable a seaman to observe the stars. And the seasonal winds, or monsoons (from the Arabic *mawsim*, meaning 'season'), blow in the same direction for regular periods each year. In winter the monsoon winds blow from the northeast, and in the summer they come from the southwest. A sailing craft can therefore make a relatively safe crossing in one direction or the other. Having discovered this wind cycle, early seamen made use of it by sailing in time with the seasons.

The Chinese histories refer to an expedition of AD 98 to Rome, and say that with favourable winds, a sea voyage to the west would take three months, whereas with a contrary wind it would take up to two years. The writer must mean the monsoons. The Greek geographer Strabo tells of an Indian shipwreck-survivor Hippalus who, landing in Egypt, was cared for by an ambassador named Eudoxus. To show his thanks, Hippalus guided the ambassador on a voyage to India, using the seasonal winds. This was about 110 BC, and by then Arabs and Indian seafarers already knew the monsoon winds well.

East meets West

The Indian Ocean was an important meeting place between the East and West. Until the 7th century, Indian and Arab traders acted as 'middlemen' in trade between the Mediterranean (by way of Egypt and the Red Sea) and East Africa in the west, and the East Indies and Southeast Asia in the east. Perfumes, spices, gems and Chinese silks came westward. Africa exported rhinoceros horn, ebony and ivory. India was rich in silver and gold, and the best pearls came from Sri Lanka (Ceylon). Even plants, such as palm species and bananas, reached Africa from Asia across the sea.

13 Links with Iron Age Africa

This rock picture (below) of a person playing a pipe shows the music coming out as tiny dots. The drawing comes from Pahi in Tanzania.

The map (right) shows southern and east-central Africa, with the main Iron Age sites.

The hunting scene (below) shows people with bows and arrows chasing an antelope. It comes from Msana in Zimbabwe.

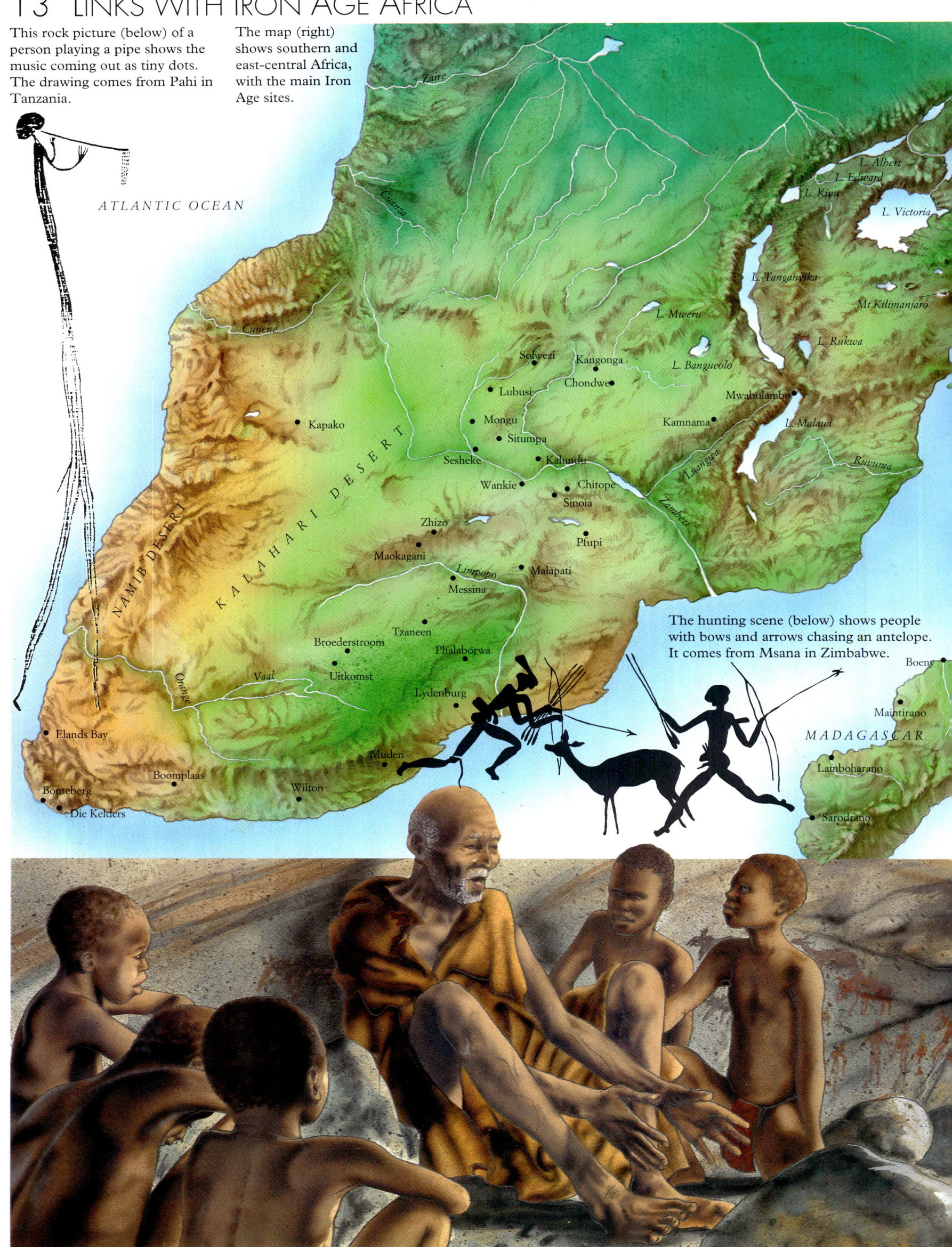

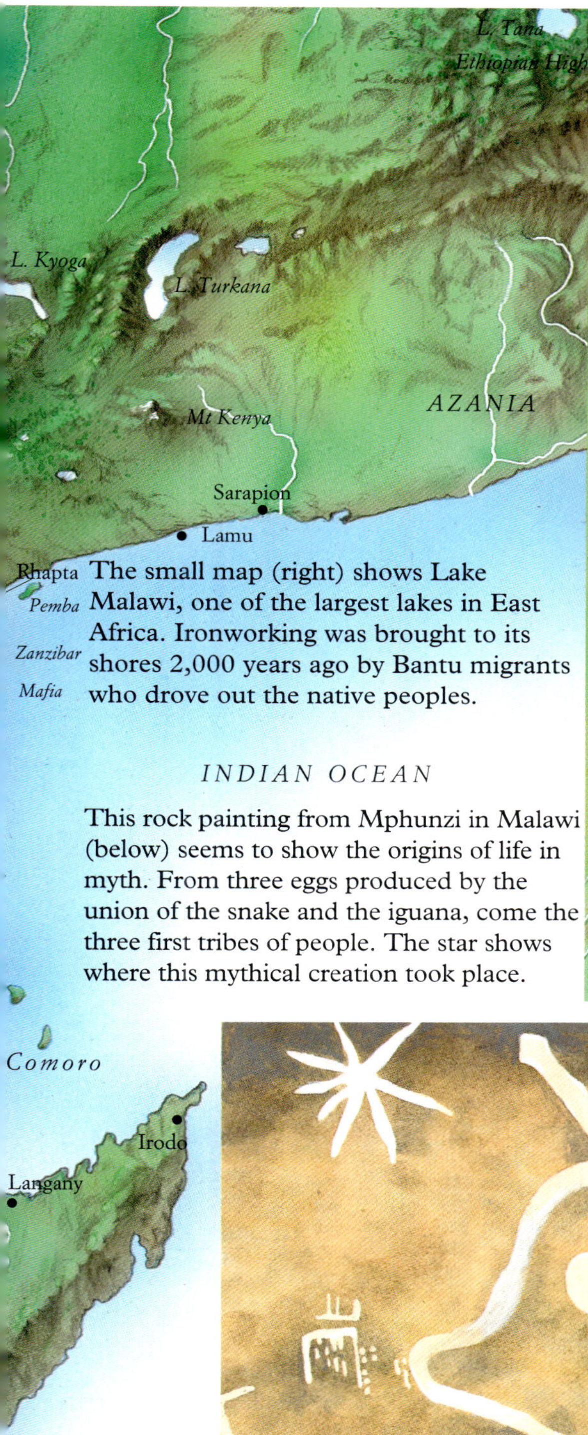

The map (below) shows the main African migrations of people at the start of the modern era, when Iron Age technology was spreading.

+ ironworking sites before AD 400

The small map (right) shows Lake Malawi, one of the largest lakes in East Africa. Ironworking was brought to its shores 2,000 years ago by Bantu migrants who drove out the native peoples.

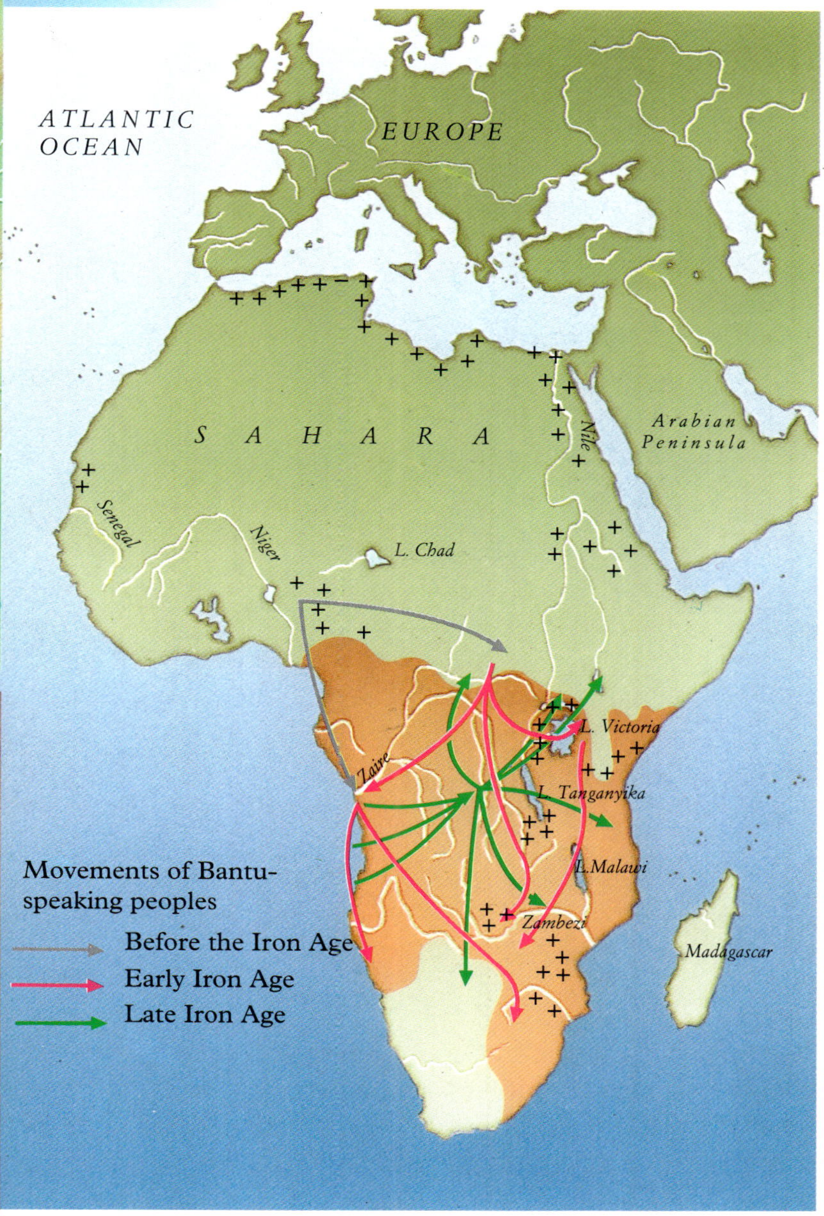

This rock painting from Mphunzi in Malawi (below) seems to show the origins of life in myth. From three eggs produced by the union of the snake and the iguana, come the three first tribes of people. The star shows where this mythical creation took place.

Movements of Bantu-speaking peoples
→ Before the Iron Age
→ Early Iron Age
→ Late Iron Age

13 Links with Iron Age Africa

This terracotta figure of a person kneeling comes from Bwari, Nigeria. It is an example of Nok art, a style common between AD 400 and 1200.

At the start of the 1st millennium BC, sub-Saharan Africa was in the Stone Age. For a time, between 3000 and 2000 BC, the Sahara had 'greened' during a period of wetter climate. Then dry conditions returned. Only a few people lived on the great grasslands or dense forests of central and southern Africa. They were hunter-gatherers, moving in small groups after the animals they hunted. They used bows and poison-tipped arrows, and traps for catching large animals. People living near lakes and rivers caught fish. But most of their food was gathered, in the form of roots, fruits, leaves and berries. Rock paintings show men armed with bows, and women using sticks to dig for roots.

Iron Age Africa

This part of Africa did not have a Bronze Age, and the Iron Age was slow to appear. There are few sites to help archaeologists uncover Africa's past, and in most areas no written records of these ancient times, so we can only guess at how ironworking was developed. Stone tools continued to be used, even after iron had come into use.

Most experts believe that iron technology had reached Africa by the 500s BC. The knowledge may have come from the north, from Egypt, or from Arabia by way of the kingdoms of Kush and Axum. Or central and southern Africans may have discovered ironworking for themselves, while making pottery in kilns.

The Bantu migrations

Farming now became widespread, along with pottery, and a typical village architecture of cylinder-shaped huts with conical thatched roofs. The main unifying feature was language. One language-group became common across half the continent. These related languages used the word *Bantu* for 'people', and the term has since been used for the people who belonged to this language group. The Bantu people were not one tribe.

Many experts have seen a link between the spread of Bantu languages in central and southern Africa, and the appearance of iron there, with the resulting change in people's lives. If the Bantu did have iron, this would explain their rapid success over such a large area. Some were herdsmen, others farmers who used iron tools to till the fields. They very quickly imposed their way of life on the hunter-gatherers whose territory they moved into.

This was a colonization by technology, not by war. The Bantu took with them their tools, their ironworking skills, and their seed-sowing knowledge. Small family groups cleared land for crops and built homes. After a few seasons, they moved on to find fresh land. The Bantu lived alongside the peoples of the plains and forests, teaching them their ways and their language.

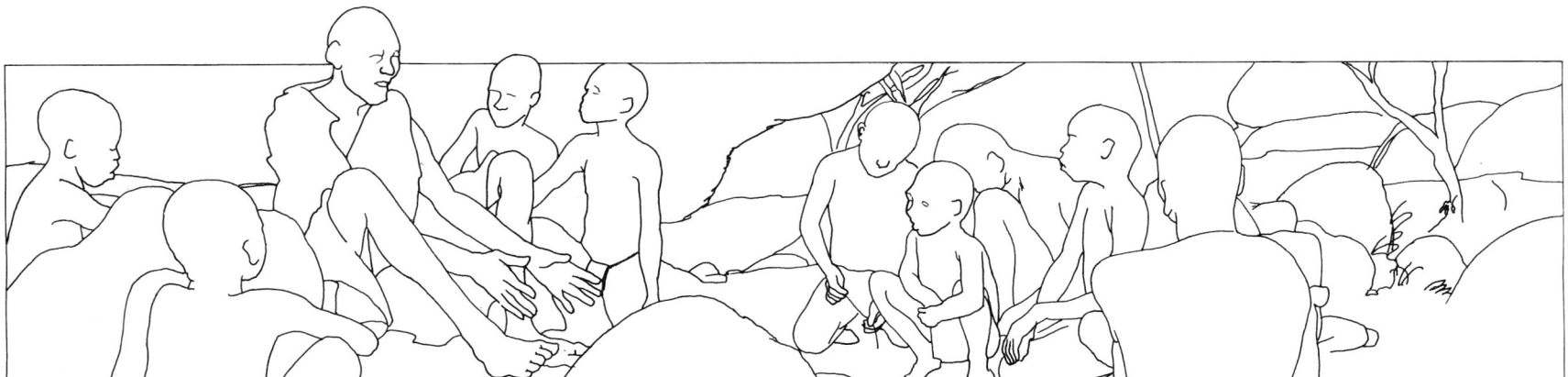

The scene below (shown in colour on pages 52/53) shows a Bantu elder teaching a group of youngsters. On the walls of the cave in which the lesson takes place are paintings of animals. In caves near Lake Nyasa in Malawi are cave paintings which are the most ancient cultural record of this region. The paintings give us clues as to what the ancient Bantu believed about myths, how the world was made, and how they and the people before them lived.

The caves were meeting places. These youngsters have come to listen and learn. Their teacher is an old man, full of stories and memories. They have no written books. Everything is spoken aloud, and remembered. The most valuable teachings were inscribed on the walls of the cave, as pictures. This made the caves sacred places. Possibly boys were allowed in them only when they were old enough to be initiated as full members of the tribe.

This picture (left) of people fishing in a lake comes from a rock painting in Lesotho. The people are using spears and harpoons, and are fishing from rafts, one of which is clearly anchored.

The scene (below) shows a battle, between men with bows and arrows, and shields. To the left is a wounded animal, possibly representing the cause of the quarrel. The painting was found in a cave in Cape Province, South Africa.

Wealthy states and trade with Asia

The first sub-Saharan state of any real importance was Ghana, a kingdom that arose in the 3rd to 4th centuries AD. News of its wealth spread to the Middle East. Ghana grew rich through trade. Its position between the Niger and Senegal rivers in West Africa helped its people to control trade in gold from the west and in luxury goods, horses, foods and salt from the north.

Not all of central-southern Africa came under Bantu influence. Northern Uganda, most of Kenya and central-northern Tanzania were influenced by the civilizations of the Nile and of Ethiopia. Ethiopia's great Kush kingdom, originally a farming and herding state, became an important commercial link between Africa, the Middle East and India. The western coast of Kush was dotted by settlements where people traded with merchants sailing across the Indian Ocean to Asia. In this way, contacts between Africa and Asia were developed.

Another rock painting from South Africa (above) shows herdsmen with their cattle.

14 The Contribution of Asia

This panel (right) in red-lacquered wood was made in Han China. The symbol in the centre of the disc at the top represents the two aspects of life, according to Taoism, *yin* and *yang*. The black element (*yin*) and the red (*yang*) represent opposite but interdependent expressions of reality. *Yin* stands for the passing of a mountain into shadow, and so by analogy, for night, darkness, cold, winter and the colour black. *Yang* is the passing of the mountain into sunlight, and stands for

This silver beaker (right) is called a *rhyton*, and ones like it are shown on many Greek vases from the 5th century BC. Made of silver, with traces of gold, its base combines as a handle in the shape of a baby goat or deer.

day, light, heat, summer and the colour red. Each contains part of the other, as shown by the way the symbol is constructed: everything is cyclical, people and nature are interacting. The eight barred signs around the *yin/yang* symbol are known as 'trigrams'. The Chinese believed that by arranging these signs in various ways, as taught in the *I Ching* of Confucian thought, profound meanings could be understood. The tiger (shown at the bottom) is a symbol of energy (*Chi*). It manifests *yin* and *yang*, as shown by its eyes – one black, one red.

The map shows Asia as it was 2,000 years ago, with its main communication routes over land (in red), and by sea (in green). The spread of Buddhism is shown in yellow.

14 The Contribution of Asia

The tomb of Cyrus the Great, ruler of the Persian empire. The building is 10 metres (33 feet) high, of simple design, with a sloping roof and stepped surround.

The ancient history of Asia is marked by the appearance of great and powerful civilizations, which shaped the entire continent. After Persia (early 500s BC) came India (first with the teachings of Buddha and then with the Maurya empire in the 400s BC). China meanwhile was a massive influence in thought, art and technology, and in government organization from the 200s BC. Asian philosophies, such as Buddhism, Confucianism and Taoism, spread far.

Asia's influence on other regions

Asian technology was exported to other regions, and international trade across land and sea can be said to begin with Indian and Chinese merchants. Close by the developing and comparatively stable cultures there were numerous nomadic peoples, with very different ways of life. The migrations of these nomads brought great changes to Asia. They included the Indo-Europeans who moved east in the 2nd millennium BC, the inroads made by Medes and Persians in Mesopotamia, and the arrival of the Aryans, who probably overran and destroyed the civilizations of Harappa and Mohenjo-Daro in the Indus Valley.

The nomads from central and northern Asia were a troublesome force to the great civilizations of the continent, but also an important link between one culture and another. They did not follow fixed trade routes, like merchants, but their movements nevertheless left permanent results. Their fighting methods, for example, changed the traditional military strategy of the Chinese, while their love of naturalistic (lifelike) art was imitated by other, more 'civilized' peoples. Only Japan was left largely untouched by these continental migrations until the early centuries AD, when the Iron Age began on the Japanese islands – long after it had started elsewhere in Asia.

East-West trade

Southeast Asia and Indonesia were areas influenced by both Chinese and Indian culture. The geographic position of these regions made them important links in sea trade between the Far East and Africa and the Middle East. Exchanges of goods brought remote regions, such as East Africa, in contact with Asian civilization, with the possible transmission of new ideas (such as ironworking).

As well as trading across the sea, Asian merchants also

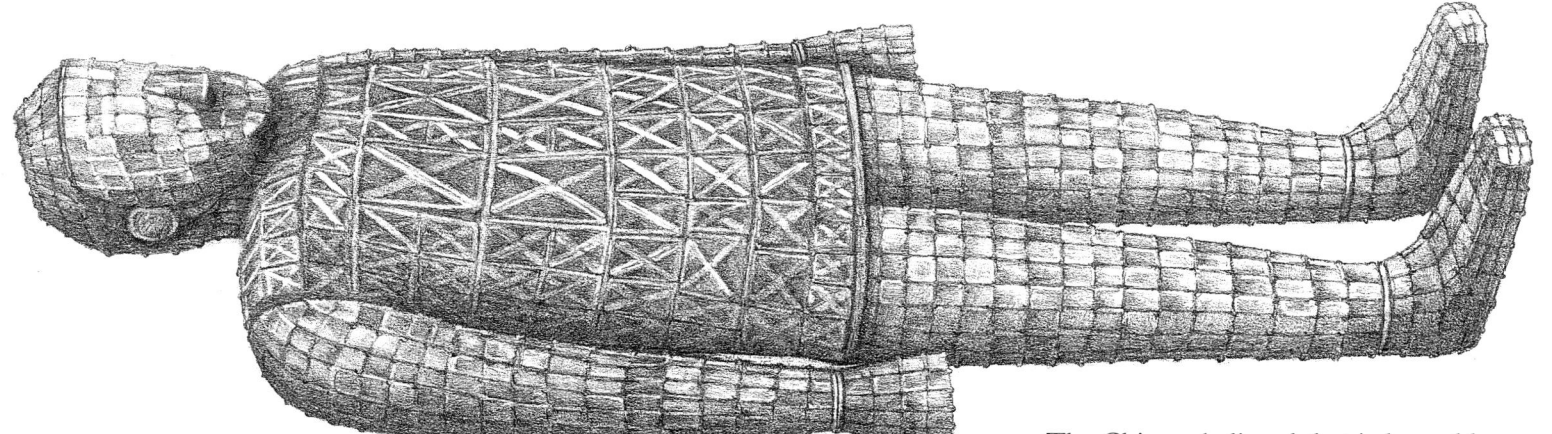

The Chinese believed that jade could preserve a body after death. The Princess Tou Wan was buried wearing a suit made of 2,256 pieces of jade (shown here). People who could afford only a few pieces of jade were buried with them covering body openings (mouth, eyes and so on) so that the slow ebbing of the life spirit was not disturbed by unlucky influences.

This figure (left) of a Chinese fish-seller, preparing fish for sale, comes from a Han tomb.

a)

b)

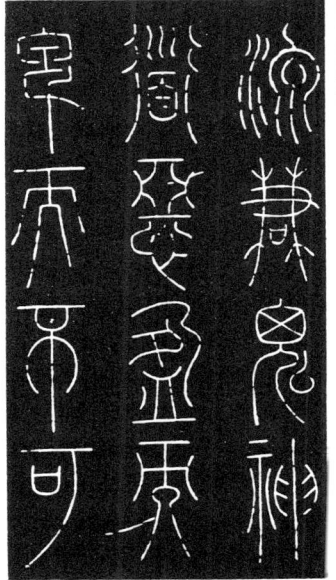

These are examples of Chinese writing. On the left (a) are standard characters from the Qin empire, on the right (b) the official script of the Late Han period.

This carving (below left) is a relief of the Hindu sun god Surya, made in the 10th century.

The bronze figure with a lamp (below) came from a Dong Son tomb.

made immense land journeys. The most famous trade route of all was the Silk Road, a long and dangerous route that linked the Far East with the European West. The great western and eastern civilizations were brought to touching point. No longer was the Great Wall the limit for the East, nor the Mediterranean the limit for the West.

Great ideas and religions

Asia also produced great ideas and religious teachings. Within a few hundred years, the world was enlightened by the teachings of Zoroaster, Buddha, Confucius and Lao-tzu, as well as by the great thinkers of Greece, by the Hebrew tradition, and later by the founders of Christianity and Islam.

From the 500s BC, humanity seemed to be entering a new era of geographic and technical discovery, as well as a time of new moral and religious conviction. Ancient myth and tradition remained central to many people's lives, but for many these old beliefs began to take on a more purely symbolic value. Individuality and personal responsibility within society were becoming part of human experience. In this great development, which continues to influence the modern world, Asia played a major part.

Glossary

Portrait of Han Yu (768-824) in ceremonial dress. One of the leading figures of Confucianism, this celebrated prose writer was a fierce opponent of Buddhism.

ablution religious ritual, practised by Hindus especially, whereby the body or part of the body is washed to purify both body and spirit. Hindus consider the waters of the Ganges river to be most sacred.

absolute ruler a king or other sovereign who has total authority, taking all the state's powers to himself.

alchemy the search for a means of turning base metals such as lead into gold.

annals collection of yearly historical chronicles or writings. One of the main sources of historical information about China and its neighbours.

Aramaic language originally spoken in Syria, which later spread throughout the Middle East and western Asia.

archaeologist scientist who studies the past by examining evidence of ancient settlement, such as tombs, ruined cities, buried objects, plant remains, bones, shells and other items.

Aryan describes people who speak an Indo-European language.

ascetic someone who practises self-denial, such as fasting (going with little or no food and drink) to attain spiritual fulfilment.

Brahmin a member of the Hindu priestly caste.

bronze a metal alloy (mixture) of copper and tin. Used for making tools and weapons from about 3500 BC.

caravan a group of traders travelling together for protection, with their goods loaded onto pack animals such as horses, camels, donkeys and oxen.

caste social group closed to people outside it; to belong to a caste, a person is born into it. The caste system is still part of Indian society.

character in writing, a symbol standing for an object or idea.

chariot two-wheeled wagon, used either as a lord's carriage or for battle. Chariots were pulled by two or four horses.

clan social group made up of families related by common ancestors.

creed system or statement of religious beliefs.

cult system of religious belief, practised by a group or sect, and often of a mystical or secretive nature.

cuneiform type of writing in which the characters are wedge-shaped, made by pressing a tool into soft clay or wax.

divine of a god, or of the gods.

dynasty series of rulers belonging to one family, descending in line (though not always father-to-son) from the founder.

edict order from an emperor or king, or other important ruler, which must be obeyed by everyone living within his or her territory.

ethics philosophical ideas about how to tell good from evil, and how to live a moral life.

feudal society in which vassals serve a lord in return for his protection.

find something discovered by an archaeologist, such as a fragment of pottery, a bone, an old coin, or simply some holes in the ground where the posts of a timber building once stood.

flood plain area covered and made fertile by the floodwaters of a river and its tributaries.

horde a large group, used to describe a mass of nomad warriors following their leader in search of new lands.

irrigation watering dry farmland by taking water to the fields from a river by means of canals and ditches.

investiture transfer of land from a ruler to a subject lord (known as a vassal). This was a feature of feudal society in Asia and Europe; the giving of land bound the vassal to the ruler by a duty of honour and obligation.

jade hard semi-precious stone, which can be green, brown, white or yellow. It can be carved to make ornaments and jewellery. The green form of jade was most highly prized.

junk Chinese sailing vessel, made in various forms and sizes, and used for trading along rivers and across oceans. Junks are still found today in Asia.

kami gods and spirits revered by the ancient Japanese.

kinship blood relationship; people of one family are of the same kin.

kshatriyas member of the Hindu ruling or warrior caste.

legal of the law. In China, Legalism was a code that became important in government.

loess windblown deposits of fine silt that wash into rivers. Yellow loess from the Asian deserts is responsible for the colour of the Huang He river in China.

loin cloth simple form of clothing worn by men, consisting of a strip of cloth wrapped around the hips to protect the sexual organs.

meditation a state of deep, concentrated thought, clearing the mind of trivial things in order to become receptive to spiritual and religious truths.

monsoon seasonal winds in the Indian Ocean that bring rain to western India, and used by sailors for regular voyages between Asia and the Middle East and Africa.

myth ancient story about gods and heroes. Many myths may have begun as an account of a real incident, person or great event, which retold over and over again becomes a symbolic explanation of past and present.

Neolithic period of prehistory also known as the New Stone Age, in which people used

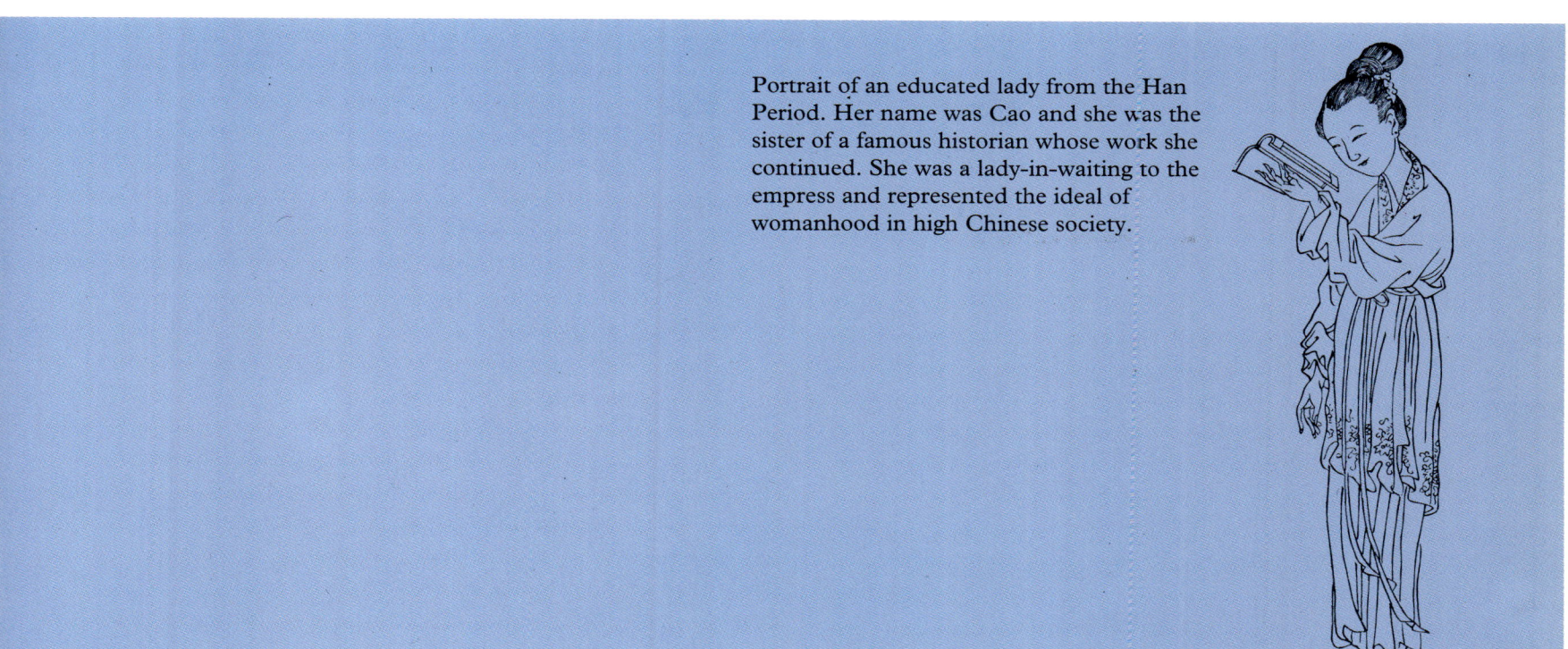

Portrait of an educated lady from the Han Period. Her name was Cao and she was the sister of a famous historian whose work she continued. She was a lady-in-waiting to the empress and represented the ideal of womanhood in high Chinese society.

smooth stone tools, began to grow crops and rear animals, and made pottery.

nomads people who have no permanent homes, but wander with their flocks and herds, seeking new pastures.

oligarchy political system in which power rests with a few rich and strong individuals.

oracle a person, place or thing considered to be a medium of divine revelation. People consulting the oracle received answers to their questions from an attendant priest or soothsayer. Leaders in the ancient world often consulted oracles before taking decisions about making war, marrying, going hunting, and so on.

outpost a frontier post or a group of soldiers positioned some distance away from the main army.

outrigger canoe light craft used in Asian and Pacific waters; often a dugout canoe with a single sail, and a second smaller hull for extra stability. The forerunner of the modern catamaran.

pack animal domestic animal used to carry loads on its back. Camels, horses, donkeys, oxen, yaks and elephants were all used in this way in ancient times.

philosopher thinker or wisdom-seeker, a person who contemplates the basic questions of existence such as 'what is good?', and teaches others.

pilgrim person travelling to visit a religious centre, such as a shrine.

province region of a state ruled by a governor, responsible to the head of state. A local government district.

relic any part of the remains of a person or thing, often kept as an object of reverence.

relief type of sculpture in which figures are slightly raised from the background, so that they stand out – a feature of Persian and Indian sculpture.

ritual religious or solemn ceremony, in which things are said and done in a particular, unchanging way.

sacrifice an offering to a god, to obtain the god's goodwill or forgiveness. Burials of kings were sometimes accompanied by sacrifices of servants and animals who were killed to accompany the dead ruler into the next world.

samurai medieval Japanese 'knights', who followed a military code of honour, and who were inspired by the earlier invaders of Japan.

Sanskrit Indo-European language, spoken in India from the 10th century BC and used for official documents.

satrapy province of the Persian empire, ruled by a governor known as a satrap.

seal stone or metal cylinder engraved with an image or symbol, which is imprinted into clay or wax when the seal is pressed into it. Used like a signature, to show that a document or command had the ruler's authority.

shintai places, people and animals that contained the kami (gods) of the ancient Japanese and were therefore sacred to them.

shrine place sacred to a god or an ancestor, where people bring offerings (such as food, flowers, gifts) and pray.

site in archaeology, a place where remains of ancient human settlements or other remains have been discovered.

soapstone a grey-brown mineral, a form of talc, which is soft enough to be easily carved.

soothsayer a person who is believed to be able to interpret oracles, and foretell the future through signs and omens such as shooting stars, comets, flights of birds and so on.

spices plants found in hot countries (such as pepper, cloves and cinnammon) which have long been valued as flavourings and preservatives of foods.

steppes treeless, grassy plains of central Asia, home to nomad herdsmen.

stupa dome-shaped tomb of an Indian ruler or some other great person, used also to house the ashes of dead Buddhist priests and holy relics.

stylize to portray something in art by simplifying it and reducing it to its essential elements.

subcontinent large area of land that is recognizably distinct from the continent of which it is part and which has distinctive physical or cultural features. For example, the Indian subcontinent is part of Asia.

Sumerian person or language of the ancient civilization of Sumer in Baylonia.

Taoism philosophical ideas based on the teachings of the Chinese thinker Lao-tzu.

terracotta kind of pottery, an unglazed brownish-red earthenware, made by baking a mixture of sand and clay.

tribute a tax or compulsory gift sent by a subject ruler to his overlord. The Chinese emperors expected to receive tributes from rulers of weaker, neighbouring lands.

tumulus plural tumuli; a mound of earth and stones, piled up above a burial place.

Vaishyas peasant farmers and traders in the Hindu caste system.

vassal someone owing duty to a lord, in the feudal social order.

Vedic describes the sacred texts of ancient India, the Vedas; also used to refer to the Hindu religion.

yurt tent-like home of steppe nomads, made from light wooden poles and coverings of felt and animal skins.

INDEX

Map references are in roman type, picture references are in *italic* type and text references are in **bold** type.

A
Adamgarh 8
Adana 12
Aden, trade 48
Aduli, Asian contact with 56
Afghanistan: Indo-European migration to **10**
    invasions of **23**
Africa, Iron Age 52-53, **54-55**
Agni (Aryan god) *10*, **11**
Agta (tribal group) 41
Ahar 4, 8
Ahicchatra 16
Ahura Mazda (Persian god) **15**, *15*
Ajanta 20, 21, 57
Aksu 44
Alamgirpur 4, 8, 16
Alchemy, Taoist interest in **31**
Aleppo 12
Alexander the Great **19**, **23**
Alexandria, Asian contact with 56
Alexandria-Kandahar 44
Alimurad 4
Alosigni, trade 49
Altai mountains 44
Amaravati 17, 20, 21
Amri 4, 9
Amu Darya river 44
Ancestors, cult of **39**
Andaman Islands 21, 49
Anga, religions 9
Angara river 45
Angkor 57
    Bronze Age site 40
Angkor Borei (Bronze Age site) 40
Anhsi 57
Animal-rearing, Indus Valley 7
Annam 57
Anshan, king of **14**
    seal of *15*
Antioch 12
    Asian contact with 56
    trade 48
Anuradhapura 57
Anyang (ancient Chinese site) 24, 29, 35
    economic zone **27**
Anyi (ancient Chinese site) 24, 33
Apologos, Asian contact with 56
Arab traders **51**
Arabia: Persian province 12
    trade 15
Arabian Peninsula 4
    trade routes and ports 48-49
Arachosia 13, 16
    trade 15
Aral Sea 56
Aramaic language **14**
Arbela 12
Arbuda 20
Architecture: Iron Age Bantu **54**
    Japanese **39**
Arikamedu 41
Armenia: Persian province 12
    trade 15
Art: influence of nomad **58**
    Japanese **39**
    Nok **54**
Artaxerxes, palace and tomb of *12*
Aru (Spice Island) 51
Aryan India **10-11**
    expansion of **10-11**
    first kingdoms and states **10-11**
Aryans: conquest of India 7, 8
    cultural influence **58**
    invasion of Sri Lanka **22**
    northern Indian states **18**
    sacred writings *see* Vedas
    social system *see* Caste system
Asandivate, founding of **10**
Asia: influence on other regions **58**
    most powerful civilizations **58**
    see also Central Asia; Southeast Asia
Asoka, emperor **15**, **19**
    and the Tamils **22**
    extent of empire 17
    pillars of *19*
    son **22**
Assur 12
Assyria: Persian province 12
    trade 15
Atharvaveda *11*
Athens 12
Atlantic Ocean, early sailors **50**
Australia 40, 49
Avanti 16, 17, 20, 21
    annexed by Magadha **19**
    religions 9
Axes, bronze: Chinese **26**
    Dong Son period **43**
    Indo-European *8*
Axum (kingdom), trade routes and ports 48
Ayodhya 17
Azania: Iron Age sites 53
    trade routes and ports 48

B
Babylon/Babylonia: Asian contact with 56
    city 12
    Persian conquest 12, **14**
    trade 15
Bactra 13
Bactria 13
    coin *23*
    conquest of **23**
trade 15
Baikal, lake 45
Bala Kot 4, 9
Balearic Islands 56
Bali 49
Balkhash, lake 44, 57
Baluchistan 4
    earliest settlements 4
Bampur 13
Banteay Prei Nokor (Bronze Age site) 40
Bantu: Iron Age sites 53
    migrations 53, **54**
    teachings and beliefs **52-53**, **54**
'Barbarian' invasions **47**
Barbaricum 56
Barygaza 57
Barynza, trade 49
Battles: Greek/Persian **14**
    southern African **55**
Bay of Bengal 57
    trade routes and ports 49
Beaker, silver 56
Bei-ti, 7th cent. movements 45
Beijing (Chinese capital city) 35
Beikthano (Bronze Age site) 40
Benares 17
Berenice: Asian contact with 56
    trade 48
Bhagatrav 4, 9
Bhils 41
Bisitun 13, **14**, 15
Bo Hai 28
    archaeological sites 24
Boats: bridge made of *24-25*, **26**
    Japanese **39**
    see also Canoes; Junk
Bodh Gaya 17, **18**
Boeny (Iron Age site) 52
Bonteberg (Iron Age site) 52
Books, Chinese: destruction of **34**
    rewriting of **35**
Boomplaas (Iron Age site) 52
Borneo 40, 49, 57
Borobudur 57
Borsippa 12
Boxian (ancient Chinese site) 24
Brahma (Hindu god) 20
Brahmagiri 8, 16
Brahmanism 20
    spread of 9
Brahmaputra river 44, 57
Brahmins 8, **11**, *11*
British Isles 56
Broederstroom (Iron Age site) 52
Bronze Age: Central Asian migrations 44-45
    Chinese **26**
    ritual vessels *25*, *27*
    Southeast Asia **42**
    sites 40
Buddha **18**, *19*, **59**
Buddhism: Asoka and **19**, *19*
    in Japan **39**
    in Southeast Asia **43**
    in Sri Lanka **22**
    Korean missionaries **39**
    schools of **18**
    spread of 17, **23**, **56-57**
    teachings **18**
Buildings: Han peasants' house **35**
    Harappa **4-5**, 6
    Japanese Iron Age **38**
    Mohenjo-Daro house **6**
    Southeast Asian **40-41**, **42**
    steppe nomads *see* Yurts
    see also Architecture
Bullock cart **8-9**, **10**
Burial mounds: Japanese Iron Age **37**, **38**
    steppe nomads **46**
Burma 40
Buru (Spice Island) 51
Byzantium 48
    Asian contact with 56

C
Cai (Chinese city-state) 25, 28
Cakala 16
Calendar, Japanese **39**
Cambodia 40
Cambyses, ruler of Persia **14**
Camels: Chinese use of *32-33*, **34**
    steppe nomads and **46**, *47*
Cana, Asian contact with 56
Canal system, Qin dynasty 28
Candle-holder, Dong Son period *43*
Cangwu (Chinese city) 33
Canoes: Annam culture 41
    Sri Lankan **50**
Cao (Chinese state) 28
Cappadocia (Persian province) 12
    trade 15
Caravans, Chinese *32-33*, **34**
Caria (Persian province) 12
    trade 15
Carts: Indus Valley **27**
    steppe nomads **46**
    see also Bullock Cart; Ox-carts
Caspian Sea, Asian contact with 56
Caste system **11**, **20-21**, **22**
Cavalry: Chinese: horses for 33
    terracotta **34**
    Persian *15*
    steppe nomads **47**
Celebes (Spice Island) 49, 51, 57
Central Asia, migrations from 44-45
Ceram (Spice Island) 49, 51
Ch'un Ch'iu (Chinese book) **35**
Chad (Lake), Bantu settlement 53
Cham (Southeast Asian state) 41
Champa, kingdom of **43**
Chandoli 16
Chandragupta Maurya **19**
Chang Jiang (Yangtze) 32, 35, 45, 57
Changsha (Chinese city) 33
Changye (Chinese city) 32
Chanhu-Daro 4, 9
Chansen (Bronze Age site) 40
Charax, Asian contact with 56
Chariots: Chinese hunting *35*
    Indo-European *8*
Chedi, religions 9
Chen (Chinese city-state) 25
Chenchu (tribal group) 41
Chenla, kingdom of **43**
Chera (southern Indian kingdom) 16, 17, 20, 21, **22**
China: Central Asian wars **47**
    cultural influence **58**
    defensive walls 29
        see also Great Wall of China
    first civilization **26**
    imperial cities 35
    influence on Southeast Asia **42-43**
    invasions of northern India **23**
    Japanese embassy to **39**
    main archaeological sites 24
    main communication routes 57
    migrations 45
    origin of name **34**
    population density 32
    status of kings **26**
    time chart of main events **24-25**
    trade routes and ports 49
        use of monsoon winds **51**
        with Southeast Asia **42**
    unification of 28
    see also Spring and Autumn Period; Warring States Period
Chitope (Iron Age site) 52
Chokojiyama 36
Chola (southern Indian kingdom) 16, 17, 20, 21, **22**
Chondwe (Iron Age site) 52
Cilicia 12
Circumnavigation of the Eritrean Sea (Egyptian book) **50**
Citadel, Mohenjo-Daro 7
Cities: Indus Valley **4-5**, 6
    see also specific names
City-states: Indus Valley **6-7**
    Zhou empire 25
Civil service, Chinese **35**
Clans, federation of **38**
Class systems: Indus Valley civilization **4-5**, 6, 7
    see also Caste system
Clothing: Chinese: court costume *31*
    jade suit **58**
    Persian-style *15*, **23**
    steppe nomads **44-45**, **46**
Clysma, Asian contact with 56
Co Los (Bronze Age site) 40
Coins/coinage: first made of gold **23**
    see also Currency
Colour: Indo-European classes and *8*
    Japanese government system **39**
Communications: importance of Indonesian islands **43**
    main Asian routes **56-57**
    Persian empire **14-15**
Confucianism 30
Confucius (Chinese philosopher) **30**, *31*, **59**
Copper mines, Shang dynasty **27**
Corsica 56
Craftspeople (Indo-European class) *8*
Cravasti 17
Creation myth, Malawian **53**
Crete 56
Crops: Indus Valley civilization 7
    Southeast Asian **42**
Cult objects, Japanese **39**
Cuneiform 7
Curparaka 17
Currency: as evidence of sea trade **50**
    Indian **23**
    Persian empire **15**
Cyaxares (Median leader) **14**
Cyrenaica (Persian peovince) 12
Cyrus the Great: expansion of empire **14**
    tomb **58**

D
Dabar Kot 4, 9
Dai, 7th cent. movements 45
Daifang (Chinese city) 39
Damascus 12
Dancer, 1st cent. Indian *23*
Darius I (the Great) **14-15**
    empire 12-13
    palace *12*, *15*
Dascyliu 12
Deccan 20
    ruling families **22**
    trade routes 49
Demetrius, king, coin of *23*
Deng (Chinese city-state) 25, 28
Dengzhou (Chinese city) 39
Desalpur 4
Di Xin (Shang king) **26**
    Overthrow of **27**
Die Kelders (Iron Age site) 52
Diet, steppe nomads **46**
Ding-ling (Central Asian state) 45
Dingxiang (Chinese city) 33
Doab, earliest settlements 4
Dong Son culture, Annam 40, *41*, **42**, *43*, 59
Dong-hu, 7th cent. movements 45
Donghai (Chinese city) 33
Drachma (northern Indian coin) *23*
Drainage canals, Mohenjo-Daro 7
Drangiana (Persian province) 13
Dravavati (Southeast Asian state) 41
Dravidians: 1st millennium BC 9
    invasion of Sri Lanka **22**
Drums/drumming, Southeast Asian 41, **42**, *42*
Dunhwang 44
Dynasties: Chinese **26**
    Indian **19**, **22-23**
    see also specific names
Dzao (Shang city) 27

E
East China Sea 57
East Indies: as trading centre **43**
    colonization of Madagascar **50**
Eastern Huns 45
Ebetsu 37
Ecbatana 13, 15
    Asian contact with 56
Economy: Han dynasty **35**
    Zhou dynasty **27**
    see also Trade/trade routes
Egypt: Asian contact with 56
    Persian province 12
    trade 15
        with Indus Valley civilization **6-7**
Elam (Persian province) 13
    trade 15
Elands Bay (Iron Age site) 52
Emperors, Chinese: divinity of **34**
    first *see* Shi Huang-di
Entertainers: Han dynasty *35*
    Japanese *39*
    see also Music
Ephesus 12
    Asian contact with 56
Eran 16
Eudoxus (Egyptian ambassador) **51**
Eurasian Steppe, migrations and states 44-45, **46-47**
Europe: Asian contact with 56
    Indo-European migration to **10**
Execution, sacrificial **27**
Exploration, early accounts **50**

F
Farming: Chinese philosophy **34**
    Indus Valley civilization 7
    Iron Age African **54**
    Shang dynasty **26**
    Southeast Asian **42**
    spread in India **5**
    sub-Saharan **55**
    see also Animal-rearing; Peasant farmers
Feng (Zhou city) 25
Fenhsiang (Chinese city) 28
Fish-seller, Chinese **59**
Fishing, sub-Saharan **55**
'Five Kings of Wa' **37**
'Flying horse' *33*
Forest civilization/cultures 5
    Southeast Asia **40-41**, 41, *42*
Four Noble Truths **18**
Fu-yu (Central Asian state) 45
Funan, kingdom of **43**
Funayama 36

G
Gandhara (Persian province) 13, 16, 17, 20
    religions 9
    trade 15
Gang-zhu (Central Asian state) 45
Ganges river/valley 57
    Aryan settlement **8-9**, **10**, *10*
    early settlements 4, **6**
    importance to Hindus **20-21**, **22**
Garuda 20
Gautama, Siddharta *see* Buddha
Gautamiputra (emperor), size of empire **22**
Gaza 12
    trade 48
Ghana, kingdom of **55**
Gherra: Asian contact with 56
    trade 48
Gobi Desert 45
Gods: Aryan *10-11*, **11**
    Hindu **20-21**, **22**
    Persian **15**, *15*
Gong (ancient Chinese site) 24
Government: Aryan **10**
    basis of Qin **34**
    centralization of Chinese **34**
    Han dynasty **35**
    Indo-European class *8*
    Indus Valley civilization 7
    Japanese **39**
    Persian **14-15**
        language of **14**
    Qin dynasty **31**
Governors, Persian provincial *see* Satraps
Grazing lands, nomad search for **44-45**, **46**
'Great Hero' *see* Mahavira
'Great powers' of the world **23**
'Great Vehicle' *see* Mahayana Buddhism
Great Wall of China 29, 33, **34**, **47**
Greece: Asian contact with 56
    Chinese trade with **35**
Greeks: name for China **34**
    see also Alexander the Great; 'Indian-Greeks'
Guanghan (Chinese city) 32
Guiyang (Chinese city) 33

Gujarat, earliest settlements 4, **6**
Guli (Chinese city) 33
Guzheng 44

H
Hadda 44
Hadramut, trade routes and ports 48
Hafit, trade 48
Hainan 49, 57
Hala, emperor **22**
Halmahera (Spice Island) 49, 51
Hami (Central Asian state) 45
Han (Chinese city-state) 25, **27**, 28
Han dynasty: periods **35**
 see also Han empire
Han empire 32
 peace treaties with Huns **47**
 symbols of life *56-57*
 territories 45
Han Fei (Qin minister), Legalist document **34**
Handan (ancient Chinese site) 24
Hangzhou (Chinese city) 39
Haniwa figures *37*, **38**, *38*
Hanzhong (Chinese city) 32
Hao (Zhou capital city) 25, **27**
Haranka dynasty **19**
Harappa 4, **6-7**, 8, 9
 plan of **7**
Harappa civilization **6**
 destruction by Aryans **10**
 timespan **6**
Harihara (Southeast Asian god) *43*
Harran 12
Hastinapura 16
Hecatompylos, trade 48
Henei (Chinese city) 33
Herodotus, on the Persian empire 12
Hili, trade 48
Himalayas 44
Hinayana Buddhism **18**
Hindu (Persian province) 13, **15**
Hindu Kush 4
Hinduism **20-21**
 gods *59*
 in Southeast Asia **43**, *43*
 pilgrimages **20-21**, **22**
 Satavahanas and **22**
 see also Vedas
Hippalus (Indian sailor) 51
Hiraide 36
Hmawza Sriksetra (Bronze Age site) 40
Hoa-Binh (Bronze Age site) 40, **42**
Hokkaido (island of Japan) 37
Hongshao (Zhou city) 25
Hongtong (ancient Chinese site) 24
Honshu (island of Japan) 36, 39
Horses: Aryan use of **8-9**, **10**, **11**
 Chinese supplies *33*
 Japanese 36, **38**
 steppe nomads 44-45, **46**, *46*, *47*
 see also Saddles
Hsiangfen (Chinese city) 28
Hu (steppe tribe), migration **46**
Huan (Chinese city-state) 25
Huang (Chinese city-state) 25
Huang He (Yellow river) **26**, 45, 57
 archaeological sites around 24-25
 changes in course of 25
 cities around 25
 Stone Age settlement **26**
Huaxian (ancient Chinese site) 24
Human sacrifice, Shang dynasty *26*, **27**
Hun-zhu, 7th cent. movements 45
Hungfung (Chinese city) 28
Huns *see* Xiongnu
Huns 29
 7th cent. movements 45
 ancestors **46**
 Central Asian wars **47**
 conquest of **47**
 migrations 44-45, **46**
 organization of kingdoms **47**
Hunter-gatherers: Saharan 54
 Southeast Asian 41, **42**
Hunting: Chinese **35**
 Iron Age African *52*
 Sumatran 40-41, **42**
 see also Fishing

I
I Ching (Chinese book) **35**, *57*
Idraprastha **16**
Ignu (Aryan god) **11**
Inariyama 36
India: 2nd-1st cent. BC peoples and kingdoms **20-21**
 Aryans in **10-11**
 Chinese trade with **35**
 cultural influence 58
 Dravidian and Aryan 9
 effect of Indo-Europeans **10-11**
 influence on Southeast Asia **42-43**
 kingdoms 20
 main communication routes 57
 spread of farming and town life 5
 trade **15**
 routes and ports 49
 with Southeast Asia **42**
 with the West **50-51**
 valley civilizations 4
 see also Aryan India; Northern India; Southern India
'Indian-Greeks' *see* Indo-Greeks
Indian Ocean: exploration of **50**
 trade routes and ports **48-49**
Indo-Europeans: cultural groups **10**
 cultural influence 58
 eastern branch *see* Aryans
 in southern India **22**
 origins **10**
 social divisions *8*
 see also Aryans
Indo-Greeks 44
 and the Scythians **23**
Indo-Scythians 44
Indochina 40
 trade routes and ports 49

Indonesia 40
 cultural influences 58
 early states 41
Indra (Aryan god) *11*
Indraprastha 16, 17, 21
Indus river/valley 4, 16, **56-57**
 early settlements 4, **6**
 importance as trade route **6**
Indus Valley civilization 5, **6-7**
 3rd millennium BC 4
 daily life *4-5*, **6**
 disappearance of 7
 invasions **23**
Ionia (Persian province) 12
 trade **15**
Iran 4
 Chinese trade with **35**
Iranian plains, Indo-European migration to **10**
Irodo (Iron Age site) 53
Iron Age: African **54-55**
 main sites **52-53**
 Japanese **38**, 58
Ironworking, development in Africa 53, **54**
Irtysh river 44
Ishim river 44
Issus 12
Issyk-Kul, lake 44
Ito (Japanese city) 39
Iwasakiyama 36
Iwatoyama 36

J
Jainism **18-19**
Jaio (Chinese city-state) 25
Janamejaya (Indian ruler) **10**
Japan 49
 3rd-7th cent. AD **36-37**
 Chinese idea of 39
 invasions of *36-37*, **38**, *38*
 isolation of **38**
 main communication routes 57
Java 40, 49, 57
Jerusalem 12, **15**
Jhukar 4
Ji (Chinese city) 28, 29, 33, 45
Jian (Chinese city) 33
Jiangxia (Chinese city) 33
Jianwei (Chinese city) 32
Jiaozhi (Chinese city) 32
Jimo (ancient Chinese site) 24
Jin (Chinese city) 28
 7th cent. movements 45
Jinan (ancient Chinese site) 24
Jinguji 36
Jinyang (Chinese city) 28
Jiu-hura-Shan 57
Jiuzhen (Chinese city) 32
Jo-Jiang (Central Asian state) 45
Ju (Chinese city-state) 25
Judeirjo-Daro 4
Julu (Chinese city) 33
Jumna river 9
 Aryan settlement **11**
Junk, Chinese **28-29**, *30*, *51*

K
K'ung Fu-tzu *see* Confucius
Kabu (Southeast Asian state) 41
Kaifeng (Chinese capital city) 35, 39
Kalibanga 4
Kalinga 16, 17, 21
Kalundu (Iron Age site) 52
Kami (divine spirits) 39
Kamnama (Iron Age site) 52, 53
Kandahar 13
Kangonga (Iron Age site) 52
Kanishka, king **23**
Kapilavastu 17
Kara Shahr 44
Karnata 20, 21
Kashgar 57
Kashmir 20
 Indo-European migration to **10**
 religions 9
Kasi 17
 religions 9
Kausambi 9, 17
Kauva dynasty **23**
Khairkhana 44
Khambhat, Gulf of 4
 trade centre on **6**
Khartoum, trade 48
Khmer empire **43**
Khmer Tahi (tribal group) 41
Khotan 57
Khwarezm (Persian province) 13
 trade **15**
Kinzheng 45
Kiui-mi (Central Asian state) 45
Kizil 44
Knope (Iron Age site) 53
Koganezuka 36
Kokand 57
Kokubumji 36
Koldihawa 8
Korea 57
Kosala 17
 religions 9
Kot Diji 4
Kota Cina (Bronze Age site) 40, 41
Koyahan (Japanese city) 39
Krishna (Hindu god) *43*
Kshatriyas *8*, **11**
Ku Bua (Bronze Age site) 40
Kuala Selensing 41
Kucha 44
Kumi 44
Kurgan 45
Kuru 9, 16
 alliance with Pancala **10**
Kush, kingdom of, trade with Asia **55**
Kushan empire 20, **23**
 coin *23*
 origins **46**
Kusinara 17
Kyushu (island of Japan) 36, 39

L
Laccadive Islands 20
Lamboharano (Iron Age site) 52
Lamu, trade 48
Langany (Iron Age site) 53
Languages: Indo-European influence **10**
 of Persian empire **14**
 spread of Bantu 54
Langya (Chinese city) 33
Lanzhou 57
Lao-tzu (Chinese philosopher) **31**, *31*, *59*
Laos 40
Larsa 13
Legalist document (Qin dynasty) **34**
Leu-lan, 7th cent. movements 45
Leucecome, Asian contact with 56
Lhasa 57
Li Chi (Chinese book) **35**
Limpopo river, Iron Age sites 52
Lin-zhu, 7th cent. movements 45
Liu Bang (Han leader): rebellion against Qin **34**
 see also Han Gaozu
Lob Nor river 44
Loess, importance to Chinese settlement **26**
Long-men 57
Lothal 4, 8, 9, 20, 21
 importance to trade **6**
Loulan 44
Lu (Chinese city-state) 25, 28
Luangwa river, Iron Age sites 52
Lubusi (Iron Age site) 52
Lukchun 44
Lumbule Hill (Iron Age site) 53
Lun yu (book by Confucius) *31*
Luolang (Chinese city) 33, 39
Luoning (ancient Chinese site) 24
Luoyang (Chinese capital city) 25, **27**, 33, **35**, 39
 trade 49
Luzon 49, 57
Lydenburg (Iron Age site) 52
Lydia (Persian province) 12
 Persian conquest of **14**
 trade **15**

M
Macedonians, and the Scythians **23**
Madagascar: Asian voyages to **50**
 Iron Age sites **52-53**
Madyadesh, religions 9
Magadha (Aryan state) **10-11**, 17, **18**
 dynasties **19**
 religions 9
Maha-Kosala 20, 21
Mahavira **19**
Mahayana Buddhism **18**
Maintirano (Iron Age site) 52
Maka 13
 trade **15**
Malacca, straits of, importance to trade **43**
Malapandaram (tribal group) 41
Malapati (Iron Age site) 53
Malawi, Lake: Bantu settlement 53
 Iron Age sites **52-53**
Malayan Peninsula 40
Malaysia: main communication routes 57
 trade routes and ports 49
Maldive Islands 20
Maokangi (Iron Age site) 52
Maracanda 56
Marathon, battle of **14**
Margiana 13
Maru, religions 9
Mask, Balinese *42*
Master K'ung *see* Confucius
Matara, trade 48
Mathura 16, 21
 street scene *23*
 trade 49
Matsumoto 36
Matsuura (Japanese city) 39
Maurya empire 16
 collapse of **22**
Mauryan dynasty **19**
 imperial procession *19*
Maya, dream of **16**
Medes: cultural influence 58
 extent of empire **14**
Media (Persian province) 13
 trade **15**
Mediterranean Sea: Asian contact with 56
 early sailors **50**
Memphis 12, **15**
 trade 48
Mencius (Chinese philosopher) **30**
Mentawai 49
Merv 13, 56
Mesopotamia/Mesopotamian civilization 4, 5
 trade with Indus Valley civilization **6-7**
Messina (Iron Age site) 52
Metalwork, Southeast Asian **42**, *42-43*
 see also Ironworking
Mianchi (ancient Chinese site) 24
Migrations: Bantu 54
 Indo-European **10**
 steppe nomads 44-45, **46**
Miletus 12
Min Yue (independent Chinese kingdom) 33
Mindanao 49
Mining, Shang dynasty **27**
Miran 44
Misool (Spice Island) 51
Mitra (Aryan god) **11**
Mohenjo-Daro 4, **6-7**, *6*, 8, 9
 destruction by Aryans **10**
 plan of citadel **7**
 streets **7**
Mongu (Iron Age site) 52
Monks, Buddhist **16-17**, **18**, *18*
Monsoon winds **48-49**
 importance to trade **51**
'Moon of Bali' *41*
Moral code, Chinese **34**
Moscha, trade 48
Muang Bon (Bronze Age site) 40
Muang Fa Daed (Bronze Age site) 40
Muang Sing (Bronze Age site) 40

Muden (Iron Age site) 52
Munda (tribal group) 41
Muro Miyayama 36
Music, Iron Age African *52*
Muza, trade 48
Muziris 57
 trade 49
Mwabulambo (Iron Age site) 52, 53
Mytilene, Asian contact with 56

N
Na (Japanese city) 39
Nagariunakonda 41
Nan Yue (independent Chinese kingdom) 33
Nanda, kingdom of **19**
Nandi (Hindu god) **20-21**, **22**
Nanhai (Chinese city) 33
Nanjun (Chinese city) 33
Nanking (Chinese capital city) **35**
Nanyang (Chinese city) 33
Nara 36, 57
Narmada 21
Nasik 21
Navdatoli 16
Neanderthal people **42**
Nei Huang (Shang city) 27
Neolithic *see* New Stone Age
Nevasa 16
New Guinea 40
New Stone Age, northern steppe **46**
Nichya, religions 9
Nicobar Islands 49
Niger river, Bantu settlement 53
Nile river, Bantu settlement 53
Nineveh 12
 destruction of **14**
Nintoku (emperor), tomb of *37*, **38**
Nippur 12
Niya 44
Nirvana **18**
Noh 8
Noin Ula 45
Nomads: Chinese protection against *see* Great Wall of China
 invasion of Zhou empire **27**
 migrations from Central Asia **44-45**
 see also Steppe nomads
Northern India: early states 17
 Greek influence **23**
 invasions **22-23**
 states **16-17**
Nubia, trade **15**

O
Ob river 44
Obi (Spice Island) 51
Oc Eo (Bronze Age site) 40, 41
Oceanus (Greek god) *50*
Oceo 57
Oman: Asian contact with 56
 trade routes and ports 48
Opis 12
Oracles, Shang dynasty **26**
 bones *24*, **26**
 tortioseshell **26**, **27**
Orange river, Iron Age sites 52
Ormuz, Asian contact with 56
Osaka 36
Otsukayama 36
Ox-carts: Chinese *24-25*, **26**
 Indus Valley **27**
Ox teams **47**
Oxus river *see* Amu Darya river
Ozuka 36

P
Pa (Chinese state) 28
Pacific Ocean 57
 first sailors **50**
Pack animals: Chinese *32-33*, **34**
 steppe nomads **47**
Pagan (Bronze Age site) 40
Paiyampalli 16
Palawan 49
Palmyra 12
Panai 49
Pancala (Aryan state) 9, **11**, 16
Pandu Rajar Dhibi 8
Pandya (southern Indian kingdom) 16, 17, 20, **22**
Parikshita, King **10**
Parthia/Parthians (Persian province) 13
 and the Scythians **23**
Pasargadae 13, **15**, *15*
Patala, trade 49
Patalene 20, 21
Pataliputre 17, 21, 57
Pattala 57
Peasant farmers (Indo-European class) *8*
Pei (Chinese city) 33
Pemba, trade 48
Persepolis 13, **15**
 royal residences *12-13*, **14**, **15**
 plan of *12*
Persia/Persian empire: Asian contact with 56
 cultural influence of 58
 extent of **15**
 Indo-European conquest **10**
 main communication routes 56
 new capital **15**
 organization of **12-13**
 reorganization of **12-13**, **14-15**
 trade: goods traded **15**
 routes and ports 48
 with Indus Valley civilization **6-7**
Persian Gulf, Asian contact with 56
Peshawar 44
Petra: Asian contact with 56
 trade 48
Pfuti (Iron Age site) 52
Phalaborwa (Iron Age site) 52
Phasis 12
Philippines 40, 57
Philosophy: importance in China **30**, *30*
 of Confucius **30**
 of Lao-tzu **31**
 of Mencius **30**
 of Taoism **31**
 of Xunzi **30**

63

Phimai (Bronze Age site) 40
Phoenicia/Phoenicians: trade 15
  trading ships *48-49*, *50*
Phopo Hill (Iron Age site) 53
Pi, archaeological sites 24
Pi disc *28*
Pillars of Asoka *19*
Pingyin (ancient Chinese site) 24
Populations: 2nd cent. China 32
  migrations from Central Asia 44-45
'Powerful warrior' *see* Wu Wang
Prachya, religions 9
Pragiyotisha 17
Pratisthana 20, 21
Priest-king, Mohenjo-Daro *5*
Priests: Indo-European class *8*, **11**
  Indus Valley civilization **7**
  interpreting the oracles **26**
  Persian empire *15*
Punjab 20
  earliest settlements 4
Purushapura 16

Q
Qi (Chinese city-state) 25, **27**, 28
Qin (Chinese city-state) 25, **27**, 28
Qin dynasty **27**, **34**
  chief minister *see* Shang Yang
  conquests 28
  government structure *31*
  unification of China by 28
Qingdao (ancient Chinese site) 24
Qiufu (Shang city) 27
Qu (Chinese city-state) 25
Qufu (Chinese city) 29
Quyang (ancient Chinese site) 24

R
Rajagriha 17
Rajasthan: earliest settlements 4, **6**
  religions 9
Ramagiri 20
Rangpur 4, 9, 16
Ravi river **6**, 44
Rawak 44
Rean 16
Red river basin, conquest by China 42-43
Red Sea: Asian contact with 56
  trading route *48-49*, *50*
Religions **59**
  early Japanese **38-39**
  importance in China *30*
  Indian *16-17*, *18*, **18-19**, *20*
    spread in 9
  Shang dynasty **26**
  Vedic society **11**
  see also specific religions
Rhagae 13
Rhapta (Iron Age site) 53
  trade 48
Rhyton 56
Rice-cultivation, beginnings **42**
Rigveda *11*
Rivers: Qin control of Chinese *28*
  see also specific rivers
Rizhao (ancient Chinese site) 24
Rock paintings: Iron Age African *52-53*, **54**, *54*, *55*
Rojadi 9
Rojdi 4
Rome/Roman empire 48
  Asian contact with 56
  Chinese contact with **51**
  invasions **47**
Ruicheng (Chinese city) 28
Rulers: first Zhou **27**
  Indian **10**
  Indo-European class *8*
  northern Indian **19**
  Persian **14**
  Southeast Asian concept **43**
  see also Emperors; Kings *and specific names*
Rupar 4

S
Saba, trade 48
Sacred cow *9*
Saddles, Siberian *44*
Sadhu 20-21, *22*
Sagartia (Persian province) 13
  trade 15
Sahara, Iron Age people **54**
Sais 12
Saitobaru 36
Saka 44
Sakaeura II 37
Saki, 7th cent. movements 45
Salawati (Spice Island) 51
Samarkand *see* Maracanda
Samaveda *11*
Sambor Prei Kuk (Bronze Age site) 40
Sanchi 20, 57
Sandhanawala 9
Sangala 44
Sanskrit **43**
Sarapion, trade 48
Sardinia 56
Sardis 12, 15
  Asian contact with 56
Sarmatians **46**
  migrations 44-45
Sarodrano (Iron Age site) 52
Satavahana 20
Satavahana dynasty/empire 21, **22**
Satraps/Satrapies, Persian 12-13, *12-13*, **14-15**, *14*
Scholars (Indo-European class) *8*
Science/scientists: Chinese books **34**
  early Chinese **31**
Scythia/Scythians: Chinese trade with **35**
  invasion of northern India **23**
  migrations 44-45
  Persian province 13
  trade 15
Sea of Japan 36-37, 39
Seals: Indus Valley civilization 5, **6-7**
  Persian empire *15*
Sekijinyama 36
Selenga river 45
Seleucia, trade 48
Senegal river, Bantu settlement 53
Servants (Indo-European class) *8*
Sesheke (Iron Age site) 52
Seventeen Articles (Japan) **39**
Shaka dynasty: coin *23*
  invasion of northern India **23**
Shan (ancient Chinese site) 24
Shan Yu (Hun title) **47**
Shan-shan (Central Asian state) 45
Shang (Chinese city-state) 25, 45
Shang Di (Shang god) **26**
Shang dynasty **26**
  main archaeological sites 24
  overthrow of **27**
Shang Yang (Chinese minister): effect of reforms by *28*
  Legalist doctrine **34**
Shangan (China's capital city) **35**, 45, 57
  plan of *32*
  trade 49
Shanggu (Chinese city) 33
Shanghe (Chinese city) 32
Shangjun (Chinese city) 33
Shangye 45
Shanyang (Chinese city) 29
Shen (Chinese city-state) 25, 28
Sheng (Chinese state) 28
Shengpu (Chinese city) 29
Shi Huang-di, emperor of China 29, **34**
  tomb *34*
  wall built by *see* Great Wall of China
Shih Ching (Chinese book) **35**
Shikashima (Japanese city) 39
Shikoku (island of Japan) 36
Shimanosho Ishibutai 36
Shintai (receptacles for the spirits) **39**
Shinto **39**
Ships: Chinese *see* Junk
  Phoenician *48-49*, *50*
Shishunaga dynasty **19**
Shiva (Hindu god) *20*, *21*
  see also Harihara
Shotoku, Prince **39**, *39*
  reforms **39**
Shouchun (Chinese city) 33
Shu (Chinese city-state) 25, 28, 29, 32
Shu Ching (Chinese book) **25**
Shudras *8*
Shuga dynasty **23**
Si Maha Pot (Bronze Age site) 40
Si Thep (Bronze Age site) 40
Siberia, migrations through **46**
Sicily 56
Sidon 12
Sien-pi empire **47**
  Central Asian wars **47**
  territories 45
Silk Road 33, *32-33*, *34*, **35**, **59**
Simhala *see* Sri Lanka
Sind 16, 20, 21
  earliest settlements 4
  religions 9
  trade routes and ports 49
Sinhalese, origin of **22**
Sinoia (Iron Age site) 52
Sinope 12
Sippar 12
Situmpa (Iron Age site) 52
Siu-yan, 7th cent. movements 45
Sixian (ancient Chinese site) 24
'Small Vehicle' *see* Hinayana Buddhism
Society, divisions of: Indo-European *8*, **11**
  Shang dynasty **26**
  Yamato **38**
Sogdiana (Persian province) 13
  trade 15
Soldiers: Chinese *24-25*, *26*
  Han army *35*
  Japanese *37*
  see also Warriors
Solwezi (Iron Age site) 52
Somnath 16
Song (Chinese city-state) 25, **27**, 28
Soothsayers: Shang dynasty *24*, **26**
Sopatma 57
Sotka-Koh 4
South China Sea 57
Southeast Asia: influences on **42-43**
  cultural **58**
Southern Huns 45
Southern India, Indo-Europeans reach **22**
Spice Islands 51
Spring and Autumn Period, Zhou dynasty **27**
  China at end of 28
Sri Lanka 16, 17, 20, 21, 22
  invasions of **22**
  main communication routes 57
  trade routes 49
Steppe nomads: ancestors **46**
  camp *47*
  cultural influence **58**
  northern migrations 44-45, **46**
  source of wealth **46**
  wars **47**
Stone Age: Chinese settlement **26**
  sailors **50**
  Southeast Asia **42**
  see also New Stone Age
Strabo (Greek geographer) **51**
Sukhothai 57
Sula (Spice Island) 51
Sulawesi 40
Sumatra 40, 49, 57
  forest dwellers *40-41*, *42*
Sumba 49
Sunda, strait of, importance to trade **43**
Surashtra 20
Surya (Aryan god) *11*, *59*
Susa 13, **15**, 15
  Asian contact with 56
  trade 48
Sutkagen-Dor 4

T
Tabriz: Asian contact with 56
Taiwan 28, 49, 57
Taiyuan (ancient Chinese site/city) 24, 33
Takehara 36
Takkola 57
Taklamakan Desert 44
Tamil/Tamils 20, **22**
Tamralipti, trade 49
Tan (Chinese city-state) 25, 28
Tang (Shang king) **26**
Tang-shan 57
Tang-shi-huai (Sien-pi leader): conquests 45
  size of empire **47**
Tanganyika, Lake, Bantu settlement 53
Tangyin (ancient Chinese site) 24
Tanimbar (Spice Island) 51
Tanis, trade 48
Tao Teh Ching (book by Lao-tzu) **31**, *31*
Taoism **30**, *31*
  aspects of life *56-57*
  key book *31*
Tarim river 44
Tarsus 12
Tasaday (tribal group) 41
Tashkent 56
Tawi Silaim, trade 48
Tax system: Persian empire **15**
  Shang dynasty 27
Tax-gifts *see* Tribute
Taxila, kingdom of 16, 20, 21, 44
  destruction of **23**
  trade 49
Technology, spread of: Bantu 53, **54**
  from Asia **58**
Tekkalakota 16
Tetradrachma (northern Indian coin) *23*
Thailand 40
  states **43**
  toolmaking and farming **42**
Tharro 4, 9
Thebes 15
  trade 48
'Thinai' **34**
Tibet *see* Xizang
Timor 49
Tin mines, Shang dynasty 27
Tokhary, 7th cent. movements 45
Tokoro Chashi 37
Tombs: Chinese *34*, *58*
  Japanese *37*
  Persian *58*
  Vietnamese *59*
Tomi, Asian contact with 56
Tong (Chinese city-state) 25
Tonkin 40
Tools, Stone Age **42**
Tou Wan, Princess: burial *58*
Town life, 3rd millennium BC 5
Trade/trade routes 56-57
  Chinese 33
    philosophy **34**
    ports *28-29*, *30*
    silk **35**
  East Indies and **43**
  East-West 56-57, **58-59**
  Han dynasty 32
  Indian Ocean 48-49, *48-49*, **50-51**, *50*
  Indus Valley civilization **6-7**
  Japanese **39**
  Kushan control of **23**
  Mediterranean and East African **51**
  Persian empire 15
  Southeast Asian *40-41*, 41, **42**, *42*, **43**
  spices *51*
  sub-Saharan **55**
  see also Silk Road
Trade goods: Indian Ocean **51**
  Persian empire 15
  Spice Islands *51*
  see also Tribute
Traders (Indo-European class) *8*
Transoxiana 44
Trapezus 12
Tribute: Persian empire 12-13, *12-13*, *14*
  Shang dynasty 27
'Trigram' *56-57*
Tripuri 16
Tso Chuan (Chinese book) **35**
Tumuli *see* Burial mounds
Turfan 44, 57
Tyre 12
  Asian contact with 56
Tzaneen (Iron Age site) 52

U
U Thong (Bronze Age site) 40
Ubsu Nur river 44
Udichya, religions 9
Udozuka 36
Uenodai 36
Uighur people 44
  Huns and **47**
Uitkomst (Iron Age site) 52
Ujjayini 16, 17, 20
'Untouchables' *20-21*, *22*
Ur 13
Urfa 12
Uruk 13
Utnur 8
Uttar Pradesh, earliest settlements 4, **6**

V
Vaal river, Iron Age sites 52
Vaishyas *8*, **11**
Varna 8
Varuna (Aryan god) **11**, *11*
Vasa 9
Vatsa 16
Vedas (sacred writings) **11**
  structure *11*
Vedda (tribal group) 41
Vedic religion, spread of 9
Victoria, Lake, Bantu settlement 53
Vietnam 40
  bronze figure *59*
Vima Kadphises, king *23*
Vishnu (Hindu god) *20*
  see also Harihara

W
Wa, Kingdom of 39
Wagons: Indus Valley civilization 6
  see also Carts
Waigeo (Spice Island) 51
Wang Mang, Han usurper **35**
Wankie (Iron Age site) 52
Warfare: Hun tactics **47**
  influence of steppe nomads 58
Warring States Period, China *25*, **27**, 28
Warrior-democracy, Hun **47**
Warriors: Aryan *8-9*, *10*
  Indo-European class *8*, **11**
  Persian *15*
Way of Virtue, The see Tao Teh Ching
Weapons: Han dynasty *35*
  Indus Valley civilization 7
  Iron Age African *52*
  Saharan Iron Age **54**
  Shang period *26*
  steppe nomads **47**
  sub-Saharan *55*
Wei (Chinese city-state) **27**, 28
  archaeological sites 24
Wei Zhi (Chinese account of Japan) 39
Weights, Indus Valley civilization **6-7**
Wenxi (ancient Chinese site) 24
Western Huns 44
Western Satrapy 20
Wetar (Spice Island) 51
Wieng Sra (Bronze Age site) 40
Wilton (Iron Age site) 52
Winka (Bronze Age site) 40
Women, status of steppe nomad **46**
Writing: Chinese: Qin and Han *59*
  early Chinese **26-27**, *27*, *29*
  modern Chinese *29*
  introduction to Southeast Asia **43**
  Japanese **39**
  see also Cuneiform; Vedas
Wu (Chinese city-state) 25, 28
Wu Wang (Chinese prince), overthrow of Shang dynasty **27**
Wu-sun (Central Asian state) 45
  7th cent. movements 45
Wuwei (Chinese city) 32, 45
Wuyuan (Chinese city) 33, 45

X
Xerxes, palace and gate of *12*
Xi (Chinese city-state) 25
Xia dynasty **26**
Xian (Chinese city-state) 25
Xihe (Chinese city) 33
Xing (Chinese city-state) 25
Xinxiang (ancient Chinese site) 24
Xiongnu (steppe nomads) *see* Huns
Xizang 4, 44
  main communication routes 57
Xu (Chinese city-state) 25, 28
Xun (Chinese city-state) 25
Xunzi (Chinese philosopher) **30**

Y
Yajurveda *11*
Yama (Aryan god) *10*
Yamanoshita 36
Yamatai (Japanese city) 39
Yamato region, Japan **38**
Yan (Chinese city-state) 25, **27**, 28
Yang-Yue (Chinese city-state) 25
Yangcheng (ancient Chinese site) 24
Yanling (Chinese city) 28
Yanmen (Chinese city) 33, 45
Yarang (Bronze Age site) 40
Yayoi period (Japan) **38**
Yenisey river 44
Yin and *yang 56-57*
Yin Yang (Shang city) 27
Yisheng (Zhou city) 25
Yiwu 44
Yizhou (Chinese city) 32
Yong (Chinese city-state) 25
  archaeological sites 24
Yongcheng (ancient Chinese site) 24
Yotkan 44
Youbeiping (Chinese city) 33
Yue (Chinese state) 28
Yue-zhi, 7th cent. movements 45
Yueh-chih: in Bactria **46**
  Indian conquests **23**
Yulin 45
Yun (Chinese city-state) 25
Yunzhong 45
Yurts *44-45*, *46*
  transporting *47*
Yutai (Shang city) 27
Yuzhang (Chinese city) 33

Z
Zaire river, Bantu settlement 53
Zambezi river: Bantu settlement 53
  Iron Age sites 52
Zanzibar trade 48
Zariaspa 56
Zhang (Shang city) 27
Zhao (Chinese state) 28
Zhe-shi (Central Asian state) 45
Zhending (Chinese city) 33
Zheng (Qin warrior king) *see* Shi Huang-di
Zhenjiang (Chinese city) 39
Zhizo (Iron Age site) 52
Zhongking (Chinese capital city) 35
Zhou (Chinese state) 28
  archaeological sites 24
Zhou dynasty/empire 25, **27**
  phases of **27**
  vase *25*
Zhu (Chinese city-state) 25, **27**, 28
Zhuang-zi (Chinese philosopher) **31**
Zhuofang 45
Zhuwo (Chinese city) 28
Zichuan (Chinese city) 33
Zizhuan 45
Zoroaster **59**
Zu (Chinese city) 28